From Knowledge to Beatitude

Grover A. Zinn, Jr.

EDITED BY
E. ANN MATTER &
LESLEY SMITH

From Knowledge to Beatitude

ST. VICTOR, TWELFTH-CENTURY SCHOLARS, AND BEYOND

Essays in Honor of Grover A. Zinn, Jr.

University of Notre Dame Press
Notre Dame, Indiana

Copyright © 2013 by University of Notre Dame
Notre Dame, Indiana 46556
www.undpress.nd.edu
All Rights Reserved

Manufactured in the United States of America

Library of Congress Cataloging-in-Publication Data

From knowledge to beatitude : St. Victor, twelfth-century scholars, and beyond ; essays in honor of Grover A. Zinn, Jr. / edited by E. Ann Matter and Lesley Smith.
    pages cm
  Includes bibliographical references and index.
  ISBN-13: 978-0-268-03528-0 (cloth : alk. paper)
  ISBN-10: 0-268-03528-8 (cloth : alk. paper)
  1. Theology—History—Middle Ages, 600–1500.   2. Spiritual life—Christianity—History of doctrines—Middle Ages, 600–1500.
3. Bible—Criticism, interpretation, etc.—History—Middle Ages, 600–1500.
4. Saint-Victor (Abbey : Paris, France)   5. Hugh, of Saint-Victor, 1096?–1141.
6. Paris (France)—Intellectual life.   I. Zinn, Grover A.   II. Matter, E. Ann.
III. Smith, Lesley (Lesley Janette)
  BT26.F76   2012
  230'.20902—dc23
                                                                    2012036990

∞ *The paper in this book meets the guidelines for permanence and durability of the Committee on Production Guidelines for Book Longevity of the Council on Library Resources.*

Contents

Abbreviations ix

List of Illustrations xi

Grover Zinn: An Appreciation xv
RAYMOND CLEMENS

Preface xix

1   Maps and Plans in Medieval Exegesis: 1
     Richard of St. Victor's *In visionem Ezechielis*
     CATHERINE DELANO-SMITH

2   An Illuminated Manuscript of Writings by Hugh of   46
     St. Victor (Paris, Bibl. Mazarine, Ms 729)
     WALTER CAHN

3	The Twelfth-Century Church of St. Victor in Paris: A New Proposal WILLIAM W. CLARK	68
4	*Decor Domus Domini*: Innocent II's Privilege for the Abbey of St. Denis, May 9, 1131 THOMAS WALDMAN	86
5	*Lectio exhortatio debet esse*: Reading as a Way of Life at the Twelfth-Century Abbey of St. Victor FRANKLIN T. HARKINS	103
6	Robert Amiclas and the Glossed Bible LESLEY SMITH	131
7	Preaching by Word and Example HUGH FEISS, OSB	153
8	"Transgressing [its] measure . . . trespassing the mode and law of its beauty": Sin and the Beauty of the Soul in Hugh of St. Victor BOYD TAYLOR COOLMAN	186
9	Contemplation as "Speculation": A Comparison of Boethius, Hugh of St. Victor, and Richard of St. Victor DALE M. COULTER	204
10	*Synderesis* and Conscience: Stoicism and Its Medieval Transformations MARCIA L. COLISH	229
11	The Spirituality and Theology of Beauty in Hugh of St. Victor DOMINIQUE POIREL	247

12	*Iam cor meum non sit suum*: Exchanging Hearts, from Heloise to Helfta BARBARA NEWMAN	281
13	Hildegard of Bingen's Theology of Revelation RACHEL FULTON BROWN	300
14	Returning Crusaders: Living Saints or Psychopaths? JEREMY ADAMS	328
15	Christ or Antichrist? The Jewish Messiah in Twelfth-Century Christian Eschatology FRANS VAN LIERE	342
16	Medieval Women Visionaries in the Renaissance: Jacques Lefèvre d'Étaples' *Liber trium virorum et trium spiritualium virginum* (1513) RAYMOND CLEMENS	358
17	Heart Calls to Heart: The Importance of the Love between the Lover and the Beloved in *The Mystical Ark* and *Wachet auf!* E. ANN MATTER	384

Grover A. Zinn: Selected Publications	396
Bibliography	399
List of Contributors	443
Index	448

Abbreviations

AASS	Acta Sanctorum
BAV	Biblioteca Apostolica Vaticana
BnF	Bibliothèque nationale de France
BEC	Bibliothèque de l'École des chartes
CCCM	Corpus Christianorum, Continuatio Mediaevalis (Turnhout: Brepols, 1967–)
CCSL	Corpus Christianorum Series Latina (Turnhout: Brepols, 1954–)
CSEL	Corpus Scriptorum Ecclesiasticorum Latinorum (Vienna, 1866–)
GCS	Griechischen christlichen Schriftsteller der ersten drei Jahrhunderte

MGH	Monumenta Germaniae Historica
PG	Patrologia Graeca, ed. J.-P. Migne, 162 vols. (Paris, 1857–66)
PL	Patrologia Latina, ed. J.-P. Migne, 221 vols. (Paris, 1844–64)
RTAM	Recherches de théologie ancienne et médiévale
SAEMO	Sancti Ambrosii episcopi mediolanensis opera
SC	Sources chrétiennes (Paris, 1942–)

Illustrations

Fig. 1.1. Richard of St. Victor, *In visionem Ezechielis*. Plan for chapter 2 of Richard's treatise showing the general layout of the Temple complex. Redrawing taken from *Patrologia Latina* volume 196 to aid identification of the buildings mentioned in this essay. The Temple (*templum*), which contains the sanctuary and the innermost sanctuary, or Holy of Holies, is sometimes itself referred to as the sanctuary. West is at the top. 10.5 × 14.5 cm. Reproduced with the permission of the British Library.   12

Fig. 1.2. Richard of St. Victor, *In visionem Ezechielis*. Plan for chapter 16 from a late twelfth-century manuscript showing the Temple proper with the altar of incense in the main room or sanctuary. The measurements of the door jamb ("five cubits here," "five cubits thence") accord with those given in Ez 40:48. West is at the top. 20 × 12 cm. Oxford, Bodleian Library, Ms Bodl. 494, fol. 158v. Reproduced with the permission of the Bodleian Library.   14

xii   Illustrations

Fig. 1.3. Richard of St. Victor, *In visionem Ezechielis*. Plan for chapter 12 from a thirteenth-century manuscript showing the eastern part of the Temple complex from the sanctuary threshold to the outermost gate. The stream emerges as a single course to flow eastwards, passing the altar of holocausts to the south (on its right), but then divides into four so that each kitchen (*locus coquine*) is supplied with water. North is at the top. 30.5 × 21cm. Paris, BnF, Ms lat. 2165, fol. 50r. Reproduced with the permission of the BnF.   17

Fig. 1.4. Richard of St. Victor, *In visionem Ezechielis*. Plan for chapter 12 in an abridged version of the treatise made, possibly in Paris, for personal use. The plan replicates faithfully almost every detail of its exemplar, whether this was BnF, Ms lat. 2165 (see fig. 1.3) or another. Note the three signs indicating the direction of slope in the outer precinct have been added. The inner and middle gates are shown in the plan, the outermost one in elevation (and in fig. 1.3). Late twelfth or early thirteenth century. West is at the top. Approx. 22 × 15.5 cm. Durham, Cathedral and Chapter Library, Ms A.III.22, fol. 5r. Reproduced with the permission of Durham Cathedral and Chapter Library.   20

Fig. 1.5. Plan of Ezekiel's Temple, with the four-branching stream described by Richard of St. Victor, drawn in ink on an endleaf in a Bible probably made in Paris about 1240–50. Richard's plan has been extended to the west to include the entire Temple complex, with the three buildings adjacent to the Temple proper. East is at the top. Approx. 16 × 16 cm. Oxford, Brasenose College, Ms 5, fol. 443r. Reproduced with the permission of the Principal and Fellows of Brasenose College, Oxford.   23

Fig. 1.6. Plan of Ezekiel's Temple, with Richard of St. Victor's four-branching stream supplying the kitchens, drawn in ink on an endleaf in an early thirteenth-century French Bible and showing the whole Temple complex, as in Oxford, Brasenose College, Ms 5 (see fig. 1.5). Extra details here include several flights of steps, described in the Bible, which are also reminders of the sloping land. In red ink, with black writing, on a blank folio at the end of the volume. West is at the top. 25 × 25 cm. Oxford, Bodleian Library, Ms Laud Lat. 9, fol. 458v. Reproduced with the permission of the Bodleian Library.   24

Fig. 1.7. Richard of St. Victor, *In visionem Ezechielis*. Map of Canaan for chapter 20, entitled *Descriptio seu divisio totius terre promissionis*. Red ink lines with black writing. Early thirteenth century. 22 × 18 cm. Oxford, Bodleian Library, Ms Bodl. 459, fol. 37v. Reproduced with the permission of the Bodleian Library.   27

Fig. 1.8. Nicholas of Lyra, *Postilla litteralis super totam bibliam* (1323–32). Plan of the Temple proper for Ezekiel 47, with the sanctuary stream in a single course throughout. The copyist drew the stream passing to the right of the altar of holocausts (Ez 47:1–2), which here is the north side, and then corrected his error by exchanging the cardinal direction for north (*Aquilone*) and south (*Auster*) to give the illusion that the plan accords with the biblical description of what Ezekiel saw as he looked eastward. Early fourteenth century. 35.5 × 25 cm. Oxford, Bodleian Library, Ms Canon. Bibl. Lat. 70, fol. 165v. Reproduced with the permission of the Bodleian Library.   31

Fig. 2.1. Creation of Heaven and Earth (Paris, Bibl. Mazarine, Ms 729, fol. 13r). Used with the permission of the Bibliothèque Mazarine.   52

Fig. 2.2. Creation of the Angels (Paris, Bibl. Mazarine, Ms 729, fol. 38v). Used with the permission of the Bibliothèque Mazarine.   53

Fig. 2.3. Marriage (Paris, Bibl. Mazarine, Ms 729, fol. 137r). Used with the permission of the Bibliothèque Mazarine.   54

Fig. 2.4. Construction of a church (Paris, Bibl. Mazarine, Ms 729, fol. 214r). Used with the permission of the Bibliothèque Mazarine.   55

Fig. 2.5. Heavenly Bridegroom (Paris, Bibl. Mazarine, Ms 729, fol. 247r). Used with the permission of the Bibliothèque Mazarine.   57

Fig. 2.6. Dialogue of the Soul and Reason (Paris, Bibl. Mazarine, Ms 729, fol. 230r). Used with the permission of the Bibliothèque Mazarine.   58

Fig. 2.7. Faustus (Vendôme, Bibl. mun. Ms 34, fol. 90v). Used with the permission of the Institut de recherche et d'histoire des textes.   60

Fig. 2.8. David fighting the lion, David and Goliath (Paris, Chambre des Députés, Ms 2, fol. 164r). Used with the permission of the Bibliothèque de l'Assemblée nationale.   63

Fig. 3.1. View of the north flank of Saint Victor, detail of the church after Mérian, *Topographia Galliae*.   70

Fig. 3.2. View of the west end and north side of Saint Victor, detail of the church, after Mérian, *Topographia Galliae.* 71

Fig. 3.3. Foundations excavated by Grimault in 1931 (letters added) after Willesme, "Saint-Victor au temps d'Abélard," fig. 4. 72

Fig. 3.4. Reconstructed plan of Saint-Victor by Grimault, 1931, detail after Grimault, "Rapport présenté sur les fouilles effectuées place Jussieu." 73

Figure 16.1. Title page from Jacques Lefèvre d'Étaples, *Liber trium virorum & trium spiritualium virginum.* Paris: Henri Estienne, 1513. Image courtesy of the Rare Book and Manuscript Library, University of Illinois at Urbana-Champaign. 366

RAYMOND CLEMENS

Grover Zinn
An Appreciation

Grover Zinn made being a professor appear like a seamless extension of his own personal curiosity. He did his own research, made his own translations, reacted to the political situations around him, and actively shared his thoughts along the way with eighteen- to twenty-two-year-olds, making us believe that we could follow our natural inquisitiveness where it might lead. He shared his passion for medieval religion with many students who, no doubt, remember his classes fondly. For a small group—among them, some of those in this volume—he did more. His published works provided a model of creative and interdisciplinary scholarship long before interdisciplinary became a catchphrase. In his teaching and his translations he inculcated deep respect for primary sources and the need for all scholars—even undergraduates—to have before them the documents of an earlier age. In his mentoring, he treated undergraduates as if we were scholars, giving us the confidence to pursue our own ideas.

Grover taught very much as he wrote. One of Grover's earliest and most influential articles, "Mandala Symbolism and Use in the Mysticism of Hugh of St. Victor," published in 1973, illustrates the sort of creativity students often saw in class. In it, Grover compared Tibetan Buddhist practices of mandala construction with the mystical ark that Hugh of St. Victor described in his *De arca Noe morali* and *De arca Noe mystica*. The article did several things at once. It compared Eastern and Western religious practices without privileging either one, and it did so without any attempt to connect the two traditions through any sort of textual mediation. It relied, instead, on an almost structuralist analysis, but one that was deeply committed to historical context. As Grover writes: "Symbols live within a particular environment; they are not abstract elements."[1] Treating images as seriously as texts, submitting both to the same analysis, the article examined how images functioned to focus concentration and memory as part of a larger mnemonic for the benefit of novices in their respective orders. Interestingly, he was able to do all this despite the fact that there are no surviving images of Hugh's *arca*, only a textual description of what it was meant to look like.

Grover fostered interdisciplinary work in his students as well. He encouraged them to look for connections between various writings, emphasizing that these spiritual works were not written in a vacuum but were part of a conversation that took place often over two or three hundred years between people from very different intellectual environments, but driven by common concerns, such as how to love God properly, how to use pagan texts for Christian ends, or what it meant to be created in God's image.

In the classroom, Grover's love of his subject was palpable. No class ever reached the end of a syllabus because Grover would follow one tangent after another, giving the material depth that the readings alone didn't inspire. He was clearly fascinated by religion and how it was practiced, and his enthusiasm was infectious. Grover's insistence that students read primary sources, usually in their entirety rather than as excerpts, was complemented by his publications, particularly his translation of several of Richard of St. Victor's works for the Paulist Press' Classics of Western Spirituality series.[2] His volume was one of the first in that now-illustrious series that has done so much to bring noncanonical or lesser-known figures to the attention of English-speaking medievalists, and has allowed teachers to have students read the original sources rather than rely on secondary literature to describe and characterize these writers. Grover's translation was one of the first to make any of Richard's works available in English, and his brief biography of Richard gives historical context to a thinker previously little known and hugely overshadowed by his predecessor at St. Victor, Hugh (on whom Grover is also expert).[3] Grover's commitment to bringing more of these texts into classroom use has been realized through his editorship of the Victorine Texts in Translation series, which has already seen three volumes in production.

Grover's classes were also shaped by his desire to challenge his students with the most recent scholarship. In one seminar he taught in 1987 he assigned both Caroline Bynum's *Holy Feast and Holy Fast: The Religious Significance of Food to Medieval Women* (1986) and Barbara Newman's *Sister of Wisdom: St. Hildegard's Theology of the Feminine* (1987), selecting both before either had become required reading for medievalists. In that same year he brought Barbara Newman to campus to lecture on her book; the following year he brought Bernard McGinn to campus. He seemed to know all the established as well as the rising stars, and he brought them to Oberlin College. In a sleepy college town and at a liberal arts college not near any large university, Grover assigned cutting-edge material and brought nationally acclaimed scholars, and together with Marcia Colish and Jeffrey Hamburger, he challenged undergraduates to do original research, making Oberlin, somehow, a small center of medieval scholarly activity.

The essays in this volume speak to Grover Zinn's passion for medieval history and are a testament to his teaching and mentoring over the years. They reflect Grover's insight about the conversations medieval authors had with one another over disparate times, and his interest in lesser-known figures as well as canonical authors. They also reflect the love of learning that Grover inspired in all his students, both published and not. He has kept the conversation moving forward, with harmony.

NOTES

1. Zinn, "Mandala Symbolism," 318.
2. Zinn, *Richard of St Victor*.
3. Clare Kirchenberger published several treatises and parts of the *Benjamin minor* (*The Twelve Patriarchs*) and the *Benjamin Major* (*The Mystical Ark*) in her

Richard of St Victor, but Grover was the first to offer a full translation of both. Kirchenberger also includes the first English translation of Richard's *Of the Four Degrees of Violent Charity.* Grover's was the first translation in English of any part of Richard's *De Trinitate* to appear in print until Boyd Taylor Coolman and Dale M. Coulter edited *Trinity and Creation,* and Ruben Angelici published *Richard of St. Victor: On the Trinity.*

Preface

Few times and places in Christian history have left a legacy of intellectual, imaginative, and artistic splendor comparable to that of twelfth- and thirteenth-century France. The founding of the Abbey of St. Victor in Paris by William of Champeaux in 1108 was the beginning of a period of intellectual fervor that was ended only by a new beginning: the foundation of the University of Paris in the late twelfth century, an institution originally formed by St. Victor and two other Parisian schools. The noted scholars of St. Victor, especially Hugh, Richard, and Andrew, set many of the most important intellectual trends of medieval Christianity. These men were Augustinian canons who lived a mixed life of contemplation, learning, and interest in the wider world. St. Victor was thus home to Hugh's important advances in biblical studies, Richard's soaring mystical theology, and Andrew's openness to ideas from the Jewish intellectual tradition—though elements of each can be found in the work of all three. The career of Grover A. Zinn has in large part focused on these scholars and their sources, and we offer here a collection of essays on related topics as a book honoring his contributions to the field.

The title of this volume, *From Knowledge to Beatitude*, is a quotation from Hugh of St. Victor's *Didascalicon*. It illustrates Hugh's belief that the knowledge of the schoolroom was only the first step—albeit an essential one—in a longer journey towards wisdom, which came with deeper knowledge of God. The aim of all intellectual life was the beatific vision, and so learning that did not have that as a goal was worthless. Everyone who knows Grover Zinn will recognize this as his philosophy, too: knowledge for its own sake is dusty unless it contributes towards the development of the whole person.

Nevertheless, Hugh—like Grover Zinn—believed that the first step could not be overlooked: indeed, he famously noted, "Learn everything; later you will see that nothing is superfluous." The house of knowledge could not be built without foundations, and these were laid down by considering the literal meanings of texts. Thus it seems appropriate that our volume begins with four essays that examine the material culture of the Abbey of St. Victor. Catherine Delano-Smith's opening essay begins with some of the manuscripts made at St. Victor, in particular, the copies of Richard of St. Victor's *In visionem Ezechielis*. Drawing on her knowledge of the study of medieval maps and diagrams, she underlines the important point that, without the maps and other drawings found in medieval manuscripts (and yet often overlooked in studies and editions), readers using modern printed versions cannot understand the texts in the same way that medieval readers did. Her focus on Richard of St. Victor's *In visionem Ezechielis* brings this argument directly into the world of medieval biblical commentary studied by Grover Zinn, and reminds us that reading and commenting on the Bible was the cornerstone of the life of St. Victor's scholars and their primary means of working.

Walter Cahn's contribution considers the interest of probably the most important of St. Victor's scholars, Hugh, in religious imagery in the broadest sense, including placing manual arts on the same level as intellectual pursuits. This elicits a comparison to Suger, abbot of the royal church of St. Denis, just outside Paris. Although Cahn cautions that Suger had a greater urgency than Hugh about issues of visual representation, it has been suggested that both Hugh and Suger held conceptions of art influenced by the writings of

Ps.-Dionysius. Focussing once more on contemporary (medieval) materials, Cahn calls our attention to a manuscript of the works of Hugh, Paris, Mazarine MS 729, that includes part of his commentary on the Ps.-Dionysian *Celestial Hierarchies*. It is the work of an extraordinary artist whose identity (like so many of the Middle Ages) is unknown, but that is certainly worthy of further research.

Moving to the abbey itself, William Clark's essay reexamines the sources for the construction of St. Victor and concludes that this edifice, which has totally vanished from the Parisian landscape, was of an "audacious" size, larger and longer than every church in Paris except the cathedral until the expansion of the rival churches of St. Denis and St. Germain-des-Prés in the mid-twelfth century. Thomas Waldman's essay on the 1131 Privilege of Pope Innocent II to the Abbey of St. Denis argues that this document supported Abbot Suger's plans for the magnificent expansion and decoration of his edifice. The survival of historical materials, even those as big as a church, is always a matter of chance, especially in a country famed for its anticlerical revolution. The disappearance of St. Victor must be a matter of regret for historians; but it illustrates how fortunate we are to have the textual evidence of the vivid life that its Augustinian canons lived.

The next set of four essays shifts to life and learning in twelfth-century Paris, although St. Victor remains a particular focus. Franklin Harkins highlights Grover Zinn's analysis of the educational works of Hugh of St. Victor, as he taught the novices of St. Victor that study and prayer belonged together, just as the literal sense of scripture could reveal the tropological, or moral, meaning of the biblical text. Lesley Smith tells the story of a little-known twelfth-century Parisian master, Robert Amiclas, who left twenty volumes of glossed biblical texts to the English Cistercian abbey of Buildwas. The annotations and corrections in these manuscripts give a clear picture of one Parisian master's care to collect an up-to-date version of glossed books of the Bible in the period before a standard *Glossa ordinaria*. This effort shows some important aspects of glossed Bibles in Paris during the glory days of St. Victor, even though the volumes survive in one collection only because they were transported to rural Shropshire. Reminding us that the life of the Victorine community was one of pastoral involvement as well as scholarship, Hugh Feiss opens a consideration of canons as part of the new pastoral initiatives of the reforming church of the twelfth century. Feiss shows that the canons were involved in preaching as well as in prayer and meditation, and that this preaching, especially when directed to the laity rather than to fellow religious, did not follow the tradition of literal interpretation of the biblical text for which the school is so famous. Feiss' essay makes us consider whether the academic strictures of the classroom had a place in the canons' practical ministry, or whether the two sides of their community were kept apart. Finally, Boyd Taylor Coolman shows how Hugh of St. Victor developed an understanding of the beauty of the soul in relationship to the ideal of measure—not only the measure expected of all religious in bodily comportment, but also of intellectual measure.

Our third set of essays considers twelfth-century spirituality and learning in ever-broader circles. Some of these focus on an inherited philosophical or spiritual tradition, such as Dale Coulter's comparison of contemplation as "speculation" in Boethius and Hugh and Richard of St. Victor, Marcia Colish's tracing of the Stoic idea of *synderesis*, or first principles, in relation to conscience to the thirteenth century, and Dominique Poirel's explication of the influence of Ps.-Dionysius in Hugh of St. Victor's spirituality and theology of beauty. Barbara Newman and Rachel Fulton Brown both focus on medieval women visionaries, Newman on the *topos* of the mystical exchange of hearts from Heloise to the nuns of Helfta in the thirteenth century, and Fulton Brown on Hildegard of Bingen's concept of revelation as a coherent, even systematic theology.

The final four essays range farther afield in their guiding questions, and in some cases also in chronology. Jeremy Adams considers the reactions of several important ecclesiastical figures of northern France, including Suger of St. Denis, to the violent behavior of some returning soldiers of the First Crusade, arguing that these varied reactions set the stage for "the reformist monastic attitude toward violence that affected decisively so much of medieval history in the aftermath of the millennium." He shows us that the twelfth century cannot be characterized solely in terms of "renaissance," which make it seem a time of such positive and innovative growth. Expansion and confidence had an equally dark side, which found an outlet in violence and psychopathy. Frans Van Liere also considers an aspect of the Crusades, evaluating their effects on Christian understanding of medieval Jewish expectations of the coming of the Messiah who would overturn Christian hegemony. Although the scholars of St. Victor may have studied the prophets with Jewish scholars, Van Liere points out that they did not see, nor wish for, the same things, and that, in fact, mutual study could lead to polemic as well as understanding. The apparent openness of some Victorines scholars to Jewish ideas can be deceptive, if we imagine that it took place in a context of toleration and acceptance.

Returning to Hildegard of Bingen, Raymond Clemens demonstrates how in 1513 the Humanist scholar Jacques Lefèvre d'Étaples published the first printed edition of Hildegard's *Scivias* in a work entitled *Liber trium virorum et trium spiritualium*, perhaps primarily as part of an attack on scholasticism, but with the result of making a space for the serious study of women (and some men) visionaries, the origin of our modern Hildegard of Bingen industry. Clemens' focus on the material culture of the book—albeit now the printed page—takes us full circle from Delano-Smith's consideration of Victorine manuscripts. But Ann Matter lets us finish with a musical coda: her essay wanders all the way to the eighteenth-century Lutheran spirituality evident in Johann Sebastian Bach's Cantata 140, *Wachet Auf!* to show the far-reaching influence of the mystical treatises of twelfth-century authors such as Richard of St. Victor.

These are, then, a varied set of essays, on topics ranging from the exegetical school of twelfth-century St. Victor and medieval glossed Bibles to the medieval cultural reception of women visionaries, preachers, and crusaders. The thread they have in common is Grover Zinn's careful attention to the connection between medieval spirituality and biblical studies, where these ideas originated, and their lasting influence in Christian culture. They take us from Hugh of St. Victor's foundation—material culture—to the "beatitude" of a wider understanding of Victorine culture and its lasting legacy. They are offered to him with gratitude for the ways in which he has encouraged so many scholars to follow their ideas with confidence and joy.

The editors are grateful to soon-to-be-Dr. Brian Fitzgerald for his calm, careful, and cheerful help, especially with the bibliography. Andrew Zinn gave us permission to use his lovely photograph of his father as our frontispiece. We are also grateful to the William R. Kenan, Jr. Foundation for subvention of some of the expenses involved in the production of the book, particularly of the images.

CATHERINE DELANO-SMITH

1 Maps and Plans in Medieval Exegesis
Richard of St. Victor's *In visionem Ezechielis*

Drawing for explanation was nothing new in the Middle Ages. A millennium or so earlier, classical authors had illustrated their scientific and didactic treatises with drawings to aid understanding and memorization.[1] How many of the medieval copies we read today contain the original author's design, as opposed to a copyist's insertion or amendment, is unclear. The most reliable indication of authorial intent is an explicit reference in the text to an accompanying illustration, since the verbal allusion tends to continue to be copied even when the drawing is omitted and the space for it closed up. Whether the drawing matches the author's intent in every detail is another matter; later copyists were liable to update the drawing in the light of the knowledge or opinions of their day.[2] Just occasionally, however, there is every reason to believe that the drawings that have come down to us do indeed follow the author's originals, either because the manuscript is an autograph or because circumstantial evidence has led to scholarly consensus that the surviving illustrations convey exactly, or essentially, the author's intentions. The maps, plans, and elevations in Richard of St. Victor's treatise on the book of the prophet Ezekiel, *In visionem Ezechielis*, are a case in point.

The existence of twenty-two manuscripts of the full text of Richard's treatise on Ezekiel, together with one extract, can be confirmed at the time of writing (see appendix 1).[3] All contain illustrations or (in one case) spaces for illustrations (see appendix 2), fifteen in total, consistently positioned.[4] Not every drawing has been completed, nor is every manuscript intact.[5] Furthermore, stylistic variations within some manuscripts suggests that the labor of illustration may have been shared out, with maps and plans produced by one scribe or artist and elevations by another.[6] Overall, though, and despite minor stylistic differences, the illustrations form a cohesive, predictable, and generally complete corpus. Only one figure from the middle of the work, to which we shall return, is consistently missing in all but two of the twenty-two full manuscripts.[7]

The focus in this essay is on Richard of St. Victor's plans and map, rather than the elevations to which Walter Cahn has already paid particular attention (see appendix 2).[8] I begin, however, with a discussion of what visual exegesis involves and a summary of the salient aspects of Christian exegetical drawing before the twelfth century before focusing on Richard's plans of the visionary Temple and his map of Canaan restored to the Israelites. I conclude with reference to Nicholas of Lyra's drawings for Ezekiel.

DRAWING FOR EXPLANATION

Exegetical drawing is by definition intimately related to the text of the commentary. Unlike narrative illustration, which may be integrated with the scriptural text, exegetical drawing belongs to writings *about* the Holy Word and is confined to glosses, postils, and treatises. Within such commentary, each drawing is placed as close as possible to the specific comment to which it relates. In one sense, thus, the exegetical drawing duplicates what was written. In another sense, the visual directness of the exegetical drawing's schematic style, and its unambiguous message, ensures instant and efficient communication between author and reader.

In general the tendency today is to amalgamate reference to exegetical and other didactic illustrations into the single word "diagram," to avoid the ponderous "in diagrammatic style."[9] However it is expressed, we are referring to a visually economical construct in which everything is reduced or distilled to the barest minimum consistent with the efficient communication of the point being made: content is minimal; lines are straight or boldly curving, shorn of all irregularity or aesthetic fussiness; and potentially distracting content is eliminated. In essence, drawing for explanation is drawing in answer to a specific question that the reader has asked, or is being encouraged to ask, as part of the discourse. The question may be implicit in the title, if there is one, or explicit in the text or context.

Diagrammatically styled maps and plans are by definition topological constructions. Accuracy of contiguity—not size, direction, or shape—is the critical factor; mathematical scale and angle are irrelevant. As long as that which is next to something is shown as next to it, the map or plan is accurate. This is not to say that scientific precision has to be completely ignored. If the author wants it, dimensions can be given alongside the relevant lines or in an adjacent note. Otherwise they are in the text. Thus, in the seventh century, in his *De locis sanctis*, Adamnán supplied what he said were Arculf's firsthand measurements from the Church of the Holy Sepulchre in Jerusalem, saying that Christ's tomb as measured with the hand had been found to be seven feet long and that the side of the sepulchre was about three palms high.[10] Richard of St. Victor included a geometrical diagram in *In visionem Ezechielis*, with angles labelled A, B, C, D, etc., to demonstrate how the buildings of Ezekiel's Temple could be accommodated to the sloping ground of the mountain, explaining his calculations in the text below the diagram.[11] In 1168 the Jewish exegete Maimonides annotated his profile of Herod's Temple with figures, giving the height of the terraces that rose from outside the outer wall to the Holy of Holies on the summit of the mountain.[12] In other instances, a general impression of relative height or distance sufficed. Richard reminded his readers: "For when we look at lines drawn in proportion to the measurements . . . , it is easily inferred."[13] Later, Nicholas of Lyra was likewise always anxious to convey the correct "proportions," given the problems, as he repeatedly pointed out, of rendering three-dimensional features on a flat surface (*in plano*).[14]

In contrast to such emphasis on literal measurement, the labelling of cardinal points in exegetical drawing only sometimes had a literal role. The function of the map of Canaan for Joshua 13–19 was indeed a geographical exposition of the location of the tribal territories in relation to boundaries and major natural features (the Jordan River, Sea of Galilee and Dead Sea) and the relative positions of major settlements (such as Jerusalem and Jericho) as described in the text. In such cases the cardinal directions are needed not only to match the drawing to the text but also to indicate which way up the map is placed on the page. (Which way up a local or regional map is presented has no intrinsic importance, and maps were orientated in any direction up to the later sixteenth century.) The same may be said of the map of Canaan envisioned by Ezekiel (Ez 45 and 48), which shows an idealistic division of the land amongst the Twelve Tribes. Elsewhere, however, and notably in discussions of the layout of Moses' Tabernacle (Ex 40), the disposition of the tribes around the Tabernacle in the desert (Nm 2–3), and Ezekiel's Temple (Ez 40–47), the labelling of the wind directions had allegorical significance.[15]

Gregory had followed Augustine in associating the earthly cardinal points with things of the spiritual realm, noting that the north, source of glacial winds, symbolised the spirit of evil; the east evoked the light shed by Christ over the whole world; and the south, the life-giving heat of the Holy Spirit.[16] For Bede, the north designated "that multitude of the Gentiles that did not cease to languish in the darkness and cold of unbelief right up to the time of the Lord's incarnation."[17] For Nicholas of Lyra, it was the direction from which came misfortune in the form of "the Babylonians (Chaldeans) who would enter Judea . . . as prophesied by Isaiah and Jeremiah."[18] The repeated emphasis on the east in the scriptures in connection with the Tabernacle and the Temple was no accident, and the careful labelling of the cardinal directions in Richard's plans of the Temple conveyed deep symbolism: the east faces not only "the sun's rising" but also the point of entry of "the bright presence of the God of Israel," whose presence lit up the entire earth in splendor.[19]

Unwary or uninitiated readers, in the past as today, may find the typical exegetical map or plan, with its uncompromising straight lines, emptiness, and "lack of realism," a visual disappointment.[20] On occasion one gets the impression that a particular medieval illustrator strove to disguise his despair over such artistic inelegance by minimizing the didactic and emphasizing instead the decorative role of the drawings he had been set to copy for a presentation volume.²¹ In general, though, the integrity of exegetical drawing in theological commentary was respected. Even magnificently illuminated copies of Nicholas of Lyra's *Postilla litteralis* do not usually attempt to disguise the fact that the illustrations they contain were all created for exegesis, not for ornamentation, although the passing of time meant that later illuminators may not always have understood the exegetical significance of their work.

BEFORE RICHARD OF ST. VICTOR

The earliest pointer to the use of drawing in Christian writing on a biblical topic dates from about 302 CE when Eusebius, bishop of Caesarea, was completing his major historical work "On the Place-Names in Holy Scripture" (*Onomasticon*). In the preface to the fourth and only surviving book, Eusebius tells the reader that his text contained, in addition to a list of names of peoples outside the Holy Land, an "engraving" of ancient Judea "from the information given in the Scriptures, with its division amongst the Twelve Tribes," and a "figura" or plan of Jerusalem and its Temple with comments explaining the sites.²² Nothing survives of Eusebius' map or plan, nor of anything identifiable as a derivative, but it may be assumed, given the essentially historical nature of the whole work, that the map of Judea showed the tribal territories as allocated by Joshua after the Israelites' conquest of Canaan (Jo 35) and that the city plan represented the Herodian Temple, destroyed by the Romans in 70 CE. Although the *Onomasticon* was not a textual commentary so much as a historical account supported by lists of place-names, it may also be speculated that the style of Eusebius' cartography would have been diagrammatic, at least to some extent.

Not every biblical plan was necessarily exegetical in function. The role of the plan in the front of the mid sixth-century *Codex Amiatinus*—a compound of two plans, one of the Tabernacle of Moses with all furnishings and utensils in place (Ex 40), the other the encampment of the tribes around the Tabernacle in the desert (Nm 2)—is unclear.²³ The illumination matches the relevant biblical descriptions as regards content and layout, but it is not part of an exposition or commentary; the codex contains only the Holy Scriptures. The plan's position at the front of the codex suggests it may have been an aid to contemplation, much as were the later carpet pages of Sephardic Bibles that also depicted the Tabernacle utensils.[24] Nor was every late antique exegetical drawing after Eusebius confined to Latin commentators. In Egypt, at much the same time as Cassiodorus was working on his Great Pandect in southern Italy, the supposed author of the lavishly illustrated *Christian Topography* (c. 547/549), Cosmas Indicopleustes, showed the uncovered Tabernacle and utensils in one plan and the disposition of the tribes around it in their desert encampment in another.[25]

Enough has survived to indicate that exegetical drawing in the Latin West was regular practice for those so inclined throughout Late Antiquity and the Middle Ages. Evidence for lines of transmission, however, is missing and usually disconnected. Not one given to drawing in explanation, Bede illustrated neither his treatise on the Tabernacle (*De tabernaculo, c.* 720) nor that on Solomon's Temple (*De templo, c.* 725) despite having had plenty of opportunity to study Cassiodorus' Tabernacle plan (or at least the version being prepared in his own monastery for the Codex Amiatinus). The three plans in his work on the holy places (*De locis sanctis*, 702/3) came, with some modification, from Adamnán's late-seventh-century treatise of the same title.[26] Yet also originating (possibly) in the eighth century is the earliest known surviving exegetical map of the land of Canaan, the *Figura terre repromissionis*, which represents the historical division of Canaan (Jo 15) in typically diagrammatic style.[27] And a plan of the Tabernacle for Exodus 40 made at Kirkham, Lincolnshire, in the twelfth century recalls that in the Codex Amiatinus.[28] But no Christian commentary on the whole Bible, such as the Gloss (widely used by scholars by 1150) and the commentaries by Stephen Langton (before 1228) and Hugh of St. Cher (available in full probably by, or soon after, 1240) was illustrated until Nicholas of Lyra's *Postilla litteralis* (1323–32).

EXEGETICAL MAPPING BETWEEN EUSEBIUS AND RICHARD OF ST. VICTOR

What is known is that a small number of Christian exegetes in the twelfth and thirteenth centuries turned to their Jewish counterparts to shed light on the interpretation of the Bible by reference to the Hebrew text and to a

Jewish authority on the Hebrew Bible and the Talmud, the commentaries of Rabbi Solomon ben Isaac, better known as Rashi (1030/40–1105). In so doing, they were likely to encounter Rashi's exegetical drawings.

Rashi made liberal use of drawing as an aid in explanation.[29] Mayer Gruber has identified at least eight maps and plans in addition to portrayals of the Tabernacle utensils, the architecture and furnishings of Solomon's Temple, the representation of Jericho as a labyrinth, and several other subjects, which were all originally keyed into the text.[30] Amongst these were two maps of the historical Canaan for the book of Joshua and two maps of the visionary Canaan for the book of Ezekiel, the second of which was used by Richard of St. Victor. Although Rashi did not produce a drawing of Ezekiel's Temple for his commentary, he did at some stage send a plan to the rabbis of Auxerre.[31] Later than Rashi, and roughly contemporary with Richard of St. Victor, was Maimonides (Moses ben Maimon, 1135–1204) another leading Jewish commentator whose autograph manuscript (dated 1167/8) contains ten plans, three cross-sections, and five other figures within the twenty or so folios devoted to the *Middot* (*Measures*) of the apartments and furnishings of the Herodian Temple.[32] In view of the contact between Jewish and Christian scholars at the abbey of St. Victor in Paris, it is not surprising how many of the Jewish illustrations passed into Christian biblical commentary through Richard.

RICHARD OF ST. VICTOR'S DRAWINGS

Richard's *In visionem Ezechielis* is devoted to the third of Ezekiel's great visions, that of the Temple. The treatise opens with a lengthy introduction in which Richard explains his approach to the book as a whole and says something about the prophet's first vision of the four wheels and four beasts, the usual subject of commentary on the book of Ezekiel up to then (notably by Gregory in the fourth century and, at St. Victor in Richard's day, by Hugh and Andrew). It closes with some verses from Ezekiel and interlinear gloss relating to the reapportionment of Canaan amongst the Twelve Tribes on their return from exile in Babylon. Nineteen of the twenty numbered chapters comprising *In visionem Ezechielis* are devoted to the Temple itself. Likewise, all Richard's drawings relate in some way to that structure. The map of

Canaan at the end provides the wider context for Temple and city, and is an integral element of both Ezekiel's verbal account and Richard's cartographical exegesis.

It is generally accepted that Richard of St. Victor was responsible for all the drawings in his treatise on Ezekiel, and indeed the consistency with which they are reproduced in manuscript after manuscript must surely confirm Richard's imprimatur, or at least respect for his authority. In the early part of the treatise each drawing is unambiguously keyed into the text. Phrases such as "We represent the shape of these things that we have already described in this manner" or, more fully, "for the greater clarity of what has been said, and what needs to be said, we here bring together in one figure all that has been said in separate parts above," as well as the brief "as in this manner," introduce seven of the eight figures before chapter 15.[33] After the geometrical diagram that comes early in chapter 15, however, Richard stops this practice and none of the following elevations is so introduced, nor is the plan of the sanctuary, the lateral view of the altar, or the map of Canaan.

Richard makes no secret of the primary function of his drawings, which is to convince the reader of the truth of his statements. The geometrical figure used to show his method of calculating the angles involved in building on steeply sloping land is introduced as "proof" of his argument: "For the present, we give some evidence by which anybody, no matter how simple, can satisfy himself of the truth of our assertion."[34] In other cases, the persuasion is subtler: if "we present the argument to the eye" and it can be "inferred" by the reader "from the drawn lines," the reader is more likely to understand and accept the point being made.[35] Convincing the reader was important to Richard. Concluding his illustrated exposition of the eastern gate he remarks: "If anyone by chance would accuse me of prolixity in this exposition, let him consider, I beseech, whether he is right in so doing. But to speak the truth, I would rather be fastidious for the more subtle [reader] than obscure for the slower in mind, especially in such an obscure matter in which almost everything that is said needs proof rather than exposition."[36]

Did Richard lack self-confidence, or was he simply realistically appreciating the challenge of attempting what Gregory had proclaimed to be impossible, namely, to arrive at a literal understanding of the book of Ezekiel? For the Christian Richard in the mid-twelfth century (and Nicholas of Lyra in the 1320s), as for the Jewish Rashi in the eleventh century, a satisfactory allegorical interpretation of the Bible could come only from a sound grasp and good understanding of the text's literal meaning. Moreover, for all three scholars, understanding the literal meaning of passages detailing complex spatial relationships demanded visual as well as written exegesis, and all three expositions are, as we have noted, liberally illustrated.[37] Ten of Richard's drawings are ichnographic (that is, drawn as if viewed from vertically above), four are cross sections or elevations, and one is the geometrical diagram already mentioned (see appendix 2). The architectural elevations show the façade and one side of the eastern gatehouse, the side of the building that lay to the north of the Temple, and the altar of holocausts. Cahn has suggested that Richard's "coordination of the plan with the frontal and lateral elevations for the Temple gatehouse" was "unprecedented as a method of architectural representation" and not generally practised until Leon Battista Alberti's time.[38]

It is evident from the text of Ezekiel that visual thinking had come naturally to the prophet. Quite apart from the "seeing" of visions, Ezekiel early on recounts how he was instructed in his second vision to create a drawing and a three-dimensional model in order to demonstrate the besieging of the city by its enemies: "go and get a tile; set it before thee and make marks on it, to represent the city of Jerusalem. . . . And therewithal get thee an iron-cooking pan, that shall make a ring of iron between thee and this city of thine; look closely as thou wilt, here is the siege complete" (Ez 4:1–3).[39] Ezekiel spent many years in exile in Babylon, and it is not unreasonable to suppose that he would have been well acquainted with ancient Mesopotamian mapmaking. This has been suggested by Helen Rosenau, who sees the prophet's verbal description as based not only on an existing ground plan but also inspired by plans such as the measured outline of a Temple inscribed on the tablet held by the statue of Gudea, prince of Lagash (c. 2141–22 BC).[40] In similar vein, Mayer Gruber hypothesises that a cuneiform map of the ancient Egyptian province of Canaan lay at the origin of Rashi's maps for Joshua 34.[41]

THE TEMPLE PLANS

Representations of the Tabernacle and the different Temples are often confused. The earliest historical structure was the portable tented Tabernacle of Moses that housed the ark of the covenant during the Exodus. Once the

Israelites had settled in Canaan, the ark was placed in the innermost sanctum of the stone Temple built by King Solomon in Jerusalem. After the destruction of Solomon's Temple by the Babylonians in 586 BCE, a second Temple was erected. The third historical Temple was Herod's, constructed in the last century BCE. Ezekiel's Temple was probably no more than a vision, a mental construct, although some of its features could have been inspired by what was remembered of the first Temple. In ancient Judaism, where the Temple was the central cultic institution, representations of the Temple referred invariably to the Herodian building.[42] Even Rashi, who drew a plan of the Tabernacle (for Ex 35) and elevations of Solomon's Temple (for 3 Kings), left no detailed ground plan of that first Temple.[43] Likewise, the drawings in Maimonides' commentary concern Herod's Temple.[44] In Christianity, where the Temple held a special place, it was its symbolic significance that mattered more than whether it was Solomon's or Herod's building. For Augustine, it was a "type and figure of the future Church and the body of the Lord," signifying the faithful.[45] For Bede, whereas "the Tabernacle is the time of the synagogue (that is, of the ancient people of God)," "the Temple signifies the Church."[46] Bede also likened the Tabernacle to the present Church and the Temple to the future Church.[47]

Richard of St. Victor was concerned neither with Moses' Tabernacle nor with either of the great historic Temples (Solomon's or Herod's), but with the mountain-top complex envisioned by Ezekiel and described in confusing, and at times contradictory, detail in Ezekiel 40–47.[48] This Temple was so extensive that it resembled a city with the Temple proper—containing the sanctuary (*sanctum*) and the Holy of Holies (*sanctum sanctorum*)—at its heart. The overall structure of Richard's treatise is logical enough. He proceeds from the general—the outlines of the three precincts or courts—to the detail of the inner rooms, by way of the eastern gatehouse, before returning to the general to close by setting the whole complex into its broader territorial context within the Holy Land in the final chapters (Ez 47–48). Within this framework, discussions of further details, such as the kitchens (chap. 12) and the altar of holocausts (chap. 19), are interpolated, together with the appropriate illustrations.

Richard's plans vary in their complexity. Several are simple. His first figure (for chapter 1) gives the basic arrangement of three precincts or courts, from outermost (into which the common people were allowed) to innermost (accessible only to priests). Another (figure 4, introduced towards the end of chapter 3) is also simple. It outlines the outer wall with a gate on three of the sides. The gates, rendered in profile and shown as rectangular in some manuscripts or with rounded arches in others, are surmounted by a tower with windows, conical roof, and, inevitably, a round finial. Other plans are comparatively detailed. Figure 2 (introduced in the final sentence of chapter 1) gives the layout of the eastern part of the middle court. It depicts a T-shaped arrangement of rectangles and squares indicating the relative positions of the main buildings, their monumental gates and entrances, and the paved areas in between. At the bottom of the plan (no orientation is given) is a *porticus* that we take to be the eastern gate (Ez 40), to which Richard devoted a good deal of attention. He illustrated his discussion with three plans and two elevations in chapters 15 and 17 and explained his calculations of the architectural angles involved in constructing such an edifice on a steep slope with reference to the geometrical diagram.[49]

Richard's third figure, another detailed plan introduced at the end of chapter 2, shows what lay beyond the eastern gate (fig. 1.1). From this gate the reader is led into a large paved area (*pavimentum stratum lapide*) flanked on both sides by a row of fifteen rooms or parlors (*gazophylacia*), not differentiated in this diagram. This is the outer court (*atrium exterius*) of other plans. At the far end, at right angles to the yard and its parlors, ran a paved alley (*via*) overlooked by further rows of parlors that linked the northern and southern gates of the inner precinct. It was interrupted in the middle by the small court (*atrium interius*, in which, we learn from the other plans, stood the altar of holocausts) of the inner gatehouse (*porticus interior*) that provided access, to those for whom it was permitted, from the main paved yard to the Temple proper (*templum*). The interior layout of the Temple is not indicated on this diagram, nor is the altar of incense that stood in the middle room, the sanctuary, beyond which was the Holy of Holies at the western end. Outside the Temple proper lay two free-standing houses (*domus australis, domus aquilonis*, respectively). Behind the Temple, between it and the precinct wall, was a third independent building (*aedificium separatum*) with a vestibule at each end. There is no western gate in the wall of the precinct, but the identification of the other three (*porticus orientalis, porticus australis, porticus aquilonis*), like that of the two free-standing houses, confirms the orientation.

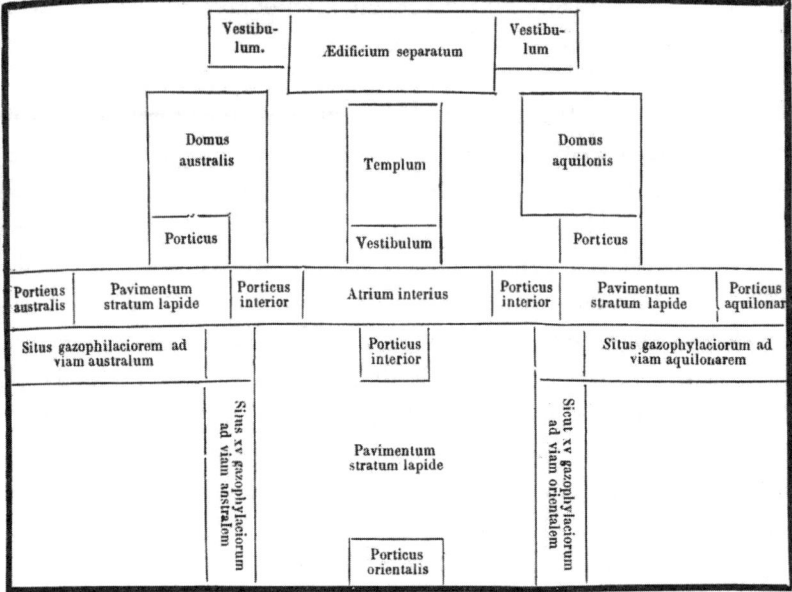

Figure 1.1. Richard of St. Victor, *In visionem Ezechielis*. Plan for chapter 2 of Richard's treatise showing the general layout of the Temple complex. Redrawing taken from *Patrologia Latina* volume 196 to aid identification of the buildings mentioned in this essay. The Temple (*templum*), which contains the sanctuary and the innermost sanctuary, or Holy of Holies, is sometimes itself referred to as the sanctuary. West is at the top. 10.5 × 14.5 cm. Reproduced with the permission of the British Library.

After detailed discussion of the eastern gate, illustrated by a further three ground plans, Richard turns to the inner parts of the complex (chaps. 8–14), reaching the sanctuary—the heart of the Temple and the climax of both Ezekiel (Ez 41:4: *hoc est sanctum sanctorum*) and *In visionem Ezechielis*— only three-quarters of the way through chapter 15. These chapters include a description of the tables on which offerings were to be placed and sacrifices offered (chap. 11) and of the kitchens where the sacrificial victims were to be washed and prepared for the ceremonies (chap. 12). A plan is alluded to at the end of chapter 12, but is not normally present in the manuscripts, and the text in most manuscripts runs straight on with the heading for chapter 13. Thus, after the geometrical diagram and the two elevations of the eastern gatehouse, the next plan comes at the end of chapter 15. This shows the Temple proper and is often accorded a full page, despite its relatively simple design (fig. 1.2).[50] It represents a rectangular structure subdivided into three rooms: the Temple vestibule; the relatively spacious main Temple area with the altar of incense (*altare incensi*) in the center; and, finally, the innermost holy of holies (*sanctum sanctorum*). As is Richard's style, the diagram is uncluttered, and labelling (often incomplete) is kept to a minimum. *In visionem Ezechielis* ends with a drawing of the altar of holocausts and the map of Canaan, for Richard neither discussed nor illustrated the nameless city, with its twelve tribal gates, with which Ezekiel concludes (Ez 48:30–35) and that Nicholas of Lyra would later illustrate.

Although nearly every known manuscript of *In visionem Ezechielis* lacks a plan for chapter 12, or even space for one, there is no doubt that Richard not only intended one but had indeed produced one. In the first place, the unambiguous reference to the plan in the final sentence of the chapter is preserved in every manuscript I have seen. Richard declares: "And of all these things of which we have spoken we express the form and model in a very new and large plan so that [all] may be seen there."[51] In the second place, an essentially identical plan is extant, in its correct place, in three manuscripts: Paris, BnF, lat. 2165, fols 40r–70r; Vatican City, BAV, Reg. Lat. 277, fols. 1r–34r; and Durham, Cathedral and Chapter Library, A.III.22, fols 2r–7r.[52]

It is difficult to say why the plan is consistently missing—omitted without space left for it—from so many manuscripts, despite the textual reference. Possibly a hint is contained in the subject matter discussed in the chapter the plan illustrates (chap. 12), which is usually headed "On the kitchens."[53] The chapter opens with Richard's observation that the kitchens were not shown on any earlier plans, although they could have been. He follows this with a quotation from Ezekiel 46:23: "and here under an open roof kitchens were built." The critical point for Richard, however, comes from a different chapter, Ezekiel 40:38, in which reference is made to the need to purge and wash animals destined for sacrifice. To the practical-minded canon, bent on a literal exposition, such washing, and all preparation of meat, implied an adequate water supply. The question, then, was where were the kitchens located, and from where did the water come?

The only water mentioned in scripture in connection with Ezekiel's vision of the Temple is the stream described in Ezekiel 47. The first two verses

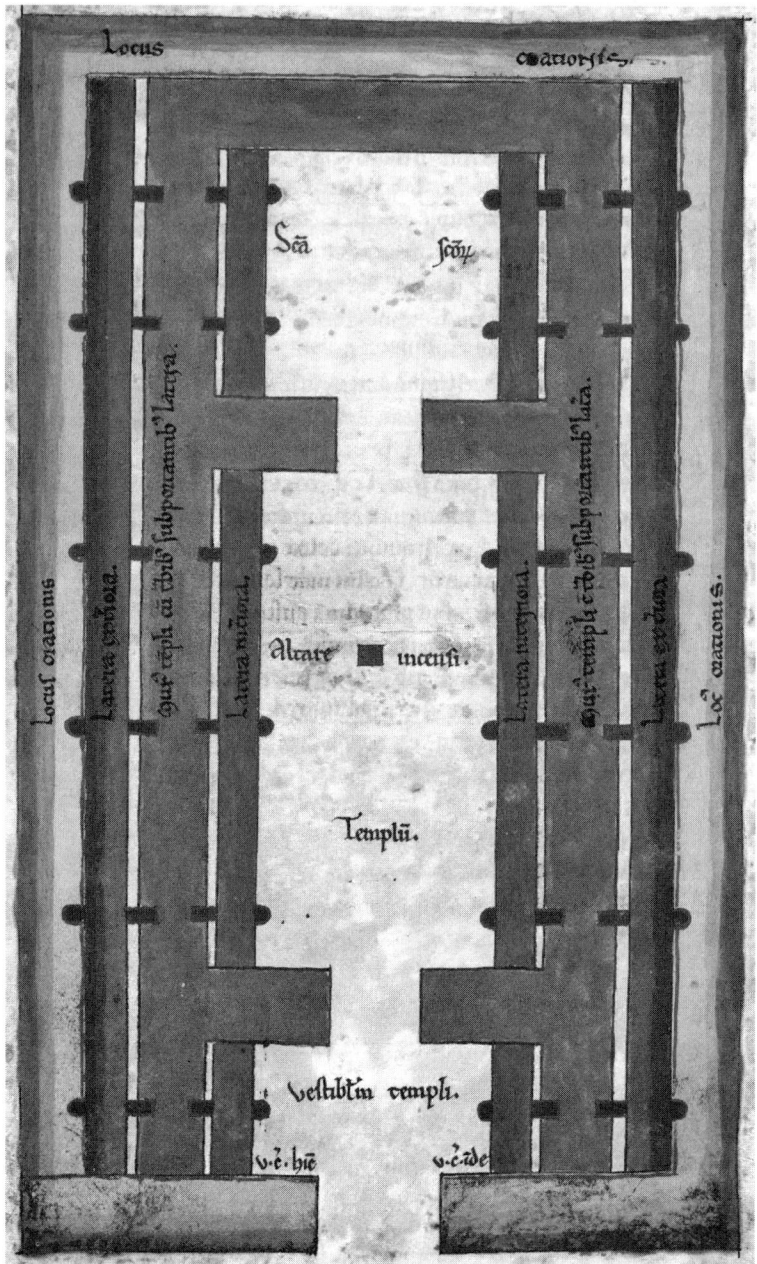

Figure 1.2. Richard of St. Victor, *In visionem Ezechielis*. Plan for chapter 16 from a late twelfth-century manuscript showing the Temple proper with the altar of incense in the main room or sanctuary. The measurements of the door jamb ("five cubits here," "five cubits thence") accord with those given in Ez 40:48. West is at the top. 20 × 12 cm. Oxford, Bodleian Library, Ms Bodl. 494, fol. 158v. Reproduced with the permission of the Bodleian Library.

of that chapter relate how the prophet was shown how the waters that emerged from beneath the threshold of the Temple sanctuary to flow "eastwards . . . somewhat to the Temple's right, so as to pass by the southern side of the altar [of holocausts]" and out, eventually, through the eastern gate of the Temple complex, all the time gaining velocity and volume. As they flowed across the countryside, the deserts were transformed into fertile land and the water of the Dead Sea became sweet and rich in fish. For the church fathers and other early expositors, Ezekiel's sanctuary stream was the River of Life, a type for Christ's baptism, an allegory for salvation, and a symbol of the paradise to be regained.[54] More to the point here, however, is that the scriptural waters were without fail interpreted as constituting a *single* stream.

Richard's problem was to find an explanation of the way water reached each of the several (as he interpreted the scriptural text) kitchens in the Temple complex. To him, the source was obviously the sanctuary stream, except that one stream alone could not possibly reach all the kitchens, which lay in different directions and different precincts. Accordingly, Richard divided the stream, explaining:

> We make that water that issues from the Temple flow down in this atrium and descend on the right of the altar. But around the lower [parts] of the atrium we divide [the water] into four, and we lead it through the middle of the kitchens, so that it should pass through in front of the parlours (*gazophylacia*) so that there should be somewhere to wash the holocaust, as it is written: *and through each gazophylacium an entrance with the fronts of gates, and there they shall wash the holocaust* [Ez 40:38].[55]

Appreciating that his interpretation contradicted traditional exegesis and patristic authority, Richard stressed the novelty of his drawing, underlining — as quoted above — the fact that the plan was most new (*novissima*) and drawn large (in an *exemplar latius*) so that all could be shown clearly.[56] The plan for chapter 12 thus shows the eastern part of the Temple complex, from the threshold of the Temple proper at the top by the altar of holocausts, with the inner and outer eastern gatehouses, the kitchens (eight, according to Richard), and the sanctuary stream divided into four branches and forming a double-stemmed T as it passes through the Temple complex. A single stream is shown emerging from the sanctuary to pass to the right of the altar (as one looks, as if with Ezekiel and his guide, from the sanctuary towards the eastern gate), after which it divides into two. The two branches then divide again, diverging so that each of the outermost branches sweeps along the alley towards the northern and southern gates respectively after passing through first one kitchen and then another. The other two branches continue eastwards in parallel courses, passing first through the kitchens of the inner gatehouse, then along the sides of the outer, paved courtyard, and through the kitchens of the middle gatehouse.

Richard appears not to have completed his text by the time he died in 1173. The final chapter (chap. 20) of *In visionem Ezechielis* is uncharacteristically brief and contains only some of the material needed for the fuller exposition implied by the map that accompanies it in most manuscripts. Five verses (Ez 45:1–5) describing the future layout of the sanctified central portion of the land are quoted, with interlinear comment, but there is nothing on the dimensions of the whole country (Ez 45:6–8) or, even more critically, on the order and dimensions of the twelve tribal strips (Ez 48:1–29), also depicted on the map. One possibility is that completion of the branched-river plan for chapter 12 had been held up longer than the map for chapter 20, which is present in fourteen of the twenty-two full-length manuscripts (including Troyes, but not Paris, BnF, Ms lat. 14516). As already noted, that Richard intended from the outset to have a plan for chapter 12 is unquestionable, for the sentence describing it is present in every manuscript. Can we learn anything about the chronological order of production of the twelfth-century manuscripts of *In visionem Ezechielis* that will enable us to explain the missing illustration?[57]

As Richard promised, the map's size allows everything to be easily seen. The three manuscripts containing it form a group inasmuch as they alone contain the map, but they all differ in some way. Paris, BnF, lat. 2165 is a substantial codex containing a number of treatises, still in its medieval binding. It is catalogued as early thirteenth century and of unknown provenance. *In visionem Ezechielis* occupies folios 40r–70r. The plan is fully integrated into the manuscript. It is placed exactly where it should be, that is, immediately after the sentence announcing it, which here is at the bottom of a verso folio (fol. 55v); the plan occupies the entire following recto folio, thus facing the sentence announcing it, and the text continues on the next verso with chapter thirteen. As warned by Richard, the plan is indeed large (30.5 × 21 cm) and all details are clearly presented (see fig. 1.3). Indeed, it is one of the more arresting images in any *In visionem Ezechielis* manuscript I have seen. The

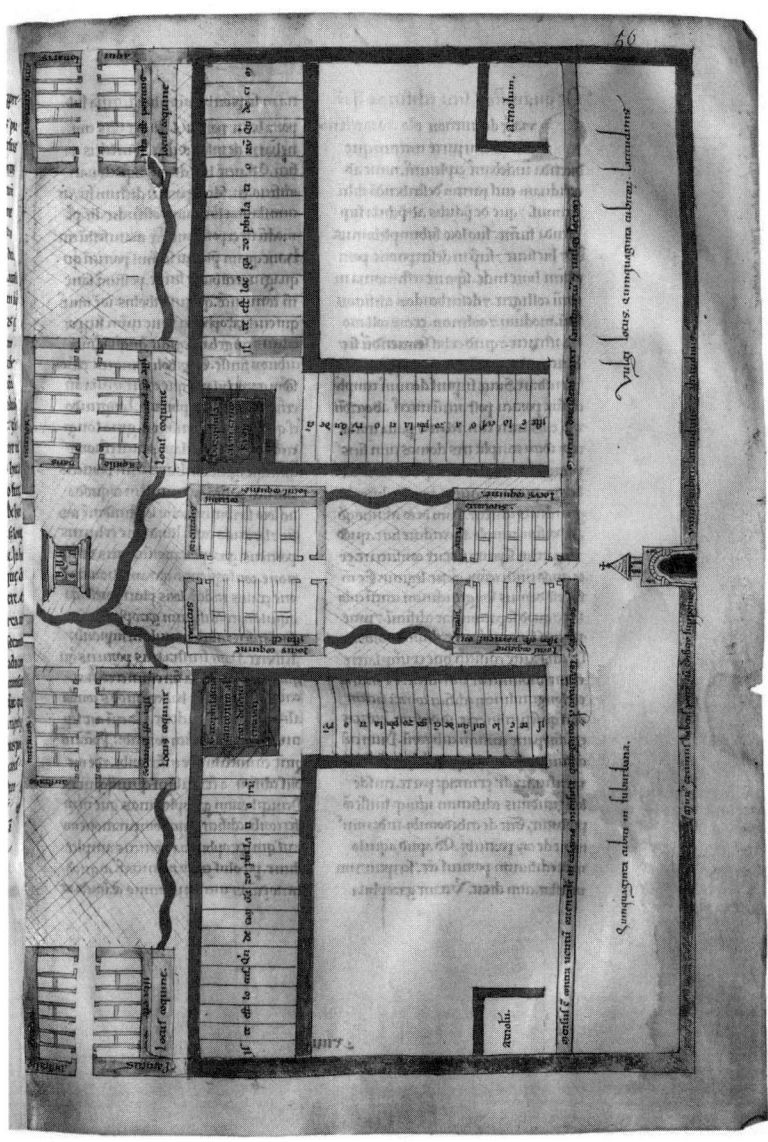

Figure 1.3. Richard of St. Victor, *In visionem Ezechielis*. Plan for chapter 12 from a thirteenth-century manuscript showing the eastern part of the Temple complex from the sanctuary threshold to the outermost gate. The stream emerges as a single course to flow eastwards, passing the altar of holocausts to the south (on its right), but then divides into four so that each kitchen (*locus coquine*) is supplied with water. North is at the top. 30.5 × 21cm. Paris, BnF, Ms lat. 2165, fol. 50r. Reproduced with the permission of the BnF.

layout is bold, and the bright colours, similar to those used on the other diagrams in the manuscript, have been deployed to emphasise different parts of the Temple complex. The four streams are in an eye-catching blue. Under the paint, the labelling of each of the eight kitchens (*locus coquine*) is legible.

Vatican City, BAV, Reg. Lat. 277 is another folio-sized codex, containing only *In visionem Ezechielis* (fols 1–32r). It was described in 1945 by André Wilmart, who gave chapter titles and the numbers of the folios on which illustrations occur, including folio 20 with its "very large picture" (17 × 25 cm) on a bifolium.[58] What Wilmart did not explain is that the bifolium is folded down the centre and bound into the codex in a manner that conceals the image inside. As the text continues uninterruptedly from folio 19v to 21r, it is not inconceivable that the plan could have been overlooked, especially by a reader in haste. The plan is identical to that in BnF, lat. 2165 except that there are no rivers and it appears to have been drawn with a little less attention to detail. But it includes something not on the Paris version— a sign used in three places to indicate, presumably, the direction of slope on the southeastern side of the Temple complex.[59] The sign is composed of a rough semicircle from which an arrow points downslope. No such signs are indicated on BnF, lat. 2165, but they are present (more neatly executed) on the third example of the plan, that in Durham, A. III.22.

The manuscript in Durham Cathedral and Chapter Library could not be more different from either BnF, lat. 2165 or BAV, Reg. Lat. 277. It is not a formal copy of the whole of *In visionem Ezechielis*, with carefully executed illustrations, but an extract on a few ill-shaped vellum leaves (fols. 2r–7v) now bound into a codex also containing the glossed books of Ezekiel and Daniel. These seven homely folios form, as Richard Gameson has put it, a self-contained booklet written by a single scribe on "conspicuously low quality parchment in a compact, highly abbreviated academic or glossing hand."[60] It was evidently made as economically as possible. Moreover, the scribe appears to have known exactly what he wanted from the illustrated exemplar from which he was copying, namely, only the chapters relating to the Temple and only the plans. He omitted the prologue, the final chapter, the four elevations, the geometric diagram, and the map of Canaan. He obviously copied the plans as he progressed, for they are tightly embedded within his writing in the expected positions. The plan for chapter 12, too, is placed where it should be with regard to the text. Richard's comment that it was an unusually large figure is respected even here, rough though the sketch is; at 6 × 4.5 cm the figure is much larger than any of the others in the booklet (fig. 1.4). The essentials of the layout are faithfully replicated, and the three signs indicating direction of slope are present in the same places as on BAV, Reg. Lat. 277. As on the other two versions of the plan, each of the eight kitchens is labelled and, as on the plan in BnF, lat. 2165, the branches of the boldly represented stream pass *through* the kitchens, not by them.

Jochen Schröder has suggested that the texts in the two earliest manuscripts, BnF, lat. 14516 (used to produce the edition in PL 196), and Troyes, MAT, 544, fols. 1–36, represent two different stages of Richard's thinking on Ezekiel recorded in a longer and a shorter version respectively.[61] The suggestion appears to be supported by a number of corrector's marginal insertions in Oxford, Bodleian Library, Ms e Mus. 62, at least eleven of which are headed *in alio libro* (in the other book). Since the text of Ms e Mus. 62 seems to me to conform to PL 196, this "other book" presumably contained the shorter recension that Schröder speculates may have been released before BnF, lat. 14516.[62] If we recognize as a group the three manuscripts containing the chapter twelve plan, we may also have to think in terms of *three* separate recensions of Richard's work. According to Schröder, too, Richard may have been working on his Ezekiel treatise much earlier than is usually assumed, possibly even in the early 1150s, when the manuscript that is now Troyes 544 appears to have arrived at Clairvaux abbey. The unavailability of Richard's figure 8 in the earliest stages of transmission, and subsequent diversity in details such as the indication of slope, would thus come as no surprise.

The omission of the four-river plan from so many manuscripts may be more puzzling, however, than at first thought. On the surface of it, all could be explained as a function of transmission: once the first two, authorial manuscripts (Troyes, MAT, 544; BnF, lat. 14516) left St. Victor without the plan, copies were likely to have been made in rapid succession, without space being left for the plan for chapter twelve. Questions niggle, though. Why was Richard so late in producing this one plan, especially when he was able to make sure the map of Canaan was present for the final chapter even before he had completed the text for that chapter? Was the four-river plan a particularly demanding creation, more so than the map of Canaan, which was (as described below) essentially a Latinized version of an existing Hebrew map? Above all, what exactly was the controversy—for controversy there

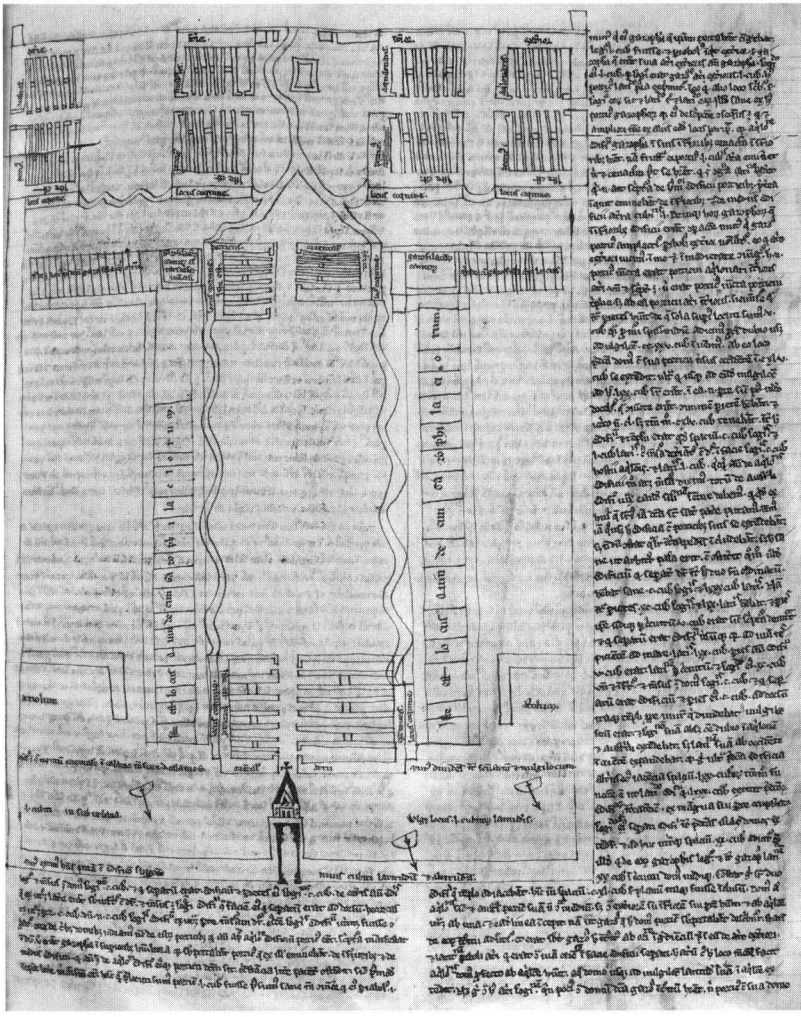

Figure 1.4. Richard of St. Victor, *In visionem Ezechielis*. Plan for chapter 12 in an abridged version of the treatise made, possibly in Paris, for personal use. The plan replicates faithfully almost every detail of its exemplar, whether this was BnF, Ms lat. 2165 (see fig. 1.3) or another. Note the three signs indicating the direction of slope in the outer precinct have been added. The inner and middle gates are shown in the plan, the outermost one in elevation (and in fig. 1.3). Late twelfth or early thirteenth century. West is at the top. Approx. 22 × 15.5 cm. Durham, Cathedral and Chapter Library, Ms A. III.22, fol. 5r. Reproduced with the permission of Durham Cathedral and Chapter Library.

certainly was, as Nicholas of Lyra later makes clear—about the number of kitchens and the division of the sanctuary stream? Did colleagues at St. Victor voice objections?

It would be tempting, without reading Richard's argument in chapter twelve, to see his four-branched stream as an allusion to the symbolic or allegorical significance of four, starting from the Four Rivers of Paradise (Gn 2).[63] The Victorine's concern with Ezekiel's Temple vision was, however, exclusively literal. A fourfold division of the sanctuary stream was the only way Richard could find to make sure all the kitchens he had decided on were provided with a supply of water that would ensure the ceremonial cleanliness insisted on by the prophet. Some scholars, such as Hugh of St. Cher (d. 1263), were happy to follow Richard's line of argument. The exact date of Hugh's *Commentarius super totam bibliam* is uncertain, not least as short versions of parts of it seem to have been circulating, probably amongst students in Paris, before the entire work was complete or finalized in the early 1240s.[64] Hugh provided no illustrations, but his verbal exegesis of Ezekiel 47 is explicit and matches almost exactly Richard's plan for chapter 12 of *In visionem Ezechielis*:

> This river, as some say, is divided into four rivulets. One flowed to the kitchens of the southern porticoes; another flowed to the kitchens of the northern porticoes; two others flowed to the kitchens that were on the two sides of the oriental porticoes. And these two rivulets proceeding from the whole building on the eastern side came together into one; and similarly the other two rivers issuing from the whole building: one on the northern side, the other on the southern, bent back their courses towards the east and came to the two other rivers.[65]

Richard's version does not show the separate branches doubling back to join up again into the single stream that, as Hugh goes on to relate, "thus made the torrent in which the prophet walked, first up to the ankles, second up to the knees, and third, up to his kidneys."[66]

Richard's four-river plan for chapter 12 may not have been in the main recensions of *In visionem Ezechielis*, but it does seem to have been more widely known than might be suspected from the three known examples just described. An extended version, showing more to the west of the sanctuary threshold (the rest of the sanctuary, the three adjacent buildings, and the walls of the middle and outer courts), is found on otherwise empty folios at the end of two thirteenth-century Bibles, both now in Oxford: Bodleian Library, Ms Laud Lat. 9 (where the plan was drawn to my attention by Grover Zinn), and Brasenose College, Ms 5. Both Bibles appear to have originated in France, although it is impossible to say if the plans were executed there or in England. The plan in Ms Laud Lat. 9 measures 25 × 25 cm drawn in red ink with labelling in black (fig. 1.5). It is the only such addition in the volume. It occupies the upper half of the verso of the final leaf of a large folio volume said to date from the middle of the thirteenth century and to have been "very early in England."[67] Brasenose, Ms 5, is, in contrast, a small quarto volume with leaves of thin vellum, a format that was becoming popular in Paris from the final decades of the twelfth century onwards as a relatively affordable and conveniently portable Bible for students or, later, the preaching and teaching friars.[68] On spare leaves added at the end of Brasenose 5 are found, first, two full-page maps, in the usual diagrammatic style; one of the historical Canaan (Jo 35) and the other Richard's version of the map of the visionary Canaan restored to the returning Israelites (Ez 48). Both maps are enlargements of marginal diagrams found earlier in the volume adjacent to the relevant text (fols 32r and 281r respectively). Then, on folio 443r, in red and black ink with the rivers in blue, comes the plan of Ezekiel's Temple (fig. 1.6). The three drawings, and the incomplete and unlabelled outline of the Temple on the verso of folio 443, appear to be in the same hand as the annotations and cross-references that pack the margins of the Bible text.[69] Lesley Smith's conclusion is that all the drawings in the volume are related to the written annotations, would seem to have been made within a generation of the making of the Bible, and are likely to date from the third quarter of the thirteenth century, possibly as early as c. 1250.[70]

The Laud and Brasenose plans are strikingly similar to each other, despite differences in orientation. The one in Ms Laud Lat. 9 has west at the top, so that the stream is drawn to the left of the altar in order to respect the scriptural description that it went to the altar's right (as the observer faced east) and south. In the east-orientated Brasenose 5 plan the stream is drawn to the right of the altar, which is also the southern side. Both plans show eight kitchens, labelled *culina* on Brasenose 5, *coquina* on Laud Lat. 9 as on Durham, A.III.22, and BnF, lat. 2165, but on Brasenose 5 the individual

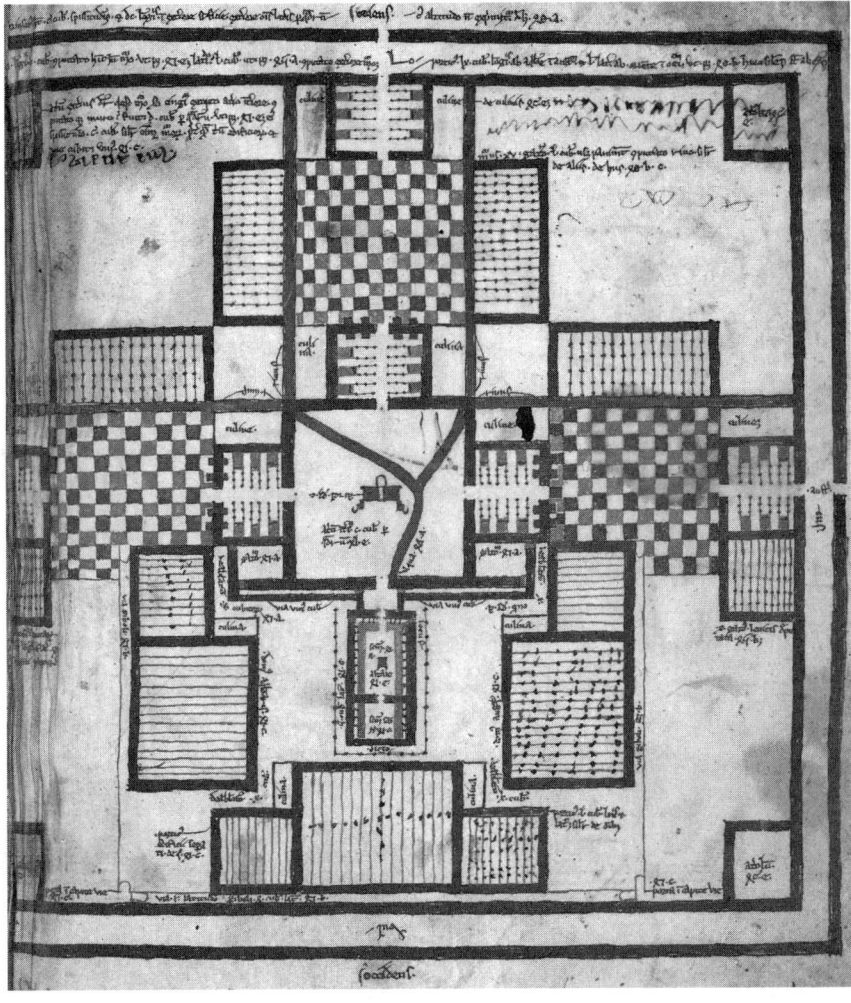

Figure 1.5. Plan of Ezekiel's Temple, with the four-branching stream described by Richard of St. Victor, drawn in ink on an endleaf in a Bible probably made in Paris about 1240–50. Richard's plan has been extended to the west to include the entire Temple complex, with the three buildings adjacent to the Temple proper. East is at the top. Approx. 16 × 16 cm. Oxford, Brasenose College, Ms 5, fol. 443r. Reproduced with the permission of the Principal and Fellows of Brasenose College, Oxford.

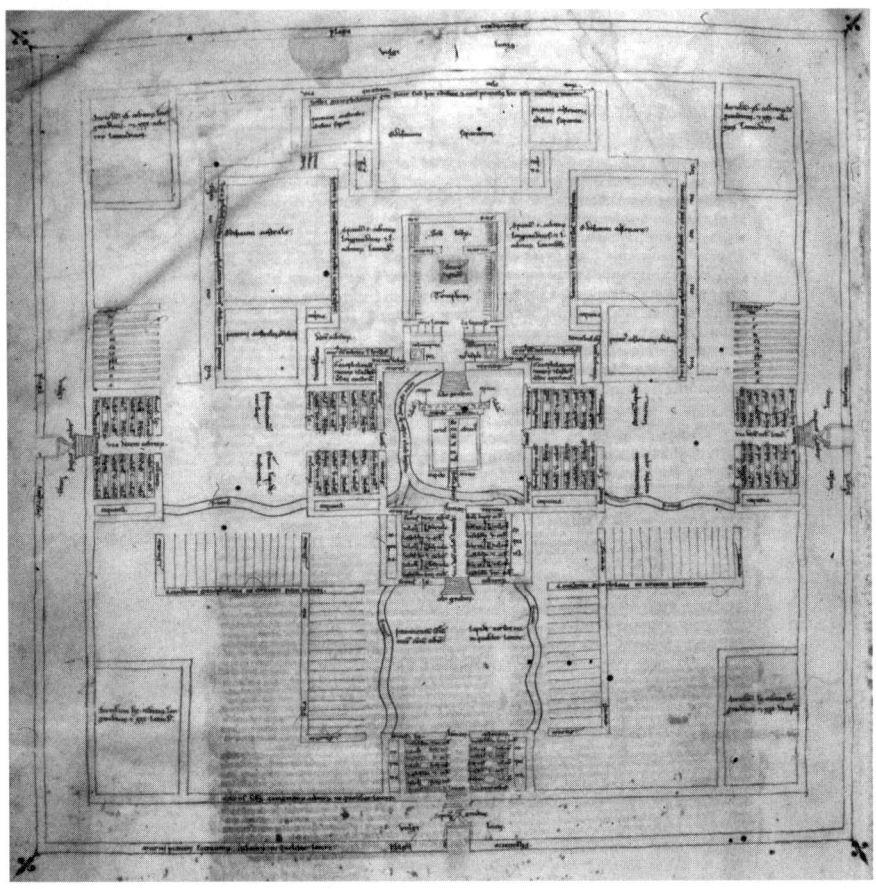

Figure 1.6. Plan of Ezekiel's Temple, with Richard of St. Victor's four-branching stream supplying the kitchens, drawn in ink on an endleaf in an early thirteenth-century French Bible and showing the whole Temple complex, as in Oxford, Brasenose College, Ms 5 (see fig. 1.5). Extra details here include several flights of steps, described in the Bible, which are also reminders of the sloping land. In red ink, with black writing, on a blank folio at the end of the volume. West is at the top. 25 × 25 cm. Oxford, Bodleian Library, Ms Laud Lat. 9, fol. 458v. Reproduced with the permission of the Bodleian Library.

branches of the stream pass alongside, not through, them. Other minor differences include the labelling of each of the branches as *fluvius*, the omission on Brasenose 5 of the gatehouse in the outermost precinct, and the portrayal on the Laud Lat. 9 plan of several flights of steps. The Laud Lat. 9 plan also has rather more annotation. Given these differences, it is unlikely that either plan was copied directly from the other or that they were executed in concert, which raises the possibility that there must have been a prototype, presently unknown, that would provide a direct link with Richard's plan for chapter 12 of *In visionem Ezechielis*.

THE MAP OF CANAAN RESTORED

The final drawing in *In visionem Ezechielis* is a map of Canaan for Ezekiel 48, present in all but five of the full-length manuscripts for which the final pages are not missing.[71] Chapter twenty (which must be seen as unfinished) is comprised of a series of phrases from Ezechiel 45:1–5 with interlinear commentary, but lacking any reference to the other verses also germane to the discussion and the map (Ez 45:6–8 and Ez 48:1–29). If the text of the chapter is incomplete, though, the map was certainly finished. It follows the scriptural text closely. In Ezekiel 45:1–8 the layout of the central sanctified strip that was to be set aside for the Temple and the city, together with the land needed to support the priests and the princes, is described, with measurements. The external boundaries of the whole territory are described in Ezekiel 47:13–23, and those of each of the twelve tribal allotments are given in Ezekiel 48:1–29. Richard gave his map the title *Descriptio seu divisio totius terrae promissionis* ("Description or division of the whole promised land").

In the majority of manuscripts, the map of Canaan fits neatly on a full page, usually after chapter 20, but in two cases it has been drawn separately on a larger sheet that was then inserted at the appropriate place. In the Cambridge manuscript (Corpus Christi College, 315, fol. 113r), where the map measures overall some 22 × 27 cm, it spreads over two folios glued together before drawing, folded, and then bound into the volume along the left margin to form the final folio of the work. Folding, however, took place before all the ink was dry, with the result that the words indicating the Levites' portion (*primitie levicarum*), which were written across the fold in blue, are imprinted in reverse on the opposite sides of the fold. The verso is blank. In BnF, lat. 3438, fol. 81r, the map has been drawn to fit a smaller format (18.5 × 25 cm). It, too, is on a centrally folded bifolium, which has been bound in along the left edge.[72] In all cases, east is at the top of the page, so that the tribal allocations are shown as vertical strips (fig. 1.7).

It is not difficult to identify Richard's model for his map of Canaan. Jewish exegetes had always had a practical need to know the exact boundaries of the area to which Judaic law applied, and Rashi had drawn two maps to demonstrate the historical allocation of tribal lands after the Israelites' conquest of Canaan (Nm 34:3, 11).[73] He had also created two maps for the book of Ezekiel. One represents only the central strip of sanctified land (Ez 45:1–5) and shows the Temple and city separated (a utopian ideal, which never came to pass), with the portions allocated to the Levites, the priests, and the prince between. The other shows the whole of Canaan with the tribal portions in a succession of east-west strips of equal size to north and south of the sanctified section. It was this second map that Richard took for *In visionem Ezechielis*, substituting Latin captions for Rashi's Hebrew. This may have been the first occasion on which a Christian had drawn a map for Ezekiel 48, for the traditional emphasis in Christian exegesis, from Eusebius onwards, had been on the historical event of the Israelites' arrival in the promised land under the leadership of Joshua and the original tribal allotments as described in Numbers 35.

Rashi had orientated his map of Canaan so that north was at the top and the tribal strips run horizontally across the page. Richard put east at the top of his map, with the result that on close copies of his map the strips are vertical.[74] Both Rashi and Richard followed the description in Ezekiel 48 of the future reallocation of land, which was to give each tribe a portion of equal dimension and shape reaching across the country, from the Mediterranean coast to the desert, in such a way as to give each a share of the country's varied terrain and economic resources. Seven tribal allotments lie to the north of the broad central strip of sanctified land, and five to the south.[75] The central strip is divided in the opposite direction into three main compartments, with the easternmost and westernmost labelled as the princes' land.[76] The compartment in the middle is again divided into three. The central unit is labelled the Levites' land; the southern unit contains the city and its suburbs

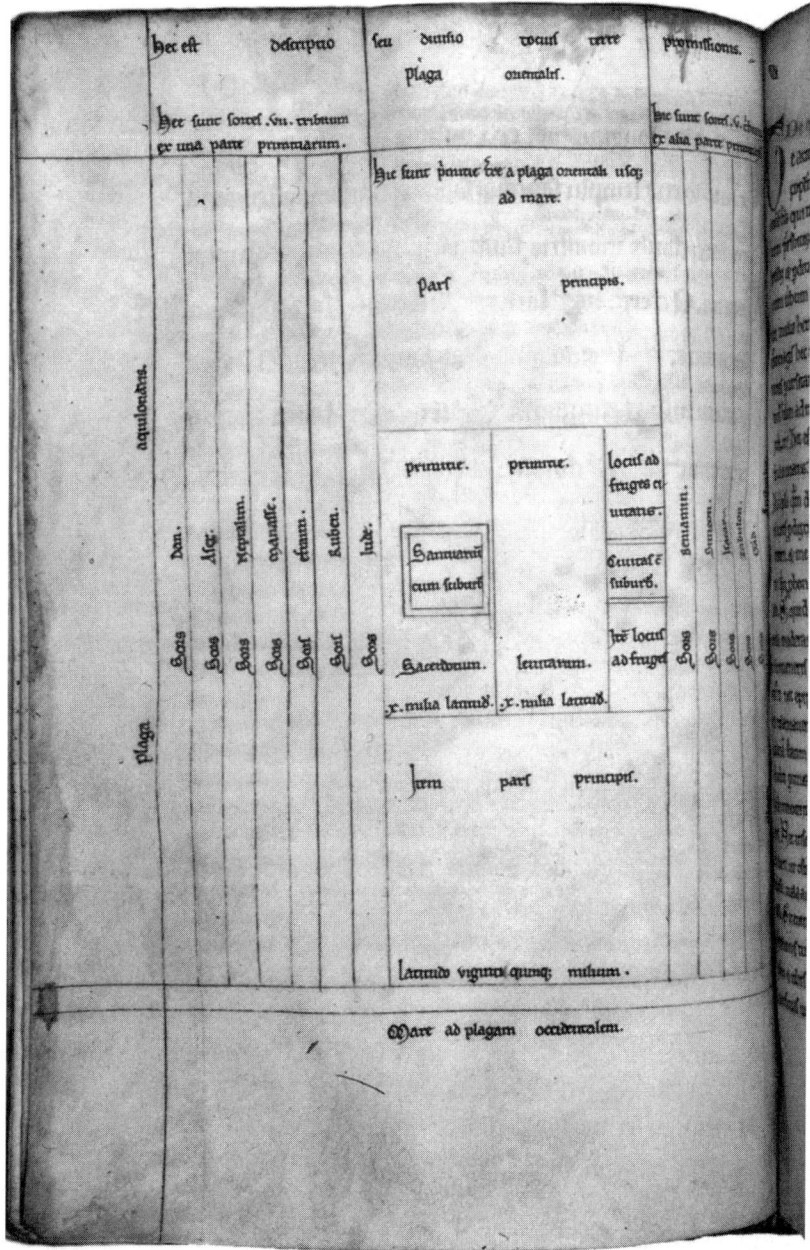

Figure 1.7. Richard of St. Victor, *In visionem Ezechielis*. Map of Canaan for chapter 20, entitled *Descriptio seu divisio totius terre promissionis*. Red ink lines with black writing. Early thirteenth century. 22 × 18 cm. Oxford, Bodleian Library, Ms Bodl. 459, fol. 37v. Reproduced with the permission of the Bodleian Library.

(represented as a square) surrounded by the cities of refuge (*locus ad fuges civitates*); and the northern unit contains the Temple and its suburbs surrounded by the priests' land.[77] In many manuscripts, Temple and city are outlined with double lines; in all, the biblical measurements for all these central units are noted.

AFTER RICHARD

To judge from extant manuscripts, medieval copiers of Richard's map of Canaan for Ezekiel followed their models faithfully, especially for the layout of the central strip, unlike those responsible for Rashi's map, where errors were frequently made.[78] It would be interesting to identify the exemplar used by Richard, just as it would be useful to be able to establish a Judeo-Christian stemma for all late-twelfth- and early-thirteenth-century copies of the map for Ezekiel 48. For example, Richard's version is also found on folio 442v of the Brasenose 5 Bible, between the map of the historical Canaan and the Temple plan, with annotations similar to those made in Latin on a Hebrew map in Rashi's commentary in Oxford (Corpus Christi College, Ms 6, fol. 59a). On the Brasenose 5 map, an extra strip, parallel to the northernmost tribal territory (Dan), contains a number of place-names (*Betsaliam, Seddada, Emath, Barotha, Damate*), a reference to *via Betsaliam*, and two short texts separated by a short vertical line that signifies the boundary between *Emath* to the west and *Damate* to the east.[79] *Betsaliam*, we learn from Eusebius, was in the territory of Benjamin, well to the south of the country, beyond the sanctified central portion, and a thin, rather scratchy ink line, representing the *Betsaliam* road, links the word with the tribal strip. Although many of the places named in that additional strip were indeed in the north, their arrangement was not so much geographical as an aide-memoire inserted in a convenient place on the map. On Rashi's map, a Christian scholar, no doubt struggling with the Hebrew words, added the same and other names—*Hetelon* (or *Betsaliam* again?), *Sedada, Herriat, Berothac, Siberiam, Hasar Hatican*, and *Dameset*—along the margin.[80]

Richard's maps and plans continued to circulate in the thirteenth century, but there continued to be individuals like Hugh of St. Cher who preferred not to provide drawings, even for a literal exposition of the scriptures. It was Nicholas of Lyra who brought the long and somewhat scattered tradition of visual exegesis together in one great work, the *Postilla litteralis super totam bibliam*, compiled between 1323 and 1332. From the printed editions of Nicholas' *Postilla litteralis*, the practice of using illustration in exegesis passed, together with many of the medieval diagrams themselves, into the writings of sixteenth-century reformers, most famously Martin Luther and John Calvin.[81]

Like his twelfth-century predecessors, Nicholas consulted Jewish as well as Christian scholars before arriving at his own interpretation of the matter in hand, and in nearly a third of his diagrams the rabbinical version is portrayed next to the Christian. As in *In visionem Ezechielis*, most of Nicholas' illustrations are keyed into the text, either with an immediately preceding phrase (such as "here follows a figure" or "so that this is better understood it is expressed as a figure") or an allusion embedded more distantly in the relevant postil.[82] Of around forty subjects illustrated by Nicholas, fifteen are depicted in plan.[83] A century later, Paul of Burgos included three of his own diagrams in his critical comments on the *Postilla litteralis* in his *Additiones* (1429).[84]

Although Nicholas acknowledged some of his sources, it is not always clear where the boundary lies between those and his own thinking. At the start of his commentary on Ezekiel 40, however, he expanded on the disagreement between Jews and Christians and between the "Latins" themselves. He named specifically Richard of St. Victor, Hugh of St. Cher, and the preacher as yet unidentified "brother Gerard of Provins, the Friars Minor," for the different ways in which they described and expounded the Temple vision.[85] Nicholas found the difference unsurprising. In his words:

> the description of this building is very obscurely rendered in the text. And also our translation seems to differ a lot from the Hebrew truth. It would be a very lengthy business to repeat all their statements, and to show where they [the expositors, Hebrew and Latin] go wrong.

So he gives "what seems to me most consistent with the text."[86]

At Ezekiel 47, Nicholas comes to the problem of the sanctuary stream. He contradicts Richard of St. Victor and Hugh of St. Cher:

Concerning this, it is to be noted that the Latin expositors say that before they leave the inner atrium these waters are divided into four rivulets, one of which goes to the kitchens at the southern porticoes, before their exit from the inner atrium. Another goes to the kitchens of the northern porticoes. The other two go to two of the sides of the eastern porticoes where, according to them, the kitchens are similarly disposed. And these four rivulets, after coming out of the eastern gate of the outer wall, turn back and come together into one.[87]

After considering detailed objections, Nicholas is decisive: "And so I say with the Hebrews that these waters proceed by one river from the place of origin to the exit from the external wall."[88] His plan for Ezekiel 47 accordingly shows a single stream (fig. 1.8). He also avoids identifying any kitchens, the number and location of which had evidently been much in question. On Nicholas' plan, the rooms identified as kitchens on Richard's four-river plan are either simply omitted or, if they are shown (as in the case of those by the eastern gatehouse), they are called simply "rooms" (*thalami*).

Nicholas' *Postilla litteralis* was immensely popular, and hundreds of copies were made, although by no means all were illustrated. However, not all scribes or illustrators (or those who transferred Nicholas' drawings onto wood blocks for the new printed editions) had as sound a grasp of the cardinal points as is necessary to produce a correct plan for Ezekiel 47. They understood that the stream should always be shown to the *right* and to the *south* of the altar, as the scriptural text says. Some, however, failed to grasp the implications of choosing to orientate their version of the plan with west at the top of the page instead of east, in which case (as the person responsible for the plan in Ms Laud Lat. 9 had fully understood) the stream has to be drawn to the *left* of the altar (as the reader sees it) if it is to pass by on the south. Mistakes were made. Like the Laud Lat. 9 plan, figure 1.8 has west at the top, but the stream is shown passing the altar on the right, the side indicated by the cardinal direction written in the right hand margin as south. However, south on a west-orientated map has to be on the left side. Exactly what went wrong here can only be conjectured, but it is likely that not only had the plan been laid out on the page but that the stream had also been drawn before the error was realized. This left the scribe with only one way out of the embarrassment: to invert the directions for north and south on

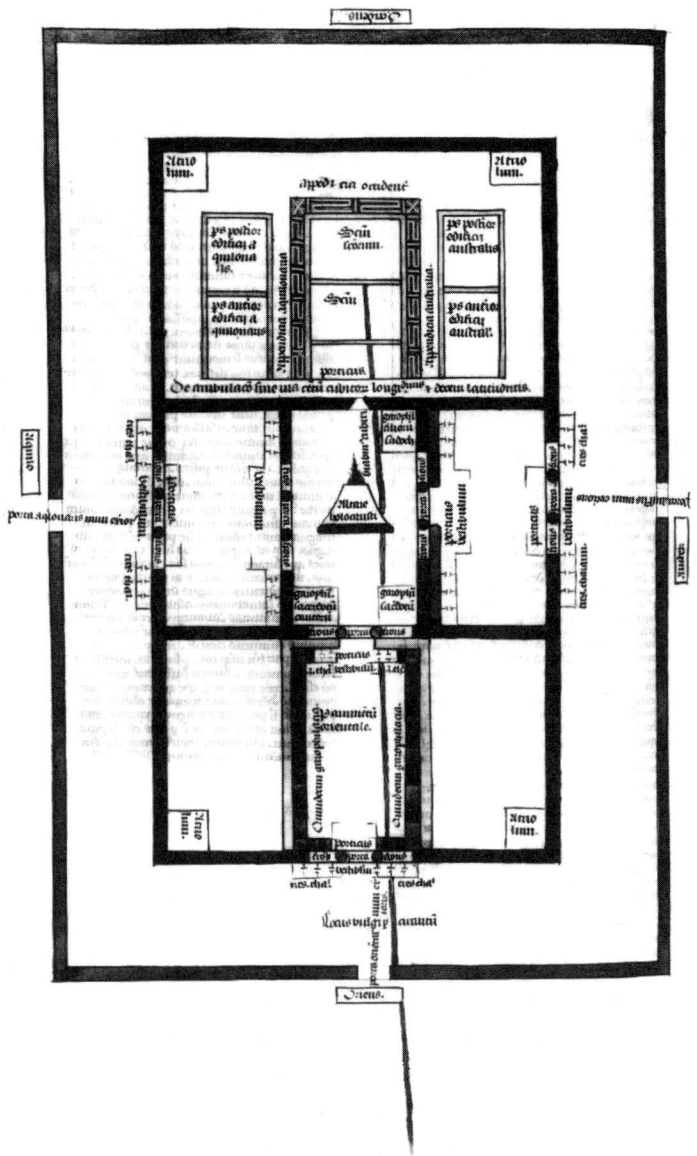

Figure 1.8. Nicholas of Lyra, *Postilla litteralis super totam bibliam* (1323–32). Plan of the Temple proper for Ezekiel 47, with the sanctuary stream in a single course throughout. The copyist drew the stream passing to the right of the altar of holocausts (Ez 47:1–2), which here is the north side, and then corrected his error by exchanging the cardinal direction for north (*Aquilone*) and south (*Auster*) to give the illusion that the plan accords with the biblical description of what Ezekiel saw as he looked eastward. Early fourteenth century. 35.5 × 25 cm. Oxford, Bodleian Library, Ms Canon. Bibl. Lat. 70, fol. 165v. Reproduced with the permission of the Bodleian Library.

the plan to give the impression of scriptural accuracy, despite being wrong both geographically and according to the text of Ezekiel 48:1–2.

Nicholas placed all his diagrams as close as possible to the relevant text. For the last of his diagrams for Ezekiel—the unnamed city described in 48:30–35—he could have adapted almost any contemporary representation of a city as a notional image, a common practice in his day. Instead he kept to the simple and straightforward textual description as his guide to his visual representation in plan. The outline is thus a simple square, each side of which is interrupted only by three tribal gates. The interior, about which nothing is said in the scriptures, is left empty. In the first illustrated printed edition of the *Postilla litteralis*, published by Anton Koberger in Nuremberg in 1481, however, the city is portrayed in bird's eye perspective, with high walls—and an interior packed with buildings, a practice that continued to the end of the sixteenth century.[89]

By the time Nicholas of Lyra had completed the *Postilla litteralis* and Paul of Burgos had contributed his extra diagrams, scholars and theologians in the Latin West would have known for which books of the Bible they could expect an illustrated commentary. They would also have known exactly which passages of the scriptural text might refer to an accompanying figure. And, given the basic principles of drawing for explanation, they would have had a reasonable idea of what that figure might look like. Later in the sixteenth century—by when geographical maps constructed on mathematical principles and with places positioned on the map according to astronomical observation (latitude and longitude) had become generally and widely familiar—the disciplined format of the diagrammatic map employed to such impressive effect by Rashi, Richard of St. Victor, and Nicholas of Lyra, and respected in the main by early printers of the *Postilla litteralis*, was abandoned. Instead, attempts were made to adapt them to the naturalistic style of geographical image, constructed on the new "scientific" principles of Ptolemy's *Geography*, which was becoming increasingly familiar to a wide readership. However, what the new image gained in pictorial familiarity, to the benefit of readers who were now predominantly nonclerical and even nonacademic, it lost in theological truth. Pierre Eskriche's rendering in 1568 of Richard of St. Victor's map of Canaan for Ezekiel 48 portrays a realistically styled, and increasingly familiar, coastline for the Holy Land, but Ezekiel's strictly egalitarian strips are of every size and shape, and far from equal in area.[90]

Rosamund McKitterick has suggested that Carolingians made use of the written word "to organise, control and challenge the world."[91] How much more powerful a tool for directing and forming religious thought, we may suggest, would have been Rashi's, Richard of St. Victor's, and Nicholas of Lyra's visual exegesis in their day. Think of the impact that Richard's plan for chapter 12, as we find it today in BnF, lat. 2165, must have had on at least some of his readers, who might otherwise have been prepared to turn a blind eye to a written description of an offending feature, the diversion of the sanctuary stream to the kitchens. And how much would drawings such as those in Richard's *In visionem Ezechielis* have been valued by their medieval readers as a potent way of "making God seem human."[92]

NOTES

I have accumulated a huge debt over the years to a great many people for their advice and assistance. To all I am immensely grateful. Some people are named in the notes, but I should express individual thanks here to Mayer Gruber, P. D. A. Harvey, E. M. Ingram, the late R. A. Markus, Lesley Smith and, not least, Grover Zinn himself, who originally invited me to write this paper and to whom I happily dedicate it.

1. Weizmann, *Ancient Book Illumination*, 154; Murdoch, *Album of Science*.

2. For an example of such updating see Hiatt, "The Map of Macrobius before 1100."

3. Appendix 1 updates the lists given in: Cahn, "Architectural Draughtmanship in Twelfth-Century Paris"; idem, "Architecture and Exegesis"; Schröder, *Gervasius von Canterbury*, 1:157; and Goy, *Die handschriftliche*, 114–18. I have inspected eleven originals (those in Cambridge, Durham, Oxford, and Paris), and microfilm or online reproductions of two (Vatican City, Troyes), and have relevant information on all the other manuscripts, for which I am greatly indebted to the kind attention of archivists and librarians at Arras, Cambrai, Karlsruhe, Prague, Toulouse, Troyes, Vatican City, Wrocław, and Zwickau. I am also grateful for the information, by telephone, that the manuscript listed by Schröder, *Gervasius von Canterbury*, and Goy, *Die handschriftliche*, at Vitry-le-François, Bibliothèque municipale, Ms 42, was destroyed in the Second World War.

4. I am grateful to Jocelyne Deschaux for the information that Toulouse, Bibliothèque municipale, Ms 206, has empty spaces only. The discovery of the hitherto unrecorded plan discussed in this article means that the total number of illustrations created by Richard for *In visionem Ezechielis* has also had to be revised.

5. Manuscripts with missing folios include Oxford, Bodleian Library, Ms Bodl. 459, fols. 1v–37v, which lacks two folios containing three illustrations of the Temple (figs. 10, 11, 12; see appendix 2) and some text, and Oxford, Bodleian Library, Ms e Mus. 62, fols. 75r–106r, which lacks one folio with text and two Temple illustrations (figs. 2 and 3). In both manuscripts the loss predates the numbering of the folios. Ms e Mus. 62 contains several corrector's notes, the first (fol. 75r) explaining that *Hic liber non est emendatus nisi secundum exemplaria duo mendosa, quia aliud non habuimus* ("This book has not been corrected except by comparing the text to two poor exemplars, because we have nothing else"), although whether the omissions can be attributed to the faulty exemplar is less clear. The map of Canaan, normally placed at the end of the whole work and thus on the last folio, was clearly never intended to be included in Ms e Mus. 62, where a new work, *De hoc monticulo dixit Ysaias*, starts after the final line of *In visionem Ezechielis*. The manuscript in Zwickau (Ratsschulbibliothek, IV, 1) may also be incomplete, as only eight drawings are reported; I am grateful to Lutz Mahnke for this information.

6. As in Paris, BnF, Ms lat. 14516, where the plans are neatly drawn and lightly colored, but the elevations on fols. 240r, 240v, and 248r are heavily colored, sometimes giving an exceptionally strong show-through. Indeed, fol. 240v (the verso of fig. 10) is blank, as if the scribe had refused to use it. With Schröder, *Gervasius von Canterbury*, 1:161, however, I see no reason for supposing, as does Cahn, "Architecture and Exegesis," 59, that this, and a second folio (together with a space at the end of a half-column of text) were intended for "at least two additional illustrations"; Ms lat. 14516 seems an unusually disorganized production, and it is more likely that a division of labor led to misunderstandings between scribe and illuminator.

7. It is also included in the extract preserved in Durham, Cathedral and Chapter Library, Ms A. III.22.

8. Cahn, "Architectural Draughtmanship in Twelfth-Century Paris," "Architecture and Exegesis," "Notes on the Illustrations of Ezekiel's Temple Vision."

9. The classic modern example of a diagrammatic map is Harry Beck's map of the London Underground system (first published in 1933). On the principles of such maps and plans, see Delano-Smith, "Smoothed Lines and Empty Spaces," and "To Whom the Map Speaks."

10 Adamnán's "De Locis Sanctis," 229. See also Wilkinson, *Jerusalem Pilgrims*, 93–116, 193–97, and plates 1–6. For a critical assessment of Adamnán, see O'Loughlin, *Adomnán and The Holy Places*.

11. Richard of St. Victor, *In visionem Ezechielis*, 15 (PL 196:575).

12. Tractate Middoth: Oxford, Bodleian Library, Ms Pococke 295, fol. 288v. I am indebted to Ilana Tahan for translation of the Hebrew annotations. For a facsimile, with introduction by Sassoon, see *Maimonidis Commentarius in Mischnam*. The treatise forms part of the Kodashim, the fifth Order of the Mishna; see *The Jewish Encyclopedia*, 8:618.

13. "Cumenim lineas proportionali commensuratione modificatas aspicimus . . . facile est subintelligere," Richard of St. Victor, *In visionem Ezechielis*, 6 (PL 196:549).

14. "It should be known, however, that this figure, and the others following, are not always protracted in the exact proportions that are given here." ["Sciendum, tamen, quod haec figura, et aliae sequentes non semper sunt protractae praecise in illa proportione que dicitur hic."]: Nicholas of Lyra, *Postilla litteralis*, Ez 40:6. Nicholas is here referring to the walls of the Temple; in Genesis he makes a similar comment about the dimensions of Noah's Ark.

15. On the significance of cardinal direction in Nicholas of Lyra's plan of the desert encampment (Nm 2–3), see Catherine Delano-Smith, "Redesigning the Medieval Exegetical Map."

16. Augustine, *Epistolae*, 2.22.5 (PL 33:561); Gregory, *Homiliae in Ezechielem prophetam*, 2.1.6 (PL 76:939).

17. Bede, *De tabernaculo*, 2.6 (PL 91:460).

18. Nicholas of Lyra, *Postilla litteralis*, Ez 1.

19. Ez 43:1.

20. In many archival records and catalogues, the presence of non-narrative illustration is passed over in total silence or only inconsistently mentioned. Neither Neubauer, *Catalogue of the Hebrew Manuscripts*, nor Beit-Arié, in his *Supplement of Addenda and Corrigenda* to it, mention illustrations, even where these are present in some quantity, as, for example, in Bodleian Ms Pococke 295, which contains eighteen drawings, large and small, almost one on every page.

21. As in New Haven, Yale University, Beinecke Library, Ms 640; Cambrai, Bibliothèque municipale, Ms 290-293; and Cambridge, University Library, Mss Dd.7.7–10, all copies of Nicholas of Lyra, *Postilla litteralis super totam bibliam*, dating from the mid-fourteenth, late-fourteenth, and mid-fifteenth centuries respectively. The illuminator of Beinecke Ms 640 adorned each diagram and filled the margins, and sometimes entire columns, with exuberant foliage and scrolls (e.g., Ezekiel, fols. 176r, 179v, 196r–v, 198v, 200v). The Cambrai illuminator, who also framed the diagrams with leaves and sprays, transformed the Temple plans into three dimensional representations in which all sense of spatial relationship is lost. In the Cambridge manuscript, radically redesigned diagrams (e.g., Exodus, fols. 80v and 81v, the curtains and boards of the tabernacle; fol. 83v, the high priest; III Kings, fol. 241r, elevation of Solomon's Temple; Ezekiel, fol. 147v, elevation of the eastern gatehouse; fol. 153r, elevation of the Temple facade) match nothing in any of the early (mid-fourteenth-century French) manuscripts I have seen.

22. In Eusebius' work, "engraved" (καταγράφή) was rendered by Jerome as *delineatio*, and "plan" (τυπος ... εικονα διαχαξας, lit. iconic likeness) as *figura ... insculpta imagine*. It is generally accepted that in both cases Eusebius was indicating a map of one type or another. For the preface in the original Greek and Jerome's Latin, see Klostermann, *Eusebius Onomastikon*, 11:1.

23. Bruce-Mitford, "The Art of the Codex Amiatinus," misleadingly refers to the plan as showing "the Temple" (meaning Solomon's Temple) rather than the Tabernacle. Other examples of similar misunderstandings are given by Corsano, "The First

Quire of the Codex Amiatinus," esp. 9, n. 25. It is generally agreed that Cassiodorus had derived his ideas, if not the drawing itself, from Jewish sources, most notably Josephus, *Antiquities*, 3.6. Bede gives an idea of how Cassiodorus interpreted part of the structure in *De templo* 2.17.2: see Bede, *Bede: On the Temple*, 66. Cassiodorus is an example of an early writer for whom drawing was a ready aid to explanation; see Gorman, "The Diagrams in the Oldest Manuscripts of Cassiodorus' *Institutiones*." Gorman suggests Cassiodorus' drawing of geometrical shapes and solids were incorporated into manuscripts of the *Etymologiae* by Isidore of Seville (41 and plates 4–8).

24. Gutmann, "Return in Mercy to Zion"; Narkiss, "A Scheme of the Sanctuary," esp. 15.

25. For reproductions of these two plans, see Wolska-Conus, *Cosmas Indicopleustes*, 1:89 and 1:193. A list of the more than ninety separate illustrations is given in the same volume, 158–71. For a recent assessment of the work, see Kominko, "New Perspectives on Paradise," and further references therein.

26. Reproductions of Adamnán's four plans may be found in Adomnán, *Ádamnan's "De Locis Sanctis*," and in Wilkinson, *Jerusalem Pilgrims*, and Bede's versions in Bede, *Bede: A Biblical Miscellany*.

27. Paris, BnF, Ms lat. 11561, fol. 43v. O'Loughlin, "Map and Text," plate 1 (reproduction) and fig. 1 (transcription). The manuscript in which the map is found, a treatise on Joshua, dates from the mid-ninth century. Apart from towns, only the Lebanon Mountains are named; the Mediterranean Sea is indicated by a broad straight line. All other lines are also straight (only the Jordan curves boldly, like a hockey stick, into an attenuated Dead Sea), and content is restricted to a scatter of rectangular place-signs with their names and the names of the tribes.

28. London, British Library, Add. Ms 38817, fol. 2r.

29. Gruber, "Light on Rashi's Diagrams," gives seven "lines of evidence" for the drawings being Rashi's own work. Two such lines include the many references in medieval manuscripts of his commentaries to the letter Rashi sent to the rabbis of Auxerre saying, "I will make you drawings and send them to you," and the comment of Rashi's grandson (Rabbi Samuel son of Meir) that his grandfather had furnished his commentary on Numbers 34 with maps: see Delano-Smith and Gruber, "Rashi's Legacy," and Kedar, "Rashi's Map of the Land of Canaan."

30. The formulaic phrase linking text and image came to be dropped by copyists when the drawing was missing and the empty space seemed to have no function, leaving a continuous text: see Gruber, "What Happened to Rashi's Pictures?" The first printed edition of Rashi's commentaries must have been made from such an exemplar, and knowledge of the full complement of Rashi's maps and plans was lost until recently. Mayer Gruber is preparing a systematic and comprehensive investigation and recording of the illustrations.

31. The plan was rediscovered by Jordan S. Penkower, who includes it in his commentary on Rashi, *Bible: Miqraot Gedolot HaKeter, Ezekiel*, 322. I am indebted to Ilana Tahen for help with this reference.

32. Oxford, Bodleian Library, Ms Pococke 295. Wischnitzer, "Maimonides' Drawings of the Temple," refers to Maimonides' drawings as technical rather than, as in this article, exegetical.

33. "Horum itaque quae iam descripsimus formam huius modi repraesentamus": *In visionem Ezechielis* (PL 196:535); "ad maiorum dictorum dicendorumque evidentiam, omnium quae superius per partes prolata sunt formam in unam figuram colligere, ut intuentis amimus eorum omnium locum, situm et numerum, qualitatem, quantitatem, proportionem facile possit ex eius contemplatione colligere" (449–550); "in hunc modum" (534). I am grateful to the late R. A. Markus for the Latin translations in this essay.

34. "Dabimus interim huis rei aliquod documentum, per quod possit quivis quantumlibet simplex assertionis nostrae capere experimentum" (PL 196:575).

35. "sub occulis repraesentemus" (PL 196:546); "facile est subintelligere ab hac linearum deductione" (449).

36. "Si quis me fortassis in hac nostra expositione prolixitatis arguat, videat, obsecro, quam recte id faciat. Sed ut verum fatear malo subtillioribus fastifiousus, quam tardioribus obscurus, praesertim in tam obscura re, ubi pene omnia quae dicuntur probatione indigent potius quam expositione" (PL 196:549–50).

37. I am grateful to Patricia Stirnemann for confirmation that there are no drawings in Hugh of St. Cher's *Postilla super totiam Bibliam* (1498–1502). The woodcuts in an early printed edition of Hugh's work are from blocks originally created for Nicholas of Lyra's *Postilla litteralis*, already published by the same printer, Anton Koberger.

38. Cahn, "Architecture and Exegesis," 66–67.

39. Translation from the Vulgate (Burns & Oates, publishers to the Holy See, 1945, 1955).

40. Rosenau, *Vision of the Temple*, 19. Cooke, *The Book of Ezekiel*, 430. For a reproduction of statue and plan, see Millard, "Cartography in the Ancient Near East," 109, figs. 6.2 and 6.3. For the hitherto unsuspected wealth of surviving clay-tablet maps and plans, as well as an exposition of Gudea's plan, see Francesca Rochberg, "The Expression of Terrestrial and Celestial Order in Ancient Mesopotamia," esp. 9–34.

41. Gruber, "The Sources of Rashi's Cartography."

42. The foundational document of Rabbinic Judaism, the Mishnah (compiled c. 220 CE), with its utopian description of what ought to be, also almost consistently refers to Herod's Temple. Philo, in the first century CE, and Josephus, whose writings bridge the gap between the functioning of Herod's Temple and its destruction by the Romans in 70 CE, interpreted the Temple as a cosmological symbol. Eventually, hope for a restoration of the destroyed Temple became integral to Jewish understanding of the role of the long-awaited Davidic Messiah, and representations of the Temple came to symbolise that coming. I am grateful to Mayer Gruber for these observations.

43. I am indebted to Mayer Gruber for his comment that "Rashi's drawings for Solomon's Temple (I Kings) are the least familiar; many manuscripts otherwise rich in

his drawings lack the architectural figures, even where the introductory formula remains in the text, and show only details such as the brass lavers." Some idea of Rashi's drawings for Solomon's Temple may be gained from Nicholas of Lyra, who relied heavily on Rashi for his comparative illustrations. The plan sent by Rashi to the rabbis of Auxerre (see notes 29 and 31 above) was of the inner courts of Ezekiel's temple.

44. Oxford, Bodleian Library, Ms Pococke 295. For reproductions of some of the Temple plans from different manuscripts, see Wischnitzer, "Maimonides' Drawings of the Temple." Rosenau, in "The Architecture of Nicholas de Lyra's Temple Illustrations," 294–304, and in *Vision of the Temple*, 35, refers to Maimonides' plan as of Solomon's Temple. Maimonides may have completed his commentary in Fostat, Egypt (and sent it to scribes for multiple copying) in 1168, five years before Richard's death. Sassoon describes Maimonides' working methods in detail in "The Development of the Text," in *Maimonidis Commentarius*, 1:17–18.

45. Augustine, *Enarrationes in Psalmos*, 126.2, quoted from Hodder, "New Treasures and Old," esp. 239.

46. Bede, *De tabernaculo*, 2.1, quoted in full in Bede, *Bede: On the Tabernacle*, "Allegory and History," esp. 119, which also gives the Latin.

47. Bede, *Bede: On the Tabernacle*, "New Treasures and Old," 239.

48. Apart from conflicting measurements, the biblical terminology is sometimes misleading. Richard himself comments on the use of *porta* to mean the entire portico instead of entrance gateway (e.g., "hic porticum sub nomine portae designat," PL 196:545), as pointed out by Coulter, *Per visibilia*, 93–94. For a helpful guide to the biblical text of Ezekiel, with a plan of the Temple, see Carley, *The Book of the Prophet Ezekiel*, esp. 267–321. See also Joyce, *Ezekiel*, and Cooke, *The Book of Ezekiel*.

49. In contrast, the northern gatehouse (Ez 42) is illustrated only by a side elevation, which also portrays the projecting gallery at the top of the building and the steep rocky slope on which the gatehouse was built (chap. 17) In Paris, BnF, Ms lat. 2165, fol. 66r, the projecting gallery is missing. The layout of outer and inner eastern gates appears to be identical.

50. As in Oxford, Bodleian Library, Ms Bodl. 494, fol. 158v; Cambridge, Corpus Christi College, Ms 315; Paris, BnF, Ms lat. 14516 (reproduced in Cahn, "Architecture and Exegesis," 61); and in Migne's edition (PL 196:585–86).

51. "Horum omnium quae diximus in novissima, et magna figura, sicut ibi videri potest, formam et exemplar latius expressimus" (PL 196:566).

52. The discovery of this plan brings the total number of Richard's drawings for *In visionem Ezechielis* to fifteen (see appendix 2). I am immensely grateful to Massimo Ceraso of the Vatican Library and Susan L'Engle of the Vatican Film Library, St. Louis University, for their generous assistance during the protracted closure of the Vatican Library for refurbishment, and to Joan Williams of the Cathedral and Chapter Library, Durham, for her similarly kind assistance.

53. "De coquinis," expanded in PL 196:565, to "De coquinis quae subter porticus fabricatae erant et de atrio interiori" ("On the kitchens that were built under the porch and on the interior court").

54. See, for example, Carley, *The Book of the Prophet Ezekiel*, 5.

55. "In hoc atrio facimus aquam illam, quae de templo egrediebatur decurrere, et a dextro altaris descendere. Circa atrii vero inferiora in quatuor eam secamus, et per medias coquinas traducimus, ita ut per ante gazophylacia transeat, ut sit ubi holocaustum lavari queat, quaemodum scriptum est: *Et per singula gazophylacia ostium in frontibus portarum, et ibi lavabant holocaustum,*" emphasis in original (PL 196: 566).

56. In Richard of St. Victor's day the epithet "new" would have been striking, if not audacious. "New" ceased to be a "dirty word," Beryl Smalley pointed out, only gradually over the 150 years between 1100 and 1250: Smalley, "Ecclesiastical Attitudes to Novelty."

57. Differences in two other illustrations—in BnF, lat. 2165, and BAV, Reg. Lat. 277—suggest the illustrations in these manuscripts, if not the manuscripts themselves, cannot be directly related to each other (or to any manuscript from the two main recensions). In both the Paris and Vatican manuscripts, the geometrical diagram (appendix 2, fig. 9) is, as already noted, accompanied by a column of squares and triangles, but only in BnF, lat. 2165, does figure 13 (elevation of the northern gatehouse) lack the projecting gallery found on every other known example of this figure, and which is unlikely to have been omitted accidentally, for lack of space on the page.

58. Wilmart, *Codices Reginensis Latini*, 2:78–80.

59. The steepness of the ground, discussed in chapter 15, is usually shown in the elevations of the eastern and northern gatehouses (Richard's figures 11 and 13). In Troyes, MAT, Ms 544, however, the ground is flat in both diagrams.

60. Personal communication, January 28, 2009. I am most grateful to Richard Gameson for his kind help.

61. For Cahn, "Architecture and Exegesis," 54, BnF, lat. 14516 was written during Richard's lifetime, but Schröder, *Gervasius von Canterbury*, 160, agrees only that it dates from the last decades of the twelfth century. I am indebted to Hanna Vorholt for her assistance with Schröder's text.

62. From a reference in a letter from the sub-prior John and from the dedication in Richard's *De Concordia temporum* to Bernard of Clairvaux that Richard's works were in demand at Clairvaux (the provenance of Troyes, MAT, Ms 544), Schröder, *Gervasius von Canterbury*, 170, is led to conclude that "a special transmission of an early version of a text that the author later revised thus seems plausible."

63. Fourfold exegesis in the twelfth century is discussed by Esmeijer, *Divina Quaternitas*, 13, who refers in this connection to Augustine, John Cassian, and Rabanus Maurus. See also Tuell, "The Rivers of Paradise," in which only modern scholarship is discussed.

64. Patricia Stirnemann suggests that most of the work was composed between 1225 and 1235, when Hugh was still in Paris, and that the postils (which would include those on Ezekiel, which are in the oldest extant manuscript) may have been circulating amongst students before 1240s: P. Stirnemann, "Les manuscrits de la *Postille*."

65. "Iste rivus ut dicunt quidam: in quattuor rivulos scindebatur. Unus fluebat ad coquinas porticuum australium, alius fluebat ad coquinas porticuum aquilonarium,

duo alii fluebant ad coquinas quae erant in duobus lateribus porticuum orientalium. Et hi duo rivuli de toto aedificio procedentes ex parte orientali ad unum veniebant. Et similiter alii duo rivuli exeuntes de toto aedificio, unus ex parte aquiloni, alius ex parte australi, reflectebant cursum suum ad orientem & conveniebant ad alios duos rivulos orientales." Hugh of St Cher, *Postillae*, Ezekiel 47.

66. ". . . sic faciebant . . . torrentum . . . in quo propheta traducitur, primo usque ad talos, secundo usque ad genuo, tertio usque ad renes." Hugh of St Cher, *Postillae*, Ezekiel 47.

67. Pächt and Alexander, *Illuminated Manuscripts*, I, entry 527. The plan is here described as showing the "Temple in Jerusalem."

68. Glunz, *History of the Vulgate*, 269–70, identified Brasenose, Ms 5, as an example of "the art of producing small and convenient volumes" of the whole Bible, on thin vellum and with small writing. However, he thought Brasenose 5 was made in Oxford, a suggestion queried by Lesley Smith, who sees Paris as the place of manufacture, and to whom I am grateful for this and other comments on the format and origin of the volume. Alexander and Temple, *Illuminated Manuscripts*, entry 181, have evidently followed Glunz for their description and identify the plan as showing "Solomon's Temple." On "student Bibles" in general, see De Hamel, *History of Illuminated Manuscripts*, esp. 118–20. For a colored reproduction, see my "The Exegetical Jerusalem," Plate 1.

69. Lesley Smith, personal communications since 2006, sees these annotations, which are mostly scriptural cross-references, as notes made by a mendicant (possibly Dominican) as an aid to his Bible study. The underlying interest, revealed in other forms of visual aids in the text besides the maps, would seem to have been in the literal meaning of the scriptures.

70. Lesley Smith, personal communication, September 30, 2011. The annotations and the maps and plans could be the work of its first user.

71. The absence of the map of Canaan from BnF, Ms lat. 14516, explains why it did not get into any early printed edition of *In visionem Ezechielis* or into PL 196.

72. For a reproduction, see Sed-Rajna, "Rashi's Diagrams," 156, and fig. 11.

73. For the maps for Numbers 34:3, 11, see Delano-Smith and Gruber, "Rashi's Legacy," 30–35.

74. In manuscripts of Rashi's commentary the plan is inconsistently orientated on the page, often according to the space available, as was common with maps as book illustrations. In early printed editions of the map of Canaan (Ez 48) in Nicholas of Lyra's *Postilla litteralis*, south is at the top.

75. Dan, Asser, Nepthali, Manasse, Ephraim, Ruben, and Judah to the north of the central portion, with the leading tribe Judah in the privileged position of being next to the sanctified strip; Benjamin, Simeon, Issachar, Zebulin, and Gad to the south. The maps in *In visionem Ezechielis* are consistent in their orientations, as in all other details.

76. The term "prince" was used in Ezekiel as a deliberate rejection of "king," which by then had been brought into disrepute: personal communication from Mayer Gruber, May 19, 2007.

77. City and Temple were to be kept apart, for the princes had been accused of appropriating the Temple's land. The cities of refuge, in which anyone who had committed manslaughter could take shelter, are listed in Joshua 20:7–8.

78. Paris, BnF, Ms Hebreu 161, for instance, has six strips on either side of the central section, and out of eleven manuscripts I have noted five variations from the usual arrangement. For errors in Vienna, ONB, Ms Hebraica 220 (one of the lines defining the territory of Gad in the south is missing and the central strip has four compartments instead of three), see Sed-Rajna, "Rashi's Diagrams," esp. 153–54. Sed-Rajna considered the drawings in two of the Paris manuscripts of *In visionem Ezechielis* (BnF, lat. 3438, and nouv. acq. lat. 1791) to be "faithful copies" of Rashi's (p. 156) although she does not say which of the Hebrew exemplars she has in mind.

79. Betsaliam, Zedad, Hamath, Berathah, Damascus. I am grateful to Paul Harvey for the transcriptions and to Rehav Rubin for modern spellings.

80. Probably Hethlon, Zedad, Hamath [Antioch], Berathah, Sibraim, Hazar-hatticon, Damascus. I am again grateful to Paul Harvey for the transcriptions and to Rehav Rubin for the modern spelling. The additions to Oxford, Corpus Christi College, Ms 6, fol. 59a are in an ink different from the original map and the rest of the text and represent notes made by a Christian scholar relating to his own interests.

81. Exegetical maps for the New Testament were introduced with the Reformation; see Delano-Smith, "Maps as Art *and* Science"; Ingram, "Maps as Readers' Aids"; and Delano-Smith and Ingram, *Maps in Bibles*. On changes to the styling of exegetical maps, and the addition of new map subjects in the reader's aids in Geneva (Protestant) editions of the Bible from 1559, see Delano-Smith, "The Exegetical Jerusalem."

82. "sequitur figura," "ista melius intelligantur expressi ea hic in figura."

83. Nicholas of Lyra provided twelve architectural plans, two geographical plans (the desert encampment and the city of Ezekiel's vision), and one map (Canaan restored). Plans and elevations are combined differently from manuscript to manuscript and in the various printed editions, which makes it difficult to arrive at a definitive total. Similar differences as well as variations in the illustrations themselves are found even in the four manuscripts considered "contemporary" (made before Nicholas' death in 1349); see my "The Exegetical Jerusalem," n. 14.

84. Paul of Burgos (born *c.* 1351) had converted from Judaism and was appointed archbishop of Cartagena in 1405 and of Burgos in 1415. He savaged Nicholas' rabbinical references and interpretations. Strachan, *Early Bible Illustrations*, 22–23, suggested that the mathematically inclined Paul altered the perspective of some of Nicholas' drawings, and changed the stance of Aaron the high priest, but this has not been established. Strachan seems to have based his chapter on Nicholas of Lyra on a single manuscript (Cambridge, University Library, Ms Dd.7.7–10, dated *c.* 1440) which does not contain Burgos' *Additiones* and in which, as already remarked in n. 21 above, some plans are presented in unusual and not always appropriate

format. A chronologically ordered census of all drawings in every manuscript is badly needed, if comparisons between manuscripts are to be valid.

85. What work by Gerard of Provins (diocese of Sens, France) Nicholas of Lyra could have consulted is at present unclear. A sermon by Gerard is included in a fourteenth-century manuscript (London, British Library, Ms Arundel 275, fols 45v–47v), and reference to a payment to him of "xxxv L." is made in a manuscript originally from Provence now in the University of Salzburg Library (M. III.24).

86. "Nec est mirum de dictis variationibus: quia descriptio huius ædificii valde obscuram traditur in textu. Et etiam translatio nostra in multis discrepare videtur ab Hebraica veritate. Omnia vero eorum dicta repetere, & ubi deficere videntur improbare; . . . qui videtur mihi magis consonus literae."

87. "Circa quod sciendum, quod expositores Latini dicunt quae istae aquae ante suum egressum de atrio interiori dividuntur in quatuor rivulos, quorum unus vadit ad coquinas porticuum australium. Alius ad coquinas porticuum aquilonarium. Alii duo ad duo latera porticuum orientalium, ubi similiter secundum eos ponuntur coquinae. Et isti quatuor rivuli post eorum egressum de porta orientali exterioris muri reflectuntur & conveniunt in unum."

88. "Et ideo dico cum Hebraeis, quod aquae istae per unum rivum procedunt de loco originis usque ad exitum de muro exteriori."

89. For a reproduction of the two versions referred to here, see figure 6 in my "The Exegetical Jerusalem." For an example of a sixteenth-century transformation of the exegetical plan into three-dimensional view, with realistically portrayed structures within the walls, see the woodcut in Pinto, *Hieronymiani in Ezechielem*, 527, amongst other examples.

90. Eskrich's map is reproduced in Delano-Smith and Ingram, *Maps in Bibles*, fig. 36. In the sixteenth century, maps for explanation in vernacular Bibles aimed at the general reader were adapted to look geographically "realistic," while maintaining an exegetical function: see Delano-Smith, "The Exegetical Jerusalem."

91. McKitterick, "The Carolingian Church and the Book," 71.

92. Southern, *Medieval Humanism*, 37.

APPENDIX 1: LIST OF EXTANT MANUSCRIPTS OF RICHARD OF ST. VICTOR, IN VISIONEM EZECHIELIS

Complete text

Arras, Médiathèque municipal (formerly Bibl. mun.), 703 (622), fols. 66r–111v

Cambrai, Médiathèque municipal (formerly Bibl. mun.), 305, fols. 240r–257v

Cambridge, Corpus Christi College, 315, fols. 76r–113r (new foliation)

Karlsruhe, Badische Landesbibliothek, Aug. perg. 214, fols. 47r–85v

Oxford, Bodleian Library, Bodl. 459, fols. 1v–37v (folios missing in middle)

Oxford, Bodleian Library, Bodl. 494, fols. 128r–166v

Oxford, Bodleian Library, e Mus. 62, fols. 75r–106r (folios missing in middle)

Paris, BnF, lat. 2165, fols. 40r–69r

Paris, BnF, lat. 3438, fols. 37r–81r

Paris, BnF, lat. 3848, fols. 73r–92v

Paris, BnF, lat. 14516, fols. 207r–252r

Paris, BnF, lat. 16702, fols. 63r–84r

Paris, BnF, nouv. acq. lat. 1791, fols. 1r–39r

Prague, Nàrodni Knihovna eské Republiky (National Library of the Czech Republic), XIV. D. 20, fols 196r–221r

Toulouse, Bibliothèque de Toulouse, 206, fols. 108r–199r (lacks final chapter)

Troyes, Médiathèque de l'Aggolomération Troyenne, 544, fols. 1r–30r

Vatican City, Biblioteca Apostolica Vaticana, Chigi B.VII.106, fols. 253r–217v

Vatican City, Biblioteca Apostolica Vaticana, Lat. 1053, fols. 152r–186r

Vatican City, Biblioteca Apostolica Vaticana, Lat. 13014, fols. 52v–71v

Vatican City, Biblioteca Apostolica Vaticana, Reg. Lat. 277, fols. 1r–34 (includes three additional folios with duplications of some drawings)

Wrocław, Bibliotheka Universytecka, IF 232 (259), fols. 23v–50r

Zwickau, Ratsschulbibliothek, IV,1, fols. 27r–46r (?complete)

Extract

Durham, Cathedral and Chapter Library, A.III.22, fols. 2r–7v

Notes

Vitry-le-François, Bibliothèque municipale, 42, was destroyed in World War II. The first printed edition (Paris, Jean Petit, 1518), from which the *Patrologia Latina* edition was taken, contains only thirteen illustrations; the plan for chapter 12 and the map for chapter 20 are both missing, as they are from the other early printed editions (1534, 1592).

44 Catherine Delano-Smith

APPENDIX 2: LIST OF ILLUSTRATIONS IN RICHARD OF ST. VICTOR, IN VISIONEM EZECHIELIS

K = referred to in text

Chapter 1

Figure 1. Plan of the three walled precincts. K
Figure 2. Plan showing the eastern side of the outer precinct, with paved court and parlours (*gazophylacii*) on each side, that is, from the eastern gate (*porticus*) to the inner court (*atrium interius*). K Fig. 1.1 in this volume.

Chapter 2

Figure 3. Plan of the whole of the inner court, from the eastern gate as in fig. 2, but here with the temple proper (*templum*), the two adjacent houses (*domus australis* and *domus aquilonis*), and the independent building to the west of the temple proper, between it and the wall of the inner precinct (*aedificium separatum*). K

Chapter 3

Figure 4. Plan of the outer wall, with the three gates (northern, southern, and eastern) in elevation. K

Chapter 4

Figure 5. Plan outlining the two sides of the eastern gatehouse and the passageway (*transitus, vel via, vel medium vestibulum*) between them; with measurements.

Chapter 5

Figure 6. Plan of one side of the eastern gatehouse with the three rooms (*thala*) and the vestibules at each end (the seven parts of the ground floor); with measurements. K

Chapter 6

Figure 7. Plan of the whole complex of the eastern gatehouse, showing the rooms and vestibules on both sides of the central passageway; with measurements. K

Maps and Plans in Medieval Exegesis 45

Chapter 12

Figure 8. Plan of the eastern part of the inner court, from the eastern gate to the threshold of the temple proper, with parlours (*gazophylacii*) to show the location of eight kitchens (*coquinis*) and the sanctuary stream divided into four branches. Missing in all except two manuscripts of the full text and one containing an extract. K. Figs. 1.3 and 1.4 in this volume.

Chapter 15

Figure 9. Circular geometrical diagram for the calculation of angles. Two manuscripts add a column of squares and triangles in margin. K
Figure 10. Elevation showing the façade of the eastern gatehouse.

Chapter 16

Figure 11. Elevation showing the side of the eastern gatehouse, with land sloping down steeply from the right.
Figure 12. Plan of the temple proper (*templum*), with the interior divided into vestibule, main temple area, and holy of holies (*sanctum sanctorum*), and the altar of incense in the middle of the central room. This diagram is sometimes referred to in modern literature as the sanctuary plan. Some plans have few measurements, others give measurements for passages along the side walls.

Chapter 17

Figure 13. Elevation of the northern gatehouse, with projecting gallery (*deambulationis*) normally on left, and land sloping down steeply from left to right. In one manuscript the gallery projection is omitted.

Chapter 19

Figure 14. Elevation of the altar of holocausts.

Chapter 20

Figure 15. Map of Canaan, *Description seu divisio totius terrae promissionis*, with the sanctified central strip, containing the temple, city, and lands of the Levites (the priests) and the prince, flanked by the strips allotted to the twelve tribes, seven to the north and five to the south. K. Fig. 1.7 in this volume.

WALTER CAHN

2 An Illuminated Manuscript of Writings by Hugh of St. Victor (Paris, Bibl. Mazarine, Ms 729)

Hugh of St. Victor (d. 1141) has in the past one hundred years come to occupy a persistent, if somewhat episodic, place in the historiography of medieval art. Although his concern with issues of visual representation are not those articulated, with perhaps greater urgency, by Bernard of Clairvaux or Abbot Suger of St. Denis, his large body of writings touch incidentally on a variety of topics related to the arts in their contemporaneous setting or through the lens of modern interpretation. Thus, the dignity accorded to the mechanical arts in the decisive formulation of his *Didascalicon* (II, 20–27) places manual activity on a par with intellectual pursuits, displaying a particular interest in skills such as weaving, sewing, woodworking, or masonry construction, and, elsewhere, in ship building.[1] On a more conceptual plane, Hugh gave renewed currency to the parallel instituted by Pope Gregory the Great between the procedures of biblical exegesis and the stages of construction, in which the literal meaning figures as the foundation, the moral dimension as the walls set upon it, and the anagogical or tropological interpretation as the decorative features of the completed structure.[2] Hugh was intimately familiar with the use of diagrams for demonstrative purposes, employed in his treatise *De tribus maximis circumstancii gestorum*, and put to use with much greater ambition and unprecedented complexity in his reconstruction of Noah's Ark as a kind of theological *Weltmodell*.[3] An anonymous treatise of descriptive geography, plausibly attributed to him, which seems to have contained a map of the world, further documents this diagrammatic strain in his work.[4]

Hugh's influence on the monumental arts has been detected in a variety of contexts. As in many instances within a historiography reaching back to the nineteenth century, Emile Mâle's classic book on religious art in thirteenth-century France gave a decisive impulse in this direction, though Mâle's reliance on the authority of Migne's *Patrologia* led him to attribute to Hugh some writings now thought to be the work of other authors.[5] In more recent times, Hugh's theology has been assumed to stand behind the then-novel program of Nicholas of Verdun's Klosterneuburg altar, with its tripartite exegetical scheme of *ante legem, sub lege*, and *sub gratia*.[6] M.-L. Thérel discerns his influence on the theme of the Assumption of the Virgin as embodied in the tympanum of the central doorway of Senlis Cathedral.[7] But the great number of topics addressed in Hugh's large written oeuvre and the wide diffusion that these writings achieved, first in the twelfth century and again toward the end of the Middle Ages, has made him a "relevant" point of reference for commentary on questions of religious imagery in the broadest sense.

Much scholarly energy has been expended on the question of the origins of Gothic architecture, as epitomized by the reconstruction of the ancient abbey of St. Denis undertaken in the reign of Abbot Suger, and strikingly memorialized by his writings. How these texts help us to understand the intentions of the builders and the underlying esthetic of the new edifice remain the subject of some contention. Erwin Panofsky, who translated Suger's writings and commented on them, thought the monument to exhibit a metaphysics of light, which Suger distilled from an immersion into the mystical tracts of Ps.-Dionysius the Areopagite.[8] Later authors have not denied this claim, but have predicated Suger's response to these difficult writings on the existence of intermediaries, or have sought to embed this Parisian reception of the Dionysian corpus within a wider context, from which Suger, not himself a profound theologian in any sense, might have drawn inspiration. Otto von Simson was the first to propose that Ps.-Dionysius was mediated for Suger and his contemporaries by Hugh of St. Victor's *Commentary on the Celestial Hierarchy*, a view suggestively elaborated by Grover Zinn, while Suger's indebtedness to the spirituality of the Victorine milieu more generally has been propounded by Conrad Rudolph and other writers.[9]

Hugh's now rather large profile as a significant figure for the understanding of the art of his time stands in some contrast to the paucity of works that can be tied more directly to his life and career. Save for his epitaph, transmitted to us by late sources, his tomb in the cloister of St. Victor has long ago vanished, along with nearly all material traces of the abbey. The diagrammatic construction described in the treatise now called *Liber de formatione arche*, on whose elucidation much ink has been spilled, has not been found among the some fifty-three copies of the work that have thus far been identified, and may well have been a rhetorical figure only, as some commentators have surmised.[10] Setting aside *De sacramentis Christianae fidei*, his longest and most systematic work, Hugh's writings, catalogued in an *Indiculum* by Abbot Gilduin of St. Victor (d. 1155) tend to be relatively short. Their diffusion, which began in the lifetime of the author, took the form of collections of such pieces, reflecting a particular, though not always easily discernible, interest, or only the availability of a particular text model.[11] The placement of the tract *De institutione novitiorum*, which is the first item in a number of these collections, including the manuscript to be dealt with in further detail below, perhaps reflects such a deliberate choice, since its contents seem well suited for such an introductory purpose.

Founded in 1113, St. Victor, like other newly established reformed houses, did not have a reserve of older books or the benefit of an existing scribal practice. But the value that it placed on learning and its setting in the shadow of a growing university in Paris must have made the acquisition and production of books a priority. From the *Liber ordinis* of the abbey, we learn that the canons copied books for their own use, but also turned to professional scribes in the city to supplement these in-house efforts.[12] It is not easy to differentiate the productions realized in the abbey from those obtained *pro precio*, as indeed both shared in a common culture marked by the rise of a demand of an academic public for books of biblical commentary and prescholastic literature, increasingly fed after the middle of the century by lay ateliers. Such as it has come down to us, the rich library of St. Victor is undoubtedly not fully representative, either of its original contents or of the holdings of comparable religious houses.[13] Liturgical books, on which greater care and often luxurious decoration were lavished, are virtually absent, and a three-volume Bible with ornamental initials of good if not spectacular quality, now divided between the Bibliothèque nationale de France and the Mazarine Library, is the only manuscript of some decorative elaboration from the first half-century of the abbey's existence to which we can point.[14] On the other hand, the library of St. Victor was substantially enriched over time by donations of books from clerics who, having studied in Paris, eventually became members of the community or sought to benefit from the prayers of its members.

Manuscripts containing Hugh's writings or those of other Victorine authors were of course designed primarily for study rather than display, and they customarily received from their scribes only a modest embellishment of drawn and painted ornamental initials. Richard of St. Victor's *Commentary on Ezekiel* is in this respect an exception, in that it received at the outset a series of ground plans and elevations illustrating the author's literal interpretation of the prophet's visionary temple on the mountain, which are explicitly called for in Richard's text, and reproduced in later copies of the work.[15] The general trend in Paris was also, from the second half of the twelfth century onward, toward a more spartan or unadorned presentation of philosophical and theological texts, just as Gothic architecture, reacting against the exuberance of Romanesque decorative carving, resorted increasingly to ornament of an abstract character. Allowance made for the inevitable lacunae in our evidence, one would therefore look in vain in this Parisian setting for productions of Victorine writings with more than a very modest visual interest. A distinction must be made, however, between Paris and copies of these texts made elsewhere, especially in older Benedictine houses, where different canons obtained, or where the personalities and reputations of the Parisian masters assumed something like the status of the traditional *auctoritates*. Images of Hugh of St. Victor, who was sometimes referred to as *alter Augustinus*, and portrayed as an author engaged in writing or addressing a group of disciples, thus adorn a number of manuscripts containing his works from different parts of Europe, and the reception of other *moderni*, among them Peter Lombard and Peter Comestor, followed a similar pattern.[16]

The manuscript of works of Hugh of St. Victor that is the subject of this paper also reflects the rapid diffusion of his writings in an older monastic setting, and it is the only example known to me among the considerable number of surviving copies of his literary production that is fully illuminated. It is a volume, preserved in the Mazarine library (Ms 729), containing the following texts: *De institutione novitiorum* (fols. 1r–11r); *Liber de sacramentis* (11r–197r); *De archa Noe morali* (197r–221r); *Liber de formatione arche* (221r–229v); *De vanitate mundi* (230r–247r); *De amore sponsi ad sponsam* (247r–249v); *De tribus diebus* (249v–260v); *Adnotationes elucidatoriae in threnos Jeremiae* (260v–263v); *De verbo incarnato collatio I* (263v–264v); *Commentariorum in hierarchiam Sancti Dionysii Aeropagiticae* (264v–292r), the latter extant through the words "*Laudabimus inquam, principium omnis hierarchiae scientiae*" near the beginning of book 5. The manuscript, sporting an unassuming nineteenth-century binding, has suffered some damage. The initial Q of the opening text, which perhaps featured a portrait of the author, has been excised, along with the initial of book 7 of *De sacramentis* (fol. 56r), and, as noted above, roughly half of the last item in the volume, which probably covered some twenty-five to thirty folios, is missing. The work was first mentioned and summarily, if not altogether accurately, described in Auguste Molinier's catalogue of the manuscripts of the Mazarine, and its contents have been more recently exploited for the editions of *De tribus diebus* by D. Poirel and the treatises on Noah's Ark by P. Sicard, who have assigned to it the *siglum* Pm².[17] According to Molinier, the volume comes from the library of the Jacobins, the Dominican house founded upon the arrival of the friars in Paris in 1217, which indicates that this was not the site of its creation. It was acquired by the Mazarine, like the rest of the medieval holdings of the library, from one of the *dépots* established in the aftermath of the French Revolution to which books of religious houses of the capital that had been suppressed were consigned before being dispersed to public collections of the city.[18] The date of the manuscript is not known, but Patricia Stirnemann places it on stylistic grounds between the years 1140 to 1150, a judgment with which I concur.[19]

Though written with care in a late-Romanesque book hand, there are irregularities in the treatment of the material, a sign that the transmission of this collection of texts, some of which only recently composed, others perhaps still not yet having reached their definitive state, was by no means straightforward. One is thus surprised to find summaries (*capitula*) only for books 3, 5, 6, and 7 in the first part of *De sacramentis* (fols. 26r, 38r, 45v, 55v–56r). *Incipits* are sometimes present and sometimes not, or take different forms, and the same is true for *explicits*, as in the case of the two treatises on Noah's Ark, which shade into one another without a break, or *De verbo incarnato*, which similarly follows the preceding text unannounced. The *Commentary on Jeremiah's Lamentations* is incomplete, the matter on hand corresponding to no more than nine of a total sixty-seven columns in the printed version of the *Patrologia*, while Hugh's authorship is given for some items (*De archa Noe morali, De vanitate mundi, De tribus diebus*) but not for the other pieces in the volume. Beyond what inferences can be drawn from a detailed examination of the manuscripts, the correspondence of Priors William of Ourscamp and Guarinus of St. Albans and St. Victor, both of whom sought to obtain copies of the writings of Richard of St. Victor for their communities, sheds a glancing light on the processes of textual transmission involved.[20]

The illumination of the Mazarine codex was carried out by a single painter, and takes the form of figurative and ornamental initials placed at the head of the different pieces collected in the volume and their subdivisions, while flourished letters in red and blue grace the body of the text throughout. Although a fluent and experienced performer, the artist must have faced a certain challenge, for which there was no precedent. The results by no means adhere to a strict and predictable plan, but a certain rough pattern in his procedure can be discerned. Ornamental initials, including several hybrid designs featuring acrobatic, clambering figures (fols. 249v, 264v) outnumber figurative ones, but with a certain degree of alternation. For the most part, the figurative imagery draws on an existing repertory rather than ad hoc invention, in all probability taking guidance, for the choice of subject, from the rubricated chapter headings. Thus, the discussion in the first part of *De sacramentis* of the Creation (*prima pars exameron in opera conditionis*) displays in the opening initial the Lord dividing the heavens from the earth (fig. 2.1), followed in due course by the creation of the angels (*De creatione*

Figure 2.1. Creation of Heaven and Earth (Paris, Bibl. Mazarine, Ms 729, fol. 13r). Used with the permission of the Bibliothèque Mazarine.

Figure 2.2. Creation of the Angels (Paris, Bibl. Mazarine, Ms 729, fol. 38v). Used with the permission of the Bibliothèque Mazarine.

angelorum) (fig. 2.2) and of Adam (*De creatione hominis*), familiar subjects of biblical illustration, while the more ecclesiological content of the second part is highlighted by initials showing a bishop and two disputing clerics (*De potestate spirituali et eius corona*), the dedication of a church (*De dedicatione Ecclesiae*), a scene of marriage (*De sacramento conjugii*) (fig. 2.3), and the anointing of the sick (*De unctione infirmorum*), all subjects customarily found among the illustrations of books of canon law.

Figure 2.3. Marriage (Paris, Bibl. Mazarine, Ms 729, fol. 137r). Used with the permission of the Bibliothèque Mazarine.

Figure 2.4. Construction of a church (Paris, Bibl. Mazarine, Ms 729, fol. 214r). Used with the permission of the Bibliothèque Mazarine.

This is also the likely source of the arresting depiction of the construction of a church that rather unexpectedly singles out for attention the fourth chapter (fifth as given in our manuscript) of the following tract in the volume, *De archa Noe morali*, introduced and accounted for by the heading *Ubi et unde et cum quo et qualiter edificanda sit domus dei* (fig. 2.4). In other instances, the illuminator, faced with the challenge of an unfamiliar assignment, fell back on well-ingrained habits. The initial that marks the beginning of the *Commentary on the Celestial Hierarchy* of Pseudo-Dionysius provided the occasion for a portrait of this obscure sixth-century author, conventionally reinvented here as a bishop or abbot discoursing from an open book. The letter I, that marries form with content in a single standing figure, is a familiar motif in Romanesque book illumination, and the painter of the Mazarine manuscript twice makes use of it, first as an emblem of the incarnate Word (*De Sacramentis*, 2.1) and again as a personification of the Bridegroom that marks the beginning of the short treatise *De amore sponsi ad sponsam* (fig. 2.5).

De vanitate mundi, the fifth item in the anthology, drew from the illuminator a more unusual composition, that cannot be so easily accounted for on the basis of a reliance on stock imagery or force of habit. The treatise in its denunciation of worldly pursuits and pleasures reveals its derivation from the words of Ecclesiastes, whose opening phrase "Vanitas, vanitatum" constitute the biblical source of the disabused tone characteristic of the literary genre that bears the label *De contemptu mundi*.[21] The composition of this piece, of which forty-seven copies survive—twelve datable in the twelfth century—seems to have been laborious, and questions raised by its genesis and transmission have not all been resolved.[22] The work consists of four books and, like a number of Hugh's writings, is cast in the form of a dialogue between interlocutors identified in some manuscripts (and the edition of the *Patrologia*) with the letters D and I, which have been thought variously to stand for *Discipulus* and *Magister*; *Docens* and *Interrogans*; or Dindimus, King of the Brachmanes, and one Indaletus, similarly cast in the respective roles of teacher (or wise man) and student, who are the protagonists (along with another speaker named Sosthenes) of another composition by the author, *Epitome in philosophiam*. It has also been noted that the content of books 3 and 4 differs from that of the first two books, which alone treat the topic announced by the title, and might originally have been conceived as independent compositions. Mazarine 729, in any case, omits this more "normative" second part, which was perhaps not available to the scribe, and substitutes for it part of another tract by Hugh in dialogue form, *De sacramentis legis naturalis*.[23]

In our manuscript, as in an undetermined number of copies of *De vanitate*, including what is thought to be the earliest known version (BnF, Ms lat. 15139), which stems from St. Victor, the speakers in the dialogue are identified as A and R (in the minuscule form of these letters), or *Anima* and *Ratio*,

Figure 2.5. Heavenly Bridegroom (Paris, Bibl. Mazarine, Ms 729, fol. 247r). Used with the permission of the Bibliothèque Mazarine.

Figure 2.6. Dialogue of the Soul and Reason (Paris, Bibl. Mazarine, Ms 729, fol. 230r). Used with the permission of the Bibliothèque Mazarine.

the Soul and Reason.[24] The initial is a circle, thickly outlined in grey-green and light blue, and set within a matte gold square (fig. 2.6). The hollow of the letter houses a crowded and roughly symmetrical composition which juxtaposes two separate, differently scaled components somewhat awkwardly brought together: a bearded, bust-length figure set in a roundel that nearly fills the lower half of the space and, framing it, the dialogue carried on by gesticulating female personifications of the Soul and Reason, the first given visual form as a long-haired naked figure, the second dressed in long robes and chastely veiled. A distych in red letters that appears above the initial describes and comments on the subject: "Hic species anime depingitur et rationis / Mundus adest etiam de quo fit lectio presens" (Here are depicted the Soul and Reason / Present is the world also, which is the subject of this lesson). Explanatory sets of verses of this kind, most likely added after the completion of the manuscript, are found in the margins adjoining two other historiated initials of the manuscript, the first near the creation of the heavens and the earth (*De sacramentis* 1.1),[25] the second commenting on the Lord's formation of Adam (1, part 6).[26]

The confrontation of a pair of female figures, one of them naked and the other clothed, may in Western art, and especially in the Renaissance and Baroque periods, bear the connotation of a radical contrast between Virtue and Vice.[27] But in the initial at hand, we deal rather with a more benign allegorical engagement between two complementary, if unequal moral agents, Reason giving instruction based on knowledge and experience to an innocent Soul seeking wisdom, as in the idealized relationship between Master and Pupil. Although the scene in general terms partakes in the tradition of dialogue images, whose origin has been traced back to Late Antiquity,[28] making visible the embodied Soul as an active protagonist suggests that there are links between the image of Mazarine 729 and the poetic evocation of the Soul's joys and travails in the Psalms. Among the literal illustrations of the ninth-century Stuttgart Psalter and, later, the initials of the Psalter of St. Albans, the Psalmist or his Soul addressing his supplication to the Lord is thus portrayed as a conversation between a lively, naked figure and a fully dressed interlocutor.[29]

Who is the wide-eyed, staring figure in the roundel, and what is its relation to the dialogue of *Anima* and *Ratio*? A possible visual clue might be lodged in his curious headgear, a wide grey cap with a golden border resembling an inverted saucer that sits tightly on the skull. In Mazarine 729, it figures once again as an attribute of the Bridegroom at the beginning of the following piece, *De amore sponsi ad sponsam*, where the object exhibits a small excrescence at the top (fig. 2.5), as it does in another manuscript illuminated by the painter, where a similar cap is worn by St. Augustine's opponent, the heretic Faustus (fig. 2.7).[30] It takes a plainer, more

Figure 2.7. Faustus (Vendôme, Bibl. mun. Ms 34, fol. 90v). Used with the permission of the Institut de recherche et d'histoire des textes.

rounded form in the figures of Moses, Job, and one of the Hebrews addressed by St. Paul in a Bible that is now preserved in the library of the Chambre des Députés (Assemblée nationale),[31] but it is also worn by one of the Romans in a copy of Gilbert de la Porrée's commentary on the Pauline Epistles,[32] as well as the husband in a scene of marriage found in a volume of Peter Lombard's *Sentences*.[33] For some of these figures at least, the peaked hat (*pileus cornutus*) that functions as an identifying sign in the representation of Jews might have been found appropriate, but it must be said that the version favored by the painter does not closely resemble the form of this headgear, admittedly quite variable, typically seen in late-Romanesque and Gothic art.[34] We seem to deal thus with an attribute that confers on the wearer a mark of distinction, but not a specific identity, and if there is anything that describes this group of figures, among which both biblical and extrabiblical subjects are found, it is its decidedly miscellaneous character.

Although an elaborate incipit—the most extended in the manuscript—names Hugh as the author of *De vanitate*, the figure lacks the clerical tonsure and canonial vestments that are invariable aspects of his portraiture. On the other hand, the weighty presence of the figure, its solemn demeanor, and the golden circle that frames it and effectively detaches it from its surroundings were no doubt designed to endow it with a certain measure of significance. Perhaps we should think of it as a personification of *Mundus*, (the World or worldliness), *presens*, according to the distych, whose distinctive headgear should be read as a piece of showy finery.[35] Or it might have been intended as an authorial portrait in a generalized sense, justified to a degree by the fact that the text itself makes no mention of the writer nor explicitly names anyone else. One might also speculate that the figure was designed to represent the author of Ecclesiastes, which furnished the inspiration for Hugh's commentary. This hypothesis raises other objections, which are pertinent though not altogether unanswerable. Ecclesiastes proclaims its author, the Preacher (as he is also known), to be "the son of David, King of Jerusalem" (Eccl 1:1), a fact noted and elaborated upon by Hugh in his *Didascalicon* (IV, chap. 3), as well as in his *Homilies on Ecclesiastes*,[36] which appears to cite that work. In line with this royal ancestry, depictions known to me thus generally show him wearing a crown, as does our painter in the initial which adorns the text in the Chambre des Députés Bible.[37] But there are exceptions, in which a more neutral treatment of the subject occurs, and the figure in the Mazarine manuscript, where neither his name nor royal status are mentioned, might well be one of them.

The localization of the manuscript happily poses fewer difficulties, as it has been possible through the collective efforts of scholars over the past decades to assemble a small but coherent body of work illuminated by the same painter. Along with a fair amount of leaf gold, left unpolished, he works in a distinctive range of opaque colors, pink, powder blue, and a kind of grey tinged with green predominating, while forms are sharply outlined in black and shaded by means of parallel striations. Figures display a characteristic and more or less uniform physiognomy, with staring eyes, small pinched mouths, and beards marked in the middle by a sharp vertical cleft. One of the books in the series, the already-mentioned copy of Augustine's *Contra Faustum*, was written by a scribe named Aubertus and bears the ex-libris of the abbey of La Trinité at Vendôme,[38] and three other manuscripts illuminated by the same hand or exhibiting traces of his style stem from the same library: copies of Gilbert de la Porrée's commentary on the Epistles, Peter Lombard's *Sentences*, and an Epistolary.[39]

Penelope D. Johnson, whose book on the abbey includes a brief sketch of manuscript illumination at Vendôme, proposes to call him "the gold leaf artist" in order to distinguish his work from the more sober manner of earlier local productions.[40] His style has close connections with the book illumination of nearby Tours, a much older and long-established center of manuscript production, and a Gregory *Moralia in Job* from the cathedral of that city should perhaps be counted among his works, as Jean Porcher suggested.[41] He contributed several initials to a homiliary of unknown provenance preserved in the Arsenal Library, the remnant of a multivolume set, which would seem to be the earliest manuscript in which his hand is found.[42] With its comprehensive décor of historiated and ornamental initials, the Bible of the Chambre des Députés is the most important work that can thus far be attributed to him (fig. 2.8). It came to its present repository from the library of Nigeon (Minim friars of Passy, or of Chaillot), established on the western fringes of Paris after 1483, and it is known earlier to have been in the possession of a notable in Bourges, but its place of origin, too, remains for the moment unknown. Future discoveries, one may hope, will help to shed additional light on the painter's career.

Figure 2.8. David fighting the lion, David and Goliath (Paris, Chambre des Députés, Ms 2, fol. 164r). Used with the permission of the Bibliothèque de l'Assemblée nationale.

NOTES

1. Hugh of St. Victor, *Didascalicon de studio legendi*, ed. Buttimer, 38 ff., and English translation by Taylor in Hugh of St. Victor, *Didascalicon*, 74–79. On the mechanical arts and Hugh's important place in the history of the concept, see Sternagel, *Die artes mechanicae*, 67–77. In the preparation of this essay, I have benefited from the advice and suggestions of Patricia Stirnemann, here gratefully acknowledged.

2. *Didascalicon*, VI, 2–3. De Lubac, *Exégèse médiévale*, 2:41–60. In the wake of Hugh's reiteration of this conceit, it is taken up with slight variation in Peter of Poitiers' *Allegoriae super tabernaculum Moysis* (see Moore, *The Works of Peter of Poitiers*, 97); Peter Comestor, *Historia scholastica* (PL 198:1053–54); Adam the Scot (or Dryburgh), *Allegoriae in universam Scripturam sacram* (PL 112:849–50); John of Kelso, *De Tripartito Tabernaculo* (PL 198:623); Alain de Lille, *Sermones octo*, V (PL 210:209); Gerald of Wales, *Symbolum electorum*, ep. 24 (in his *Opera*, ed. Brewer, 1:271–72); Caesarius of Heisterbach, *Dialogus miraculorum*, Dist. I, chap. 1, p. 57.

3. I borrow the expression from Ehlers, "Arca significat ecclesiam." A schema of Hugh's *opus conditionis* is reproduced and described by W. Green, "Hugh of Saint-Victor," and further discussed by Zinn, "The Influence of Hugh of Saint-Victor's *Chronicon*." On Hugh and the diagrammatic tradition, see further Obrist, "Image et prophétie," and Carruthers, *The Book of Memory*, 231–39 and *passim*.

4. Gautier Dalché, *La "Descriptio mappe mundi."*

5. Mâle, *L'art religieux du XIIIe siècle*, translated as *Religious Art in France*, 9, 12,13, 103, 108, and *passim*.

6. Röhrig, *Der Verduner Altar*, 26 ff, and Buschhausen, "The Klosterneuburg Altar," 20–25.

7. Thérel, *Le triomphe de la Vierge-Église*, 294–99 and *passim*.

8. Panofsky, *Abbot Suger*, 18–20.

9. Simson, *The Gothic Cathedral*, 120 ff. Zinn, "Suger, Theology, and the Pseudo-Dionysian Tradition," 33–40. Rudolph, *Artistic Change at St.-Denis*. This view has been contested on various grounds by Markschies, *Gibt es eine "Theologie,"* and Speer, "Is There a Theology of the Gothic Cathedral?" 65–83. See also on this question the judicious overview of this question by Poirel, "Symbolice et anagogice," in Poirel, ed., *L'Abbé Suger* as well as the papers of Erlande-Brandenburg and Sicard in the same volume.

10. Holding that the diagram of the Ark described by Hugh is a literary fiction only are Evans, "Fictive Painting in Twelfth-Century Paris," and Carruthers, "Moving Images in the Mind's Eye," esp. 292 ff. That Hugh's demonstration was accompanied by a graphic image of some sort is maintained, among others, by Ehlers, "Arca significat ecclesiam"; Sicard, *Diagrammes médiévaux*; Rudolph, *"First I Find the Center Point"*; and Gautier Dalché, *La "Descriptio mappe mundi,"* 17, who writes "Il

est certain qu'il représenta sur les murs ou le sol du cloître de Saint-Victor un dessin complexe revêtu de couleurs destiné à servir de support à ses explications."

11. On the manuscript evidence of Hugh's writings and their diffusion, see Goy, *Die handschriftliche Überlieferung*, and the review of that book by Châtillon, "La transmission de l'oeuvre de Hugues de Saint-Victor."

12. *Liber ordinis Sancti Victoris Parisiensis*, and the commentary by Jocqué, "Les structures de la population claustrale," esp. 74–81 on the role of the *armarius* (chap. 19), as well as the analysis in d'Alverny, *Bibliothèque nationale*, xi and following.

13. Ouy, *Manuscrits de l'abbaye de Saint-Victor*.

14. Paris, BnF, Mss lat. 14395 and 14396, completed by Paris, Bibl. Mazarine, Ms 47. See Cahn, *Romanesque Bible Illumination*, p. 278, no. 94, and Stirnemann, "Où ont été fabriqués les livres de la Glose," 266 and 279, n. 34.

15. Paris, BnF, Ms lat. 14516, fols. 207–52. Cahn, "Architecture and Exegesis." Since the publication of my article, a fuller list of manuscripts of this text has been given by Goy, *Die handschriftliche Überlieferung*, 114–18. Also see the chapter by Delano-Smith in this volume

16. Poirel, "Alter Augustinus." An anthology of portraits of Hugh in manuscripts is found in Sicard, *Hugues de Saint-Victor et son école*, pls I–V.

17. 292 fols., 2 cols., 42 lines, 377 x 256 mm. Two older shelfmarks: 1156 and 410 (fol. 1r). Molinier, *Catalogue des manuscrits de la Bibliothèque Mazarine*, 1:338–39. It should be noted that the foliation of the manuscript, a somewhat irregular medieval one in Roman numerals up to fol. 214, another of the nineteenth century to the end of the volume, has led to some confusion. This is reflected in the differences between the description of the contents by Molinier, Goy, *Die handschriftliche Überlieferung*, who follows him; and my own, which attempts a more accurate enumeration. The manuscript was included in a small exhibition of the library designed to accompany the colloquium *1108–2008: L'influence de l'école de Saint-Victor de Paris au Moyen Âge* (Paris, Collège des Bernardins, 24–27 Sept. 2008) with a catalogue prepared by C. Giraud and P. Stirnemann, entitled "Le rayonnement de l'école de Saint-Victor: Manuscrits de la Bibliothèque Mazarine." The text, kindly made available to me in proof by Patricia Stirnemann, is found in the published text on pages 653–66, where our manuscript figures with a brief description as no. 9 on p. 658.

18. On the library of the Jacobins (Dominicans of the Rue St. Jacques), see Franklin, *Les anciennes bibliothèques*, 1:191–96, and on the foundation of this convent, Schenkluhn, *Architektur der Bettelorden*, 29–31 and *passim*.

19. Giraud and Stirnemann, "Le rayonnement de l'école de Saint-Victor." Poirel, *Livre de la nature*, 110, dates the manuscript on the authority of Stirnemann in the years 1140–1150, and "vers 1140–1155" in his edition of Hugh of St. Victor's *De tribus diebus*, 47, while Sicard's edition of Hugh's *De archa Noe* and *Libellus de formatione arche*, 43, has "vers 1140–1150." Lalou, Rabel, and Holtz, "Dedens mon livre de pensee ...," 34, prefer a date "vers 1160" for two Vendôme manuscripts illuminated by the same hand, on which see further below.

20. An issue perspicuously explored in the introductory remarks of Châtillon, *Trois opuscules spirituels*, 23–27.

21. PL 176:703–40, and Hugh of St. Victor, *De vanitate mundi*, ed. Müller, 26–48. On the substance of the work and its background, see Stammler, *Frau Welt*, 14 ff.; Schlette, *Die Nichtigkeit der Welt*, 67–103; Sieben, "Vanité du monde," esp. 263–64, and the brief commentary of Poirel, *Hugues de Saint-Victor*, 115–17. Stammler, *Frau Welt*, 18 and 92–93, n. 48, notes the wide currency in the theological literature of the wordplay *mundus immundus*, which opens Hugh's treatise.

22. Hauréau, *Hugues de Saint-Victor*, 93–94. Hugonin, *Etude critique*. Baron, *Science et sagesse*, 179–81.

23. The borrowed material encompasses roughly two-thirds of the printed text (PL 176:17–42) from the beginning through the phrase "ubi et quando et qualia bella gesserint quomodo vicerint, quae postremo praemia victoria consummata perceperint" at the top of col. 33.

24. Another dialogue between the Soul and Reason, is attributed to Adam of Dryburgh, *Soliloquium de instructione animae libri II.*

25. "Hic celum terramque creat deus omnium creatorum / Ut placat ista facit sol(um) et ex nichilo" (fol. 13r).

26. "Dissimilem cunctis animantibus: ipse creator / Sic hominem format vivificatque deus" (fol. 45v).

27. Panofsky, *Herkules*, 42 ff. and 150–66.

28. Saxl, "Frühes Christentum und spätes Heidentum," and Bloch, "Eine Dialogdarstellung."

29. Stuttgart, Württemb. Landesbib. MS fol. 23, fols. 10r (Ps 9:14–15); 30r (Ps 24:4); 50v (Ps 38:10, 12); 55r (Ps 42:4–5); 67r (Ps 54:20–23); 70v (Ps 58:1, 4), on which see the facsimile edition *Der Stuttgarter Bilderpsalter Bibl. fol. 23 Württembergische Landesbibliothek*, and Bischoff, Eschweiler, Fischer, and Mütherich, "Der Inhalt der Bilder," 55–150, in the accompanying commentary volume. In the St. Albans Psalter (Hildesheim, St. Godehard), see the initials of Psalms 27:7, 56:2, 72:21, 114:4, 118:1, 118:28, 118:73, and 118:109, in Pächt, Dodwell, and Wormald, *The St. Albans Psalter*, Pls. 50d, 58b, 63b, 75a, 76a, 77, 79a, and 80a.

30. Vendôme, Bibl. mun., Ms 34, fol. 90v.

31. Paris, Bibl. de la Chambre des Députés, Ms 2. Coyecque and Debraye, *Catalogue général des manuscrits*, 3–6. Cahn, *Romanesque Manuscripts*, 26–27, no. 15.

32. Vendôme, Bibl. mun. Ms 23, fol. 1r.

33. Vendôme, Bibl. mun. Ms 61, fol. 256r.

34. Sansy, "Chapeau juif ou chapeau pointu?" 349–75, with earlier bibliography, 350, n. 2.

35. Stammler, *Frau Welt*, 16–17, for symbols of *mundus*, and Gsodam, "Welt, Fürst der Welt, Frau Welt."

36. Hugh of St. Victor, *Didascalicon* (IV, 3 and 8), Taylor trans., 103, 109–10. Hugh of St. Victor, *In Salomonis Ecclesiasten homiliae XIX* (PL 175:115–16).

37. Paris, Bibl. de la Chambre des Députés, Ms 2, fol. 194r.

38. "Liber sancte Trinitatis Vindoci. Hanc librum scripsit Aubertus quem modo finit" (fol. 167r).

39. See above, nn. 32 and 33, and Vendôme, Bibl. mun., Ms 115 (Epistolary).

40. Johnson, *Prayer, Patronage, and Power*, 148. Lalou, Rabel and Holtz, "*Dedens mon livre de pensee*...," and Giraud and Stirnemann, "Le rayonnement de l'école de Saint-Victor: Manuscrits de la Bibliothèque Mazarine," refer to him as "Maître de Vendôme."

41. Tours, Bibl. mun., Ms 321. See the exhibition catalogue, *Manuscrits à peintures du VIIe and XIIe siècle*, 85, no. 235.

42. Paris, BnF, Arsenal, Ms 471. Martin, *Catalogue des manuscrits*, 1:315–20. The decoration of this manuscript is the work of two or more hands, our painter's share of the work beginning on fol. 111v, and includes as well the fine initial on fol. 134v (*Passio S. Vincentii*), the only historiated one in the volume. Granboulan, "De la paroisse à la cathédrale," 52, n. 28, citing F. Avril's opinion, adds to the list of attributions the decoration of a Sacramentary of Chartres or Tours (BnF, Ms lat.1096). The two painted ornamental initials (fols. 81v, 82r) in this otherwise rather undistinguished volume seem to me the work of a related, though different hand.

WILLIAM W. CLARK

3 The Twelfth-Century Church of St. Victor in Paris
A New Proposal

Evidence of the first church at the Abbey of St. Victor in Paris is, to say the least, minimal. It is almost inversely proportional to knowledge of the order, its founding, its famous philosophers, scholars and writers, and its impact on the intellectual life of Paris.[1] Nevertheless, gathering and examining the meager data of the church reveals the broad outlines of the building and some of its most prominent features that, in turn, provide clues for its dating (in the absence of solid evidence from the documents) and its relationship to twelfth-century architecture in Paris.[2] Careful consideration of this evidence suggests that St. Victor did not assume its grandest form until the abbacy of Gilduin (mid-1130s–1150), and that this church was of grander proportions than its Parisian rivals St. Denis and St. Germain-des-Prés, second only to the cathedral of Notre Dame as the longest and widest church of twelfth-century Paris.

Four categories of evidence constitute the starting point for this investigation, requiring a blend of art history, archaeology, and history to create an image of that early church. The effort is complicated because the first church was mostly replaced, following the collapse of the high vaults in 1517, by the construction of a new church, the cornerstone of which was laid on December 18, 1517.[3] In turn, this never-completed structure disappeared from the landscape of Paris in the aftermath of the French Revolution. The four categories include: (1) early engraved views; (2) pre-Revolutionary plans; (3) drawings of excavated sections of foundations; and (4) modern plans incorporating some of the excavated evidence.

THE VISUAL EVIDENCE

The least known category of evidence is the visual, specifically two mid-seventeenth-century engraved views by Jean Marot, the details of which show the exterior of the church directly from the north (fig. 3.1), and from the northwest (fig. 3.2).[4] Marot's prints were carefully copied several times by Silvestre and Mérian, among others. The view of the north side (fig. 3.1) includes, to the left of the sixteenth-century church, the twelfth-century bell tower and its stair vise, the spiral staircase used to access the upper stories. The tower had four stories: the lower three with single arched openings on each face, the top with double openings and a modest spire. This elevation makes it comparable to surviving twelfth-century towers, from St. Germain-des-Prés and Sainte-Geneviève in Paris to Chartres and St. Denis and the numerous examples cited below. The view from the northwest (fig. 3.2) mostly shows the sixteenth-century church, but includes a surviving section of the twelfth-century facade, analyzed below. An idea of the early building begins to emerge when these views of the church are studied together with the second category of evidence, specifically the ground plan drawn by Petit-Radel and Bénard in 1791,[5] and, the third, the evidence from the sporadic archeological investigations of the site conducted between 1899 and 1968,[6] especially the twelfth-century foundations located in 1931 (fig. 3.3).[7]

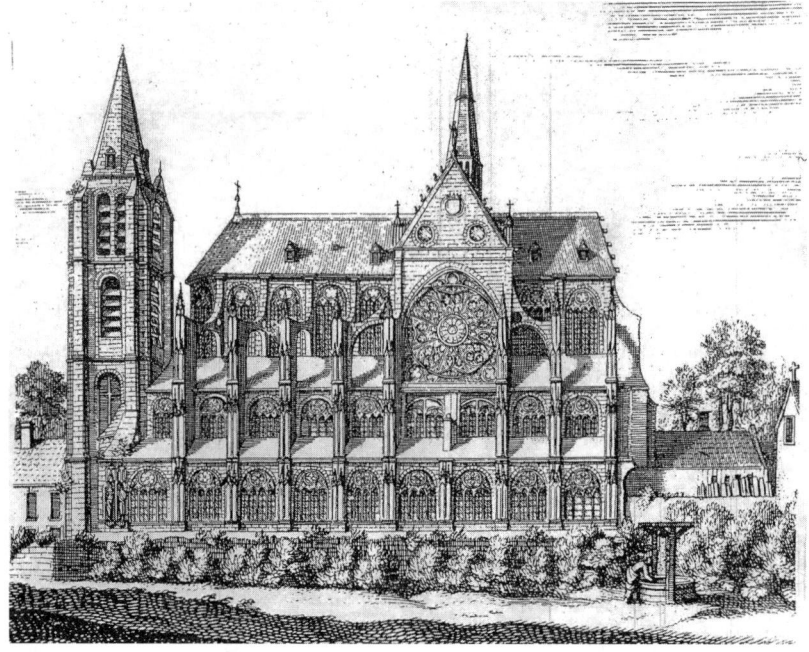

Figure 3.1. View of the north flank of Saint Victor, detail of the church after Mérian, *Topographia Galliae*.

These were combined with the 1791 plan in a second 1931 plan by Grimault (fig. 3.4).[8] Unfortunately, none of the excavations produced decorated or carved pieces that might have been useful for suggesting dates. The few pieces that emerged—all from periods long after the twelfth-century—were analyzed by Willesme in 1979.[9]

The 1931 excavations unearthed four distinct foundation masses separated from one another by the walls of the *halle aux vins* constructed in the early nineteenth century. These big chunks of masonry were carefully recorded in a plan by Grimault (fig. 3.3). In a second, larger plan he partially adapted these excavated foundations to the 1791 plan at ground level (fig. 3.4). Thus the two plans do not agree with one another at several points. The foundations (fig. 3.3), which appear to have shifted in the ground either during the post-Revolutionary destruction or the nineteenth-century construction that severed their connections, revealed the partially buried crypt (C),

Figure 3.2. View of the west end and north side of Saint Victor, detail of the church, after Mérian, *Topographia Galliae*.

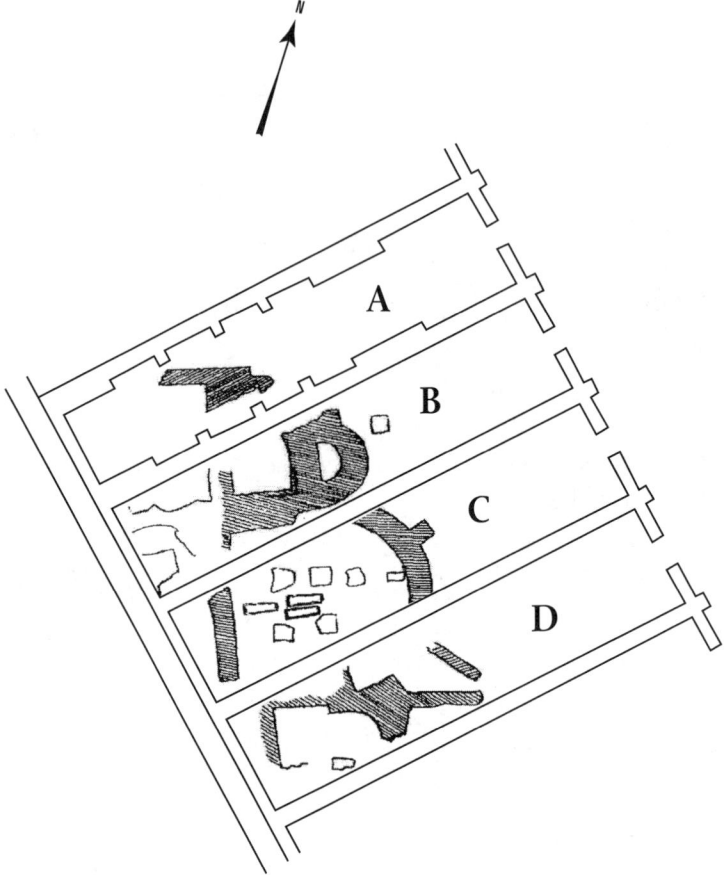

Figure 3.3. Foundations excavated by Grimault in 1931 (letters added) after Willesme, "Saint-Victor au temps d'Abélard," fig. 4.

a semi-circular apse with a square bay in front of it, five of the six supports for the upper level, and the foundations of the two ground-level apsidal chapels (B and D) that flanked it. Thus, the ground level had a classic tri-apsidal plan reflecting the crypt and the chapel foundations: over the crypt a larger, slightly elevated center chapel (the choir of the twelfth-century church) flanked by apsidal chapels. This tri-apsidal east end had three floor levels: the crypt, which, by the age of the masonry, Grimault identified with the first chapel

The Twelfth-Century Church of St. Victor in Paris   73

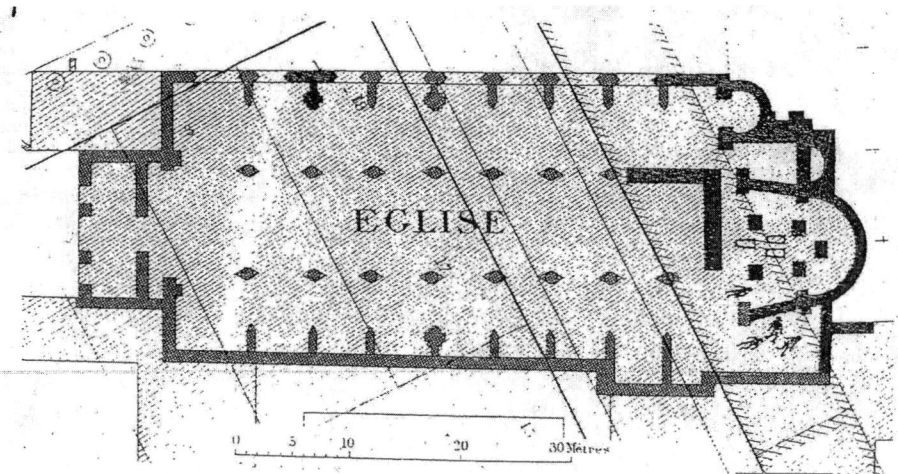

Figure 3.4. Reconstructed plan of Saint-Victor by Grimault, 1931, detail after Grimault, "Rapport présenté sur les fouilles effectuées place Jussieu."

on the site; the next level up, the ground-level flanking chapels, whose heavy foundations are twelfth-century; and lastly, the raised floor level of the new altar area, built over the the crypt and doubtlessly reached by front or side stairs. In addition, there was a smaller, partly circular foundation (A) flanking the north side of B. A was the stair vise opening off the east wall of the north transept arm and providing access to the second level of the tower over chapel B, both of which are visible in figure 3.1.

The most important discrepancy between the two plans (figs 3.3 and 3.4) is that Grimault chose to ignore his excavated evidence of the crypt and the flanking chapel foundations and instead imposed the plan of the sixteenth-century center chapel on the crypt. The crypt consisted of an almost semicircular apse with a square bay before it, as indicated by the parallel east-west walls of the foundations, rather than the trapezoidal space of the sixteenth-century chapel still evident in the 1791 plan. Upstairs the twelfth-century altar area occupied the space of the apse and the square bay in front of it. Hurtaut described two tall, rib-vaulted spaces (bays?) with windows.[10] In addition, the foundations of the south chapel (D) revealed an apse and a square bay in front of it, elements Grimault arbitrarily omitted in his second plan (fig. 3.4). The differences between the foundations of the two chapels suggest a shift of "D" in the landfill, as well as the fact that this chapel was destroyed during the reconstruction of the cloister and the library east of it in the sixteenth century. Judging by the thickness of the foundations (D), in comparison with the somewhat more extensive foundations of the north chapel (B), it is possible that D also carried a tower over the apsidal chapel similar to that erected above B and shown in the Marot prints. This would link the plan of the original east end to that series of plans with two towers flanking the center apse, a disposition present at St. Germain-des-Prés already in the eleventh century and still seen in numerous other examples, from Morienval to St. Leu d'Esserent.[11] Such a possibility should not be ruled out because the early records do not mention any towers. Knowledge of the single tower at St. Victor comes only from the seventeenth-century prints.

Unfortunately, there is no evidence for the precise location of the high altar, dedicated to St. Victor, in the twelfth-century church. Given the raised floor level over the crypt, it is most likely that the high altar was also along the line between the apse and the square bay or centered in the square bay. Hurtaut's *Dictionnaire*, in reality an early guidebook, mentions two upper, rib-vaulted bays and staircases on either side descending to the crypt chapel.[12] Additional stairs would have been located at the west end leading up to the altar area.

The second 1931 plan (fig. 3.4), like its 1791 source, indicates that the sixteenth-century church was expanded to the north to increase its width; thus, its east-west axis no longer matched that of the twelfth-century church. That axis, however, can be determined from the axis of the crypt and the chapel above it. The width of the early church was established along that original axis and limited by the original cloister on the south side. The twelfth-century church probably had a slightly projecting transept, suggested by the expanse of the two easternmost chapels on the south side of the sixteenth-century nave and by the presence of a corner of the original wall in the foundations on the north side (A). The combined east-west width of the two sixteenth-century chapels suggests that the original crossing bay and both transept arms might have been rectangular along the east-west axis. Within limits, we can speculate on the width of the choir and nave, but there is no reliable way to estimate the width of the side aisles (although they might have reflected the width of the two eastern apsidal chapels) nor can we determine the number of bays in the nave and aisles.[13] The overall length of the nave and aisles can be established, however, from the survival of part of the western wall of the early church that was still visible in the seventeenth-century Marot prints showing the facade (figs. 3.1 and 3.2). As at Montmartre, the canon's choir must have extended well into the nave and might well account for the length of the nave itself.

The center section of the facade shown in figure 3.2, was part of the original west end. It shows a lower west wall framed by pier buttresses at the two corners and surmounted by a triangular gable, the bottom edge of which is marked by a carved cornice. By the mid-seventeenth century the gable was truncated to fit within the roofed extension to the west end of the new nave. As shown, the facade wall is wider than the original nave, yet not wide enough to encompass the nave and side-aisles. The corner pier buttresses indicate that the wall was most likely part of a shallow narthex built in front of the nave. In turn, there was a low, double-gabled, vaulted porch before the narthex.[14] The discrepancies between the views—figure 3.1 shows the side (and thus the depth) of the narthex and porch, seen from the front in figure 3.2—and the plan (fig. 3.4) is explained by changes made between c. 1650 (the date of the prints) and 1791 (when the Petit-Radel and Bénard plan was drawn).

Nonetheless, because both the 1791 and 1931 plans were drawn to scale, we can estimate some of the original dimensions of the twelfth-century church, just as we have reconstructed some of its features from the prints and the archeological evidence. The interior length from the inner wall of the center chapel to the inner wall surface of the narthex is about 65 m. The width of the crypt between the straight walls excavated by Grimault in 1931 was about 10 m. This, in turn, suggests that the width of the altar area, the crossing, and the nave was also about 10 m, while the overall transept width was about 27.5 m. The distance between the centerline of the nave arcade and the wall of the sixteenth-century cloister indicates that the south side aisle was a little more than 5 m wide, assuming the new cloister followed the line of the twelfth-century cloister wall. The north side aisle might have been somewhat wider because there was no limit to its width. It must be noted that these are centerline measurements because we have no idea of the size, plan, or number of the nave piers and, therefore, can only speculate that the nave walls would have been thicker and would have required heavier supports for the vaulted superstructure.

If the proportions and the height of the west wall shown by Marot are reliable, then we can estimate that the nave vaults might have been as much as 20 to 22 m tall; if the narthex was shorter than the nave, then the vaults could have been taller, although it is doubtful. The crypt, with its six piers (in parallel rows of three each, as opposed to Grimault's decision to include only five) supporting the floor of the altar area, could have had a barrel vault, although the square bay raises the possibility of a groin vault, as in the ground level chapels. The rest of the church, like the altar platform, was rib-vaulted. The nave elevation would have consisted of either two or three stories, either main arcades with clerestory windows above them or, given a height of 20-plus meters, with a second level inserted between arcades and windows. Second story openings, even small ones, would have permitted air circulation between the aisle vaults and roof.

DOCUMENTS AND DATES

The original documents, including the foundation charter granted by Louis VI in 1113,[15] provide the historical context into which we should place the construction of St. Victor. The brilliant analysis of the historical situation and the political and ecclesiastical maneuvering in Paris during the early years of St. Victor, published by Bautier in 1991,[16] has stood the test of time and leaves little to be done, save for the study of the immense number of internal documents from the abbey, especially the donation charters. That project is daunting, to say the least. In his lengthy lists of the surviving documents, Bonnard noted, for example, over one hundred cartons of documents related just to the donation of income and lands in and around Paris.[17] The scope of the archival holdings is so vast that Bonnard himself, despite his disclaimer to the contrary, seems to have used only the summaries assembled between 1625 and 1659 by Jean de Thoulouse in the Annales,[18] or the latter's abbreviated version, the Antiquités.[19] Unfortunately, the Antiquités, although intended for publication, was never printed, and only the Abrégé de la fondation de l'abbaye de St Victor de Paris,[20] a single folio, was published in 1640. Thus, we are left with Bonnard's (questionable) endorsement of the accuracy of Jean de Thoulouse, but with nothing that can be used to confirm this. In short, much of the internal history of the abbey, especially its financial resources and properties, awaits thorough analysis and publication.

More than previous scholars, Bautier consulted the original documents, as well as the many published charters, and the voluminous evidence on twelfth-century Paris in general.[21] His astute observations of the situation have created the context into which we can place the construction of the first church. That context is crucially important because not a single known document, published or unpublished, makes specific reference to the construction of the twelfth-century church, other than the note in Gilduin's obituary that it had been built during his abbacy (1113–55).[22] The situation is further complicated because the 1113 foundation charter mentions an extant "chapel" of St. Victor on the site: "ecclesia Beati Victoris qui iuxta Parisiorum civitatem sita est."[23] Bautier cited earlier references to a "cella vetus" (old cell or chapel) and pointed out that, in the total absence of a cult of St. Victor in northern Gaul in the early Middle Ages, this might have been a corruption of "cella Victurina" that became "cella vetus sancti Victoris." Because no relic of St. Victor of Marseille is known in Paris prior to 1115, Bautier suggested other possible saints named Victor who might have been commemorated by an oratory or chapel in the Merovingian cemetery, such as an early bishop of Paris or another of Le Mans, among others. When, in 1108, Guillaume de Champeaux resigned as archdeacon of the cathedral and moved to the site with eight companions, they would have repaired, refurbished and possibly even expanded this earlier funerary chapel for their worship. Guillaume's election and consecration as bishop of Châlons-en-Champagne (formerly, Châlons-sur-Marne), where the foundation charter for St. Victor was issued by Louis VI between May 21 and August 2, 1113, left behind only a small community in Paris.

In 1981, Willesme argued, as have others before him, that the new church of St. Victor was probably begun in the 1120s, but there is no evidence to support this assertion.[24] The financial recovery of St. Victor, like that of most of the other religious institutions in Paris, seems to have begun only after the decision of Louis VI to settle, more or less permanently, in Paris circa 1130. Although the abbey reached a low point in 1134, when only eighteen canons remained, it grew to great prominence, as Bautier demonstrated, in the half-century from 1135 to 1185.[25] His systematic analysis of the sociopolitical turmoil of the period provides persuasive evidence that church construction most likely began after 1135, during the "golden age" of St. Victor, the period that witnessed the extraordinary development in the intellectual life at the abbey and its profound impact on intellectual life in Paris.[26]

THE ARCHITECTURAL CONTEXT

The tri-apsidal plan, the slightly projecting transept, and the tower or towers above the eastern chapels are all features that appeared regularly in Parisian religious architecture from the 1130s.[27] In fact, a date for the beginning of construction circa 1135–40 accords well with Bautier's analysis of the financial recovery and expansion that benefitted all of the major Parisian religious establishments, old and new. While all of the features listed above appeared in the eleventh-century abbey church of St. Germain-des-Prés, they became more common in the twelfth century. The royal nunnery of St. Denis, Notre Dame, and St. Pierre, founded on Montmartre by Queen Adelaide de Maurienne and Louis VI in 1134, offers the closest contemporary comparison of features with St. Victor. Both churches had tri-apsidal plans with nonidentical side chapels; towers above the bay in front of the northern apse (if not over both chapels); slightly projecting transepts with nearly square crossings; and (probably, in the case of St. Victor) rectangular nave bays with rib-vaults. In fact, there are a number of similar contemporary and slightly later churches that share these same features in Paris (St. Marcel, St. Julien-le-Pauvre, St. Germain-de-Charonne, St. Denis de la Chapelle, even Sainte-Geneviève, St. Martin-des-Champs, and St. Germain-des-Prés, among others) and to the south and east of Paris (Marolles-en-Brie, Notre-Dame at Château-Landon, St. Loup-de-Naud, Bransles, and St. Hilaire at St. Thierry in Champagne, to cite but a few).[28] Given these similarities, the archeological and visual evidence firmly place the church of St. Victor in the Parisian/Ile-de-France architectural context from the mid-1130s until the 1150s, during the abbacy of Gilduin.

In the final analysis, however, it is the audacious size of St. Victor that is its most striking feature. Some 65 m long, it was exceeded in length and overall size only by the cathedral. Not until the extensions at St. Denis (to about 99.5 m) and the addition of the chevet at St. Germain-des-Prés (to about 72.3 m) did its rivals exceed its projected length. And the combined nave and aisle width of 20–22 m made St. Victor second only to the cathedral as the widest church in Paris. If, as Bautier put it, its origins remain obscure and the circumstances of its foundation problematic, the new church of St. Victor displayed a grandeur that matched the abbey's place in the intellectual firmament of Paris during the twelfth century.

NOTES

It is a pleasure to present this project to Grover Zinn, Jr., a true friend and valued colleague. When Grover asked me about the first church, about 1983, my knowledge of it was limited, to say the least. Now in all humility, I have tried, a quarter century later, to answer his question. Special thanks to Vivian P. Cameron, Thomas G. Waldman, and Clark Maines for their advice and, above all, their questions.

1. The major studies are most recently cited in Berndt, "Bibliographie"; see also Teske, *Die Briefsammlungen*, for a study of the collections of letters by prominent Victorines. The only study devoted to the church of St. Victor is the unpublished dissertation of Willesme, "L'abbaye de Saint-Victor de Paris," from which he has published six articles (and one unpublished paper), all listed in the bibliography of this volume. Also, none of his publications focuses specifically on the twelfth-century church. Aspects of it are mentioned in Willesme, "L'abbaye de Saint-Victor"; "Saint-Victor au temps d'Abélard"; "L'abbaye Saint-Victor de Paris: L'église et les bâtiments"; "Histoire et l'architecture de l'abbaye Saint-Victor."

2. Bautier, "Paris au temps d'Abélard," and, especially, "Les origines et les premiers développements," give the best analysis of the historical evidence and the sociopolitical situation of twelfth-century Paris. The architectural context is analyzed by Willesme, "Histoire et l'architecture de l'abbaye Saint-Victor," and W. Clark, "Context, Continuity."

3. Willesme, "L'abbaye Saint-Victor de Paris: l'église et les bâtiments," and "L'abbaye Saint-Victor de Paris sous la Révolution," give a good resumé of the later history of the church, as does Biver and Biver, *Abbayes, monastères et couvents*. The Bivers wrongly identify their plate 30 as St. Victor. The church shown is the Bernardins. See also Christe, *Eglises parisiennes*, and Boussard, *De la fin du siège de 885–886*. The first stone of the new choir was laid by the abbot on the same day. Construction of the new church, which was never completed, was followed by the rebuilding of the canon's dormitory, the cloisters, and the abbey walls. Reconstruction of the infirmary and refectory followed in 1531 and 1535, respectively.

4. Marot, *L'architecture françoise*, plates 41 and 42, are the two views included here in copies after Marot, made by Mérian; see Mérian, *Paris et l'Ile-de-France*. Marot's originals were published by Willesme, "L'abbaye de Saint-Victor." Other engraved views are not included in this discussion because they do not contain information useful to the analysis of the early church. Interestingly, the view of the flank of the church, our fig. 3.1, was copied in the later eighteenth century; see Biver and Biver, *Abbayes, monastères et couvents*, plate 30.

5. The plan was published by Willesme, "Saint-Victor au temps d'Abélard," as fig. 3. The original is in the Archives Nationales, Q2121, liasse no. 7. The archives also house a plan of the abbey made in 1765: AN, NII, Seine 163, cited in the unpublished Willesme, "L'abbaye de Saint-Victor de Paris," at p. 101, n. 1.

6. For the excavations, see, in chronological order: Sellier, "Communication relative aux vestiges de l'ancienne abbaye Saint-Victor," and idem, "Rapport dur les fouilles de démolitions"; Magne, "Rapport présenté au nom de la 2e Sous-Commission"; Grimault, "Rapport présenté sur les fouilles effectuées place Jussieu," and idem, "Compte-rendu de la visite effectuée aux fouilles de la place Jussieu"; and M. Fleury, "Communication sur les fouilles"; as well as the analyses by Lamy-Lasalle, "Saint-Victor"; Périn et al., *Collections merovingiennes*; and Busson, *Carte archéologique de la Gaule*.

7. The drawing is published by Willesme, "Saint-Victor au temps d'Abélard," fig. 4. The original is housed at the Rotonde de la Villette, in the archives of the Commission de Vieux Paris, Dossier 189, pièce 18.

8. The complete plan is published in Grimault, "Rapport présenté sur les fouilles effectuées place Jussieu," and in Willesme, "L'abbaye Saint-Victor de Paris: L'église et les bâtiments," fig. 2.

9. Willesme, "L'abbaye Saint-Victor de Paris sous la Révolution," catalogs the "finds" from the excavations.

10. Hurtaut, *Dictionnaire historique de la ville de Paris*. A description of the stairs descending to the crypt is found in Thiéry, *Guide des amateurs*.

11. For a view of St Germain-des-Prés before the twin towers were truncated, see Plagnieux, "L'abbatiale de Saint-Germain-des-Prés," 9, fig. 3.

12. Hurtaut, *Dictionnaire historique de la ville de Paris*.

13. If the proportions of the bays resembled those of the contemporary nun's church on Montmartre, then the nave had five or six bays, most of which would have been included in the canon's choir. For Montmartre, see W. Clark, "Context, Continuity," with bibliography.

14. Such porches are common in the region to the northeast of Paris in the area from Soissons to Reims and north to Laon.

15. The charter was well known to early scholars of the history of the abbey and is often quoted by them. The first attempt to create an accurate version was that of Lasteyrie, *Cartulaire général de Paris*, but the standard edition is that of Dufour, *Recueil des actes de Louis VI*. His splendid analysis was available to Bautier before publication.

16. Bautier, "Les origines et les premiers développements."
17. Bonnard, *Histoire de l'abbaye royale*, xxiii–xxx.
18. The analysis of the contents of each of the manuscript volumes made by Delisle, "Inventaire des manuscrits latins de Saint-Victor," is indispensable for an understanding of their contents. J. de Thoulouse, *Annales abbatialis ecclesiae sancti Victoris Parisiensis*, Paris, Bibliothèque nationale de France, Mss latins 14368–14374 and 14679–14683.
19. J. de Thoulouse, *Antiquitatum regalis abbatiae sancti Victoris Parisisensis libri duodecim*, Paris, Bibliothèque nationale de France, Mss latins 1437514376 and 14677–14678.
20. Thoulouse, *Abrégé de la fondation de labbaye S. Victor*.
21. Out of the numerous articles of Bautier on medieval Paris, Bautier, "Paris au temps d'Abélard" and idem, "Les origines et les premiers développements," are the most important for this study. The complete list is given in Boussard, *De la fin du siège de 885–886*. Among the older historians of Paris, Corrozet, *La fleur des antiquitez*, and de Breul, *Le theatre des antiquez*, hardly mention St. Victor. Bonfons, *Les fastes antiquitez*, is one of the earliest to use the foundation charter and to recount the history of the abbey in terms of its most illustrious members, establishing the pattern followed, albeit in greater detail, by Brice, *Description de la ville de Paris* (1684), and Felibien, *Histoire de la ville de Paris*, among others. Even Sauval, *Histoire et recherches*, and Lebeuf, *Histoire de la ville* (1883; orig. pub. 1754–58), evidenced little interest in the church itself, other than to recount the sixteenth-century building sequence and to discuss the many works of art displayed throughout the abbey. Hurtaut, *Dictionnaire historique de la ville de Paris*, was apparently the first to discuss the surviving parts of the original church. He even mentioned the rib vaults over the early altar area, while Thiéry, *Guide des amateurs*, added references to staircases descending into the crypt.
22. Bautier, "Les origines et les premiers développements," quotes the appropriate section.
23. Bautier, "Les origines et les premiers développements." See also the lengthy analysis by Dufour, *Recueil des actes de Louis VI*, including a discussion of the meaning of the word "ecclesia" in this context.
24. Willesme, "Saint-Victor au temps d'Abélard." The assertion is repeated in Willesme, "L'abbaye Saint-Victor de Paris: l'église et les bâtiments."
25. Bautier, "Les origines et les premiers développements."
26. Bautier, "Les origines et les premiers développements." See also Jocqué, "Les structures de la population claustrale," for a discussion of numbers and the organization of St. Victor.
27. See Gardner, "L'église Saint-Julien de Marolles-en-Brie," and W. Clark, "Context, Continuity."
28. See Collin et al., *Champagne romane*; Prache, *Ile-de-France roman*; and Oursel et al., *Nord roman*; as well as Gardner, "L'église Saint-Julien de Marolles-en-Brie," and Clark, "Context, Continuity," for a sense of the regional contexts of

St. Victor, and for the buildings mentioned in the text. Willesme, "Histoire et l'architecture de l'abbaye Saint-Victor de Paris," surveys features of St. Victor in the regions mentioned, as well as the Orléanais.

APPENDIX 1: THE BUILDINGS OF THE ABBEY OF ST. VICTOR:
A COLLECTED BIBLIOGRAPHY

This appendix has been included with this chapter in order to provide a bibliography of the relatively specialized material on this topic to scholars in other branches of medieval studies.

Bautier, R.-H. "Les origines et les premiers développements de l'abbaye Saint-Victor de Paris." In *L'abbaye parisienne de Saint-Victor au moyen âge*, edited by Jean Longère, 23–52. Biblioteca Victorina 1. Turnhout: Brepols, 1991.

———. "Paris au temps d'Abélard." In *Abélard en son temps: Actes du Colloque international organisé à l'occasion du IXe centenaire de la naissance de Pierre Abélard (14–19 mai 1979)*, edited by Jean Jolivet, 21–77. Paris: Les Belles Lettres, 1981.

Berndt, R., ed. "Bibliographie." In *Schrift, Schreiber, Schrenker: Studien zu Abtei Sankt Viktor in Paris*, edited by Rainer Berndt, 321–62. Corpus Victorinum, Instrumenta 1. Berlin: Akademie Verlag, 2005.

Biver, Paul, and Marie-Louise Biver. *Abbayes, monastères, et couvents de Paris: Des origines à la fin du XVIIIe siècle*. Paris: Éditions d'histoire et d'art, 1970.

Bonfans, P. *Les fastes antiquitez et choses plus remarquable de Paris*. Paris, 1607.

Bonnard, Fourier. *Histoire de l'abbaye royale et de l'ordre des chanoines réguliers de St-Victor de Paris*. 2 vols. Paris, 1904, 1907.

Boussard, Jacques. *De la fin du siège de 885–886 à la mort de Philippe Auguste*. 2nd ed. Nouvelle histoire de Paris, esp. 209–21. Paris: Diffusion Hachette, 1997.

Brice, Germain. *Description de la ville de Paris et de tout ce qu'elle contient de plus remarquable*. 4 vols. Paris, 1684.

———. *Description de la ville de Paris et de toute ce qu'elle contient de plus remarquable, reproduction de la 9e edition (1725)*. Edited by Pierre Codet. Centre de recherches d'histoire et de philologie de la IVe section de l'Ecole pratique des Hautes-Etudes V. Hautes Etudes médiévales et modernes 12. Paris: Minard; Geneva: Droz, 1971.

Busson, Didier. *Carte archéologique de la Gaule 75: Paris*, 380–82. Paris: Académie des Inscriptions et Belles-Lettres, 1998.

Christe, Y. *Églises parisiennes actuelles et disparues*, 17–18. Paris: Éditions Tel, 1947.

Clark, William. "Context, Continuity, and the Creation of National Memory in Paris, 1130–1160: A Critical Commentary." *Gesta* 45 (2006): 161–75.

Collin, Hubert, et al. *Champagne romane*. La Pierre-qui-Vire: Zodiaque, 1981.

Corrozet, Gilles. *La fleur des antiquitez de la noble et triumphale ville et cité de Paris.* Paris, 1532; repr. Paris, 1874.
de Breul, Jacques. *Le théatre des antiquez de Paris.* Paris, 1639.
Deslisle, L. "Inventaire des manuscrits latins de Saint-Victor." *Bibliothèque de l'école des chartes* 30 (1869): 1–79.
Dufour, Jean, ed. *Recueil des actes de Louis VI, roi de France (1108–1137).* Vol. 1, 173–80. Paris: Académie des Inscriptions et Belles-Lettres, 1992.
Duval, Noël, et al. "Paris." In *Topographie chrétienne des cités de la Gaule des origines au milieu du VIIIe siècle,* edited by Nancy Gauthier and J.-C. Picard, vol. 8, *Province ecclesiastique de Sens (Dugdunensis Senonia),* 97–129. Paris: De Boccard, 1992.
Félibien, M. *Histoire de la ville de Paris.* Rev. and exp. ed. Edited by G.-A. Lobineau, 5 vols. Paris, 1725; abr. ed. 1735.
Fleury, Michel. "Communication sur les fouilles à l'émplacement de l'abbaye de Saint-Victor (5e)," séance du 1 avril 1968. In *Procès-verbaux de la Commission du vieux Paris,* 34–36. Paris, 1968–69.
Gardner, Stephen. "L'église Saint-Julien de Marolles-en-Brie et ses rapports avec l'architecture parisienne de la generation de Saint-Denis." *Bulletin monumental* 144 (1986): 7–31.
Grimault, A. "Compte-rendu de la visite effectuée aux fouilles de la place Jussieu," séance du 9 mai 1931. In *Procès-verbaux de la Commission du vieux Paris,* 87–93. Paris, 1931.
———. "Rapport présenté sur les fouilles effectuées place Jussieu," séance du 28 fevrier 1931. In *Procès-verbaux de la Commission du vieux Paris,* 64–68. Paris, 1931.
Hurtaut, P.-T.-N. *Dictionnaire historique de la ville de Paris et de ses environs.* Vol. 1, 106–21. Paris: Moutard, 1779.
Jocqué, Luc. "Les structures de la population claustrale dans l'ordre de Saint-Victor au XIIe siècle: Un essai d'analyse du 'Liber Ordinis.'" In *L'abbaye parisienne de Saint-Victor au moyen âge,* edited by Jean Longère, 53–95. Bibliotheca Victorina 1. Paris: Brepols, 1991.
Lamy-Lasalle, Colette. "Saint-Victor." In *Les anciennes églises suburbaines de Paris (IVe–Xe siècles),* edited by Elisabeth Chatel et al. Memoires de la Fédération des sociétés historiques et archéologiques de Paris et de l'Ile-de-France 11 (1960): 17–282, esp. 160–64.
Lasteyrie, Robert de. *Cartulaire général de Paris I (528–1180),* 187–90 and passim. Paris: Imprimerie Nationale, 1887.
Lebeuf, Jean. *Histoire de la ville et de tout le diocèse de Paris.* Revised by Adrien Augier and Fernand Bournon, 1:334–43. Paris, 1883–93.
Magne, C. "Rapport présenté au nom de la 2e Sous-Commission," séance du 7 decembre 1912. *Procès-verbaux de la Commission du vieux Paris,* 243–48. Paris, 1912.

Marot, Jean. *L'architecture françoise, ou, Recueil des plans, élévations, coupes et profils des églises . . .*, plates 41 and 42. Paris, 1727.

Mérian, Gaspar. *Topographia Galliae*. 13 vols. Frankfurt, 1655; repr. as *Paris et l'Ile-de-France*, edited by M.V. Paris, 1986.

Oursel, Hervé, et al. *Nord roman*. La Pierre-qui-Vire: Zodiaque, 1994.

Périn, Patrick, et al. *Collections merovingiennes*, 174–78. Catalogues d'art et d'histoire du Musée Carnavalet 2. Paris: Musée Carnavalet, 1985.

Plagnieux, Philippe. "L'abbatiale de Saint-Germain-des-Prés et les débuts de l'architecture gothique." *Bulletin monumental* 158 (2000): 6–86.

Prache, Anne. *Ile-de-France romane*. La Pierre-qui-Vire: Zodiaque, 1983.

Sauval, Henri. *Histoire et recherches des antiquités de la ville de Paris*. Vol. 1, 408–9. Paris: Charles Moette, 1733.

Sellier, Charles. "Communication relative aux vestiges de l'ancienne abbaye Saint-Victor," séance du 13 avril 1899. *Procès-verbaux de la Commission du vieux Paris*, 113. Paris, 1899.

———. "Rapport sur les fouilles de démolitions exécutées du 10 octobre au 14 novembre 1901," séance du 14 novembre. *Procès-verbaux de la commission du vieux Paris*, 168–72. Paris, 1901.

Teske, Gunnar. *Die Briefsammlungen des 12. Jahrhunderts in St. Viktor/Paris*. Studien und Dokumente zur Gallia Pontificia 2. Bonn: Bouvier, 1993.

Thiéry, L.-V. *Guide des amateurs et des étrangers voyageurs à Paris*.Vol. 2, 158–61. Paris, 1787.

Thoulouse, Jean de. *Abrégé de la fondation de l'abbaye S. Victor lez Paris*. Paris, 1640.

———. *Annales abbatialis ecclesiae sancti Victoris Parisiensis*. Paris, Bibliothèque nationale de France, Mss. latins 14368-14374 and 14679-14683.

———. *Antiquitatum regalis abbatiae sancti Victoris Parisisensis libri duodecim*, Paris, Bibliothèque nationale de France, Mss. latins 14375-14376 and 14677-14678.

Willesme, J.-P. "L'abbaye de Saint-Victor." In *La montagne Sainte-Geneviève*, edited by Musée Carnavalet, 146–51. Paris: Musée Carnavalet, 1981.

———. "L'abbaye de Saint-Victor de Paris." Unpublished diss., 3e cycle, University of Paris-IV, 1979.

———. "L'abbaye Saint-Victor de Paris: L'église et les bâtiments, des origines à la Révolution." In *L'abbaye parisienne de Saint-Victor au moyen âge*, edited by Jean Longère, 97–115. Bibliotheca Victorina 1. Paris: Brepols, 1991.

———. "L'abbaye Saint-Victor de Paris sous la Révolution et la dispersion de son patrimoine." *Bulletin de la société de l'histoire de Paris et de l'Ile-de-France* 106 (1979): 133–53.

———. "Histoire et l'architecture de l'abbaye Saint-Victor de Paris du XIIe au XVIe siècles." Unpublished paper intended for presentation at the International Congress for Medieval Studies at Kalamazoo in 1984.

———. "Les origines de l'abbaye de Saint-Victor de Paris à travers ses historiens des XVIIe et XVIIIe si siècles." *Bulletin philologique et historique du Comité des travaux historiques et scientifiques* 58 (1977): 101–14.

———. "Saint-Victor au temps d'Abélard." In *Abélard en son temps: Actes du Colloque international organisé à l'occasion du IXe centenaire de la naissance de Pierre Abélard (14–19 mai 1979)*, edited by Jean Jolivet, 95–105. Paris: Les Belles Lettres 1981.

———. "Saint-Victor et la famille victorine (XIIe–XIIIe siècle)." In *Naissance et fonctionnement des réseaux monastiques et canoniaux*, 175–94. Travaux et recherches 1. Saint-Etienne: Centre européen de recherches sur les congrégations et ordres monastiques, 1991.

THOMAS WALDMAN

4 Decor Domus Domini
Innocent II's Privilege for the Abbey of St. Denis, May 9, 1131

THE VISIT OF INNOCENT II TO ST. DENIS

It was at Rouen on May 9, 1131 that Pope Innocent II granted to the abbey of St. Denis and Suger, its abbot, a general confirmation of its privileges and possessions.[1] To a great extent, this privilege recapitulated material found in earlier papal privileges for the abbey, but because the privilege was drafted at the abbey, it can give us insights into the monks' aspirations, and it also helps us to understand Suger's thinking about art in a church building.

In one of the most well-known passages in his *Life of Louis* VI, Abbot Suger tells how on Wednesday of Holy Week, April 15, 1131, Innocent II had come to St. Denis.[2] The pope had left Rome following the schism that ensued after the death of Honorius II in February 1130.[3] With the followers of the antipope, Anacletus II, in control of the city, Innocent had gone first to

Pisa and Genoa, before coming to France to seek the support of the French king and clergy.[4] The French recognized Innocent's rights at a council held at Étampes in October, and it was Suger whom King Louis VI chose to bring the news to the pope, who was at Cluny by late October.[5]

Suger was well aware of how important this support was to the pope, and he would have been aware of the long tradition—dating back to Pope Stephen II's visit to St. Denis in 754—of the close bonds between the papacy and the French kingdom.[6] He also knew of the papacy's special ties to the abbey, special ties that had been enunciated in a series of papal privileges from the eighth century on.[7] So it was not surprising that he was probably instrumental in arranging for the pope to celebrate Easter at the abbey. The papal visit took place with all the pomp and ceremony that was unique to the papal court. Mounted on a white horse—with the barons and castellans of the abbey acting as grooms holding the reins—the pope was wearing the phrygium or tiara, an imperial ornament like a "helmet, surrounded by a circle of gold."[8] He was followed by the members of the papal court, who were mounted on horses of different colors, but all with white blankets, singing hymns of praise.

On Maundy Thursday, Innocent gave out presents, "more Romano," and he followed the offices on Good Friday and the Easter Vigil with the monks. On Easter morning, he "secretly" went out to the Church of St. Denis-de-l'Estrée.[9] The Romans threw money at the large crowds to keep them away, the trees were adorned with precious hangings, and the streets were strewn with branches. Returning to the basilica, the pope celebrated mass, with Suger assisting, in a church "shining with golden crowns and glistening with the splendor of gems and pearls a hundred times more precious than gold."[10] The following day the procession was repeated to the church of St. Rémi, and though Suger does not say so, with probably the same ceremony.[11] Suger emphasizes the splendor of the processions rather than any liturgical function, but it should be noted that it was during the rogation processions of the Easter season that the monks made a circuit of town churches, including St. Denis-de-l'Estrée and St. Rémi.[12]

The pope remained at St. Denis for three more days before going on to Paris. He then visited other churches in France that helped supply his needs, probably with money and hospitality.[13] He visited Pontoise, Gisors, Rouen (where he issued the privilege for St. Denis) and Beauvais before settling at Compiègne on May 26.

THE PRIVILEGE OF MAY 9, 1131

Innocent's privilege, the original of which is in the Archives Nationales (Museé AE III, no. 140), can profitably be compared to another privilege of Innocent II, issued in 1142, that is printed in *Diplomatique Médiévale*.[14] A comparison of the two privileges shows that the privilege for St. Denis conforms to what was, by the twelfth century, standard papal chancery practice. The privilege, recently edited by Rolf Grosse for the *Papsturkunden in Frankreich*, is printed such that it is easy to see what in the privilege is new and what is copied from earlier privileges, particularly that of Calixtus II in 1119.[15] The privilege is witnessed by the pope, whose name appears between the rota and the monogram *Bene valete*. It was granted "per manum" of Cardinal Haimeric, the papal chancellor, and was witnessed by three cardinal bishops, five cardinal priests, and three cardinal deacons.[16]

The privilege was written by the papal chancery (the papacy did not allow charters to be written outside the chancery and be submitted for sealing), though it was not unusual for papal privileges to be drafted by the beneficiary, and this is certainly the case for the privilege for St. Denis.[17] (There were, however, royal charters of Louis VI that were both drafted and written at the abbey.)[18] This can clearly be seen in two principal ways: from the abbey's possessions, which are based on *acta* in the abbey's archives, and from phrases which appear in other of Suger's writings. The possessions are described thus:

1. In pago Metensi [Metz]
2. Monasterium Argentolium, quod situm est in pago Parisiacensi [Argenteuil]
3. In episcopatu Aurelianensis [Orléans]
4. Ad comitatem Vilcassini [Vexin]
5. Vicariam quoque et omnimodam iustitiam ac plenariam libertatem . . . sicut subscriptis terminis distinguitur [Lendit]

Before discussing these five groups individually, it should be noted that all of these possessions were added to the abbey's holdings after Suger became abbot in 1122, and they are arranged geographically. Dietrich Lohrmann pointed out that this is the first time in a privilege for St. Denis that possessions are individually identified, and he also pointed out that they are found in descending order of their distance from the abbey.[19] Though direct evidence is lacking, it seems likely that the abbey's muniments were arranged geographically, as was to be the case in the abbey's later cartularies.[20]

The charters that were the sources for the possessions (1–5) are as follows:

1. Mainard, count of Mörsburg, returned these possessions to St. Denis in 1125, and Suger absolved Count Albert of Mörsburg in the same year. The order of the possessions in Mainard's charter is identical to that in the bull, showing that Suger followed the order of the charter in the text prepared for the pope.[21]
2. The description of the location of Argenteuil is found in the charters of Louis the Pious/Lothair and Louis VI that confirmed St. Denis' possession of the priory.[22]
3. The act of Louis VI, now lost, is mentioned by Suger in his *Gesta*.[23]
4. The county of the Vexin is mentioned in Louis VI's celebrated charter of 1124. That charter mentions that the king holds the county "in feodum," and Suger used similar language in his *Vita Ludovici VI*.[24] Louis' charter was not only drafted by the beneficiary, but was even written at the abbey.[25] However, in confirming the grant of the county of the Vexin made by Louis VI in 1124, the privilege adds a significant phrase, "quoniam his [sic] possidet, cuius nomine possidetur," which is based on the *Digest*, 42, 18, 2, praef. It is not clear, as Lohrmann noted, if this phrase was supplied by the abbey or the papacy, but as all of the other phrases come from abbatial sources, the former case seems likely.[26] In any case, it is a very early use of the *Digest* in northern France, and it most likely came from extracts from the *Digest*, rather than the *Digest* itself.
5. The description of the grant of the Lendit is taken from the charter of Louis VI with a couple of changes. "Sicut certa metarum distinctione terminavimus" is changed to "subscriptis terminis distinguitur" and "Sequane videlicet" to "videlicet Sequane"; the added reference to Aubervillers is also taken from Louis' charter.[27]

The rest of the "dispositio" of the privilege is taken from earlier papal privileges for the abbey, which had confirmed St. Denis' possessions and liberties, particularly those that freed it from any royal or episcopal control. Most of these rights had been enunciated in a series of royal and papal privileges (authentic and false) and were no longer a subject of significant controversy.[28]

If, moreover, we look at the preamble, we can see the use of language that is similar if not identical to that used in several of Suger's writings. (The initial phrase will be discussed later on.) The parallel passages are in italics; line numbers are indicated in parentheses.

> (1) Ecclesia namque Dei, que non sine multo *sudore* et *labore* temporaliter peregrinator in terris pro illius amore et desiderio, que perpetuis et inconcussis gaudiorum premiis fruetur in caelis, religiosa et honorabilia loca, que Deo dicata sunt et eius famulatui mancipata, attentius reveretur et diligit. Ea igitur ratione nos, qui ex commisso nobis a (5) Deo apostolatus officio *curam* et *administrationem* ecclesiarum omnium *gerimus, famosum* et nobile beati Dionisii monasterium imperatorum et *regum munificentia* et *liberalitate* ditatum affectione paterna diligimus et, ne *pravorum* hominum molestetur incursibus defensamus. Quocirca, dilecte in Domino fili Sugeri abbas, quem fidelem et devotum beato Petro sancteque Romane aeclessie certis indiciis experti sumus, cuius (10) etiam *industria* et *sollicitudine* in prefato beati Dionisii monasterio gratam Deo religionem *reformatam* esse *comperimus, rationabilibus* tuis postulationibus gratum prebemus *assensum*.

> [And so the church of God, which journeys on earth, not without much sweat and labor, for the love and desire of [God], and which enjoys perpetual and unbroken rewards of bliss in heaven, attentively cherishes and reveres honorable religious places that are dedicated to God and entrusted to his service. And so for this reason, we exercise the care and administration of all churches through the apostolic office entrusted to us by God, and we cherish with paternal affection the famous and noble monastery of the blessed Denis, endowed by the munificence and generosity of emperors and kings, and we defend it lest it be injured by the incursions of evil men. Therefore, beloved in the Lord, Suger, son and abbot, whom we have learned through certain indications to be faithful and devoted to blessed Peter and the Holy Roman Church, and by whose industry and care we have discovered that the religious observance, pleasing to God, in the aforementioned monastery of the blessed Denis, has been reformed—we offer our grateful assent to your reasonable demands.]

The following are the related passages from Suger's works:

1. *Ord.* 3, providere labores et certaminium sudores
   Vita Ludovici, p. 182, labores sumptuoso sudore
   Vita Ludovici, p. 270, laborem continuato sudore
5. *Ord.* 65, curam gerere
5. *De cons.* 108, sancta ecclesie tanta preficere administrationi
6. *De cons.* 59, famosus rex Francorum Dagobertus
   Gesta 341, famosa beati Dionisii villa
   Vita Ludovici, p. 4, Gloriosus igitur et famosus rex
6. *Ord.* 98, imperatorum . . . multa liberalitate, larga munificentia
   Gesta 495, antiqua regum liberalitate
   Gesta 638, liberalitate regum
7. *Gesta* 171, pravorum . . . infestacionem
10. *Gesta* 393, industria prelatorum
    Ord. 70, sollicitudine votiva
    Gesta 15, bene zelantem sollicitudinem
11. *Ord.* 99, ad salutem animarum . . . reformare
    Ord. 137, reformare studiose laboravimus
    Gesta 136, ut reformaretur ibi religionis ordo
    De cons. 66, auxilium . . . comperisset
    Gesta 16, rationabilibus eorum petitionibus assensum exhibentes[29]

Perhaps all writers use certain characteristic words and ideas repeatedly in their works, but Suger, in particular, does this. Whole sections of the *Gesta* and the *De Consecratione* repeat one another, so it is not surprising that he later reused words and ideas found in the privilege of 1131.

REFORM AND CONSTRUCTION AT ST. DENIS

By 1131, Suger had more on his mind than recovering possessions for the abbey, and there are two themes in this bull that specifically reflect Suger's concerns and ideas. The first is the idea of "reform," a word that is seldom associated with Suger—and when it is used, it is usually with some skepticism. Suger, however, was known to be both strict and caring toward the monks, and in the earliest charter we have from his abbacy, 1122–24, he makes several important changes to the liturgy.[30] His improvements to the psalmody and his cleaning up of the lax behavior in the monastery is part of the reason for Bernard of Clairvaux's laudatory letter of 1127, and there is no reason to assume that Bernard's praise was not sincere.[31] In this context, the phrase in the bull, cited above, "cuius etiam industria . . . comperimus," reflects Suger's own awareness of the significance of these reforms. Lindy Grant makes the point that Suger's ordinances for the regulation of the monastic life reflect the influence and prestige of the ordinances of Abbot Hilduin, the great ninth-century abbot.[32] This is consistent with his great desire to repair and restore to their former glory the objects that Charles the Bald had given to St. Denis.[33] *Renovatio/restoratio* of lands, objects, and the monastic life went hand in hand for him, and nowhere is this more evident than in his desire to restore and to glorify the basilica of the saints.

The second theme, indeed, was that Suger had been actively planning for the reconstruction of the abbey church. As noted below there is evidence that he was working on the west end in the late 1120s, and certainly the church glistening with gems and gold that greeted the pope is probably the result of the refurbishment that Suger undertook on becoming abbot. With this point of view and conscious of the splendor of the abbey's ancient treasures, which dated from the time of its greatest benefactor, Charles the Bald, Suger was proposing an aesthetic that would counter that enunciated by Bernard and the Cistercians. Bernard's view had been articulated in the *Apologia* addressed to William of St. Thierry; this was written around 1125 and was likely known at St. Denis not long after.[34]

There is a large literature on Bernard of Clairvaux's attitude to art.[35] Much of the discussion has focused on whom Bernard had in mind when he wrote chapters 28 and 29 of the *Apologia*, where he criticized the "incorrect" use of images in various monastic houses, and most of the discussion about Suger has been based on what he wrote in chapter 33 of his *Gesta*.[36]

The papal privilege of 1131 can help us consider this question as it appeared many years before the completion of the work on the church and Suger's description of it. Innocent's privilege begins by paraphrasing Psalm 25:8, "Decor domus Domini diligendus est et locus habitationis glorie eius attenta diligentia et reverentia honorandus." This verse is not used in any other papal privilege before that time, and its use here indicates its importance at St. Denis.[37]

At the beginning of the twelfth century work began at St. Denis to repair and paint the walls, and repair various utensils used in the liturgy. By the mid-1120s, at the same time that Suger was increasing the abbey's possessions, work was begun at the west entrance to the church. Suger had written in a charter of 1125 that he was devoting two hundred pounds that he was receiving from the town of St. Denis "ad introitum monasterii beati Dyonisii renovandum et decorandum."[38] Sumner Crosby thought that this referred to the gates of the abbey, but Suger used the same word "introitum" to refer to the entrance to the church.[39] Also in 1124, Louis VI had said that his devotion to the saints followed that of his ancestors by whose munificence the abbey was "amplificatam et decoratam."[40] With the recovery of the priory of Argenteuil and its possessions in 1129, the financial resources were mostly in place to enable the abbot and the monks to proceed with the enlargement of both the west and east ends of the church.[41] At the time of the pope's visit in April 1131 construction was probably underway at the west entrance, and so the pope probably used the north portal entrance at the time of his visits to St. Denis-de-l'Estrée and St. Rémi. So the psalm phrase "Decor domus" takes on an additional importance when we remember what was happening at the abbey. Unfortunately, Suger's description of the pope's visit to St. Denis does not tell us what planning or construction was taking place at the time. We are told that the pope and his entourage made processions to the churches of St. Denis-de-l'Estrée and St. Rémi, and it is likely that the processions returned to the church through the north portal, the entrance that faced the town.

According to Conrad Rudolph, by the beginning of the twelfth century the allegorical interpretation of Psalm 25 as seen in the works of Augustine and Cassiodorus was giving way to a more literal understanding of the verse.[42] Both types of interpretation can be found in this period. Allegorical interpretation can be seen in letters of Ivo of Chartres. One, written 1094–95 to a certain Robert says that God will complete the temple that He began in his heart. A second to Hugh, archbishop of Lyon, in 1098 says that to love the "decorem domus dei" is to love the church—that is, take care of and protect it—with special care.[43] On the other hand, William of St. Thierry, writing in 1131, still cites the psalm in an allegorical sense.[44]

Innocent's privilege, however, uses the psalm in a different sense. Three papal letters that cite the psalm in this period reinforce this change clearly.

They are a letter of Honorius II, 1125–28, asking for money to construct the church of S. Pietro in Pistoia; and two letters of Innocent II, one to Hugh, archbishop of Rouen, on June 27, 1131, asking for money to repair the church at Noyon that had recently been damaged by fire, and the other, on May 4, 1131, to the bishop of Osma, stating that "loving the beauty" of the house of the Lord, Innocent desires to build a church there.[45]

Finally, the last example in this sequence. In the fall of the same year, 1131, the Benedictine abbots of the province of Reims issued a series of capitula aimed at "reforming" various monastic practices, and in response, Matthew, the cardinal bishop of Albano, wrote a heated and sarcastic criticism. Responding to the abbots' zeal, the cardinal reminded them that Moses had adorned the Tabernacle and Solomon the Temple, and Christian emperors, kings, and abbots had endowed their churches with their treasures. With the Psalmist, he says, they are justly able to sing, "Domine, dilexi decorum domus tuae et locum habitationis gloriae tuae," and because of this, "the celestial kingdoms are believed to have been promised them."[46] However, it appears that Matthew of Albano is carrying the argument further than Suger is willing to go, at least in 1131. Rather, Suger is combining three old ideas: that the abbot will protect the rights and possessions of the church entrusted to him; that the monastic life will be lived in accordance with the standards of the Rule; and that to honor the Lord is to build His church.

SUGER AND BERNARD OF CLAIRVAUX

The papal privileges and the letters cited above were not the only works of the 1120s to quote Psalm 25, for so, too, did Bernard of Clairvaux in the *Apologia* addressed to William of St. Thierry.[47] The *Apologia*, written circa 1125, in a combative and satirical style, is concerned principally with the reform of the monastic life, praising the discipline and simplicity of the Cistercians against the "excesses and frivolities" of other (unnamed) monks. The work was immensely popular, and it was probably known at St. Denis not long after it was written.[48] Because chapters 28 and 29 are the fullest discussion of the uses of art in churches in the twelfth century, and because the psalm cited by Bernard is the same as that used in the preamble to Innocent's privilege, it is worthwhile looking at what relation there is between these works, and if they shed light on the relationship between Suger and Bernard and their respective aesthetics.

There is only one explicit contact that we know of between the two men in this period, and that is Bernard's Letter 78, discussed above. This letter is dated 1127, and though Bernard praises Suger's "reform," he says that he knows of it by hearsay.[49] Conrad Rudolph has shown how the tradition came about of seeing the *Apologia* as an attack on Cluny, and it is of course possible that Bernard is condemning various attributes that he considers to have no place in the monastery (he contrasts them with what is permissible in a cathedral), and that he is not thinking of any particular place.[50] And because of the close dating of the *Apologia* and the letter, there is no reason to think that Bernard has St. Denis in mind. But even if this was the case, there are reasons, I believe, to think that the letter was read with concern and trepidation at St. Denis. Bernard was a towering—even frightening—figure, before whose words great laymen and powerful ecclesiastics trembled. So if we cannot discern Bernard's attitude to St. Denis (though based on the ideas expressed in the *Apologia* he would have been critical of the expense and magnificence of the new church), I think we can discern some of what the monks thought. First of all, by using Psalm 25 in the papal privilege, which had been given at the time when the pope had visited the "glistening" church, where work had already begun, Suger is placing himself among those monks who, while believing in reform, yet wished to adorn their churches in a style worthy of glorifying (in their view) the Lord. As Yves Christe suggestively wrote, "The black Benedictines did not think that beauty was an obstacle to spiritual meditation; on the other hand their churches were open to laymen, and of the numerous monasteries, those in particular that were the most decorated, were also the most frequented pilgrimage sites."[51]

That Suger does not stand alone in 1131 can be seen when we look at the exchange of polemics (mentioned above) between the Benedictine abbots of the province of Reims and Matthew of Albano. If reform meant a stricter observance of the Rule, the abbots' approach was a much more radical one. Though the texts that we have from these abbots mainly concern the liturgy and the life of the community, Matthew's letter and William of St. Thierry's response to it, both of which quote Psalm 25, make it clear that they disagree on the appropriate construction and decoration of churches. This is a much bigger subject than can be treated here, but it would appear that the "debate" was a complex one, even for St. Bernard.[52] I would suggest that a large number of Benedictines favored a monastic life free from outside control, and one devoted to a strict observance of the Rule, but did not wish to abandon elaborate decoration of buildings, objects, or manuscripts.

Suger's activities in the 1130s are not always clear, but he must have been involved with the new construction. However, he did not forget what Bernard had written, and in his own writings he explicitly shows that there is another way to render thanks to God. In several of his works, he paraphrases or uses the exact words of Bernard; but whereas Bernard had used these words to criticize and to censure work that echoed the "antiquum ritum Judaeorum," Suger exalted in his achievements and his creation of the objects for the service of the Lord.[53]

This is not to say that Suger is writing "contra" the *Apologia*, but it is notable that he quotes Bernard's words back to him, in works written many years later: "immensas altitudines, immoderatas longitudines, supervacuas latitudines, sumptuosas depolitiones, curiosas depictiones."[54] So, too, in the *Ordinatio* of 1140, he explicitly says that he raised revenues for the support of the "exteriorum pauperum," and whereas Bernard had deplored the skill of the workmen and the glistening gems and stones and lamps, these are the very qualities Suger reports with enthusiasm at the time of the pope's visit.[55] Bernard had scorned that the "Fulget ecclesia parietibus, et in pauperibus eget"; whereas Suger was to recount later how the pope had come "ad sanctorum basilicam . . . splendore fulgurantem."[56]

There are three more references to Psalm 25 in Suger's *oeuvre*, and together they give a vivid sense of his thought, not on art, but rather on how he saw himself in relation to the "decorem domus Dei." After he finished the construction he described what it meant to him, and to others, who would celebrate mass in the new "oratorium" of Saint Romain; they would feel, he said, recalling the psalm, "dum sacrificant, eorum in celis sit habitatio, cognorunt."[57] In contrast to this, he used the next verse in the psalm to portray his own unworthiness, and how for that reason he hastened to join the beginning to the end, the Alpha to the Omega. The Psalmist had said that he had cherished the "decorem" of the house of the Lord, "ne perdas cum impiis animam meam et cum viris sanguinum vitam meam."[58] I think we must take this attitude sincerely as we must take the penitential postures of himself that Suger placed around the church.[59] Finally, at whatever point he started thinking about the dedication of the new church, he would have been aware that Psalm 25, *Iudica me*, was part of the liturgy for the dedication of a church. The ceremony was described in several manuscripts that were in the monastery library, and the liturgy was outlined in the eleventh-century gradual, now Paris, Bibl. Mazarine, Ms 384.[60]

This discussion has wandered, perhaps too far, from the privilege of Innocent II, but returning to the privilege makes several things clear. For Suger, enhancing the church, reforming the monastic life, and protecting the monastery's rights and possessions are part of *one* enterprise, to serve the "nobilis ecclesia" of St. Denis. Many modern commentators have discussed Suger as the patron of his church and "his" patron, [Pseudo]-Denis. They have forgotten how influenced Suger was by history. He loved to read the chronicles, he spent his youth pouring over the charters, and, recalling the abbey's ancient lineage from the time of Dagobert, he tried to recreate the splendor and riches of St. Denis at the time of its greatest benefactor, Charles the Bald.[61]

PRETERITORUM ENIM RECORDATIO FUTURORUM EST EXHIBITIO (*GESTA* 847)

There are two contemporary endorsements on the back of Innocent's privilege: "Pancarta" and "Pancarta Innocentii pape II°." This is a very interesting use of this term for, strictly speaking, this privilege does not reproduce the diplomatic form of the charters it uses, as a *pancarta* usually does.[62] Moreover, as noted above, in contrast to *pancartae* produced by other monastic beneficiaries, this privilege, though drafted at St. Denis, was written by the papal chancery in conformity with its normal practices. These endorsements, however, are an indication that the monks of St. Denis saw this privilege as a recapitulation of the abbey's possessions and rights, and perhaps they also indicate that, if needed, this privilege could be produced in lieu of the original charters it summarized.[63]

In this sense, the privilege looked to the past, for it confirmed the abbey's rights, secured over many centuries as they relate to pope, king, and bishop. The new great increase in wealth and the maintenance of its special status would allow St. Denis once again to assume an eminent, maybe even preeminent, position among the abbeys of northern France. To a great extent, it had recovered the stature and brilliance it had last enjoyed at the time of Charles the Bald.

But this privilege, drafted at the abbey, did more than that: it looked to the future as well. Many of Suger's writings are hard to date precisely, and they were probably revised over many years. But this privilege can be precisely dated, and it shows, I believe, that by 1131 Suger was planning for the culmination of the restored wealth and prestige to be a magnificent resting place for the saints. The use of Psalm 25:8, moreover, places his program for St. Denis, from its inception, firmly in the tradition of the construction and decoration of churches by the black Benedictines.

NOTES

1. The privilege is printed, with bibliography and commentary, in *Papsturkunden in Frankreich*, no. 35, 148–51. The privilege is Jaffé-Wattenbach, *Regesta Pontificum Romanorum*, 7472 (5361). I would like to thank Messieurs Luc Requier and Ghislain Brunel at the Archives Nationales, Paris, for the photograph of the privilege and their responses to my questions about it. I would also like to thank Elizabeth A. R. Brown, William W. Clark, Rolf Grosse, Eric Knibbs, Guy Lobrichon, Edward M. Peters, Robert Somerville, and Benoît-Michel Tock for their advice on particular points.

2. Suger, *Vita Ludovici Grossi Regis*, ed. Waquet, 262–66 (hereafter *Vita Ludovici*).

3. For a summary of the schism, Robinson, *The Papacy*, 69–76.

4. *Vita Ludovici*, 259, n. 5.

5. *Vita Ludovici*, 260–61. For Etampes, see Grabois, "Le Schisme de 1130 et la France"; *Vita Ludovici*, 258–66; Grosse, "Saint-Denis und das Papsttum," 228; and Gasparri, "L'abbé Suger de St Denis et la papauté," 75–78.

6. *Vita Ludovici*, 258–59.

7. Innocent's privilege says that it is confirming privileges of previous popes, among others, Zacharias, 742–51 (*Papsturkunden*, no. 1, 61–64), a forgery; Stephen [II] (ibid., nos 2a–5, 64–77), some of which are false.

8. *Vita Ludovici*, 264; Robinson, *The Papacy*, 20–21, notes "The papal crown was especially associated, as Bruno of Segni observed, with 'great processions'" and "the ceremony served a didactic purpose, teaching those of the faithful who were unacquainted with 'the Roman custom' something of the nature of papal authority."

9. Almost nothing is known of the church of St. Denis-de-l'Estrée (Wyss, *Atlas historique de St Denis*, 209). The priory lay about 800 m to the west of the abbey church, so the papal procession (assuming it went directly there) was not a long one.

10. *Vita Ludovici*, 264. The phrase, which will be discussed more fully below, is: "Perveniens vero ad sanctorum basilicam, coronis aureis rutilantem, argenti et plus cencies auri preciosarum gemmarum et margaritarum splendore fulgurantem."

11. For St. Rémi, see Wyss, *Atlas historique de St Denis*, 208. The church situated outside the walls lay about 800 m to the east of the abbey church.

12. Robertson, *The Service Books of the Royal Abbey of Saint-Denis*, 259; Foley, *The First Ordinary of the Royal Abbey of St.-Denis*, 248–52, 404–9. The three rogation days normally took place before Ascension Thursday, but perhaps because of the presence of the papal court, these similar processions took place on Easter and Easter Monday. Also, though Suger mentions only two churches, it is certainly possible that they were the termini of the processions, which had made a tour of the town, as was the practice in the thirteenth century. Also, see Foley, *The First Ordinary of the Royal Abbey of St.-Denis*, 259–60.

13. *Vita Ludovici*, 264. "Exinde Galliarum ecclesias visitando et de earum copia inopie sue defectum supplendo"; Robinson, *The Papacy*, 283.

14. Guyotjeanin, Pycke, and Tock, *Diplomatique médiévale*. The privilege of Innocent II for the abbey of St. Feuillien de Roeulx, November 27, 1142, is transcribed and discussed, 169–71, and reproduced, 168, plate 13. It includes a discussion of the dating, external and internal characteristics, and diplomatics commentary.

15. See n. 1 above. Based on the photograph of the verso of the privilege, the leaden bulla, formerly attached by silk cords, still exists, but it is no longer attached.

16. Robinson, *The Papacy*, 94. "Probably the most powerful chancellor of the twelfth century was Haimeric, cardinal deacon of S. Maria Novella, who held the office from 1122 until 1141. Haimeric did not himself become pope, but he was the pope-maker who contrived the election of two of the popes whom he served, Honorius II and Innocent II." For the growing importance of the cardinals under Innocent II, ibid., 104–5.

17. Guyotjeanin, Pycke, and Tock, *Diplomatique médiévale*, 228, and 228–29 for a discussion of the drafting of documents. For acts created outside of the chancery, Tock, "Auteur ou impetrant?" esp. 222–29.

18. Gasparri, *L'écriture des Actes de Louis VI*, 18, 21.

19. Lohrmann, *Kirchengut im nordlichen Frankreich*, 177–78.

20. Grosse, "Remarques sur les cartulaires," 285.

21. Mainard's charter (Paris, AN, K 22, no. 4[1]) is printed in *Monuments historiques*, no. 397. Suger's absolution of Count Albert is printed in Suger, *Oeuvres*, 2:174–77. For a discussion of St. Denis' possessions, Parisse, "St Denis et ses biens," esp. 250–51.

22. Dufour, *Recueil des Actes de Louis VI, roi de France*, no. 281, for the charter of Louis VI, and *Recueil des Historiens des Gaules et de la France*, 6:542 for the diploma of Lothair/Louis the Pious. Also see the edition and discussion in Waldman, "Abbot Suger and the Nuns of Argenteuil."

23. Suger, *Gesta*, 292; compare Dufour, *Recueil des Actes de Louis VI*, App. II, no. 18, 472–73.

24. Dufour, *Recueil des Actes de Louis VI*, no. 220. *Vita Ludovici*, 220. See Barroux, "L'Abbé Suger et la vassalité du Vexin en 1124."

25. Gasparri, *L'écriture des Actes de Louis VI*, 18, 21.

26. Lohrmann, *Kirchengut im nordlichen Frankreich*, 237.

27. Dufour, *Recueil des Actes de Louis VI*, no. 220, esp. 465.

28. For a bibliography on this subject, see *Papsturkunden*, pp. 9–20.

29. The cited passages come from Suger's *Vita Ludovici, Gesta, Ordinatio*, and *De consecratione*.

30. For his attitude to monks see, among various passages, Suger, *Sugerii Vita*, 2:308, 325–26; for liturgy, 156–67.

31. Bernard of Clairvaux, *Lettres*, letter 78, 368–99. Admittedly, the principal reason for the letter is to seek Suger's assistance against Stephen of Garlande.

32. Grant, *Abbot Suger of St-Denis*, 186–87. It should be noted that Suger's *Ordinatio* follows the style of Hilduin's.

33. Among others, the altar panel, cross, and candelabra; Suger, *Gesta*, 340, 354–55, 362.

34. Bernard of Clairvaux, *Apologia ad Guillelmum Abbatem*, 63–108. Chapters 28–29, which treat art in the monastery, are on 104–7. An English translation is in Rudolph, *The "Things of Greater Importance,"* 232–87. Lobrichon, "Chronologie des oeuvres de saint Bernard de Clairvaux," 33. There are two versions of the *Apologia*, the first 1123–24 (?), the second 1125 (?).

35. Besides Rudolph, *The "Things of Greater Importance,"* see idem, "The Scholarship on Bernard of Clairvaux's *Apologia*," and "Bernard of Clairvaux's *Apologia* as a Description of Cluny," where he reviews these passages and criticizes the viewpoint that Bernard is describing Cluny.

36. Rudolph, *"Things of Greater Importance,"* 33, and *Artistic Change at St Denis*, 26–31.

37. It was used in a privilege of Adrian IV for Santa Maria de Reno, March 17, 1155; *Regesta Pontificorum Romanorum* 6853. The privilege for St. Denis is ibid., 5361. The psalm verse is: "Domine dilexi decorem domus tuae et locum habitationis gloriae tuae."

38. Suger, *Oeuvres*, 2:171.

39. Crosby, *The Royal Abbey of Saint-Denis*, 124. Suger, *Gesta*, 1:727, reads "Accessimus igitur ad priorem valvarum introitum,"; "in introitu valvarum," ibid., 1:730; "in amplificatione corporis ecclesie et introitus," ibid., 733; and "principali porte in introitu ecclesie," ibid., 1173.

40. Dufour, *Recueil des Actes de Louis VI*, no. 220, 465.

41. Suger lists the possessions in *Gesta*, 270. It was among the richest of the abbey's possessions.

42. Rudolph, *The "Things of Greater Importance,"* 32. Augustine, *Enarrationes in Psalmos*, 149. "Domus Dei ecclesia est; adhuc habet malos, sed decor domus Dei in bonis est, in sanctis est . . . ergo quia dilexi decorum domus tuae, id est, omnes qui ibi sunt et gloriam tuam quaerunt."

43. Ivo of Chartres, *Epistolae (Correspondence)*, ed. Leclercq, 138, 282.

44. William is writing in response to Matthew of Albano's letter of 1131 to the Benedictine abbots of the province of Reims; William of St. Thierry, *Responsio Abbatum*, 348. See Ceglar, "Guillaume de Saint-Thierry," and "The Chapter of Soissons."

45. The letter of Honorius is in *Regesta Pontificorum Romanorum*, 7335 (5277), PL 166:1286. Letter to Hugh of Rouen, ibid., 7481 (5367), PL 179:98. Letter to bishop of Osma, ibid., 7470 (5359), PL 179:92.

46. *Epistola Matthaei Albanensis Episcopi* in Bur, ed., *Saint-Thierry*, 331.

47. Bernard of Clairvaux, *Apologia ad Guillelmum Abbatem*, 106.

48. I am grateful to Guy Lobrichon for his advice on this subject.

49. Bernard of Clairvaux, *Lettres*, letter 78, 368. "Exiit sermo bonus in terram nostram," a paraphrase of Luke 7:17. For an overview, see Führer, "Suger et Bernard de Clairvaux." See also, Constable, "Suger's Monastic Administration," 19–20, who is more skeptical: "The accounts given by the two men [Abelard and Bernard] must be taken with a grain of salt." However, Constable does note Suger's desire "for good order" and that "Suger's writings show, however, that the reform (in spite of Bernard's feeling account of the devotional exercises at St. Denis) was along the lines more of strict black Benedictine monasticism. . . . With these two features—an orderly but not uncomfortable life and a long liturgy—Suger combined a third feature of old, black Benedictine monasticism: a concern for conspicuous display, both in charity and in building and decoration." If my emphasis is different, my analysis of Innocent's privilege has led me to a similar conclusion.

50. Rudolph, *The "Things of Greater Importance*," "The Scholarship on Bernard of Clairvaux's *Apologia*," and "Bernard of Clairvaux's *Apologia* as a Description of Cluny."

51. Christe, "À propos de l'*Apologia* de Saint Bernard," esp. 9.

52. Ibid., "He [Bernard] was not opposed to the harmony of proportions, to architectural beauty or the poetry of the liturgical hymns. He preferred, however, for the monks a sacred art that was not too marred by material seductions, or was not the object of a distraction or the pleasure of the senses, in order that the beauty of a cloister or church might not be an obstacle to supernatural searching" (my translation).

53. The phrase "antiquum ritum Judaeorum" appears in Bernard of Clairvaux, *Apologia ad Guillelmum Abbatem*, 104. Suger turns this passage around at *Gesta*, 1043–49, where he says that as the golden objects were used for the blood of cows and goats at the order of God and his prophets, how much more fitting it is to use precious objects for the blood of Jesus Christ; see Suger, *Gesta*, 328–70.

54. *De cons.*, 410 "ad altitudinis cacumen produceretur"; *De cons.*, 287 "longitudinis et latitudinis pulcritudine innitereur nobilitare"; *Gesta*, 709 "pictoribus eas aptare et honeste depingi"; *Gesta*, 1171–75 "vitrearum . . . varietates . . . de manu exquisite depingi fecimus"; *De cons.*, 123 "in tanta tamque sumptuoso opere profecimus." We should note that as, I believe, Suger is reflecting the words of the *Apologia*, then it is the second redaction that was known at St. Denis, for in the first,

instead of "latitudinis" is written "amplitudinis"; see Bernard of Clairvaux, *Apologia ad Guillelmum Abbatem*, 104, n. 13.

55. The phrse "exteriorum pauperum," comes from Suger, *Ordinatio*, 49. Also see Suger, *Gesta*, 180, where Suger is conscious of the effects of the high cost of food on the "pauperibus." For Bernard's comments, see his *Apologia ad Guillelmum Abbatem*, 105: "Ponuntur dehinc in ecclesia gemmatae, non coronae, sed rotae, circumseptae lampadibus, sed non minus fulgentes insertis lapidibus. Cernimus et pro candelabris arbores quasdam erectas, multo aeris pondere, miro artificis opere fabricates, nec magis coruscantes superpositis lucernis, quam suis gemmis." Suger's report of the visit is in *Vita Ludovici*, 264. Also see Suger, *Gesta*, 988, where Suger praises the "artifices, and the "mirabili anaglifo opere," and 1208, "mirafico opere."

56. Bernard of Clairvaux, *Apologia ad Guillelmum Abbatem*, 105; *Vita Ludovici*, 264.

57. Suger, *Gesta*, 742–43.

58. Ibid., 725. Because of the repeated use of the psalm by Suger, I think this is a more likely reference than 2 Sm 16:7 as in ibid., p. 318.

59. Maines, "Good Works, Social Ties, and the Hope for Salvation."

60. Robertson, *The Service Books of the Royal Abbey of Saint-Denis*, 221–22, suggests that Ordo 41 of the *Ordines Romani*, *Ordo Quomodo ecclesia debeat dedicari* (*Les Ordines Romani de Haut Moyen Âge*, 4:340–49) was compiled for the dedication of St. Denis in 775. The ritual for the dedication of a church, including the psalm *Iudica me* is found in Paris, Bibl. Mazarine, Ms 384, fol. 196v (facsimile in Maître, *Graduel de l'abbaye royale de St Denis*). A similar liturgy is found in Foley, *The First Ordinary of the Royal Abbey of St.-Denis*, 496 ("In dedicacione ecclesiae beati Dyonisii"), and it was certainly the one that was followed by Suger.

61. Suger, *Sugerii Vita*, 304–5, "erat illi historiarum summa notitia." Suger, *Gesta*, 116–17, as Suger recounts how he "found" the foundation charter for Argenteuil. See the important article of Morelle, "Suger et les archives," esp. 117–30. There are many references to the generosity of Charles the Bald; for example, Suger, *Gesta*, 970, describing the altar frontal.

62. For a discussion of *pancartae* and similar charters of confirmation, see Bates, "Les chartes de confirmation et les pancartes normandes," and for papal confirmations, Tock, "La diplomatique sans pancarte" esp. 136–38.

63. For the various types of *pancartae*, Parisse, "Les pancartes," esp. 26–27.

FRANKLIN T. HARKINS

5 Lectio exhortatio debet esse
Reading as a Way of Life at the Twelfth-Century Abbey of St. Victor

Of the many contributions that Grover Zinn has made to current scholarly understanding of the twelfth century, one of the most significant is the light he has shed on the holistic vision of learning and living that prevailed at the Abbey of St. Victor.[1] In honor of Zinn's work highlighting the harmony among liberal arts education, secular and sacred history, scriptural exegesis, liturgy, ethics, contemplation, and spirituality at St. Victor, this chapter aims at an analysis of Hugh of St. Victor's understanding of the necessary correspondence between sacred reading and Christian living. Our treatment will be tripartite. First, against the dual backdrop of the ancient understanding of philosophy as a way of life and of Christianity as the philosophy *par excellence*, we will consider Hugh's teaching on scriptural reading and its ethical end as presented in the *Didascalicon on the Study of Reading*.

Informing Hugh's notion that sacred reading should issue forth in a particular way of life is Gregory the Great's building metaphor: history or literal reading is the foundation on which the superstructure of allegorical reading must be built, whereas tropology is the beautiful coat of color that adorns the exterior of the edifice.[2] Second, we move from the *Didascalicon*'s theoretical teaching to Hugh's practical instructions concerning how to lead a virtuous life in *De institutione novitiorum*. Finally, we will view the Victorine's teaching in *De institutione* through the lens of modern reader-response criticism in an effort to further elucidate the transformed and transformative way of life toward which scriptural reading ought to aim.

For Hugh of St. Victor, it is important that the reader of scripture be more than just learned.[3] Thus, it is not conducive to the student's objective to become so carried away by the desire for knowledge that, preoccupied with reading more and more, he never moves on to putting what he has read into action.[4] Hugh teaches that the reading of Sacred Scripture is intended to encourage or edify (*aedificare*, lit. "build up"), not preoccupy (*occupare*).[5] "For the Christian philosopher, reading ought to be an exhortation [*lectio exhortation debet esse*], not a preoccupation, and it ought to feed good desires, not destroy them," he maintains.[6] According to Hugh, the *Christianus philosophus*, as one who reads the biblical text, gains knowledge of God's sacrificial love from it, and consequently is inspired to live a life in imitation of this divine virtue. It is no coincidence, of course, that Hugh envisions the ideal reader of scripture as a "Christian philosopher." In so doing, he demonstrates his debt to the ancient understanding of philosophy as a way of life that grows out of the reading of authoritative texts.

Pierre Hadot has demonstrated that one of the fundamental aspects of philosophy in the Hellenistic and Roman periods was its character as a way of life.[7] In antiquity, philosophy consisted not primarily in conveying specialized knowledge or an abstract theory, Hadot argues, but rather in learning to live in a certain way. It was not simply a specific moral code or type of conduct, however. Rather, philosophy was "a mode of existing-in-the-world, which had to be practiced at each instant . . . the goal of which was to transform the whole of the individual's life."[8] This way of being in the world was practiced by means of a number of spiritual exercises.

In Hadot's view, the Christian domestication of ancient *philosophia* is what is ultimately responsible for the modern understanding of philosophy as "a purely abstract-theoretical activity."[9] He points specifically to the development of scholastic theology, which jettisoned the spiritual exercises that had always been at the heart of philosophy, both pagan and Christian alike:

> [The transition of philosophy from a way of life to a strictly theoretical activity] seems to be the result of the absorption of *philosophia* by Christianity. Since its inception, Christianity has presented itself as a *philosophia*, insofar as it assimilated into itself the traditional practices of spiritual exercises. We see this occurring in Clement of Alexandria, Origen, Augustine, and monasticism. With the advent of medieval Scholasticism, however, we find a clear distinction being drawn between *theologia* and *philosophia*. Theology became conscious of its autonomy *qua* supreme science, while philosophy was emptied of its spiritual exercises which, from now on, were relegated to Christian mysticism and ethics. Reduced to the rank of a "handmaid of theology," philosophy's role was henceforth to furnish theology with conceptual—and hence purely theoretical—material. When, in the modern age, philosophy regained its autonomy, it still retained many features inherited from this medieval conception.[10]

Whatever the truth of Hadot's claims, Hugh of St. Victor wrote and taught during the period just prior to these developments. Hugh envisions reading in the liberal arts and in Sacred Scripture as together constituting a single *philosophia* that sets the postlapsarian reader on the way toward salvation or restoration to the image of God.[11] More importantly for our present purposes, however, Hugh understands the reader as ultimately attaining this restoration not by reading alone (whether in the arts, scripture, or both), but rather by living out what he learns in these studies—that is, by reenacting what he reads. Indeed, the Victorine master teaches that the philosophy according to which the student pursues and loves that Wisdom, Word, and Reason who is the second Person of the Trinity consists of both study and action.

Centuries before Hugh and his particular Christian appropriation of *philosophia*, the ancient pagan philosopher's task was the pursuit of the wisdom or reason that is immanent in the cosmos. The Stoic wise man, for example, was he whose thoughts, will, and actions completely coincided with this ordering principle of the universe. For such a philosopher, this represented the achievement of wisdom, which was understood as "nothing more than the vision of things as they are, the vision of the cosmos as it is in the light of reason, and . . . the mode of being and living that should correspond to this vision."[12] "Should" is the operative word here, as seeing and living according to cosmic reason (i.e., knowing and loving wisdom) was always an ideal state, virtually inaccessible to human beings. Although the various philosophical schools diverged considerably in their visions of the world and their corresponding styles of life, they all agreed that it was nearly (if not utterly) impossible for a human being to arrive at wisdom. This is precisely why every school considered wisdom a transcendent norm that ultimately coincided with the rational idea of God.[13]

Nonetheless, thinking and living according to wisdom was the ideal spiritual state or goal toward which the philosopher constantly sought to move. Philosophers in every school sought to make progress toward the ultimate goal of wisdom by participating in various spiritual exercises. These represented training for the philosophy student's mind or soul, analogous to physical exercises for an athlete's body. In general, the spiritual exercises of ancient philosophy consisted of meditation and self-control.[14] By the first, the student learned to see and think about the cosmos in accordance with wisdom; by the second, he practiced living out what he had learned.

The most important of the practices was meditation, which could take any number of forms. Primarily meditation meant "the memorization and assimilation of the fundamental dogmas and rules of life of the school."[15] Hadot explains how this kind of purely rational exercise aimed at and accomplished the complete transformation of the student's worldview: "Philosophical meditation on the essential dogmas of physics, for example the Epicurean contemplation of the genesis of worlds in the infinite void or the Stoic contemplation of the rational and necessary unfolding of cosmic events, can lead to an exercise of the imagination in which human beings appear of little importance in the immensity of space and time."[16] This meditation or contemplation depended on such intellectual exercises as reading, listening, research, and investigation. The student meditated on what he had read, listened to, researched, and investigated in order that he might always have a certain worldview and rule of life always "at hand,"[17] enabling him consciously and intentionally to live out the teachings of his school at any and every moment, whatever the circumstances.

Meditation was closely connected, then, to the subsequent category of spiritual exercises that Hadot terms "self-control," consisting of the practices of attention, self-mastery, and the accomplishment of duties (i.e., action). The practice of attention was characterized by a constant vigilance and presence of mind, an absolute consciousness of oneself in light of philosophical principles. The great Stoic Epictetus (c. 55–c. 135 CE) provided a summary statement of attention when he taught: "You must not separate yourself from these general principles; don't sleep, eat, drink, or converse with other men without them."[18] By virtue of such attention, the student was aware of what he ought to do at each moment and fully willed the actions he performed. Thus, the practice of attention was intended to lead quite naturally to self-mastery and proper action. By engaging in this entire plan of spiritual exercises, the student of ancient philosophy transformed his seeing, thinking, and living. And by means of this transformation, he moved ever closer toward the transcendent state of wisdom.

In Neoplatonism, which Augustine would use to construct a Christian philosophy that found its way into the medieval West, the stages of this spiritual progress corresponded to different degrees of virtue.[19] Porphyry (c. 234–c. 305 CE), the student of Plotinus (204–270 CE) and editor of his *Enneads*, systematically arranged his master's work according to the stages of spiritual advancement in virtue. First, the student's soul was purified by its gradual detachment from the body. Second, he gained knowledge of, and subsequently moved beyond, the visible things of the world. Finally, his soul was converted toward the Intellect and the One.[20]

Plotinus, Porphyry, and other Neoplatonic thinkers understood spiritual exercises as indispensable to the student's progress from corporeal attachment to knowledge of material things to conversion toward the Intellect. The first stage consisted of strict asceticism, including a vegetarian diet. The second required extensive reading, meditation, and contemplation. And all three, but particularly the third stage, demanded that the student live out what he had learned. In short, the student was challenged both to internalize and to externalize Neoplatonic teaching in such a way that it became, as Porphyry taught, his "nature and life."[21] As his nature, the student was to have the Neoplatonic vision of the world deep within his being, and in his life he was to show forth what was deep within. Plotinus used the visually striking metaphor of sculpting to describe the interior-exterior dynamic at work in the philosophical life of virtue:

> If one wants to know the nature of a thing, one must examine it in its pure state.... When you examine it [the soul], then, remove from it everything that is not itself; better still remove all your stains from yourself and examine

yourself, and you will have faith in your immortality. . . . If you do not yet see your own beauty, do as the sculptor does with a statue which must become beautiful: he removes one part, scrapes another, makes one area smooth, and cleans the other, until he causes the beautiful face in the statue to appear. In the same way, you too must remove everything that is superfluous, straighten that which is crooked, and purify all that is dark until you make it brilliant. Never stop sculpting your own statue, until the divine splendor of virtue shines in you.[22]

Hugh of St. Victor invokes a similar metaphor—namely, that of painting the exterior of an edifice with beautiful colors—to describe the virtuous living-out of Christian teaching that has been internalized. Furthermore, just as the various intellectual exercises prepare the students of pagan philosophies for the practical exercises of attention, self-mastery, and the accomplishment of duties, so too do the exercises of reading or instruction (*lectio sive doctrina*) and meditation (*meditatio*) enable the students at the school of St. Victor to engage productively in the prayer (*oratio*) and performance (*actio*) that leads to the contemplation (*contemplatio*) of God.[23]

In his teaching on this point, Hugh draws on a lengthy and rich tradition of Christian writers who understood and presented Christianity as a philosophy like others in antiquity.[24] This tradition of viewing the Christian faith within a broad philosophical framework dates back to the second-century apologists, most notably Justin Martyr (c. 100–c. 165 CE). In an attempt to make a reasoned defense of the faith in the face of pagan critics, the Apologists set Christianity over against pagan philosophy by describing it as "our philosophy" and *the* philosophy par excellence.[25] Whereas Greek philosophers had limited access to the eternal Logos, this very Word or Reason of God had revealed himself to Christians in the Incarnation, the Apologists maintained. If philosophy meant living in accordance with the law of reason, then Christians, who lived in obedience to the commandments of the incarnate Logos, were exemplary philosophers.[26]

It was under the influence of the Greek patristic tradition that monasticism continued to be described and understood as a philosophy throughout the Middle Ages.[27] As a *philosophia*, medieval monasticism combined the ancient pagan and patristic connotations of the term—namely, it was a way of life oriented toward divine reason or wisdom, which became incarnate in

Jesus of Nazareth. In the twelfth century, Bernard epitomized this perspective in seeking to form the monks at Clairvaux in the "disciplines of celestial philosophy."[28] Similarly, Bernard's student Guerric of Igny (d. 1157) proclaimed in a homily on the Feast of St. Benedict: "Blessed also are you, my brothers, who have enlisted in the discipline of wisdom and in the school of Christian philosophy."[29] Jean Leclercq has noted the close connection between the terms *philosophia* and *disciplina* in medieval monasticism. Specifically, *disciplina* denoted a particular type of education or formation that the monk would seek to put into practice as a way of life or *philosophia*.[30]

In the first half of the twelfth century, the relationship between *disciplina* and *philosophia* may be best understood as that between knowledge and love. Thierry of Chartres, a contemporary of Hugh of St. Victor, defined *philosophia* as "the love of wisdom. Wisdom, however, is the complete apprehension of the truth [*integra comprehensio veritatis*] of the things that exist, which [apprehension] is not attained or barely attained unless [the student] loves."[31] For Christian theologians and masters such as Thierry and Hugh, "the truth of the things that exist" is ultimately none other than the very Truth or Wisdom of God who creates and restores all things. It is in knowing and particularly in loving this divine Wisdom that human beings come to engage in philosophy most fully and profoundly.

For almost two thousand years, from the middle of the fourth century BCE to the late sixteenth century CE, pagan philosophy was generally understood as a way of life that grew out of various exegeses of a small number of texts written by "authorities," most notably Plato and Aristotle.[32] Hadot links this protracted period of "exegetical philosophy" to the existence of philosophical schools whose principal aim was to preserve and transmit the thought, writings, and lifestyle of the founder or master. The writings of each school's founder served as the basis for instruction, and a master or teacher determined the order in which these works were to be read and interpreted.[33] Thus, the proper *ordo* in reading was a significant emphasis of all ancient philosophical schools.

The parallels in the Christian tradition, particularly in medieval monasticism, are striking. Certainly from the late first century CE, adherents of Christianity read, heard, and attempted to live out the truth that had been divinely revealed in their Sacred Scriptures. For Christians, God himself was the *auctor*, and therefore the *auctoritas*, behind scriptural truth. It was primarily to God's sacred text, rather than to the writings of Plato or Aristotle, that Christian thinkers and exegetes went to learn how to arrive at the knowledge and love of wisdom. Even during the High Middle Ages, when scholastic theologians broadened their reading and commentating to include the newly discovered works of Aristotle, the writings of Boethius, and the *Sentences* of Peter Lombard, Sacred Scripture remained the first and most important textual authority. Furthermore, other authoritative texts that became foundational for various forms of religious life in the medieval period, such as the *Rule of St. Benedict* and the *Rule of St. Augustine*, were intended and understood principally as commentaries on Scripture and manuals for living out the wisdom revealed therein.

According to Hugh of St. Victor, the postlapsarian Christian philosopher is the virtuous or just man of *Didascalicon* V.9, who trains his life (*exercetur vita*) by means of the successive spiritual exercises of reading, meditation, prayer, and action.[34] His knowing and loving having been disordered, he must engage in these exercises in a particular order so as to be reordered according to the original order with which humans were created. Hugh is primarily concerned with the exercises of reading (*lectio*) and action (*operatio*), which must be practiced in that order. The pursuit of knowledge by means of *lectio* is for the beginner, whereas the pursuit of virtue by means of *operatio* is the purview and obligation of the learned student. The student who begins with reading (as all should) must advance to action when he is sufficiently erudite. By contrast, the unlearned student must not skip over reading in his desire for the virtuous life. This is so because, as Hugh explains, "instruction . . . is the beginning of discipline" for "those who are still to be educated [*doctrinam quae principium est disciplinae incohantibus*]."[35]

Hugh's Latin is significant. The context suggests that he is using *disciplina* not in the strict sense of "a branch of study," but rather more broadly as "training," particularly "moral training," and even as "orderly conduct based on moral training."[36] His principal aim in *Didascalicon* V.8–9 is to demonstrate the proper *ordo* in the spiritual exercises: to teach that those students who have devoted themselves to perfection must advance from reading to the practice of virtuous living, ordering their conduct according to what they have read.[37] Hugh emphasizes the absolute dependence between students' living and reading by describing beginners with the present participial form of the verb *incohare*, which literally means "to start making or forming (a building or other structure)."³⁸ So "Christian philosophers" cannot begin to build, form, or order their lives morally without first reading Sacred Scripture. They know the things they should do only after reading the narrative of things God has already done. They must begin, then, with *historia*, the first discipline of sacred reading. On this foundation, they build the edifice of faith on successive sacraments throughout history by means of *allegoria*. Finally, they paint the building's exterior with the beautiful colors of the moral life by means of *tropologia*. Let us now turn to a consideration of how Hugh instructed the student-readers at St. Victor to decorate their lives with the splendor of virtue.

FOR HUGH, TROPOLOGY IS NOT SIMPLY OR FINALLY A *DISCIPLINA legendi*, in other words, a branch of study pertaining to reading; rather it is a *disciplina vivendi*, that is, a method of moral training that is to be lived out. This helps to explain why he devotes so little space to it in his handbook on reading, the *Didascalicon*. By contrast, however, in his treatise on the formation of novices at St. Victor, *De institutione novitiorum*, Hugh provides thorough instructions on how to lead a virtuous life. Indeed, having been written sometime before 1125, shortly after the *Didascalicon*, *De institutione novitiorum* takes up right where the enchiridion on reading leaves off.³⁹

From the opening lines of his instructions to the novices, Hugh strikes the keynote of love as the way back to God: "Because, brothers . . . you have converted from the vain things of this world . . . toward him who has made you, . . . it is right that you now learn the very road [*uiam*] by which you will be able to arrive at him whom you seek."⁴⁰ Like Augustine's road of the affections, Hugh's road here is a way of life that leads to God and to eternal beatitude.⁴¹ But a fallen human being can arrive at beatitude only through virtue, that is, by living a good life. And only discipline orders the human person's life according to virtue. In fact, according to Hugh, "the discipline of God orders [the human being] into his end because, reforming the human fully and perfectly through virtue, it leads him through to beatitude."⁴² Finally, or firstly on the student's journey to God, discipline is a product of knowledge, which is gained by reading or through instruction. Thus, in *De institutione*, Hugh understands the process whereby fallen human beings are reordered and return to God through the lens of Psalm 118:66 (Vulgate), "Teach me goodness and discipline and knowledge."⁴³

Based on these scriptural words, the Victorine divides the road back to God into three segments: "The road to him consists of knowledge, discipline, [and] goodness. Through knowledge [the novice or student] goes to discipline; through discipline he goes to goodness; through goodness he goes to beatitude."[44]

De institutione is perhaps most profitably read as an extended tropological commentary on Psalm 118:66 in which Hugh invites his student-novices at St. Victor to learn the truth of this scriptural verse, internalize it, and in turn live it out in the world. The Victorine master asks his students to actively respond to the psalmist's words here as if they were their own. He sets out to encourage them toward such a lived response by praising them for the conversion of life into which they have already entered, showing them that this is but a continuation of that initial response: "You have believed the commandments of the one saying, 'If you want to be perfect, go and sell all that you have and come and follow me, and you will have treasure in heaven' [Mt 19:21]. You have done what he commanded, you have hoped for what he promised; now ask from him what is useful for obtaining it."[45] And what is useful for obtaining it is, according to Hugh, knowledge, discipline, and goodness, in that order.

Hugh understands secular reading and the first two disciplines of sacred reading (viz., history and allegory) as instructing the mind with knowledge, whereas the scriptural discipline of tropology adorns it with virtue.[46] Because the goal of all reading at St. Victor was to lead the reader to live out what he had read, Hugh could properly describe the abbey school as "a school of the virtues."[47] It is noteworthy that from its earliest beginnings the Abbey of St. Victor understood and intended itself as a *schola uirtutum*. For example, an extant letter from a student from Germany pursuing his education and formation at the nascent abbey under William of Champeaux speaks highly of the latter's holiness of life and skill in teaching the virtues. It is significant that the student begins his praise for William by noting the admirable manner in which "on a past Easter he gave up all his possessions to live in some poor little church to serve God alone," where he would receive all students who came to him free of charge.[48] The knowledge that William imparted was "good" and, because it was "knowledge with love," it "edified" his students. In short, the student maintains that his teaching "uprooted vices [and] planted virtues."[49]

Another letter, from Hildebert of Lavardin (1055/56–1133) to William himself, continues this emphasis on the master's teaching and living virtue. After having served as director of the cathedral school at Le Mans (appointed 1091), as bishop of Le Mans (elected 1096), and as archbishop of Tours (elected 1125), Hildebert retired to St. Victor, where he apparently came to know William well.[50] In his letter to William, Hildebert writes:

> My soul rejoices and exults in your conduct and conversion, giving thanks for these acts of grace to him from whose gifts you have at long last decided to begin philosophy. For what you have done until now did not savor of philosophy. You merely gathered knowledge from philosophers; you did not bring forth in yourself beauty of conduct. But now you begin to draw out from it [the beauty of manners] the pattern of good behavior like honey from the comb.[51]

Hildebert clearly understands William's teaching at St. Victor as informed by and informing his own way of life, in other words, as constituting a philosophy. As with Hugh after him, William's Christian philosophy is a life of beautiful conduct or sweet behavior that has been, like honey from a comb, carefully drawn out of the body of knowledge that he has acquired. For Hildebert, William's own beauty of conduct and the way his instruction aims to inculcate the same in the students at St. Victor together distinguish his newfound *philosophia* from the mere gathering of *scientia* in which he previously had been engaged as head of the cathedral school of Notre Dame.

These words of Hildebert help to illuminate Hugh's description of Sacred Scripture as a honeycomb that seems dry on the outside but is filled with sweetness inside.[52] The knowledge that scripture teaches — particularly by means of the first discipline of *historia*, the narrative of deeds done in this present earthly life — often strikes the reader as lifeless, boring, and having nothing to do with eternal salvation. Yet inside, at the levels of *allegoria* and *tropologia*, the reader finds spiritual sweetness. With tropology, in particular, the reader imitates the humble love of God revealed in the biblical narrative, thereby bringing out (quite literally) from the text the sweet honey of virtue that leads to eternal beatitude. Young men from all over Europe came to St. Victor during the 1120s and 1130s to study with *Magister Hugo* and to enroll as novices, at least in part because of his reputation as someone who himself had drawn the honey of virtuous living out of the scriptural comb and who was adept at instructing others in doing the same.[53]

In *De institutione*, Hugh seeks to help the novices at St. Victor extract the honey of virtue from the instructional comb by imparting the "knowledge that pertains to formation in living rightly and honestly [*scientiam, que ad institutionem recte et honeste uiuendi pertinet*]."[54] There are several ways that the novice or student should gather this knowledge and integrate it into his very self, namely, by reason, by instruction, by example, by reading and meditating on Sacred Scripture, and by constantly inspecting his own works and moral conduct.[55] Each of these exercises, like those of the ancient philosophical schools, partly (*partim*) contributes to the complete moral formation of the individual. The first is reason, according to which the student diligently considers and discerns what he ought to do in every action, in every place, in every time, and in relation to every person.[56] It is significant that these categories of action parallel nearly exactly the "circumstances" that the student of scripture is to learn about biblical history according to Hugh's *Chronicon* (viz., the who, what, when, and where).[57] In Hugh's view, "the sacred and divine mysteries ought to be implemented" in every action of the student.[58]

This is, of course, closely related to the final way of gaining knowledge of right living, namely, constant vigilance regarding one's own works and moral conduct. This entails probing one's thoughts in addition to one's outward speech and actions.[59] Each day the student is to "call his life to judgment [*uitam suam ad iudicium uocat*]": when he rises in the morning, he ought to consider what he did during the night; and when he goes to bed in the evening, he ought to consider his actions throughout the day.[60] The goal of this continual *circumspectio*, for Hugh, is to achieve a complete correspondence or transparency between one's inner self and outer life.[61] Indeed, Hugh makes clear that this scrutinizing of one's outer life is—like all of the other activities by means of which one obtains knowledge, namely, reasoning, learning, imitating the exemplary lives of the saints, and reading and meditating on scripture—an activity performed by the student's heart.[62] In the prologue to his *Chronicon*, which marks the beginning of his pedagogical program, Hugh describes the student's heart as a "treasure-chest" (*archa*) in which the immortal treasures of wisdom are to be stored.[63] Here in *De institutione*, he brings his educational plan full-circle: the ark of wisdom that has been built in the human heart—from memory-training to liberal arts study to the foundation of history to the edifice of allegory—must be perfected by the application of a beautiful coat of colors that the student shows forth through virtuous living.

C. Stephen Jaeger has argued that this identification of physical appearance and action (the outer life) with the state of the inner life is a defining characteristic of the cathedral school culture of the eleventh and twelfth centuries.[64] One manifestation of this desire for inner-outer correspondence was what Jaeger describes as "pedantic caution in the regulating of behavior," exemplified (in his view) in the customary of the Victorine community, the *Liber ordinis Sancti Victoris Parisiensis*.[65] Whereas the *Liber ordinis* may appear to be little more than a rather cumbersome set of trivial regulations to a modern reader far removed from its medieval religious context, for those twelfth-century canons who sought to live according to it the *Liber ordinis* represented the order of outward discipline that was necessary for the virtuous ascent to God and to eternal happiness.[66]

Another important purpose of the canon's outer discipline was to teach those around him by example. To the extent that canons regular had a particular charism that distinguished them from monks in the twelfth century and beyond, theirs was "to teach by word and example" [*docere verbo et exemplo*].[67] This charism was part and parcel of a new outward-looking orientation that was characteristic of the changing face of spirituality and religious life during "the long twelfth century," from around 1050 to 1215.[68] As a canon regular firmly rooted in this context, Hugh stresses the novice's obligation to provide a good example in his outward behavior or discipline. In his consideration of "what one should do in every place," he teaches: "And, although a person ought in no place to desert his discipline, it ought however to be preserved more diligently and more solicitously where being neglected it will cause scandal to many and being maintained it will be an example for good imitation."[69]

According to Hugh, the novice or student becomes an example for good imitation by imitating examples of good imitation himself. For the master, then, the third way of gaining knowledge to live rightly is by imitating the example of the saints. We have already seen how imitating the humble and loving example of God himself forms or orders fallen readers of scripture according to virtue. Saints are simply those who have imitated the example of the incarnate Word most profoundly. Thus, if readers are to imitate the Word,

Wisdom, or Image of God, and thereby be re-formed or reordered according to it, they must imitate the saints. Invoking a powerful visual image from antiquity, Hugh explains: "Why do you think, brothers, that we should imitate the life and behavior of the good, if not because by imitating them we are re-formed to the likeness of a new life? Indeed, in these saints, the form of the likeness of God has been pressed out [or expressed; *expressa est*], and for that reason when we are imprinted with them by imitation we too are formed according to the image of this same likeness."[70] The master goes on to explain that just as the wax into which a seal is pressed must be made soft in order to receive the form or image of the seal, so too must the hardness of human pride be softened by humility in order for the student to be re-formed into God's image through the impression of the lives of the saints.[71] The analogy of the seal impressed in wax teaches a final lesson that returns us to Hugh's emphasis on the correspondence between the inner and outer life. Namely, just as the seal is pressed into the wax and then the figure becomes visibly and outwardly displayed in the ring or thing having been formed, so too should the *imago Dei* that is re-formed in the inner self through reading the lives of the saints be made visible in outward behavior.[72]

In *Didascalicon* V.7, Hugh briefly treats the saints as contributing to the student's knowledge of virtue. Here, the saints provide the bridge between learning "by example [*exemplo*]" and "by instruction [*doctrina*]." Whereas one learns by example through reading the lives or deeds (*facta*) of the saints, reading the words they wrote (*dicta*) pertaining to discipline teaches by instruction.[73] Hugh takes up learning by instruction in chapter six of *De institutione*, where (as in his consideration of the example of the saints) he again draws a sharp Augustinian contrast between humility and pride. To the novices, he proclaims: "Since, therefore, you have come to the school of the virtues [*scholam uirtutum*] for instruction, you ought to know that hereafter verbal combat in no way pertains to you, because the study of spiritual instruction requires listeners not litigants."[74] Even before he can begin instruction in virtue, then, the novice must be able to practice the humble virtues of silence and deference. Hugh again underscores the inner-outer connection in explaining that discordant and disrespectful speech originates in a prideful heart: "There is no doubt that dispute and verbal combat always arise from a deadly root. Unless the heart had swollen first with pride inside, outside the tongue would have by no means loosed itself from its guard of humility [to go] into verbal insult."[75]

In his insistence on a constant vigilance concerning proper speech, Hugh stands as an important precursor to what Carla Casagrande and Silvana Vecchio have described as "the century of the sin of language," which they identify with the period from 1190 to 1260.[76] During this time—from the late-twelfth to the mid-thirteenth century—preachers, moralists, canonists, theologians, and others concerned with proper Christian behavior appear particularly animated by a preoccupation with the sins that humans commit in speaking.[77] The degree to which these Christian thinkers were so preoccupied is evident in their insistence that any word to be spoken first be subject to the traditional "list of circumstances," most often codified either in a series of questions (who, what, where, when, why, how) or in specific categories corresponding to these questions (namely, person, event, place, time, cause). Indeed, in his *Liber de doctrina loquendi et tacendi* (c. 1250), Albertano of Brescia maintains that the list of circumstances fulfils for speech the same function that a grammar or primer plays for writing, namely, it dictates standards, imposes prohibitions, and resolves doubtful questions.[78]

The list of circumstances, which plays a central role in the pedagogy of Hugh of St. Victor, enjoyed great success throughout the Middle Ages in such diverse cultural and literary domains as rhetoric, ethics, penitential literature, and exegesis. For example, the Victorine master—following Gregory the Great and Bede—used the scheme of circumstances as a fundamental mode of interrogating the biblical text and the history that it recounts.[79] Under the influence of Hugh, however, the use of the circumstances was also extended from the formal structures of literature and exegesis to the realms of personal behavior and moral formation. Casagrande and Vecchio explain: "With Hugh of St. Victor, this schema becomes a discipline, the *disciplina in locutione*, an articulated body of rules to follow, an integral part of a more general discipline of behavior that aims at a radical reform of the manners of the external man in view of attaining interior perfection and a relationship with God."[80] As these words make clear, the final purpose of the aforementioned correspondence between the inner life and outer life of Hugh's pupil is the interior perfection that is requisite for union with the deity.

For our present purposes, however, what is most significant is how Hugh's utilization of the circumstances in *De institutione novitiorum* serves to return his reader full-circle to scriptural *historia* as the principal locus of personal transformation and restoration. Hugh teaches the reader of the sacred text to begin by internalizing the basics of salvation history—"the foundation of the foundation," as he describes it—by memorizing the three most important circumstances of things having been done, namely, the persons, places, and times. The penultimate goal of this internalization of *historia* is the uniquely personal externalization of these deeds done in time by means of the discipline of living rightly (the end of *tropologia*), which stipulates the what, where, when, why, and how of every aspect of behavior and speech. The student of Christian philosophy is trained to embody the love that is signified in scripture in order that ultimately he might thereby be led back to God by means of virtuous living. By an ordered reading and living of the sacred text, Hugh's disordered student is finally reordered toward beatitude. He instructs his students thus: "When you read Sacred Scripture, therefore, carefully consider what is said there to incite you to the love of God, to the contempt of the world, to the avoidance of the traps of the enemy, and to what serves to nourish good loves and to destroy evil desires."[81] Just as in the *Didascalicon*, so too here in *De institutione* Hugh teaches that the reader should pay attention to how scripture instructs concerning virtue. He should seek to be formed by the text's precepts rather than encumbered by its questions.[82] Hugh's instructions for reading here are aimed at experienced students, specifically those who have already built the firm foundation of *historia* and erected the edifice of *allegoria*. Furthermore, his hearers have presumably demonstrated their capacity to begin to live out the love signified in scripture by their enrollment as novices at St. Victor. At this advanced stage of religious reading, their task is to seek out and respond to the scriptural text's moral teaching, as Hugh explains: "But you, brothers, who have already entered the school of discipline, first ought to seek in divine reading what instructs your moral conduct toward virtue [*quod mores uestros ad uirtutem instruat*] rather than what sharpens your understanding toward subtlety [*quod sensum acuat ad subtilitatem*]."[83]

The knowledge of appropriate moral conduct should ideally come to fruition in outward discipline, which is "a good and upright way of life, which is the same as not doing evil. . . . Similarly, discipline is the well-ordered movement of all one's body parts and an appropriate disposition in every facet of life and in every action."[84] For Hugh, not only does the inner state of the mind or heart determine the outer movement or disposition of the body, discipline on the outside stabilizes and strengthens the mind or spirit.[85] Thus, the interaction between scriptural reading and Christian living establishes something of a self-perpetuating cycle according to which *scientia* gained through well-ordered *lectio* animates a correspondingly well-ordered bodily response in the form of virtuous living, which in turn prepares and nourishes the mind to be further instructed in wisdom. Outward discipline, then, is utterly indispensable to the Christian life and to Hugh's pedagogical program, which explains why he provides detailed instructions on how to maintain discipline in dress, conduct, speech, and eating.[86]

At a number of points throughout his treatment of discipline, Hugh presents these instructions as growing out of scriptural texts, using his own tropological exegesis of scripture to teach his students how they ought to read the sacred text for moral living. For example, in teaching that discipline always ought to be maintained in gesture, Hugh maintains that many passages of scripture denounce inordinate gestures that arise from the inner corruption of the soul.[87] One such is Isaiah 3:16–17: "And the Lord said: Because the daughters of Zion are haughty and have walked with outstretched necks and wanton glances of the eyes, and have made noise with their feet as they moved along in step, the Lord will make bald the crown of the head of the daughters of Zion and the Lord will strip away their hair."[88] That the daughters of Zion walked with outstretched necks and glancing eyes indicates arrogance (*arrogantia*), according to Hugh's reading. That they made noise with their feet as they walked indicates lasciviousness (*lasciuia*). That the Lord will make the crowns of their heads bald and strip away their hair indicates the punishments for such arrogance and lasciviousness, respectively.[89] After explaining that the following verses (vv. 18–24) relate the divine punishment for the luxury of precious clothing, Hugh concludes: "See how diligently he [Isaiah] enumerates all the signs of vanity in order to show how severely God prohibits those things in which human beings think there is no or very little fault."[90]

A second example appears in Hugh's consideration of the discipline that one should maintain in speaking.[91] In speech, the student ought to pay attention to five things, according to Hugh: what is said, to whom it is said, how it is said, when it is said, and where it is said.[92] Here again the Victorine orders his treatment of discipline according to the traditional circumstances so that his students might similarly order their speech according to these easily-memorable categories—categories according to which they have already learned the basic narrative of salvation history recounted in the biblical text.

Hugh begins discussing when a certain thing is to be said by affirming: "There is a time when nothing should be said, and there is a time when something should be said, but there is never a time when everything should be said."[93] This significant moral truth comes, according to Hugh, directly from Ecclesiastes 3:7b, "tempus tacendi et tempus loquendi." Hugh reads these five brief scriptural words to mean that the time to be silent should always precede the time to speak by virtue of the fact that silence teaches the student the appropriate time to speak. "For this reason," he explains, "Solomon does not say, 'There is a time to speak and a time to be silent,' but rather, 'There is a time to be silent and a time to speak,' because first, as was said, in silence the manner of speaking is chosen, which afterwards is expressed by the voice during the time to speak."[94]

This interpretation exemplifies Hugh's understanding that *tropologia* is always firmly grounded in *historia*: that is, that scripture's moral teaching directly depends on the basic narrative of the sacred text and its first meaning. For Hugh, the actual word order in Ecclesiastes 3:7b truthfully reflects the order in which King Solomon spoke, and is crucial in instructing the reader morally. And such instruction, in turn, indicates how the reader is to order his speaking. By actively responding to or embodying such moral instruction, the reader acquires discipline, which leads to goodness and to beatitude. Hugh intends his program of reading not only to begin at the level of *historia*, but to continue at this level, even as the reader progresses to tropology.

THROUGHOUT HIS DISCUSSION OF *DISCIPLINA* IN *DE INSTITUTIONE*, Hugh aims to elucidate how tropological reading is actually to do its transformative work in the reader. In the final part of this essay, we shall view Hugh's practical teaching in *De institutione* through the lens of modern reader-response criticism in an effort to shed further light on the Victorine's understanding of sacred reading as directed toward a particular way of life.

Reader-response theory, a school of literary criticism that emerged in the 1960s and 1970s, seeks to provide a corrective to the notion that a text possesses an objective meaning, determined once and for all, and that the reader's purpose is to discover this singular inherent meaning.[95] It highlights the role of the reader and the process of reading rather than the author or the text itself in the determination of meaning. Each reading of a text is a performance, and meaning is an event. According to Stanley Fish, the reader's response is not *to* the meaning of a text; rather, the reader's response *is* the meaning.⁹⁶ Hans Robert Jauss states:

> A literary work is not an object that stands by itself and that offers the same view to each reader in each period. It is not a monument that monologically reveals its timeless essence. It is much more like an orchestration that strikes ever new resonances among its readers and that frees the text from the material of the words and brings it to a contemporary existence.⁹⁷

Throughout his writings, from the beginning of his pedagogical program in the *Chronicon* to his moral instruction in *De institutione,* Hugh of St. Victor seems to share the basic assumption that literary meaning is forged when the text comes to be in the reader and thereby assumes "a contemporary existence." That he goes to such great lengths in the *Chronicon* Prologue to teach his students to memorize the entire Psalter intimates as much. Hugh makes clear in both the *Chronicon* Prologue and *De institutione,* however, that the ultimate goal of internalizing the scriptural text is the subsequent externalizing of it through teaching, living, or teaching by living. The meaning of the biblical text is neither primarily nor finally found on the leaves of parchment that the reader initially encounters; rather, it takes shape in the mind or heart of the reader. By means of historical and allegorical reading, the ark of wisdom is built inwardly; and by means of tropological reading, the edifice shows forth its beautiful coat of color.

Simply because reader-response criticism prioritizes the reader does not mean, its proponents are quick to point out, that the meaning or comprehension of a text is completely arbitrary or utterly subjective. This is so because every text has what Jauss calls a "horizon of expectations" in the historical moment of its appearance that determines to some degree the ways in which it will be received. "A literary work," Jauss explains, "even when it appears to be new, does not present itself as something absolutely new in an informational vacuum, but predisposes its audience to a very specific kind of reception by announcements, overt and covert signals, familiar characteristics, or implicit allusions."⁹⁸ More broadly speaking, textual production and reception always take place in what Fish calls an "interpretive community" with a set of shared interpretive assumptions and strategies. "[M]eanings are the property neither of fixed and stable texts nor of free and independent readers but of interpretive communities that are responsible both for the shape of a reader's activities and for the texts those activities produce."[99] According to Fish, communication between a text or author and a reader happens not because the two share a language in the sense of apprehending the meanings of individual words and the rules for combining them, but rather because "a way of thinking, a form of life" unites them and implicates them "in a world of already-in-place objects, purposes, goals, procedures, [and] values."[100]

The astute reader—whether medieval or modern—observes that from the opening lines of its Prologue, *De institutione* is squarely situated within an interpretive community of Augustinian canons regular that shares a common understanding of the scriptural text and its transformative potential. Hugh's readers "have converted from the vain things of this world" toward God and "now [seek to] learn the very road [*uiam*] by which . . . [they] will be able to arrive at him."[101] As our foregoing analysis suggests, these words alone grow out of and presuppose "a world of already-in-place objects, purposes, goals, procedures, [and] values" established largely by the life and writings of Augustine and the Augustinian tradition through the time of Hugh's work. Through the reading and hearing of Augustine's own written works (as well as scripture) as part of their regular routines, the students at St. Victor constructed a "horizon of expectations" that they brought to the reading of both *De institutione* and the scriptural text to which it referred them. At the heart of this structure of expectations stood the conviction that God's revelation in Sacred Scripture calls the reader to a particular mode of existence to which he ought to respond faithfully, and that the reading of and response to the scriptural text can and should lead to spiritual transformation.

Hugh and his Victorine students gleaned this view of scripture and the transformative power of sacred reading from, for example, such works of Augustine as *Confessiones*. At the heart of Augustine's understanding of the relationship among reading, loving, and restoration stands his firm belief that the scriptural narrative of things past (*praeteritorum narratio*) is efficacious in nourishing and strengthening charity and in conquering and extinguishing cupidity in the reader.[102] It is important to note that his certainty in this regard grows, in large part, out of his own powerful experience of the close connection between reading and conversion of life as recounted in book 8 of *Confessiones*. What is abundantly clear about Augustine's account of his conversion here is that he understands and intends his own personal narrative as an imitation of the master narrative found in scripture (and of other personal narratives of conversion that are themselves imitations of the biblical narrative).[103]

The parable of the prodigal son (Lk 15:11–32), in particular, is the scriptural lens through which Augustine rereads the story of his past life in *Confessiones* 1–9.[104] Like the prodigal son, Augustine had wandered far, in love, from his heavenly Father and found himself roaming the streets of the earthly city, loving the things of this world as ends in themselves. For years, Augustine's cupidity and pride (i.e., disordered loving) prevented his return to God on the road of the affections.[105] His *Confessiones* is the story of his journey from the earthly city (i.e., the love of self and the world to the exclusion of God) back to the heavenly city (i.e., the love of God to the exclusion of self and the world), where he was welcomed with mercy, forgiveness, and beatitude.

Augustine relates that even prior to his conversion or return to God he believed that God had established the way of eternal salvation in Christ and in the Sacred Scriptures.[106] His confidence in the salvific power of scripture grew as he heard of others who had been converted to the Catholic faith and way of life by reading sacred texts.[107] Furthermore, Augustine affirms that when his friend Simplicianus narrated the story of Victorinus' scripture-induced conversion, he himself "was inflamed toward imitation"—the very purpose of Simplicianus' narration.[108]

In the midst of these interconnected narratives of reading and conversion to ordered loving, Augustine recounts his own story of transformation or restoration by reading.[109] When he was in the garden of the rented house he was sharing with his friend Alypius, a tremendous tumult began to rage in Augustine's heart. He struggled greatly within himself and was tormented. He desired to be converted to the truth and to the service of God, on the one hand; yet he was wholly unwilling, on the other. His loves pulled him in opposing directions. It was during his weeping and bitter sorrow that he heard a voice repeating, "Take up, read; take up, read" (*Tolle lege, tolle lege*).[110] Recalling the story of Antony's conversion upon reading and applying directly to himself Christ's words in Matthew 19: 21 ("Go, sell everything you have, give to the poor and you will have treasure in heaven; and come, follow me"), Augustine believed *tolle lege* to be a divine command to open the "book of the Apostle" that he had nearby and read the first passage he found. He snatched up the book, opened it (seemingly) randomly, and read the first words upon which his eyes fell: "Not in rioting and drunkenness, nor in debauchery and lewdness, nor in arguing and jealousy; but put on the Lord Jesus Christ and make no provision for the flesh in its desires" (Rm 13:13–14). Augustine relates that he needed to read no further, as these words filled his heart with the light of certainty and dispelled all the darkness of doubt. By means of these words, he was converted from cupidity to charity, from self-love to the love of God. These scriptural signs began to effect and build up in him the ordered love that they signified.

It is significant that Augustine concludes the story of his restorative reading experience in *Confessiones* 8 by recounting the way in which it, in turn, inspired Alypius to read and be converted.[111] Augustine tells his reader that immediately after his own reading from the book of the Apostle, he narrated his experience to Alypius, who wished to know exactly what he had read. When Augustine showed him the passage, Alypius looked further in the text to Romans 14:1, "Receive the one who is weak in faith," and applied it to himself. Thus, Alypius associated himself with Augustine's decision and good purpose. Furthermore, he began to love Augustine with the love of use (*uti*) in order that the newly reordered Augustine might lead him to the enjoyment (*frui*) of God. In short, both Augustine and Alypius embarked on the road to restoration by reading the scriptural narrative and living out the ordered love that it both signified and effected. And they sought to give their own narratives meaning by integrating them into the ongoing story of God's salvific deeds throughout history.

With the "horizon of expectations" of Hugh of St. Victor's students having been shaped by precisely such narratives and the larger theological and spiritual worldview that they presuppose, the Victorine master undoubtedly intended his own *De institutione* as an impetus to a similar sort of transformative reading of and response to scripture. Furthermore, just as Augustine constructed the narrative of his own conversion in the language of scripture and intended it to become part of the ongoing narrative of salvation history, so too does Hugh want his students to model their own moral behavior on both the sacred text and the lives of such saints as Augustine. Hugh provides a set of detailed directives in *De institutione* precisely because, as a theological and spiritual master, he understands how difficult such an imitation of these sacred narratives can be. Yet, this is the very challenge of moral reading, as Hugh notes in the *Chronicon* Prologue: "It rightly receives the name 'tropology,' that is converted language or replicated speech, because we certainly turn the language of a foreign narrative toward our own instruction when, by reading the deeds of others, we conform ourselves to their example of living."[112]

According to reader-response theory, any narrative or text is always to a certain degree "foreign" to the reader and vice-versa. We might profitably understand Hugh of St. Victor's pedagogical program as a kind of broad-based theological and spiritual initiation into the particular "interpretive community" that would make comprehension and concretization of the scriptural text both possible and transformative. The various elements of the Victorine master's educational program—namely, establishing the basic outline of salvation history in memory, studying the liberal arts, learning certain doctrines or "sacraments" of the Christian faith, reading the lives and writings of the saints, inculcating an understanding of Christianity as the true philosophy or way of life—seem to aim at the formation of the reader's mind or consciousness in such a way that the narrative of Sacred Scripture might be perceived as less "foreign." For example, the memorization of secular and sacred history that Hugh seeks to cultivate in the *Chronicon* and the Ark treatises prepares the reader well for the "transfer" of the scriptural text at the fundamental level of historical reading. Similarly, the basic instruction on the sacred mysteries in *De sacramentis* provides structures of comprehension that are indispensable for proper allegorical reading. And it is such fruitful reading at the levels of history and allegory that prepare the reader to respond appropriately to the sacred text at the level of tropology. In concretizing or living out the love signified in scripture, the reader moves closer toward restoration and in so doing participates in the ongoing history of salvation.

NOTES

1. See, e.g., Zinn, "Mandala Symbolism," "*Historia fundamentum est*," "Hugh of St. Victor and the Art of Memory," "History and Interpretation," "Exegesis and Spirituality in Richard of St. Victor," and "Hugh of St. Victor's *De scripturis et scriptoribus sacris.*"

2. On Hugh's adoption of Gregory's building metaphor, see Harkins, *Reading and the Work of Restoration*, 139–40 and 167–69.

3. *Didascalicon de studio legendi* (hereafter *Did.*) V.6, ed. Offergeld, 338 (hereafter FC 27). All translations of *Did.* will be my own. My complete translation of *Did.* can be found in Harkins and van Liere, eds., *Interpretation of Scripture*, 61–201.

4. *Did.* V.7 (FC 27:340).

5. Augustine also uses the verb *aedificare* in conjunction with the language of love to describe scripture's purpose in the reader. See, e.g., *De doctrina christiana*, 1.36.40 (CCSL 32:29).

6. *Did.* V.7: "Christiano philosopho lectio exhortatio debet esse, non occupatio, et bona desideria pascere, non necare" (FC 27:340).

7. The following discussion relies heavily on P. Hadot, *Philosophy as a Way of Life*.

8. Ibid., 265.

9. Ibid., 107–8.

10. Ibid., 108–9. Compare Swanson, *The Twelfth-Century Renaissance*, 104–38, for a discussion of the major transitions in philosophy and theology during the twelfth century. Swanson's notion that two categories of philosophy coexisted in this era seems to confirm what Hadot describes as the emptying of philosophy's spiritual exercises. Namely, Swanson maintains that one approach understood philosophy as a practical transferable "skill" with vocational application, whereas the other envisioned philosophy as an "intellectual act, a way of thinking about, and thinking through, significant problems of existence" (105).

11. See Harkins, *Reading and the Work of Restoration*, 112–36.

12. P. Hadot, *Philosophy as a Way of Life*, 58.

13. Ibid., 57–59.

14. Ibid., 59.

15. Ibid., 59.

16. Ibid., 59.

17. Ibid.

18. Epictetus, *Discourses* 4.12.7, in *Epictetus: The Discourses*, trans. Oldfather. Compare P. Hadot, *Philosophy as a Way of Life*, 84.

19. P. Hadot, *Philosophy as a Way of Life*, 99–101.

20. Ibid., 99–100.

21. Porphyry, *On Abstinence* 1.29; P. Hadot, *Philosophy as a Way of Life*, 100. For text and French translation see Porphyry, *Porphyre: De l'abstinence*, ed. and trans. Bouffartigue and Patillon. For an English translation see Porphyry, *Select Works of Porphyry*, trans. Taylor.

22. Plotinus, *Ennead* 1.5.7.10.28–32 and 1.6.9.8–26; P. Hadot, *Philosophy as a Way of Life*, 100. For text see Plotinus, *Plotinus: Enneades*, ed. Henry and Schwyzer. For an English translation see Plotinus, *Plotinus: Enneads*, trans. Armstrong.

23. See *Did.* V.9 (FC 27:348–50).

24. See P. Hadot, *Philosophy as a Way of Life*, 126–44.

25. Justin Martyr, *Dialogue with Trypho* 8.1. For a consideration of Christianity as a philosophy in early Christian apologetic literature, see Malingrey, "*Philosophia*," 107–28.

26. See Justin Martyr, *Second Apology* 2.13.3; and *First Apology* 1.46.1–4.

27. Leclercq, "Pour l'histoire de l'expression 'philosophie chrétienne'"; P. Hadot, *Philosophy as a Way of Life*, 129; and Leclercq, *Love of Learning*, 100–1.

28. *Exordium magnum Cisterciense*, PL 185:437; Leclercq, *Love of Learning*, 101.

29. "Beati et vos, fratres mei, qui in disciplinam sapientiae, et christianae scholam philosophiae nomina dedistis." *Sermo in fest. S. Ben.* 1.4, my translation (PL 185:101B); Leclercq, *Love of Learning*, 102.

30. Leclercq, *Love of Learning*, 101–2.

31. "Philosophia autem est amor sapientiae; sapientiae autem est integra comprehensio veritatis eorum quae sunt, quam nullus vel parum adipiscitur nisi amaverit." Jeauneau, "Le *Prologus in Eptatheucon* de Thierry de Chartres," 174. For similar definitions, see Baron, "Hugonis de Sancto Victore *Epitome Dindimi in philosophiam*," esp. 130.

32. P. Hadot, *Philosophy as a Way of Life*, 71.

33. Ibid., 71–72. Hadot explains: "We still have some of the writings in which Platonists gave advice on the order in which Plato's dialogues were to be read. Thus, we can tell that from the fourth century BC on, Aristotle's logical writings were arranged in a definite scholastic order—the *Organon*—which would not change until modern times" (p. 72).

34. *Did.* V.9: "Quattuor sunt in quibus nunc exercetur vita iustorum et, quasi per quosdam gradus ad futuram perfectionem sublevatur, videlicet lectio sive doctrina, meditatio, oratio, et operatio" (FC 27:348; Taylor, 132). Hugh understands *contemplatio* as a fifth stage that is the fruit of the first four.

35. *Did.* V.8 (FC 27:346).

36. See *disciplina* in *The Oxford Latin Dictionary*.

37. *Did.* V.8. Hugh teaches the advanced student: "Exercitium tibi esse potest lectio, sed non propositum. Doctrina bona est, sed incipientium est. Tu vero te perfectum fore promiseras, et ideo tibi non sufficit, si incipientibus coaequaris" (FC 27:348).

38. See *incohare* in *The Oxford Latin Dictionary*.

39. On the dating of *De institutione novitiorum* [hereafter *De inst. nov.*, providing page numbers in the Feiss et al. edition], see van den Eynde, *Essai sur la succession et la date des écrits de Hugues de Saint-Victor*, 113–15 and table 1; and Feiss at al., *L'oeuvre de Hugues de Saint-Victor*, 1:10–11.

40. *De inst. nov.* Prol., 18. All translations of *De inst. nov.* will be my own.

41. Ibid.; compare *De doctrina christiana*, 1.4.4 (CCSL 32:8).

42. *De inst. nov.* Prol., 18.

43. *Ibid.* Ineke van 't Spijker has noted that this treatise can be read as a sustained exegesis on this psalm. See van 't Spijker, *Fictions of the Inner Life*, 61–70, here at 63.

44. *De inst. nov.* Prol., 20.
45. Ibid.
46. See *Did.* V.6 (FC 27:36–38).
47. *De inst. nov.* 6. To his students, Hugh declares: "Ad scholam uirtutum erudiendi acceditis,", 36; n.b.: the chapter numbers that I will use for Hugh's treatise are taken not from the Latin itself but rather from the facing French translation of Feiss and Sicard. For ease of reference I have chosen to use these instead of the line numbers given in the Latin.
48. *Udalrici codex*, Ep. 160: "Qui cum esset archidiaconus fereque apud regem primus, omnibus quae possidebat dimissis, in praeterito pascha ad quandam pauperrimam ecclesiolam, soli Deo serviturus, se contulit; ibique postea omnibus undique ad eum venientibus gratis et causa Dei solummodo," 286; all translations my own. On St. Victor as a "school of the virtues" in the twelfth century, with particular reference to this letter, see Jaeger, *Envy of Angels*, 244–68, and "Humanism and Ethics."
49. *Udalrici codex*, Ep. 160: "Quod videlicet bonum sapientiae, quando cum munda intentione quaeritur et suscipitur, merito ab omnibus discretis summum et creditur et habetur. Scientia enim, ut ait apostolus, sine caritate inflat, scientia vero cum caritate aedifficat [sic]. Vicia enim eruit, virtutes inserit," 286–87.
50. For a brief biography of Hildebert see Harris, "Hildebert of Lavardin."
51. Hildebert of Lavardin, *Epistolae*, Ep. 1: "De conversatione et conversione tua laetatur et exsultat anima mea, illum prosequens actione gratiarum, cujus muneris est, quod nunc tandem philosophari decreveris. Nondum enim redolebas philosophum, cum ex acquisita philosophorum scientia, morum tibi minime depromeres venustatem. Nunc autem sicut e favo mellis dulcedinem, sic ex ea bene agendi formulam expressisti" (PL 171:141A); the translation is Jaeger's (see *Envy of Angels*, 245).
52. See *Did.* IV.1 (FC 27:270) and V.2 (FC 27:320–22).
53. See Jaeger, *Envy of Angels*, 246, who quotes Lawrence of Westminster on his choice of Hugh as a master: "With all possible dispatch I chose that excellent and unique doctor, and I embraced his teaching with supreme diligence, since the moral excellence of his life [*vitae honestas*] decorates his learning, and the saintliness of this teacher illuminates his polished doctrine with beauty of manners [*morum venustate*]." It must be noted that between 1100 and 1140, roughly the period of Hugh's life, the student population of Paris swelled from about one hundred (all associated with the cathedral school of Notre Dame) to between two thousand and three thousand associated with at least twenty-five different schools in and around the city; see Jaeger, *Envy of Angels*, 239, and Southern, "The Schools of Paris and the School of Chartres," esp. 119. Hugh and other renowned masters were largely responsible for this rapid growth.
54. *De inst. nov.* 1, 22.
55. Ibid.
56. Ibid.
57. See Harkins, *Reading and the Work of Restoration*, 14–41, and the treatment of the "list of circumstances" below.

58. *De inst. nov.* 2: "In omni actu, hoc est qualiter sacra et diuina mysteria impleri oporteat," 22.
59. *De inst. nov.* 9, 44–48.
60. *De inst. nov.* 9, 46.
61. Van 't Spijker, *Fictions of the Inner Life*, 65.
62. At the close of his consideration of self-scrutiny and of knowledge more generally, Hugh affirms: "Quisquis cor suum in huiusmodi studio exercet, existimo quod cito ad illam bonam et salubrem scientiam perueniat, quam, sicut supra diximus, ad seruandam disciplinam et bonitatem psalmista dari sibi postulabat," *De inst. nov.* 9, 48.
63. *Chronicon* Prol., in W. Green, "Hugo of St. Victor," 488.
64. Jaeger, *Envy of Angels*, 9–10 and 244–68.
65. Ibid., 10. The *Liber ordinis* has been edited by Jocqué and Milis and can be found in CCCM 61.
66. Jaeger provides an example of this modern perspective when he writes: "The customary of the community of St. Victor at Paris spins every moment of the day into a web of regulations, seemingly trivial ones: how to hold the soup bowl, what direction to swing the legs when climbing into bed—along with minute prescriptions for greater issues like receiving and training novices, welcoming guests, and arranging the liturgy"; *The Envy of Angels*, 10.
67. See, e.g., Bynum, *Docere Verbo et Exemplo*; eadem, *Jesus as Mother*, 22–58; Zinn, "The Regular Canons," 218–28; and Chase, *Contemplation and Compassion*, 22–25, who observes: "The twelfth century rediscovered the concept of *gestus* ('behaviour' in gesture, bearing, and humility) as an important aspect of teaching by example. Hugh of St. Victor, in fact, writing for novices, wrote a unique treatise on the meanings attached to details of exemplary behaviour. Such behaviour was intended to both reflect and teach the apostolic life" (24).
68. Bynum, *Jesus as Mother*, 22.
69. *De inst. nov.* 3, 24.
70. *De inst. nov.* 7, 40). Compare *Did.* I.1 (FC 27:114–16).
71. *De inst. nov.* 7, 40–42.
72. *De inst. nov.* 7, 42.
73. *Did.* V.7 (FC 27:338–40).
74. *De inst. nov.* 6, 36.
75. Ibid.
76. Casagrande and Vecchio, *Les péches de la langue*, esp. 13.
77. Ibid., 17.
78. See ibid., 65.
79. See Harkins, *Reading and the Work of Restoration*, 14–41, and Casagrande and Vecchio, *Les péches de la langue*, 65–68.
80. Casagrande and Vecchio, *Les péches de la langue*, 69.
81. *De inst. nov.* 8, 44.
82. Ibid.

83. Ibid.
84. Ibid., 10, 48.
85. Ibid., 50.
86. Ibid., 11–21, 50–98.
87. Ibid., 12, 58.
88. My translation from the Vulgate.
89. *De inst. nov.* 12, 61–62.
90. Ibid., 62.
91. He treats this general theme in ibid., 13–17, 74–90.
92. Ibid., 74.
93. Ibid., 16, 82.
94. Ibid., 84.
95. See, e.g., Jauss, *Toward an Aesthetic of Reception*, and *Aesthetic Experience and Literary Hermeneutics*, trans. Shaw; Iser, *The Act of Reading*; and Fish, *Is There a Text in This Class?*
96. Fish, *Is There a Text in This Class?* 3.
97. Jauss, *Toward an Aesthetic of Reception*, 21.
98. Ibid., 23.
99. Fish, *Is There a Text in This Class?* 322.
100. Ibid., 303–4.
101. *De inst. nov.* Prol., 18.
102. *De doctrina christiana* 3.10.15 (CCSL 32:87). Cf. *De doctrina christiana* 1.36.40 (CCSL 32:29).
103. See Stock, *Augustine the Reader*, 75–111.
104. See, e.g., *Confessiones* 1.18.28 (CCSL 27:15–16) and 2.4.9 (CCSL 27:21–12). In the introduction to her translation, Boulding writes: "Like other Fathers of the Church, Augustine was vividly conscious of the entire mystery of salvation as embodied in a story that runs from Genesis to Revelation but still continues. He was himself caught up in it, for like the prodigal son, he had wandered far off into a land of unlikeness, but the journey home brought him to a recovery of the lost image and likeness to God with which book 13 is concerned. It is a story still unfolding in the faithful and in the Church, and in it we are all participants" (Augustine, *The Confessions*, 30).
105. See, e.g., *Confessiones* 2.3.6–8 (CCSL 27:20–21).
106. *Confessiones* 7.7.11 (CCSL 27:99–100).
107. See ibid., 8.2.3–3.6 (CCSL 27:114–17) and 8.6.13–15 (CCSL 27:121–23).
108. Ibid., 8.5.10 (CCSL 27:119–20).
109. The following summary is taken from *Confessiones* 8.8.19–12.30 (CCSL 27:125–32).
110. Ibid., 8.12.29 (CCSL 27:131).
111. Ibid., 8.12.30 (CCSL 27:131–32).
112. *Chronicon*, Prol., in W. Green, "Hugh of St. Victor," 491.

LESLEY SMITH

6 Robert Amiclas and the Glossed Bible

No reader, entering a book-lined room, can resist looking at what is on the shelves: we think we know someone better when we know their books. This curiosity can be extended to whole communities by the burgeoning study of medieval library inventories, and it is especially enticing when we can see a collection expand and contract over time. On the whole, medieval libraries were small and, given the expense of buying manuscript books or the protracted labor of copying them, the collections of individuals were even smaller. Much to scholars' disappointment and frustration, the evidence of contemporary book lists cannot always be matched with extant volumes today. The eminent Paris theologian Peter Lombard, for example, left his books to Notre Dame; we have the list, but none of those volumes has been identified among surviving manuscripts, and so a fascinating potential source of evidence for the working methods of a twelfth-century scholar is lost.[1]

However, although Peter's books are unknown, we do have books with a link to a less-celebrated Parisian master. Although the name Robert Amiclas barely appears in the medieval record, he was a contemporary of Peter Lombard and of the school of St. Victor in its heyday. Even better, the twenty volumes associated with him are examples of that most characteristic product of the mid-twelfth-century book trade, the Glossed Bible or *Glossa ordinaria*.[2] And best of all, the books are evidence not only *that* he read them but of *how* he read them: all twenty are annotated in Robert's own hand (see table 6.1). They comprise a unique record in the Western Middle Ages of a named scholar working on an extensive group of biblical texts, and especially of the new and fashionable Gloss.

Although we have evidence of Robert only from Paris, the twenty volumes he wrote in once formed part of the medieval library of the modest Cistercian abbey of Buildwas in Shropshire. Forty-nine manuscripts survive from Buildwas, making it the largest surviving English Cistercian collection from the Middle Ages.[3] Unfortunately, we have no medieval inventory to link to the extant volumes. The *Registrum Anglie* (the fourteenth-century Franciscan union catalogue of books in monastic houses) lists 111 texts (not books) at Buildwas, of which only eighteen can be identified among the surviving codices, giving an idea of how much else must have been there.[4] Fifteen of the extant forty-nine books were certainly made at Buildwas (according to their modern cataloguer), although up to another ten may have been. The surviving books are by and large an unremarkable collection of patristic theology, lives of the saints, and pastoralia—except for Robert's annotated Glosses, nineteen of which are now in the Wren Library at Trinity College, Cambridge, donated to the college by John Whitgift (Master of Trinity and Archbishop of Canterbury) at the end of the sixteenth century.[5] From the evidence of a deed used as a pastedown in one of the volumes (Ms B.2.6), they appear to have remained at Buildwas until at least the late fifteenth century. The single book of Robert's that we know was not kept with the others (the Gloss on the Canonical Epistles and Revelation) was bought by Shrewsbury School from a London dealer in the early seventeenth century.[6] We have no idea how it came to be separated from the other books, or to find its way to London. Robert's *ex libris*—*Iste liber est magistri Roberti Amiclas*—appears in only one of the volumes (Ms B.1.11: Matthew and Mark); the others have been linked with him by M. R. James and Jenny Sheppard, by comparing the handwriting of the annotations to the *ex libris*.[7]

Table 6.1. Robert's Glossed books, ordered by date. Alternate dates are from Sheppard, *The Buildwas Books*.

Shelfmark	Gloss format	Biblical book	Origin	Date (Sheppard, if different)	Ex libris
TCC B.1.10	Simple	Matthew	French	1140	—
TCC B.1.34	Simple	Acts	French	1140	Buildwas
TCC B.1.12	Simple	Luke	French	1140–50	—
TCC B.1.39	Simple	Ecclesiastes, Song of Songs, Leviticus (part), Tobit	?French	1140–50	Buildwas
TCC B.1.31	Simple	Leviticus	?French	1140–50	Buildwas
TCC B.1.14	Simple	Deuteronomy	?French	1140–50 (12mid)	Buildwas
Shrewsbury School 12	Simple	Canonical Epistles, Revelation	French	1140–50 (12mid)	Buildwas
TCC B.1.13	Early transitional	Proverbs, Ecclesiastes	French	12mid	—
TCC B.1.11	Simple/early transitional	Matthew, Mark	??French	1150–	Robert & Buildwas
TCC B.1.36	Simple/early transitional	John	French	1150	Buildwas
TCC B.1.33	Transitional	Matthew (partial)	French	1150	—
TCC B.2.6	Simple	Exodus	Prob. English	1150+	—
TCC B.1.6	Simple	Pauline Epistles	English	1150+	—
TCC B.1.35	Early transitional	Numbers	?French	12¾ (1150)	Buildwas
TCC B.1.32	Transitional	Wisdom	French	12¾ (1150)–	—
TCC B.3.15	Early transitional	Kings	?English	12¾ (1150–60)	Buildwas
TCC B.3.16	Early complex	Joshua, Judges, Ruth	?French	12¾ (1160)	—
TCC B.2.15	Simple	Isaiah	English	12¾ (1160)	Buildwas
TCC B.1.1	Transitional-complex	Jeremiah-Lamentations	French	12¾ (1160+)	Buildwas
TCC B.4.3	Simple	Minor prophets	West Country; but painter French?	12¾ (1160+)	Buildwas

ROBERT AMICLAS

Who was Robert Amiclas, and what can we know about him? Rod Thomson has convincingly argued that Robert was a teaching master of theology and the arts at Paris in the twelfth century, using as evidence references to a Robert Amiclas in William of Tyre's *Historia Ierosolymitana* and in the *Metamorphosis Goliae*.[8] Thomson argues, rightly I think, that this Robert is neither Robert Pullen nor Robert of Melun, as had been previously suggested, but a separate and identifiable master. Dating these sources (and thereby dating Robert's career) is problematic: the earliest possible date for the *Metamorphosis* is 1142, but a date in the mid-1150s would also be possible.[9] A Master Robert Amiclas is also named in a document leasing a property in Paris from the Templars. Again, dating is uncertain, ranging from about 1165 to about 1175. The lease gives the property to Master Robert Amiclas *and his heirs*, and there would be nothing to stop Robert from having been a married man.[10] From the age of some of the Buildwas books, I am inclined to agree with Thomson's earlier dating, and to think that Robert was a master by the 1140s. But even if the later dating were correct, Robert would still have been teaching in Paris in the third quarter of the twelfth century, which is precisely the period when the Gloss was at its most popular as a teaching text in the Paris schools. It is not clear where he himself studied or who his master might have been, although possibilities in Paris would include the school of St. Victor and its master, Hugh; Gilbert de la Porrée, who was a particular proponent of teaching with glossed texts; Robert Pullen; and Alberic of Reims, another name linked to the early Gloss.

Amiclas is an unusual name, but one not unknown in the twelfth century. It refers to the figure of a boatman—*pauper Amiclas*—in Lucan's poem *Pharsalia* (a text encountered in the arts course). By the twelfth century it had become a nickname meaning a poor man. Rod Thomson suggests that Amiclas in this case is a clever, punning way of translating the English surname "Poor," or variants such as Poer and Poore.[11] Englishmen surnamed Poor included the illegitimate brothers Herbert and Richard, who were bishops of Salisbury and Durham. Five people named Poor are mentioned in early documents from Hereford Cathedral (whose diocese included Buildwas).[12] Thomson surmises that Robert was an Englishman who had studied and taught in Paris, and who came home to retire to Buildwas, bringing at least some of his books with him. Although Buildwas, which was founded in

1135, would probably not have existed when Robert left for Paris originally, by the time he returned it would have been under the energetic abbacy of Ranulf (1155–87), a period when the house and its library flourished.

When might Robert have come to Buildwas? A possible clue lies in another Buildwas book—this time one actually made at the abbey. It is a copy of the Gloss on the books of Leviticus and John (a very unusual pairing), which is dated to 1176.[13] Leviticus and John can each be found separately among the Glosses Robert annotated, both copies probably written in France. If Robert and these books were already at Buildwas in 1176, it seems perhaps less likely that a volume containing only these two texts would have been written there. Certainly, if Robert was already a teaching master in Paris in 1142, and we place his birth at about 1110, a retirement date after 1176 is possible.

Thomson's picture of Robert's retirement to Buildwas, bringing these twenty Glossed books with him and leaving them to the abbey library when he died, is very attractive, and for the rest of this paper I shall proceed as though it were indeed the case. But as so often with medieval evidence, the truth is tantalizingly just out of our grasp. All we can really know is that Buildwas possessed twenty Glossed books with annotations by Robert Amiclas, his hand identified by his *ex libris* in one of them. Robert may never have come to Buildwas; he may not have been English; or he may only have owned a single book and annotated others that were already at Buildwas. Nonetheless, the most straightforward reading is that Robert owned at least the French-made books, and retired with them to Buildwas where, if he did not already own the English-made books, he either found them in the library, acquired them himself, or got the abbey to do so; and he continued with his annotations. For simplicity, I shall continue to refer to them as Robert's books, although only one has Robert's *ex libris* and twelve have the *ex libris* of the abbey.

THE GLOSSED BOOKS

Putting aside all speculation, what we can say is that a collection of twenty extant Glossed books written in by one scholar is unique. What can they tell us? Table 6.2 reveals both surprising inclusions and surprising omissions. The oddest omission is a Glossed Psalms. Psalms was a perennial favorite, the earliest book to be glossed, and a ubiquitous teaching text. Genesis, also

Table 6.2. Glossed books owned by Robert of Amiclas

Robert owned	Did not own
	Genesis
Exodus	
Leviticus (+ an extra copy of 11:1–45)	
Numbers	
Deuteronomy	
Joshua	
Judges	
Ruth	
1–4 Kings	
	Chronicles
	Psalms
Tobit (Gloss not supplied)	
	Esther
	Judith
Proverbs	
Ecclesiastes (2 copies)	
Song	
Wisdom (7:23 to end)	
	Ecclesiasticus
	Job
Isaiah	
Jeremiah-Lamentations	
	Ezra-Nehemiah
	Ezekiel
	Daniel
Minor Prophets	
	Maccabees
	[Baruch]
Matthew (2 copies + extra copy of 1:1–7:27)	
Mark	
Luke	
John	
Acts	
Pauline Epistles	
Canonical Epistles	
Revelation	

missing, was a common Gloss, and is often found either with the rest of the Pentateuch (which is here) or else in a pair with Exodus. One of the earliest and most common *groups* of Glossed books to circulate is the so-called Sapiential books: Proverbs, Ecclesiastes, Song of Songs, Wisdom, and Ecclesiasticus. Robert is missing only Ecclesiasticus, probably the least surprising lacuna, but he is also missing Job, which often travelled with the Sapiential books and, as one of the earliest books to be glossed, a common Glossed volume in its own right; one would expect him to have it. Similarly found in a group are the biblical biographies: Tobit, Judith, Esther, and Ruth. Here, Robert has Ruth as part of Joshua and Judges (Ruth could travel with either the single heroines and hero, or with Judges), and he also has a copy of Tobit, although only the biblical text is present: it was ruled for a Gloss that was never supplied. It is *not* surprising to find Robert missing Chronicles (which was probably not glossed until late in the twelfth century) or Maccabees (c. 1200), or Baruch, which was never glossed. Neither is the lack of Daniel and Ezekiel strange: scholars often had copies of only two of the four major prophets, and Isaiah and Jeremiah-Lamentations was the more common pair. We know, too, from Abelard's comments in the *Historia calamitatum* that Ezekiel was not a popular book on which to lecture.[14] Robert has a complete set of New Testament Glosses, including three copies of Matthew, which was a common text. His New Testament pairings of Matthew with Mark and Acts with Revelation were common sets of fellow-travellers. The Buildwas copy of Leviticus and John, on the other hand, is an odd pairing, and Robert notably did not write in it.

The books comprise an almost completely Glossed copy of the Bible; but they do not form "a set"—that is, a group of books together making up a single Glossed Bible, made in the same workshop or to the same specifications, closely resembling one another. This is not surprising. No sets of the Gloss, in this sense, survive from the Middle Ages, and it may be that few were ever made. Those that were would have to be thirteenth-century at least, since before that time the Gloss was not complete. Robert's books range in date from the 1130s to the 1170s, although he did not necessarily acquire them in date order.[15] His copies come from both France and England, although again he need not have acquired all the French books in France, since copies of the Gloss were quickly available in England. Robert has multiple copies of only Ecclesiastes and Matthew. Ecclesiastes, a small book, is rarely found on its own, so it is reasonable that, in acquiring other biblical books, Robert ended up with more than one copy. His three manuscripts of Matthew comprise two full copies and one partial copy. The partial copy contains a fuller text of the Gloss than the others, one of which also has the Gospel of Mark—and so we might see the three copies as filling different requirements in the collection.

CONTEXT

To own this number of Glossed books was unusual for a single scholar, especially so early in the Gloss' history. However, it was an almost equally unusual collection for an institution, or at least for one as modest as Buildwas, which does support the argument that, if the books were not all Robert's own, his was the impetus behind their acquisition. And, *pace* his nickname, if even the majority belonged to him, he cannot have been a poor man. Robert has the texts of twenty-five biblical books, counting the four books of Kings and the twelve Minor Prophets as one each, respectively. Who can we look to in comparison? Thomas Becket left sixty-nine books to Canterbury, including Glosses on twenty-six biblical books. Peter Lombard, head of the cathedral school at Notre Dame and latterly bishop of Paris, left the cathedral his Glossed books, which comprised the whole of the New Testament, the Pentateuch, the Psalms, the Major and Minor Prophets, Wisdom, the Song of Songs and Ecclesiasticus, Job, Esther, Tobit, and Judith (a total of twenty-six biblical books). Peter is known as both a teacher who used Glossed books and a moving force behind the introduction of Anselm of Laon's Glossed biblical texts into the mainstream Paris schools. Master Robert of Adington or Edington, near Morpeth, who had been a theology student in Paris probably in the 1180s, left his books (containing thirty-five biblical books plus Lombard's *magna glosatura*) to Durham when he died around 1200. Robert, dean of Arras, gave his Glossed books (twenty volumes) to the Cistercian abbey of Ourscamp, with a contract allowing him to use them during his lifetime, but not to sell, pledge, or give them away, nor take them outside the monastery. We know of few other twelfth-century owners on this sort of scale, and those we do know of are often specifically honored for their gift of books. For instance, Master Ralph of Reims donated his thirty-one biblical books (along with Peter Lombard's *magna glosatura* on the Psalms and Pauline Epistles) to Canterbury when he died in 1194; for doing so, he appears in the Canterbury necrology and is given the rites of an archbishop. Similarly, Ralph of Canterbury gave twenty-one Glossed volumes to St. Augustine's Abbey, Canterbury, and is accorded special honors in its necrology.[16]

ROBERT'S OTHER BOOKS?

At the end of Trinity College, Ms B.1.6 (fol. 131v), is a list of books in Robert's hand:

> Epistolas Pauli, Lucam, Iohannem, Ecclesiasten, Cantica Canticorum, Apocalypsin, Epistolas canonicas, Tobiam, Sacramenta Ivonis, Librum cintillarum, Teodulus glosatus, Exempla versificandi, Tractatus de scientia lune, Tabulam Gerlandi, Tabulam Rimachie, Glosulas Petri maiores et minores, Glosula de Iuvenali.

Ms B.1.6 is Robert's copy of the Glossed Pauline Epistles (the first text mentioned in the list), so it seems possible to assume that the other biblical books mentioned are Glossed books as well. Along with these, we can recognise Ivo of Chartres' *Sermones de sacramentis* and Defensor of Ligugé's popular *Liber scintillarum*, a florilegium on biblical themes. The rest have been identified by Rod Thomson and Charles Burnett as texts from the trivium and quadrivium that could be used for arts teaching in the schools.[17] Assuming that the biblical books listed are Glosses, can we identify them among Robert's books as Ms B.1.6 itself (Pauline Epistles); Ms B.1.36 (John); Ms B.1.12 (Luke); Ms B.1.39 (Ecclesiastes, the Song of Songs, Leviticus, and Tobit) or Ms B.1.13 (Proverbs and Ecclesiastes) or both; and Shrewsbury School, Ms 12 (canonical Epistles and Revelation)? All of these except Ms B.1.6 itself are French books from the mid-twelfth century. Could the list be a record of the core books Robert brought with him from Paris? This would be more likely if the list were written in a French-made book, and not an English one. If it *is* Robert's booklist, it is a very small group—only four glossed volumes apart from Ms B.1.6. Moreover, it does not contain the earliest of Robert's books, Ms B.1.10 (Matthew), nor Ms B.1.11 (Matthew and Mark) with Robert's *ex libris* in it. On the other hand, it is a very good small collection of typical early Glosses, since it contains the Pauline Epistles (though still no Psalms), two Gospels, Sapiential books, and the common early pairing of Revelation and the canonical Epistles—just the sort of books being taught in the biblical classrooms of the schools. Thomson suggests it might constitute Robert's wish list of books he did not yet own, but it is odd that this would be written in an English book, when the volumes we are able to identify are French and generally earlier than Ms B.1.6 where the list is found. Robert of Adington, whom we came across earlier donating his Glossed books to Durham, at one point kept his books at St. Victor in Paris, for safe-keeping: we have the list of those he deposited there.[18] Might this list be something similar? The presence of the arts texts does suggest these were books Robert had in Paris and used for teaching; but he appears not to have brought them with him or left them to Buildwas, perhaps like scholars who on retirement keep their research books but sell or give away others they have only used for teaching and are not going to use again.

WHEN DID ROBERT GET THE BOOKS?

One of the things that makes this Buildwas collection so interesting is that many of them date to relatively early in the history of the Gloss: about half of the twenty date from around 1150 or before, and are French (or probably French) copies. One, Robert's earliest glossed book, Ms B.1.10 (Matthew), probably dates to between 1130 and 1140 at the latest. It is not a copy of what became the standard Matthew Gloss; its text is similar to the Gloss but not identical—what Beryl Smalley called "gloses périmées."[19] Another glossed Matthew, Ms B.1.11, is similarly an early type, and Robert may have been picking up copies at the time of the Gloss' introduction into Paris and its schools, before it was standardized. Some of the French books share scribes (e.g., Mss B.1.31 and B.1.14; B.1.39 and Shrewsbury 12; and B.1.36 and B.1.11), showing they were made at or for the same scriptorium: in the case of the Gloss at this time, this would not have been a monastic scriptorium but a commercial dealer.

Glossed books were made in three different formats, which in Paris succeeded one another over time. The earliest Glosses are laid out in a "simple," rigid, three-column format; from the 1150s, the three-column system begins to break down, giving a transitional layout; and finally, from about the mid-1160s, Glosses are made in a virtuoso "complex" format, in which not an inch of space is wasted on the page. Eleven of the Buildwas copies are simple format, and another five are early types of the transitional format; only two are laid out in anything close to the complex format—none is the full complex type. Since it is probably not until about 1160 or slightly later (really with the full takeover of the complex layout in Paris) that the text of the Gloss stabilized in its first common redaction, these Buildwas copies are interesting examples of its early history.

The copies written in English hands are amongst the latest of the Buildwas Glosses, and yet they are all laid out in simple format or in one case a primitive type of transitional layout. This is probably because the exemplars the English scribes were using were older, simple-format copies imported from France. Parisian scribes moved over to the more complex layouts, but this transition did not occur immediately, nor perhaps at all, in other places, where older books continued to be copied. So, for example, Ms B.4.3, a Glossed Minor Prophets, written in England with elaborate "Channel style" decoration, dating from after 1160, is nevertheless laid out in the simple format. The complex format was difficult to master, and some less adept scribes may have decided that they should stick with something they knew they could execute successfully. Jenny Sheppard, cataloguer of the Buildwas books, suggests that Ms B.1.32 (Wisdom) is an example of a scribe who started out trying to write the newer format but gave up part way through.[20] We know it was a complicated job: Abbot Simon of St. Albans (1167–83) ordered a programme of book production designed to bring the abbey library up-to-date with the latest works, commissioning copies of Glossed books of both the Old and New Testaments.[21] As well as choosing the best scribes (*electissimos scriptores*) at the abbey itself, he provided for a "special scribe" (*scriptorem specialem*) to be hired to do the work.[22]

The five English (or possibly English) Glosses are all made according to the older layouts: Exodus, Kings, Isaiah, the Pauline Epistles, and the Minor Prophets; of these only the Pauline Epistles is in Robert's booklist. If the abbey already possessed these (English) books before Robert arrived, it was lucky that none overlapped with volumes that he already owned, and it does seem more likely that he or they acquired the books in England after he came to Buildwas, to fit in with his collection. Although the first Glossed books were made in France for use in the schools, copies were made in England (and found their way into monasteries) relatively early on, often made for (or at the behest of) masters who had come back from studying in France and entered religious life. For example, at Bury from about 1150, the contents of the library show the influence of Paris-trained masters who had joined the monastic community, and who brought new ideas about what sorts of books should be taught and read; one, master Samson, was elected abbot in 1182. Bury has thirty-three Glossed volumes of the second half of the twelfth century.[23] At Buildwas, abbot Ralph may have played a similar role, if on a smaller scale.

ROBERT'S ANNOTATIONS

Although his *ex libris* appears in only one of the volumes, Robert wrote in all twenty of the Buildwas Glossed books. Sometimes he did more than make annotations: Ms B.1.13 is a Glossed copy of Proverbs and Ecclesiastes, which by the time it reached Robert was missing its last two quires of Ecclesiastes. He completed the copying of both the text and the Gloss, and as a separate action when the copying was finished, corrected and annotated them both. However, the Buildwas collection also includes a copy of Tobit (Ms B.1.39), ruled for a simple-format Gloss, although with changing column width for individual pages, which the scribe seems to have carefully copied from his exemplar. The text is complete, but the Gloss is missing. Given that he finished Ecclesiastes, we might expect Robert to supply the missing Tobit Gloss; but he does not. This suggests that although Robert could obtain a copy of the Ecclesiastes Gloss (there was indeed one in the Tobit volume, Ms B.1.39), he did not have access to an exemplar of the Tobit Gloss that he could copy. This may make it marginally less likely that Robert brought Ms B.1.39 with him from Paris, since there he could surely have at least borrowed a copy of the Tobit Gloss to complete the text, had he wanted to.

It would also seem that Robert tried not to repeat himself. Ms B.1.33 is a Glossed Matthew, with a rather fuller version of the Gloss than that in Ms B.1.11, but only extant up to chapter 7, verse 27. Robert has annotated Ms B.1.33 throughout, but his annotations to B.1.11 only start after 7:27, where the other ends. We cannot know if he had access to Ms B.1.33 before Ms

B.1.11, or whether he preferred it for its fuller Gloss. Similarly, for Ms B.1.39 (Ecclesiastes, Song of Songs, part of Leviticus, and Tobit), he annotates only the Song of Songs. Might this be because he had already annotated Ecclesiastes and Leviticus in Mss B.1.13 and B.1.31, and Tobit, as we have seen, had no Gloss?

What Robert does not attempt to do in the Tobit volume is to supply a commentary of his own in the space left for the Gloss. Nor does he annotate each of his Glossed books to the same extent. In fact, I judge that most of what we can see Robert doing in the manuscripts is bringing them closer to what had come to be the standard text—bringing them up to date, where his copy contains a rather earlier version of the Gloss text.[24] He does this by amending the texts, by adding missing text and glosses, and occasionally by erasing or cancelling what is there already. He is very careful and diligent in these corrections, even to the extent of adding punctuation or altering what was already there. Making sure the text is clear is important to him. On Leviticus 1:10, for example, the standard gloss reads "*Unde Heremias. Ego quasi agnus.*" In Robert's copy, Ms B.1.31, *Heremias* has been copied as the abbreviation *IER*, which one would normally expand to read *Hieronymus* (Jerome); and so for clarification Robert has corrected it to *Ieremias* in the margin; he does the same thing again in Ms B.1.33, in the Gloss on Matthew. On Exodus 20:5, the standard Gloss reads "*Lapidee vero fuerunt tabule,*" but *vero* has been left out of Robert's copy, Ms B.2.6. He adds it in the text; but because the reading is still not very clear, he repeats it in the margin. He even does this in the Exodus Gloss (Ms B.2.6) when the text has been slightly blurred by a drop of liquid falling on the page: he writes the uncertain word again in the margin. In Ms B.3.15 (Kings), the scribe has written *Idē*, which Robert has expanded in the margin to *Idem*, to avoid it being read as *Id est*.

The changes may also result from a presumed scribal error, such as when (in the Exodus Gloss, Ms B.2.6) he alters *perfectione* to *professione*: this looks like a case where the scribe has wrongly expanded an abbreviation, and Robert corrects it. He is not only worried about making changes when they alter the meaning. Robert corrects his copy when it and the standard text have the same basic meaning, but he wants to bring his text closer to the standard. For example, his copy of Leviticus 1:11, in Ms B.1.31, originally read "*faciem enim domini appellat sancta sanctorum,*" which Robert has corrected to *"facies enim dei sanctum sanctorum dicitur,"* to follow the standard text. When the text of his copy is good, as, for example, in Ms B.1.14 (Deuteronomy), there are very few amendments and additions: Robert does not seem interested in making notes for the sake of it—or, indeed, for any other higher scholarly purpose.

Most interestingly, he is concerned with the *ordering* of the individual glosses, and especially of the prologues or prothemata, so that they conform to the standard pattern. Each of the biblical books or groups of books in the Gloss is preceded by one or more prefaces, but what these were, and what order they followed, was not stable until at least the middle of the twelfth century; the beginning of a Gloss was often a favorite place for making changes. Robert wants to make sure that the order of the prefaces in his copies follows the established form, and to do this he uses tiny letters to indicate in what order the prologues and individual glosses should be read. His method is a simple alphabetical one: he places a tiny *a* next to the prologue or gloss to be read first, then a *b* next to the second, *c* the third, and so on; the reader skips from letter to letter, confident of following the correct order. Robert orders prologues in Ms B.1.34 (Acts) and Ms B.2.15 (Isaiah), and individual glosses in Ms B.1.39 (Song of Songs), Ms B.1.6 (Pauline Epistles), and Ms B.1.33 (Matthew). In this last, on folios 1v–2r, Robert has added a five-line missing prologue in the lower margin, across both pages, and then put in the tiny letter *n* to make clear where it fits (fourteenth) with the other prologues. As well as tiny letters, Robert also uses tiny (Arabic) numbers, for numbering the ten plagues of Egypt, for example (Ms B.2.6, Exodus)—adding the numbers in the margin, so that it is easier to follow the points in the Gloss text. Again, in the Exodus manuscript, he uses a tie mark to signal that an individual gloss should ideally have been placed further down the page, so that it is in a more logical position vis-à-vis the text and the other glosses.

Robert occasionally adds his own textual clarifications. He adds "OR" superscript over attributions of individual glosses to "Adamantius" (in Ms B.3.16: Joshua, Judges, Ruth), to make it obvious that Adamantius and Origen are one and the same—Adamantius being a nickname meaning "indestructible." He also correctly gives credit to Gilbert of Auxerre, who was known as "the universal," for some of the prologues. For example, in Ms B.1.31 (Leviticus) the text attributes a prologue to Rabanus Maurus, but Robert rightly adds "*G. universalis*" in the margin as a correction; he similarly notes "*Gislebertus*" in the margin of Ms B.1.14 (Deuteronomy). Robert is aware of how easily confusion can arise from abbreviated names: in Ms B.1.11 (Matthew and Mark), "*Iohe b*" in the gloss has been expanded to "*baptista*" in the margin.

For most of his interventions, Robert must have had access to other copies of the Gloss, and this is confirmed when he uses *alia* or *alii* to introduce some of his correcting notes, for example in Ms B.1.11, although in the Deuteronomy Gloss (Ms B.1.14) he seems not always to agree: "*alii non vixerit sed melius non virerit.*" Moreover, these are copies that Robert somehow recognized as more authoritative than his own, and this suggests also that they were probably later French copies, with an updated text. How did he make the decision on authority, and where did the comparison copies come from? Did he amend the manuscripts in Paris, where there would have been an ample supply of current versions, or was it a retirement project, with books borrowed from another house, and returned when he had brought the Buildwas volumes up to date? The availability of copies and exemplars is something we need constantly to bear in mind. It is an obvious but crucial point that, without an exemplar, Robert could not make his alterations. The twelfth-century scholar Andrew of St. Victor, who went from Paris to be prior of Wigmore in Hereford, laments "my poverty" in the number and type of books available to him.[25]

In addition to these amendments, the manuscripts have been changed to make them easier for readers to use. It seems to me likely that Robert made these alterations too, although their nature—lines and tie marks (*signes de renvoi*), on the whole—makes them hard to pin down as the work of any one hand. Simple-format manuscripts of the Gloss can be difficult to read because they do not provide a number of desirable reader-aids, such as signs to make it clear which individual gloss belongs to which part of the biblical text—often a matter of guesswork. Some later readers of these Glosses tried to rectify these deficiencies, and it may be that Robert saw something similar in another manuscript. Like many of these readers, he uses a volley of different tie marks to make links between text and gloss, and to clarify which column of gloss follows on from which. Sometimes he uses the old-fashioned method of direct lines drawn from gloss to text—or from a correction to the text it is correcting.[26] The tie marks are also used to put in chapter divisions, which are generally missing in early copies of the Gloss.[27] The lack of chapter numbers is another of the odd exclusions that makes early copies of the Gloss so annoying to use, and they were often added by later readers. To complicate the picture, at the point when early copies of the Gloss were made, biblical chapter and verse divisions were not yet standard (which must be at least part of the reason why they are missing in the first place), and in some places the standard divisions do not correspond to those Robert adds (for example, in Ms B.1.11). If this work on the manuscripts is not Robert's own, nevertheless, the fact that it is there shows that at least one other of the annotators of these manuscripts was a careful reader interested in Glossed texts.

Where they are in evidence—and there do not seem to be many of them—Robert's own comments are not very deep; they confirm the impression given by William of Tyre that he was not in the front rank of teachers. Often he adds little more than short explanatory phrases, often starting *vel* or *id est*, and linked to the Gloss text by tie marks. For example, one of the prologues to the Matthew Gloss in Ms B.1.33 reads, "*Et genus humanum quadrifida morte peremptum.*" Robert wants to explain what these four types (*quadrifida*) might be, and links the word to a marginal note detailing the four types of law which can be broken: "*transgressione precepti in celo. legis naturalis. mosayce. Evangelii.*" Again, to a prologue to Leviticus (Ms B.1.31), which explains that the book begins where Exodus left off—"*Unius enim et eiusdem diei opus in utroque continetur*"—Robert adds the note, "*quia istoria indivisa.*" He also seems inclined to add occasional spiritual readings of the text. For instance, again in Leviticus, to "*Nebulosa enim fere semper haec pars est,*" he notes, "*scilicet nubilo ignorantie*"; or, a little further on, to "*contemplationi fuit necessaria,*" he adds, "*spirituali intellectus*"; and he expands the Gloss on Mark, chapter 1 (Ms B.1.11), which refers to "*mandata moralia,*" by adding a reference to the beatitudes, "*beati pauperes spiritu, etc.*" These notes show he was actively engaged in reading, but with either not very much to say himself or a disinclination to say it by writing in these books. In her article on Robert's books, Jenny Sheppard says, "The annotations are, in fact, precisely the type likely to have been made by a man who used the book to teach," adding that the amended punctuation (e.g., in Ms B.1.11) suggests the text was being prepared to be read aloud in a classroom.[28] But looking at the annotations as a whole, it does not seem to me that Robert's interventions are necessarily a teacher's preparation, except in the wider sense that he is taking a set of texts that were still in flux and bringing them to the standard of what might be termed the latest edition. Robert is clearly very good at what we might call the "administration" of the text, to make it easier to read, and he is pedantically careful about working through the manuscripts: it must have taken him a considerable period of time and concentration to compare his copies to the more recent versions and make his amendments.

REVISING THE TEXT

The Glossed Bible was primarily a schools text—it was born out of schools teaching in Laon and came to prominence in the Paris schools by about 1140. If, as Thomson argues, Robert was teaching in the 1140s, he was in Paris just when the Gloss was becoming established as a classroom tool. At this stage, not all of the Bible had been glossed, and the texts (and certainly the prologues to the books) were not entirely stable; nor was the layout. In the succeeding twenty years, both content and layout underwent revision, until they reached a reasonably static period from the 1160s until the end of the century. Around half of Robert's books date from before this standardization of the text. Although, at least at the beginning of its life, the Gloss was associated with teaching masters, copies soon found their way into monasteries, often because masters joined religious houses or retired there, bringing their books with them. We know almost nothing (yet) about if and how Glossed books were used in the monastery. English houses acquired books from France and began to copy them themselves. When their copies contained earlier stages in the history of the text and its layout, they extended the life of these versions beyond what would have been acceptable in the cutting-edge theology schools of Paris. Perhaps these earlier versions could be bought cheaply, if the new owner was prepared to put in the work required to bring them up to date?

Although it is tempting to see Robert's books as comprising a set, they do not in fact form one. The history of the glossing of each of the books (or groups of books) of the Bible is different, and we cannot treat them all in the same way. For example, it is unsurprising that Robert's Glossed Kings is a relatively late, English copy, for these history books were not commonly taught in the schools, and their Gloss was one of the last to be completed; Robert surely did not need it when he worked in Paris. However, it is surprising that, when Robert acquired his English copy of Exodus to go with

Table 6.3. Buildwas books in addition to the Amiclas Glosses (from Sheppard, *The Buildwas Books*)

Shelfmark	Text	Date	Origin
Oxford, Christ Church 88	Augustine sermons on John	1167	Buildwas
London, Lambeth 109	Gregory, *Moralia in Iob*	c. 1160–70	Buildwas
Cambridge, Trinity, B.14.5	Gregory, *Cura pastoralis*	c. 1160–70	Buildwas
Cambridge, Trinity, B.1.3	Gregory sermons on Ezekiel	c. 1160–70	Buildwas
Cambridge, Trinity, B.1.4	Gregory, *Dialogues*	c. 1160–70	Prob. Buildwas
Cambridge, Trinity, B.3.8	Jerome on Blessed Virgin Mary and saints lives	c. 1160–70	Buildwas
London, BL, Add. 11881	*Vitae sanctorum*	c. 1170	Prob. Buildwas
Cambridge, UL, Ii.2.3	William of Malmesbury, *De gestis regum anglorum*	c. 1170	Prob. Buildwas
London, BL, Harley 3038	Glossed Leviticus and John	1176	Buildwas
Cambridge, UL, Add. 4079	Missal fragment	c. 1175–80	Prob. Buildwas
Oxford, Balliol 229	Patristics	c. 1180	Buildwas
Edinburgh, NLS 6121	Patristics	c. 1180	Buildwas
Cambridge, Pembroke 154	Cyprian, Peter of Blois, etc.	c. 1180	England/Buildwas?
Oxford, Bodl. Lib., Bodl. 395	Isidore, *Etymologies*	s xii^{ex}	Buildwas
Cambridge, St John's D.2	Aelred, *Speculum*, Rabanus, *Cena Cypriani*	s. xii^{ex}	Buildwas

Table 6.3. (cont.)

Shelfmark	Text	Date	Origin
Oxford, Bodl. Lib., Bodl. 730	Cassian	s. xii^{ex}	Buildwas
Cambridge, Trinity, B.2.30	Vitae sanctorum	s. xii^{ex}	Buildwas
London, Lambeth 107	Hugh of Fouilly, *De claustro*	s. xii^{ex}	Prob. Buildwas
Oxford, Bod. Lib., Bodl. 371	Peter Chanter on Kings/Chronicles	s. xii^{ex}	?France
Oxford, Balliol 39	Nequam on Song of Songs	s. xii^{ex}/xiii^{in}	Unknown
Oxford, Balliol 40	Nequam on Song of Songs	s. xiii^{in}	Prob. Buildwas
Oxford, Balliol 150	Bernard, *Sermons*	s. xiii^{in}	Buildwas
London, London 73	William of Newburgh; sermons, etc.	s. xiii^{in}	Poss. Buildwas
Cambridge, Trinity B.1.29	Jerome on Song of Songs; Glossed Pauline Epistles; Andrew of St Victor on Kings, etc.	s. xii^{in}/xiii^{in}	?N. France
Cambridge, Trinity O.7.9	Comestor, *Sermons*; Nequam, Boethius, etc.	s. xii^{mid}–xiii	? France? Unknown
London, Lambeth 488	Sermons; Aelred; etc.	s. xiii	Various, inc. Buildwas
London, Lambeth 457	Letters (Jerome, Seneca)	s. xiii^{in}	Various, inc. Buildwas
London, Lambeth 456	*Artes*, inc. Boethius	s. xiii	Various, inc. Buildwas
London, Lambeth 477	*Pictor in carmine*, etc.	s. xiii^{mid-ex}	Poss. Buildwas
Oxford, Balliol 35A	Peter Lombard on Psalms	s. xii^{ex}	?N. France
Oxford, Balliol 173B	Peter Lombard on Pauline Epistles	s. xii^{ex}	? N. France

his French Leviticus, Numbers, and Deuteronomy, he did not also manage to acquire the more common and interesting Gloss on Genesis. The presence of his *English* copy of the Pauline Epistles only points up how odd it is that he did not already have a French version, along with a Glossed Psalter, since these two texts were virtual twins, and ubiquitous teaching texts.

Robert's marginal and interlinear notes are tiny, and the identification of his hand in amendments to punctuation and additions of tie marks or connecting lines depends a great deal on minute details, such as variations in color of ink, along with an acquired "feel," born of long looking, for Robert making his way through a text. Jenny Sheppard has done sterling work in tracking Robert in these twenty books. Simply finding a Paris master systematically writing in so many linked texts raises hopes of what we will learn about the elusive working methods of the twelfth-century masters, but in the end it seems to me that we learn less than we would wish. Robert's own notes in the manuscripts are few, and they seem not to venture beyond short, commonplace explanations. Is this a reflection on Robert, or on the work of the schools and the quality of most of the students? The volumes are perhaps more interesting for the history of the Glossed Bible, since they appear to show us a medieval scholar recognizing the existence of a "later edition" of what is often (wrongly) characterized as an unchanging text, and altering his own editions to conform to it. In a society before printing—and perhaps in a backwater like Buildwas—there was no other way.

NOTES

1. Peter Lombard, *Sententiae*, 19*–20*.

2. By "Glossed Bible" here I mean to refer to what is often called the *Glossa ordinaria* or Gloss on the Bible—copies of one or more biblical books laid out in a distinctive fashion, containing the entire and continuous biblical text with, alongside but separate from it, a commentary, drawn in the main from patristic and early medieval exegetes. The origin of these books is associated with Master Anselm and his school at Laon, although they do not become common until the Gloss was adopted by teachers at the schools of Paris, around 1140. Some biblical books were not complete until at least this point, and the text of the Gloss continued to be revised until about 1200. See Smith, *The Glossa ordinaria*. I shall use upper case

"Gloss" to refer to the whole text, either of a single book ("Glossed Jeremiah") or the whole Bible, and lower case "gloss" to refer to the individual comments.

3. What were originally forty-nine medieval volumes at Buildwas now survive as fifty-one codices, three of which were once a single volume. For the history of the abbey see the entry for Buildwas in Gaydon et al., *A History of the County of Shropshire*, 2:50–59. On the abbey library see Sheppard, *The Buildwas Books*; Robert's Glossed volumes are nos. 32–51.

4. *Registrum Anglie*.

5. James, *A Descriptive Catalogue of the Manuscripts of Trinity College, Cambridge*.

6. It is now Shrewsbury School, Ms 12; see Sheppard, *The Buildwas Books*, no. 51.

7. See Sheppard, *The Buildwas Books*, lvi–lviii and figure 30, and "Master Robertus Amiclas."

8. Thomson, "Robert Amiclas," esp. 238–39.

9. Thomson has a good summary of the dating problems; he favors the earlier dating of the texts, which would establish Robert as a teaching master by 1141 at least: Thomson, "Robert Amiclas."

10. See ibid. Robert's heirs need not, however, have been an immediate family, and indeed the phrase may be conventional.

11. Poole, "The Masters of the Schools at Paris and Chartres," esp. 244–46; and Thomson, "Robert Amiclas."

12. See Thomson, "Robert Amiclas," n. 27, with a reference to the Hereford Episcopal *Acta*.

13. Now London, British Library, Harley Ms 3038: see Sheppard, *The Buildwas Books*, no. 9. Although, like all of Robert's books now at Trinity College, this manuscript is not in its original binding, both Leviticus and John were written by the same scribe, which strongly suggests that they were always together.

14. Peter Abelard, *Historia calamitatum*, lines 164–240, describes the whole of Peter's time at the school of Laon.

15. I am grateful to Michael Gullick for discussion of the dating and localization of the manuscripts, and I have taken account of his dating, along with that of Sheppard and Thomson, alongside my own inspection of the manuscripts. Generally speaking, dating any manuscript to within a decade is hubristic, but I am as confident as possible that the manuscripts fall within the fifty-year range and—perhaps more importantly—that their relative dating is as given in table 6.1.

16. De Hamel, *Glossed Books of the Bible*, 10–13, for references to these examples.

17. Thomson, "Robert Amiclas," 241–42. The other trivium books are: Theodulus, *Eclogae*, and Juvenal, *Glosulas*, both grammar and rhetoric textbooks; an *exempla versificandi*, an early copy of the genre of exempla for teaching grammar (possibly the *Ars versificatoria* by Matthew of Vendôme or Bernard Silvester's *Ars*

poetica); and Peter Helias' glosses on both parts of Priscian's grammar. The quadrivium books are: an unidentifiable *de scientia lune* (perhaps a set of lunar tables such as that by Walcher of Malvern); and two sets of *tabulae*, one to Gerlandus' *Compotus*, the other to a treatise on rhythmomachy (winning and losing proportions). Thomson and Burnett judge this to be a fairly standard list of texts.

18. For Robert's list of deposited books (*repositi apud sanctum Victorem*) see Mynors, *Durham Cathedral Manuscripts*, 78–79.

19. See Smalley, "Les commentaires bibliques de l'époque romane."

20. The same scribe wrote Mss B.1.36 and B.1.11, but he used different layouts for each.

21. "After he had been made abbot he continued to have written fine books and volumes of both the Old and New Testaments, glossed and corrected (*authentica*), faultlessly finished, which we have not seen bettered": Thomson, *MSS from St Albans*, 1:51–62, on Simon, here at 52. For the Latin text see *Gesta abbatum monasterii Sancti Albani*, 1:184.

22. *Gesta abbatum monasterii Sancti Albani*, 1:192.

23. Thomson, "The Library of Bury St Edmunds Abbey," and *Books and Learning in Twelfth-Century England*, esp. 30–34.

24. I am referring glibly to a more "standardized" version of the Gloss here in order to leave an enormous can of worms unopened. The evolution of the Gloss up to its first "steady state" version in the middle of the twelfth century is recognised by Gloss scholars, but the virtual absence of modern critical editions of any parts of the Gloss makes it impossible to point to a standard text for comparison. Mary Dove describes the changing nature of the text well in the introduction to her edition of the Song of Songs Gloss: *Glossa Ordinaria*. I have used the Adolph Rusch *editio princeps* of the Gloss (*Biblia cum glossa ordinaria* [Strassburg, 1480–81]; *Biblia latina cum glossa ordinaria: Facsimile Reprint of the Editio princeps, Adolph Rusch of Strassburg 1480/81*, ed. Froehlich and Gibson) to make my comparisons, since it is recognized as a reasonable reflection of the state of the text in the mid-twelfth century and is also easily available.

25. ". . . *mee paupertati que non potest semper pre manibus vel commentarios vel libros habere glosatos consulo . . . et quasi in unum corpus succincte compingens*"; Andrew of St Victor, general prologue to the Prophets, quoted in Smalley, "Andrew of St Victor," 371.

26. We can see these additions in Mss B.1.31, B.1.35, B.1.39, B.2.15, B.1.11, and B.1.33, for example.

27. For example, in Mss B.1.1, B.2.6, B.1.35, B.1.1.

28. Sheppard, "Master Robertus Amiclas," 281.

HUGH FEISS, OSB

7 Preaching by Word and Example

Estuaries, peninsulas, and other locales where currents from different sources mix ordinarily become very fertile and productive, and that was the case with the Abbey of St. Victor, located on the edge of Paris. There the traditional forms and contents of the meditative theology of the monasteries met the emerging methods and questions of the theology of the schools; there the customs and practices of the monastic tradition mixed with efforts to reform ordained ministry and preaching; there the deliberate marginality of the monastic tradition mingled with involvement in the political life of the capital.

The author of the anonymous *Libellus de diversis ordinibus*, which was likely written around 1150 by a canon regular in the area around Liège, devotes a section to "canons who have their houses near the activities of men, such as the canons of St. Quentin-in-the-Field and St. Victor." He writes that these canons regular live on the borders of the world of men and sojourn there as strangers. The canons, some of whom are ordained to various orders, live near other men, so that their life might call others to conversion. The author of the *Libellus* describes how canons of St. Victor and similar communities aimed to serve others both by example and by pastoral care. The abbot kept some canons in the cloister of the mother church so that they could devote themselves to interior things or to care for their brothers, guests, or pilgrims; others he sent to a dependency or a parish where they were to teach and guide the people by example, preaching, and pastoral care. All the canons, at the mother church or in dependencies, prayed for God's people as well as for themselves.[1] In a sermon, Richard of St. Victor confirms the abbey's liminal status: his community dwelt where the secular life ends and the spiritual life begins.[2]

In a similar vein, Jacques de Vitry, who was connected with the Augustinian canons at Oignies before becoming bishop of Acre and later a cardinal, wrote in the *Historia occidentalis* (1221–25):

> There are some other congregations of canons regular, devout, humble, and beloved of God, called canons of St. Victor. They are so named because this martyr of God is the patron and advocate of those in whom the beginnings of this order shone brightly. The first and foremost community of this saintly religious group is situated outside the walls of Paris at a church called St. Victor. Like a light of the Lord placed on a stand, it enlightens to the knowledge of God and enflames to the love of God not only the nearby city, but also distant regions in all directions.[3]

The canons of St. Victor thus combined a monastic way of life with ordained ministry; they taught by word and example: some of them studied, taught, preached, and administered sacraments.

ST. VICTOR AND REFORM

Only twenty-three years separated the death of Pope Gregory VII (d. 1085) from the foundation of St. Victor by William of Champeaux about 1108. In resigning his ecclesiastical positions and embracing the life of a canon regular, William was entering into a broad-based reform movement in the church. The murder of Thomas of St. Victor in 1133 by opponents of church reform is symptomatic of the seriousness of this effort. The struggle to bring clergy, and especially communities of canons, under a religious rule that enforced celibacy, dispossession of private property, and obedience to a religious superior, was a central component of this reform movement, of which St. Victor, and other congregations of regular canons, such as Arrouaise (fl. 1090) and Premontré (fl. 1120), were leading proponents.

The customaries and constitutions of regular canons were much influenced by the customaries of existing Benedictine communities and the new Cistercian movement that flourished pari passu with the canons regular for the next hundred years or more. Thus the *Liber ordinis* of St. Victor draws on monastic sources and gives few hints of any involvement in pastoral ministry or education. Perhaps the *Liber ordinis* did not treat pastoral activities because it was written for use in a wide variety of settings, from small dependencies of St. Victor to other abbeys that engaged in different or few pastoral works. In any case, we know St. Victor was an important school that educated clerics, both extern students and members of the community of St. Victor. One of the primary aims of such an education was to enhance not just the virtue (*disciplina virtutis*) of the clergy, but also the quality of the pastoral care they provided, in particular their preaching (*doctrina veritatis*). By their way of life (*exemplo*) and in their teaching and preaching (*verbo*) the canons of St. Victor aimed to be models of pastoral care. Their preaching, which was not confined to the cloister at St. Victor, was itself an example for other preachers.[4]

THE *ORDO* OF ST. VICTOR

In 1134, when Pope Innocent II wrote about assigning a prebend in the cathedral of Paris to St. Victor, he said that St. Victor "was outstanding in the observance of a regular order and church discipline with the result that now—thank God—many churches in various places have benefited by learning from its praiseworthy way of life."[5] Before the pope wrote this, only one monastery is attested to have adopted the *ordo* of St. Victor and received an abbot or canons from St. Victor. In 1131, Bishop John of Séez introduced canons regular from St. Victor into his cathedral chapter. When John died, his brother Arnulf (Bishop of Lisieux, 1148–81) and St. Bernard intervened with Pope Eugene III to make sure that John's successor, Girard (1148–57) made profession as a regular canon before becoming bishop. In subsequent years, many churches introduced Victorine canons. In France it was usually bishops who installed them in or near their see cities; in the Anglo-Norman realm it was more often members of the nobility who introduced the Victorines. Sometimes an abbot was sent to reform an existing community according the Victorine *ordo*; in other cases, several companions accompanied him. Sometimes bishops sent men to St. Victor to learn the way of life there and then return to introduce that *ordo*, described in the Victorine *Liber ordinis*, into their communities.[6] Other communities, dependent priories and cells, were an integral part of the community of St. Victor.

PASTORAL MINISTRY IN DEPENDENCIES OF THE ABBEY

The Abbey of St. Victor had many dependencies that were subject to the mother abbey. The most important of these dependencies were priories, which had parochial or economic functions. By the mid-thirteenth century, twenty-five churches and chapels were in the possession of the abbey. Many of these churches had previously been under lay control. In some cases, the Abbey of St. Victor built new churches or established new parishes. It is clear that the Victorine canons sent to these parochial churches served as pastors exercising *cura animarum*. Victorine canons assigned to parishes were expected to observe as much of their rule and the common life as possible. To make this possible, several canons were sent to live at each church.

More than half of the churches entrusted to St. Victor were connected with priories subordinate to the abbey, the oldest of which were Puiseaux and Amplonville. By the middle of the thirteenth century, St. Victor had at least fifteen dependent priories. A special set of regulations was composed for them.[7] According to these statutes, each priory received a specified sum annually for its operating expenses. Puiseaux received twenty pounds, Fleury-en-Bière, ten pounds, and the other priories, 100 solidi. Once a year, over three days, the priors of the fifteen priories were to make a report to the assembled chapter of St. Victor. Each prior had at least three canons in residence; sometimes (e.g., Villiers-le-Bel in 1161) the number reached eight.[8]

There are some obvious conclusions to be drawn from the existence of these priories. A canon of St. Victor could expect to spend some of his life in a priory. There he had an opportunity to learn managerial, leadership, and pastoral skills that would qualify him for leadership roles at St. Victor or in another abbey. However, since so many canons were involved in temporal administration, there may also have been a danger that they would be administrators more than men of prayer. Canons of St. Victor had to be prepared to move from the large, well-endowed, academically vibrant abbey in Paris to priories or other abbeys and back again. There must have been a sharp contrast between the solemnity, formality, and intellectual life of St. Victor and the simpler life in the priories. However, the Victorines were reformers with a mission to promote clerical reform by word and example. Their presence in abbeys and priories away from Paris was integral to that mission.

PREACHING IN VICTORINE LIFE

Preaching, along with poetry and letter-writing, was one of the rhetorical arts increasingly practiced and then systematically studied during the twelfth and thirteenth centuries.[9] St. Victor did not produce a systematic treatise on preaching, but the importance of preaching to the Victorines is evident. The library of the abbey included a store of homilaries, and the sermons of Richard of St. Victor and other Victorines were gathered in collections.[10] At the daily chapter meeting, a sermon by the abbot or someone else followed the reading of the martyrology and rule. The private reading that the canons did during the day probably included homilies. According to the *Liber ordinis*, the reading done during meals in the refectory included homilies of Origen on the Old Testament, Augustine's *Explanations of the Psalms*, Gregory the Great's *Moralia on Job* and *Exposition of Ezekiel*, as well as other sermons suited to each part of the liturgical year.[11]

Among the sermons from twelfth-century St. Victor that have been preserved, those of four canons of the abbey are particularly noteworthy: Richard, Achard, Walter, and Godfrey. The following sections will examine their theory and practice of preaching more closely and consider briefly the efforts of Maurice de Sully, bishop of Paris and friend of the abbey, to improve preaching.

RICHARD OF ST. VICTOR

From Prayer to Preaching

Guigo II, a Carthusian, describes four elements that are both intertwined and successive in a devout Christian life: reading, meditation, prayer, and contemplation.[12] This fourfold path is that of a strictly enclosed, Carthusian monk. The Victorines sometimes expanded the list. For example, Richard of St. Victor (d. 1173) wrote:

> We do our threshing by reading and meditating, we gather the vintage by praying and contemplating, and we sow by action and preaching. This is the correct and proper order: first, by reading we learn and by meditating discern what we should afterwards do or avoid. But since we cannot by ourselves accomplish the good things we have learned, we must first seek divine help by pouring out prayers, and then we can usefully hasten to the good things to be done.[13]

Elsewhere Richard writes disapprovingly that some people do not make space for the works of the contemplative life, which include reading, meditation, prayer, and divine contemplation, or for the works of the active life, which include preaching and other ministries. He cites Gregory the Great to the effect that no one should completely neglect the needs of his neighbor in favor of contemplation of God, nor should he neglect the contemplation of God because of the needs of his neighbor.[14] The two lives are intimately connected: what one read, took to heart (*meditatio*), prayed over (*oratio*), and contemplated was to be put into action in one's own Christian life and to be shared through teaching and preaching. In his sermons and elsewhere Richard speaks of the importance and craft of preaching and about the duty and qualifications of preachers.

THE *LIBER EXCEPTIONUM* AND PREACHING

Richard of St. Victor's *Liber exceptionum* is an interesting text, divided into two books. In the first book, chapters on the division of the arts, the study of scripture, and geography are followed by seven chapters on history from

Adam down to Richard's own time. The second half of the book devotes nine chapters to the allegorical meaning of the Old Testament, the tenth chapter contains twenty-seven sermons, and the final four chapters discuss the allegorical and tropological meanings of the gospels. Thus, though Richard's interest is in the spiritual senses of the scriptures, he arranges his book on an underlying historical grid.[15] The preface to the second book tells of the benefits which follow from reading the Holy Scriptures: adroitness in meditation, perseverance in prayer, fervor of devotion, and clarity in heavenly contemplations; in short, in a favorite Victorine phrase, knowledge of the truth and love of the good. Richard concludes: "Receive, brother, this second part of our notes, which you requested, as a kind of platter prepared for your soul, so that by it you may grow spiritually."[16] This could suggest that the contents of Richard's book were meant solely for the reader's personal growth.

However, commenting on Matthew 25:14–30, the parable of the talents, Richard says the servant who buried his talent in a field signifies false Christians who have received knowledge from God but out of fear or disdain will not increase it by preaching it to others who, if they heard that preaching, could multiply what they heard by deed and word. Even someone who knows only a little can bestow that little by preaching. Others, though appointed to the ministry of preaching, do not make the effort to read and meditate on the scriptures in the resources readily available in libraries, homilaries, commentaries, and treatises.[17]

Richard ends the first part of the *Liber exceptionum* with a description of the allegorical meaning of the armaments of the Maccabees, which include the spear of prayer and the bow and arrows of preaching.[18]

If the *Liber exceptionum* is a set of notes intended not just for personal edification but also to prepare readers for the ministry of preaching by word and example, that would account for the puzzling presence of the twenty-seven sermons in chapter ten of book two. On this hypothesis, the way to use in preaching the biblical allegories that precede and follow the twenty-seven sermons would be illustrated by the twenty-seven sermons.[19] For example, in *Liber exceptionum* 2.13.22, Richard says this of the parable of the workers in the vineyard (Mt 20:1–10):

> "The kingdom of heaven is like the head of a household, who went out early in the morning to hire workers for his vineyard." The householder is God;

the vineyard is the church; the workers are prelates; the hours of the day are ages of the world;[20] the hiring of the workers is the making of prelates and also the sending of preachers; the evening of the day is the end of the world; the salary of a denarius is the retribution of the heavenly kingdom. Again, the householder is God; the vine is the soul; the workers, our senses; dedication to work, the exercise of virtues; the hours of the day, the ages of man; the evening, the end of life; the payment, eternal beatitude. About the cultivators of this vine and their payment, a certain poet speaks thus:

> The vine was cultivated, the cultivators sought rewards;
> Their labor was not equal, but the gifts were equal.
> The one who came last, at the giver's call,
> Received as much as the one who had come earlier.
> Thus God shows that no matter when we come
> To set about the work, we may be certain of his gift.[21]

In this note on the parable, Richard offers both an allegorical interpretation, which applies the passage doctrinally, in this case to the church and in particular to church leaders and preachers, and a tropological or moral interpretation applied to the individual Christian.

The fifteenth sermon of *Liber exceptionum* 2.10.15, gives only a moral interpretation of the parable, in which Richard concentrates on the cultivation of the vines.[22] The field is the human heart, which is to be plowed by a threefold compunction arising from awareness of our sins, consideration of God's gifts, and pondering on the foretaste of future goods. By divine grace, the vine is planted by good desires, so that it may grow in good and bring forth branches, leaves, flowers, and fruit. The branches are trained when we humble our thoughts. The leaves are good action; the scent of the flowers is a good reputation. The fruit is a good conscience aware of justice. A denarius is the reward of eternal life, which consists in seeing God through contemplation and tasting God through love.

The *Sermones centum*

The twenty-seven sermons included in the *Liber exceptionum* 2.10 form the first part of a collection known as *Sermones centum*, which was printed in

Migne, *Patrologia latina* 177, among the works of Hugh St. Victor. Since the first twenty-seven appear to be Richard of St. Victor's work, the likelihood is that all one hundred come from his pen, although that is not certain.

The first three of these sermons are about the Jerusalem and the Old Testament tabernacle, both of which are images of the church and the soul, because they are dwelling places of God.[23] The first sermon begins from the physical features of the church and refers them to the church constituted by the faithful in Christ. Hence, it is concerned with the allegorical meaning.

> The individual stones are the faithful who are squared off and firm, squared off by the stability of their faith, firm by virtue of their patience. The mortar is charity, which adjusts, joins, and unifies each, and makes them the same shape so that no discord causes disagreement among them. The foundation is the prophets and the apostles as it is written . . . [Eph 2:20] The walls are the contemplatives who are next to [Christ], the foundation that is above; they abandon earthly things and cling to heavenly ones. . . . The roof is made up of those who are active, near to earthly activities, who because of their imperfection are less intent on heavenly things and who administer earthly things to meet the need of their neighbors. The length of the holy church stands for temporal duration; the width for the multitude of people; the height for the difference in merits. . . . The church is built upward when the priestly order is placed over the laity, the episcopal order over the priestly, and above this the archiepiscopal, and finally, above all, the pope, the bishop of the Romans. The sanctuary stands for the order of virgins; the choir for the order of the continent; the nave for the order of the married. . . . The atrium stands for false Christians, who are sanctified in so far as they are baptized, but are full of rotten cadavers, because they are full of the corruption of vices. . . . The altar is Christ, upon whom we offer not only the sacrifice of good deeds but also the offering of prayers. . . . The tower is the name of God. . . . The bells are preachers, who speak the word of God. The glass windows are spiritual people through whom divine knowledge illumines us. The interior whitewash signifies purity of heart; the exterior paint, purity of the body. The twelve candles are the twelve apostles, who preached the banner of the cross and faith in the passion of Christ to the four parts of the world.[24]

Just as the church building, Jerusalem, and the tabernacle all symbolize the church built of living stones, so they signify the soul also. In *Sermon* 2, Richard takes up this tropological sense.

> The stones of this tabernacle are the individual virtues that are polished through exercise and are unmoved by vices because of their stability. The mortar is charity that connects, unites, fits together, and contains the other virtues. The foundation is Christ. . . . The soul has walls through contemplation of heavenly goods. Separated from earthly affections through contemplation, it inheres more closely to Christ, its foundation. It has a roof through good action, through which it gives to the needy temporal goods for the sake of eternal goods. Its length is faith, through which it believes to be true all that God has done himself or through angels or through men from the beginning or is going to do until the end. It has height through hope, through which it is lifted up from the terrestrial to the celestial, from the transitory to the eternal, from the visible to the invisible, from the corporeal to the spiritual. The soul has width through charity, through which it is stretched to the right and the left, to the right to friends who are to be loved in God and to the left to enemies who are to be loved for God's sake. It has a sanctuary, insofar as it is made in God's image. As in the church building nothing is more worthy than the sanctuary, so in the soul nothing is more holy, noble, or excellent than the divine image. It has a choir, insofar as it is made in God's likeness. . . . It has a nave through its senses . . . an atrium through its flesh . . . an altar which is its heart . . . glass windows which are the spiritual senses, through which it is enlightened by the ray of the divine sun and freed from the blindness of its ignorance. . . . It has bells through the preaching by which it calls those far away to the worship of God. . . . Its high priest is the Holy Trinity. Try, dear brothers, each one of you . . . to become the tabernacle of God so that God may deign to dwell in it.[25]

For the canon regular, the task is so to grow in virtue in the church of the soul that, as a minister of the church, he can make Christ known by word and example. In another sermon, which is addressed to priests, Richard says the priest must announce to the people the things that are God's. The human being is doubly rooted in God: as God's image, it can know the truth; as God's likeness, it can love the good. All this is lost or damaged through sin.

Priests see the people dressed nicely for church on Sunday and feasts, but interiorly they may be ugly. And that could be the fault of their priests. Taking as his starting point Isaiah 18:2, Richard admonishes the clergy:

> "Go, swift messengers (*angeli*) to an unruly and wounded people, to a fearsome people, after which there is no other, a people waiting and downtrodden whose rivers devastate its lands." Behold, dearest brothers, the divine office enjoined on us. Behold the care, the solicitude and the work of priests. Behold the devout but dangerous task imposed on them. "Go swift messengers." The prophetic, nay, the divine word admonishes us in this passage, not to disdain the ministry divinely enjoined on us, not to cast off the holy burden, not to neglect the people entrusted to us, a people formed in the image and likeness of God and redeemed by the precious blood of Christ. . . . Go, therefore, messengers, by preaching, not by sinning. Go to a deformed people, so that you may make it beautiful in form by the word of salvation. Don't go so that by the deformity of its sin you will make yourselves like it. Christ ate with sinners, in order to join them to himself in good. . . .
>
> What do the people await? Your word, your example, your patronage, and divine help and gift through your solicitude and ministry. They await your word in order to be taught; your example in order to be formed; your patronage in order to be defended; and divine help and gift through your solicitude and ministry in order to be freed from evil and justified in the good. . . .
>
> "Go, therefore, swift messengers," and "preach to a formidable people."; fulfill your ministry.[26]

In a sermon for the feast day of saints, Richard comments on the four verbs in Wisdom 3:7–8: "they shall shine (*fulgebunt*), and shall dart about (*discurrent*) as sparks through stubble; they shall judge (*judicabunt*) nations and rule (*regnabunt*) over them. These four actions pertain respectively to shining virtue, energetic preaching, judgment at the resurrection, and reigning in heavenly happiness. Of preaching he says:

> A spark is small in size, and it has brightness and heat. The name "sparks" symbolizes preachers, the holy apostles and the successors of the apostles, who are small through the virtue of humility, bright through knowledge of

the truth, warm through love of virtue.[27] They are rightly said to dart about like sparks in the stubble field. They darted through the gentile world which like stubble was empty of all truth, full of vanity, sterile and fruitless in every good work, shaken by every wind of doctrine; darting through it, I say, they freed it from pride by their preaching. Showing it that it was ash and would return to ash, so that it might rise as a good planting, they reduced it to burning embers, so that it might rise as a good planting. . . . Thus we see shepherds of animals in wooded pasture lands burn dry grasses with fires, and when those have been burned, other green grasses come up which are suitable for pasturing animals. But (and this should not be said without sorrow), see how in places in which by the labor of the apostles and their successors, when the stubble had been burned, fruitful crops arose, in these places, I say, stubble again has grown up because of our laziness and now has practically filled the Lord's field. For what are the impure, the fornicators, the avaricious, the thieves, the grasping, and whoever else are separated from God and joined to the devil by other such depravities? What, I ask, are they, if not sterile, fruitless stubble tossed around by the demons' suggestions as though by various winds in every depraved direction? Why then are we inert with idleness? Why do we [not] dart about by preaching? Why do we not enflame every sort of wicked persons with our teaching, in order to make them good? But woe to us wretched men, because there are many darting about, but few preaching. We go through towns, castles, and villages, but we exert ourselves very little in warning sinners and converting souls. The world is full of priests, and if there be any who hears some good, there is no one who repeats it. We read in the book of the *Dialogues* that a certain holy man always took with him books that contained holy words. Wherever he went he watered the meadows of minds from those books. Let us blush, brothers, over our sloth; let us attend to the studied zeal of the holy fathers, whose sons we ought to be and whose life we ought to imitate. Let us light the stubble; let us correct the wicked from their depravities. And well did he say first "they shone," and then "they darted," because first we must shine with virtues and then teach them to others, as it is written: "Because Jesus began to act and to teach" [Acts 1: 1].[28]

In another sermon, Richard says there are two principal means by which a prelate with authority over others discharges his responsibility: the example given by his deeds and the words of his preaching, in that order. There are many pastors who, though they are thought to live good lives, desist from the word, or do not know how to speak, or neglect it. They should be imparting a fourfold teaching to those subject to them: faith in the Trinity, how to govern the five senses of the body, the six corporal works of mercy, and the seven principal virtues.[29]

Richard explains in *Sermon* 28 the tropological meaning of Jerusalem. It is a city on a hill, and one goes up the hill in seven stages. First comes faith, then hope, then charity, then the other virtues, especially those described in the Beatitudes, then good works, then preaching (he again cites Acts 1:1), which is done through word and miracles, and finally one ascends from preaching to contemplation.[30]

Like the prophets and apostles, clergy must preach against faults, for to remain silent when one could have rebuked is to consent to evil.[31] Each should dispense to others what he has been given. "Preaching should be fitted to the will, capacity, and utility of each, so that it is useful to all, harms no one, and penetrates between all vices like a two-edged sword."[32]

> For when the holy doctors preach, they give birth not for themselves, but for the Lord, because when by teaching they give birth to spiritual offspring, they seek not their own praise, but Christ's. . . . They have two interior shoes: knowledge of the truth and love of virtue, and two others that are evident externally, the word of preaching and the example of good works. . . . The teacher in the church should be distinguished by both his life and by his teaching, so that we use not our own words, but those of the holy fathers.[33]

One principle underlying Victorine exegesis and so Victorine preaching was enunciated by Hugh of St. Victor: Sacred Scripture is different from other writings in that in it not only do the words refer to things, but the things themselves signify still other things. Or to put it another way, the words of the literal sense refer to objects that in their turn have spiritual meanings.[34] An example of this principle is Richard's sermon for the Nativity of the Blessed Virgin, which also serves to illustrate the place that Mary had in Victorine preaching:

> Like a thornbush producing a rose, Judea gave birth to Mary. Brothers, the ancient people, the Israelites, were like a tree, which had its roots in

Abraham, which produced a trunk in Isaac and Jacob and grew upward, and in the twelve patriarchs and their offspring produced many branches and twigs. This people, because of the richness of faith and justice of Abraham, Isaac, and Jacob, and others who were born of them, deserved to be called an olive tree and a vine in certain biblical passages. However, because of the wickedness of some, indeed most, of those who succeeded them, this people can be compared most of all to a thornbush. To show their former goodness and their subsequent wickedness, the Lord says through Jeremiah: "I planted you as a chosen vine, an uncontaminated seed. How have you turned bad and become a wild vine?" And shortly later Jeremiah writes: "A bountiful olive tree, beautiful, fruitful, comely—the Lord called your name."[35] . . .

But because we have said how the Jewish people can be compared to a thornbush, let us also say how blessed Mary may be signified by a rose, that is, the flower itself. One can distinguish four things in a rose: nature, form, color, and fragrance. By nature the rose is cold, its form is spread out, its color is white or red, its scent is pleasing. Therefore, its nature signifies the elimination of evil habits, its form signifies charity, its color, purity and passion or more correctly compassion, its odor, good reputation. All of these attributes, except bodily passion, rightly befit Mary, whose birth we celebrate today. Among other obvious attributes which I will pass over in silence because they are well known, Mary had the virtues of compassion, because as it is written, a sword of sorrow pierced her soul. . . . What is more merciful than Mary, who is called the "Mother of Mercy" by all the faithful and experienced as such by all who call on her with true faith. . . .

Let us imitate the Blessed Virgin Mary, especially with reference to what we said earlier about [the attributes of] the rose. Let us extinguish the flames of our vices in accord with its cold nature, and in keeping with its form let us expand our hearts wide in loving God and neighbor. Let us be red, if not by pouring out of blood for Christ, at least by having compassion on his weak members. Let us be sweet smelling, by everywhere diffusing a good reputation. Let us avoid the wickedness of the Jews [spoken about above] by turning from evil, and let us imitate the holiness of the Blessed Virgin Mary by doing good, so that by her merits and prayers we may merit to avoid damnation and merit to attain beatitude. May Jesus Christ, Our Lord, who is God, blessed forever, deign to grant us this.[36]

The allegorization of the rose was part of the exegetical and homiletic tradition which was practiced by the fathers and the monastic theologians of the early Middle Ages, a tradition in which Richard was steeped. But the systematic analysis of the nature and qualities of the rose reflects the sytematic guides to allegorizing called *distinctiones*, which became popular in late twelfth- and thirteenth-century academic preaching as sermon aids. Thirteen of the *Sermones centum* are for feasts of the Blessed Virgin, which is indicative of the extent to which she was venerated at St. Victor.[37] The reference to her compassion is indicative of an increasing emphasis in medieval devotion.[38] This particular sermon is an example of a technique Richard used often: first, he offers a summary of the points he is going to make, then develops them, then summarizes again. In this way, the allegorical development serves to help the hearer remember the outline and main points of the sermons.

Preachers knock down the specious arguments of philosophers, just as the trumpets of Josuah knocked down the walls of Jericho. However, once purified, philosophical wisdom, eloquence, and teaching can be incorporated into "our ministry of divine preaching."[39] In fact, the *Sermones centum* do not cite pagan philosophers very often, but Richard does like to quote from poets. His citations include both pagan authors and Christian poets.[40] However, these quotations are few compared to quotations from the Bible. Many of the sermons explicate a biblical passage given at the beginning, but Richard weaves in quotations and allusions from many biblical books as he develops his theme. It is evident that *lectio* and *meditatio* (including memorization) of the Bible were an important part of his life.

ACHARD OF ST. VICTOR

Achard of St. Victor (d. 1170) was a contemporary of Richard. He was abbot of the community at St. Victor from 1155 until he became bishop of Avranches in 1161. Fifteen of his sermons have survived. The first twelve are relatively brief. The last three are longer, and are in effect treatises, perhaps expansions of sermons. In *Sermon 15*, on Lent, he writes of seven deserts that the canon regular must cross and seven acts of dispossession, which correspond to the seven gifts of the Holy Spirit. The canon regular deserts mortal sin out of fear of the Lord; then he deserts the world in order to give himself to God in religious life; then he deserts the enticements of the flesh and self-will. In the fifth desert, he submits reason to faith. Achard spells out at length ten mysteries that must be accepted by faith. In the sixth desert, the canon deserts activities aimed at bestowing four benefits on his neighbors: bodily sustenance, protection, teaching, and consolation. He easily enters into the peace of God, and sees all things in God. In the light of God,

> he easily apprehends in what great darkness, the world, which he has under his feet, lies; in his ecstasy, he says truthfully "everyone is a liar" [Ps 116:11]. He sees without obstruction, as though from a high mountain, how great was the affliction that depressed and oppressed his brothers and sisters in Egypt as they slaved for Pharaoh "with mortar and brick" [Ex 1:14]. He cannot be unmoved by compassion, because, after being brought into the wine cellar by the spouse [Sg 2:4], he is inebriated with love so that he wants everyone to be as he is. He remembers the One who, being free of all, made himself the slave of all, not seeking what was his but what belonged to the many.[41]

Preaching is one expression of this compassion toward others. In his sermon for the Feast of All Saints, Achard insists on Christ, the Truth, as the touchstone of preaching:

> Those who have been so enlightened by truth and so rooted in truth are capable of enlightening and building up others: to enlighten them to know truth, to build them up to love truth; to enlighten them through teaching, to build them up to love truth; to enlighten them through teaching, to build them up through exhortation. Both pertain to preaching. . . . We must recognize whether people have been sent by truth to preach by the following signs: if they do not teach or advise anything not taught and advised by truth, according to truth and for the purpose that truth teaches and advises—that is, only what is required, and in accord with what is required, so that all things in their preaching are in harmony with truth—that is, matter, form, and cause—so that they preach only the truth, in accord with the truth, and for the sake of the truth. In the ministry of preaching, the

apostles of truth must be fully involved in the fight against the adversaries of truth, sustain many things at their hands, and even contract something of the dirt and dust of common human life on the soles of their feet.[42]

Hence, preaching is an expression of compassion to which the contemplation of divine love leads, and the heart of preaching is Christ, who is Truth incarnate. This is borne out in Achard's *Sermon 2*, the first of two he preached on the feast of the dedication of a church.[43] The sermon is too long to reproduce here, but a condensed version will illustrate Achard's preaching practice.

In the first section of the sermon, Achard draws his theme from Psalm 19:4–5: "He pitched his *tent* in the *sun*, and like a *bridegroom* he will proceed from his bridal chamber." The visible sun generates light and heart. It can stand for spiritual people who shine and are ardent in themselves and illumine others with their knowledge and inflame them with their love. "They illumine others by the word of preaching and inflame them by the example of their good lives."

Christ is a more sublime sun, who has received from the Father splendor and warmth in himself, although not from himself. Christ is

> "sun of righteousness" [Mal. 4:2], "the splendor of glory," [Heb. 1:3], "the brightness of eternal light" [Wisd. 7:26], "the light that illumines every person coming into the world" [John 1:9] who in his very nature and essence possesses splendor and warmth. . . . All holy people receive from the fullness of this sun so that they too may be suns, always shining and ardent in themselves, but not always sending out their rays to illumine others. . . . They are hesitant not because they do not love God and neighbor, but because they are afraid they will destroy themselves through the arrogance which comes from praise.

And so the visible sun stands allegorically for Christ and for Christians who derive light and heat from Christ and pass it on to others.

In the second paragraph, Achard says God pitches his tent in such people. We are "pilgrims and strangers" (Lv 25:47; Ps 39:12; 1 P. 2:11, etc.). Armies camp in tents, and God fights for us against the flesh, the world, and the devil. Only God's help will enable us to overcome these enemies.

Occasionally God leaves us on our own and lets us "be wounded by the enemy's spears," so that we will know our weakness and "attribute every triumph of victory to divine grace."

In the third paragraph, Achard says the tent is mobile because human beings never remain in the same state. They are either advancing toward God or they are retreating when God abandons them momentarily so that they may know themselves. The good things God gives us in this life pertain to the tent; the good things of heaven pertain to the temple, where

> eternity will replace time, rest will replace labor, sight will replace faith [2 Cor 5:7], and beatitude will replace righteousness. Then will we leave the tabernacle and enter the temple of God—or rather, we ourselves will be the temple and house of God. He will dwell in us and we in him when we contemplate his beauty without interruption, enjoy his love without satiety, and are satisfied with his sweetness without any want.
>
> In this house will be various portions and dwelling places (Jn 14:2). God will dwell in the bodies of the saints through immortality and the brightness of incorruption as in the outer part of the house; he will dwell in both soul and spirit as in the interior part of the house; he will dwell in the mind as though in a bridal chamber. Since his image and likeness reside there, he will pour himself directly into the mind itself, and he will offer himself to be shared in the fullness of knowledge and love. Then will the bride be joined to her spouse, and they will become two, I do not say in one flesh, but in one spirit [Gn 2:24; 1 Cor 16:16–17].

In the final paragraph of this sermon, Achard says that in heaven the totality of the faithful will be God's temple, but so will each of the saints in soul, mind and body. The dedication of the temple of the soul occurs in the exodus of its death; the dedication of the temple of the body, symbolized by the octave death of the feast, occurs when what is corruptible puts on incorruptibility.

This sermon revolves around three words in the quotation from Psalm 18 (19): sun, tent, and bride. Achard considers all three spiritual senses: allegorical (or doctrinal: Christ, the church, grace), tropological (avoidance of pride; love of neighbor; struggling against the world, the flesh, and the devil), and anagogic (the heavenly temple). Here and generally, however,

Achard's use of allegory is somewhat more restrained than Richard's. Partly for that reason, Achard weaves fewer scripture quotations and allusions into his text, though in this short sermon Achard cites all four gospels, at least seven epistles, six psalms, and three other Old Testament books.

Both Richard and Achard wrote strikingly original works on the Trinity, in which they appealed primarily to reason rather than to the authority of the scriptures or church teaching.[44] Achard's interest in the Trinity shows itself when he situates Christ in relation to the Father, before speaking of how Christians participate in Christ's knowledge and love. Achard also wrote a treatise *On the Distinction of Soul, Spirit, and Mind*, in which he spells out the differences and relations of these facets of the human being that are referred to in the third paragraph of *Sermon* 2.[45] Hence, Achard's sermons draw on carefully thought out theoretical foundations.

Achard uses commonplaces of twelfth-century theology when he refers to the human being's spiritual self as God's image and likeness, the world, the flesh and the devil, knowledge that illumines and love which enflames, mystical marriage, and joy without satiety. For educated listeners, such terminology would have suggested rich associations.

Like Richard, Achard stresses both personal holiness (shining and ardent in oneself) and the need to minister to others. Spiritual people "illumine others by the word of preaching and inflame them by the example of their good lives." Which is what Blessed Achard did by his life and preaching and urges his audience to do in this sermon.

WALTER OF ST. VICTOR

Walter, who succeeded Richard of St. Victor as prior of St. Victor after the latter's death in 1173, died in 1180. Walter may, in fact, have been older than Richard. Walter is notorious as the author of the pamphlet *Contra quatuor labyrinthos Franciae*, a vehement attack on Peter Abelard, Peter Lombard, Peter of Poitiers, and Gilbert Poreta (de la Porrée), whom Walter considered heretics.[46] Walter was a preacher steeped in the writings of his Victorine predecessors, particularly Hugh and Richard, and he was a committed defender of some of their Trinitarian and Christological ideas. Walter several times says he would prefer not to preach, but, in Jean Châtillon's estimate,

Walter was not devoid of talent and he has an impressive place in the series of Victorine preachers from the second half of the 12th century whose homilies have come down to us. His language and style do not lack either warmth nor elegance; his exegesis is sober, and if he sometimes is a little strident, something for which he has been severely reproached, he is before all concerned to provide his brothers with a spiritual teaching of undeniable worth, nourished by theology and constantly rooted in Scripture.[47]

In the Victorine collection of thirty-six sermons that he edited, Fr. Châtillon identified twenty-one sermons that he regarded as certainly the work of Walter of St. Victor, and he thought it probable that six others, given as anonymous in the collection, were Walter's also.

In his second sermon, for the solemnity of Easter, Walter begins by pleading his lack of skill as a preacher:

> "Christ has died for our sins and he has risen for our justification" [Rom 4:25]. You know, my dearest brothers, that I have not yet managed this kind of speaking. Hence, I am afraid to give this sermon to you on so great a solemnity, especially since I am unskilled both in speaking and in knowledge. You who are wise and spiritual do not need either my teaching or my exhortation "because your only master is Christ" [Jn 14:26], whose anointing teaches you about all things. Still, put up "a little while with my ignorance, and support me" [2 Cor 11:1]. I prefer to seem foolish rather than to be found disobedient or rebellious. I have faith in him who made "light shine from the darkness" [2 Cor 4:6], who "illumines the blind" [Ps 145:8] and opens the mouths of the mute, who gives "speech and wisdom, whom all the enemies of truth cannot resist" [Lk 21:15], who "has died for our sins and risen for our justification" [Rom 4:25].[48]

And in the last of the anonymous sermons, which is probably Walter's, we read:

> "I am the way, the truth, and the life" [Jn 14:6]. Brothers, you have already experienced that I have not yet mastered this form of speaking. Hence my heart quakes whenever this duty is enjoined on me. For I am unskilled in words and very hampered in speech; I labor at saying things. Moreover,

you are already saturated, already filled up, already rich in every discourse. You have a great abundance of words; I have a great scarcity. Hence, I am afraid to address you, because "the saturated soul will walk all over the honeycomb" [Prv 27:7]. But if I have collected anything from the crumbs falling from the tables of the rich [Mt 15:27; Lk 16:21], reason says to serve it to the hungry poor, the starving and the thirsty, because "the hungry soul takes the bitter as though it were sweet" [Prv 27:7].

But remember, brothers, you to whom God has given wise and learned speech, that "the kingdom of God" not in speaking but "in virtue" [Mk 8:39], and so there is more need for the example of holiness than the word of preaching. The Lord implied as much mystically when he was hungry and came to the barren fig tree and did not "find anything except leaves" [Mt 21:18–19; Mk 12:14]. He cursed it, and immediately it withered. What is this barren, fruitless, cursed, and withered fig tree? It is a man who has words, but not deeds. When we see people who say good things and do bad ones, we usually say: "The voice is indeed the voice of Jacob, but the hands are the hands of Esau" [Gn 27:22]. Such people who talk but do not act are barren, autumnal, twice dead trees. But you, brothers, leave behind the barren trees and raise the eyes of your mind [Jn 4:35] to the fruitful tree, the tree of life [Rv 2:7; 22:4, 22], the medicinal tree, the green tree, the tree whose foliage is able to cure the peoples and whose fruit, as the bride says, is "sweet to my taste" [Sg 2:3]. This green tree has brought forth three leaves, the words that I put forward: "I am the way, the truth, and the life" [Jn 14:6].

The only-begotten of God who was truth and life according to his divinity, became for us the way according to his humanity, not only because he showed us the way of salvation and the path to heaven by the example of his holiness and the word of his preaching, but even more because he gave us by grace the strength to follow and imitate him.[49]

It is difficult to know whether Walter really felt inferior to the canons to whom he was preaching, or was merely expressing a humility *topos*. In any case, he was a better preacher than these disclaimers would suggest.

Walter's preaching is Christocentric, but he is also eloquent about the role of the Holy Spirit.[50] In a sermon on a responsory used in the divine office for Pentecost, Walter begins by distinguishing the old and new covenants, one written on tablets of stone, the other in minds through understanding and in hearts through love. God's promise of this second covenant was fulfilled on Pentecost. The Holy Spirit, who is the light in and from himself, from his very being pours into the hearts of the faithful the fire of divine love and into their minds the splendor of divine knowledge. The Father created human nature as a receptacle for divine grace. Sin sullied this receptacle, but Christ cleansed and freed it. The Son came to remove what was old and to set free, the Spirit came to give newness, beatitude, and charismatic gifts, especially wisdom (which includes love) about divine things and knowledge about human things and beatitude. Knowledge of the truth restores the image of God in us; love repairs the likeness of God.

> In all the members of Christ, the Holy Spirit effects these two things: knowledge of the truth and love of virtue. There is one body of Christ, which consists of the head and members. Christ is the head [1 Cor 12:27; Eph 5:30] and has the fullness of grace and truth [Eph 4:15; Jn 1:16]. Christians are the members, receiving from the fullness of the head.[51]

The church is the woman clothed with the sun, with the moon (of earthly things) beneath her feet (Rv 12:1). The Holy Spirit has removed the veil that covered her eyes, and she can gaze upon God's glory and be transformed into God's image (2 Cor 3:18). In contrast to those who love the world with immoderate desire and seek human glory, those who have the Spirit of God are led to internal and eternal peace, to the paternal light, to brightness beyond beginning (*superprincipalem*), to the contemplation of the highest Trinity.[52]

Walter derives the terms "paternal light" and "brightness beyond beginning" from Ps.-Dionysius, by way of the translation of John Scotus Eriugena and probably the commentary of Hugh of St. Victor as well.[53] Ps.-Dionysius' influence among the Victorines reached its apogee in the works of Thomas Gallus, who was sent from St. Victor to the Victorine monastery in Vercelli (d. 1246).[54]

GODFREY OF ST. VICTOR

Godfrey was born between 1125 and 1130 and studied as a secular cleric from 1144 to 1155; he died after 1194. He studied the liberal arts at the school of the Petit Pont, founded by Adam of Balsham (*Parvipontanus*).

Then Godfrey studied and taught theology; his theological training seems to have been oriented toward the Bible and the fathers, rather than to the methods and concern of the new schools, although he was well acquainted with them. Like his friend Stephen of Tournai, he may have studied law at Bologna. Between 1155 and 1160 he entered St. Victor, thus entering at a time of disturbance, under the incompetent Abbot Ernisius. Maurice of Sully, the bishop of Paris, wrote to William, archbishop of Sens:

> You are well aware of what great and harmful confusion Brother Ervisius [sic], the former abbot of St Victor, brought to his church and all the brothers who are recognized to have excelled the rest both in religious life and in learning.[55]

Perhaps Godfrey was one of these. Or maybe his humanistic interests were unacceptable to Walter of St. Victor who succeeded Richard as prior in 1173.[56] In any case, Godfrey found himself assigned to a priory.

Godfrey returned to the abbey about 1185/86, and served there as sacristan. Godfrey was a poet and musician, a preacher, and a theologian. Godfrey wrote two works, *Fons philosophiae* and *Microcosmus*, that display the encyclopedic interests of Hugh of St. Victor.[57] An early seventeenth-century Victorine author says that the library at St. Victor had thirty-one sermons of Godfrey's. In fact, thirty-two of his sermons seem to have survived. They have not yet been published in their entirety, but published excerpts indicate Godfrey's preaching style.[58] He refers to his sermons in his *Microcosmus*, and in it he speaks of those who accept the "vocation of preaching or other various strong and exemplary actions."[59]

One of Godfrey's sermons, preached on All Saints' Day, takes as its starting point Revelation 7:9–10: "I saw a great crowd that no one could count from all nations, tribes, peoples, and tongues standing before the throne and in the sight of the Lamb. They were clothed with white stoles, there were palm branches in their hands, and they were shouting with a loud voice: 'Salvation from our God sitting on the throne and from the Lamb.' If the feast of one saint gives us great joy, how much greater is the joy which is ours from this feast of all the saints. However, sin has weakened our capacity for these joys just as it has weakened our desire for them."

Godfrey then traces the history of the introduction and spread of the Feast of All Saints, which aims to lift the higher eye of the mind toward the true city of believers and its joys. Leaving aside those who are not born yet, this city made of living stones is composed of three sorts of members: (1) some have arrived there and rest in peace; (2) others are moving toward it as travelers (*viatores*), exiles, and soldiers; (3) others are no longer traveling, but are in a place of punishment, because they died, freed from guilt of sin but not from its penalty. These are the poor or the beggars of the city. There will come a final time when all these will be gathered into one place and one perfect state of joy.

John saw this city better than others, and he shared what he saw with his comrades. He saw 144,000, which stands from the twelve tribes (12 x 12) and perfection (1000). Then he saw an inestimably greater number from all the nations. Godfrey thinks John saw the heavenly city with all his interior senses, both cognitive and affective, and not just with his intellect.

The city John saw is identical with the gathering of all God's saints. The Savior is its walls. It is the eighth day of eternity, beyond the flow of time, the stable vision of the Trinity (2 x 2 x 2). In his description of the heavenly city, John indicates its qualities. It is a crowd (*turba*), but one that is secure; no one there disturbs (*turbat*) another. Second, he refers to its greatness (*magna*) or dignity, which is the opposite of the quantitative magnitude of fallen Babylon. Third, the city is boundless; its citizens are countless, except to God. Fourthly, it is very diverse (from all tribes). The city is the queen, clothed in variety, who stands next to the king (a reference that can also be applied to the Blessed Virgin).

In addition to these first four properties of the heavenly city, there are four still more glorious ones. The fifth is that, standing before the throne (by metonomy, the throne is the One on the throne) and the lamb (who saved us by his blood), the citizens of the heavenly city enjoy the eternal vision of their Creator and Redeemer. Sixth, they wear the two stoles of impassibility of body and soul. Seventh, they have at hand (*in manibus*) the happy memory of what they suffered on earth for Christ. Finally, they praise God endlessly for their victory as we do today on this feast. Whether the praise that the saints will render there in union with the praise of angels will be bodily, we cannot know now.

Godfrey discusses the heavenly banquet, where some (the king, queen, and magnates) are served, others serve and eat, while some others hope to receive the leftovers. The first are wholly inside; those in the second group go in and out; the third group is outside. Those in the second group go in through interior contemplation and out through compassion. They carry food in; they carry alms and leftovers out to the poor. The king and his fellow banqueters eat for enjoyment (*delectatio*), the servers eat for sustenance (*confortatio*), the poor to be revived (*refectio*). Christ, Mary, and all the saints are those resting at the banquet; we are the servers who are progressing; the poor are those in purgatory (*purgatoriis*), hastening to the banquet.

On the first day we prepare ourselves to serve by fasts, prayers, almsgiving, and other acts of charity. Today, the second day, if we are worthy we serve the king and queen and their guests. We bring them the food of praise, obedience, and good works, especially today, the Feast of All Saints. The seven-day hours of the Liturgy are the principal dishes brought to the king, the queen, and the saints who have advanced there by the sevenfold grace of the Holy Spirit. The nine readings and responses of the night office are the main dishes of the nine orders of angels. The twelve readings refer to the Trinity and the angels. The feast occurs night and day, because there it is eternal day. There are also lesser dishes, such as devout prayers, holy meditations, pure contemplations, holy readings, ministries of the divine word, and careful listening to them. Among all of these dishes, the most excellent of all is the Eucharist, the food that is the lamb and the drink that is his blood.

In this sermon, the ecclesiological concerns of the Victorines are evident, and so, too, is their balancing of ministry (compassion) and prayer (contemplation). In the *Fountain of Philosophy* Godfrey wrote a section on "the City of God, or the Church," which contains some of the themes of this sermon: Jerusalem a city of living stones, surrounded by a strong wall; Christ the cornerstone; a diversity of members:

> At this riverbed is a City situated
> Blessed town, Jerusalem, widely celebrated;
> City built of living stones, City animated!
> Girt with noble mound and walls strongly crenellated.
> . . . .
> Founded on a Corner-stone, structure safe from reeling,
> Marvelous the novelty that she is revealing.
> . . . .
> All the people of this town widely are selected:
> Races quite diversified into one collected.[60]

Missing, though, in both the sermon and the *Fountain* is any emphasis on preaching. In the *Fountain*, Godfrey describes the canons regular, his own entry into St. Victor, and how he was formed as a canon. The canons fulfill the cleric's role by reciting the divine office, working, and reading. On the other hand, Godfrey concludes the *Fountain* with

> Much about this God-Man then (or, on God) receiving,
> I drank in, within my heart a deep thirst relieving;
> No good to lie hidden here: if some way achieving,
> I shall publish these things to all who'll be believing.[61]

Preaching looms larger in the *Microcosmus*, which Godfrey wrote during his years at a priory (1173–85). It is a complex, encyclopedic work, which Françoise Gasparri describes as moral theology, inspired by Platonic cosmology, based on the Bible, centered on Christology, and structured as a commentary on the six days of creation. In it Godfrey is positive toward human nature and pagan moralists and the arts. Speaking of good prelates, he says they preach by word and example.[62]

The *Microcosmus* exists in only two manuscripts, one written and annotated in Godfrey's own hand, the other a copy that he corrected himself.[63] Other Victorine manuscripts have jottings in Godfrey's handwriting of his musical compositions and sermon notes. These jottings include two self-portraits. One, in a manuscript of the *Fons philosophie*, shows him as a young canon, seated, holding a book. The other is at the beginning of a collection of his sermons. He is older, dressed for choir in a black cape and surplice, standing between the two pillars of the Temple of Jerusalem. This is Godfrey the preacher, author of the sermons that follow. It is inscribed with the opening words of his sermon for the beginning of Advent: "I am standing upon the watchtowers of the Lord continuously throughout the day, and I am on watch through the nights. I watch over God's encampment."[64]

MAURICE OF SULLY

Maurice of Sully was born of a humble family at Sully-sur-Loire about 1120. He went to Paris about 1140 and received a good education. He was a cleric by 1147, a deacon by 1150, and in 1159 he became one of the archdeacons of Paris. When Peter Lombard died in 1160, Maurice was chosen to succeed him as bishop of Paris. Maurice of Sully had very close ties with the monastery of St. Victor. He issued a number of acts on its behalf, entrusted to it the work of his chancery, and had a house there where he stayed often. He entered the community before he died there in 1196, and he was buried in the choir of the abbey church.[65]

Maurice of Sully was an energetic and able pastor, who undertook the reconstruction of the administrative center of his diocese on the Ile de la Cité and began the construction of the cathedral of Notre Dame.[66] Like the Victorines he was committed to pastoral renewal, and like them he promoted good preaching. To that end, he authored a collection of sermons for the people. There are forty manuscripts that contain some portion of these seventy-one sermons. The collection is divided into three sections, each with a prologue. The prologue to the first section is an exhortation on preaching addressed to priests. The second sermon is a brief commentary on the creed, and the third is a commentary on the Our Father, much of it taken from Richard of St. Victor's *Liber exceptionum*. There follow twenty-five sermons on the liturgical year from the Feast of the Circumcision until Pentecost. The second section has sermons for the Sundays from Pentecost to Christmas. The third second contains sermons for specific feasts and saints.[67]

The long prologue (*Sermon* 1) includes borrowings from Gregory the Great's *Dialogues* and almost the entirety of *Sermon* 23 of Richard of St. Victor's *Liber exceptionum* and *Sermones centum*, which was discussed above. Richard and Gregory are two of Maurice's main sources throughout the collection. In this first sermon, Maurice of Sully says that priests entrusted with the care of souls need to do three things: live a holy life, be educated and discerning, and preach continuously. The priest should have homilies for all the Sundays of the liturgical year and for feasts and saints' days. He should be insistent and constant in preaching by word and example. Like Godfrey of St. Victor, Maurice thinks of the preacher as someone who stands upon a high mountain proclaiming God's word with patience and learning.[68]

All the sermons we have discussed so far have been in Latin. At St. Victor it was possible to preach or read Latin sermons, but when the canons were preaching to people at parish churches and rural priories they would have had to speak in French if they wished to be understood.[69] With Maurice of

Sully's sermons, we see how the translation from Latin to French occurred. His sermon collection exists in both Latin and French. Two facts suggest that he wrote the sermons first in Latin: the Latin manuscripts are older than the French ones, and there does not seem to be any obvious reason for translating French sermons into Latin. However, if Maurice of Sully wrote the sermons in Latin, he intended them for the use of priests who would preach to the people. There is nothing of the lecture hall or the theological disputation in the sermons: they are clear and practical. The French translations vary somewhat from the Latin originals. The French versions omit supporting biblical references; they are more clearly organized and make clear the transitions from one part to another; they often have a conclusion which restates the theme announced at the beginning; and the sins and vices listed differ, because the French versions emphasize external acts more than internal dispositions.[70]

PREACHING AT THE BORDER

St. Victor was a contributor to the renewal of church and society in the twelfth century. The canons of St. Victor lived a monastic life, but within that framework they exercised pastoral ministry both at the abbey and its dependencies. Their ministry included teaching, preaching, and acting as confessors. It is clear that they took preaching very seriously, and the many examples of their sermons that have survived show that they were expert preachers.[71] At St. Victor as elsewhere during the twelfth century, sermons were most often focused on moral teaching and exhortation.

The Victorines' sermons have characteristics of both the monastic and academic milieus. Since most of their surviving sermons were preached to their fellow Victorines, they can tell us something about the interests of the canons of the monastery. However, Richard's *Liber exceptionum* seems to be closer to Maurice of Sully's effort to provide models, guidance, and encouragements for priests responsible for preaching to the people. Although Hugh of St. Victor emphasized the primacy of the literal sense, and in his biblical commentaries Andrew of St. Victor expounded it exclusively, the sermons of the Victorines are not expositions of the literal meaning of biblical texts. Often they are satisfied to preach on a single line of scripture, or even a single image or word. Their use of *distinctiones* and *exempla* is not as thoroughgoing or automatic or mechanical as it became in the work of some sermons of the next century.[72]

NOTES

1. *Libellus de diversis ordinibus*, 73–97.
2. Richard of St. Victor, *Sermones centum* 72 (PL 177:1130D): "We dwell between the border of the spiritual life and the border of the secular life. We hear . . . games, shouts, songs, and the tumults of men."
3. Jacques de Vitry, *Historia occidentalis*, ed. Hinnebusch, 137: "Sunt alie canonicorum regularium devote et humiles et amabiles deo congregationes qui Sancti Victoris canonici nominantur, eo quod predictus dei martyr patronus et advocatus sit eorum, in quibus huius ordinis primordia claruerunt. Primus siquidem et precipuus huius sancte religionis conventus extra muros parisiensis civitatis in ecclesia que dicitur sancti Victoris, quasi lucerna domini supra candelabrum posita, non solum propinquam civitatem sed remotas circumquaque regiones et ad dei cognitionem illuminat et ad caritatem dei inflammat."
4. On pastoral ministry by monks and canons regular in the twelfth century see Constable, *The Reformation of the Twelfth Century*, 227–39; and for monks, Henriet, *La parole et la prière*, 207–23.
5. ". . . in observatione regularis ordinis et ecclesiasticae disciplinae clarescere, adeo, quod sua laudabilis institutionis magisterio in diversis partibus iam ecclesiae multae—Deo gratias—proferunt." Cited by Teske, *Die Briefsammlungen*, 232.
6. Exact information on monasteries affiliated with St. Victor is wanting, but Teske, *Die Briefsammlungen*, 232–36, lists eighteen that were founded by about 1165. Two of these, St. Augustine, Bristol, and Wigmore, were in England, and by the early thirteenth century they had founded a half dozen or more houses in England and Ireland.
7. Martène, *De antiquis ecclesiae ritibus*, 3:817–20, cited by Schoebel, *Archiv und Besitz*, 253.
8. On the dependencies of St. Victor, see Schoebel, *Archiv und Besitze*, 239–54. Earlier in his study (85–227), Schoebel studies each of the priories individually as he surveys the possessions of St. Victor.
9. Ziolkowski, "Latin and Vernacular Literature," 663.
10. Châtillon, "Sermons et prédicateurs victorins."
11. Longère, *La prédication médiévale*, 64. The relevant passages are in *Liber ordinis* 19 ("De officio armarii"), 33 ("De hora capituli"), 48 ("De lectione mensae"), ed. Jocqué and Milis, 82, 156, 211–14. Longère, *La prédication médiévale*, 140, notes that collections of homilies, though they continued to be inspired by the

fathers of the church, are witness to a very evident effort of renewal, personal redaction and pastoral adaptation.

12. Guigo II, *Scala claustralium*, 1–12, ed. Colledge and Walsh, 82–108.

13. Richard of St. Victor, *Apprehendet messis*, ed. Hauréau, 116–17: "Legendo et meditando metimus, orando et contemplando vindemiamus, operando et predicando seminamus. Et est hic quidem rectus ordo et competens, ut primum vel per lectionem discamus, vel per meditationem discernamus quid postmodum agere vel vitare debeamus. Sed quia, que scimus bona per nos implere non sufficimus, prius oratione fusa divinum adjutorium impetrare debemus, et tunc ad bona agenda utiliter properamus." I have modified Hauréau's text slightly in the light of a forthcoming edition by Chris Evans and me. This and other short exegetical texts by Richard of St. Victor are associated in manuscript tradition with his notes on the psalms. In other places Richard does not include preaching in his lists of the these interrelated activities; e.g., *Liber exceptionum* 2.7.13, ed. Châtillon, 325; *De contemplatione* [*Benjamin major*] 4.14, PL 196:151A–C; *Nonnullae allegoriae tab. foed.*, PL 196:193A; *Sermones centum* 56, PL 177:1066BC, 1067D. Hugh of St. Victor gives variations of this list, but does not include preaching: see *Didascalicon*, 5.9, ed. Buttimer, 109–10; *De meditatione*, 46. On the other hand, in *Sermones centum* 85 (PL 177:1169) Richard says "we should consider, whether, following [St. Augustine's] example, we love the word of God by reading, meditating, expounding, preaching, according to the grace given us" ("Attendamus, an verbum Dei, ejus exemplo, legendo, meditando, tractando, praedicando, secundum gratiam nobis datam, diligimus").

14. Richard of St. Victor *Liber exceptionum*, 2.13.3, ed. Châtillon, 481.

15. Ibid., 1, prol., ed. Châtillon, 97: "the meanings of the allegories and tropologies arranged according to the underlying historical sequence" ("sensus allegoriarum et tropologiarum secundum subjacentis lineam historie dispositarum").

16. Ibid., 2, prol., ed. Châtillon, 213. On the meaning of *exceptiones*, see ibid., 68–69.

17. Ibid., 2.23.2, ed. Châtillon, 479–81.

18. Ibid., 1.9.4, ed. Châtillon, 371.

19. Longère, *La prédication médiévale*, 66, notes that the final four chapters of the *Liber exceptionum* on the gospels originated in sermons. *Sermones centum* 28, 29, and 30 are inserted in those chapters. Parts of *Sermons* 61, 62, 70, 71, and all of *Sermones centum* 88–90 are found elsewhere in the *Liber exceptionum*. On these correspondences see Châtillon, "Le contenu, l'authenticité et la date."

20. Richard outlines the six ages of the world and of human life in *Liber exceptionum*, 2.11.3, ed. Châtillon, 442, in an allegory of the six water jars at Cana.

21. Ibid., 2.13.22, ed. Châtillon, 494. The poem is generally attributed to Hildebert of Lavardin who, when William of Champeaux retired to St. Victor, wrote to urge him to continue teaching there and not put his light under a bushel basket.

22. Ibid., 2.10.15, ed. Châtillon, 404–6.

23. Ibid., 2.10.1–3, ed. Châtillon, 375–81 (=*Sermones centum* 1–3, PL 177:902A–907D).
24. *Liber exceptionum*, 2.10.1, ed. Châtillon, 375–76 (PL 177:901–3).
25. Ibid., 2.10.2, ed. Châtillon, 377–78 (PL 177 903–5).
26. Ibid., 2.10.23, ed. Châtillon, 418, 421, 422, 423 (= *Sermones centum* 23, PL 177:941–946). See further discussion in Old, *The Reading and Preaching of the Scriptures*, 3: 319–22. I discovered this book after I had completed the first draft of this study. Old discusses *Sermones centum* 1, 2, and 23 because he too is interested in Richard's theology of preaching.
27. Richard often uses threefold divisions in his sermons; see Old, *The Reading and Preaching of the Scriptures*, 309–12.
28. *Sermones centum* 32 (PL 177:973–74).
29. Ibid., 35 (PL 177:983).
30. Ibid., 39 (PL 177:1001–2).
31. Ibid., 71 (PL 177:1125).
32. Ibid., 93 (PL 177:1191A).
33. Ibid., 57 (PL 177:1070).
34. For example, Hugh of St. Victor, *De scriptures et scriptoribus sacris* 3 (PL 175:12); *De sacramentis christianae fidei*, Prol. 5 (PL 176:185).
35. On the Jews in Victorine theology, see R. Moore, *Jews and Christians*. Moore finds that Richard was less open to Jewish scholarship than was Hugh, and more likely to express anti-Jewish sentiments.
36. *Sermones centum* 65 (PL 177:1102D–1103A, 1104C–1105A, 1105CD).
37. See Adam of St. Victor, *Quatorze proses*.
38. Fulton, *From Judgment to Passion*.
39. *Sermones centum* 71 (PL 177:1124AB)
40. Ibid., 4 (PL 177:910D–911A); 38 (PL 177:996D, 998B); 54 (PL 177:1060B); 72 (PL 177:1130B); 73 (PL 177:1133C); 74 (PL 177:1135C); 83 (177:1164D–1165A). See also Courcelle, "La culture antique." One place where Richard does invoke some technical distinctions from logic and grammar is the beginning of the long sermon "On the Sending of the Holy Spirit" (PL 196:1017D–1020B).
41. Achard of St. Victor, *Sermon* 15, 35, trans. Feiss, 347. The Latin text of Achard's sermons is found in Achard of St. Victor, *Sermons inédits*.
42. Achard of St. Victor, *Sermon* 14, 15–16, trans. Feiss, 281–82. The close nexus between contemplative union with God and compassion for others is stressed in Richard of St. Victor's *On the Four Degrees of Violent Charity*. Latin text in Richard of St. Victor, *Les quatre degrés de la violente charité*, 114–15, 171–77. See also Godfrey of St. Victor's sermon on the Feast of All Saints, discussed below.
43. Achard of St. Victor, *Sermon* 2, trans. Feiss, 149–54.
44. Richard of St. Victor, *De Trinitate*, and *La Trinité*; Achard of St. Victor, *L'unité de Dieu et la pluralité des creatures*. Book 3 of Richard's *De Trinitate* has been translated by Grover Zinn, in Richard of St. Victor, *The Twelve Patriarchs*,

371–97. There is a complete translation by Christopher P. Evans in Coolman and Coulter, *Trinity and Creation*. For an English translation of Achard's treatise, see Achard of Saint Victor, *Works*, trans. Feiss, 375–480. There is an extensive secondary literature on Richard's theology of Trinity. For Achard's Trinitarian thought see Ilkhani, *La philosophie de la création chez Achard de Saint-Victor*, 60–160.

45. English translation in Achard of St. Victor, "On the Distinction of Soul, Spirit, and Mind."

46. Walter of St. Victor, *Contra quatuor labyrinthos Franciae*, 187–335. Glorieux, "Mauvaise action et mauvais travail."

47. Walter of St. Victor, *Sermones ineditos triginta sex*, 8–10. See Châtillon, "Sermons et prédicateurs victorins."

48. *Sermo* 2, in Walter of St. Victor, *Sermones ineditos*, 19. For other such declarations both in the sermons assuredly attributed to Walter and in the anonymous sermons that are likely his, see Walter of St. Victor, *Sermones ineditos*, 238–39.

49. *Sermo anonymus* 8:1–2, in Walter of St. Victor, *Sermones ineditos*, 283.

50. See Châtillon, "Une ecclésiologie médiévale," where Jean Châtillon observed that the Victorines' theology was deficient in pneumatology.

51. *Sermo* 3, in Walter of St. Victor, *Sermones ineditos*, 29–30.

52. Ibid., 26–32.

53. Hugh of St. Victor, *In hierarchiam coelestem S. Dionysii*. See, for *superprincipalem* and *paternum lumen*, 2:1 (PL 175:933B–934B).

54. For a bio-bibliographical orientation see *Lexikon des Mittelalters*, 8:719.

55. Godfrey of St. Victor, *Le Microcosmus de Godefroy de Saint-Victor*, 29, citing Martène and Durand, *Veterorum Scriptorum*, 6:253–54.

56. Godfrey's career and writings have been greatly clarified by the studies of Françoise Gasparri. For a summary and references see her "Philosophie et cosmologie"; the previous paragraph derives from 119–23, 140–41.

57. Godfrey of St. Victor, *Fons Philosophiae*; translation in idem, *The Fountain of Philosophy*. Idem, *Le Microcosmus de Godefroy de Saint-Victor*. See also idem, "The *Preconium Augustini* of Godfrey of St. Victor," ed. Damon.

58. Delhaye, "Les sermons de Godefroy de Saint-Victor."

59. Ibid., 195; Godfrey of St. Victor, *Le Microcosmus de Godefroy de Saint-Victor*, 131.

60. Godfrey of St. Victor, *Fons philosophiae*, lines 497–500, 505–6, 521–22; *Fountain of Philosophy*, 57–58.

61. Godfrey of St. Victor, *Fons philosophiae*, lines 833–36; *Fountain of Philosophy*, 70.

62. Gasparri, "Philosophie et cosmologie," 124–25, 138–44.

63. Paris, BnF, Mss lat. 14515 and 14881. See Ouy, *Les manuscripts de l'abbaye de Saint-Victor*, 2:277, 611.

64. Gasparri, "Godefroid de Saint-Victor," 58.

65. Longère, "Maurice de Sully," 27, 30.

66. Erlande-Brandenburg, "Le grand dessein de Maurice de Sully."

67. Longère, "Maurice de Sully," 45–51. There is a shorter collection of sermons for the people, which several manuscripts plausibly attribute to Maurice of Sully.

68. This summary is based on the Old French version of Maurice's sermon in Dobson, *Maurice of Sully* (excerpts Latin version), 79–82. For further discussion of Maurice of Sully's sermon collection, see Old, *The Reading and Preaching of the Scriptures*, 322–29.

69. Preaching in the vernacular was required by the Council of Tours (817). See Longère, "Maurice de Sully," 69.

70. Spieralska, "Les sermons attribués à Maurice de Sully."

71. See the comment of Jean Longère in Michel Lemoine, "L'abbaye de Saint-Victor," 118: À Saint-Victor "plus on avance dans le XIIe siècle, plus on assiste à un renforcement de sa dimension pastorale. . . . Ils ont toujours apporté beaucoup d'attention à la predication. . . . Grâce aux Victorins, on a beaucoup de sermons conservés, venant d'eux, mais aussi d'autres prédicateurs du XIIe siècle."

72. In identifying the characteristics of the Victorine commitment to preaching and of their surviving sermons, I have been aided by Mark Zier, "Sermons of the Twelfth-Century Schoolmasters and Canons."

BOYD TAYLOR COOLMAN

---

8 "Transgressing [its] measure... trespassing the mode and law of its beauty"

Sin and the Beauty of the Soul in Hugh of St. Victor

> "'The *Beautiful*' includes, for Platonists, all that is worthy of love and admiration. It is thus impossible to separate æsthetics from ethics and religion."
> —Inge, *The Philosophy of Plotinus*

"May our Lord grant that you, as lovers of spiritual beauty, may observe all these things."[1] Thus concludes the so-called *Rule of St. Augustine*, as it was known to Hugh of St. Victor in the twelfth century. A twelfth-century commentary on this rule, long attributed to Hugh, the *Explanation of the Rule of St. Augustine*, avers that "the soul must observe the beauty of justice" and that adherence to the rule is possible only for those who "have a true love of justice, which constitutes the spiritual beauty of the soul."[2] That Hugh of St. Victor himself spoke often of the beauty of the soul has not gone unnoticed among students of his thought.[3] Yet more remains to be said. This theme is, of course, found in the Christian traditions to which Hugh is an heir, especially that stemming from Augustine.[4] As is often the case, though, with this *"alter Augustinus"* Hugh's treatment is distinctively his own, and this originality appears in the association of beauty with justice. Though this is perhaps jarring to a modern ear, justice is the foundation upon which Hugh constructs an aesthetic dimension in his moral theology. More precisely, Hugh links beauty and justice through a third, perhaps even more surprising, term: measure (*mensura*). For this Victorine, the soul's beauty consists in its justice, and justice is in part a function of proper measure in desire, thought, and act. With this conception, Hugh offers a distinctively aesthetic account, not only of the moral beauty of the soul, but also of creation, sin, and salvation.

THE BEAUTY OF THE SOUL

From its inception, the Abbey of St. Victor was known for its concern for the inculcation of virtue. Hugh himself was praised for "the moral beauty of his life (*vitae honestas*)," which "decorates his learning" and "illuminates his polished doctrine with the beauty of virtue."[5] Hugh, moreover, turns frequently to comparisons with artistic shape and image, which by imitation of exemplary individuals are sculpted and impressed, both upon the outer comportment of the body and especially upon the inner form of the soul. As Hugh observes in his *De institutione novitiorum*: "When [saintly men] act in such a way as to arouse the admiration of human minds, then they appear as exquisite sculptures. What stands out in them should be recreated inwardly in us."[6] In his *Didascalicon*, he lays out a philosophy of life, a discipline of living well (*bene vivendi disciplina*), which he consistently describes in terms of moral beauty.[7] An aesthetic conception of virtue is thus evident at St. Victor.[8]

References to the soul's beauty litter Hugh's works: "Of [the soul], the prophet longed to see the beauty," he notes in *Noah's Ark*.[9] Elsewhere he says: "God speaks to the soul in two ways: either as a prostitute or as a spouse; either as deformed or as beautiful; either as a sinner or as one justified. He rebukes her deformity; he praises her beauty."[10] In one of his most popular spiritual writings, the *Soliloquy on the Earnest Money of the Soul*, where Hugh employs a nuptial framework to reflect on the soul's relationship to its divine Spouse, the theme is quite prominent.[11] The soul's spiritual, invisible beauty, a comeliness that surpasses "the grace and beauty of all visible things," is the Creator's gift to the creature which crowns all other gifts.[12] The soul's "singular comeliness" makes her the beloved spouse of the divine Bridegroom; and the spouse's beauty is but a reflection of the divine beauty, which she must love in return.[13] The soul's beautification, moreover, is central to the ethicospiritual thrust of the dialogue. In creation, the soul has been given not only *esse* but *pulchrum esse*, not only being but beautiful being.[14] But this has been lost in the Fall and must now through various means be restored, including the sacraments, good works leading to virtue, and even scripture.[15]

In the *Soliloquy*, Hugh is preoccupied with the soul's beauty—or lack thereof. The soul's present state is one of defiled beauty, corrupted integrity, dispersed comeliness.[16] The Fall entailed the "loss of beauty" when "the confusion of ugliness contorted" the soul.[17] Hugh wistfully mourns the soul's lost state: "You do not know how vile you have been in the past, how polluted, how deformed and squalid, how unkempt and dissipated, plainly a horror and an enormity to all."[18] Despite these rhetorical flourishes, however, the precise nature of spiritual beauty remains unclear. Hints emerge along the way—wisdom, virtue, ordered desire—but a fuller account must be sought elsewhere in Hugh's corpus.[19]

MEASURE: THE BEAUTY OF ORIGINAL JUSTICE

In his *On the Sacraments*, the systematic fruit of his mature thought, Hugh's discussion of the creation of rational creatures (humans and angels) offers a more substantive account of the soul's beauty, now in terms of justice and measure.[20]

Hugh's account of prelapsarian creation describes a highly differentiated world. Rational beings are arranged in hierarchical gradations of power, subtlety, wisdom, and freedom, such that each has its proper "measure, mode, and end."²¹ Hugh finds this arrangement to be aesthetically pleasing, since "in the composition and order of the universe that diversity is beautiful in which less good is not evil and different good is greater good."²² Elsewhere, Hugh employs the triad from Wisdom 11 to describe how all things have been made in "number, weight, and measure," each having "its established boundary and end."²³ In that sense, the expression of infinite divine power is confined by the boundaries of created things: "for this reason if the power of the Creator is compared with the measure and mode of his works, then without a doubt it is declared to be limited by end and measure."²⁴

This measured diversity pertains not only to their initial creation—establishing creatures as certain kinds of things, with distinct boundaries and unique modes of being—but also to their consummation. Each has its appropriate end in God. Hugh sees rational beings emerging out of the primal chaos with a certain form, which, good and beautiful as it is, is nonetheless capable of, and indeed summoned to, a higher degree of form and beauty.²⁵ In Hugh's words, the creature must move from *esse* to *pulchrum esse*, from being to beautiful being. The upshot of this is that all rational creatures are called to a unique, specific, and proper realization of *pulchrum esse*, in accordance with what Hugh consistently refers to as the creature's own measure. This achievement differs according to the measure of the creature's nature and capacity. As he says elsewhere, God rested on the seventh day "in order to promise us future rest, if we should be zealous to do good and perfect works according to our own measure and mode."²⁶ Again, it is fitting, says Hugh in yet another work, for the Creator to reform the creature in a manner congruent with its original "measure, mode, and order."²⁷ Hugh finds all this aesthetically pleasing. "The beauty of the universe," he argues, is completed precisely in this: "that all things, not in one and the same way, but individually according to their various and multifarious order and grade are recalled to communion with the divine goodness."²⁸

THE LOSS OF ORIGINAL BEAUTY AS THE LOSS OF MEASURE

For Hugh, the calling to realize a measured beauty is the backdrop for the drama of original sin. Stationed, as it were, between nonbeing and beautiful being, the creature could either turn toward evil through sin or turn toward good through justice.²⁹

Hugh's account of the Fall focuses less on the literal act of eating fruit and more on the interior dynamics of the soul yielding to temptation. As he says, if we wish to consider where sin came from or what sin itself is, "which vitiates good nature and takes away its beauty and integrity," we must consider the "quality of the interior person."[30] His analysis here is complex and psychologically fine-grained. Originally, he argues, the creature had a desire for justice, that is, a desire to will the good in all things.[31] Yet in sinning, the creature ceased to will the good. How, asks Hugh, can this have occurred, since the creature's just will was God-given? His answer hinges on the notion of measure. Answering one rhetorical question by another, Hugh responds: What else can be said, he asks, except that the human person "willed something *outside the measure* in which alone was justice?"[32] What does this mean? Adapting Augustine's distinction between use and delight to his own purpose, Hugh asserts that God had prepared two kinds of goods for rational creatures: temporal ones, to be used, and eternal ones, to be enjoyed. But justice did not consist merely in using and enjoying the right things. Neither use nor enjoyment per se is just. Hugh adds this qualification: both use and enjoyment had to be done *well*. Hugh notes that the first humans were never commanded *not* to desire what the forbidden fruit contained, that is, God-likeness, knowledge of good and evil, and eternal life.[33] Rather, as he explains, "a measure was defined for the human person" according to which it should use temporal goods and enjoy eternal goods *well*.[34]

The measure of using well differs from that of enjoying well. Just use is fourfold, requiring not only the proper object, but also the proper time, manner, and extent.[35] By contrast, since for Hugh it is self-evident that God should be enjoyed as much as possible, right delight was only twofold: proper time and manner.[36] On these, Hugh elaborates: Proper manner was the desire to be like God "according to the imitation, as befits a creature," not "inordinately," "according to equality, which exceeds creaturely capacity." Proper time was only after the human being had "completed its obedience."[37] In Eden, Hugh concludes, the first humans exceeded proper measure on both counts:

> In this therefore was the injustice of man: that he extended his desire beyond measure, both according to quality, when he wished to be made like

his Creator, and according to time, when he hastened to forseize reward before merit. When, therefore, he desired the highest good, he desired good but he did not desire *well*, because he sought to seize this both immoderately and unreasonably.³⁸

As noted, Hugh stresses that nowhere were the first humans told that they should not desire what the forbidden fruit contained: knowledge of good and evil, or life. The sin was failing to submit to the divine dictate regarding degree and timing. Original sin then was a violation of proper measure: it was excessive desire and irrational haste.³⁹ In short, the rational creature was rapacious and impatient. The primal failure was not so much a wrong act, but an act done wrongly; not a bad deed, but a deed badly done.

Hugh sums up the results of this primal injustice by equating the violation of measure with lost beauty: by "averting itself (*avertenti se*) and transgressing measure (*transgrediendi mensuram*)," the rational creature became "shameful" (*turpis*), "depraved" (*prava*), and "disordered" (*inordinata*); "issuing forth" (*effluens*), it no longer "held fast to (*non tenens*) the mode and law of its beauty (*modum et legem pulchritudinis suae*)."⁴⁰ Here, "transgressing measure" is a refusal to hold creaturely poise; a failure to maintain creaturely composure, a violation of creaturely boundaries:

> Every vice takes its origin from nature; since vice is nothing other than natural affection [having gone] beyond order and measure: it transgresses order, when it is moved toward that which it ought not [to be moved]; it exceeds measure, when it is moved more than it ought [to be moved].⁴¹

In short, sin is a failure to preserve due measure, proper mode, and right order in being and acting, the results of which Hugh consistently construes in aesthetic terms: after the Fall, the soul no longer has "its form or comeliness or beauty, for which it should have been loved and brought to glory."⁴² (This thinking even finds its way into Hugh's numerical symbolism. The number nine, falling short of the perfection of the number ten, indicates an imperfection due to lack. Conversely, the number eleven, exceeding ten, indicates a certain excess of perfection, signifying "transgression beyond measure.")⁴³

THE MEANING OF MEASURE

What more can be said about this transgression of measure and resulting loss of beauty? Wound up in Hugh's summary are the basic strands that I would like now to unravel. While Eden's loss of measure pertained to the soul's delight in God, the same principle has a broader application in his theology. For Hugh, measure is a multifaceted stone, which I hope now to rotate.

Playing a rather minor role in Hugh's theology is the sense of trespassing a hierarchical boundary. In his commentary on the *Celestial Hierarchy* of Ps.-Dionysius, Hugh suggests that every participant in a hierarchy must function in a manner befitting its status, so that nothing trespass its "assigned mode, measure, and proper order (*ut praeter modum, et mensuram ab ipso assignatam et ordini suo debitam*)."[44] This, though, is rather muted in Hugh's theology, rarely appearing outside of the commentary.

To trespass measure has another sense for Hugh: a failure to maintain posture and poise. Here, Hugh's dictates regarding the comportment of the novice canons, found in his *On the Instruction of Novices* (*De institutione novitiorum*), are illustrative: "In those things which are right," he tells them, "maintain mode and measure."[45] Everything, he continues, should be done "in that mode and measure in which it ought to be done," that is, "no more and no less and not otherwise than is necessary." No act should "exceed the limit of temperance (*temperantiae limitem*) or the form of decorem (*formam honestatis*)," such as laughing with one's teeth apart.[46] When eating, one should "maintain mode and measure," so as to eat "slowly and not with too much haste."[47] Such actions are "neither contrary to decorum nor beyond necessity."[48] In resuming the consumption of food after fasting, there is always the temptation to "exceed mode and measure," and so to "expand into superfluity."[49] The overall sense here is the need to seek a golden mean, to maintain or hold a proper measure or modulation in action (*mensuram et modum tenere, rationis moderamen*).[50] In the *Didascalicon*, interestingly, Hugh can give this a musical depiction: there is a music in human beings (*musica humana*), which is "in those activities (the foremost among them are mechanical) which belong above all to rational human beings and which are good if they do not go beyond measure, so that avarice or appetite are not fostered by the very things intended to relieve our weakness."[51]

Loss of measure has yet another sense for Hugh, namely, a failure to maintain a kind of intellectual restraint in the pursuit of knowledge. This emerges most clearly in his *Homilies on Ecclesiastes*. Discussing the temptation to exceed his own intellectual limits, Hugh observes of himself: "there was not then any consideration of the truth in me, which might correct and constrain me, lest I attempt to exceed my held measure (*tentarem mensuram meam*), nor presume to desire those things that are not given to human beings to know and investigate."[52] The failure to maintain this intellectual discipline is to yield to the temptation of Augustinian *curiositas*:

> The occupation of curiosity [is] that by which the mind extends itself to illicit things, and attempts to search into and to investigate that which it is either unfitting or dangerous to know: and that is the worst occupation, since, when it is dilated beyond measure, it either captures the affection and inflates the soul through vain/empty knowledge; or if it is not strong enough it wearies the soul through dilation and desperation.[53]

Elsewhere, accordingly, discussing the various kinds of meditative thought, Hugh will advise: "Lest therefore the soul be embittered by evil, let it patiently endure its impossibilities; lest [the soul] be occupied by evil, it must not extend its possibilites beyond its measure."[54]

Similarly, Hugh's descriptions of moral virtues often appeal to the importance of measure. The desire for necessary things, for example, if not disciplined, can become excessive, mutating first into cupidity and then to iniquity. "Vice is nothing other than the natural affection outside of order and above measure."[55] As a remedy for this, desire must be "ordered according to measure, and measure according to justice."[56] "The fecundity of the virtues," he says, "must be encircled, guarded, and constrained, lest in their multiplication, they are relaxed beyond the measure of justice (*metas justitae*)."[57] In one place he suggests that the soul should not "transcend the measure of justice in compassion."[58] Negligence of measure in virtue, by contrast, risks moral dissolution.[59] For him, the soul seems constantly on the verge of releasing its grip on proper measure, to experience a kind of moral relaxation. "Through incontinence," a once stable and secure mind is "relaxed to the point of ugly deformity."[60] This is graphically illustrated in Hugh's discussion of David's son Amnon, who raped his sister. Amnon's appetite was moved to excess, when he "relaxed the love for his sister all the way to the point of the desire of the flesh."[61] In this, the notion of moral poise or balance presents itself as an apt characterization: "The *habitus* of the virtues gathers those virtues into unity, lest they flow out or draw back from the unity of concord."[62] For Hugh, to maintain measure is to hold fast and cling to virtue in the face of pressures to release and relax.

Perhaps incorporating all the prior meanings is Hugh's description of the forfeiture of measure as an "issuing forth" (*effluens*), adumbrated variously above. The sense here is that of liquid excess, of superfluity. This notion stands behind one of his favorite images for the dissipation and dispersion of both desire and thought, resulting from sin: overflowing water, rushing floods, dispersing rivulets.[63] Vice, he says, emerges when valid needs are allowed to exceed "mode and measure" and "expand into superfluity." "Luxury is a slippery and slackening prostitution of the mind toward the body, descending from impure desires."[64] Elsewhere, this sense of measure pertains to both desire and thought. In his treatise on *Noah's Ark*, Hugh describes this in relation to the soul's love: before the Fall, the soul "remained one in the love of the One," but then it was "divided into as many channels as there were objects that it craved, once it had begun to flow in different directions through earthly longings."[65] Again: "the desire for the world is likened, therefore, to waters because it is liquid and slippery . . . because it makes those who pursue it unstable and disintegrated."[66] One of Hugh's *Homilies on Ecclesiastes* makes a similar point regarding intellectual endeavor. The vice of curiosity, wherein the mind reaches forth to illicit things and excessive investigations, results in either vain self-inflation or desperate fatigue. Such a mind dissipates (*dissipat*) and pours itself out (*illaqueat*); it is distended (*distendantur*) and dilates (*dilatat*) beyond measure (*ultra mensuram*).[67] Again: "I descended therefore *into the worst occupation, which God gave to the sons of men, so that they might be* 'distended' *into them*, and I dispersed my soul into all things, and in thought I began to run about through everything, that I might seek and investigate concerning everything under the sun: and I was not up for it."[68]

Finally, in a way that seems to recapitulate the others, loss of measure for Hugh entails the loss of creaturely integrity. Vice "vitiates good nature and takes away its beauty and integrity."[69] Hugh's language above of distension and dilation suggest a distortion of the creature's proper dimensions and thus its form, through the loss of measure. The result is a kind of grotesque enormity and ugly deformity of the soul. As he notes in a discussion of lost measure, evil is "that which was sought without measure," and thus, for the rational will, evil was "not to be what it ought to have been."[70] For this reason, Hugh continues, it "does not have its form or comeliness or beauty, for which it should have been loved and brought to glory."[71] Ultimately, it is this that seems to prompt Hugh to define the soul's beauty by measure, for measure is beautiful because it is the essence of proportion, integrity, and comely form.

THE CHRISTOLOGICAL RETURN TO MEASURE

In light of the foregoing, a particular aspect of Hugh's account of Christ becomes more intelligible. In the so-called Ark treatises, he engages in a moral-mystical reading of the symbol of Noah's Ark, which is meant among other things to be a symbol of the soul itself, as it is healed and restored. From the perspective of measure, several aspects of these treatises gain additional interest. First, Hugh is preoccupied with the proper measurements of the Ark, with getting the literal dimensions just right, so that they may become that of the soul:

> Let us consider the measurements of the ark, and how they may be realized in us. . . . This is the ark that you must build. These are the bounds of your fathers, which it is not lawful for you to pass. . . . Rest then within these walls. . . . Storm and tempest rage outside, if you issue forth in any direction at all you will be wrecked. If you . . . exceed the height . . . you go beyond . . . you transgress the measure.[72]

Second, for Hugh, the Ark is constructed like a pyramid that narrows to a perfect square at the top, the measure of a cubit. This symbolizes not only the ultimate integration and unity of the soul, but also Christ, who, I suggest, is construed in some sense as the true measure of the soul. "[Christ] was at once perfect, and yet *never overflowed*."[73] In his earthly life, Hugh notes, Christ made right use of both his body and his soul. In his body, he did not desert patience; in his soul, his compassion never exceeded the measure of justice.[74] So, Hugh observes, "Growing in this way, both in the knowledge of the truth and in the merit of virtue, spiritually we strive towards conformity with [Christ] and 'the measure of the age of his fullness' [Eph 4:13]."[75]

GOOD FORM

For Hugh of St. Victor, sin is the creature's transgressing of its measure, the measure that is the mode and law of both its beauty and its justice. This is more than trespassing a boundary: it is a failure to maintain (*non tenens*) a certain moral-intellectual composure or poise; a superfluity (*effluens*), dissipation, and dilation, a deforming relaxation. It is a violation of integrity and form, and thus beauty. Ultimately, the impression emerges that for Hugh the spiritual life is to be executed in the manner of something like a singer holding a note. Even where he makes no explicit mention of measure, Hugh is everywhere concerned with proper limits, with fitting modes of being, with a sense of proper modulation and moderation, balance, equilibrium, and timing. All of this, moreover, seems to flow from a concern with the composure, integrity, and, finally, comely form. In short, for our Victorine, spiritual beauty consists in proper measure in desire, thought, and act.

NOTES

1. Ps.-Hugh of St. Victor, *Expositio regulae S. Augustini* (PL 176:923A): "Donet Dominus ut observetis haec omnia tanquam spiritualis pulchritudinis amatores."
2. Ibid. (PL 176:924A): "qualiter pulchritudo justitiae debeat observari"; and 897C: "amorem justitiae, quae est spiritualis pulchritudo animae."
3. For Hugh's aesthetics see Bruyne, *Études d'esthétique médiévale*, 2:203–50; Karfíková, "*De esse ad pulchrum esse*"; and Coolman, "*Pulchrum Esse*."
4. See Eco, *Art and Beauty*, 9–10.
5. This pursuit of virtue extended even to the level of manners, comportment, dressing, eating, and gesturing; see Jaeger, *The Envy of Angels*, 246.
6. Hugh of St. Victor, *De institutione novitiorum* 7 (PL 176: 933B–C), cited in Jaeger, *The Envy of Angels*, 259.
7. William of Champeaux, the founder of the order, was praised for his pursuit, not of mere knowledge, but of the beauty of virtue (*morum venustatem*) and the form of living well (*bene agendi formula*); Jaeger, *The Envy of Angels*, 245.
8. Ps.-Hugh of St. Victor, *Expositio Regulae* (PL 176:897C): "Nostrae divitiae, nostra pulchritudo, boni mores sunt." Cited in Jaeger, *The Envy of Angels*, 461, n. 66.
9. Hugh of St. Victor, *De archa Noe*; English translation in Hugh of St. Victor, *Hugh of St. Victor: Selected Spiritual Writings*, trans. by a religious of the Community of St. Mary the Virgin (CSMV). Cited as *Archa Noe*, book and chapter, followed by page and line number in Sicard's edition, and by CSMV and page. Except

"Transgressing [its] measure . . . trespassing the mode and law of its beauty"   197

where noted, all translations are from the CSMV edition. Here, *Archa Noe* 1.4 (ed. Sicard 8.65; CSMV 50).

10. Hugh of St. Victor, *De amore sponsi* (PL 176:989B–C): "*Loquar*, inquit, *sponsae meae*. Duobus modis loquitur Deus ad animam. Aliter ad fornicariam, et aliter ad sponsam. Aliter ad foedam, aliter ad pulchram. Aliter ad peccatricem, aliter ad justificatam. Illius foeditatem increpat, hujus pulchritudinem laudat."

11. Hugh of St. Victor, *De arrha animae*, in *L'oeuvre de Hugues de Saint-Victor I*, ed. and trans. Feiss, et al.; English translation in Hugh of St. Victor, *Soliloquy on the Earnest Money of the Soul*, trans. Herbert. Cited hereafter as *Arrha*, followed by page and line number in the Feiss et al. edition and by the page number in Herbert's translation.

12. *Arrha* (Feiss 230.76–77; Herbert 15): "quae specie tua omnino visibilium decorem et pulchritudinem vincis."

13. *Arrha* (Feiss 234.128; Herbert 16): "singularis décor." *Arrha* (Feiss 234.126–27; Herbert 16): Of the Bridegroom's beauty, Hugh remarks, "one so beautiful, so handsome, so elegant and extraordinary" ("tam pulcher, tam formosus, tam elegans, tam unicus in tuo aspectu").

14. *Arrha* (Feiss 252.413; Herbert 23): "But he has given us more for we have received not merely existence, but a beautiful and fair existence. Just as our being surpasses nothingness through existence, so does it through its beauty of form surpass the indeterminate. And as existence is pleasing, so ordered existence is even more pleasing." ("Nunc autem amplius dedit, quia dedit non solum esse, sed pulchrum esse, formosum esse, quod quantum superat nihil per existentiam, tantum antecedit aliquid per formam, in quo multum placet id quod est, et amplius id quod tale est.")

15. *Arrha* (Feiss 270.680f; Herbert 31): "Next you put on the garments of good works and by the fruit of almsgiving, with fasts and prayers, with holy vigils and other deeds of piety you become arrayed as though with the finery of the most varied kinds." ("Deinde vestimenta bonorum operum induis, et fructu eleemosynarum, cum jejuniis et orationibus, cum sacris vigiliis, aliisque operibus pietatis, quasi quodam vario ornatu decoraris.")

16. *Arrha* (Feiss 256.456–57; Herbert 24). ". . . lest you destroy such a gift, lest you defile such an ornament, lest you corrupt such a beauty" ("ne tale donum perderes, ne tale ornamentum foedares, ne tantum decorem corrumperes"). Again: *Arrha* (Feiss 256.465; Herbert 24): "You have corrupted your integrity, you have defiled your beauty, you have dispersed your ornament." ("Corrupisti integritatem tuam, foedasti pulchritudinem tuam, dispersisti ornatum tuum.")

17. *Arrha* (Feiss 256.459–60; Herbert 24). ". . . ne te cum damno amissae pulchritudinis simul torqueret confusio foeditatis."

18. *Arrha* (Feiss 262.563; Herbert 28): "nescis quam foeda prius fuisti, quam polluta, quam deformis et squalida, discissa et dissipata, omni horrore et enormitate plena."

19. *Arrha* (Feiss 254.455–56; Herbert 24): "Externally He adorned you with the senses, within He enlightened you with wisdom, giving the one as an outer garment,

the other as inner garb. His gifts of the senses are, as it were, precious and resplendent jewels for display, and the faculty of wisdom within is like the natural beauty of your countenance. Indeed your attire far surpasses the beauty of any gems and your countenance is the most beautiful of all." ("Sensibus foris decoravit, intus sapientia illustravit. Sensus dans quasi exteriorem, sapientiam quasi interiorem habitum. Sensus quasi quasdam gemmas fulgentes appendens exterius, sapientiam quasi naturali pulchritudine faciem vultus tui decorans intus. Ecce ornatus tuus, omnium gemmarum vincit pulchritudinem, ecce facies tua omnium formarum superat decorem.")

20. Hugh of St. Victor, *On the Sacraments of the Christian Faith (De sacramentis)*, trans. Deferrari. Cited hereafter as *Sacr.*, followed by book, part, and section numbers, and cited with PL reference followed by page number in Deferrari's translation.

21. *Sacr.*, 1.5.12 (PL 176:251C; Deferrari 80).

22. *Sacr.*, 1.5.9 (PL 176:250D; Deferrari 79).

23. Hugh of St. Victor, *Super Canticum Mariae*, 66.597–68.59): "Certum est enim quod omne quod factum est in numero, et pondere et mensura, legitimum terminum et finem suum habet."

24. Ibid., 68.599–601: "et idcirco si ad operis mensuram Creatoris potentia, modumque componitur, ipsa procul dubio, et fine et mensura terminari declaratur."

25. Hugh consistently locates the status of original creation as suspended between absolute nonbeing, on the one hand, and a perfected state of created being (typically described as *pulchrum esse*, beautiful being), on the other. See *Archa Noe* 1.2 (Sicard 4.33–37; CSMV 46): "This was, therefore, the one, true good of man, to wit, the full and perfect knowledge of his Maker—full, you must understand, after that fullness which he received at his creation, not after that which he was to receive hereafter, when his obedience was fulfilled."

26. Hugh of St. Victor, *De sacramentis legis* (PL 176: 20D): "ut nobis si secundum modum et mensuram nostram opera bona et perfecta facere studuerimus, requiem futuram promitteret."

27. Hugh of St. Victor, *In hierarchiam caelestem S. Dionysii* (hereafter, *In hierarchiam*) (PL 175:1007A–B): "hoc scilicet proprium illi est, vocare ea, quae sunt, ad communionem suam, ut hoc est, sicut unicuique eorum quae sunt, definitur vel dispensatur ex propria analogia, id est mensura, et modo, et ordine."

28. *In hierarchiam* (PL 175:1007B–C): "Nam in hoc ipso pulchritudo universitatis perficitur, quod non uno et eodem modo omnia, sed singula quaeque secundum ordinem et gradum suum varie, ac multifariam ad communionem divinae bonitatis revocantur, ut in eo quod non deseruntur, compleatur opus bonitatis; in eo vero, quod varie disponuntur ad decorem et pulchritudinem omnium opus sapientiae perficiatur."

29. See *Arrha* (Feiss 254.423f; Herbert 24): "As He took us to himself in love, so He also wished to make us like himself. Therefore, having granted both existence and beautiful existence to us He also granted us to live such that we might both

excel by our essence that which does not exist and also excel by our form those things which are disordered or not well-composed." ("Dedit ergo nobis esse, et pulchrum esse; dedit et vivere, ut praecellamus et iis quae non sunt per essentiam, et iis quae inordinata aut incomposita sunt, per formam.")

30. *Sacr.*, 1.7.10 (PL 176:291B; Deferrari 125).

31. He begins by introducing a distinction on which the whole discussion pivots. From the beginning, says Hugh, God placed two things in the soul "by which his whole nature might be ruled and led to the fulfillment of its end," i.e., *pulchrum esse*, namely "the desire for the just and the desire for the beneficial"; *Sacr.*, 1.7.11 (PL 176:291B; Deferrari 125).

32. *Sacr.*, 1.7.12 (PL 176:292D–293A; Deferrari 127).

33. *Sacr.*, 1.7.15 (PL 176:293C–294A; Deferrari 127–28).

34. *Sacr.*, 1.7.13 (PL 176:293A; Deferrari 127).

35. *Sacr.*, 1.7.14 (PL 176:293A–B; Deferrari 127).

36. Hugh's analysis of the fall of angels (*Sacr.*, 1.5.29 [PL 176:259D; Deferrari 87]) proceeds similarly. Angels too sinned by exceeding measure (*extra mensuram*), which Hugh describes as moving toward illicit objects. To the rational mind (*mens rationalis*) certain licit objects were assigned, movement toward which was "according to measure" (*secundum mensuram*) and was accordingly movement "according to justice" (*secundum justitiam*).

37. *Sacr.*, 1.7.15 (PL 176:293C; Deferrari 127–28). A similar discussion is found in Hugh's *De sacramentum legis*. (PL 176:26B): "D. What therefore is justice? M. Measure in desire for the beneficial. D. What is the desire of justice? M. The love of measure. D. What then does it will, so that it ceases to will this? M. It wills something beyond measure. D. And was it not sin to will this? M. It was not sin because it willed this, but because of the measure of willing in willing this, that it let go of the desire of justice. D. What did it will beyond measure? M. It desired likeness to God." ("D. Quid est ergo justitia? M. Mensura in appetitu commodi. D. Quid est appetitus justitiae? M. Amor mensurae. D. Quid ergo voluit ut hoc velle desineret? M. Voluit aliquid extra mensuram. D. Nunquid et hoc velle peccatum non fuit? M. Non quod hoc voluit peccatum fuit, sed quod hoc volendo mensurae volendi, id justitiae appetitum amisit. D. Quid voluit extra mensuram? M. Similitudinem Dei appetiit.")

38. *Sacr.*, 1.7.15 (PL 176:294A; Deferrari 128) ; emphasis added.

39. *Sacr.*, 1.7.6 (PL 176:289B; Deferrari 123). Here, vice is excess: Gluttony is "immoderate desire to eat"; vain glory is "inordinate desire to excel"; avarice "excessive passion for holding and possessing."

40. *Sacr.*, 1.7.21 (PL 176:296D; Deferrari 131): "the beauty and dignity of reason appear in this, that it checks its affection from inordinate things."; and *Sacr.*, 1.5.29 (PL 176:258A–B; Deferrari 88): "Hoc itaque malum factum est voluntati avertenti se et transgrediendi mensuram, quod turpis facta est et prava et inordinata, effluens et non tenens modum et legem pulchritudinis suae."

41. Hugh of St. Victor, *Elucidationes Variae* (PL 177:501C–D): "*Unde vitium originem trahat?* Omne vitium ex natura originem trahit; quia non est aliud vitium, quam affectus naturalis praeter ordinem et supra mensuram: ordinem transgrediens, quando movetur ad ea quae non debet; mensuram excedens, quando movetur plusquam debet."

42. *Sacr.*, 1.7.16 (PL 176:294C; Deferrari 129).

43. Hugh of St. Victor, *De scripturis et scriptoribus sacris* (PL 175:22C): "Secundum modum porrectionis numeri significant, ut septenarius ultra senarium requiem post operationem. Octonarius ultra septenarium, aeternitatem post mutabilitatem. Novenarius ante denarium, defectum intra perfectionem. Undenarius ultra denarium, [significat] extra mensuram transgressionem."

44. *In hierarchiam* (PL 175:994C).

45. Hugh of St. Victor, *De institutione novitiorum*, ed. and trans. Feiss, et al. Hereafter cited as *Inst.*, followed by page and line number. Here, *Inst.*, 6 (38.311–314): "Proinde, fratres charissimi, linguam vestram a superfluitate non solum inanium verborum restringite, sed in ipsis etiam quae recta sunt mensuram et modum tenete, et in collatione sanctorum magis auditores quam doctores esse eligite."

46. *Inst.*, 12 (72.834–74.840): "Secunda est custodia disciplinae in gestu, ut unumquodque membrum id quod facit, eo modo atque mensura faciat quo faciendum est, id est nec plus nec minus, nec aliter quam oportet, faciat. Quatenus in actu suo sic et dirigatur et moveatur, ut in nulla unquam parte temperantiae limitem aut formam honestatis excedat, hoc est (ut id paucis exemplis probemus) ridere sine apertione dentium."

47. *Inst.*, 21 (98.1224–1230): "Temperantiam manducandi intelligimus in eo, si tractim homo et non cum nimia festinatione comedat; ubi nos quidem quantum fieri potest modum et mensuram omnes tenere suademus, legem tamen nullam dare praesumsimus, quia, sicut jam supra diximus, alius sic et alius sic. Haec vobis, fratres, de scientia et disciplina interim nos diximus: Bonitatem vero orate ut vobis det Deus. Amen."

48. *Inst.*, 20 (96.1193–1203): "Deinde sequitur custodia disciplinae in eo quantum quis sumere debeat, cujus mensura haec mihi esse videtur, ut neque contra honestatem neque supra necessitatem. Non omnis venter idem capit, alius sic contentus, alius vero sic. Cui minus sufficit, iste priusquam ad turpitudinem edacitatis perveniat, in superfluitatem offendit; cui multum opus est, in eo saepe honestas comedendi laeditur, etiam priusquam ad superfluitatem veniatur. Ergo ille cui parum satis est, magis superfluitatem caveat; ille tero cui multo opus est, magis ad honestatem attendat, quia neque ille nisi temperantiae metas transierit, ad turpitudinem veniet, neque iste nisi prius honestatis oblitus fuerit, in superfluitatem impinget." ["Whence there follows the custody of discipline with respect to how someone ought to eat, the measure of which seems to me to be, that it neither be contrary to beauty nor beyond necessity. For not every stomach has the same capacity, one is contented thus, but not another. The one to whom it suffices less, he comes ahead of

time to the ugliness of gluttony; to the one who needs more, in him often the beauty of eating is ruptured, also before he comes to superfluity. Therefore the one who is satisfied with little guards more against superfluity; but the one for whom much is needed, attends more to beauty, since he only arrives at beauty in trespassing the boundary of proportion/temper and before the beauty was sullied, he impinges on superfluity."]

49. Hugh of St. Victor, *De meditatione*, trans. [French] by Baron. Hereafter cited as *Meditatione*, followed by line numbers in Baron's edition. All translations are mine. Here, *Meditatione* (Baron 54.135–39) "Sed quia modum et mensuram transeunt, excrescunt in superfluitatem. Ut verbi gratia cum post famem cibus sumendus immoderate appetitur, et post abstinentiam in sumendo edulio mensura non tenetur."

50. See Jaeger, *The Envy of Angels*, 259.

51. Hugh of St. Victor, *Didascalicon*, ed. Buttimer; *The Didascalicon of Hugh of St. Victor*, English trans. Taylor. Here, *Disdascalicon*, 2.12 (Buttimer 32.23; Taylor 69): "Quae sensibilibus communis est, alia in operationibus: quae specialiter rationalibus congruit, quibus mechanica praeest; quae si modum non excesserint bonae sunt, ut inde non nutriatur cupiditas: unde infirmitas foveri debet."

52. *In Salomonis Ecclesiasten homiliae* 7 (hereafter, *In Eccl.*) (PL 175:160A): "*Quod perversi difficile corrigantur*, etc. Vis, inquit, scire quam difficile perversi corrigantur? Cape me. Ego hodie tibi omnium exemplum fiam. Nam et ego aliquando perversus fui et non intellexi ipse perversitatem meam; sed putavi me rectum esse, et recte agere quando *proposui in animo meo quaerere et investigare sapienter de cunctis quae fiunt sub sole*; nec erat tunc aliqua consideratio veritatis in me, quae me corrigeret et cohiberet; ne excedere tentarem mensuram meam, neque appetere praesumerem quae non sunt data hominibus scire et investigare."

53. *In Eccl.*, 5 (PL 175:157C): "Occupatio autem curiositatis qua se mens ad illicita extendit, et instat scrutari et investigare quod ei scire aut non convenit, aut noxium est: ipsa est pessima occupatio, quia, dum se dilatat ultra mensuram, aut affectum capit, et animum per inanem scientiam inflat; aut si apprehendere non valet per dilationem et desperationem fatigat."

54. *Meditatione* (Baron 56–58.180–83): "Ne igitur male amaricetur animus, suam impossibilitatem patienter sustineat: ne autem male occupetur, possibilitatem suam extra mensuram suam non extendat."

55. *Sacr.*, 1.7.31 (PL 176:301D; Deferrari 136): "This is what is called concupiscence of the flesh itself, namely, the natural desire or affection transgressing order and going beyond measure (*mensuram transcendens*)—transgressing order when it moves toward those things to which it ought not to move; going beyond measure (*mensuram transcendens*), when it moves otherwise than it ought."

56. Hugh of St. Victor, *Elucidationes Variae* (PL 177:628B–C) : "*De tribus viis. Utinam dirigantur viae meae!* etc. [Ps 118] Via hominis mutabilis est, et ad diversa inflectitur; hoc est, vel ad viam Dei vel ad viam diaboli. Si enim necessitas intorquetur ad cupiditatem, et cupiditas ad iniquitatem, via hominis flectitur ad viam

diaboli. Si autem diriguntur ad mensuram, et mensura ad justitiam, via hominis directa est ad viam Dei. Propterea ait: *Utinam dirigantur viae meae* etc."

57. *In hierarchiam* (PL 175: 1145D): "Sensus est: Quod zona quae lumbos et umbilicum, in quibus est seminativum propagationis, ambit et constringit, significat custodiam fecundarum virtutum: quae custodia ipsas virtutes ambit, et custodit, vel constringit, ne in sua multiplicatione extra metas justitiae relaxentur, aut diffluant."

58. Hugh of St. Victor, *De quatuor voluntatibus in Christo* (hereafter, *Quat. volunt.*) (PL 176:844B): "animus in compassione justitiae mensuram non transcendit."

59. Hugh of St. Victor, *Adnotatiunculae elucidatoriae in threnos Jeremiae* (PL 175:279D–280A): "Propter quod necesse est ut semper solliciti simus, ne nos per accepta dona virtutum, aut superbia elevet, aut negligentia dissolvat."

60. *In Eccl.*, 12 (PL 176: 200D): "Vena sollicitudo reprehenditur, ut male secura mens per torporem, et otium, et incontinentiam ad turpitudinem relaxetur."

61. Hugh of St. Victor, *Elucidationes Variae* (PL 177:501D): "*Unde vitium originem trahat?* In David propter indigentiam: appetitus movebatur ad ea quae non debuit, quando esuriens panes sanctificatos concupivit [1 Kgs 21]. In Amnon filio ejus propter vehementiam movebatur plus quam debuit, quando Thamar sororis suae dilectionem usque ad carnis libidinem relaxavit [2 Kgs 13]."

62. *In hierarchiam* (PL 175:1145D): "quod habitus virtutum ipsas virtutes in unum congregans, ne diffluant sive ab unitate concordiae recedant."

63. *In Eccl.*, 7 (PL 176:196C–D): "Novissime sequitur in dispositionis ordine opus tertiae diei, ut congregentur aquae quae sub coelo sunt in locum unum, ne carnis desideria fluxa sint, et ultra metam se necessitatis expandant, ut totus homo ad statum naturae revocatus, et secundum ordinem rationis dispositus, in locum unum omne desiderium colligat, quatenus et caro spiritui, et spiritus subjectus sit Creatori."

64. Hugh of St. Victor, *De fructibus carnis et spiritus* (PL 176:1002A): "Luxuria est ex immundis descendens desideriis lubrica et effrenata mentis corporisve prostitutio."

65. *Archa Noe*, 1.1 (Sicard 5.46–50; CSMV 47).

66. *Archa Noe*, 3.12 (Sicard 103.14–17; CSMV 139).

67. *In Eccl.*, 5 (PL 176:157B–C): "De dictorum verborum Ecclesiastae litterali et morali expositione. Et dedit hanc occupationem pessimam filiis hominum ut distendantur in ea. Occupatio enim est distractio et illigatio mentium quae avertit et dissipat et illaqueat animas ne cogitare pervaleant ea quae salutis sunt, et ideo occupatio. . . . Occupatio autem curiositatis qua se mens ad illicita extendit, et instat scrutari et investigare quod ei scire aut non convenit, aut noxium est: ipsa est pessima occupatio, quia, dum se dilatat ultra mensuram, aut affectum capit, et animum per inanem scientiam inflat; aut si apprehendere non valet per dilationem et desperationem fatigat."

68. *In Eccl.*, 7 (PL 176:160A–B): "Descendi ergo in *occupationem pessimam* quam *dedit Deus filiis hominum, ut* distendantur *in ea*, et dispersi animum meum in omnia, et cogitatione coepi per cuncta discurrere, ut quaererem et investigarem de cunctis quae fiunt sub sole: at non valui."

69. *Sacr.*, 1.7.10 (PL 176:291B; Deferrari 125).

70. *Sacr.*, 1.7.16 (PL 176:294A; Deferrari 128); and *Sacr.*, 1.7.16 (PL 176:294B; Deferrari 128).

71. *Sacr.*, 1.7.16 (PL 176: 294C; Deferrari 129). This last phrase links up nicely with the *De arrha animae*, which sought to recover the lost beauty as the basis for being loved by the Bridegroom.

72. *Archa Noe*, 2.2 (Sicard 34.32-56; CSMV 74–75).

73. *Archa Noe*, 1.8 (Sicard 12.79; CSMV 53).

74. *Quat. volunt.*, (PL 176:844B): "Nunc ergo mutabilitate sua bene utrumque utitur, si et caro in passione patientiam non deserit, et animus in compassione justitiae mensuram non transcendit."

75. *Archa Noe*, 2.11 (Sicard 46.90–95; CSMV 86).

DALE M. COULTER

9 Contemplation as "Speculation"
A Comparison of Boethius, Hugh of St. Victor, and Richard of St. Victor

Following late antique thinkers like Augustine, Boethius, and Ps.-Dionysius, the Victorines framed the mystical life as a hermeneutical journey in which the individual learned to read correctly God's two books of scripture and creation. By rediscovering the wisdom woven into the fabric of the created order and contained within scriptural texts, the Victorine reader participated in a divine pedagogy, the point of which was to bring humanity to its ultimate end. In his earliest works (for example, *De tribus diebus, Didascalicon*), Hugh built the educational program of St. Victor around this idea, which Richard continued to use as a basis for a more systematic understanding of mystical ascent. Such a program was "scientific" and humanistic for its day insofar as it concerned forming faithful interpreters who could extract the appropriate meaning out of both books in order to reconstruct a coherent picture of life that enabled humans to fulfill their purpose.

One of the key ideas central to forming faithful interpreters may be viewed through the Victorine use of the term "speculation" (*speculatio*) and its connection to the medieval term for mirrors (*speculum*). As Javelet observes, "*The word 'speculation' is not reserved for spiritual introspection*: speculation concerns the spiritual observation of all the simulacra of nature and grace. *It embraces the entire visible world as that which resembles the invisible.* Speculation is the vision of the truth through the medium of a mirror *by the mediation of likenesses. In a broad sense all speculation is sacramental.*"[1] The adjective "sacramental" captures how the entire physical universe functions as a divine language that communicates God's purpose and nature. "Speculation," with its close connection to contemplation (*contemplatio*), communicates the process by which individuals can come to understand the universe as a reflection of God, the *simulacra* or images and shades of the divine reflected in the mirror of creation, as Javelet puts it. By examining the term *speculatio* in its Victorine milieu, one can see how study, prayer, and contemplation were all part of the same fabric, the intention of which was to peer into the mysteries (*sacramenta*) of life and, through penetrating the wondrous depths of God's two books, glimpse the being of God. A figure no less than Bonaventure would attempt to harness the Victorine approach of forming faithful interpreters as a means of integrating Aristotelian ideas into Christianity in the late thirteenth century.[2]

What complicates any discussion of the Latin term *speculatio* is the difficulty of rendering it into English. It is not exactly what is normally meant by speculation, and yet there is a sense in which it retains the idea of conjecture. *Speculatio* denotes an imaginative construction of reality that is more than merely hypothetical, in which one supposes what may be the case. Instead, it is, as Javelet notes, a vision of reality. Another way of translating the term could simply be "contemplation," and I employ this rendering in the first part of the essay. Contemplation also involves a kind of sight or vision, because to contemplate is to bring something before the mind and to gaze at it or to examine it. However, the Victorines determined that *speculatio* involved a different kind of vision than *contemplatio*, which makes contemplation a rather useless English equivalent. A third possibility, which I employ in my discussion of Hugh and Richard, is simply to render it "reflection."

Once again, this has limitations, but it underscores the mirroring effect occurring in the mental activity. *Speculatio* is a contemplative reflecting upon the created world, which itself mirrors the divine Artist. From this perspective, the world is sacramental through and through. Each of these ways of rendering *speculatio* identifies shades of meaning that unlock the Victorine use of the term, even though they all fall short of its richness.

What these various meanings point toward is a process of "extraction" in which the meaning "in" created realities must be drawn out. One might consider Richard's image of a hummingbird that remains suspended over this or that flower in order to extract the nectar. This is how the mind functions in *speculatio*. It extracts meaning by reflecting upon the created world, which is itself deemed to be a reflection of divinity. Such a process assumes that divine wisdom is woven into the very fabric of creaturely existence. In Hugh of St. Victor's words, created realities (*res*) are God's own language.[3] The world is indeed a book in which divine wisdom communicates itself to those who have "ears to hear." In order to support such a claim, I wish to draw on the Boethian background to Hugh and Richard, before turning to discuss their use of *speculatio*.

THE BOETHIAN BACKGROUND OF THE TERM

There are three contexts in the Boethian corpus that illumine the uses of *speculatio* important for Hugh and Richard. The first context connects *speculatio* to wisdom, eventually identifying it with theoretical philosophy; the second further specifies its function by attaching it to *theologia*, which concerns analyzing forms as distinct from material bodies (what Boethius calls intellectible things); and the third uses the term in relation to a discussion about universals. A brief examination of each of these contexts provides the background for the evolution of the term in Hugh and Richard.

Examination of Boethius' understanding of the term commences with the opening dialogue of his first commentary on Porphyry's *Isagoge* where Boethius discusses philosophy as involving a kind of friendship with wisdom. Such a relational connection to wisdom is possible because wisdom is a living mind (*vivax mens*) and the sole pattern (*ratio*) for all things, not simply knowledge of how to live or act in the world. This neoplatonic deification of wisdom highlights how wisdom shares its divinity with individual souls. Boethius builds upon his claim of a relational dimension by suggesting that "love of wisdom" (philosophy) involves an illumination connected to the rational soul's act of understanding that attracts the soul.[4] Illumination of the truth is also an attraction for the truth that is analogous to the attraction between two persons in friendship. In essence, Boethius is transmitting the idea of philosophy as a way of life the purpose of which, as Hadot argues, is "to form people and to transform souls."[5]

The discussion advances to a more detailed analysis of how souls participate in divine wisdom, beginning with a general division into truth and action, which Boethius connects to the Aristotelian division of philosophy into theoretical and practical. For Boethius, the Latin adjectives *speculativa* and *contemplativa* are the equivalent of the Greek term *theōrētikē*, while *activa* is the Latin equivalent of *practikē*. The pursuit of philosophy through its branches explains how wisdom gives birth to truth amidst human contemplations and thoughts (*speculationum et cogitationum*) and brings forth holy chastity in human action.[6] Chadwick suggests that Boethius establishes *speculatio* as the Latin translation of *theoria*, which involves gazing at incorporeal natures as distinct from material bodies.[7] The individual ascends from the material to the immaterial through *speculatio*. In this scheme, contemplation is not distinct from critical analysis, but advances its gaze through such mental exercises. Boethius thus places the Aristotelian division of philosophy into a neoplatonic framework to show how philosophy cultivates a love for and pursuit of the divine mind as a critical dimension of the soul's quest for wisdom.

In his *De Trinitate* book 2, Boethius identifies the threefold division of theoretical philosophy as physical science (*naturalis*), mathematics, and theology. Physical science deals with the forms of bodies and their matter, which cannot be separated from these forms. It analyzes moving bodies, like the earth, asking how form takes on motion when joined to matter. Mathematics gazes at (*speculatur*) the forms of bodies without matter, though these forms cannot be really separated from matter. In other words, mathematics helps one consider form abstracted from its material shape. Theology investigates pure form (*vere forma*) apart from all matter, and as such deals with the divine substance. Boethius envisions an upward ascent in his divisions beginning with an analysis of form and matter as a whole, then form separated from matter, and finally pure form without any association to matter. Each division not only signals a different kind of analysis but also requires higher levels of thinking.

The threefold division in the *De Trinitate* corresponds to the threefold division that Boethius provides in the first commentary on the *Isagoge*.[8] He divides theoretical philosophy into intellectible things (*intellectibilia*), intelligible things (*intelligibilia*), and natural things (*naturalia*). Natural things refer to the knowledge of corporeal bodies that Boethius terms physiology; intelligible things refer to celestial works, sublunary beings, and human souls; intellectible things refer to divinity and therefore cannot be apprehended by any of the senses. One can see that natural, intelligible, and intellectible primarily designate grades of being within a neoplatonic metaphysical hierarchy. In addition, they refer to domains of knowledge, that is, subdisciplines under the broader category of theoretical philosophy. Consequently, each level of being has its corresponding discipline of investigation, which Boethius had clearly indicated with the division of theoretical philosophy into physical science, mathematics, and theology.

In the *Consolation*, Boethius articulates what Marenbon has called the Modes of Cognition Principle to correspond to the levels of being and subdisciplines of theoretical philosophy.[9] The immediate context is Lady Philosophy's explanation of the compatibility of divine foreknowledge and future contingents. She suggests that a common mistake is when individuals think that knowledge stems from the object grasped rather than the capacity of the knower (*secundum cognoscentium facultatem*). The same object can be perceived in four different ways: sensation, imagination, reason, and understanding. Sensation perceives the material shape; imagination examines the shape apart from matter; reason examines the universal form instantiated in multiple individuals; and understanding moves beyond forms to simple Form itself with the clear vision of the mind (*pura mentis acie*). The first three modes of cognition belong to humans, while Lady Philosophy reserves the final mode for God alone; and yet, the fact that she provides a definition of eternity in order to show Boethius precisely how God grasps all things simultaneously suggests that humans can, with help, participate in the final mode. It is through the modes of cognition that humans are designed to participate in wisdom as they move through the levels of being (physical, intelligible, intellectible) by way of the subdisciplines of theoretical philosophy (physics, mathematics, theology).

Boethius says that the intellectible "consists of searching into the contemplation of God and the incorporeality of the rational soul and the consideration of true philosophy."[10] *Speculatio* is here further specified as an activity of theology. Elsewhere, Boethius refers to someone who can grasp divine eternity as a *speculator divini* and notes that *speculatio mentis divinae* liberates human souls from earthly concerns, bringing a greater degree of freedom to them than they previously had.[11] These references not only connect his use of *speculatio* to the third branch of theoretical philosophy, which is concerned with pure form and thus God himself, but also imply that intellectual progress requires moral progress from the transitory to the permanent; there is indeed a kind of friendship at work.

The final context where Boethius uses the term concerns a discussion about universals in the first commentary of the *Isagoge*. When seeking to answer the question of whether genera and species genuinely exist or are merely conceptual categories of the human intellect, he addresses how the human mind moves from corporeal to incorporeal things. He states, "Since the human rational soul is multiform, it understands objects subjected to the senses through the nature of the senses and from these things—which have been conceived by a kind of contemplation—it secures a way for it to understand incorporeal things."[12] Boethius uses *speculatio* to describe how the rational soul (*animus*) abstracts universals from particulars. The particular reflects the universal, which in turn the rational soul conceptualizes in a kind of mental reflection in order to come to an awareness of the universal. There is a continuous mirroring effect throughout the process grounded in the imprinting of an imaginative depiction of a created form upon the mind.

In this brief description of Boethius' use of *speculatio*, three contexts have been examined that help to determine how the term functions in Hugh and Richard. First, the term underscores how the divine mind communicates truth to the human mind through a relational connection that engenders a kind of friendship and fosters a way of living in the world. Conscious awareness of the truth stems from an active reflection upon created things themselves and the way they mirror other realities. Second, the term refers to the theoretical branch of science in which it becomes synonymous with *contemplativa*. In this context, it summarizes the entire process of moving from an examination of form and matter, to an examination of form apart from matter, and finally to an examination of pure form. Third, the term explains the process of "extracting" a universal from a particular. The particular reflects the universal, which is in turn reflected in the rational soul. All of these uses point toward a method of moving upward through a process of "extraction" that culminates in an exploration of God himself. The individual branches of theoretical science aid this process along the way by providing the tools necessary to understand an object in relation to its level of existence. These uses become important for Hugh and Richard as they look for a method to explore theological ideas.

THE USE OF *SPECULATIO* IN HUGH OF ST. VICTOR

Hugh utilizes a narrow range of meaning for *speculatio*. Surprisingly, the term finds little prominence in *De sacramentis* where one would expect it, if it were an important part of Hugh's methodology as a whole. Instead, his most sustained use of it is primarily in *Expositio in Ecclesiasten*, and this treatment remains brief. One must examine two alternative contexts to find what shaped Hugh's own idea of *speculatio*: the *Didascalicon*, where the term has strong Boethian influence, and the commentary on the *Celestial Hierarchy*, where Hugh must interpret its meaning within the Dionysian treatise. These two works define the boundaries of Hugh's exploration of the term, indicating that they should be examined first before moving to the treatment in *Expositio in Ecclesiasten*. Though restrictive, my claim is that Hugh builds upon Boethian ideas to define *speculatio* as a process of reflection upon the created world as a means of ascending in the mind to God. This understanding of the term allows Hugh to hold together study of the liberal arts and sacred scripture as *didascalia*, a participatory learning process that allows the individual to gaze at divine wisdom by becoming virtuous and wise. In his own way, Hugh continues the ancient understanding of philosophy as a way of life.

The *Didascalicon*

Since *speculatio* largely retains its Boethian shape in the *Didascalicon*, it requires only a brief examination. As a means of investigating the truth, Hugh suggests how *speculatio* aids the restoration of the image of God in humanity. Examining the specific function of each "science" or art reveals further how it aids the process of discovery. In this second sense, *speculatio* is part of theoretical science as the means of peering into the divine life. Exploration of these two uses of *speculatio* help to demonstrate how Hugh manipulated what he received from Boethius.

The first context reveals that Hugh identifies *speculatio* with the pursuit of truth and virtue guaranteed by wisdom, which the term philosophy encapsulates. The term enters Hugh's discourse in a lengthy quotation taken from Boethius' first commentary on Porphyry's *Isagoge*. The purpose at this point in Hugh's argument is to reinforce wisdom's role of giving birth to the truth of our contemplations and deliberations.[13] Hugh also uses the term to show how humans participate in the restoration of divine likeness through "the contemplation of truth and the exercise of virtue."[14] Wisdom remains central to this restoration because humans reflect the divine through wisdom and justice. As Hugh states, "The integrity of our nature, however, is attained in two things—in knowledge and in virtue, and in these lies our sole likeness to the supernal and divine substances."[15] Divine wisdom intersects with the mind to produce human wisdom through the enterprise of actively reflecting on the truth.

Hugh also divides wisdom into two parts: understanding (*intelligentia*) and knowledge (*scientia*).[16] Understanding encompasses both theoretical science as the "investigation of truth" and practical science as the "consideration of morals."[17] Here Hugh uses the Boethian term *speculativa* to define the activity of theoretical science. The consistent application of *speculatio* to theoretical science is further illustrated when he tells the reader that theoretical science "strives for the contemplation of the truth."[18] *Intelligentia* functions as a higher faculty in humanity that makes learning (*didascalia*) possible because it is a point of contact between the divine and human.[19] One might also think of the "understanding" as a higher level of thinking within the rational soul.

In the *Didascalicon* Hugh attempts to be consistent with Boethius' use of the term *speculatio* by maintaining its connection to wisdom and truth. *Speculatio* is a mental activity in which the divine generates understanding through a learning process that unfolds as part of the domain of theoretical science. Intelligence emerges from aptitude (*ingenium*) through inquiry. Hugh retains the Boethian division of theoretical science, with the highest branch focused upon God and spiritual creatures. It is the place where intelligence emerges as the understanding attempts to penetrate what is hidden through a process of reflection. Thus *speculatio* not only identifies a method of investigating divine things, but the very activity of *speculatio* is itself a reflection of the divine because it is wisdom at work in the human mind.

The Commentary on the *Celestial Hierarchy*

When he confronts the Dionysian system in his commentary, Hugh is once again faced with the term *speculatio*. By examining the three areas where Eriugena's translation forces Hugh to provide some interpretation for *speculatio*, a clearer picture of its semantic range emerges. It becomes evident that the term indicates some type of vision, whether inward or outward, of an object. Furthermore, this vision seeks to comprehend the object in question by defining it in ways that are understandable to the human mind. These semantic uses provide the parameters for its operation and so move one closer to the meaning Hugh associates with the term.

Hugh first attempts to explain the statement, "I think, therefore, that the first task must be to set forth what we think the contemplation of every hierarchy is."[20] He offers his interpretation of the statement: "[Dionysius] calls contemplation a definition because the definition of a thing is like a mirror where its nature is perceived, as for instance, the nature of a body seems to be the image opposite it in a mirror."[21] A definition, then, functions as a kind of reflection of the object being defined. Hugh suggests that a definition can function in a more general sense when it takes into account the generic features of an object, or it can function more narrowly when it refers to a specific set of features. Defining a hierarchy as angelic provides an example of the latter because it only refers to a specific type of hierarchy and does not encompass human hierarchies. In explaining what the contemplation of a hierarchy might be, Hugh has further refined his understanding of *speculatio* to include a process of defining an object or term either generally or specifically.

Hugh's exposition of chapter 7 of the *Celestial Hierarchy* provides another glimpse at his understanding of the term.[22] The chapter in question concerns the explanation of the hierarchy that exists closest to God himself. The Latin text of the *Celestial Hierarchy* identifies these angelic beings as "those who contemplate sensible symbols or gaze at intellectual ideas, not as those directed back to the divine from the diverseness in the contemplative vision of the Sacred Writer; rather, as those filled with the higher light of all immaterial knowledge."[23] For Hugh, Ps.-Dionysius is emphasizing how the highest ranks of angels know God by direct illumination; and yet Hugh also interprets this passage as implying two ways in which illumination occurs, either through the mediation of sensible symbols or the inward perception of intellectual ideas.

Sensible symbols are "material signs—whether in creatures, in the scriptures, or in divine sacraments—set forth to depict invisible realities."[24] To contemplate such symbols is to know by divine illumination their mystical signification or the invisible truth to which they point. To describe the highest orders of angels as "those who contemplate sensible symbols" (*contemplativas sensibilium symbolorum*), then, is to indicate how these beings perceive God through the immediate and direct awareness of the truth embodied in the symbol. The illumination in question concerns the meaning of an external object, and thus Hugh considers it as outward in focus. Conversely, to describe such angels as "those who gaze at intellectual ideas" (*intellectualium speculativas*) is to indicate how they perceive God through the pure and unclothed truth (*puram et nudam veritatem*). By "pure and unclothed truth" Hugh means that there are no material signs in which the truth is packaged. One might consider how Hugh thinks of spiritual interpretation. Literal interpretation involves going from the human words to the realities intended by the human author (words to things). Spiritual interpretation begins with the realities the human author intended and then asks whether they do not point beyond themselves to other realities (such as moral, theological, or eschatological realities). To contemplate sensible symbols is to receive direct illumination as to what "other realities" those symbols point to, but Hugh suggests that one could also perceive the truth without any material pointers to serve as symbols. The truth is no longer "clothed" in material symbolism. The adjective *contemplativas* (contemplatives, those who contemplate) refers to perception through symbol whereas *speculativas* ("speculatives," those who gaze at) refers to perception without symbol. Both adjectives underscore how divine illumination works with rational beings to reveal the truth, albeit in different ways.

The final place where Hugh uses *speculatio* comes in an exposition of chapter 8 of the *Celestial Hierarchy*, which addresses the second hierarchy of dominions, powers, and authorities. The text of the *Celestial Hierarchy* states, "we should now move into the middle rank of celestial intellects: by exploring as much as is possible, with eyes directed beyond this world, those dominions and the truly mighty sights (*speculamina*) of divine powers and authorities."[25] The key word is *speculamina* or "sights," which Hugh interprets as *speculationes vel contemplationes*. Since the idea of vision is implicit in *speculamina*, Hugh suggests that the desire to explore these "sights" presents two possibilities: either an investigation of the dignity of these creatures by means of "speculations" and contemplations or an investigation of the angels' contemplative vision of God. Hugh does not decide which option is best, instead simply leaving the decision to his reader. What is important is the connection between exploration and the terms used. Both *speculatio* and *contemplatio* function as synonyms to represent a type of vision that emerges from an exploration of some object, in this case either God or angelic beings.

Though Hugh is faced with a different textual tradition within which *speculatio* is used, nevertheless he retains the basic sense behind the term. It is a kind of vision closely connected to contemplation. This vision emerges from the intellectual activity of forming (or having formed by divine illumination) an idea or concept. As an extension of this basic meaning underlying *speculatio*, Hugh indicates that it can refer to the definition of an object. A definition is a way of looking at an object because it reflects the qualities and attributes of the object in question. As the discussion turns to *Expositio in Ecclesiasten*, the idea of vision will remain the driving element behind the term and its use.

Expositio in Ecclesiasten

At the beginning of the first homily on Ecclesiastes, Hugh provides two different sets of terms to explain how Solomon perceives the world as a wise man. The first set of terms—*cogitatio, meditatio, contemplatio*—point toward a kind of mental activity by which an individual perceives an object and then handles that information. The second set of terms—*meditatio, speculatio, contemplatio*—elaborates upon the function of the first set. Hugh's juxtaposition of these two sets reveals how *speculatio* ought to be understood in the present context.

The first set of terms concerns three visions of the rational soul (*rationalis animae*). Prior to making this claim Hugh indicates that an initial consideration (*consideratio*) to be made is distinguishing between the different genera of spiritual "speculations" (*speculationum*). With this statement he launches into the three visions, implying that they are the genera in question. Hugh never unpacks his meaning here, but it seems clear that the semantic range of *speculatio* can include any type of vision. *Cogitatio*, being the first vision, indicates how an image presents itself to the rational soul (*animus*) either through sense experience or through the memory. The image is initially "impressed" upon the memory. *Meditatio* is an investigation of this image that seeks to penetrate its inner meaning. This progress indicates a movement beyond the image itself through a sustained analysis of it.[26] *Contemplatio* is a free gaze of the rational soul (*liber animi contuitus*) that encompasses a variety of objects and images under one comprehensive vision. At this higher level of "thinking," the understanding becomes animated and takes on a kind of agility (*vivacitas intelligentiae*) that allows the mind to move beyond an examination of a particular image to an exploration of numerous things simultaneously. It may also indicate the relationship between an image that is examined and all of those things of which the image itself functions as a likeness.

The second set of terms (*meditatio, speculatio, contemplatio*) expands the explanation that Hugh has provided in the first set. Hugh first offers two types of *contemplatio*: the *consideratio* of creatures and the *contemplatio* of the Creator. He connects consideration of creatures to *speculatio*. While *meditatio* retains the same function as before, *contemplatio* has been expanded to incorporate *speculatio* or *consideratio*. The synonymous interplay of these two terms sets the tone for what Richard of St. Victor will do in his writings. The second list builds upon the first through an elaboration of the function of *contemplatio*. The result is a final list of four terms, which Hugh himself does not provide, but which can be inferred from the context: *cogitatio, meditatio, speculatio/consideratio*, and *contemplatio*.

When he offers a description of *speculatio*, Hugh uses the analogy of a consuming fire, which he also thinks functions well to describe Ecclesiastes' overarching purpose. Ecclesiastes, like *speculatio*, is an extended evaluation of creation centered around the theme of vanity or emptiness. A consuming fire reveals how this evaluation works and what results from it. In Hugh's extended analogy, fire symbolizes how love tames the "disturbances" of the soul.[27] When the wood is green and has not been dried out, the flame must work hard, resulting in a large amount of smoke that is an analogue to the activity of *meditatio*. With the aid of a fresh breeze of wonder (*admiratio*), the flame begins to increase and the smoke decrease until the flame's brilliance finally appears, which corresponds to the activity of *speculatio*. Hugh indicates that this movement is the rational soul (*animus*) pouring forth itself in pure mind (*pura mente*) toward the contemplation of truth. The adjective *pura* refers to the way love has focused the affections so that the passions no longer disturb the individual, causing him to lose mental acuity and focus. It is the admiration experienced through the novelty of this vision that focuses the affections and pushes the rational soul upward, renewing it and preparing it for the final surge above the transitoriness and impermanence of creation represented in *contemplatio* of the Creator.[28] The individual is indeed "caught up" emotionally in this vision. *Speculatio* involves an exploration of creation stimulated by the love enkindled through wonder at the creation itself. The rational soul is "purified" in the sense that the affections become focused and pour forth in an experience of admiration that enables the individual to rise above the creation to contemplation of the Creator.

The exploration of *speculatio* in Boethius and Hugh establishes the parameters or semantic range for the term. The basic meaning is one of vision and as such allows an association with *consideratio* and *contemplatio*, although Hugh clearly differentiates *contemplatio* from *speculatio* as different ways that vision occurs. The type of vision involves primarily an intellectual dimension yet also comprises affective elements expressed by Hugh in the idea of admiration. Boethius points toward the affective dimension by describing the connection with wisdom in terms of friendship. As an intellectual enterprise, *speculatio* entails a kind of "extraction" of meaning within created things in which their various characteristics function as symbols for some other reality. The learning process involves an attempt to move beyond materiality in order to discover the form that gives shape to it. However, this exercise is not the removal of images and flight into a purely conceptual realm so much as it is the symbolic use of images through comparison and contrast. Boethius describes this process as drawing forth a universal from a particular, or examining form and matter, form apart from matter, and pure form. For Hugh, this process concerns the construction of definitions, which are mere reflections of particular objects, or engaging the understanding to penetrate into the hidden places of an object. Theoretical science is an art that cultivates the capacity to gaze deeply at created realities (*speculativa*) because it provides the tools to aid the discovery process in the quest to examine an object. Finally, *speculatio* is a mirroring or a reflection, first, by reflecting upon an object which itself is a reflection of something deeper and, second, because its very activity is a reflection of divine wisdom. To engage in *speculatio* is participatory in the sense that the mind's reception of wisdom is a sharing of wisdom's qualities (virtue) and perception of wisdom's insights (truth). With these parameters in mind, the discussion now turns to consider Richard's own use of the term.

SPECULATIO IN THE WRITINGS OF RICHARD OF ST. VICTOR

> Although *contemplatio* and *speculatio* are usually juxtaposed and in this way often obscure and cover the proper nature of the meaning of scripture, nevertheless we more suitably and more precisely indicate *speculatio* when we perceive through a mirror, but *contemplatio* when we see the truth in its purity without any covering and veil of shadows.[29]

This quotation broadly expresses what Richard means by *speculatio* and discloses his desire to maintain its distinction from *contemplatio*, which he recognizes has not been done by other writers. The confusion brought about by the synonymous association between the terms also leads to confusion in interpretation. There are a number of interpretive issues raised by this statement that provide a way of exploring Richard's ideas about the term, such as the concept of purity or unveiled-ness (that is, with no material symbol to interpret) versus covering (that is, the truth being clothed in material symbolism). Pursuing these issues requires grounding the discussion in Richard's contrast between two kinds of individuals (*speculativa* and *contemplativa*) and his use of *speculatio* in other works, before moving to his most extensive use of the term in *De arca mystica*.

TWO KINDS OF INDIVIDUALS: SPECULATIVI AND CONTEMPLATIVI

In one of Richard's earliest works, *Liber exceptionum*, *speculativi* and *contemplativi* appear to be synonymous. Most scholars assign an early date for the work, placing it within the 1150s.[30] This would suggest that Richard composed the work while in charge of the school of novices at St. Victor.[31] In the first part, book 1, chapter 5, he discusses three kinds of "science" or arts, theoretical, practical, and mechanical, as the means to bring about the restoration of the individual from sin.[32] Much of the chapter is a redaction of Hugh's *Didascalicon*. The final sentence summarizes the meaning of the name behind each science by quoting *Didascalicon* 2.1 with one important exception. Richard quotes, "Theoretical [science] may be interpreted as contemplative (*contemplativa*), practical [science] as active, mechanical [science] as adulterate, and logic as that which concerns words (*sermocinalis*)."[33] The list shows how Hugh had altered the Boethian threefold division in order to make it correspond to his understanding of human restoration. Theoretical and practical science concerned the restoration of the soul, mechanical science the restoration of the body, and logic concerned the meaning of words necessary to understand the realities (*res*) analyzed through the other three sciences. Hugh, following Boethius, had also included the adjective *speculativa* in reference to theoretical science where Richard inserts *contemplativa*. While it is difficult to determine the reasoning behind this substitution, it suggests several possibilities: (1) Richard may not have seen any distinction between the two terms at this early stage; (2) substituting *speculativa* may indicate an attempt to begin to distinguish between the two terms. The issue must remain unresolved until other works are examined, and then it may be possible to render some judgment. What is clear is that very soon Richard began to distinguish between *speculativa* and *contemplativa* in other works.

There are four works where the adjectives *contemplativus* and *speculativus* appear in a comparison with one another: *Mysticae adnotationes in Psalmos: In Psalmum 113*; *Super exiit edictum* or *De tribus processionibus*; *De differentia sacrificii Abrahae a sacrificio beatae Mariae Virginis*; and *De arca mystica*. Chronological considerations make it somewhat difficult to examine these works in terms of a development of thought. Given the oratorical genre of certain Psalms in *Mysticae adnotationes in Psalmos* and its redaction over a period of years, the composition may be regarded as beginning earlier in Richard's life at St. Victor with the *terminus* unknown.[34] No exact date may be given for the opuscule *De differentia sacrificii Abrahae*. The extended sermon *Super exiit edictum* can more precisely be given a date somewhere between 1162 and 1173, and the *De arca mystica* assigned to the same period.³⁵ Richard's brief discussion in *De arca mystica* is very similar to that of *Mysticae adnotationes in Psalmos* suggesting that he has inserted the discussion from the Psalm into the context of the larger work. The connection between *Mysticae adnotationes* and *De arca mystica* indicates that they be examined together with *Super exiit edictum* and *De differentia sacrificii Abrahae* supplementing and filling out Richard's overall perspective.

The content of *In Psalmum 113* suggests that it may be the earliest attempt by Richard to discuss *speculativi* men as distinct from those who engage in contemplation. The discussion is based on an interpretation of Psalm 113:4, "the mountains leaped for joy like rams and the hills like the lambs of sheep," which Richard uses to describe two different kinds of men (*contemplativi* and *speculativi*) by viewing mountains as symbolic of the former and hills as symbolic of the latter. The active life is placed at the bottom of the list expanding the comparison between the active and contemplative lives into a three-tiered hierarchy of active, speculative, and contemplative. Richard's Sermon 72 uses similar imagery; however, there he identifies hills as contemplative men without any reference to *speculativi*, suggesting that no division had occurred to him at that time.³⁶

Richard begins to define the meaning of the term *speculativa* by suggesting that it identifies those men (*speculativi viri*) who examine heavenly things only through a mirror, which he defines as viewing heavenly realities through the "clouds of corporeal likenesses" (*corporalium similitudinum nubila*).³⁷ The verse under investigation, however, warrants a twofold division of *speculatio* based on lambs and sheep. Lambs represent the *speculatio* of corporeal things and sheep represent the *speculatio* of spiritual things. This division is further identified with the two lower ranks of angels in the Dionysian *Celestial Hierarchy*. Richard draws an analogy between the lower ranks of angels and individual men. Like the lower ranks of angels, *speculativi viri* contemplate the divine life but only through the higher ranks that exist above them and that form mirrors through which they may perceive divinity. While the object and goal of their vision is the same as "contemplative angels" (*contemplativa*), they must always examine this object (and so reach their goal) through a medium of some sort. Admiration or wonder (*admiratio*) reinforces the ascent by accompanying the investigation of each object. As with Hugh, wonder is the affective component that attracts and engages the mind, leading the entire person — affective and rational dimensions — toward the goal. Those men whom Richard describes as *speculativi*, therefore, move in admiration from corporeal likenesses to spiritual likenesses, and finally experience a type of ecstasy of mind (*per mentis excessus*). Yet, all of this occurs through a reflecting upon (*speculando*) something else that serves as a mirror of the divine.

A similar pattern emerges in *De differentia sacrificii Abrahae* and *Super exiit edictum*. In *De differentia sacrificii Abrahae* Richard uses the three-tiered system of active, speculative, and contemplative to describe three different lives that function as stages in the life of Abraham. The life of reflection (*speculativa vita*) and the contemplative life (*contemplativa vita*) become subdivisions of contemplation that share the same goal, although obtaining that goal either through the mediation of likenesses or through the clarity of unveiled vision.[38] The sermon *Super exiit edictum* follows a three-tiered system of speculative, contemplative, and prophetic men to explain the ascension of Christ. Richard compares speculative men to the men of Galilee in Acts 1:11 who stand on earth and gaze at Christ as he ascends to be with the Father. To stand on earth is to employ earthly and visible realities in order to know invisible realities. By using the imagination, speculative men can move from investigation of the visible to an understanding (*intelligentia*) of the invisible.[39]

The discussion in *De arca mystica* 5.14 comes in the context of the three modes of contemplation (expansion of mind, elevation of mind, and disengagement of mind) and reproduces the argument found in Richard's treatment of Psalm 113. Only two points need to be mentioned. First, in this chapter Richard sets forth the definition of *speculatio* as concerning a vision reflected by the mirror of the world. Second, the juxtaposition of Richard's examination of individuals who engage in reflection (*speculativi viri*) and contemplative individuals (*contemplativi viri*), and his subsequent formulation of a definition for contemplation and reflection, underscores their connection. Both move toward the same goal, yet arrive by different means. Individuals who engage in reflection (*speculativi viri*) encounter the divine through images whereas contemplative individuals (*contemplativi viri*) encounter it without any veil. One can see how the adjectives *contemplativus* and *speculativus* allowed Richard to formulate two distinct approaches to God that complemented the meaning Hugh had attached to *speculatio* and *contemplatio*.

Speculatio in *De duodecim patriarchis*

The work under consideration here was most likely written as part of a trilogy with *De arca mystica* and *De exterminatione mali et promotione boni*. It is clear from internal considerations that *De duodecim patriarchis* was written first with *De exterminatione mali*, building on its themes.[40] Châtillon suggests that the three works constitute a spiritual journey from Genesis (*De duodecim patriarchis*) to the ark of the covenant in Exodus (*De arca mystica*) and the crossing of the Jordan in Joshua (*De exterminatione mali*).[41] The extensive treatment of *speculatio* in *De duodecim patriarchis* and *De arca mystica* warrants an examination of both works while the minor use given to the term and the repetition of themes in *De exterminatione mali* precludes any examination.

There are four aspects of *speculatio* in *De duodecim patriarchis*. First, Richard indicates that *speculatio* points to the condescension of divine concepts to the human mind. Responding to this condescension entails a mental process of "extraction," beginning in imagination and rising through the reason and the understanding (*intelligentia*). At each stage a different "faculty" or a higher level of thinking is necessary. The term also expresses the kind of analysis that occurs during each level of mental activity and in this sense is related to *consideratio*. Finally, the term hints at the goal of this process: gaining a clearer glimpse of invisible things that are not readily accessible to the *animus*.

Richard sees the scriptures as expressing divine ideas in a way that can be grasped by the human mind.[42] The images contained in scripture act as a stimulus through their beauty rather than their deformity as in Dionysian thought.[43] The images of heavenly realities in scripture (for example, streets of gold and gates of pearl) only exist in a likeness (*per similitudinem*), they are not actually present (*per speciem*) in heaven. Scripture functions in such a way as to require *speculatio*. It is a form of accommodation to human weakness because scriptural images enable the activity of *speculatio* to occur, which enables upward ascent to divine things.

This upward ascent through the image begins with the imagination because it is the faculty of the mind that forms (*imaginari*) the image.[44] Richard further specifies the "rational imagination" as that which secures images received and constructed from sense data, as opposed to the "bestial imagination," which simply roams freely over what is seen or performed without sustaining any image of the data received. The former represents a focused mind in control of the images in its imaginary world, whereas the latter represents a mind that lacks control where images simply float freely. The imagination is the place where various images can be put together, which allows us to move beyond what each image portrays on its own. Richard gives the example of the image of gold and of a house being put together to form a gold house in the mind. This type of activity explains why a conception of the future life—either its punishment or rewards—is possible, reinforcing the need for the imagination.

In chapter 18, Richard describes the twofold *speculatio* resulting from the image formed by the imagination. The first type of *speculatio* is when reason arranges (*disposita*) the image by associating it with another image of something visible, like the example of a golden house given above. Richard identifies this process as a *consideratio* of future evils as well as a *speculatio*, which underscores the close relationship between the two terms. To gain a picture of hell, for instance, one does not have to move beyond the imagery of visible things already available, that is, a literal understanding of scripture. It is merely by associating images such as fire and darkness that the mind can have some conception of what hell may be like. Meditation or sustained thought further aids the individual in this process. The true imagination of present life allows a fictive (*fictam*) imagination of the future life. This type of *speculatio* deals with words and things on a superficial level by a process involving the mental faculties of imagination and reason and the activity of meditation or sustained thought.

The second type of *speculatio* is when the imagination becomes mixed with the understanding (*permixta intelligentia*) by moving beyond the external appearance (*speciem*) of the image to some knowledge of an invisible reality. Richard calls this process a *speculatio* of future goods. Future goods cannot be interpreted in a literal manner, and so the earthly reality described in the text must be transcended. Richard refers to this activity as a *comparatio*, since a comparison between present goods and future goods occurs, and a *translatio* because the image of visible things must point beyond itself, signifying some invisible thing. Two examples serve to depict both aspects of this *speculatio*. The visible goods of the present life can be looked at in terms of their multitude and magnitude. The multitude of visible goods that are presently enjoyed points to the amount of invisible goods that will be enjoyed in the future. Likewise, the magnitude of visible goods, such as the light of the sun, indicates the greatness of invisible goods such as the spiritual light that the angels share. As the nature of visible goods is examined, it can signify any aspect of the future and thus be translated or compared to the nature of invisible things.[45]

This brief examination of *speculatio* in *De duodecim patriarchis* underscores its importance for Richard. *Speculatio* points to the way the divine condescends to human minds by mirroring its own reality in the created universe and most particularly in scripture. By using *translatio* or *comparatio* the individual is able to move upward from the visible world toward the divine. These two ideas mine the quality found in the nature of each object to find some relationship that exists between the visible and the invisible. In *comparatio* the imagination is mixed with reason and in *translatio* it is mixed with understanding, pointing to a process of "extraction" that involves successively higher levels of thinking.

SPECULATIO IN THE DE ARCA MYSTICA

The *De arca mystica* elaborates on the idea of *speculatio* as a process of "extraction." In fact, the six genera of contemplation are more appropriately types of *speculatio* because they involve extracting meaning in order to ascend.[46] *De arca mystica* completes the picture of *speculatio* offered thus far by introducing two more facets of the term. As an activity of "extraction," *speculatio* involves investigating and drawing forth likenesses from each object being considered.

Richard expresses the process of "extraction" by employing a number of verbs (*trahere, eruere*). This activity of *speculatio* takes place on two levels. The first is the interpretation of the text of scripture with which Richard is working. By examining different aspects of the ark of the covenant, he can determine how they symbolize different levels of mental activity and different types of contemplation. Thus the first kind of contemplation is in imagination and is indicated by the pieces of wood that comprise the ark. The gold of the propitiatory, because it is solid gold rather than overlaid gold, as is the crown, indicates the fourth kind of contemplation, which does not utilize any imagination.

The second level of "extraction" is the actual ascent Richard is attempting to describe in his exegesis of the ark passage. The movement then is from visible things (first genus of contemplation/*speculatio*) to their inner structure (*ratio*; second genus of contemplation/*speculatio*), drawing out analogies for invisible things (third genus of contemplation/*speculatio*), invisible spiritual things (fourth genus of contemplation/*speculatio*), and concluding in divine things (fifth and sixth genera of contemplation/*speculatio*). The increase in mental activity enables the *speculatio* to further penetrate the object in order to draw forth the necessary likeness, which can then be applied to the next level.

SPECULATIO, MIRRORING, AND THE HUMAN MIND

Speculatio characterizes a mirroring process that may be described as "extraction" rather than abstraction. It is precisely through this process of "extraction" that divine wisdom communicates truth to the human mind, and the human mind comes to participate in that wisdom. This is how the entire created world functions as a "book" that must be read. The inner structure of the human mind is such that it can receive the "forms" of all created things. This happens as images or forms are impressed upon the memory, which serves as their organizing center. The mental image is itself a reflection of the created object. As such the mind can begin to meditate upon it and to investigate its various features. Investigation of individual features prepares the mind to extract analogies that serve as windows onto other realities. With each "extraction" and connection to another reality, an inner delight occurs that evokes wonder and drives the process onward and upward into the realm of the divine. Affective transformation in and through admiration and wonder fuels cognitive reflection and thus wisdom becomes "sweet" to the soul. Ultimately, a vision of another reality unfolds as divine wisdom intersects with human wisdom, and this vision restores the soul.

NOTES

1. "*Le mot 'spéculation' n'est pas réservé à l'introspection spirituelle*: la spéculation concerne l'observation spirituelle de tous les simulacres de la nature et de la grâce. *Elle embrasse tout le monde visible en tant qu'il ressemble à l'invisible*. La spéculation, c'est la vision de la vérité par le moyen d'un miroir, *par la médiation*

des ressemblances. Toute spéculation est sacramentelle au sens large": Javelet, *Image et ressemblance*, 377, emphasis in original. Javelet provides a discussion for the wider use of the term in the twelfth century, 376–90.

2. See Bonaventure's *De reductione artium ad theologiam* and *Itinerarium mentis in Deum*.

3. Hugh of St. Victor, *Didascalicon* 5.3, ed. Buttimer, 96; trans. Taylor, 121.

4. Boethius employs the term *animus*, which functions as a generic description of the rational dimension of the human person as opposed to the physical/bodily dimension. Thus it is shorthand for what today is called the soul or the mind with all of its cognitive and affective functions. For this reason, I translate it as "rational soul."

5. P. Hadot, *Philosophy as a Way of Life*, 20.

6. "Haec igitur sapientia cuncto animarum generi meritum suae divinitatis imponit, et ad propriam naturae vim puritatemque reducit. Hinc nascitur speculationum cogitationumque veritas, et sancta puraque actuum castimonia." (Therefore, this wisdom confers the benefit of its own divinity to all manner of souls and leads them back to the proper strength and purity of their nature. It gives birth to the truth of our contemplations and deliberations and the holy and pure chastity of our actions.) Boethius, *In Porphyrium dialogi*, PL 64:10D–11A.

7. Chadwick, *Boethius*, 131–32.

8. Ibid., 111, notes that the two separate accounts should not be thought of as contradictory.

9. Marenbon, *Boethius*, 130–35.

10. "Quae res ad speculationem Dei atque ad animi incorporalitatem considerationemque verae philosophiae indagatione componitur": Boethius, *In Porphyrium dialogi* 1.3, PL 64:11C.

11. Boethius, *De consolatione philosophiae* 5.6, ed. Goold, 428; 5.1, 392.

12. "Quoniam hominum multiformis est animus per sensuum qualitatem res sensibus subjectas intelligit, et ex his quadam speculatione concepta, viam sibi ad incorporalia intelligenda praemunit": Boethius, *In Porphyrium dialogi*, PL 64:19A.

13. Hugh of St. Victor, *Didascalicon* 1.2, ed. Buttimer, 7; trans. Taylor, 48. See full Boethian reference in n. 6.

14. "Duo vero sunt quae divinam in homine similitudinem reparant, id est, speculatio veritatis et virtutis exercitium": ibid., 1.8, ed. Buttimer, 15; trans. Taylor, 54.

15. Ibid., 1.5, ed. Buttimer; trans. Taylor, 52.

16. See ibid., Taylor's trans., 190, n. 57, for a brief explanation surrounding this distinction.

17. Ibid., 1.8, ed. Buttimer, 15; trans. Taylor, 55.

18. Ibid.,1.11, ed. Buttimer, 22; trans. Taylor, 60.

19. In *De unione corporis et spiritus*, PL 177:288D–0289C, Hugh states, "Finally, there is pure reason, beyond imagination, in which reason is lifted upward from the body to the highest point of the soul. However, when it is lifted upward from the soul to God, first there is understanding, which is reason formed from

within because the divine presence, coming together with reason, is joined to it and, informing reason from above, the divine presence creates wisdom or understanding." ("Deinde ratio pura supra imaginationem in qua ratione supremum est animae a corpore sursum. Quando autem ab anima sursum ad Deum, prima est intelligentia, quae est ratio ab interiori formata, quia rationi concurrens conjungitur praesentia divina, quae sursum informans rationem facit sapientiam, sive intelligentiam.") See also the discussion of *ratio* and *intelligentia* in Kleinz, The Theory of Knowledge, 63–86.

20. "Oportet ergo, ut existimo, primum exponere quam quidem esse speculationem omnis hierarchiae existimamus": Hugh of St. Victor, *In Hierarchiam Coelestem* 3.2, PL 175:955C.

21. "Definitionem autem idcirco speculationem vocat; quoniam definitio rei quasi speculum est, in qua ipsius rei natura cernitur, sicut in speculo natura corporis appositi imago videtur": ibid., 3.2, PL 175: 962D.

22. Ibid., 7, PL 175:1053B–1054D.

23. "Contemplativasque iterum sensibilium symbolorum, aut intellectualium speculativas, neque ut varietate sacrescribentis theoriae in divinum reductas; sed, ut omnis immaterialis scientiae altiori lumine repletas": ibid., 7, PL 175: 1053B.

24. "Sensibilia symbola materialia sunt signa, sive in creaturis, sive in Scripturis, sive in sacramentis divinis, ad demonstrationem invisibilium proposita": ibid., 7, PL 175:1053B. I take the term *demonstratio* as meaning a showing or pointing toward, not in the technical sense of logical argument.

25. ". . . transeundum, inquit, nunc nobis est in mediam coelestium intellectuum dispositionem: dominationes, illas supermundanis oculis, quantum possibile est, explorantibus, et vere potentia speculamina divinarum potestatum, et virtutum": ibid., 8, PL 175:1074A.

26. In *De meditatione*, 44, Hugh defines meditation as, "constant thought investigating the manner, cause, and reason of each thing. Manner asks what it is; cause asks why it is; reason asks how it is." ("Meditatio est frequens cogitatio modum et causam et rationem uniuscuiusque rei investigans. Modum: quid sit. Causam: quare sit. Rationem: quomodo sit. In *Didascalicon* 3.10 (ed. Buttimer, 59; trans. Taylor, 92), he states, "meditation is sustained thought along planned lines: it prudently investigates the cause and the source, the manner, and the utility of each thing." ("Meditatio est cogitatio frequens cum consilio, quae causam et originem, modum et utilitatem uniuscuiusque rei prudenter investigat.")

27. Hugh employs the Ciceronian term *perturbatio* (disturbance, agitation) for passions to describe them as negative forces.

28. "In speculatione, novitas insolitae visionis in admirationem sublevat": Hugh of St. Victor, *In Salomonis Ecclesiasten homiliae*, first homily, PL 175:118B.

29. "Quamvis enim contemplatio et speculatio per invicem poni soleant et in hoc ipso saepe scripturae sententiae proprietatem obnubilent et involvant, aptius tamen et expressius speculationem dicimus, quando per speculum cernimus, contemplationem vero, quando veritatem sine aliquo involucro umbrarumque ve-

lamine in sui puritate videmus": Richard of St. Victor, *De arca mystica* 5.14, ed. Aris, 143.

30. See Richard de St. Victor, *Liber exceptionum*, 78; Châtillon recommends the dates 1153 and 1160, with the final date being 1162 when Richard became prior. On the *Liber exceptionum*, see Dale M. Coulter, "Introduction to the *Book of Notes*" in Harkins and van Liere, *Interpretation of Scripture*, 289–96.

31. See Coulter, *Per visibilia*, 246–47.

32. The title of the chapter is *De tribus scientiis*, which could be rendered "On Three Sciences." In *Didascalicon* Hugh indicates that philosophy is the "art of arts" and, as an art, can be called a "science" (*scientia*). One could also render *scientia* in the more basic sense of "knowledge." See Hugh of St. Victor, *Didascalicon* 2.1, ed. Buttimer, 23; trans. Taylor, 61.

33. Richard of St Victor, *Liber exceptionum*, 1.5, ed. Châtillon, 1.5, 106. The quotation is from Hugh of St. Victor, *Didascalicon* 2.1 ed. Buttimer, 24; trans. Taylor, 62. Taylor notes that Hugh identified the mechanical arts as adulterate from a false connection to the Latin term *moechus*, which means adulterer. See Taylor trans., 191, n. 64.

34. A critical edition of the *Mysticae adnotationes*, retitled *Tractatus super quosdam in Psalmos*, edited with an English translation and introduction by Christopher P. Evans, is forthcoming from Brepols. In it, Evans explores most of the issues related to the work.

35. Compare Châtillon's introduction in Richard de St. Victor, *Sermons et opuscules*, xl–xlv.

36. The *Sermones centum* was compiled over a number of years. The first thirty sermons must be dated early—not later than 1160—since they are found in the *Liber exceptionum*. Sermon 40 has a quotation from Bernard of Clairvaux's *De consideratione* indicating that it must be dated after his death (1153). Châtillon, "Le contenu, l'authenticité et la date," outlines a chronology, deciding that the sermons were composed over a period of twelve to fifteen years, most likely between 1147 and 1165.

37. PL 196:337D.

38. PL 196:1055A–B.

39. Richard de St. Victor, *Sermons et opuscules spirituels*, 76, 78, 80.

40. Richard states, "elsewhere we have already indicated" in *De exterminatione mali et promotione boni* 3.6, PL 196:1106D, referring to *De duodecim patriarchis/Benjamin minor*.

41. Châtillon, "Richard de Saint-Victor," 617.

42. *De duodecim patriarchis/Benjamin minor*, 15; Richard de Saint-Victor, *Les Douze Patriarches*, 128–30.

43. In Hugh's Latin text of the *Celestial Hierarchy*, Ps.-Dionysius indicates that he would not have been led to anagogy through his examination of the angels in scripture "if the deformity had not forced us" ("nisi deformitas nos extorqueret"), *In Hierarcham Coelestem* 3, PL 175:960B, which Hugh interprets as "if the deformity of

the shape by which the angels are shown in sacred scripture had not compelled" ("nisi deformitas formationis, per quam in Scriptura sacra manifestantur, angeli, compelleret,"), PL 175:988D. It is the seemingly deformed depiction of the angels that compels the interpreter to move into anagogy rather than the beauty of the form.

    44. *De duodecim patriarchis/Benjamin minor* 17; Richard of St. Victor, *Les Douze Patriarches*, 134.

    45. Richard, following Hugh, says that things can have as many significations as they have properties: *Liber exceptionum* 2.5, ed. Châtillon, 116–17.

    46. Zinn, in his introduction to Richard of St. Victor, *The Twelve Patriarchs*, 25, notes that Richard refers most frequently to kinds of *speculatio* rather than *contemplatio*.

MARCIA L. COLISH

10 *Synderesis* and Conscience
Stoicism and Its Medieval Transformations

Conscience is a theme frequently flagged as a key aspect of the Stoics' moral philosophy. Beyond mere consciousness, our self-awareness as agents moral and otherwise, conscience specifies the ethical norms we invoke in judging our experience and acting on it. Specialists on Stoicism in antiquity have studied how members of that school think we acquire these norms, how we apply them in concrete individual cases, and how we evaluate that activity, prospectively or retrospectively. Whether the analysis depends, or not, on Ancient Stoic monopsychism has also drawn their attention. Less fully explored is the question of whether the Stoics think we can act against conscience, and if so, why and how. As these topics were appropriated by the postclassical heirs of the Stoics, this last point also included the grasp of first principles (*synderesis*) in relation to conscience. In tracking its medieval fortunes in patristic and scholastic authors, whether in Stoic or modified form, and whether attributed or not, we will note as well some of the related ideas with which this doctrine traveled.

The individual Stoic philosophers were not equally interested in the psychodynamics of self-knowledge and self-control, and they were far from consistent or systematic when they did address it, a lack of consensus duly reflected by modern commentators. Patristic and medieval authors were also selective. If, with Tertullian's *Seneca saepe noster* and Dante's *Seneca morale*, they sometimes named names, they also absorbed many Stoic doctrines indirectly, without identity-tags. If they processed Stoicism through a biblical template, they also processed the Bible through a philosophical template. The traffic was a two-way street. If and when traffic signs were posted, they were not always heeded or enforced. Some doctrines taught by the Stoics, among others, retained their vigor and identity across the postclassical divide. The Delphic injunction, "Know thyself," is a salient example.[1] Also notable in this regard are right reason or natural law as a source of universally accessible moral norms, casuistic considerations in applying them, and intentionality as the essence of the moral act. All are invoked as criteria in self-examination, in classical Latin authors who are not professed Stoics, as well as in patristic and medieval authors.[2]

If some Stoic notions survive more or less intact, others are appropriated in association with other elements, whether philosophical or theological. Critical here is St. Paul on conscience. While the Apostle defends a natural moral law whose accessibility is part of our general human endowment, he regards it as innate, inscribed on the fleshy tablets of the heart. Other biblical authors also locate ethical values in the heart. Like Paul, they often lament the ways in which we besmirch our heart and seek its repristination. They agree that a clean heart requires divine aid as well as human effort, and obedience not only to natural law but also to a divine law that may or may not coincide with it. Finally, while St. Paul acknowledges the possibility of a good conscience, for him conscience typically exposes our shortcomings, often reflecting the strife between flesh and spirit. The basic role of examination of conscience is to alert us to our sins, inspiring remorse and the wish to repent and do better. In these respects, St. Paul and other biblical authors reinforce some aspects of Stoicism on conscience while offering a striking alternative to it.[3]

The Stoics themselves present a range of options on how we acquire basic moral norms. The choices they posit include empirical evidence; innate, self-evident, or intuited principles; seminal reasons implanted at birth that become rational norms as we mature, whether more or less automatically, under the guidance of a tutelary *daimon* metaphorical or otherwise, or the teaching and example of the wise; conclusions derived from experience; the acquisition of passions compatible with reason (*eupatheiai*); analogical reasoning; or some combination of the above. In sharp disagreement with each other, scholars have assigned different weights to these possibilities, including alternatives found within individual Stoic authors.[4]

Commentators on examination of conscience, and not just on conscience itself, accent the Roman Stoics, and with good reason, if with no greater unanimity. They note that the Roman Stoics view this practice in diverse ways. Sometimes they see conscience as chastising us for our faults, sometimes as approving our moral victories. If the latter, they sometimes treat self-esteem as its goal and sometimes as a side effect of adherence to the good as an end in itself. The Roman Stoics enjoin self-examination in the morning, focusing our minds on our principles as we prepare to face the day's challenges and opportunities. They also advise retrospective examination in the evening, testing how well we have done that day. Sometimes they confine the analysis to the moment of decision making. They sometimes use forensic imagery, with conscience as our interrogator, judge, or censor. Sometimes they use therapeutic imagery. If so, they prescribe self-examination as an analgesic, an antibiotic, a palliative, a prophylactic, an upper, a downer, or a performance-enhancing drug. Context, audience, genre, and the author's general attitude or occasional tone of voice color these options, and they are rarely preclusive.[5]

The single most important Roman Stoic author on conscience in the patristic and medieval sequel is Seneca. This is not because he has a systematic theory, despite some scholarly efforts to provide him with one.[6] He is more accessible than the other Roman Stoics, and not only because he writes in Latin. For, like most people, and unlike Marcus Aurelius, he is under authority, not a *divus princeps* limited only by the burdens and hazards of empire.[7] Unlike Epictetus, he is a moderate, not an ethical rigorist. And, while inheriting a standard Stoic syllabus on conscience, Seneca enlarges it, adding topics and terminology not found in earlier or later Stoics, yielding positions that could offer a shock of recognition to patristic and medieval Christians.

The theme attracting the most scholarly debate pertinent to his later influence is Seneca on the will. His contribution here leads one prominent expositor to end his account with Seneca, presenting the Roman Stoics on the will in inverse chronological but ascending order.[8] Earlier Stoics had treated freedom of the will mainly in relation to the ineluctable laws of nature.[9] Without ignoring the cosmic dimension, the Roman Stoics shift the focus to the will vis-à-vis reason or the passions. Whatever their audience, they write in a largely hortatory vein, thus accenting a "can-do" approach, agreeing that we can indeed make the laws of nature the law of our own being.[10] The will is a function of the mind as our ruling principle (*hegemonikon*). It is not an affect or an instinct, even for Stoics who bypass monopsychism.[11] The intellectualizing of the will shifts the discussion to the relations between the will and reason. Some scholars argue for the primacy of reason over the will in Roman Stoicism. For Seneca and Epictetus, they note, once reason identifies the good, the will perforce accepts its judgment, acting on it without demur or hesitation. Commentators also observe that both authors reprise the Stoic doctrine of the vital tension responsible for a being's internal coherence (*tonos*) in explaining the will's adherence to these judgments, both initially and over time.[12] Other scholars emphasize the primacy of the will over reason in Seneca and Epictetus, seeing Seneca as a major source of Christian voluntarism or even claiming that he reduces the self as such to the will.[13]

Neither interpretation makes it possible for Seneca to posit a conflict between reason and will, or to see a bad will as occupying the same psychic space as a good will. Yet, some of the same scholars cite his point that we experience shame when we act against a good will, and that our will can waver in its objects and be divided against itself.[14] This insight explains Seneca's reframing of Chrysippus' classic image of the rolling cylinder. For Chrysippus, the cylinder necessarily describes a circular motion when it is pushed, although whether it is pushed is a matter of contingency. Seneca shifts this metaphor from physics to ethics. Removing the rolling cylinder from the context of freedom and determinism, Seneca yokes it to another example, the momentum of a runner who cannot come to an abrupt stop at the end of his course, although he wills to stop. Seneca cites this phenomenon in arguing that we cannot abandon habitual vicious behavior all at once, even when we consciously condemn and reject it; ingrained bad will continues to motivate, overlap with, and override both reason and good will.[15]

These findings suggest ways in which Seneca goes beyond other Stoics on will and conscience. He is also critically important for his use of the term *conscientia* itself. It is true that he does not use *conscientia* in the oft-cited passage in *De ira* where he describes the nightly practice of self-examination, which he says he derives from the Pythagorean Sextius. Here and elsewhere, without using this term, Seneca advises us to examine ourselves, monitoring our success in resisting vice and our progress in curing bad habits. We should also admonish ourselves for our daily failings, alerting ourselves on what to do and to resist tomorrow. When our soul, acting as observer, internal censor, and judge (*speculator, censorque secretus, iudex*), gives us a good report, we will avoid shame for our defects and sleep in peace.[16]

In passages where Seneca does use *conscientia* in treating self-examination, he also raises the issue of thwarting or mitigating someone else's vices, not only because doing so is intrinsically good, and certainly not to gain reputation, but to satisfy our own *conscientia* next time we examine it.[17] Faced with the losing proposition of urging Nero to be merciful in the *De clementia*, he argues that, while virtue is its own reward, it is also advantageous; its possession will enable the emperor to enjoy a positive examination of conscience and the approval of the gods should they call him to account that day.[18] A by-product of *bona conscientia*, he tells Lucilius, is true happiness.[19] Shifting his metaphor, Seneca also describes *conscientia* as a gatekeeper (*ianitor*). If we have *bona conscientia*, our gates are open, since we do not fear the gaze of others. We have nothing to hide. Bad conscience closes the gates, to avoid witnesses. It fears the shadows. And why is this the case? Seneca responds that we basically know right from wrong. Still, we can will an act in opposition to that knowledge as well as in its light. Acting against conscience leads to self-flagellation. Bad conscience is driven by anxiety, depriving us of what we seek the most: security.[20]

Seneca thus realizes that we can act against conscience, and that we inflict mental suffering on ourselves when we do so. Like other Stoics, he offers a miscellany of conditions promoting that negative state: unhealthy *tonos*, laziness, ignorance, inattention, complacency, moral obtuseness, bad habits, the bad example of others, and the like. They all have the effect of pushing the question one step backward rather than answering it. This issue of the etiology of conscientious decision making is one seized on by postclassical thinkers. Their analyses resonate with and amplify Seneca. Some of the most influential figures triggering medieval discussions of conscience are among the most, and the least, coherent on its psychodynamics. This paradox applies to the three most salient patristic authors in the sequel: Ambrose, Augustine, and Jerome.

Of these, Ambrose is the richest source for the range of patristic senses given to *conscientia*. He attaches three different meanings to this term. It can signify, simply, consciousness of our inner states, which a sage can perceive in himself and others. It can signify St. Paul's innate judge of sin. Conscience can also indicate the sage's tranquil awareness of his own virtue, even in the face of external criticism and misunderstanding. One of Ambrose's most widely read works, his *De officiis*, covers all these bases.[21] His commentary on Psalm 118, also influential, describes conscience—with the Psalmist—as judging our sins.[22] On the other hand, Ambrose's treatises on the Old Testament patriarchs focus repeatedly on the good conscience of the upright. These treatises originated as sermons preparing adult catechumens for baptism, hence their upbeat character. The patriarchs are models, *exempla virtutis*, whom lay converts, as new Israelites and fellow-citizens of the saints, can actually imitate. As a motivational speaker, Ambrose accents his auditors' intellectual and volitional capacities.[23] Yet, we must note that the readership of these latter works soon shrank, given the medieval replacement of adult converts from Roman paganism by Germanic chieftains and infant baptizands.

In his own way, Augustine reflects both dependence on and independence from the Stoic view of conscience and its underpinnings. With Lactantius, he is alone among early Latin Christian writers in appropriating with approval the doctrine of the *hegemonikon*. As an analogy of the Trinity, he observes, our memory, intellect, and will are activities of a single subsistent mind. While their roles are distinguishable, they are functionally interdependent. Thus, we cannot really speak of the priority of the intellect, or of the will, without falling into error on the coequal Trinitarian persons in the unity of the Godhead. *Inter alia*, this analysis alerts us to expect to find concepts such as "individual" and "person" highlighted in the first instance in medieval discussions of Trinitarian theology and Christology. Augustine follows St. Paul on conscience as the mirror of sin and goes beyond him, in his late works, in limiting free will in any but vicious choices. Despite its initial appeal, he ends by rejecting moral autarchy and Stoic *apatheia*, the freedom from irrational passions, as either desirable or attainable, redefining the norm of virtue as *caritas*, love of God and neighbor, not as rationality.²⁴ In line with that point, Augustine's fabled doctrine of the divided self is ultimately neither Pauline nor Senecan. He portrays his "O Lord, make me chaste, but not yet" state in the *Confessions* metaphorically as his simultaneous attraction to two desirable women. They represent two conflicting loves, which remain in tension in this life, in individuals and societies, like overlapping magnetic fields. Our best hope, in this life, is to order well our loves *in via*.²⁵

The third major Latin church father on conscience is Jerome. While scarcely an intellectual heavyweight, it is yet he who brings conscience and psychology together in the problematic and highly influential text that jumpstarts scholastic discussions of *synderesis* and conscience in the twelfth century. To be sure, Jerome speaks of conscience generically, and loosely, as in his commentary on the Book of Wisdom. But the key passage is in his commentary on Ezekiel, lifted most likely from Origen. This text is reprised almost verbatim in the ninth century by Rabanus Maurus and excerpted by the exegete treating Ezekiel in the twelfth-century biblical *Glossa ordinaria*. Most influentially, Jerome is quoted and the topic made canonical in Peter Lombard's *Sentences*.²⁶ The rest, as they say, is history, at least up through John Duns Scotus in the early fourteenth century, after which the theme of *synderesis* and conscience drops from the scholastic agenda, to be replaced by right reason in ethical decision making.

Jerome makes several points in his Ezekiel commentary that provide grist for the scholastic mills. Conflating Plato's subdivisions of the soul into reason, spirit, and passion, the *logikon, thumikon,* and *epithumikon,* with Aristotle's intellectual, irascible, and concupiscible faculties, he equates them, respectively, with the man, the lion, and the ox in the prophet's vision. The fourth creature in that vision, the eagle, he identifies with two terms distinct in ancient philosophy: *synderesis* (or *synteresis*) and *conscientia*. Conflating them as well, and offering no Latin translation of *synderesis*, Jerome defines *synderesis/conscientia* as the spark of reason (*scintilla rationis*) not extinguished in Cain, which inspires us to seek the good. This fourth mental faculty also enables us to acknowledge our sin when we fall, overcome by pleasure, fervor, or intellectual error. Like the eagle, it soars above the other faculties. It does not participate in their activities but corrects them when they go astray. There are notable difficulties in his account thus far. Jerome adds to them. Unlike the Cain of Genesis, his Cain does not display remorse following his sin. And, having asserted that the positive function of *synderesis/conscientia* is not extinguished, even in the worst of sinners, he observes, nonetheless, that we encounter people every day who seem to have no sense of right and wrong, and who show no compunction whatever for their misdeeds. It is easy to see why unpacking these conflations and contradictions would give Jerome's scholastic successors much to ponder.

Starting in the twelfth century, the main context in which they do so is the psychogenesis of ethical acts. The scholastics generally agree with Jerome and Peter Lombard that the *scintilla rationis* is inextinguishable. Some, taking Jerome literally, combine him with Augustine on the *hegemonikon*, arguing that the spark of reason dwells in the highest intellectual faculty.[27] But, with the advance of Aristotelianism, scholastics generally locate the spark of reason in the practical, not the theoretical, intellect. Following this line are William of Auvergne, Bonaventure, Albert the Great, Thomas Aquinas, Parisian masters of the late thirteenth century of all persuasions, and Duns Scotus.[28] Other debates flourished. *Pace* Jerome, the scholastics decided that *synderesis* and conscience are not the same thing. But how are we to understand them — as a faculty, a *habitus* or trait made connatural by exercise in Aristotle's sense, a power, a function, or an act? And, in the psychogenesis of ethical acts, what role does the will play, whether as the habitation of either *synderesis* or conscience, or in relation to the practical intellect?

In the early thirteenth century, Philip the Chancellor offers a construct that many successors accept.[29] On whether *synderesis* is a habit or a faculty, he splits the difference, calling it a *potentia habitualis*. He locates it in the will, the affective faculty, pointing us toward the good. He also grants *synderesis* a cognitive function, although not a deliberative one: a native endowment, its role is to grasp basic moral principles intuitively. For Philip, *synderesis* is infallible as well as inextinguishable in fallen humanity. Still, the faculties it informs may disobey it. Philip also distinguishes *synderesis* from conscience, and influentially so. While *synderesis* grasps the first principles of ethics, conscience applies these principles to the concrete ethical decisions made by the practical intellect and free will. In making those applications, however, conscience may be fallible.

In the second quarter of the century, John of La Rochelle largely seconds this position, although he locates *synderesis* in the intellect, not the will, and argues that conscience is an acquired, not an innate, *habitus*.[30] The followers of Alexander of Hales, who authored the text called the *Summa Halensis*, agree with Philip but add that, when it is understood simply as consciousness, conscience is neither a faculty nor a *habitus*. But it can be seen as the *habitus* enabling us to have that self-awareness and as the faculty through which we experience it. In an ethical context, they regard conscience as both innate and acquired. But they also confuse matters by stating that, while *synderesis* informs conscience, conscience itself contains innate general principles in addition to applying to concrete cases those it receives from *synderesis*.[31]

In mid-century, Bonaventure is far clearer.[32] Beginning his analysis with conscience, he states that it is a *habitus* lodged in the practical intellect. It guides the actions of the affective and operative faculty. Conscience is innate. We are all born with the capacity to grasp moral first principles when illuminated by the natural light, the *lux naturalis*. This last-mentioned qualification is important, for it situates this topic in Bonaventure's pan-illuminationist epistemology, which sees divine illumination as necessary in all modes of human knowledge. At the same time, Bonaventure regards conscience as acquired, since the information on whose basis we grasp and act on first principles also derives from sense data. Thus, conscience deals both with general ethical norms and with their practical applications. For Bonaventure, *synderesis* is also a *habitus*. It is the efficient cause of the will. Its functions vis-à-vis the will are parallel to those of conscience vis-à-vis the practical intellect. In addition to being a *habitus*, each can also be called a power (*potentia*). Since *synderesis* resides in the will, it can be impeded by voluntary foot-dragging as well as by our passions and blindness of spirit. But it cannot be extinguished. Conscience also can err, since, in guiding the practical intellect, it may make incorrect applications of general norms. This account, which accents our moral fallibility as well as the inextinguishability of our moral sense, is really the first to address Jerome's *problématique* of the unrepentant Cain and the people who seem to lack any kind of moral gyroscope, while situating the topic within Bonaventure's distinctive epistemology.

Albert the Great also offers a lucid, distinctive, and influential account.[33] He begins with *synderesis*, defined as a natural and innate habitual force (*vis cum habitu*), which furnishes inerrant and unexcogitated general moral principles to the practical intellect. *Synderesis* relays these principles to the conscience, which also inhabits the practical intellect. Conscience deals with concrete cases. It is an act, not a faculty or a *habitus*. With respect to our moral behavior, *synderesis* is the formal cause, conscience the material cause. Albert analogizes these functions to the terms of a deductive syllogism. *Synderesis* supplies the major premise. Informed by it, practical reason supplies the minor premise, addressing the major to a concrete case. Conscience then draws the conclusion, providing a judgment on our duty to perform, or avoid, the act in question.

Thomas Aquinas adds but a few refinements to Albert's position.[34] He concedes that *synderesis* can be lost, in the case of madmen and mental defectives. Otherwise, it is retained by sinners, including the damned. While he holds that, in areas of ethics pertaining to supernature, faith must join with the intuition of *synderesis* for it to be right, in areas where natural reason and natural law suffice, *synderesis* governs alone. Following Albert's syllogism analogy, he stresses that everything up to and including the judgment of conscience remains on the level of knowledge. In order to move from knowledge to act, free will must come into play. So, just as conscience can err in making specific applications of the general rules provided by *synderesis*, the will, too, may choose not to carry out the directives of conscience, whether they are correct or not. Error and sin can arise in both ways.

On the one side Bonaventure, and on the other Albert as refined by Aquinas, largely define Franciscan and Dominican teaching on this theme in the last quarter of the thirteenth century. While there are faithful followers of both positions, eclecticism is equally evident. Many contemporary scholastics, whatever their allegiances, basically slice and dice, mix and match, without adding new insights.[35] This situation holds until the arrival of Duns Scotus, the last major scholastic to treat *synderesis* and conscience. Scotus puts a distinct authorial fingerprint on this topic while incorporating insights from both mendicant schools.[36] With the Dominicans, he locates both *synderesis* and conscience in the practical intellect. *Synderesis* is both natural and innate. The moral principles it cognizes are self-evident; no Bonaventurian illuminationism is needed. Conscience applies these general principles to concrete cases. Both *synderesis* and conscience inform the will, stimulating it to choose the good when the will inclines to the good out of affection for justice. But neither intellect, knowledge, *synderesis*, nor conscience constrains the will. They are only partial causes of the will's actions. For the will can act against conscience. Even when it does not, its acts can be motivated by advantage as well as by justice—a distinction Scotus borrows from Anselm of Canterbury. The bottom line, for Scotus as for his scholastic predecessors, is that the will must act freely. Thus, while the will may be inclined to follow the advice of conscience, we have no guarantee that it will do so. This Scotist solution, nicely balancing intellectualism with voluntarism, also preserves, notwithstanding an Aristotelian scholastic faculty psychology remote from Stoicism, an echo of the Middle Stoic Panaetius' *adiaphora*, the doctrine that some things morally indifferent may be more or less acceptable, via the Ciceronian and Ambrosian doctrine of the intrinsically good and the useful, the *honestum* and the *utile*, as recast by Anselm. At the same time, Scotus shows his Aristotelian colors in citing justice as the shorthand index of virtue as an end in itself. His analysis, capitalizing on that of his scholastic forebears, offers a cogent account of how we make moral decisions, and answers the question, placed on the agenda by Seneca and problematized by Jerome, of how we can sin against conscience.

Some of the Stoics proposed the use of thought-experiments as a heuristic or rhetorical device. Concluding with one of our own, let us hypothesize Seneca's reaction were he brought back to life in the High Middle Ages to review these postclassical discussions of *synderesis* and conscience. He might well be less troubled than are some modern commentators on Seneca by the fact that some scholastics are comfortable combining innatism, self-evidence, and experience as sources of our moral norms. He would appreciate their attention to the psychodynamics of moral choice, and might even concede that their application of Aristotle's distinction between the theoretical and practical intellect is a useful addendum to his own teaching. He would be alarmed by Jerome's obfuscations and approve of the scholastics' efforts at clarification, even though *synderesis* is not a term in his own lexicon. Aware that these authors were Christians, he might yet be struck by how little their theology impinges on their handling of this particular topic. In all, most likely he would find more cause for satisfaction than dismay. While recognizing that medieval thinkers have added new instruments and a new orchestration to his score, transposing it into a new key and composing new variations, he might well conclude that many of his favorite *leitmotifs* remain fully audible, sounding, at the same time, both old and new.

NOTES

1. Courcelle, *Connais-toi toi-même*.
2. Colish *The Stoic Tradition*, 1:95–104, 136–43, 147–48, 170–71, 173, 178, 198, 209–12, 252–75, 283–89, 298–99, 302–3, 337; 2:26–33, 34, 36, 38–47, 51–54, 57, 61–62, 65–66, 68–70, 75–79, 86–87, 113–14, 117–18, 125, 127–28, 206–11, 221–25, 236, 247, 260–61, 282–90, 299–301; Blomme, *La doctrine du péché*; Delhaye, *Christian Conscience*, 24–25, 50; Verbeke, *The Presence of Stoicism*, 1–21, 67.
3. Delhaye, *Christian Conscience*, 42–49, 64–99. Both Delhaye, 50, and Verbeke, *The Presence of Stoicism*, 67, n. 97, see a carryover of the idea of conscience from Stoicism to Christianity and review the literature to date of their publications on that question. For the survival of the heart as the locus of both sin and contrition for sin in the Middle Ages, see Silvana Vecchio, "Peccatum cordis." The question of the possible influence of Stoicism on St. Paul has generated a lengthy and debated historiography, one dominated by confessional, political, and disciplinary agendas. For background on this topic, see Colish, "Stoicism and the New Testament." A more recent study, accenting Paul's use of Stoicism, Engberg-Pederson, *Paul and the Stoics*, 1–31, cites literature on this debate through the 1990s. The apocryphal correspondence between Seneca and St. Paul, while known and deemed authentic in the Middle Ages, had no influence on the topics with which this paper is concerned. On that text in the Middle Ages, see Meersseman, "Seneca maestro di spiritualità."
4. On moral norms derived from sense data albeit with a momentary lapse into innatism in Chrysippus, followed by Epictetus, many scholars have followed Sandbach, "Ennoia and Pr lepsis," at 28–30. On Chrysippean empiricism, see Gould, *The Philosophy of Chrysippus*, 62–64, 167, although he states, at 170, "Any assertions concerning the origin of moral goodness—or genuine knowledge about good things and bad things—can be but conjecture." This warning has rarely been observed. Among those convinced that Stoic empiricism rules out innatism, self-evidence, or *a priorism* of any kind, see Voelke, *L'Idée de la volonté*, 43; he also regards the *eupatheiai* as a point of transition from *oikeiosis* to mature rational *apatheiai*, at 61–65. Jackson-McCate, "The Stoic Theory of Implanted Preconceptions," sees Chrysippus on implanted moral principles as expressing a standard, not an aberrant, view, reprised by Seneca and Epictetus; but he also describes them as seminal reasons brought to fruition by analogical reasoning and as not incompatible with a *tabula rasa* epistemology in other respects. Inwood, *Reading Seneca*, 270–301, reasserts empiricism as the fundamental Stoic position yet argues for seminal reasons as implanting moral principles developed via sense experience, moral examples, and analogous reasoning. For Gill, *The Structured Self*, 132–33, 146–50, 157–62, 164–65, 181, what is innate is a universal aptitude for developing moral principles, which occurs through our complex processing of experience, teaching, and example. He in-

cludes here Epictetus, at 159–60, as versus Long, *Epictetus*, 81–82, 101–2, 113–16, who gives the strongest defense to date for fully formed innate moral norms in Epictetus; from this perspective the development of a mature moral sense is a nonevent. At the same time, Long's stress on the need to read Epictetus' ethics in the light of his theology, at 142–72, 180, 186–88, makes his "spark of the divine" view of the human soul more than a metaphor for natural human reason, seeing a tutelary divine presence supervising our moral choices as tantamount to conscience, at 186–87. Equally, however, Long argues, at 219–21, 225–27, that self-esteem governs our resistance to vicious choices for Epictetus, and that he also equates innate self-respect with conscience, thinking that instruction is needed only in the application of principles to concrete cases. On self-respect, Long follows Kamtekar, "ΑΙΔΩΣ in Epictetus," including the idea that it functions as a monitory "god within"; she sees it as a natural capacity that can be strengthened or weakened by habituation, but declines to define it either as a seminal reason or as a full-fledged norm at our birth. Agreeing on the tutelary "god within" or fragment of the deity in the human *daimon* as a function of conscience in Epictetus, Dobbin, in his commentary on his translation of Epictetus, *Discourses: Book 1*, 117–18, 188–92, 206, splits the difference among moral norms as innate ideas, as seminal reasons, and as derived from education. Marcus Aurelius is usually omitted from this debate, with good reason. As Rutherford, *The Meditations of Marcus Aurelius*, 234, 237–39, 244, observes, Marcus is all over the map in citing the sources of his own moral norms, excluding only standard *exempla virtutis* such as Socrates and Cato in preference for members of his own family, ancestors who, like himself, shouldered the burdens of empire; he is extremely vague on the nature of his *daimon*. The debate continues.

5. Kicking off the most recent round of commentary, Rabbow, *Seelenführung*, 132–40, 160–79, 180–89, emphasizes Epictetus, discussing both "orders of the day" and self-examination at the end of the day and the monitoring of both failings and moral progress. His work, however, is weakened by his use of Stoicism as the primary source for and as a *comparandum* with Christianity as exemplified by the *Spiritual Exercises* of Ignatius Loyola. I. Hadot, *Seneca* and eadem, "The Spiritual Guide," places this Stoic practice in a wider ancient tradition. P. Hadot, *Philosophy as a Way of Life*, 81–144, 179–205, notes the influence of Stoicism on early Christians, especially monastic writers, and adds the theme of thought experiments used both to test student responses in hypothetical situations and to promote a cosmic outlook on our passing concerns. He expands on this latter theme of ethics as "lived physics" in Epictetus and Marcus Aurelius in P. Hadot, *The Inner Citadel, passim* and esp. at 95–96, 181, 215, 266, 274, 307–9. Rutherford, *The Meditations of Marcus Aurelius*, 13–21, agrees that self-examination was a long-standing ancient practice and emphasizes its therapeutic aspect in Marcus. Voelke, *La philosophie comme thérapie de l'âme*, 73–106, treats Chrysippus and Marcus Aurelius on the soul but without discussing examination of conscience. Gill, "Panaetius on the Virtue of Being Yourself," focusing, unusually, on a Middle Stoic, accents the *praemeditatio futurorum malorum*

dimension of self-examination and, at 352, sees in Panaetius an element of conscious self-crafting, the moral agent's "quasi-aesthetic" appreciation of his own excellence and not just his noting of weaknesses needing correction. In idem, *Personality in Greek Epic*, 175–239, Gill emphasizes the style of self-examination from Homer to Chrysippus as an index of whether it is a dialogue between different faculties of the soul or between different options faced on the same psychic level within a unitary soul, as well as the function of this dialogue as affirming community values or not, rather than as introspection in quest of a subjective ethics. In idem, *The Structured Self*, 389–91, he accents the function in the Roman Stoics of self-examination in internalizing objective values, whether or not they accepted Ancient Stoic monopsychism. It is striking that Sorabji, *Self*, 178–79, 182, 191–95, while he notes Seneca, Epictetus, and Marcus Aurelius on daily self-interrogation, morning and evening, discusses the intra-psychic process only in connection with Proclus, at 249, 260–61, and tends to understand conscience merely as self-consciousness in these exercises. For a convincing critique of scholars who have sought to assimilate this practice, or the practice of Stoic meditation as such, to Michel Foucault's "care of the self," see Kolbet, "Athanasius, the Psalms, and the Reformation of the Self," with discussion and literature at 87-88 and in n. 15. I thank Paul Kolbet for this reference.

6. This is especially the case with Zöller, *Die Vorstellung vom Willen*. A useful corrective is Inwood, *Reading Seneca*, 102–56, who accents the multiformity of Seneca's acceptations of *voluntas*. For the most recent discussion of Seneca in the Middle Ages, referencing earlier scholarship, see Carron, "Sénèque."

7. Brought out well, with pertinent *loci* on what bothered Marcus, by Rutherford, *The Meditations of Marcus Aurelius*, 229–30; Sorabji, *Self*, 179.

8. Voelke, *L'Idée de la volonté*.

9. Most fully treated by Bobzien, *Determinism and Freedom*. See also Dobbin, on Epictetus, *Discourses*, 76, 96, 112–13, 156–57, 175, 205, 207, 228.

10. Voelke, *L'Idée de la volonté*, 96–105, 126–38; Dobbin, in Epictetus, *Discourses*, 137, 141, 142.

11. Zöller, *Die Vorstellung vom Willen*, 85, 87, 91, 106–8, 129–30, 219–32.

12. Voelke, *L'Idée de la volonté*, 17–18, 30–49, 90–95, 131–39, 161–70, 174–79, 189–99; Dobbin, in Epictetus, *Discourses*, 220; Bobzien, *Determinism and Freedom*, 250–313; P. Hadot, *Philosophy as a Way of Life*, 84; Veyne, *Seneca*, 64–65.

13. Zöller, *Die Vorstellung vom Willen*, 90–93, 130–53, 179–89, 232–54; on the reduction of the self to the will, Sorabji, *Self*, 44–45, 178, 181–85.

14. Voelke, *L'Idée de la volonté*, 172–75; Zöller, *Die Vorstellung vom Willen*, 44–45; Bénatouïl, *Faire usage*, 100–105, 109–12.

15. Noted by Bénatouïl, *Faire usage*, 100–105, 109–12.

16. Seneca, *De ira* 3.36.1–3. For the consensus reading of this passage, see P. Hadot, *Philosophy as a Way of Life*, 81–125; on this practice in Epictetus and Marcus Aurelius, see P. Hadot, *The Inner Citadel*, 95–96, 181, 266, 274, 308–9; more recently see Reydams-Schils, *The Roman Stoics*, 10, 18–20, 98. Other *loci* at

Ep. 28.10 and 83.2 are considered, from the standpoint of positive self-assessment only, by Edwards, "Self-Scrutiny and Self-Transcendence," at 29–30. For other passages on self-examination in Seneca that do not use *conscientia*, see *Ep.* 16.2, *De tranquillitate animae* 6.1, *De brevitate vitae* 10.3, 10.5; he also uses *censor* language in this last-cited work, at 10.5. More dismissive of Seneca's contribution here is Veyne, *Seneca*, 75–76.

17. Seneca, *Ep.* 3.41.

18. Seneca, *De clementia* 1.1.1: "Quamvis enim recte factorum verus fructus sit fecisse nec ullum virtutum pretium dignum illis extra ipsas sit, iuvat inspicere et circumire bonam conscientiam."

19. Seneca, *Ep.* 23.7.

20. Seneca, *Ep.* 43.4–5: "Ianitores conscientia nostra, non superbia opposuit; sic vivimus, ut deprendi subito adspici. Quid autem prodest recondere se et oculos hominum auresque vitare? Bona conscientia turbam advocat, mala etiam in solitudine anxia atque sollicita est"; *Ep.* 97.12–15: "At bona conscientia prodire vult et conspici; ipsas nequitia tenebras timet; tuta scelera esse possunt, secura esse non possunt. . . . Sed nihilominus et hae illam secundae poenae premunt ac secuntur, timere semper et expavescere et securitati diffidere; . . . mala facinora conscientia flagellari et plurimum illi tormentorum esse eo, quod perpetua illam sollicitudo urget ac verberat, quod sponsoribus securitatis suae non potest credere." See also *Ep.* 105.7. Edwards, "Self-Scrutiny and Self-Transcendence," 31, notes this point with respect to *Ep.* 43 only.

21. The *loci* in this work, illustrating the full range of applications, are collected and studied by Testard, "Observations sur le thème de la *conscientia.*"

22. See Ambrose, *Expositio in Psalmi* 118.1.9–10, ed. Petchenig. See also *Ep.* 76.17, 141.43.

23. Ambrose, *De Abraham* 2.5.22, 2.6.36; *De Isaac vel anima* 6.55, 8.79; *De Iacob* 1.7.28, 1.8.39, 2.3.12. On these works, see Colish, *Ambrose's Patriarchs*.

24. For Augustine on the *hegemonikon* and *apatheia*, see Colish, *The Stoic Tradition*, 2:206–7, 236, 221–25; on the Trinitarian analogies in the human soul, see Augustine, *De trinitate* 8–14. Medieval concepts of the individual refer literally to that which is undivided or indivisible, be it a person, divine or human, who is a *res per se una*, or any entity not capable of internal subdivision regardless of its nature and perceived relationship with other entities possessing equivalent attributes, according to the logicians. On these points see, for the twelfth-century theological applications, especially the definition of *persona* of Gilbert of Poitiers and its influence, Colish, *Peter Lombard*, 1:138–42, 151–54; for logical and other applications, see Kramer and Bynum, "Revisiting the Twelfth-Century Individual."

25. The *locus classicus* is Augustine, *Confessiones* 8.5, and 8.7 for the quotation given. On the theme of ordering charity, excellent guides remain Burnaby, *Amor Dei*, and Rief, *Der Ordobegriff*. Byers, "Augustine on the 'Divided Self,'" gives the palm to Stoicism but sees virtue and vice in Augustine as a matter of intellection

not of will or love. She thereby reprises the position of Lössl, "Intellect with a (Divine) Purpose." Sorabji, "The Concept of the Will" accents the will; while granting that Augustine made a significant contribution to the theme of the divided will derived from the Stoics, especially Seneca, he sees Maximus as the thinker who fully Christianized that concept.

26. For Jerome's generic use of conscience in the Book of Wisdom commentary, see Antin, "Les idées morales de S. Jérôme," 334. The key passage in Jerome, *Commentariorum in Hezekielem libri XIV* 1.1.6–8a, and its filiation are surveyed by Baylor, *Action and Person*, 25–42, 48–69 (although he omits Bonaventure, Albert the Great, and Duns Scotus); Delhaye, *Christian Conscience*, 106–18; Lottin, "Syndérèse et conscience aux XIIe et XIIIe siècles," in his *Psychologie et morale*, 2:103–350; Potts, *Conscience in Medieval Philosophy*, and "Conscience"; and Verbeke, *The Presence of Stoicism*, 53–70. Langston, *Conscience and Other Virtues*, 8, 23–62, reprises superficially the scholastic authors considered in this paper, but merely as a curtain-raiser for modern theories. In Hoffmann, Müller, and Perkams, ed., *Das Problem der Willensschwäche*, contributors typically treat conscience and how moral agents can act against it in the context of the weakness of will theme, starting with commentaries on the *Nicomachean Ethics* in the mid-thirteenth century. The influence of Stoicism in the Middle Ages is ignored, as in Saarinen, "Weakness of Will," ibid., 331–53 at 331, 348–49, who thinks it was a Renaissance innovation. The editors, at 17–22, hold that scholastics on conscience as studied in this volume discuss it primarily in connection with original sin. I thank Mary Sirridge for this reference. On Origen as Jerome's source, see Madec, *Saint Ambroise*, 125–27, and Kries, "Origen, Plato, and Conscience," although Kries thinks that scholastic discussions began with Aquinas. Marenbon, *The Philosophy of Peter Abelard*, 267–76, 335–36, noting the existence of the idea of conscience in Abelard, laments the fact that scholars do not give him more credit for putting the topic on the scholastic agenda. But he ignores the fact that Abelard was unaware of the Hieronymian passage that set those discussions in motion, as well as the fact that scholastics were more likely to use mainstream and accredited sources such as the *Glossa ordinaria* and the Lombard, the latter of which they could not have avoided in any case after his study was mandated by the theological faculties. For Peter Lombard on conscience, see Colish, *Peter Lombard*, 1:383. Chenu, *L'Éveil de la conscience*, 17–32, concurs with Marenbon on Abelard and elsewhere in this work treats conscience in twelfth-century authors generically as interiority, intentionalism, affectivity, and self-knowledge. For the monastic focus on conscience purely in relation to moral conversion and practical ethics, see Bertola, *Il problema della coscienza*. Neither of the latter two authors notes Jerome as a source. For the shift in the meaning of *synderesis* and *scintilla animae* to signify *grunt*, or the ground of the human soul in which mystic experience occurs in Meister Eckhart, see McGinn, *The Mystical Thought of Meister Eckhart*, 38, 40, 41, and literature cited 203–4, nn. 35, 40, 41.

27. Lottin, "Syndérèse," in his *Psychologie et morale*, 2:106–8, 123–26, 128–34, 167–72, 187–96, 301–12, 317–19. The figures Lottin treats here are Mas-

ter Udo, Simon of Bisiniano, William of Auxerre, Roland of Cremona, Walter of Château-Thierry, Richard Fishacre, John of La Rochelle, Richard Rufus, and Robert Kilwardby. He notes, at 2:105–6, that the only early scholastic to reject the inextinguishability of the *scintilla rationis* is an anonymous master in the school of Laon. But Alexander of Hales indicates conditions under which *synderesis*, as the *scintilla rationis*, may be extinguished in *viatores*. See Weber, "The *Glossa in IV Sententiarum* by Alexander of Hales," 2:105–7. Langston, *Conscience and Other Virtues*, 8, errs in claiming that conscience was not seen as a faculty in the Middle Ages. He also omits the Stoics in discussing the classical backgrounds of the doctrine of conscience.

28. Lottin, "Syndérèse," in his *Psychologie et morale*, 2:134–37, 203–301, 312–32; on Scotus, see Wolter, ed. and trans., *Duns Scotus*, 44–46, 162–66.

29. Philip the Chancellor, *Summa de bono* 1. q. 4, 4. q. 2–3, ed. Wicki, 1:101–3, 192–205. The fullest account is provided by Wicki, *Die Philosophie Philipps des Kanzlers*, 84–114, 164. See also Lottin, "Syndérèse," in his *Psychologie et morale*, 2: 138–57. On Philip's influence, see Lottin, "L'Influence littéraire du Chancellier Philippe," ibid. 6:155–60.

30. John of La Rochelle, *Summa de vitiis*.

31. *Summa Halensis Ia IIae*, tr. 1. q. 2. tit. 4. m. 1–2 = Alexander of Hales, *Summa theologica*, 2:491–500; see also Lottin, "Syndérèse," in his *Psychologie et morale*, 2:174–87. Compare Weber, "The *Glossa in IV Sententiarum* by Alexander of Hales," 105–7, quoting Alexander, in II Sent. d. 40.1.

32. Bonaventure, *Commentaria in II Sententiarum* d. 39. a. 1. q. 1–3, a. 2. q. 1–3, in *Opera omnia*, 2:897–917. See also Lottin, "Syndérèse," in his *Psychologie et morale*, 2:203–10. On Bonaventure's pan-illuminationist epistemology, its sources, and its immediate influence, see Marrone, *In the Light of Thy Countenance*, 1:29–108, 122–85, 201–50. Borgonovo, *Sinderesi e coscienza*, 31–50, 52–60, 71, includes Bonaventure only to clarify Aquinas by comparison and is concerned with medieval thought only insofar as he thinks it applicable to current Roman Catholic moral theology. I thank Tobias Hoffman for the Borgonovo reference. For an accurate overview of thirteenth-century debates on the respective roles of intellect, conscience, and will with a fine discussion of Bonaventure, see Stone, "Moral Psychology before 1277." The reader is warned that this paper by Stone proves to have been plagiarized. See Dougherty et al., "40 Cases of Plagiarism," 369.

33. Albertus Magnus, *Commentarium in II Sententiarum* d. 5. a . 6. ad 6–7, d. 24. a. 14, d. 39. a. 2; *Summa de creaturis* pars 2: *De homine* q. 71–72, in *Opera omnia*, ed. Borgnet, 27:121, 412–14, 621–22; 35:590–602. See also Lottin, "Syndérèse," in his *Psychologie et morale*, 2:174–87; Dijon, "La syndérèse selon Albert le Grand"; Perkams, "Gewissensirrtum und Gewissensfreiheit," at 35, 36, 49; Müller, "*Agere contra conscientiam.*" Cunningham, *Reclaiming Moral Agency*, 119–24, 125, considers the morality of external acts, not the psychogenesis of inner intentions, in Albert.

34. Thomas Aquinas, *Commentarium in II Sententiarum* d. 7. q. 1. a. 2, d. 24. q. 2. a. 3–4, d. 39. q. 3. a. 1–3; *In III Sententiarum* d. 33. q. 2. a. 4. sol. 4, ed. Mandonnet and Moos, 2:182–86, 609–15, 995–1005; 3:1066–67; *Quaestiones disputatae*

de veritate q. 16. a. 1–q. 17. a. 1–4, ed. Spiazzi, 1:320–25; *Summa theologiae* Ia q. 79. a. 12–13; *IaIIae* q. 19. a. 5–6, Blackfriars ed. and trans., 11:187–95; 18:61–67. See also Lottin, "Syndérèse," in his *Psychologie et morale*, 2:222–35. For a recent and judicious study balancing intellect and will in Aquinas' analysis of conscientious decisions, see Sherwin, *By Knowledge and Love*, 18–62. See also Perkams, "Gewissensirrtum und Gewissensfreiheit," 35, 36–45, 48–49, who is interested in the utility of Aquinas for a philosophical position defensible today. Some recent treatments of Aquinas on conscience focus instead on the theme that conscience obliges even if it errs; see, for example, Ghisalberti, "Figure della coscienza," at 34–38; Cavalcoli, "Autoscienza e coscienza morale"; neither author notes Thomas' view that the *scintilla rationis* can be lost, as in the insane. Borgonovo, *Sinderesi e coscienza*, 69–118, 127–28, 192–227, reiterates the analytical schema of Renz, *Die Synteresis* and is primarily concerned with the issue of conscience in relation to the virtue of prudence in the judgment of cases of conscience, with respect to heretics, the invincibly ignorant, and similar issues.

35. Lottin, "Syndérèse," in his *Psychologie et morale*, 2:236–338.

36. John Duns Scotus, *Ordinatio* 2. d. 39, in Wolter, *Duns Scotus*, 45–46, 162–66. See also Ingham, "Practical Wisdom," who notes the lack of an automatic transfer of the practical wisdom informed by *synderesis* to action in Scotus, but without commenting on the role of conscience in the psychogenesis of ethical acts in him; and eadem, *La vie de la sagesse*, with a fine discussion of Scotus' thought as a synthesis of Franciscans and Dominicans on the rational will, at 69–99, 103–8, 113–28. She sees the Franciscans in particular as important for the survival of Stoicism in this area. I thank Mary Elizabeth Ingham for the latter reference. Noone, "Duns Scotus on *Incontinentia*," 294–96, 299, 303–4, stresses Scotus' location of conscience in the practical intellect and not in the will as taught by contemporaries such as Peter John Olivi and Henry of Ghent, and his view that the intellect acts determinately, on the basis of evidence or its absence, while the will's actions are indeterminate. Compare Langston, *Conscience and Other Virtues*, 53, 59, who claims that Scotus lacks a position on conscience but who then, at 54, attributes one to him that draws on both Bonaventure and Aquinas.

DOMINIQUE POIREL

11 The Spirituality and Theology of Beauty in Hugh of St. Victor

Since there are so many paths by which one might approach the work of Hugh of St. Victor, why choose to approach it by way of the theme of beauty? The first explanation that comes to mind is that Hugh wrote a great deal about beauty, be it in nature, in man, or in God himself. This explains why, after Edgar De Bruyne's pioneering work, Lenka Karfíková dedicated her extensive and erudite thesis *Schönheit in der Theologie von Sankt Victor* to this subject.[1] However, there is a second reason. It is generally accepted that the master of St. Victor was not only one of the most brilliant theologians of his time, but also one of its greatest writers.[2] Like Bernard of Clairvaux, but with his own style, Hugh was without doubt one of the finest practitioners of the artistic rhymed and rhythmed prose, which reached its peak in the twelfth century. He was not content merely to study beauty, but actually cultivated it after his own fashion. Beyond these two reasons, there is a third that, although difficult to express, is the most essential and in fact contains, reinforces, and unites the preceding reasons. There exists between Hugh and beauty a profound and mysterious complicity that transcends the level of ideas as well as the level of words. It would be best perhaps to speak of a general "climate" of simplicity, confidence, and smiling serenity that emanates from his writings. During the first half of the twelfth century, while the princes of the church were in conflict over Investiture and the Gregorian Reform, the black monks and the white monks over the return to a stricter and more austere interpretation of the Benedictine Rule, the supporters of Innocent II and those of Anacletus over the choice of the pope, and the schools and monasteries over trinitarian orthodoxy, Hugh distinguished himself with his wise, peaceful, and benevolent view of man, nature, and himself, as though he considered in each thing above all the part of light and beauty that it contains. In other words, it seems to me that with Hugh the question of the beautiful is neither secondary nor peripheral nor incidental, but is on the contrary at the very heart of his spirituality.[3]

Let us admit that beauty often occupies a minor or even suspect place in our concerns. Whether in constructions of stone or of thought, the beautiful seldom outweighs the good or the true. We are pleased if we can supplement these with beauty, as the useful is supplemented with the pleasant; but as soon as we are forced to choose, due to lack of time or money, beauty is most often the first value on the chopping block. Against this relegation of beauty to a decorative function, Hugh of St. Victor teaches us, or rather makes us experience, that the contemplation of the beautiful can be the principle of the most rigorous intellectual inquiry as well as of the most fervent spiritual life.

As evidence of this affirmation, I propose the following plan. First we will read the *De tribus diebus*, which marvels extensively at the beauty of visible beings, including man. Next, we will explore other converging but complementary views of the beautiful and its anagogic function in other works of Hugh, notably his commentary on the *Celestial Hierarchy*. In conclusion we will examine the global significance of the beautiful in the work and thought of Hugh of St. Victor, and we will see to what extent the author's vocation as a canon regular illuminates his thinking.

This is certainly a vast and challenging project. To accomplish it would require another Hugh of St. Victor. Therefore, as often as possible I will allow him to speak for himself and will be delighted if I inspire you to reread him yourself. Let us begin by adopting the warning he addresses to the reader just prior to describing the thousand beauties of creation: "I know on one hand that everything we say will remain insufficient; but this does not mean that we should silence ourselves entirely, especially on a subject that would require us, if possible, to speak in the most harmonious fashion."[4]

THE BEAUTY OF THE WORLD AND THE BEAUTY OF GOD

Hugh of St. Victor's teaching on beauty appears simple, almost banal. It could be summarized in a few words: The beautiful leads to God. However, whereas other authors develop this thesis by quickly passing from the beauty of this material and impermanent universe to the culmination of the argument, that is to say, God the creator, Hugh takes all his time to describe visible things, not merely in passing and as necessary stepping stones to superior realities, but first of all for themselves, and with a delight that is as manifest as it is infectious. Nearly half of the *De tribus diebus* is thus given over to astonishment at the created perfections of the sensible universe. Here is a sample:

> What is more beautiful than light? Although it is colorless in itself, it is the thing that, in a certain way, colors all things by illuminating them. What is more pleasant to behold than the clear sky when it shines like a sapphire and, shedding its most agreeable light, it exposes itself to our view and delights our eyes? The sun glows red like gold. The moon shines softly like amber. Some stars blaze bright as flames while others glitter with a pink light, and still others flare sometimes pink, sometimes green, sometimes white. What can be said of jewels and precious stones? Not only are they useful, but their appearance is admirable. Behold the earth, crowned with flowers. What a pleasant spectacle she offers! How she charms our eyes! How tenderly she moves us! We see red roses, white lilies, purple violets. And among all these flowers, not only their beauty, but also their origin is admirable, that is, how divine wisdom has brought forth such splendor from the dust of the ground. Finally, the greenness, most beautiful of all, how it delights the spirit of those who contemplate it when, with each new spring, new life puts out young shoots and, standing on their stems as

though trampling death beneath their feet, they rise together toward the light, offering the very image of the resurrection to come.[5]

From the Harmonious to the Astonishing

Assuredly, this passage touches the reader of today, for the emotion that it expresses with such undeniable freshness is aligned with a modern sensibility. We have no difficulty in recognizing ourselves in this esthetic joy in the presence of the myriad splendors of nature. However, Hugh's sense of the beautiful is vaster than ours. It far surpasses the satisfaction of the spectator seated in the theater of the universe. First, because the pleasure of the beautiful is not limited to sight: hearing, smell, taste, and touch — for Hugh all the senses are doors opening to the beauty of creation:

> The pleasure we have shown that the eyes take in the diversity of colors is equal to the pleasure we find in the variety of sounds. First among these comes the sweet exchange of conversation, thanks to which men communicate with one another, telling their wills, relating the past, learning of the present, announcing the future, revealing their secrets — all to such a degree that were human life deprived of this ability, it would be comparable to the life of beasts. And what of the choir of birds? And the melodious singing of the human voice? And the sweet modes of all sounds, what is the use of recalling them? For the kinds of harmony are so numerous that thought cannot take stock of them all, neither can speech readily reveal them. And yet they are all in the service of hearing and were created for its delights. The same can be said for the sense of smell. Various kinds of incense have their fragrances, perfumes have theirs, the rosebushes, the mulberry trees, the meadows, the deserts, the undergrowth, flowers and fruits — each has its fragrance, and everything that gives off a sweet perfume and spreads pleasant scents is in the service of the sense of smell and was created for its delights. In the same way, taste and touch are imbued with various pleasures, which one can appreciate enough by analogy with the preceding senses.[6]

Among the joys that hearing procures, we have seen that the first he mentions is neither the singing of birds nor even instrumental or choral music — which would not have been surprising for a religious who is dedicated by the rule of his order to the chanting of the divine office—but rather human speech and conversation. Patrice Sicard has shown the important role that a conviviality in conformity with the rule of St. Augustine plays in Hugh's spirituality.[7] Here the fact that language enables men to communicate among themselves is not so much judged useful as it is beautiful and delightful. Beyond its informative role, language is seen as a source of harmony among men. It permits people to emerge from their inwardness in order to meet one another. It is even considered a criterion of humanity because without it, says Hugh, human life would be almost comparable to that of beasts. For the speech we are dealing with here is above all the language of friendship.

This notion of a harmonious and reciprocal exchange is not incidental to Hugh's conception of beauty, as we find it in many other examples. Those whose sense of the beautiful has been largely formed by the classical notion of beauty (that is to say, pure, sober, and slightly haughty) will doubtless have a little difficulty finding in themselves Hugh's proper sense of beauty, which above all is permeated with a kind of childlike joy in the presence of the diversity, profusion, superabundance of creation. It is not by chance that the *De tribus diebus* abounds with lists. Hugh stands before nature like a child beside a table heaped high with gifts. It is too much! It is too beautiful! And it is beautiful precisely because it is too much. There is a certain feeling of excess in his sense of beauty. However, this excess is not tantamount to disorder. The profusion becomes harmony thanks to the interchange between creatures:

> Here is the sky above and the earth below. Providence has placed stars and lamps in the sky so that they might light up all that they hang above. In the air Providence has made paths for the winds and the clouds, that their turbulence might disperse them and they might pour out the rain. In the bosom of the earth, Providence has commanded the bodies of water to gather, that here and there they might leap in all directions across their chasms, wherever Providence commands them. Providence has strewn birds in the sky, plunged fishes into the waters, filled the earth with beasts, with serpents and other sorts of creeping animals and worms. Providence has enriched the different regions, causing some to overflow with fruits, some with vineyards, others with vegetables, others with cattle, others with useful herbs, others with precious stones, others with animals and monstrous

beasts, others in varied colors, others in centers for study of the liberal arts, others in metals, others in different kinds of incense, all in such a way that there is no region that does not possess more than the others of some new and special thing, no region that cannot receive something new and special from the others.[8]

Once again we notice that among the elements of beauty in the universe, Hugh introduces the activity of men alongside the products of nature. "Centers of study" are found in the company of dye-giving plants and mineral resources. This nature whose beauty he admires is not outside of man. He is himself a part of it. If he distinguishes himself from the rest of nature, it is only by his faculty to contemplate it and therefore to contemplate himself with and in it. That is why Hugh frequently moves from admiration of the universe to admiration of the human body:

> And first of all, if you look at the mechanism of this universe, you will discover how the composition of all things has been accomplished with admirable reason and wisdom; how it is adequate, appropriate, well matched, and perfected in all its parts. Within this mechanism, not only do similar beings maintain their harmony, but even those that, created by power, are born different and incompatible gather at wisdom's command into a sort of friendship and alliance. What could be more incompatible than water and fire? Yet divine prudence has so well apportioned them in nature that not only do they not break the common tie that associates them with each other, but for all beings that are born, they procure vital nourishment so that they can subsist. What to say of the structure of the human body? The articulation of all its members follows such a mutual accord that it is absolutely impossible to find a member which does not seem to have for its function the assistance of another. Thus all of nature loves itself, and in an admirable fashion, the concord among several beings, different but reduced to unity, creates a unique harmony in them all.[9]

Hugh's notion of beauty is thus the beauty of order, but not of an unmoving order, majestic and icy as death. It is a paradoxical order that seems a victory over disorder; a living and dynamic order that does not multiply the identical and stable in a sterile manner, but that harmoniously organizes change and otherness, even in the cycle of days and nights:

Who can sufficiently admire the admirable reason with which divine providence has divided the course of time? Behold, after the night comes the day, in order that drowsy creatures may be set in motion thanks to the work. Night follows day, so that rest might cheer up those who were weary. It is not always day, nor is it always night, and the duration of night and day is not always equal, lest too great a fatigue exhaust the worn out creatures, lest continual rest ruin their nature, or lest perpetual monotony should be a cause of boredom to their spirits.[10]

It follows that among the four principal elements of which beauty is composed, Hugh mentions movement and does not even hesitate to grant it a place of "preeminence, for," as he explains, "that which is mobile is closer to life than that which cannot move on its own."[11] This little sentence, which is banal only in appearance, is rich in meaning. Through it, Hugh proclaims a typically Christian concept of beauty, in that it integrates change and time. Most Greek thinkers undervalued change and time for bearing the mark of becoming and therefore for being ontologically deficient in relation to the divine, which is not only immutable but also removed from sublunary realities that are subject to the cycle of generation and decay. Hugh, on the other hand, is not afraid to grant the most important place to that which changes, moves, becomes, is born and dies to be subsequently reborn. This is what allows him to admire, "most beautiful of all," he says, "the greening of springtime,"[12] or again the cycle of the seasons:

> First, the warmth of springtime renews in some way the world and causes it to be born. Next, the heat of summer fortifies it and leads it, so to speak, to its youth. After this, autumn arrives and the world rises towards its maturity. Finally winter follows and the world bows towards its decline. If the world always declines, it is so that it might always be renewed after its decline, for if the old did not decline and leave its state, it would, as it were, occupy the space and the new would not be able to emerge.[13]

Despite the fact that the world is ruled by stable laws, it does not cease to produce the novel, the unheard of, the astounding. Since the beautiful elicits admiration in the strongest sense, it must also be surprising. It not only quenches our thirst for esthetic emotions, but also abashes our expectation, dilates our hearts, and surpasses our hopes. That is why there is a beauty of the gigantic,[14] a beauty of extreme smallness,[15] and even, if one may say so, a beauty of ugliness.

> We admire other beings because they are in some sense monstrous or ridiculous. Yet the more distant from human reason their form is, the more easily they can move the human spirit to admiration. Why does the crocodile chew without moving its lower jaw? And how does the salamander remain unharmed in fire? Who gave sharp spines to the hedgehog and taught it to wrap itself in the fruit flung to the ground by the tornado such that, thus loaded, it produces the creaking of a cart as it moves? What of the ant that feels in advance winter's approach and fills his pantry with grain? And what of the spider that spins a web from its own entrails to trap its prey?[16]

The feeling expressed by Hugh concerning these repulsive animals is not the romantic compassion of Victor Hugo: "Because we hate them / And because nothing grants and everything punishes / Their dismal wish."[17] Hugh's is genuine admiration, rising above the mere appearances of ugliness and disorder to discover, through these negative impressions, a broader harmony—a coherence much greater than what would normally come to mind, inasmuch it makes room even for the very thing that seems to contradict it. The crocodile, the salamander, the hedgehog, the ant, and the spider are beautiful and admirable each in its own way, and this even more so because they are beautiful in a way that escapes us. It is a paradoxical beauty, which only makes sense when built on a prior confidence. If Hugh marvels thus before the totality of the real, if he finds beauty even in what seems hideous, it is because his admiration is preceded by an act of faith, in God of course, but also in life and existence in this world such as it is, since it is this one and no other that exists and that is given us to inhabit. In this way, Hugh's admiration for nature is inseparable from a sort of cosmic sympathy and a profound feeling of belonging to the created universe. This sympathy is not a mere enjoyment of the visible, but rather a joyful and trusting acquiescence.

For this reason, the *De tribus diebus* is more than an anthology of natural beauty. It is a treatise on admiration.[18] Hugh is not so much taking inventory of the wonders of creation as he is instructing his reader on how to marvel, even at the most humble realities, such as the fact that each species of tree is distinct from all others in the form, color, veins and edges of its leaves:

> Behold a leaf, how distinct its jagged outline is, how it is woven within by veins that stretch this way and that. Count one and then count another. You will discover that all that are of the same species bear the same resemblance. There are as many notches on one as there are on another, as many veins in one as in another, the same form on one as on the other, the same color on one as on the other. See how mulberries and strawberries are distinct from each other in the little seeds that crowd together all over their surface: each resembles the others, each essence, as though someone has given it an order from within, does not dare to surpass its proper limits.[19]

This accounts for the complex and strange plan of these pages on the visible universe, and for the fact that certain sections are developed at length while others are mere sketches. As Hugh says, the work is a *seminarium*, a nursery of young trees.[20] He sows seeds of admiration throughout. It is up to the reader to welcome these seeds in the proper way, to let them take root in the reader's heart that they might then bear all their fruit.

From Beauty to Wisdom

According to Hugh, another aspect of visible beauty is that it conveys meaning. When he expresses his enthusiasm for the beauty of spring verdure, the renewal of nature brings to his mind an image of the resurrection to come. Likewise, while contemplating the human body (its general contours, its four limbs as well as the hands and feet in which they terminate) he discovers in this something like a concrete resemblance to the human soul that resides in and enlivens the body:

> At the top, man is simple. Below he divides in two, for the governing part of the spirit is also simple, which is to say, reason, which looks toward the invisible, whereas the soul has two qualities, irritableness and greed, both of which move downward toward earthly things below. In the same fashion, the human body extends in the direction of its width through the arms and comes to a point at the bottom through the legs, for the spirit expands when it applies itself to activity, whereas it contracts when it inclines toward desires. Likewise, the length of the human body ends in five extremities: on each side at the fingertips, below at the toes, for whether the spirit stretches in the direction of its width, by applying itself to a task, or whether it settles

at the bottom, by following the desire of some inclination, there are five senses by which it exits to the outside world. Furthermore, the fingers are divided into phalanges at three intervals. The fingers derive from a single palm of the hand, and the toes from a single sole of the foot, because from a single sensibility are the five senses derived, in which three things can be distinguished: first the sense, then the act of sensing, then the object that is sensed. Finally on each finger or toe, we notice that the tips of the last phalanges are covered with a nail, which serves as a kind of helmet, such that wherever an obstacle is encountered when we extend our hand or take a step, the phalange has its own rampart to protect it and can thus remain unharmed by the shock. In the same way those earthly things to which our senses adhere, are like some nails. When necessary they protect us, but to the extent that they are not necessary we can trim them without feeling it, as though they were not part of our flesh.[21]

This sample of what is often called "medieval symbolism" might tempt us to smile, and after all, why not? Surely for Hugh also there was an element of play in observing such correspondences between the structure of the body and that of the soul. As in poetry, as in spiritual exegesis, the writer has in this case a great deal of freedom to create, or rather to associate. Needless to say, another writer would make different connections or would justify the connections differently. Here we find ourselves in an entirely different domain than that of deductive reasoning. Nevertheless, through these analogies, Hugh confirms his conviction in the underlying unity of the human compound. For him, the beauty of the body necessarily reflects something of the beauty of the soul. Or rather the body derives part of its beauty from the fact that it is joined to the soul, extends it, and visually materializes it and therefore resembles it after a fashion. In other words, the body is beautiful because it bears in itself more than the body.

What we have just said about human beings is equally valid for the entire universe. Nature also derives its beauty from the sense that it bears in itself something that transcends itself. Nature is like an enormous book whose letters are creatures and whose meaning is the praise of divine wisdom:

> Indeed, this entire sensible universe resembles a book written by the finger of God, that is, created by divine power, and each creature is like a

figure, not imagined according to the tastes of man, but settled according to the choice of God to manifest and as it were signify his invisible wisdom. Just as an illiterate man looks at an open book and sees figures but does not recognize letters, so too the foolish and "animal" man, who does not perceive divine things: in visible creatures, he sees the outward appearance but does not understand their purpose. By contrast, the one who is "spiritual" and can "judge all things," both sees outside the beauty of the work and understands inside how admirable the creator's wisdom is. Thus there is no one who does not find the works of God admirable since even the foolish man admires the appearance alone, while, through what he sees outside, the wise man admires the thought of divine wisdom. It is as, though given the same written text, the former values the color and shape of the characters while the latter praises their meaning and signification.[22]

Several points in this famous passage should be stressed.[23] First, when an exegete such as Hugh of St. Victor draws a comparison with a book, this is not to be underestimated: it suggests a parallel between nature and scripture. For the Bible and creation, together with inspiration and instruction, are in fact for him the two privileged means through which God reveals himself to man.[24] Now the holy books, like the universe, are concerned with the question of the beautiful. In both instances, beauty is theophanic. In addition, the wise man's view of nature is like his view of scripture: it is exegetical. Just as the biblical texts lend themselves to being read at several levels (at least the literal and the spiritual meanings), so too the universe can be seen in two ways. One remains at the level of appearances while the other attains the essence of things through their appearance.

This layering of two levels has the effect that it is up to each man either to remain at the first stage, entirely external and superficial, or to enter into a richer, more intimate, and more unified perception of scripture or of nature. The silly and "animal" man—to echo St. Paul (1 Cor 2:14)—or the "foolish" man, who says "there is no God"—to cite the words of the psalmist (Ps 13:1, Ps 52:1)—is like the illiterate man who sees only mute forms juxtaposed on the page with no apparent logic. By contrast, the "spiritual" man or the "sage" understands the meaning of what is written and, by associating one character to another, he arrives at what is called in French "reconnaissance," that is, both discovery of and gratitude for creation's author.

Now, the profuse generosity of God is such that both the foolish man and the sage have enough to marvel at nature. Being unable to transcend the level of appearances, the first can nonetheless be exultant with the beauty of creatures. The second, through what can be seen outwardly, arrives at inner divine wisdom. Does this mean that the sage closes his eyes to the world of appearances and to the beauty of the senses? On the contrary, just as the Christian interpretation of the Bible does not obviate the literal meaning but fulfills it by extending it to the discovery of the spiritual sense, so too the Christian contemplation of the universe, far from fleeing the sensory beauty of its creatures, deepens and perfects it by discovering the wisdom that underlies it.

For Hugh indeed, beauty is the radiance of wisdom. The balance of forms, the interplay of colors, the harmony of sounds, the sweetness of sensations—all manifest an inner order, that of the coherent and benevolent thought that conceived them. In order to pass from the surface to the depths, from appearance to meaning, one must see the relationships between the letters, notice connections and correspondences of all sorts that link creatures one with another and unite their individual voices (which are already melodious in their own right) in a vast symphony, the symphony of creation.

Thus there exists a deep and reciprocal relationship between wisdom and beauty. To thrill at the beauty of a thing is to admire the wisdom with which it was made, but it is also to demonstrate wisdom in oneself, it is to be sensitive to the harmony of this thing, to understand that this order manifests the thought of which it is the result. Moreover, it is to welcome this thought into oneself, to assimilate it and let oneself be transformed by it. To admire a beautiful thing is, ultimately, to commune through it with the wisdom that produced it wisely, which is to say beautifully.

Fundamentally, for Hugh, who in this matter is the heir to Augustinian exemplarism, God is beauty itself and wisdom itself. He is the summit, the cause, and the model of all created beauty, as of all created wisdom. What is more, beauty and wisdom are but one thing in him. When he creates, God creates through himself and according to himself—through himself, by his wisdom; according to himself, after his beauty. But his wisdom and beauty are only God himself, seen in the first case as the cause and in the second case as the model of all created beauty.

Since wisdom and beauty constitute one thing in God, it will come as no surprise that for Hugh, the most beautiful thing in creation, even more beautiful than light or verdure, is man. Indeed, visible beauty like that of the stars, trees, and animals manifests divine wisdom, but in an indirect and so to speak inverted fashion, as the effect refers to the cause. Therefore, in a sense, they are reflections, traces, or vestiges of divine wisdom, but they are not strictly speaking images of it. On the other hand, man, who is a rational creature, or as Hugh says, "created wisdom," actually bears within himself the image and resemblance of God.[25] Among visible beings he is the one nearest to God, and this proximity can be seen above all in his aptitude for appreciating the beauty of creation and transforming the sensory pleasure that results from this into a joy of the whole person—body and soul, intelligence and emotionality.

TO FORM OR TO REFORM BEAUTY

The *De tribus diebus*, which we have just leafed through together, is one of Hugh of St. Victor's first works. It is practically a work of his youth. The reflection on beauty that he expresses in it reappears in several later writings, with, here and there, some remarkable additions, notably in the commentary on the *Celestial Hierarchy* of Ps.-Dionysius, the *De arrha animae*, and the *De institutione novitiorum*.

The "Formific" Beauty of God

In commenting on the *Celestial Hierarchy* of Ps.-Dionysius the Areopagite, Hugh of St. Victor encounters a Neoplatonic theme, which thanks to the church fathers had been adapted to Christian theology: the theme of divine beauty, supreme and total beauty that is at once the measure and the model for all sensory beauty. In truth, the theme of divine beauty is not self-evident, since the beautiful seems linked to esthetics and sensible realities. To affirm the existence of beauty "in itself"—insensible, immaterial, and divine—is to postulate that what is beautiful in creatures does not come from them but is sensibly transposed and, so to speak, embodies a principle that comes to them from somewhere else.

We also find here another Platonic theme, the theme of participation. The beauty of God is one and unchangeable, yet it is participated in in a multiple fashion, diversely and unequally, by the numerous realities that

God has created and in which he has placed a faint echo of his own beauty. Although there is thus a certain resemblance between divine beauty and the beauty of creatures, an unbridgeable chasm still separates them. Hence this paradox: although God overrides in beauty his creatures thanks to his supreme simplicity (that is to say, from the fact that he is subject to neither otherness nor plurality nor change), nevertheless by contrast creation draws its beauty from his abundance, luxuriance, and diversity:

> The ray of divine light that illuminates those who shine spiritually, while remaining one in itself, still multiplies in a diverse fashion through the participation and distribution of gifts because he distributes and multiplies himself according to many diverse ways. Now this multiplication and variation is the beauty of the universe because, if things were not beautiful each one in a different way, they would not be supremely beautiful when seen together as a whole.[26]

Hence this asymmetric situation: what would be imperfection in God, becomes perfection in his creatures.

> For the beauty of universality is further rendered perfect in that not everything is recalled to communion with divine goodness in a single identical way, but each reality is recalled to communion according to its order and its degree by diverse and multiple fashions, so that the work of goodness might become complete, and that these realities should not be abandoned, and that the work of wisdom should be perfected inasmuch as these realities are arranged in various fashions for the grace and the beauty of all things.[27]

This reversal is not inexplicable. Fundamentally, the creator's beauty is so bright that no creature in itself could present an acceptable image of it. To manifest even a little bit of this beauty, the quality must be compensated by the quantity, the intensity by the number. The immensity of the universe is, as it were, the counterpart of the deficiency of each of its parts:

> The creation reveals its artisan, and the form of admirable works praises the beauty of their author. There is but one good and one beauty, and the

good itself is beauty itself, the sovereign good and the sovereign beauty. And in the sovereign good, all good things make but one good. And in the sovereign beauty, all beautiful things make but one beauty. Now, visible nature could not contain everything in one thing alone, and this is why numerous good things have been made, to show the unique sovereign good, and in the same way, the numerous beautiful things have been made to present the image of the unique sovereign beauty.[28]

The innumerable multiplicity of creatures is like the forward flight of the sensible world trying to bridge the infinite distance that separates the one God from his pluralistic work. Naturally, this mad race is in vain. The creature will never catch up with its creator unless God himself comes to meet it. Now to be precise, divine beauty is not only the "form," that is to say, the model of created beauty. It is also "formific," that is to say, dynamic and productive of form or of beauty. Little by little, divine beauty increases its own resemblance in the creatures that turn toward it:

> This beauty is called "formific" because it conforms to itself those which turn toward it, so that in loving true beauty they become beautiful themselves, not as in the flesh and according to the flesh, there where those who love beauty can be ugly and those who possess beauty may not be found to be good. Here, on the contrary, the one who loves possesses, and the one who loves to have begins to be.[29]

Here Hugh is articulating a law of the spiritual life, which he will return to in later works. We will come back to it also. In a certain way, man transforms himself into what he loves. Spiritual desire not only takes him outside of himself in an attempt to unite with the loved object but also changes him from within. Henceforth, in contemplating beauty, that is to say, in looking with love and by exposing himself to it as one exposes one's face to the sun, it works upon him and beautifies him. This confirms our initial claim that for Hugh beauty is neither an accessory nor a decoration but touches the very essence of things: "The one who loves possesses, and the one who loves to have begins to be."

That the beauty of creatures has its principle in the creator's beauty, and yet no sensible beauty in itself is comparable to divine beauty, raises the question: What tie links one to the other? If the beautiful is invisible in its first essence, how can we discern its trace among visible things? In other words, why is it that a beautiful spectacle moves us? By what means does the contemplation of a pleasant object procure a feeling of inner joy for our soul?

The answer is found in a sentence from the *Celestial Hierarchy*, where Ps.-Dionysius teaches that our spirit is in itself incapable of rising to the contemplation of the angelic hierarchy, unless guided there by symbols lent to all the senses. Then, he explains:

> Visible forms are images of invisible beauty. Things that smell good to our senses are figures of intellectual illumination. Material lights are an image of the effusion of immaterial light. The complications of sacred instruction are an image of a plenitude of intellectual contemplation. The orders and degrees here below are an image of the harmonious properties of the divine legions. The receiving of the most holy Eucharist is the image of the participation of Jesus, and so on in like fashion. Everything which has been transmitted to the angelic essences through a supramundane mode has been transmitted to us through a symbolic mode.[30]

In brief, there is an analogy for our spirit between the sensible and intelligible realities. In spite of their ontological difference, visible beauty can be the image of invisible beauty because both were made by God. Emanating from the same source, they share something like a family resemblance. On the basis of difference and radical inequality, they present to each other a sort of likeness and proportion, which is perceptible to the human spirit because it is itself in contact with the invisible world as well as the visible. By the corporeal senses, it receives the image of material realities. Through its spiritual faculties, it is in relation with intelligible realities. Henceforth, when the corporeal senses transmit to it an image of a visible object, it is easy for it to determine whether or not this image has an affinity with invisible realities and whether it provokes in it a feeling of joy or dejection.

> For that which is in the spirit is invisible, as the spirit itself is invisible. However, that which is invisible conceives joy, love, and emotion through visible things. The spirit loves some of them, as being similar, friends and allies. Inversely, it disdains others, detests them, flees them, goes far away from them

by love and affection and judges that they are strangers to it, that they do not suit it and bear no resemblance to it. And thus our spirit learns from its own nature that the visible is related to and resembles the invisible.[31]

The entire symbolic theology of Hugh of St. Victor is made possible by this bridge between the visible and the invisible. He himself examines its psychological and quasi-anatomical process in another work: *On the Unity of the Spirit and the Body*.[32] Two ontologically distinct spheres, the sensible and the intelligible, touch and open to one another in man thanks to his hybrid nature, half-corporeal, half-spiritual. Without the human spirit, sensible beauty would have no place to be perceived as such. After a fashion, man's original place at the hinge of the two parts of creation confers a unique vocation on him: to contemplate the beauty of the sensible universe and to marvel at it, all the while recognizing the relationship between this sensible beauty and the intelligible world to which he himself belongs through his spirit.

To Choose Beauty

In the *De arrha animae*, beauty appears less as an object of contemplation and knowledge and more as an object of love and affection. In this interior dialogue between the author and his soul, Hugh asks the latter what it loves above all. "I know," he says, "that your life is to love, and I know that you cannot be without love. But I would like you to confess to me without bashfulness what you have chosen from among all things to love." "What do you love the most?": This initial question, which runs throughout the treatise and gives it its movement and unity, could be rephrased as, "What do you find more beautiful than everything else?" since for Hugh beauty and love and joy are inextricably bound together. For him, what is lovable is beautiful and is what brings joy through fulfillment of the faculty to love. In the course of the conversation, three successive responses are proposed: the invisible world, the soul itself, and God. Certainly there is nothing very original in this ascending order, with its Augustinian flavor, rising from creation to the creator by way of the human spirit. However, what is typical of Hugh here is the effort to pass from one level to the next without rejecting its predecessor. While so many other spiritual authors would insist on denigrating the world and the soul in comparison with God alone, Hugh transcends these lower realities without denouncing them. He keeps them and integrates them in their proper place, neither more nor less, in a divine beauty that is at once both higher and wider. After reviewing the main kinds of visible beauty, Hugh thus addresses his soul:

> Tell me then, I beg you, what among all these things you have chosen for your sole object, that which alone you wish to embrace, that which you yearn to enjoy forever. I am sure that you are smitten with one of the beauties that can be seen, or if you despise them all, there is another one that you prefer to them.[33]

The soul responds by admitting its difficulty. On the one hand, nothing that it sees completely satisfies it. On the other hand, what would really fulfill it cannot be seen. "And so, until now, I float uncertain amidst my desires. I cannot be without love, but I do not find true love."[34] To solve this dilemma, the first step is for the soul to love itself, that is, to recognize its own beauty:

> If you think you must love these temporary and visible objects for a certain charm of their own that you observe in them, why not love yourself instead, you whose charm and beauty surpass all visible things? Ah! if only you would look at yourself! Ah! if only you could see your face, you would see how at fault you were for having esteemed something outside yourself to be worthy of your love! . . . Above all else, one must consider oneself and having recognized one's own dignity, in order not to abase one's love, not love beneath oneself. . . . You know, love is a fire, and fire seeks food in order to burn. But beware: do not throw onto the fire that which produces smoke and a stinking odor. Such is the power of love that you are necessarily like what you love and by the very association which produces the affection, you are transformed in some way into a resemblance of that to which your feeling ties you. Therefore consider, my soul, your own beauty and you will understand which beauty to choose.[35]

We find in those last words the rule of the spiritual life that was enunciated earlier: somehow, love transforms me into what I love. Thereafter, out of respect for myself and regard for my own beauty, I must choose as the object of my love what is most splendid and lovable. Visible things are beautiful, but they are worth less than the soul itself. If the soul shuts itself up in love for them alone, it will forget its own dignity and lower itself to their level. The antidote consists in loving oneself and, through the love of self correctly understood, to love higher than oneself, and if possible to love what is most sublime and desirable, in other words, to love God. To love God: Yes, but how, since he is invisible? Do not be put off by this:

> You have a fiancé but you do not know him. He is the most handsome of all, but you have not seen his face. He, on the other hand, has seen you, for if he had not seen you, he would not love you. Until now he has not wanted to introduce himself to you in person, but he has sent you gifts. He has offered you a betrothal gift, a pledge of love, a sign of his tenderness. If you knew him, if you saw his appearance, you would doubt no more your beauty. You would know that such a fiancé, so handsome, so accomplished, so gracious, so unique, would not have fallen in love with your appearance if he were not attracted by some feature singular and admirable among all.[36]

> My soul, what has your fiancé given you? Perhaps you are waiting and do not know what I am going to say. You think and you wonder: From whom could I have received great things? And you do not find that you possess, that you have ever received anything that you can boast of. I will therefore tell you so that you will know what your fiancé has given you. Look at the whole world and see if you can find anything that is not at your service. All of nature directs its path so that it can rush to serve you, take care of your concerns and treat you with inexhaustible prodigality, for your pleasures as well as for your necessities.[37]

The same visible world, which was set aside for an instant for the sake of the soul and God, is thus reintroduced into the loving relationship between the soul and God, as the sign and the pledge of the divine fiancé toward his beloved, which is none other than the soul of each human being. At this point Hugh's readers are bidden to choose: either we love only the visible world (more probably this means a miserable little part of that world) or they choose everything: God first and then, in addition to God, the visible world in its totality, in order to manifest, however insufficiently, the infinite superabundance of divine love.

> Ah! at least if you love these creatures, love them as inferiors. Love them as servants. Love them as gifts as the fiancé's betrothal gift, as presents from a friend, as the largesse of a lord. But do not let these affections cause you to forget what you owe him. Love creatures, not instead of him, nor with him, but because of him. Love him through them and him above them.[38]

Unfortunately it happens that man sins, making himself ugly by parceling out his desire and limiting it to sensible creatures instead of rising toward God. According to the aforementioned spiritual law, he becomes ugly by falling in love with objects that are less beautiful than himself. Is his fall irreparable? No, for the same treatise teaches the means to rise again through the life of the liturgy and the sacraments.

Being beautiful itself, the liturgy makes man more beautiful. The purpose of the sacraments, beginning with baptism, is to restore man's original splendor, which has become deformed through sin. The *De arrha animae* interprets an episode from the book of Esther (in which the beautiful Jewess prepares to visit King Ahasuerus) as a prediction in the spiritual sense of the body of methods for attaining salvation that the church makes available to souls before they are ushered into the presence of their heavenly spouse. For this they must pass through the antechamber that is the church, here described as a sort of beauty institute generously provided for his fiancées by the king of heaven:

> You do not know, my soul, you are not aware of how repulsive, stained, disfigured, filthy, ragged, and beaten down by hideous ugliness you were before. How can you demand to be ushered so quickly into the wedding chamber, a place of modesty and chastity, before at least taking the trouble to beautify yourself and to recuperate your former charms? . . . Withered as you are, it is not fitting for you to touch purity. Deformed, you cannot see beauty. Prepare yourself, put on your becoming finery. . . . Only then will you no longer blush at your former ugliness, for you will no longer have any deformity or cause for shame. Do your best first to cultivate your beauty, to adorn your face, to carry yourself upright, to correct your habits, to discipline yourself, that having done all this you might be a bride worthy of such a groom.[39]

Thus each soul is invited first to undergo the cleansing of baptism, which washes away all stains of sin. Then it is anointed with a fragrant ointment, the holy chrism of confirmation. Having been made more presentable, the soul advances to the eucharistic table to recover strength and regain a beautiful plump figure in place of the gauntness it has acquired through debauchery. After this, it dons the robes of good deeds, puts on the jewelry of alms, fasting, and prayer and is sprinkled with the perfume of virtues. Finally, taking up the mirror of Holy Scripture, the soul can contemplate and judge its face. If it soils itself again, it has the option of cleansing itself again with tears of penitence.

The Beauty of Movement and Harmony of Hearts

There is another slightly unexpected domain where Hugh finds beauty and not only observes but also recommends it: in the outward behavior of the canons regular. In *De institutione novitiorum*, Hugh provides aspirants to the canonical life with a treatise on proper comportment in a religious community.[40] Following an opening theoretical section on the way to conform to the "discipline," he examines the latter in four chapters: clothing, movement, speech, and table manners. To enhance his suggestions, he gives several life sketches of his brothers. Here for example is what he says about the wrong way to listen and speak:

> There are those who cannot listen without gaping. They open their cavernous mouths to receive the speaker's words as though the meaning had to flow to their hearts by way of their mouths. Worse are those who, when they act or listen, stick out their tongues as thirsty dogs do, and with each action turn their lips as though they were turning a mill. Others, when they speak, point their fingers, raise their eyebrows and, rolling their eyes in their sockets or staring as though they were absorbed in deep meditation, make an ostentatious show of their efforts to haul themselves up to some inner grandeur. Others wag their heads, shake their hair, fuss with their clothes and, lying on their sides, stretching out their legs, make a passably ridiculous spectacle of themselves. Others, as though only one of their ears were made for listening, twist their neck to extend just that one ear in the direction of the voice aimed at them. Others, when they look, aping I know

not what model, close one eye and open the other. Others, even more ridiculous, speak out of one side of the mouth. There are besides a thousand grimaces, a thousand pretentious airs and flarings of nostrils, a thousand pouts and contortions of the lips that deform the beauty of the face and offend the decorum of discipline. The face is in fact the mirror of discipline and one must be extremely attentive to this, as the least fault cannot be hidden by it. One must master and modify the mimicries of the face lest it be rudely hardened or lazily relaxed. It should always retain a firm softness and a soft firmness.[41]

As you have heard, Hugh denounces these bad manners because they "deform beauty." Here he speaks of the face but elsewhere makes it clear that he means the entire body. The main objective of disciplining outward behavior, the subject of this work, is to reestablish the esthetic harmony of the human person, beginning with the physique. The word "deformation" is meant to be taken in its strongest sense. Indeed, the Latin word *forma* can be translated as beauty. We must understand that in creating the human body, God endowed it with a proper "form," its particular way of being beautiful. Therefore to deform one's face or body is to stray from the divine plan and to make oneself ugly. Here as elsewhere, Hugh's plan consists in a *reformatio*, which conforms to the spiritual ideal that animated the Gregorian Reform. It is in fact a question of "reforming" the body, which is to say, returning it to the purity of its original form and restoring its primordial beauty.

Beyond this esthetic significance, discipline of movement has for Hugh a second goal, which is ethical. In fact, any reflection on good manners is concerned with the question of the connection between the outer and inner man. From this point of view, awkward bodily movements betray a disorder of passions. Like a graphologist of behavior, Hugh interprets the qualities of movements as revelations of character. To attain mastery of one's limbs, correctness of movements, and a dignified bearing, one must first attain peace and serenity of the mind. Viewed from the opposite perspective, it is possible to make progress in mastering one's passions by disciplining the body. By restraining the outward manifestations of harmful desires, they can be attenuated or even eradicated. Mimicking virtues with one's limbs can be a way of acquiring those virtues. In this way, the good manners of the Canon not only reflect his spiritual advancement, but also abet it. Soul and body are so tightly bound that a person can act indiscriminately on either one and so affect the other.

> The discipline [of the body] is a shackle on greed, a prison for wicked desires, a brake on licentiousness, a yoke for pride, and a chain for wrath. It tames intemperance, bridles frivolity, and strangles all the disorderly movements of the spirit and illicit appetites. Even as waywardness of the spirit is born of the body's disorderly agitation, so is the spirit fortified by steadfastness when the body is checked by discipline. Little by little, within, the spirit inclines toward repose when, thanks to the observance of discipline, one does not strew bad movements all around. Virtue therefore becomes complete when by the inward watchfulness of the spirit, the body's limbs are ruled by order. In fact, it is this inner watchfulness that maintains order outside in the limbs of the body. But he who loses the seat of the spirit subsequently slides outward toward fickle agitation and through his outward mobility shows that no root secures him inside.... So discipline must bind the limbs of the body on the outside so that the seat of the spirit might be consolidated inside, and that with outward watchfulness everywhere opposing inner mobility, which must be held in check, the spirit finally withdraws into itself in a stable peace. In fact, discipline bridals the movements of all the vices and to the extent that it represses wicked desires on the outside, the desire for good grows stronger on the inside, thanks to it. Gradually, with the help of habit, the same form of virtue that discipline maintains in the attitude of the body outside is impressed on the spirit.[42]

In an abbey of canons regular, the mastery of outward behavior is required not only for esthetic and ethical reasons, as a reflection and a lever for inner progress. Furthermore, it is also necessary for "political" reasons in that it affects relations between the individual canon and his whole community. Each movement, depending on whether it is beautiful or ugly, orderly or disorderly, appropriate or discordant, has repercussions on the life of the abbey. Each canon shares the responsibility for good order and harmony among brothers, and outward behavior, when it is mastered, contributes to the maintenance of brotherly charity. Good manners, which are beautiful in themselves and are the sign and support of inner peace, are translated into and also cement a more all-encompassing peace.

This is particularly true because, with their pastoral mission, canons, far more than monks, have a special responsibility to edify their neighbors "by word and by example." The canon strives at the same time for others' salvation and his own. Thus, since the body is the language of the soul, his discourse must be edifying. It is not enough to do good, he must "do good well," that is, he must do things both in the correct and exemplary way. He must keep watch not only on the rectitude of his intentions but also on the propriety and harmony of their manifestation. This concern for how one is seen by others of course has nothing to do with hypocrisy. It is not a matter of appearing virtuous when one is not, but rather of being so virtuous that one's virtue shines forth and thereby inspires virtue all around.

Esthetic, ethical, and political, Hugh's sense of beauty in outward behavior has a spiritual and quasi-theological dimension. The same correctness in movement that reconciles limb to body, flesh to soul, and individual to community, has the effect of bringing man closer to God, not only because this correctness "reforms" him according to the creator's original design, but also because by helping to reestablish peace in the soul and agreement in the community, it increases in the canon and his brothers the divine image and resemblance. Finally, ease and beauty of movement find their ultimate perfection in the actions of the liturgy, where they express the double union of many congregants in one church and the church with the Father.

A CANONICAL SPIRITUALITY OF BEAUTY?

Having examined the place that beauty occupies in Hugh of St. Victor's various writings, it is time to bind the sheaf we have gathered. We began with a lengthy examination of *De tribus diebus* (a book teeming with wisdom for those who know how to tie visible beauty to a more inward beauty) and its treatment of the superabundance of beauty in the universe. We saw how, taking a cue from Ps.-Dionysius, Hugh equates God with the simple and formific supreme beauty from which all created beauty flows. We also saw how, through his mixed corporeal and spiritual nature, man recognizes that certain creatures are beautiful by discovering that they are related to his invisible spirit and his divine finality. From listening in on the conversation between Hugh and his soul in *De arrha animae*, we saw how the search for what is most splendid and desirable leads the soul from the love of visible things, then to love of God, the divine groom, who has prepared, in the form of the church and its sacraments, all that is needed to restore the primordial beauty of the soul, withered by sin. Finally, we have seen how the novice disciplines himself to the good manners of the canons regular, and how harmony of movement can radiate on the individual and the community as a whole.

What is striking in all of this is that the theme of beauty is ubiquitous in Hugh of St. Victor's work. Sensible creatures, God, and the human body and soul—but we could also have cited the scriptures, the Virgin Mary, the church, sacred history, the liturgy, and the moral, spiritual, and sacramental life—all of these realities, whether visible or invisible, whether related to nature or grace, are beautiful to varying degrees and each in its own way— so much so that we end up asking ourselves if the notion of beauty holds any meaning. By dint of extending beauty into such disparate domains, do we not run the risk of causing it to dissolve and lose all substance?

Yet, in each domain we recognize the same concept. The beautiful is that which is in agreement with its deep essence, which is to say, in keeping with the divine plan. The beautiful thing is orderly, appropriate, and unified from what constitutes its deep identity. The beautiful therefore touches on the question of the one and the multiple. For beauty is the unfolding of the one through the multiple. Far from being a secondary or static quality, it manifests the creative action of the one and triune God. It is the radiance and glory of divine beauty shining on the realities that it brings forth from the void, giving them a form, image, or vestige of the primordial and trinitarian form.

Not only does beauty retain its unity in diverse realms, it is also what unites these realms and creates passages from one to the other. Thus, through contemplation of visible things, man advances from the beauty of nature to his own beauty and then to God's. Through contemplation of the Holy Scriptures, man assimilates the great deeds of sacred history and causes them to shine in his moral and spiritual life. Through the cultivation of appropriateness and the balance of outward behavior, he strives for inner harmony and brotherly concord. Beauty is not only what gives order to and unifies each creature and each domain of creation. It is also what gives order to and unifies all these domains among themselves.

This permits us better to understand Hugh of St. Victor's pedagogical intention. To contemplate beauty in all its facets is to rediscover the secret of the unity of being and to draw nearer to the divine model. It is to become unified within oneself and to unite with the one who is sovereignly one. In a way, this sense of beauty as harmony and unifying principle of a totality is at work, even at the strict intellectual level, in Hugh's pedagogical and theological writings. Each treatise is a renewed effort to discover in every discipline, profane or sacred, what constitutes their unity, and to assemble all the disciplines in a total and unique wisdom, identified with the search for Christ, the eternal wisdom of the Father, through the lucid and delightful assimilation of the scriptures. The *Didascalicon*, a map of knowledge, an abridgement and a summa of all the arts, was written to articulate them and harmonize them with each other. Science, as Hugh sees it, is beautiful. It is beautiful both in its parts and in its totality. Virtually encompassing all that is knowable, it resembles the book of creation, orderly to the one who gives it meaning.

Similarly, on a spiritual level, Hugh of St. Victor's plan is for the unification of the human heart, not by eliminating all his diverse and divided aspirations, but on the contrary by reintegrating them in the unique love of the divine spouse, in whom all desire and all affection regain their moral legitimacy. Seen in this way, the spiritual life is beautiful in Hugh's eyes. It is like Noah's Ark, where all the animals enter and gather in orderly fashion around the one unshakable mast that is Christ. Thus time and space, universal history and geography—all have their place in the inner ark of salvation. Every person, every thing, every event can be torn away from the instability of worldly things as soon as it finds its correct place and its own beauty in relation to Christ.[43]

If I have written so much about Hugh's conception of beauty, it is because, I believe, this conception is typically canonical. Fundamentally, Hugh defines beauty as a harmony between the part and the whole, by which the founder of the whole irrigates each of the elements. No doubt this fundamentally traditional conception would be renewed by life in a community governed by the rule of St. Augustine, who places concord and brotherly charity above all else.

We have seen, on the other hand, the important role played by the typically canonical concern for the edification of one's neighbor by word and by example, with a characteristic accent on outward behavior. Where the Cistercian monk rejects all concern for appearance or worry about what others might say, the canon regular, so says Hugh, is careful about his gestures and his entire manner of being, which he knows to be both the reflection of his soul and an unspoken message addressed to those around him—his brothers in the first place and, beyond them, all the souls that might be in his charge.

Finally we have evoked at least a little of the splendor of the liturgy and the efficacy of the sacraments as privileged means of inner beautification. The ecclesial and sacramental life, which is at the heart of the canonical vocation, then appears as the privileged conduit through which the formific beauty of God is communicated to man to restore him in his first beauty and render him even more beautiful. Is it by chance that Victorine thought, centered on the notion of the sacrament, inspired the birth and diffusion of a new architectural style (the gothic) born at St. Denis in the course of Hugh's lifetime?[44] Surely not, for it is in the church, that edifice of stone and flesh, that the vocation of the canon regular is best realized, the vocation that, according to Hugh, is to contemplate divine beauty and to allow oneself to be transformed by it and then to radiate it all around oneself unto the limits of the universe.

NOTES

This chapter was translated from the original French text by Timothy Robbins.

1. De Bruyne, *Études d'esthétique médiévale*. Karfíková, "De esse ad pulchrum esse."
2. Baron, "Le style de Hugues de Saint-Victor"; Negri, "Letture stilistica di Ugo di S. Vittore."
3. On Hugh of St. Victor, see most recently Rorem, *Hugh of Saint-Victor*. See also Sicard, *Hugues de Saint-Victor et son école*; and Poirel, *Hugues de Saint-Victor*.
4. "Scio quidem quia minus erit quicquid dixerimus, sed tamen decens non est ut ideo omnino taceamus, ibi precipue ubi, si fieri posset, maxime decenter loqui deberemus": Hugh of St. Victor, *De tribus diebus*, 11, lines 136–39. On the text, see Poirel, *Livre de la nature*. English translations of Hugh's works are by Robbins from Poirel's French translations of his edition of the Latin text.
5. "Quid luce pulcrius, quae cum colorem in se non habeat, omnium tamen colores rerum ipsa quodammodo illuminando colorat? Quid iocundius ad

uidendum celo cum serenum est, quod resplendet quasi saphirus et gratissimo quodam suae claritatis temperamento uisum excipit et demulcet aspectum? Sol sicut aurum rutilat; luna pallet quasi electrum; stellarum quaedam flammeo aspectu radiant, quaedam luce rosea micant, quaedam uero alternatim, nunc roseum, nunc uiridem, nunc candidum fulgorem demonstrant. Quid de gemmis et lapidibus preciosis narrem, quorum non solum efficacia utilis, sed aspectus quoque mirabilis? Ecce tellus redimita floribus, quam iocundum spectaculum prebet, quomodo uisum delectat, quomodo affectum prouocat! Videmus rubentes rosas, candida lilia, purpureas uiolas, in quibus omnibus non solum pulcritudo, sed origo quoque mirabilis est: quomodo scilicet Dei sapientia de terrae puluere talem producit speciem! Postremo super omne pulcrum uiride, quomodo animos intuentium rapit, quando, uere nouo, noua quadam uita germina prodeunt, et erecta sursum in spiculis suis, quasi deorsum morte calcata, ad imaginem futurae resurrectionis in lucem pariter erumpunt!": ibid., 26–27, lines 409–30.

    6. "Quot enim oblectamenta oculorum in diuersitate colorum monstrauimus, tot oblectamenta aurium in uarietate sonorum inuenimus. Inter quae prima sunt dulcia sermonum commercia, quibus homines adinuicem suas uoluntates communicant, preterita narrant, presentia indicant, futura nuntiant, occulta reuelant, adeo ut, si his careat uita humana, bestiis comparabilis uideatur. Quid autem concentus auium, quid humanae uocis melos iocundum, quid dulces modos sonorum omnium commemorem? Quia tam multa sunt armoniae genera, ut ea nec cogitatus percurrere, nec sermo facile explicare possit; quae tamen cuncta auditui seruiunt et in eius delicias creata sunt. Sic est de olfactu. Habent thimiamata odorem suum, habent unguenta odorem suum, habent rosaria odorem suum, habent rubeta odorem suum, habent prata odorem suum, habent tesqua odorem suum, habent nemora odorem suum, habent flores odorem suum, habent fructus odorem suum, et cuncta quae suauem prestant fraglantiam et dulces spirant odores, olfactui seruiunt, et in eius delicias creata sunt. Eodem modo gustus et tactus uaria habent oblectamenta, quae ex similitudine priorum satis perpendi possunt," ibid., 28–29, lines 443–62.

    7. Sicard, *Diagrammes médiévaux*, 9 ff.

    8. "Ecce caelum sursum est et terra deorsum. In caelo stellas et luminaria collocauit, ut subiecta omnia illustrarent. In aere uentis et nubibus uiam fecit, ut agitationibus suis dispersae pluuiam deorsum funderent. In gremio telluris moles aquarum recipi iussit, ut per gurgites suos hinc illincque quo nutus ferret iubentis discurrerent. Volucres in aere suspendit, pisces aquis inmersit, terram bestiis et serpentibus et aliorum reptilium uermiumque generibus repleuit. Quasdam regiones ditauit ubertate frugum, quasdam opulentia uinearum, alias fertilitate olerum, alias fecunditate pecorum, alias potentibus herbis, alias gemmis preciosis, alias animalibus et bestiis monstruosis, alias coloribus uariis, alias diuersarum artium studiis, alias metallorum, alias thimiamatum diuersis generibus, ut nulla prorsus regio sit quae non aliquid pre ceteris nouum et speciale possideat, nulla item quae non aliquid nouum et speciale ab aliis accipere queat": Hugh of St. Victor, *De tribus diebus*, 15, lines 196–210.

9. "Et primum quidem, si uniuersitatis huius machinam intueris, inuenies quam mirabili ratione et sapientia compositio rerum omnium perfecta sit, quam apta, quam congrua, quam decora, quam cunctis partibus suis absoluta; in qua non solum concordiam seruant similia, sed eciam quae creante potentia diuersa atque repugnantia ad esse prodierunt, dictante sapientia in unam quodammodo amiciciam et federationem conueniunt. Quid repugnantius esse potest aqua et igne? Quae tamen in rerum natura ita Dei contemperauit prudentia, ut non solum adinuicem commune societatis uinculum non dissipent, uerum eciam nascentibus cunctis ut subsistere possint uitale nutrimentum subministrent. Quid de humani corporis compage loquar, ubi omnium membrorum iuncturae tantam adinuicem seruant concordiam, ut nullum omnino possit inueniri membrum, cuius officium alteri non uideatur prestare adminiculum? Sic omnis natura se diligit, et miro quodam modo plurium dissimilium et in unum redactorum concordia unam in omnibus armoniam facit": ibid., 12–13, lines 152–68.

10. "Quis satis admirari potest quam mira ratione prouidentia diuina cursus temporum distinxit? Ecce post noctem uenit dies, ut torpentes motio laboris exerceat; post diem sequitur nox, ut fessos ad refocillandum quies excipiat. Non semper dies, non semper nox, non semper equalis dies et nox, ne uel immoderatus labor debilitatos frangat, uel quies continuata naturam inficiat, uel identitas perpetua animo tedium gignat": ibid., 16, lines 219–25.

11. "Sed in his quattuor motum excellentiorem locum habere dubium non est, quia uiciniora uitae sunt mobilia quam ea quae moueri non possunt": ibid., 35, lines 583–85.

12. "Postremo super omne pulcrum uiride, quomodo animos intuentium rapit, quando, uere nouo, noua quadam uita germina prodeunt, et erecta sursum in spiculis suis, quasi deorsum morte calcata, ad imaginem futurae resurrectionis in lucem pariter erumpunt!": ibid., 27, lines 426–30. The same preference for greenness can be seen in Hugh of St. Victor, *Pro Assumptione Virginis*, where it seems to have scriptural support: "Ergo intus pascua est, et ipsa est terra in qua flores apparuerunt, cuius uiror perpetuus nunquam marcescit, de quo dictum est: '*Super omne pulchrum uiride*,'" ed. Jollès, 148, lines 499–502.

13. "Primum per teporem ueris quadam innouatione mundus nascitur; deinde per feruorem estatis quasi in iuuentutem roboratur; post haec superueniente autumpno ad maturitatem conscendit; postremo succedente hieme ad defectum uergit. Iccirco autem semper deficit, ut semper post defectum renouari possit; quia nisi prius a statu suo deficerent uetera, quasi illis locum occupantibus, non ualerent exurgere noua": Hugh of St. Victor, *De tribus diebus*, 16–17, lines 228–34.

14. "Figura secundum magnitudinem attenditur, quando res quaelibet sui generis modum in quantitate excedit. Sic miramur gigantem inter homines, cetum inter pisces, grifen inter uolucres, elefantem inter quadrupedes, draconem inter serpentes": ibid., 22, lines 336–39.

15. "Figura secundum paruitatem consideratur, quando res quaelibet ceteris sui generis quantitate equari non potest, ut est succrio et tinea, termes et scinifes, et alia similia, quae inter cetera quidem animalia uiuunt, sed ceteris omnibus corporis exiguitate dispares sunt. Vide ergo quid magis mireris: dentes apri uel tineae, alas grifis uel scinifis, caput equi uel locustae, crura elefantis uel culicis, rostrum suis uel succrionis, aquilam uel formicam, leonem uel pulicem, tigridem uel testudinem? Ibi miraris magnitudinem, hic miraris paruitatem, corpus paruum magna sapientia conditum, magna sapientia cui nulla subrepit negligentia. Illis dedit oculos quos uix comprehendere potest oculus, et in tam exiguis corporibus sic omnifariam liniamenta naturae suae congrua plenissime distribuit, ut nichil uideas deesse in minimis eorum omnium quae natura formauit in magnis": ibid., 22–23, lines 340–53.

16. "Rursus alia iccirco miramur quia monstruosa quodammodo sunt uel ridicula; quorum quidem plasmatio quantum ab humana ratione aliena est, tanto leuius humanum animum in admirationem compellere potest. Quare cocodrillus manducans inferiorem molam non mouet? et quomodo salamandra in igne illesa permanet? quis dedit hericio spinas, et docuit eum ut se pomis turbine discussis inuoluat, quibus onustus incedens stridet quasi plaustrum? et formica quae hiemis superuenturae prescia granis horrea sua replet? aranea quoque de uisceribus suis laqueos nectit ut predam capiat. Isti sunt testes sapientiae Dei": ibid., 24, lines 373–82.

17. Victor Hugo, *Les contemplations*, III, 27, vv. 1–4.

18. On Hugh and admiration, see Poirel, "*Mira pulchritudo*."

19. "Vide folium, quomodo serratis dentibus per girum distinguitur, quomodo intrinsecus productis costulis huc illucque intexitur. Numera unum, numera aliud; omne quod est unius generis, unius inuenis similitudinis: tot dentes in uno quot dentes in alio, tot costulas in uno quot costulas in alio, talem formam in uno qualem formam in alio, talem colorem in uno qualem colorem in alio. Ecce quomodo mora, quomodo fraga quibusdam granulis adinuicem compactis circumquaque distinguuntur! Tale unum quale alterum, et omnis natura, quasi cuiusdam intrinsecus dictantis preceptum acceperit, nusquam terminos suos excedere presumit": Hugh of St. Victor, *De tribus diebus*, 25, lines 390–400.

20. "Meditantibus de creaturarum inmensitate, quasi seminarium quoddam iecimus; nunc ad contemplandam earum pulcritudinem transeamus": ibid., 8, lines 73–75.

21. "Sursum est homo uniformis, deorsum bifariam diuisus, quia et uniforme est principale mentis, id est ratio, quae inuisibilia respicit, et gemina est animae qualitas, ira et concupiscentia, quae deorsum ad terrena descendit. Item brachiis in latum extenditur, tibiis deorsum figitur statura humani corporis, quia et intentio operationis animum extendit, et affectus desideriorum figit. Item secundum latitudinem hinc inde per digitos manuum, deorsum per digitos pedum, in quinque finitur humani corporis protensio, quia siue in latum tendatur animus per intentionem operis, siue deorsum figatur per desiderium affectionis, quinque sensus sunt per quos foras exit. Item digiti ternis articulorum interuallis distinguuntur; qui in manibus de

una palma, in pedibus de una planta prodeunt, quia de una sensualitate quinque sensus exeunt, in quibus trina distinctione primum sensus, deinde sentire, postmodum sensibile inuenitur. Postremo in singulis digitis extremorum articulorum capita superpositis unguibus quasi galeata cernuntur, ut quocunque siue manus extenta siue pes promotus offendiculum inuenerint, ipso suo munimine protecti illesi permanere possint. Similiter terrena ista, ad similitudinem unguium foris sensibus inherentia, quasi in necessitate nos muniunt, sed quantum non pertinent ad necessitatem quasi extra carnem sine sensu precidi possunt": ibid., 17–19, lines 248–69.

22. "Vniuersus enim mundus iste sensilis quasi quidam liber est scriptus digito Dei, hoc est uirtute diuina creatus, et singulae creaturae quasi figurae quaedam sunt, non humano placito inuentae, sed diuino arbitrio institutae ad manifestandam et quasi quodammodo significandam inuisibilem Dei sapientiam. Quemadmodum autem si illiteratus quis apertum librum uideat, figuras aspicit, litteras non cognoscit, ita stultus et animalis homo qui non percipit ea quae Dei sunt, in uisibilibus istis creaturis foris uidet speciem, sed non intelligit rationem; qui autem spiritalis est et omnia diiudicare potest, in eo quidem quod foris considerat pulcritudinem operis, intus concipit quam miranda sit sapientia Creatoris. Et ideo nemo est cui opera Dei mirabilia non sint, dum in eis et insipiens solam miratur speciem, sapiens autem per id quod foris uidet, profundam rimatur diuinae sapientiae cogitationem, uelut si in una eademque scriptura alter colorem seu formationem figurarum commendet, alter uero laudet sensum et significationem": ibid., 9–10, lines 94–109.

23. I have given an interpretation of this in Poirel, "Lire le monde sensible."

24. "Quatuor modis notitia Dei cordi humano manifestatur: duobus intus, duobus foris; duobus per naturam, duobus per gratiam. Intus, per rationem et aspirationem; foris per creaturam et per doctrinam. Ad naturam pertinet ratio et creatura; ad gratiam, aspiratio et doctrina. Fuerunt ergo duo simul natura et gratia, non sola natura neque sola gratia, ne, si natura totum posset, gratia non quaereretur; aut si nichil posset, culpa excusaretur. Iudaei naturam totum posse dixerunt et gratiam non quaesiuerunt; gentiles quidam naturam nichil posse existimauerunt et culpam excusauerunt; et utrique errauerunt. Inter quatuor prima est ratio, secunda creatura, tertia doctrina, quarta aspiratio. Ratio inuestigat, creatura approbat, doctrina explicat, aspiratio confirmat fidem": Hugh of St. Victor, *Elucidationes Variae*, 1.63, PL 177:504C–505B.

25. "Primum ergo ac principale increatae sapientiae simulacrum est sapientia creata, id est rationalis creatura": Hugh of St. Victor, *De tribus diebus*, 36, lines 594–95.

26. "Diuinae claritatis radius qui spiritualiter lucentes illuminat, quamuis in se unus permaneat, participatione tamen et distributione donorum uarie multiplicatur, quoniam multis diuersisque modis distribuitur et multiplicatur. Haec uero multiplicatio et uariatio uniuersorum est pulchritudo, quoniam, nisi dissimiliter pulchra essent singula, summe pulchra non essent simul uniuersa": Hugh of St. Victor, *Super Ierarchiam beati Dionisii*, 2.1, lines 387–92, PL 175:943D.

27. "Nam et in hoc ipso pulchritudo uniuersitatis perficitur quod, non uno et eodem modo omnia, sed singula quaeque secundum ordinem et gradum suum uarie ac multiphariam ad communionem diuinae bonitatis reuocantur, ut in eo quod non deseruntur compleatur opus bonitatis, in eo uero quod uarie disponuntur ad decorem et pulchritudinem omnium opus sapientiae perficiatur": ibid., 5.4, lines 90–96, PL 175:1007BC.

28. "Monstrat creatura artificem et mirabilium operum forma speciem commendat auctoris. Vnum est bonum et una est pulchritudo, et ipsum bonum ipsa est pulchritudo, summum bonum et summa pulchritudo; et in summo bono omne bonum unum bonum, et in summa pulchritudine omnis pulchritudo una pulchritudo. Non poterat autem uisibilis natura in uno omnia continere; et ideo multa bona facta sunt, ut unum bonum summum ostenderent; et similiter pulchra multa, ut unius pulchritudinis summae imaginem demonstrarent": ibid., 9.13, PL 175:1118C–D.

29. "Quae uidelicet pulchritudo 'formifica' dicitur, quoniam sibi conformat conuersos ad se, ut pulchri fiant amantes pulchritudinem ueram, non sicut in carne et secundum carnem ubi amator pulchritudinis turpis esse potest et pulchritudinis possessor non bonus inueniri. Illic autem, qui amat possidet et esse incipit qui habere diligit": ibid., 3.2, lines 1020–25, PL 175:982C.

30. "Visibiles quidem formas inuisibilis pulchritudinis imaginationes . . . , et sensibiles suauitates figuras inuisibilis distributionis, et immaterialis luculentiae imaginem materialia lumina, et secundum intellectum contemplatiuae plenitudinis discursas sacras disciplinas, et adunati ad diuina et ordinati habitus earum quae hic sunt dispositionum ordines, et Iesu participationis ipsam diuinissimae eucharistiae assumptionem, et quaecunque alia, caelestibus quidem essentiis supermundane, nobis uero symbolice tradita sunt," Ps.-Dionysius, *Hierarchia caelestis*, PL 175:935AB.

31. "Quod enim in animo est inuisibile est, sicut ipse animus inuisibilis est; et concipit tamen ipse qui inuisibilis est ex his quae uisibilia sunt gaudium et amorem et affectum. Et diligit ex his quaedam quasi similia et amica et cognata, et prestat se illis uoluntarie et exultat in ipsis; alia autem aspernatur et odit et refugit, et longe se facit ab illis amore et dilectione, et iudicat peregrina a se esse et disconuenientia et nullam secum habentia similitudinem. Atque in hunc modum noster animus ex propria natura docetur quoniam uisibilia ad inuisibilia cognationem habent et similitudinem": Hugh of St. Victor, *Super Ierarchiam beati Dionisii*, 2.1, lines 670–79, PL 175:949D–950A.

32. Hugh of St. Victor, *De unione spiritus et corporis*.

33. "Dic ergo, obsecro, michi, quid de his omnibus unicum tibi feceris, quod singulariter amplecti, quo semper perfrui uelis. Certus enim sum quod aut horum quae uidentur aliquid amas, aut, si iam postposuisti uniuersa haec, aliud habes quae prae omnibus his diligas": Hugh of St. Victor, *De arrha animae*, 228.

34. "Sic adhuc desideriis incerta fluctuo, dum nec sine amore esse possum, nec uerum amorem inuenio": ibid., 230.

35. "Si temporalia ista et uisibilia idcirco amari debere existimas, quia illis quemdam sui generis decorem inesse conspicaris, cur teipsam potius non diligis, quae specie tua omnino uisibilium decorem et pulchritudinem uincis? O si teipsam aspiceres! O si faciem tuam uideres, agnosceres certe quanta reprehensione digna fueras, cum aliquid extra te amore tuo dignum existimabas! . . . Primum igitur necesse est ut quisquis semetipsum consideret et, cum cognouerit dignitatem suam, ne iniuriam faciat amori suo, abiectiora se non amet. . . . Scis quia amor ignis est, et ignis quidem fomentum quaerit ut ardeat. Sed caue ne id inicias quod fumum potius aut fetorem ministrat. Ea uis amoris est, ut talem te esse necesse sit, quale illud est quod amas, et cui per affectum coniungeris, in ipsius similitudinem ipsa quodammodo dilectionis societate transformaris. Tuam igitur anima pulchritudine m attende, et intelliges qualem debeas pulchritudinem diligere": ibid., 230–32.

36. "Sponsum habes, sed nescis. Pulcherrimus est omnium, sed faciem eius non uidisti. Ille te uidit, quia nisi te uidisset non te diligeret. Noluit adhuc seipsum tibi praesentare, sed munera misit, arram dedit, pignus amoris, signum dilectionis. Si cognoscere illum posses, si speciem illius uideres, non amplius de tua pulchritudine ambigeres. Scires enim quod tam pulcher, tam formosus, tam elegans, tam unicus in tuo aspectu captus non esset, si eum singularis decor et ultra caeteros ammirandus non traheret": ibid., 234.

37. "Quid dedit tibi, o anima, sponsus tuus? Expectas fortasis et nescis quid dicturus sim. Cogitas a quo quid magni acceperis, nec inuenis te aliquid tale habere aut accepisse unde gloriari possis. Dicam igitur tibi, ut scias quid tibi dedit sponsus tuus. Respice uniuersum mundum istum et considera si aliquid in eo sit quod tibi non seruiat. Omnis natura ad hunc finem cursum suum dirigit ut obsequiis tuis famuletur et utilitati deseruiat, tuisque oblectamentis pariter et necessitatibus secundum affluentiam indeficientem occurrat": ibid., 234–36.

38. "Certe si haec diligis, ut subiecta dilige, ut famulantia dilige, ut dona dilige, ut arram sponsi, ut munera amici, ut beneficia Domini. Sic tamen, ut semper memineris quid illi debeat, nec ista pro illo, nec ista cum illo, sed ista propter illum, et per ista illum, et supra ista illum diligas": ibid., 236.

39. "Nescis ergo, anima mea, nescis quam foeda prius fuisti, quam polluta, quam deformis et squalida, discissa et dissipata, omni horrore et enormitate plena. Et quomodo tam cito in illum pudoris et castitatis thalamum introduci expetis, nisi prius saltem cura aliqua et studio exculta ad pristinum decorem repareris? . . . Nec polluta debet mundum tangere, nec turpem decet pulchrum uidere. Cum autem praeparata et decenter ornata fueris, tunc demum in illum caelestis sponsi thalamum sine confusione permansura introibis. Nec te pudebit tunc priscae turpitudinis, cum nichil turpe, nichil pudore dignum habebis. Prius ergo stude formam tuam excolere, faciem ornare, habitum componere, maculas tergere, mundiciam reparare, mores corrigere, disciplinam seruare et omnibus tandem in melius commutatis digno sponso dignam sponsam reddere": ibid., 262–64.

40. On this work, see most recently Zinn, "Vestigia victorina."

41. "Sunt enim quidam qui nisi buccis patentibus auscultare nesciunt, et quasi per os sensus ad cor influere debeat palatum ad uerba loquentis aperiunt. Alii, quod adhuc peius est, in agendo uel audiendo, quasi canes sitientes, linguam protendunt, et ad singulas actiones uelut molam labia contorquendo circumducunt. Alii loquentes digitum extendunt, supercilia erigunt, et oculos in orbem rotantes aut profunda quadam consideratione defigentes, cuiusdam intrinsecus magnificentie conatus ostendunt. Alii caput iactant, comam excutiunt, uestimenta adaptando componunt, et latera cubitando, pedesque extendendo, ridiculum satis ostentationis formam fingunt. Alii quasi ambe aures ad audiendum facte non sint, alteram tantum collo detorto uoci uenienti opponunt. Alii typum nescio quem figurantes oculum inter uidendum alium claudunt, alium aperiunt. Alii maiori ridiculo cum medietate oris loquuntur. Sunt preterea mille larue, mille subsannationes et corruscationes narium, mille ualgia et contortiones labiorum, quae pulchritudinem faciei et decorem discipline deformant. Est enim facies disciplinae speculum cui tanto maior custodia adhibenda est, quanto minus si quid in ea peccatum fuerit celari potest. Temperanda est igitur facies et modificanda in gestu suo, ita ut nec proterue exasperetur, nec molliter dissoluatur, sed semper habeat et rigidam dulcedinem et dulcem rigorem": Hugh of St. Victor, *De institutione novitiorum*, ed. Feiss et al., 68–70.

42. "Disciplina est compes cupiditatis, malorum desideriorum carcer, frenum lasciuie, elationis iugum, uinculum iracundie, quae domat intemperantiam, leuitatem ligat, et omnes inordinatos motus mentis atque illicitos appetitus suffocat. Sicut enim de inconstantia mentis nascitur inordinata motio corporis, ita quoque, dum corpus per disciplinam stringitur, animus ad constantiam solidatur. Et paulatim intrinsecus mens ad quietem componitur, cum per disciplinae custodiam mali motus eius foras fluere non sinuntur. Integritas ergo uirtutis est, quando per internam mentis custodiam ordinate reguntur membra corporis. Interior namque est custodia quae ordinata seruat exterius corporis membra. Sed qui statum mentis perdit, subsequenter foras in inconstantiam motionis defluit atque exteriori mobilitate indicat quod nulla interius radice subsistat. . . . Liganda sunt ergo foris per disciplinam membra corporis, ut intrinsecus solidetur status mentis, quatinus dum undique exterior custodia interiori mobilitati coercende opponitur, tandem mens ad pacem stabilem in semetipsa colligatur. Omnium namque uitiorum motus disciplina coercet, et quantum mala desideria foris coercendo comprimit, tantum per eam bonum desiderium interius conualescit. Paulatimque eadem uirtutis forma per consuetudinem menti imprimitur, quae foris per disciplinam in habitu corporis conseruatur": ibid., 48–50.

43. I refer here to Hugh of St. Victor, *De archa Noe*. On this text, in addition to Sicard, *Diagrammes médiévaux*, see Richard of Saint-Victor, *The Twelve Patriarchs*, and Zinn, "Mandala Symbolism."

44. Poirel, ed., *L'abbé Suger*.

BARBARA NEWMAN

12 *Iam cor meum non sit suum*
Exchanging Hearts, from Heloise to Helfta

> A new heart I will give you, and a new spirit I will put within you; and I will take out of your flesh the heart of stone and give you a heart of flesh.
>
> —Ezekiel 36:26

What is it that a lover desires?

Like many of the deepest questions, this one seems easy until we think about it. Of course the lover desires the beloved. But to what end? Has love fully attained its goal when it enjoys and possesses the beloved? Or does it desire to consume and assimilate that which it loves? Does it seek, as Plato's Diotima proclaims, to "beget in beauty"? Or must perfect love be willing, as Kierkegaard thought, to renounce the beloved? In a wide swath of medieval thinking, what the lover truly desires is to *become* the beloved. Put differently, the loving couple desires to "become one."

In this essay I explore a favorite medieval expression of that desire, the metaphor of exchanging hearts. Through this transaction, one person's life and love come to animate the body of the other, so that the self is not fractured but exchanged: "he in her and she in him." Born in twelfth-century romances, the exchange of hearts had by the thirteenth century infiltrated the realm of the sacred, leaving a powerful imprint on both saints' lives and mystical writing. Beginning with some twelfth-century erotic and spiritual texts, I will trace this theme through two massive thirteenth-century books, the *Legatus divinae pietatis* and the *Liber specialis gratiae*, both produced in a large-scale collaborative effort by the nuns of Helfta. In these visionary works, a motif that normally proclaimed an exclusive heterosexual bond widens into a way of speaking about a privileged soul's intimacy with God, a passionate same-sex friendship, and a deeply grounded sense of communal solidarity.

As late as the seventeenth century, the sacred and secular poet John Donne could sing the praise of that "abler soul" that arises "when love, with one another so / Interinanimates two souls" that it "makes both one, each this and that."[1] But the medieval ideal of love as fusion is no longer in vogue—so, to understand it, we must first grasp its distance from our own culture's dominant conception of love. Our psychologies tend to represent mature love as partnership, placing a premium on the maintenance of healthy ego boundaries. Individuality must not be sacrificed to a childlike yearning for surrender, for our contemporary ideal mandates the full equality and mutuality of lovers. The blurring or permanent dissolution of boundaries is seen as neurotic, regressive, codependent. In psychoanalytic terms, love as fusion is a dangerous reversion to infantile sexuality in its pre-oedipal phase of symbiotic union with the mother.[2] Hence the metaphor of exchanging hearts can trouble us because it resists our deep belief in (and desire for) personal autonomy. The medieval ideal of "oneness" can indeed be self-destructive; it is no accident that so many of the great love stories are tragic.

Yet the permeability of the self, figured by the interchanged hearts of lovers, could enrich identity as well as destroy it. As we shall see, this is especially the case when the two lovers—God and the soul—are by definition *not* equals. In that special but paradigmatic case, the exchange of hearts became a favored way to express the New Testament doctrine of coinherence, or mutual indwelling, so forcefully stated in the writings of John and Paul. "I am in the Father and the Father in me," Jesus declares in the fourth

Gospel (John 14:11). And again, "You will know that I am in my Father, and you in me, and I in you" (John 14:20). In accord with the Evangelist, the Apostle proclaims, "it is no longer I who live, but Christ who lives in me" (Gal 2:20). This sentiment would eventually crystallize around the late medieval devotion to the Sacred Heart. It could not flourish in that context, however, until it had first been explored with zest by secular lovers.

Nowhere is the ideal of love as fusion more creatively expressed than in an early twelfth-century correspondence from the Île-de-France, now characterized as "the lost love letters of Heloise and Abelard." Unfortunately, these letters have come down to us anonymously and in fragmentary form, transmitted by a single fifteenth-century manuscript from Clairvaux. Given that the authenticity of the signed, "canonical" letters between Abelard and Heloise remained controversial for the better part of a century, it is hardly surprising that Constant Mews' ascription of these more recently discovered, unsigned letters to the same authors is yet more so.[3] Space does not permit me to discuss the complex textual issues here, but since I am inclined to accept the attribution, I will refer to the two correspondents for the sake of convenience as Heloise and Abelard.[4] My argument does not hinge on their historical identity, however, for it is their thought and language that interest me. Both lovers, especially the man, use the idiom of coinherence and express it through the image of exchanging hearts. Pressed to define love, Abelard begins by exemplifying it in a greeting: "[T]o a soul than which earth has brought forth nothing more radiant or more dear to me, from the flesh inspirited and moved by that very soul: [I offer] whatever I owe to the one by whom I breathe and move."[5] In this audacious metaphor, the beloved woman is the soul and her lover the flesh ensouled, or "inspirited," by it. He vows allegiance to her in terms that deliberately evoke the divine Spirit, which animates all flesh as he says she animates his. Yet love, as he defines it, derives from the soul rather than the flesh: "Love . . . is a certain power of the soul, not existing through itself nor content with itself, but always transfusing itself into another with a certain appetite and desire, and wishing to be made one (*idem*) with the other so that, from two distinct wills, one single thing (*unum quid*) may come to be without difference (*indifferenter*)."[6]

Naturally overflowing into the other, love seeks a union not of bodies but of wills, again echoing theological language: "whoever clings to the Lord becomes one spirit with him" (1 Cor 6:17).[7] Fused by love into one, two distinct wills become not a single *will* (which would take the feminine gender) but a single neuter "thing"—"each this and that," in Donne's words—"without difference." *Indifferenter*, a key term in Abelard's contested teaching on universals, implies concrete unanimity between the lovers: "we say yes equally, we say no equally, we feel the same about everything."[8] This definition is echoed in a later greeting, with the lapidary elegance typical of early twelfth-century letters. "Anime sue, anima eius," Abelard writes, "in una anima diu unum esse."[9] "To his soul from her soul: may we long be one in a single soul."

These philosophical lovers use the lexicon of hearts, souls, and bodies indifferently to convey their mutual indwelling. "I am wholly with you, and to speak more truly, I am wholly in you," he writes.[10] "When you left," Heloise says, "I left with you in spirit and mind, leaving nothing at home but my dull and useless body."[11] Elsewhere she bids "farewell, my heart and body and all my love."[12] But Abelard stresses oneness and coinherence even more than his beloved does. "To his lily," one greeting runs—"not the lily that fades but one whose fragrance knows no change, from her heart: [may you have] as much as it is worth with all the strength of my body and mind."[13] He enjoys the casuistry of love's paradoxes: "if there can be any alterity or division within the same body, then to the best part of his own body, divided from himself, [her lover wishes] undivided, incorrupt, and inviolate loving, and the unending sweetness of the liveliest love."[14] Here a hypothetical division of the lover's body enables the beloved, as his heart or *optima pars*, to experience a new and higher integrity. In another passage he claims, "I carry you in my whole heart. I embrace you with my inner arms; the more I drink of your sweetness, the more I thirst. In you, all my abundance has gathered itself into one; all I can do is yours. So that we may devote ourselves to one another, you are I and I am you."[15] Love's idiom of fusion accepts as equivalent the formulas of partnership (*totus tecum sum*), indwelling (*totus in te sum*), and identity (*ego sum tu*).[16] Interestingly, these formulas persist throughout the correspondence, despite tantalizing if fragmentary evidence of quarrels. We find ourselves in the riddling world of Donne's "Ecstasy" or Shakespeare's "The Phoenix and the Turtle," where "Single nature's double name / Neither two nor one was called."[17]

The heart image reaches a pitch of gothic intensity in one salutation: "You are immortally entombed in my heart, from which tomb you will never emerge while I live," Abelard writes. He goes on to echo the Song of Songs: "there you lie down, there you rest [cf. Sg 1:6]. You accompany me until sleep, and in sleep you do not forsake me. When I wake, as soon as I open my eyes I see you before the very light of day. . . . Who could deny, then, that you are truly entombed in me?"[18] This striking figure is not unique to the "lost love letters." René Nelli cites a similar image from *The Ring of the Dove*, an eleventh-century Arabic treatise on love by Ibn Hazm of Cordoba.[19] In a twelfth-century Latin correspondence preserved at Tegernsee, a nun addresses her beloved male teacher in the same way: "To you whom I hold locked in my inmost heart . . . you have powerfully pierced the depths of my heart and there you have prepared yourself a throne."[20] As a flourish, she ends her Latin letter with a love-strophe in the vernacular:

Du bist min, ich bin din:	You are mine, I am yours:
des solt du gewis sin.	you can be sure of this.
du bist beslozzen	You are locked
in minem herzen:	in my heart:
verlorn ist daz slüzzelin:	the little key is lost.
du muost immer drinne sin.[21]	You must remain there forever!

While the letters ascribed to Heloise and Abelard are exceptional in their eloquence, they share with the Tegernsee correspondence and other twelfth-century texts the axiom that love seeks not mere partnership but union, coinherence, exchange of hearts—and thereby identities. The motif would be more fully elaborated in vernacular romances, notably Chrétien de Troyes' *Cligès* and *Yvain* and Gottfried von Strassburg's *Tristan*. Later on it appears in the Occitan romance of *Flamenca*, in Chaucer's *Troilus and Criseyde*, and in countless lesser-known romances where lovers exchange hearts with abandon. In the rest of this essay, however, I will turn to religious versions of the theme. By the late twelfth and early thirteenth centuries, a fruitful marriage of *fin'amors* with the Song of Songs had eroticized religious expression to a hitherto unprecedented degree.[22] As a result, the devout soon discovered that Jesus, like a good courtly lover, was eager to exchange hearts with his brides. Although the secular writers arrived first, the two literary and iconographic traditions remained closely intertwined.

An anonymous twelfth-century author inspired by Bernard of Clairvaux and Richard of St. Victor observes: "In order for the affections of lovers to merge into one through this unitive virtue [of charity], it is necessary for the lover's heart to melt away from itself so that it can be transfused, transformed, changed into the one it loves, and united to the other—just as a drop of water infused into wine seems to lose itself completely as it takes on the taste and color of the wine."[23] Melting, merging, and migrating hearts are met frequently thereafter. St. Hermann Joseph (d. 1241), a Premonstratensian of Steinfeld and the author of a lost Song of Songs commentary, penned a devotional lyric in which he prays, in the person of the Bride:

Iam cor meum dilatatur	Already my heart expands
Et iam in te delectatur,	And already it delights in you;
Sentit vere te praesentem,	It feels you truly present,
Sentit te in se manentem	It feels you abiding in it,
Praegustat suavem gratiam.	Already it tastes sweet grace.
. . . .	. . . .
Iam cor meum non sit suum,	Let my heart no longer be its own,
Vivat tibi sitque tuum;	Let it live for you and be yours;
Sit in te et tu in eo,	Let it be in you and you in it,
Ut quiescat sic cum Deo	That it may thus find rest with God
Fiatque unus spiritus.[24]	And become one spirit [with him].

This plea for coinherence, given narrative form, would become an enduring topos of mystical hagiography. As a prelude to the exchange of hearts proper, thirteenth-century legends about the early Christian martyr St. Ignatius helped to popularize a new cult of the heart in devotional thought and practice. Vincent of Beauvais' *Speculum historiale* (c. 1245) added a brief section marked *auctor* (meaning that Vincent wrote it himself) to the martyr's existing legend: "St. Ignatius wrote twelve letters. His heart was divided in pieces and the name of Jesus Christ was found in golden letters, as we read, in each of its parts. He was said to have Christ in his heart."[25] The saint actually did write seven letters, here augmented perhaps to recall the twelve apostles (he was said to be a disciple of St. John, and one of his apocryphal letters addressed the Virgin Mary, no less). By a mystical transposition of active into passive, the letters Ignatius inscribed on parchment become letters inscribed on his heart, presumably divided into twelve pieces. Like the Eucharist, his broken heart remains whole in every fragment. Vincent of Beauvais' invention clearly piqued the interest of contemporaries, for as early as 1247, the preacher William of Savoy was citing it as an ancient miracle authenticated by Rome. To promote devotion to the Holy Name, William added the gloss that, as St. Ignatius was being tortured, he cried ceaselessly on the name of Jesus. In response to the pagans' queries, he explained that this name was written on his heart and therefore he could not be silent. So they killed him and performed an autopsy, whereupon they found the golden letters.[26] Jacobus de Voragine inserted these details into his ubiquitous *Golden Legend* (c. 1260), which quickly spread the tale throughout Europe.[27]

It was but a short step from having the name of Jesus inscribed on one's heart to possessing the heart of Jesus himself. This grace is first reported of Lutgard of Aywières (d. 1246), a Flemish Cistercian nun whose *Life*, written by her friend and disciple Thomas of Cantimpré, is contemporary with the legend of Ignatius' heart. In the Dominican friar's miracle-drenched narrative, Lutgard's exchange of hearts with Christ belongs to a series of mystical favors that include levitating at prayer, sucking from the wounds of Christ, chanting with miraculous sweetness, and oozing holy oil from her fingertips. Thomas makes this gift the culmination of a "three wishes" scenario in which Lutgard first receives, then rejects, the gifts of healing and of understanding the Latin Psalter. Finally Christ asks what she truly wants, and she replies, "'I want your heart.' 'No, rather it is I who want your heart,' replied the Lord. 'So be it, Lord . . . with you as my shield, my heart will be secure for all time.' And so a communion of hearts occurred from that time on, or rather, the union of an uncreated with a created spirit through a surplus of grace. It was this of which the Apostle says: she 'who clings to God is made one spirit with him'" (1 Cor 6:17).[28] If Thomas' chronology is accurate, which it may or may not be, Lutgard was still in her teens and had not yet made her monastic profession when this occurred. The exchange of hearts thus marks only the first stage of her love affair with Christ, rather than a state of spiritual perfection. As with earthly lovers in romance, the exchange is first of all a vow of fidelity. From this time forth, Thomas explains, Lutgard never felt the least stirring of carnal temptation, for her heart belonged wholly to her celestial bridegroom.

Whether the *Vita Lutgardis* established a model or simply marked a trend, the exchange of hearts would soon become a regular feature of women's mystical *vitae*. More than thirty women claimed or were said to have received this grace, among them Adelheid Langmann (1312–75), Catherine of Siena (1347–80), Dorothy of Montau (1347–94), Osanna of Mantua (1449–1505), Teresa of Avila (1515–82), Caterina de Ricci (1522–90), and Marguerite-Marie Alacoque (1647–90).[29] The erotic motif fits easily into the standard hagiographic model of the holy woman as bride of Christ, a model that male hagiographers almost inevitably applied to their female subjects. Interestingly, however, the largest set of medieval texts on the exchange of hearts is female-authored, proving that men did not simply invent or impose the motif. This is the vast corpus of mystical hagiography from the abbey of Helfta. Although much of this literature was written by or about Gertrude the Great (1256–1301/2), it encompasses the extensive revelations of her friend Mechthild of Hackeborn (1241–98) and the literary contributions of at least two anonymous nuns. During the long reign of Mechthild's sister, Abbess Gertrude of Hackeborn (1251–91), the wealthy Saxon abbey was a hotbed of visionary culture.

Affiliated with the Cistercians by its rule and the Dominicans by its clergy, Helfta was home from 1270 until 1282 to Mechthild of Magdeburg, a celebrated vernacular poet-mystic, who took refuge there after old age, blindness, and harassment put an end to her independent life. The former beguine dictated the last book of her *Flowing Light of the Godhead* at Helfta, so her previous visions were almost certainly known to the nuns. In one of them—early in her mystical life, as with Lutgard—Christ shows Mechthild his divine heart aglow like "red gold burning in a great fire of coals." As he places her soul within it, "the exalted Sovereign and the little waif thus embrace and are united as water and wine."[30] Here we find again the mystical metaphor so beloved of the Cistercians and Victorines. Mechthild's fiery spirit must have been a catalyst for the sisters who transcribed her revelations, for they continued to write long after she died—with the difference that, unlike the beguine, they had the ability to compose in Latin. Unique in thirteenth-century women's literature, the Helfta corpus testifies to these nuns' remarkable theological culture and Abbess Gertrude's respect for books and learning. In just over a decade—from 1289 through around 1302—the women of Helfta produced two prodigious Latin tomes, the *Legatus divinae pietatis* and the *Liber specialis gratiae*, which together fill about twelve hundred printed pages.

Traditionally, the *Liber* is attributed to Mechthild of Hackeborn, chantress and sister of the abbess, while the *Legatus* is ascribed to her younger friend, Gertrude the Great.[31] It would be more accurate, however, to describe both books as the fruits of an exceptional collaboration.[32] Written in the last years of Mechthild of Hackeborn's life, from 1291 to 1298, the *Liber* recounts her revelations as told to at least two unnamed nuns, one of whom was surely her beloved Gertrude. As for the *Legatus*, only book 2 (c. 1289) was written by Gertrude's own hand. Book 1 is a hagiographic account, while books 3–5 relate her visions in the same "as told to" genre as the *Liber*. Their authorship is unknown, and the nuns' commitment to anonymity means that the riddle of who wrote what can never be solved. More important, however, is the relationship disclosed by these braided texts. Gertrude and Mechthild, who had both entered the cloister as children, became intimate friends, sharing their most private experiences, admiring each other's gifts, praying for each other, and receiving revelations through and about one another. Both were unquestionably in love with Jesus and exchanged hearts with him; but they also loved one another, making Jesus the mediator through whom they exchanged their own hearts. Placed side by side, their books are a visionary hall of mirrors in which the same images recur, ascribed now to Gertrude, now to Mechthild, as recounted by their sister-scribes.

Anna Harrison has recently argued that the Helfta literature achieves a remarkable equilibrium between the seers' absorption in their personal intimacy with Christ and their concern to extend this union to the entire community.[33] I would go further to suggest that the two poles of private mystical union and communal solidarity are mediated by a third term, implicit but nearly always present: the deep friendship that developed between the novice mistress, Mechthild, and her most spiritually gifted protégée, Gertrude. This friendship must undoubtedly have grown—even as it was keenly tested—during the complex authorial and scribal process that produced the two books. But its intensity is clearest in the first and last books of the *Legatus*. The first relates Gertrude's early religious life as reflected in Mechthild's visions; the last describes Mechthild's deathbed experience as revealed by Gertrude's visions. Before turning to these passages, however, I will first explore the broader themes of the Sacred Heart and the exchange of hearts with Christ, which permeate both the *Legatus* and the *Liber*.

Throughout the Helfta literature, the Heart of Christ offers and signifies "experiential space" (*Erfahrungsraum*).[34] It is a reassuringly material abode of love, a powerful sign of divine abundance and interiority. Nurturing, life-giving, and infinitely resourceful, it is also a womblike shelter that may be entered through the side-wound, and like a womb, "it bleeds, it flows, it opens, it encloses."[35] Metaphorically it is compared to a lyre, a lamp, a vineyard, a furnace, and a fountain, from which flow streams of crystal, rosewater, and, of course, blood. Above all, the heart of Christ is the mystic's home. In one vision Mechthild sees it as

> a most beautiful house, lofty and very wide—within which she saw a little cottage built of cedar wood, its interior walls covered with splendid silver plate; and in the midst of it sat the Lord. She easily recognized this house as the heart of God, for she had often seen it under this form; but the cottage inside represented the soul, which is immortal and eternal, just as cedar wood is immune to rot.... And the Lord said to her, "Your soul is always enclosed thus in my heart, and I in the heart of your soul. And although you contain me in your inmost self, so that I am more intimate than any inwardness of your own, yet my divine heart towers so high above your soul that it may seem quite unattainable. That is signified by the lofty height and breadth of this house."[36]

In this image of coinherence, Christ is both inside and out—seated within the little cottage that figures the soul, and far beyond it as the great house enclosing that cottage. Mechthild's heart is both container and contained. Importantly, it is also a source of salvation for others. After entering once more into the heart of Christ, Mechthild sees "fiery rays" proceed from each of her limbs to the people for whom she has prayed.[37]

On another occasion, feeling unworthy of God's favor, she protests that she has no right even to wash the dishes in his kitchen—prompting a revelation that Christ's "kitchen" is none other than his divine heart. Just like a kitchen, the heart of God is accessible to all, both slaves and free, ready to fulfill their desires. Its "dishes" are the hearts of the saints, which the nun sees being constantly replenished with "torrents of divine pleasure" from the heart of Christ even as they constantly refill it with their gratitude.[38] Here the exchange of hearts is not private but communal, a ceaseless flood of delights flowing between God's heart and each devotee's. Gertrude made the same image her own. In one of her many exchange-of-hearts visions, she offers her heart to Christ, asking him to cleanse it with blood and water from his own heart. She then sees Christ offering her heart to the Father, united with his in such a way that the two parts form one chalice. Accepting Gertrude's prayer that her heart may stand ready at need for anyone he may wish to serve, like the flagons on a lord's table, Christ asks the Father that "this heart [may] pour out, to your eternal praise, all that my Heart contained for dispensation in my human nature."[39] This exchange of hearts is not an end in itself but a means to serve others. As Harrison has shown, the women of Helfta conceived their communal writing project as a way of enacting such symbolic exchanges in practice. Reading of her sisters' experiences should encourage the monastic reader "to become aware that she has much and . . . to want more" of God's heartfelt love.[40] Unlike the exchange of hearts in romance or in saints' lives like the *Vita Lutgardis*, where it signifies an exclusive bond, the exchange of hearts in the Helfta community is inclusive and open-ended.

One of the most frequent images is the emanation of "golden reeds" (*fistulae*) from the Sacred Heart, through which the sisters sip grace as if from straws. A *fistula* was the reed that priests used to drink from the consecrated chalice,[41] suggesting that for Gertrude, who compared Christ's heart to a chalice, this grace replaced the sacred beverage that nuns could no longer receive in communion.[42] In one vision she sees a golden pipe reaching down to her from the Sacred Heart and receives through it "an overflowing bounty of all she could desire."[43] Soon afterwards, the same grace is extended to the whole congregation. As the mystic prays for her sisters, Christ assures her that he has given each one a golden reed by which to draw all she desires "from the depths of my divine Heart."[44] Gertrude understands the reed as free will, so that those who drink most copiously from the Sacred Heart are the nuns who have most fully surrendered their wills to God, while others, more self-reliant, receive gifts with difficulty from a greater distance. Gifts from Christ's heart can even be given by proxy. Praying for a nun, Gertrude sees "a little stream of crystalline purity" flowing from the heart of God into her sister's heart.[45] She asks how this can possibly help the other, who remains unaware of it, but Christ promises that, like a slow-acting medicine, the grace will take effect in due time. In a variant on this theme, Mechthild sees rays of light extending from the heart of God into the hearts of her two scribes. Since these nuns had long been writing without her knowledge or consent, the vision reassures her that the *Liber* has indeed been written by God's grace.[46]

Within the communitarian ethos of Helfta, there seems to have been no objection to relationships that a slightly later monastic regime would stigmatize and repress as "particular friendships."[47] Mechthild and her protégée, Gertrude, clearly had such a relationship, which in the *Legatus divinae pietatis* is vividly expressed through the lexicon of the heart. Book 1 recounts a series of visions Mechthild had about Gertrude, perhaps during the younger nun's novitiate, while book 5 is a play-by-play narrative of Mechthild's death as imagined in Gertrude's visions. Both accounts were recorded by other, unnamed nuns, embedding the love triangle of Jesus, Gertrude, and Mechthild firmly in the matrix of community. No male scribes or priests are mentioned, making this work a testament of female intimacy unique in medieval literature.

The first set of visions, nested in Gertrude's *vita*, seems at first to reflect some rivalry between the two mystics. A stranger "well proven in divine revelations" comes to Helfta seeking spiritual profit and is told by Christ that the first nun who sits down beside her will be the most faithful of all. Gertrude is in fact the first, but "out of humility" she declines conversation. After her comes "Lady Mechthild, the chantress of blessed memory," whose gracious words please the stranger so much that she imagines Christ had deceived her. In response, the Lord asserts, "I am doing great things in this one [Mechthild], but much greater in the other [Gertrude]."[48] Doubtless not all the nuns would have agreed with that assessment; but who could have been the source of the anecdote? Surely not Gertrude, who could not have boasted of her own humility; nor Mechthild, whom the pious stranger would not have insulted by repeating such a message; nor the stranger (a stock figure in such tales), unless she had been sent by the devil expressly to sow discord! Rather, the tale is a literary fiction crafted by the writer to press claims for the living Gertrude's holiness, even as she gracefully nods to the saint cult already forming around Mechthild, her mentor and friend.

There follow four anecdotes in which Mechthild, probably in her role as novice mistress (*magistra*), describes her visions and dialogues with Christ about Gertrude. In the first she sees the young nun walking to and fro before the Lord, "longing ardently for the emanations from his divine Heart."[49] Next, while praying for her protégée, Mechthild sees Gertrude's heart in the likeness of a bridge, fortified on one side by Christ's humanity, on the other by his divinity, as if by two parapets.[50] This vision assures her that anyone who seeks to reach Christ by way of Gertrude will not go astray. The third vision is more intimate: Mechthild sees her friend in Christ's embrace, pressing her heart against the opening of his side wound. To explain the image, Christ tells Mechthild of the special favors he has granted Gertrude through the joining of their hearts. Her prayers for others will always be answered, no one she recommends for communion will be considered unworthy of it, and no one who hears her words "can possibly be wrong in thinking that the secret of my divine Heart is made known through what she says."[51] In the fourth exchange, Mechthild worries that the younger nun is too impulsive, but Christ reassures her that Gertrude has already attained a high degree of perfection: "I have chosen her to dwell in, so that her will, and consequently the operation of her virtuous will, are one with my Heart; she is like my Heart's right hand by which my will is accomplished."[52] The heart figures here as the self in concentrated form, the medium of union. It is directly through his heart that Christ acts and communicates, and the arresting image of Gertrude as his "Heart's right hand" revalues what Mechthild had at first seen as her friend's youthful rashness. Far from expressing envy, Mechthild must have related these flattering narratives from her sickbed, just as she revealed the visions compiled in her *Liber*. Her sister-scribes found in her memories a perfect vehicle to introduce their compilation of Gertrude's visions.

Book 5 of the *Legatus*, which deals with souls of the departed, turns the tables. In the writer's loving fifteen-page account of Mechthild's death, only Gertrude's revelations make the beloved chantress' soul transparent to her sisters. The account nowhere states that the dying Mechthild confided any experience to Gertrude; all is mediated by Christ through visions and dialogues. At one point Gertrude humbly decides not to share these revelations with the community, but Christ is displeased. So, despite her best efforts, she can see nothing more about Mechthild's soul until she repents.[53] Spiritual hoarding is not allowed, nor is a soul permitted privacy; the divine intimacies of one are meant for all to share. So we have, in effect, the story of Mechthild's death as her best friend imagined it, projecting onto her vigil every love-token from God that the sisters desired for themselves. As Mechthild is anointed in the presence of saints and angels, Gertrude sees Christ give her a honey-sweet kiss with his passionate lips. After the unction, he embraces her "so that the wound of his most sweet Heart lay open to her mouth, and from it she seemed to draw every breath that she took and exhale it once again into the same loving Heart."[54] Not the dying woman herself, but her soul, in the form of a lovely young girl (*puella valde delicata*), exhales thus into the wounded heart. Each time she does so, Christ drenches the world in a rain of grace.

Similar visions continue until the hour of consummation, when Christ wraps his bride in a mantle of light and calls to her: "Come, ye blessed of my Father, receive the kingdom; arise, make haste, my beloved, and come."[55] With this greeting, Gertrude notes, Christ was reminding Mechthild of how, a few years earlier, he had given her his heart with precisely these words as a pledge of love. The reminiscence is also a literary allusion, for it must have been Gertrude herself who had recorded Mechthild's account of that experience in the *Liber*. Hearing the Mass that begins "Come, ye blessed," Mechthild had expressed a wish to be among the happy souls who would receive such a greeting, and the Lord had promised that she would. "I will give you my heart," he added, "as a pledge that you may always have with you; and on that day when I have fulfilled this desire of yours, you will return it to me as a witness. And I give you my heart as a house of refuge, so that in the hour of your death you may pass by no way except into my heart, there to rest forever."[56] Thenceforth, says the *Liber*, Mechthild conceived a profound devotion to the Sacred Heart. Now as she lies dying, Gertrude imagines Christ asking tenderly, "And where is my gift?" In response she sees Mechthild opening her heart with both hands, "and the Lord, applying his own most holy heart to her heart, happily joined her whole being to his glory, absorbed by the power of his divinity."[57] The account ends with posthumous visions in which Mechthild, now among the blessed, enables her devotees to draw fresh gifts from the Heart of Christ.

Pious deathbeds were a staple of hagiography, but only this one lets the reader into the saint's very soul in her final hours. Gertrude was certain she knew what Mechthild was experiencing, just as Mechthild had earlier been privy to Christ's intimacies with Gertrude. Each woman in her own prayers sees her sister kissed or embraced by God, welcomed into his wound, and united with him in the bed of his heart. There is no hint of repression in these unabashed erotic visions,[58] nor does jealousy arise, for the women love each other just as they love Jesus. Here then is a love triangle with a difference. In secular romance, the woman often functions as a lens to focus a relationship between men: *Troilus and Criseyde* is as much about the friendship of Troilus and Pandarus as about the hero's fatal love.[59] What we see in the Helfta texts is a religious parallel with the genders reversed: the *Legatus divinae pietatis* celebrates the intimate friendship of Gertrude and Mechthild. Though this relationship is "lesbian-like" in its emotional intensity, to adopt a phrase of Judith Bennett, it is not celebrated for its own sake, but triangulated through the heart of Christ.[60] In the women of Helfta we see not so much the "mystical love *noir*" that Karma Lochrie discerns in the writings of Hadewijch and Angela of Foligno,[61] but an optimistic, almost utopian brand of mystical sensuality, which neither posits a conflict between divine and human love nor privileges suffering, as fourteenth-century *vitae* would do. Where male hagiographers imagined the exchange of hearts as a unique, exclusive pair-bond between a saint and Jesus, explicitly opposed to human love, the Helfta women embedded the exchange in a broad context of interpersonal and communal intimacy, setting their treatment of the theme apart from all others.

NOTES

1. Donne, "The Ecstasy," vv. 36, 41–43, in Donne, *Selected Poetry*, 113–16.
2. Bergmann, "Psychoanalytic Observations on the Capacity to Love," 32.
3. The letters were first published by Könsgen, ed., *Epistolae duorum amantium: Briefe Abelards und Heloises?*. Constant Mews reprinted Könsgen's edition with a detailed study, without the titular question mark, in *The Lost Love Letters of Heloise and Abelard*. In support of the ascription see Jaeger, *Ennobling Love*, 160–64; Ward and Chiavaroli, "The Young Heloise"; Wulstan, "*Novi modulaminis melos*"; Clanchy, "The Letters of Abelard and Heloise"; and Mews, *Abelard and Heloise*, 62–80. Peter Dronke, writing before Mews, rejects the attribution: *Women Writers of the Middle Ages*, 92–97. For arguments against Mews see Moos, "Die *Epistolae duorum amantium*," and Ziolkowski, "Lost and Not Yet Found." For a debate between Jaeger and Giles Constable, who rejects the ascription, see Jaeger, "*Epistolae duorum amantium*"; Constable, "The Authorship of the *Epistolae duorum amantium*"; and Jaeger, "A Reply to Giles Constable."

4. I have outlined my position in Newman, "Liminalities," 374–77.

5. "Anime qua nec candidius, nec michi carius terra protulit, caro quam eadem anima spirare facit et moveri: quicquid ei debeo per quem spiro et moveor." Mews, *Lost Love Letters*, Letter 24, 208. Translations are mine unless otherwise noted.

6. "Est igitur amor, vis quedam anime non per se existens nec seipsa contenta, sed semper cum quodam appetitu et desiderio, se in alterum transfundens, et cum altero idem effici volens ut de duabus diversis voluntatibus unum quid indifferenter efficiatur." Ibid.

7. On the union of wills or *unitas spiritus* as a theme in twelfth-century mysticism, see McGinn, *The Growth of Mysticism*, 213–15, 264–67. Cicero also defines friendship as a union of wills ("voluntatum studiorum sententiarum summa consensio"): *Laelius de amicitia* 15, ed. Powell, 34.

8. "Eque annuimus, eque negamus, idem per omnia sapimus." Mews, *Lost Love Letters*, Letter 24, 208–9, trans. Chiavaroli. For *indifferenter* here and in Abelard's logic, see ibid., 124–28.

9. Ibid., Letter 65, 244.

10. "Totus tecum sum, et ut verius dicam, totus in te sum." Ibid., Letter 16, 198.

11. "Te discedente tecum discessi spiritu et mente, nec aliud relictum fuit patrie, nisi corpus stolidum et inutile." Ibid., Letter 45, 224. Rhymed prose is typical of the woman's (and Heloise's) style.

12. "Vale, cor et corpus meum, et omnis dilectio mea." Ibid., Letter 18, 200.

13. "Lilio suo, non illi lilio quod marcescit, sed quod odorem mutare nescit, cor eius: quantum tota vi corporis et animi valet." Ibid., Letter 43, 222.

14. "Si in eodem corpore ulla potest esse alteritas, vel divisio, tunc divise a se optime parti sui corporis: indivisam dilectionem, incorruptam, et integram, et interminabilem vivacissimi amoris dulcedinem." Ibid., Letter 85, 264.

15. "Toto te pectore gero. Interioribus ulnis te amplector, dulcedinem tuam quo plus haurio plus sitio. Omnes copie mee in te unam se congesserunt, omne quod possum tuum est. Ut ergo operas mutuas demus, tu es ego, et ego sum tu." Ibid., Letter 77, 258.

16. On these formulas see Ohly, "Du bist mein, ich bin dein," and Morrison, "I Am You."

17. William Shakespeare, "The Phoenix and the Turtle," vv. 39–40, in Shakespeare, *Poems*, 242. Compare vv. 25–30: "So they loved, as love in twain / Had the essence but in one: / Two distincts, division none; / Number there in love was slain. // Hearts remote, yet not asunder; / Distance, and no space was seen."

18. "In pectore meo immortaliter sepulta es, de quo sepulcro me vivente non emerges; ibi cubas, ibi quiescis. Usque ad somnum me comitaris, in somno me non deseris, post somnum statim ut oculos aperio ante ipsum celi lumen te video. . . . Quis ergo negare poterit, quin veraciter in me sepulta sis?" Mews, *Lost Love Letters*, Letter 22, 204.

19. Nelli, *L'Érotique des troubadours*, 315. In Ibn Hazm, *The Ring of the Dove*, trans. Arberry, the stanza reads: "Here let her live, so long as I / Draw breath,

and when I come to die / My heart for comfort may she crave / In the dark silence of the grave," 124.

20. "[A]d te, inquam, quem teneo medullis cordis inclusum . . . tu cordis mei intima fortiter penetrasti tibique inibi, quod dictu mirabile est, sedem . . . preparasti." *Des Minnesangs Frühling*, ed. Kraus et al., 319.

21. Ohly, "Du bist mein, ich bin dein," 371.

22. Newman, "*La mystique courtoise*: Thirteenth-Century Beguines and the Art of Love," in *From Virile Woman to WomanChrist*, 137–67, and eadem, "Love Divine, All Loves Excelling," in *God and the Goddesses*, 138–89.

23. "Ut autem hac unitiva virtute in unum concurrere possint affectus amantium, cor amantis a se liquefieri necesse est, ut transfundi possit, et transformari, et in illum quem amat mutari et uniri alteri, quemadmodum aquae stilla infusa vino deficere a se tota videtur dum alterius saporem induit et colorem." Ps.-Richard of St. Victor, *De gradibus charitatis* 4, PL 196:1205D.

24. Joseph, "Iubilus de Domino Nostro Iesu Christo."

25. Vincent of Beauvais, *Speculum historiale* 10.57, cited in Polo de Beaulieu, "La légende du coeur," 303.

26. Polo de Beaulieu, "La légende du coeur," 306.

27. Jacobus de Voragine, *The Golden Legend*, 1:142–43.

28. Thomas of Cantimpré, *Vita Lutgardis Aquiriensis* 1.12, ed. Henschen, 3:193, and *Life of Lutgard of Aywières*, trans. King and Newman, 227.

29. Cabassut, "Coeurs, changement des."

30. Mechthild of Magdeburg, *The Flowing Light of the Godhead* 1.4, trans. Tobin, 43.

31. This Gertrude, whose family is unknown, was no relation to Abbess Gertrude of Hackeborn and never held monastic office. On the Helfta mystics generally see Bynum, "Women Mystics in the Thirteenth Century," in her *Jesus as Mother*, 170–262; Finnegan, *The Women of Helfta*; and McGinn, *The Flowering of Mysticism*, 267–82.

32. Voaden, "All Girls Together"; Kolletzki, "Über die Wahrheit dieses Buches"; Hubrath, "The *Liber specialis gratiae* as a Collective Work"; and Harrison, "Oh! What Treasure is in this Book?"

33. Harrison, "I Am Wholly Your Own."

34. Spitzlei, *Erfahrungsraum Herz*.

35. Voaden, "All Girls Together," 74.

36. "Post haec ostendit ei Dominus pulcherrimam domum excelsam et amplam nimis; intra quam aliam vidit domunculam factam ex lignis cedrinis, interius laminis argenteis valde splendidis coopertam, in cujus medio Dominus residebat. Hanc domum Cor Dei esse bene recognovit, quia multoties ipsum tali viderat forma; domuncula vero interior animam illam figurabat quae, sicut ligna cedrina imputribilia sunt, immortalis est et aeterna. . . . Et ait Dominus ad eam: 'Sic anima tua semper est in Corde meo inclusa et ego in corde animae tuae. Et licet in intimis tuis me contineas, ita ut intimior sim omni intimo tuo, tamen divinum Cor meum ita

excellens et supereminens est animae tuae ut omnino inattingibile videatur, quod per hujus domus celsitudinem et amplitudinem denotatur.'" Mechthild of Hackeborn, *Liber specialis gratiae* 1.19, 61–62 (all page numbers for Mechthild refer to vol. 2 of *Revelationes Gertrudianae ac Mechtildianae*). A new critical edition of this text, with German translation, is promised by Margarete Hubrath and Elke Senne. Translations are my own.

37. Mechthild of Hackeborn, *Liber specialis gratiae* 1.19, 70; compare Harrison, "I Am Wholly Your Own," 574–75.

38. "Coquina mea est Cor meum deificum, quod in modum coquinae, quae domus est communis et pervia omnibus tam servis quam liberis, semper patens est omnibus, et promptum ad cujuslibet delectamentum.... Quae [corda] singula torrens deificae voluptatis egrediens a profluvio divini Cordis copiosissima videbatur supereffluentia influere, quae rursus influentia de corde Sanctorum reinfluens cum mira gratitudine Cor Dominicum repetebat." Mechthild of Hackeborn, *Liber specialis gratiae* 2.23, 65–66.

39. "In tuam aeternam laudem, o Pater sancte, cor illud effundat quae Cor meum dispensative continuit in mea humanitate." Gertrude of Helfta, *Legatus divinae pietatis* 3.30.2, 3:134–36, and *The Herald of God's Loving-Kindness*, trans. Barratt, 2:104. Barratt's translation includes only books 1–2 (vol. 1) and book 3 (vol. 2).

40. Harrison, "Oh! What Treasure is in this Book?" 101.

41. Gertrude of Helfta, *The Herald of God's Loving-Kindness*, 2:95n.

42. On the gradual withdrawal of the chalice from the laity, see Bynum, *Holy Feast and Holy Fast*, 45, 56, 65, 118, 230; Lamberts, "Liturgie et spiritualité de l'eucharistie."

43. "Per quam fistulam mirabili modo influxit ei omnium desiderabilium affluentiam." Gertrude of Helfta, *Legatus divinae pietatis* 3.26.2, 24.

44. Ibid., 3.30.1, 132.

45. Ibid., 3.9.4, 38; Gertrude of Helfta, *The Herald of God's Loving-Kindness*, 2:44.

46. "Vidit etiam de Corde Dei tres radios tendentes in corda duarum personarum quae hunc librum scribebant; per quod intellexit quod divina inspirante et confortante eas gratia, hoc opus peragebant." Mechthild of Hackeborn, *Liber specialis gratiae* 5.22, 355.

47. This catchphrase dates back at least to the mid-fourteenth-century Dominican sisterbooks. At St. Katharinental, for example, Christ tells the prioress that those who indulge in "particular love" (*sunder minn*) cause his heart more bitterness than his passion causes her own heart. *Das "St. Katharinentaler Schwesternbuch,"* 98. It is not clear whether the main concern was unchastity or cliquishness.

48. "Magna sunt quae in illa operor, sed multo majora sunt quae operor in ista, et adhuc maxima operabor in ea." Gertrude of Helfta, *Legatus divinae pietatis* 1.3.2, 136.

49. Ibid., 1.11.9, 178; Gertrude of Helfta, *The Herald of God's Loving-Kindness*, 1:74.

50. Gertrude of Helfta, *Legatus divinae pietatis* 1.14.6, 202.

51. "... quidquid tunc loquitur indubitanter certum habebitur, quia nec ipsa nec audientes nullatenus falli possunt, quin divini Cordis mei secretum in verbo ipsius innotescat." Ibid., 1.16.1, 210; Gertrude of Helfta, *The Herald of God's Loving-Kindness*, 1:90.

52. "... ego elegi eam sic ad inhabitandum, quod voluntas ejus, et per consequens opus bonae voluntatis ejus, est Cordi meo inhaerens, quasi pro dextra, cum qua operatur quod ego volo." Gertrude of Helfta, *Legatus divinae pietatis* 1.16.2, 212; Gertrude of Helfta,, *The Herald of God's Loving-Kindness*, 1:90.

53. Gertrude of Helfta, *Legatus divinae pietatis* 5.4.10, 90–92.

54. "Peracta vero unctione, Dominus eam in amplexus amantissime suscipiens sic per biduum sustentabat, ut vulnus dulcissimi Cordis sui ad os infirmae pateret, a quo omnem flatum quem spirabat trahere et iterum in idem Cor dulcissimum emittere videbatur." Ibid., 5.4.6, 86.

55. "Venite, benedicta Patris mei, percipite regnum. Surge, propera, amica mea, et veni." Ibid., 5.4.18, 100.

56. "... daboque tibi Cor meum in pignus quod tecum semper habeas, et in die illa cum hoc desiderium tuum complevero, in testimonium mihi illud resignes. Do etiam tibi Cor meum in domum refugii, ut in hora defunctionis tuae nulla via praeterquam in Cor meum perpetuo pausatura declines." Mechthild of Hackeborn, *Liber specialis gratiae* 2.19, 156.

57. "'Et ubi est xenium meum?' Ad quod illa cor suum ambabus manibus contra Cor dilecti similiter contra se patefacti aperiens, et Dominus Cor suum sanctissimum cordi illius applicans, totam eam suae divinitatis virtute absorptam gloriae suae feliciter sociavit." Gertrude of Helfta, *Legatus divinae pietatis* 5.4.18, 102.

58. Barratt, "The Woman Who Shares the King's Bed."

59. This line of reading derives ultimately from Sedgwick, *Between Men*. See also Dinshaw, "Reading Like a Man"; Pugh, "Queer Pandarus?"; Hill, "Aristocratic Friendship in *Troilus and Criseyde*."

60. Bennett, "'Lesbian-Like' and the Social History of Lesbianisms." See also Matter, "My Sister, My Spouse."

61. Lochrie, "Mystical Acts, Queer Tendencies," 181.

RACHEL FULTON BROWN

13 Hildegard of Bingen's Theology of Revelation

This chapter offers a reading of Hildegard's *Scivias* as a work of coherent theology, structured according to a particular understanding of God. Form here is indicative of content: just as, for Hildegard, it was theologically necessary for her work to take the form of visionary revelation, so the chapter is framed as a "reading" of Hildegard's work as itself, like scripture, the Word of God. The frame is intended to startle, but it is also intended to point to Hildegard's purpose in writing her own work in the form that she did: as visions, not because she was a woman and therefore lacking in authority to speak, but rather as a witness to the way in which the Trinity has revealed itself to the world. Previous scholars have tended to suggest that the topics Hildegard addresses in the *Scivias* appear somewhat at random; my contention is that they appear purposefully in the order that they do so as to reflect the way in which the Trinity (Father, Son, and Holy Spirit) made itself known in history, through creation, the sacraments, and the virtues of the Christian soul. From this perspective, Hildegard's *Scivias* appears both as tightly structured and as rigorously argued as the other great *summae* of her day. Moreover, I would argue, Hildegard's reading of the sacraments as revelations of the Trinity as a whole offers a powerful corrective to prevailing images of twelfth-century spiritual imagination as focused primarily on the Incarnate God.

A READING FROM THE BOOK *SCIVIAS*, OR *KNOW THE WAYS*, book 1, vision 1:

> I saw a great mountain the color of iron, and enthroned on it One of such great glory that it blinded my sight. On each side of him there extended a soft shadow, like a wing of wondrous breadth and length. Before him, at the foot of the mountain, stood an image full of eyes on all sides, in which, because of those eyes, I could discern no human form. In front of this image stood another, a child wearing a tunic of subdued color but white shoes, upon whose head such glory descended from the One enthroned upon that mountain that I could not look at its face. But from the One who sat enthroned upon that mountain many living sparks sprang forth, which flew very sweetly around the images. Also, I perceived in this mountain many little windows, in which appeared human heads, some of subdued colors and some white.
>
> And, behold, He Who was enthroned upon that mountain cried out in a strong, loud voice saying, "O human, who are fragile dust of the earth and ashes of ashes! Cry out and speak of the origin of pure salvation until those people are instructed, who, though they see the inmost contents of the Scriptures, do not wish to tell them or preach them, because they are lukewarm and sluggish in serving the justice of God. Unlock for them the enclosure of mysteries that they, timid as they are, conceal in a hidden and fruitless field. Burst forth into a fountain of abundance and overflow with mystical knowledge, until they who now think you contemptible because of Eve's transgression are stirred up by the flood of your irrigation. For you have received your profound insight not from humans, but from the lofty and tremendous Judge on high, where this calmness will shine strongly with glorious light among the shining ones.

> "Arise, therefore, cry out and tell what is shown to you by the strong power of God's help, for He Who rules every creature in might and kindness floods those who fear Him and serve Him in sweet love and humility with the glory of heavenly enlightenment and leads those who persevere in the way of justice to the joys of the Eternal Vision."[1]

A great deal, perhaps even too much, has been written about the way in which Hildegard of Bingen used her visions as a way of claiming the authority, despite the fact of her female sex and lack of formal education, to speak.[2] What I would like to focus on here is the way in which they underpin her theology, that is, her thinking about God. I take my inspiration from two sources.

The first is a woodcut from the chronicle published by Hartmann Schedel in Nuremberg in 1493 in which Hildegard appears unmistakably as a woman, a virgin, in fact, with long flowing hair, alongside three of the greatest schoolmen of her own day: Gratian, Peter Lombard, and Peter Comestor.[3] Hildegard, this image seems to be suggesting, was not simply the *magistra* for her sisters at St. Disibod's and, latterly, St. Rupert's; she was, as Cardinal Pitra, the nineteenth-century editor of her works held her to be, a *magistra sententiarum*, her works comparable to Peter Lombard's own great synthesis of Christian doctrine.[4] Many modern scholars would seem to agree. As Barbara Newman observed in her introduction to the Classics of Western Spirituality translation of Hildegard's first great work, "If Hildegard had been a male theologian, her *Scivias* would undoubtedly have been considered one of the most important early medieval summas," comparable, for example, to Hugh of St. Victor's *De sacramentis Christianae fidei*.[5] For Constant Mews, it is almost an embarrassment that scholars of the twentieth century like Joseph de Ghellinck and Jean Leclercq managed to write about the theological accomplishments of the twelfth century without giving Hildegard her due.[6] For Bernard McGinn, Hildegard is no less than "the first great woman theologian in Christian history," not to mention "one of the most original apocalyptic thinkers since the intertestamental period."[7]

On what basis, other than celebrity, does one assess theological greatness? It is easy to list ways in which Hildegard herself was anxious on this account. If by virtue of deep learning, she had none, as she wrote to Bernard, abbot of Clairvaux: "Indeed, I have no formal training at all, for I know how to read only on the most elementary level, certainly with no deep analysis."[8] If on the basis of deep insight, she claimed none, as she wrote to Odo of Soissons, master of theology at Paris, comparing herself to a feather commanded by a king to fly: "And I, like the feather, am not endowed with great powers or human education, nor do I even have good health, but I rely wholly on God's help."[9] If by virtue of great influence on others' thinking, again, she had none, except, ironically, in the one way in which she expressly did not wish to have, that is, via excerpts from her work.[10] Whereas the *Scivias* (1141–51) is known to have been extant in only seventeen manuscripts, and Hildegard's other two works of theology, the *Liber vitae meritorum* (1158–63) and the *Liber divinorum operum* (1163–73), respectively in only twelve and seven, the manuscripts of Gebeno of Eberbach's *Speculum temporum futurorum* or *Pentachronon*, laboriously compiled from Hildegard's writings some forty years after her death, number in the hundreds.[11] Given such a pattern of transmission, it is, perhaps, unsurprising that even an admirer of Hildegard like Johannes Trithemius of Sponheim (1462–1516) would opine, "In all her works the blessed Hildegard proceeds very mystically and obscurely (*mistice valde et obscure*), whence her writings are scarcely understandable unless by the religious and devout."[12]

The question is whether even Hildegard's modern admirers have succeeded in lifting the veil that obscures full understanding of her theological work, particularly its structure and argument. Much as, for Gebeno and his readers, what was most important about Hildegard was her status as a prophet—her "habit of speaking obscurely"—so, for many of her modern readers, what has been most important is her status as a visionary, arguably more so than the actual content of her writing.[13] Moreover, when that content has been addressed, it is, as often as not, only thematically, in extracts, much as the masters of Hildegard's own day compiled their *sententiae* in answer to their *quaestiones* or as Gebeno anthologized Hildegard's prophecies. The assumption at present would seem to be that if Hildegard's works have anything like an argumentative structure, it is a very loose one at best—the *Scivias* contains, for example, three books, reflecting the Trinitarian nature of God—but that the visions, while comprehensive in their survey of Christian doctrine, appear in the text somewhat at random. So, for example, according to Sabina Flanagan, "The division of the *Scivias* into three major sections or 'books' reflects three different approaches to the same body of thought, rather than a logical or chronological progression, although elements of the latter are evident within the separate parts."[14] Constant Mews himself has even gone so far as to imply that whatever structure there may be in the series of visions may have more to do with Volmar, Hildegard's teacher, confidant, and secretary, "who was certainly familiar with the contemporary theological treatises and scriptural commentaries," than with Hildegard herself.[15] As a visionary, the consensus would seem to be, Hildegard thought primarily in discrete images, linked more by the repetition of certain resonant concepts or themes (*Ecclesia, Sapientia, viriditas, humanitas, iustitia Dei, lux vivens*) than by any coherent account of the mysteries of revelation. Indeed, judging as much on the basis of the current scholarship as on Hildegard's late medieval reputation, it is almost as if to credit her with a comprehensible compositional purpose would be to deprive her of the authority by which she herself claimed to speak: that her words came "not from a human being, but from the living light," that is, directly from God.[16]

Accordingly, my second source of inspiration is a definition, not of visions—Hildegard's, with a few exceptions, would seem to fall fairly comfortably in the Augustinian category of spiritual visions (seen inwardly or imaginatively through the spirit) as opposed to those seen corporeally (through the eyes) or intellectually (directly through an intuition of the mind)[17]—but of theology, taken not, to be sure, from sources that Hildegard herself might have known, like Augustine, but rather from the work of a modern academic theologian, the English Dominican Aidan Nichols. Even without the particulars of Nichols' definition, the objections at this point are easy to anticipate: how is the category "theology," not one Hildegard herself would necessarily have recognized, any less problematic than "prophecy" or "visionary experience" as a way of coming to terms with the substance of Hildegard's authorial project? Would it not be better simply to take Hildegard on her own terms and judge her writings in this way? My answer would be that, ever since Gebeno, if not, indeed, Hildegard's own lifetime, this is precisely what Hildegard's readers have consistently failed to do and that it was Nichols' definition of theology as a particular kind of task that enabled me, at least, to see how better to assess what Hildegard seemed to be trying to achieve. Nor, to return to Augustine, is Nichols' definition as far distant from the methodological categories with which Hildegard would have been familiar—such as *visio, prophetia, revelatio, doctrina*—as it might at first seem.

It is one thing, Augustine explained in his *De Genesi ad litteram*, to produce images and likenesses of things in the spirit, in Paul's terms, to "come speaking in tongues"; it is wholly another to grasp "the understanding of the sign" and, thus, to speak "in revelation (*revelatio*), or in knowledge (*agnitio*), or in prophecy (*prophetia*), or in teaching (*doctrina*)" (cf. 1 Cor 14:6).[18] Accordingly,

> less a prophet is he who, by means of the images of corporeal objects, sees in spirit only the signs of the things signified, and a greater prophet is he who is granted only an understanding of the images. But the greatest prophet is he who is endowed with both gifts, namely, that of seeing in spirit the symbolic likenesses of corporeal objects and that of understanding them with the vital power of the mind.[19]

We may compare this graduated account of the gift of prophecy with what Nichols proposes as a working (in his words, "brief and unadventurous") definition of the task of theology: "the disciplined exploration of what is contained in revelation," reading "disciplined exploration" for Augustine's "understanding with the vital power of the mind," and "what is contained in revelation" for Augustine's "symbolic likenesses" or "signs."[20]

Three things, Nichols contends, are essential to the task of theology. First, that there has been at some time in human history—for Christians above all, but not exclusively, at the Incarnation—a revelation of the one true God and that one such authentic revelation took place at the origins of the Church. Second, that it is the theologian's task to explore what is not at first obvious in the content of this revelation, "even to someone who knows and accepts the faith of the Church," thus distinguishing theology from catechism or devotion.[21] And third, that this exploration should be disciplined, that is, ordered or structured on the basis of some aspect of revelation to which it relates everything else, for example, grace (Augustine), the coming forth of creatures from God and their return to him (Aquinas), or human beings as the image of God (Rahner).[22] Key here, for my purposes, is the link Nichols proposes between revelation and order.

Everything that human beings know about God, that is, God as transcendent, personal, and free, depends on revelation. Conversely, "the self-revelation of God is unthinkable" unless God is transcendent, that is, having an other to whom he can show himself; personal, that is, having a someone to reveal in something; and free, that is, neither, as with pantheism, revealed automatically through the emanation of the world nor, as with deism, incapable of showing himself further even if he wanted to. For revelation to occur, human beings must, in their turn, be open to transcendence, not only "intellectually capable of grasping God's self-revelation," but also willing to be drawn to—and to love—the goodness, truth, and beauty of God.[23]

The theologian's task is to interpret this revelation, that is, God's showing of God to the world, as it comes to humanity through scripture, tradition, and the events of history. In this task, the theologian may find it helpful to invoke questions, concepts, and ways of looking at things formulated philosophically, for example, questions about human existence and the nature of the self (the preserve of anthropology, psychology, and ethics), about the world and the reality of which the self is a part (the concern of cosmology and history), about existence as such and what makes it possible (the problem of ontology).[24] Such questions may touch on the existence and concept of God. Indeed, Nichols points out, "the typical form of the proclamation of a revealed religion . . . presupposes that people already have some notion of God." What the theologian (or preacher or missionary) does is to offer new insight into the character of the God his or her audience already worships.[25] In theological terms, such insight (that is, ordering) is necessary not, as many critics have alleged, in order to restrict people's imagining of God, but rather because revelation always already exceeds the capacity of any human system, such as theology, to contain it. It (revelation) is, in one of Nichols' most illuminating metaphors, the King to the Queen of any given theological principle of order and to the Jack of any given philosophical principle of order. And what is the Ace? "The mystery of God in himself. We cannot assume," Nichols cautions,

> that divine revelation tells us everything there is to know about God's being and purposes. It tells us enough for our needs and more than enough. [But] behind historic revelation there lie the unknown depths of the divine essence. . . . Beyond even revelation there lies the vision of God, which is not for wayfarers but for those who have arrived at the assembly of the angels.[26]

Hildegard of Bingen was a visionary, which should mean, if we take at all seriously the first of Nichols' claims concerning the possibility and historicity of revelation, that she was the recipient of showings of God by God. She was also, if we take Augustine's distinction between spiritual seeing and the understanding of signs, a great prophet, because she not only received showings from God but was also granted the power of interpreting the things she had seen. Did she order her revelations such that we might likewise recognize her as a theologian? My argument is that she did, but not, as others have suggested, simply with reference to recurrent concepts or themes. Rather, the fact of her visions was itself substantive to her theology; her methodology was part and parcel of her argument about the divine. From this perspective, the particulars of her imagery, that feature of her writings hitherto most singled out for its creativity and originality, whether her invocation of the feminine or her appeal to images from nature, were largely subordinate to the overriding message of her theology: the self-revelation of the Trinitarian God.

That scholars have hitherto neglected this message, insisting instead that "Hildegard is more interested in the relationship of God to creation than in the doctrine of the Trinity as such," says more, I would argue, about their interests than hers.[27] It is not just, as Bernard McGinn has pointed out in a recent essay on "Theologians as Trinitarian Iconographers," that works like the *Scivias* and the *Liber divinorum operum* contain striking representations of the Trinity: a bright light suffusing a glowing fire pouring over a human figure; a great purple-black pillar with three sharp, metallic edges; a human figure with shining face holding a lamb and the face of an old man emerging from a chaplet on its head.[28] Nor is it just, as Constant Mews has shown, that Hildegard was inclined, more so than her contemporaries, to metaphors taken from the natural world—stones, flames—in her exposition of the faith.[29] (She also invokes, in the same chapter of the *Scivias* [2.2], the analogy of the sound, meaning, and breath of human words.) Rather, her concern throughout all of her works, but most particularly, as I hope to show here, in her theological *summa* the *Scivias*, is with how the Trinity is revealed, not only in history, as part of the economy of salvation, but also by way of its powers or virtues within the human soul.

HILDEGARD OFFERS HERSELF AS A WITNESS TO THIS MYSTERY. As she asserts at the outset of the *Scivias*, in the so-called "Protestificatio" of her method: "Behold! In the forty-third year of my earthly course, as I was gazing with great fear and trembling attention at a heavenly vision, I saw a great splendor in which resounded a voice from Heaven, saying to me: 'O fragile human, ashes of ashes and filth of filth, say and write what you see and hear'" (*dic et scribe quae uides et audis*).[30] The echoes in this passage of the command given to John the Divine at the outset of the revelation on Patmos (*quod vides scribe in libro et mitte septem ecclesiis*, Rv 1:10) have often been noted, nor were they lost on Hildegard.[31] Just as John "saw and heard" (Rv 5:11, 8:13, and 22:8) that which he recorded in his book, so Hildegard both "saw" the splendor of heaven and "heard" a voice from heaven telling her what she should write in hers. Later in life, Hildegard experienced a vision in which she identified herself explicitly with John in his capacity as evangelist, again emphasizing the way in which her knowledge of God came directly from God:

> For my knowing (*scientia*) was changed into another mode in which, as it were, I did not know myself. It was as if the inspiration of God were sprinkling drops of sweet rain into my soul's knowing, just as the Holy Spirit filled John the Evangelist when he sucked from the breast of Jesus the most profound of revelations, when his understanding was so touched by sacred divinity that he revealed hidden mysteries and works, saying: "In the beginning was the Word . . ."[32]

Whereas John, however, received the mystery of the "true light (*lux vera*) that illumines every person coming into the world" (Jn 1:9), that is, the Word, Hildegard received the mystery of the "living light (*lux vivens*) that illumines what is obscure."[33] Mews has noted that the phrase *lux vivens* appears nowhere in the databases of the *Patrologia latina* or the *Corpus christianorum* prior to Hildegard, nor does it appear in scripture as such, although there are potential echoes in Job (33:28, 30).[34] Even more intriguing is Hildegard's own exegesis of her experience of John's knowing of the Word, from the same vision quoted above:

> For it was the Word, which before all created things had no beginning, and after them shall have no end, which summoned all created things into being. He brought his work into being like a smith causing his work to shower sparks. In this way, what was predestined by him before ever the

world was, appeared in visible form. Therefore man is the work of God along with every creature. But man is also said to be the worker of the Divinity and a shadow of his mysteries, and should in all things reveal the Holy Trinity, for *God made him in his image and likeness* [Gn 1:26]. So, just as Lucifer for all his malice could not bring God to naught, so too, he shall not succeed in destroying the human race, however much he tried to with the first man.[35]

Insofar as Hildegard saw herself, in McGinn's words, "as a female version of the Beloved Disciple," she did so with a twist.[36] John saw God as Word; Hildegard, seeing perhaps even more clearly than the eagle-eyed John, even unto the "living light," saw God as Trinity.

The purpose of the *Scivias* is to reveal this mystery by showing the ways in which God as Trinity has manifested himself to the world: first, as God, through creation; second, as Trinity, through the Incarnation; and third, in his justice, through the virtues of the human soul. The first vision of the first book, from which our opening reading was taken, sets the scene. God appears to Hildegard spiritually, that is, by way of images, in the form of one enthroned in glory from whom sprang forth many living sparks (*uiuentes scintillae*), an image that modern scholars, following the early twentieth-century historian of science Charles Singer, have been inclined to read as evidence of the "scintillating scotomata" of migraine but that would likely have resonated for many of Hildegard's contemporaries with John's description of the "one like the Son of Man" whom he saw "in the midst of the lampstands" and who spoke to him in a "voice like the sound of many waters" (Rv 1:12–15).[37] (Perhaps John too experienced what we would call migraines?) As with John, the voice that Hildegard heard gave her a mission:

> Cry out and speak of the origin of pure salvation until those people are instructed, who, though they see the inmost contents of the Scriptures, do not wish to tell them or preach them, because they are lukewarm and sluggish in serving the justice of God. Unlock for them the enclosure of mysteries that they, timid as they are, conceal in a hidden and fruitless field.[38]

Whether or not Hildegard knew it, the Benedictine abbot Rupert of Deutz (*c.* 1075–1129) had made a similar defense of his own Spirit-inspired exegesis of scripture in the prologue to his own commentary on the Apocalypse of St. John (1119–21), in which he argued that "the field of the sacred scriptures is common to all confessors of Christ and by no law (*iure*) can license to treat them be denied, provided faith is preserved."[39] Scripture, Rupert went on to explain in his last major work, *De glorificatione Trinitatis et processione sancti Spiritus* (1128), is a field "open to all" in which is hidden a treasure, "namely, the glorious distinction of the persons of the Holy Trinity," and yet, Rupert continued, this field has all too often been dug solely for what it says about the person of the Son, when "in that same place is hidden the mystery of the whole Trinity."[40] Hildegard would tend to agree. As she would put it in the fourth of the six visions of book one, "Miserable are they who worship the Devil, not knowing God. How? Because they do not adore one God in Trinity and do not seek to know the Trinity in Unity. So let the one who wishes to be saved be unwavering in the true Catholic faith" (I.4.30).

All but the first of the six visions in book one treat God as revealed—yet all too often misunderstood—in the "visible and temporal" things of the world: the creation of the angels, Adam and Eve, Lucifer's fall, and the continuing generation of humanity through marriage and birth (vision 2); the firmament, sun, moon, stars, and clouds, envisioned in the figure of a great cosmic egg (vision 3); the soul, its powers and proper relationship to the body (vision 4); the Synagogue (vision 5); and the armies of angels, "all singing with marvelous voices all kinds of music about the wonders that God works in blessed souls" (vision 6). The resonances with Paul's letter to the Romans (1:18–20) are here unmistakable—and, indeed, paraphrased by Hildegard in the explanation of vision three:

> For the wrath of God is revealed from heaven against all impiety and injustice (*iniustitia*) of those who by injustice suppress the truth. For what can be known about God is plain to them, because God has shown it to them. From the creation of the world his eternal power and divinity, invisible though they are, have been understood and seen through the things he has made. So they are without excuse; for though they knew God, they did not honor him as God or give thanks to him, but they became futile in their thinking. (New Revised Standard Version, with changes)

In Hildegard's words: "God, Who made all things by His will, created them so that His Name would be known and glorified, showing in them not just the things that are visible and temporal, but also the things that are invisible and eternal. Which is demonstrated," as the divine voice explained to her, "by this vision you are perceiving" (I.3.1).

This theme of *iniustitia* as the failure to recognize God in his works recurs throughout book one: those who, being learned in the scriptures, should be responsible for teaching the way to salvation fail to do so "because they are lukewarm and sluggish in serving God's justice" (I.1). Lucifer fell because he mistook his own beauty for the wholeness of the divinity; God, in his turn, would have been unjust if he had not cast Lucifer and his angels down "and reduced their impiety to nothing" (I.1.2–3). Human beings, when they give themselves over to fornication "cast aside the mirror of God and sate [their] lust at will," rather than, as they should, recognizing themselves as made "in the image and likeness of God" (I.2.22, 29; Gn 1:26). "Now tell me, O human," the heavenly voice demands in vision two,

> What do you think you were when you were not yet in soul and body? Truly you do not know how you were created. But now, O human, you wish to investigate Heaven and earth, and to judge of their justice in God's disposition, and to know the highest things though you are not able to examine the lowest; for you do not know how you live in the body, or how you may be divested of the body. (I.2.30)

Foolish are those who attempt to discern the future by means of God's creatures, "casting Me [God says] aside, worshipping the frail creature instead of [their] Creator" (I.3.20). Even worse are they who seek the magic arts by way of the Devil: "O human!," God cries, "I have sought you by the blood of My Son, not in malicious iniquity but in great justice; but you forsake Me, the true God, and imitate him who is a liar" (I.3.22).

Accordingly, the soul laments in vision four: "I should have been a companion of the angels, for I am a living breath, which God placed in dry mud; thus I should have known and felt God. But alas! When my tabernacle saw that it could turn its eyes into all the ways, it turned its attention toward the North; ach, ach! and there I was captured and robbed of my sight and the joy of knowledge, and my garment all torn" (I.4.1). It was to restore this sight and knowledge to the soul that, as book two of the *Scivias* will make clear, the Trinity "showed itself to the world" by way of the Incarnation of the Son

(I.4.8). The Synagogue, although "the mother of the Incarnation of the Son of God," nevertheless "did not look on the true light, since she held the Only-Begotten of God in despite" (I.5.1, 5). Thus, "she conceals the works of justice under the apathy of her laziness," much as those learned in scripture chastised in vision one. The angels, however, "blessed in the power of God, make known in the heavenly places by indescribable sounds their great joy in the works of wonder that God perfects in His saints," thus showing forth at the same time the proper disposition of the human body and soul in service of God (I.6.11). At this point, however, even Hildegard's otherwise so penetrating vision was limited, able to see the angels in only their grossest form (wings and eyes). As her voice explained: "there are many secrets of the blessed spirits that are not to be shown to humans, for as long as they are mortal they cannot discern perfectly the things that are eternal" (I.6.10).

BOOK TWO OF THE *SCIVIAS* OPENS WITH A VISION OF THE LIVING God who, by way of the Word's incarnation, death, and resurrection, "showed Man the way from death to life" (II.1.15), and yet it is not the Word that is the focus of the subsequent six visions of the book. Rather, "somewhat illogically," as Barbara Newman has put it, not to mention unexpectedly for those more accustomed to the credal structuring of the elements of Christian doctrine adopted by Peter Lombard in his *Sententiae*, this vision of the Word's sending His brightness into the world is followed immediately, in vision two, by an explanation of the relationship among the three persons of the Trinity, "perhaps," as Newman notes, "because the Trinity was first revealed to humankind through the incarnation."[41] This, I would argue, is precisely Hildegard's point. Her purpose in this second book is not, as one might expect from her opening vision of God's assumption of human flesh or from writings of her contemporaries like Bernard of Clairvaux or Aelred of Rievaulx, to foster in her readers compassion for Christ in his suffering humanity. Nor is it the case that in failing to do so Hildegard was somehow, in Sabina Flanagan's words, "arrested at an earlier stage in spirituality, where Christ was viewed solely as a triumphal king and just judge."[42] Rather, for Hildegard, what mattered was the way in which the Incarnation of the Word of God was the work of the whole Trinity, even unto the three days that the "noble body of the Son of God, born of the sweet Virgin" spent in the tomb "to confirm that there are three Persons in one Divinity" (II.1.15). The vision of the Trinity in Unity follows upon the vision of the Incarnation of the Word in book two precisely because the revelation of the Trinity followed upon the revelation of the Incarnate Word in time. In Hildegard's words (or, rather, the words of the living Light):

> These three Persons are one God in the one and perfect divinity of majesty, and the unity of Their divinity is unbreakable; the Divinity cannot be rent asunder, for it remains inviolable without change. But the Father is declared through the Son, the Son through Creation, and the Holy Spirit through the Son incarnate. How? It is the Father Who begot the Son before the ages; the Son through Whom all things were made by the Father when creatures were created; and the Holy Spirit Who, in the likeness of a dove, appeared at the baptism of the Son of God before the end of time. (II.2.2)

Hildegard was not alone in her interest in the Trinity. Indeed, I have argued elsewhere—and in emendation of much of my earlier work—that it was, in fact, the whole of the Trinity, not just the suffering of the Son, that was the devotional and theological focus of her day.[43] We might think here, for example, of Bernard of Clairvaux's great clashes with Peter Abelard over the metaphors he used to talk about the persons of the Trinity and with Gilbert of Poitiers over his distinction between the *id quod* of God's concrete individuality and the *id quo* of his divinity. These were debates, I would now argue, as much about the proper worship of God (devotion) as they were about philosophical categories (logic or reason); it was in this context that Bernard so famously insisted against Abelard's and Gilbert's excessive Trinitarian subtleties, that all the faithful need to do to find God is believe and know that Christ dwells in their hearts, whether or, more likely, not they are able to grasp the mysteries of the eternal and blessed Trinity with their minds.[44] Hildegard (not to mention Gilbert and Abelard) would beg to disagree. As she explained to bishop Eberhard of Bamberg, who had written to her in the hope that she might help him in his own debate with Gerhoch, provost of the Augustinian house at Reichersberg, over Peter Lombard's position on Christ:

> Eternity is the essential quality of the Father. . . . Equality is the essential characteristic of the Son. . . . The connection between eternity and equality

is the Holy Spirit. . . . [It] is like a blacksmith who unites the two materials of bronze and makes them one through fire. It is a sword brandished in every direction. The Holy Spirit reveals eternity and enkindles equality, joining them into one. The Holy Spirit is fire and life in eternity and equality, because God lives.[45]

Stone (cool dampness, solidity to the touch, sparkling fire), flame (brilliant light, red power, fiery heat), word (sound "that it may be heard," meaning "that it may be understood," breath "that it may be pronounced"): these were the images that Hildegard invoked in book two of the *Scivias* in her explanation of the triune nature of the divinity not simply because she favored images taken from the organic or, as with the blacksmith, artisanal world over the logical or political analogies of the philosophers (for example, Abelard's bronze seal), but rather because, in her theology, the creation of the world was the originary theophany. In similar fashion, and in the proper course of time, it was the incarnation of the Son that revealed God as triune, in which theophany humanity now participates not only biologically, as Adam and Eve, through the generation of children, but also spiritually, through the sacraments. This latter revelation through the sacraments is the topic of book two, visions three through six.

The first of the sacraments is baptism, "the sacrament of the true Trinity," through which the Church (*Ecclesia*) becomes the "virginal mother of all Christians, since by the mystery of the Holy Spirit she conceives and bears them, offering them to God so that they are called the children of God" (II.3.10, 12). "For," Hildegard goes on to explain, "in holy baptism Heaven opens and that Blessed Trinity appears to the baptized, so that the faithful person may receive the knowledge of how to worship the One God in the true Trinity, Which truly appeared in the first sacrament of baptism" (II.3.14). It is for this reason that it is necessary for there to be three persons present at the font, supporting the one to be baptized: the priest "who pours the water on him" and the godparents "who give the words of faith for him." As the voice from Heaven put it:

In the baptism of My Son, I the Father thundered, which the priest reenacts when he gives the benediction for the washing; and the Holy Spirit was seen in the form of a gentle animal [the dove], whose place is held by the man who speaks to and teaches the person to be baptized in simplicity of heart; and My Son was present to be baptized in the flesh, which is symbolized by the woman who stands by in the sweetness of a nurturer in the place of the sweet Incarnation of My Only-Begotten. (II.3.32)

The second of the sacraments, symbolized in vision four as a immense round tower of white stone with three windows at its top from which shone forth so much brilliance "that even the roof of the tower . . . showed very clearly in its light," is confirmation, the anointing with the chrism of the Holy Spirit. "This tower that you see," Hildegard's divine voice explained, "represents the flaming forth of the gifts of the Holy Spirit, which the Father sent into the world for love of His Son, to enkindle the hearts of His disciples with fiery tongues and make them stronger in the name of the Holy and True Trinity . . . for the ineffable Trinity is manifested in the outpouring of the gifts of the power of the Holy Spirit" (II.4.1, 3). Those baptized but not confirmed have only brightness but no color, for they have been cleansed but not yet set on fire. The Son "received baptism in His body and thus sanctified it by His flesh," but it was the Holy Spirit coming down on the disciples after the ascension that "illuminated the world in fiery ardor, confirming all justice in the hearts of [the] disciples and revealing to them what had before been hidden." Thus, confirmation supports the Church like a tower, "for this is the testimony the Holy Spirit gave to the Church, that death cannot resist the justice of God" (II.4.8).

The third of the sacraments or mysteries of the Trinity is the vow of virginity that the religious (priests, but especially monks and nuns) make to God. This mystery is symbolized, in vision five, by a number of figures with their heads covered in white veils marked by "the likeness of the glorious and ineffable Trinity . . . which shows," the divine voice explained, "that these people's minds firmly and strongly uphold the honor of the celestial and glorious Trinity." Further, from the likeness of the Trinity "sculpted" (as Hildegard described it) on the veils, golden rays went forth to various other figures standing round those wearing veils, some of whom wore miters on their heads and pallia on their shoulders, "for the ineffable Trinity unceasingly works the miracles of Its profound wisdom among the faithful who seek virtue and flee the seductions of the Devil" (II.5.7). Although Hildegard does not say as much, the implication is clear: those whose minds, like

Hildegard and her nuns, were veiled in constant contemplation of the Trinity outshone even those holding the "glory of higher offices in the world," namely, the bishops who, although they did not lose "the ornament of virginity" in their service, nevertheless were not necessarily as focused on the mystery of God as those who, like Hildegard and her nuns, held no such formal obligations to preach.

The fourth and last of the sacraments is that of the altar (vision six). On the one hand, as Hildegard's opening account of her vision makes clear, this sacrament is that by which Jesus Christ, the true Son of God, dowers himself to the Church "with His crimson blood" (II.6.1).[46] On the other, it is the sacrament above all by which God reveals himself to be worshipped—and experienced—as Trinity. As God himself explained through Hildegard:

> I the Father sent My Son into the world, physically born of the Virgin, that through Him I might redeem you from the perdition of death; so that I might dwell in you and you in Me, since My own Son underwent the Passion and gave you His flesh to eat and His blood to drink. Hence you shall eat this sacrament devotedly for your salvation and feed blessedly upon it; and thus, through the oil of My mercy, the hunger of your souls' perdition shall be satisfied. For My Son brought you penitence as a medicine for your wounds, and My Son's Bride was adorned with all justice and truth. And therefore you shall faithfully praise My name; for I am one God in true Trinity, and I govern you and display My wonders in you, miraculously snatching you from the power of the Devil. (II.6.9)

The sacrament itself as celebrated daily at the altar is shot through with Trinitarian significance. Just as baptism requires the presence of three persons at the font, so at the altar, three things—bread, wine, and water—must be offered in honor of the Trinity. "If," the divine voice warned, "any of these three is lacking, the Trinity is not truly worshipped, for the Father is understood by the wine, the Son by the bread, and the Holy Spirit by the water" (II.6.44). "Everywhere else I give My grace to My elect by the exchange of the gifts of the Holy Spirit, but here in this sacrament I show Myself wholly: My Son in Me and I in Him, and the Holy Spirit in Us, and We in Him, One in Divinity, as the body and soul and powers of anyone make up one living person. Therefore," the voice warned once again, "let anyone who approaches this sacrament take care not to come in such a state as to offend the glory of Divinity" (II.6.50). Accordingly, the remainder of the commentary on this vision is given over to the preparation of the communicants, including women and priests. The final vision of the book, number seven, concerns the deceptions of the Devil and the dangers of misusing the sacraments, as well as the struggles and temptations of those who, "although greatly fatigued by their struggles, do not cease to worship the true and ineffable Trinity" (II.7.15).

THE THIRD BOOK OF THE *SCIVIAS* IS AT ONCE THE LONGEST (thirteen visions, as many as in the first two books combined) and the easiest—thanks to its explicit diagrammatical structure—to read. Although often described, and labeled as such in the Classics of Western Spirituality translation of the work, as an account of the history of salvation symbolized by a building, it might more accurately be described as an account of the revelation of God's justice in the powers (*virtutes*) of the soul. It is, as it were, a psychology of salvation figured as the construction of the heavenly Jerusalem. Once again, the key lies in Hildegard's understanding of the Trinity as revealing itself to humanity through the Incarnation of the Son. Vision one hearkens back to the opening vision of the *Scivias* as a whole. "I looked toward the East," Hildegard relates. "And there I saw . . . a royal throne, on which One was sitting, living and shining and marvellous in His glory, and so bright that I could not behold Him clearly" (III.1.0). "This," she explains, "is the Living God, Who reigns over all things, shining in goodness and wondrous in His works. The deep mystery of His immense glory can never be perfectly contemplated by anyone, unless faith allows that person to comprehend and bear Him, as a seat contains and surrounds its owner" (III.1.3). The purpose of visions two through ten in book three is to prepare this four-square seat for the soul on the mountain of Faith rooted in the Fear of the Lord (vision two).

The construction begins in the northeast with the tower of the anticipation of God's will, which first arose with Abraham and the circumcision (vision three). This tower is inhabited by five virtues, corresponding to the five senses, for "just as a person's senses do not work by themselves, but the person with them and they with the person," so the virtues—Celestial Love, Discipline, Modesty, Mercy, and Victory—work with the soul, worshipping

God "in human deeds with equal devotion" (III.3.3–4). Inside the building and just below the tower stand Patience, wearing a three-sided crown, "glowing red like a hyacinth, for she was the first crowned through faith in the Holy Trinity," and Longing, carrying a cross with an image of the Savior (III.3.12–13). To the north of this tower stands the pillar of "the ineffable mystery of the Word of God," divided into three sides—Law, Grace, and the exposition of scripture—with edges sharp as steel (vision four). At its base stands the virtue of the Knowledge of God, while at its top shines a light in which appears a dove, "with a gold ray coming out of its mouth, shedding a brilliant light on the pillar," as the divine voice explains, "for in the heart of the radiant Father, in the brilliance of the light of the Son of God, burns the Holy Spirit, Who comes from on high and declares the mysteries of the Son of the Most High to redeem the people seduced by the ancient serpent" (III.4.14). The jealousy of God occupies the north corner of the building in the figure of a great three-winged head, symbolizing at once the immovability of God's justice and the expansion of the power of the Holy Trinity in judgment over all human deeds (vision five).

Between the north and west corners of the building runs the triple wall of the Old Law, inhabited by eight virtues clustered in three groups: three standing near the north corner looking at the wall (Liberality, Abstinence, and Piety), three near the west, likewise looking at the wall (Peace, Truth, and Beatitude), and two at the same end looking toward the pillar of the true Trinity in the west (Discretion and Salvation) (vision six). The wall runs as it does from the north, that is the time of Abraham and Moses, to the west, that is "the open declaration of the true Trinity in the true and Catholic faith, when the Son of God was sent into the world by God the Father," so as to symbolize both the foreshadowing in the Old Law of the Incarnation by which the Trinity was revealed and, by way of various images that appear in arches along the wall, that those who rule according to human law do so as representatives of the justice and mercy of God (III.6.9–11). The great purple-black pillar of the Trinity anchors the building in the west, much as the description of the pillar occupies the central vision of the book (number seven of thirteen). Its core is a parable about a certain lord who owned a flint and who "decided to command a numerous people to do a necessary thing, both personally and through messengers." When, predictably, those messengers failed to do their work, the lord "used his flint to produce a violent fire, which ran through those messengers with such heat that all their veins were inflamed," and so at last they remembered and understood the lord's message and went forth to communicate it to the people. The lord, of course, is the Father Almighty, and the flint that he struck was the fire of the Holy Spirit, which, "because the true Word had become incarnate . . . came openly in tongues of fire," set alight the apostles "so that with their souls and bodies they spoke in many tongues" and at last remembered "with perfect understanding" everything that Christ had taught them that previously they had recalled only with "sluggish faith and comprehension" (III.7.7).

To the south of the pillar of the Trinity stands a "great and shadowed pillar" with a ladder running from bottom to top, "on which," Hildegard relates, "I saw all the virtues of God descending and ascending, laden down with stones and going with keen zeal to do their work" (vision eight). These climbing virtues include, most notably, Humility, Charity, Fear, Obedience, Faith, Hope, and Chastity. At the top of the pillar stands the Grace of God, admonishing humanity to wake from sin and allow her to "polish and refine them without ceasing [like the finest cut stones], that they may rightly and fitly be placed in the heavenly Jerusalem" (III.8.8). The pillar itself symbolizes the humanity of the Savior; it supports the ladder of the virtues because it is in Christ that all the virtues "work fully and are openly manifested" (III.8.9–13). There are seven of them to represent the seven gifts of the Spirit (cf. Is 11:1–3), "for it was by the overshadowing of the Holy Spirit that the glorious Virgin conceived the Son of God without sin, sanctified by these holy virtues; they were clearly shown in God's Only-Begotten and illumine the hearts of the faithful as if in His form" (III.8.14).

The tower of the Church stands to the south of the pillar of the humanity of the Savior because the Church arose when the Incarnation was accomplished (III.9.7). It is constructed from "living stones enkindled by the fire of the Holy Spirit" and fortified by seven bulwarks, the Spirit's seven gifts (III.9.8, 12). In front of the tower, towards the center of the building, stand seven white marble pillars, likewise symbolizing the seven gifts, surmounted by an iron dome. On the top of this dome, stands Wisdom (*Sapientia*), her head shining "like lightning, with so much brilliance that you cannot look directly at it; for God, Who is terrible or mild to every creature, sees and judges all things as a human eye assesses what is before it, but no human can understand fully the profound mystery of the Divinity" (III.9.25). In her turn, Justice, standing alongside the marble pillars, explains how Lucifer was thrown down at the beginning of time, just as the Antichrist will fall at the end of time, so that "then it will be known Who is the true God; it will be seen Who He is, Who has never fallen" (III.9.2). Fortitude and Sanctity stand ready to either side of her "to repel the advances of the Devil" and "adorn [the good] in the heavenly host" (III.9.28–29).

IN THE TENTH VISION OF BOOK THREE, THE SON OF MAN ADDRESSES the people of the world, chiding them for not even wanting to open their eyes to see "how good [their] souls could be" (III.10.1). Despite having been given the knowledge of good and evil and thus the power to master themselves and to love God in truth and justice, they despise good and do evil, and so they will be judged. Nor is it theirs to question the judgment of God, when they cannot, except insofar as God allows, see into the secret of divinity "with [their] mortal minds," any more than they can look on divinity "with [their] mortal eyes" (III.10.5). And yet, they have been offered a treasure, indeed, "the best of treasures, a vivid intelligence," by their Creator, "who loves [them] exceedingly" and who commands them "in the words of His Law to profit from [their] intellect in good works, and grow rich in virtue, that He, the Good Giver, may thereby be clearly known." Once again, we see how, for Hildegard, what is at stake in not only her visions, but also in the experience of vision as such, is the knowledge of God, now, however, made manifest not only through the Incarnation of the Son but, potentially, in all humanity, through the virtues inspired in them by the Holy Spirit. Thus, the Son of Man admonishes them:

> Hence you must think every hour about how to make so great a gift as useful to others as to yourself by works of justice, so that it will reflect the splendor of sanctity from you, and people will be inspired by your good example to praise and honor God. And when you have justly multiplied it to advantage, this praise and thanksgiving will come to the knowledge of God, Who by the Holy Spirit inspired these virtues in you. (III.10.9)

At the foot of the Son, the virtues Constancy, Celestial Desire, and Compunction of Heart stand together in their devotion to the power of the Trinity, "[manifesting] God in those people who magnify Him in their works"

(III.10.21–22), while, to the north, Contempt of the World "holds fast the fresh and beautiful shoot of blessed virtues, bathed in the breath of the Holy Spirit" (III.10.26) and, to the south, Concord "longs for the vision of eternal peace" (III.10.27).

It remains only to pave the building with "the strength of pure faith," which, shining with a calm splendor, like white glass,

> supports and expands the work and the city of God, shining pure and clear in its candor and mirror-like simplicity. Faith watches and builds the city of God with all the works done in her. And so when people begin to do good works with a calm and bright intention, they touch God; and when they perfect the works, their souls are saved and they know Him profoundly. For when the work is accomplished, faith herself shows the devotion with which each soul has sought God. (III.10.28)

Thus God completes the fortress of the soul, expels all pagans, Jews and false Christians from the Church, and confounds the work of the Devil. It is, likewise, at this point, that Hildegard, as author of the *Scivias*, makes her inspiration—and model for writing—clear. In her words: "But the great and beautiful work of God, in the height of His supreme goodness, shines out clearly amid this dark misery to anyone who seeks it, as the beloved Evangelist John testifies by divine revelation, saying: 'And he took me up in the spirit to a great and high mountain; and he showed me the heavenly Jerusalem, coming down out of Heaven with the glory of God'" (III.10.30–31, citing Rv 21:10–11). Hildegard, it has been suggested, saw herself as an *alter Johannes*, witnessing to the revelation of God by way of the visions that she received. Here, she makes good on her claim, unlocking the mysteries in his vision that mortal eyes had not, hitherto (in Hildegard's reading), had the virtue to see. "Oh, how beautiful are your eyes," Hildegard heard the One Who sat on the throne at the beginning of book three say to her, "which tell of divinity when the divine counsel dawns in them!" (III.1.0). Now, at the end of her great ten-part vision of the building of God's justice in the soul, she is at last able to explain how it is that she sees:

> The Holy Spirit lifts up the spirit. How? The Holy Spirit, by Its power, draws the human mind out of the heavy flesh, that it may share in the vision of

the Spirit, whose eyes are not obscured by the blindness of carnal pleasure, and Who sees the inner things. What does this mean? The Holy Spirit lifts the human spirit upward to the mountain of heavenly desires, that it may clearly see the works to be done in the Spirit, the great works of God. (III.10.31)

It is these "great works of God" of which Hildegard's *Scivias* is a record, the great works that she, by the power of the Holy Spirit working in her, was able, waking, not in "dreams, or sleep, or delirium," to see. Her experience and understanding is itself the testimony to the authenticity of her visions because it is through just such workings in creation, in the sacraments, and in the virtues that God makes himself known to the soul. It is for the same reason that she—and her readers—may be assured that her visions come not from the Devil or her imagination, but from God. "And thus," Hildegard's exegesis of John's vision of the heavenly Jerusalem concludes, "the work of the Spirit is shown to the faithful and holy souls. The heavenly Jerusalem is to be built spiritually, without the work of physical hands, through work given by the Holy Spirit.... And so by this revelation the eyes of the spirit see and know that by the inspiration of the Holy Spirit righteous human works appear before God in the regions of Heaven" (III.10.31).

THE COMPOSITION OF THE *SCIVIAS*, AS HILDEGARD WOULD have it and I hope to have shown, was one such work. How much this work depended on sources other than direct inspiration from God—for example, the second-century *Shepherd of Hermas* for its depiction of the building by the virtues of the tower of the Church; Rupert of Deutz's own visionary inspiration for his exegetical work, likewise his emphasis on the self-revelation of God through history—should not distract us from the complexity and coherence of Hildegard's theological construction.[47] Peter Lombard, *magister sententiarum*, was far more explicitly dependent on others' work, and yet he was recognized for centuries as a great theologian, even if his reputation is only just beginning to be revived today.[48] Rather, such comparisons should caution us that, in looking for Hildegard's "originality" (still our contemporary criterion for "greatness"), we should look as much to the structure of her works as to her imagery. It is not just that Hildegard crafted novel metaphors for talking about the mystery of the Trinity or proposed novel readings of particular passages of scripture that makes her worth our attention. Nor is it the fact of—or claim to the reality of—her visions, however much they fascinated her contemporaries and titillate us.[49] Nor, I would venture to suggest, is it her gender or sex, except insofar as it mattered for her reputation; to judge from her visions, it had relatively little impact, except insofar as she was human, on her relationship to God, although I am willing to concede this point provisionally, awaiting further work on her most likely intellectual model, Rupert. It is, rather, that, as a human being "made in the image and likeness of God," she ventured both to see God and to explain what she had seen so that others might understand; that she was, in fact, a theologian and deserves to be read as such, much as Hartmann Schedel's fifteenth-century chronicle suggested she should be.

That others accepted her extraordinary visions as proof of her authority to speak should not distract us from the role that they play in her theology, as a reflection of the way in which she understood God, revealing himself through his works. To be sure, her imagery throughout her works, as has often been noted, is fresh and unusually rich, but, again, it is there for a purpose, as part of a whole. To focus overmuch on her use of feminine personifications as such or on the variety of images she invokes to discuss a particular point of doctrine is, as it were, to mistake the creature for the Creator, to worship the object made as opposed to contemplating its reasons for being. More bluntly, her images need to be read in context: the Trinity as a pillar anchoring the building of the soul, Wisdom atop her iron dome witnessing to the mystery of the divine. We should take it as a sign of our own inattentiveness and lack of vision if her images do not, as so often has been claimed, make sense. To be sure, they are, as Trithemius cautioned, "mystical and obscure" if we read them piecemeal, abstracted from the larger argument of which they are a part. Why imagine the Trinity as a pillar any more than as a stone or a flame? Here, it would seem, is one instance in which it does matter that Hildegard was a woman. As Barbara Newman has shown, even Hildegard's biographer Theoderic of Echternach (who, unlike Gottfried of St. Disibod, the editor of her autobiographical memoir, had never met her) felt compelled to describe her works as "subtle" and "obscure," requiring great effort to comprehend.[50] Some years later, Gebeno of Eberbach cemented this reputation through his florilegium of her "prophecies": "Many people," he remarked in his prologue, "dislike and shrink from reading

St. Hildegard's books because she speaks obscurely and in an unusual style, not understanding that this is a proof of true prophecy.... The fact that she speaks in an unusual style is a proof [Hildegard would doubtless appreciate the irony] of the true finger of God, the Holy Spirit."[51] My purpose in this essay has been a simple one: to restore Hildegard's visions to their context by offering a reading of the *Scivias* as a work of theology, ordered, as all works of theology arguably are, around a particular aspect of revelation. For Hildegard, far more than concerns with her own authority, this ordering principle is the possibility and necessity of revelation itself, if human beings are to know anything about God; it embodies the necessity of her visions as revelations from God.

Thanks largely to Gebeno's editing, the final three visions of the *Scivias*, rather than the work as a whole, made Hildegard's reputation as a prophet. We may read them here as a commentary on her own concerns for the reception of her work. Having labored for the better part of ten years (1141–51) on a work of great theological insight, Hildegard justifiably hoped that her work might be accepted as such. As she observed in vision eleven, in her description of the signs accompanying the seventh epoch, approaching the end of time:

> But now the Catholic faith wavers among the nations and the Gospel limps among the people; and the mighty books in which the excelling doctors had summed up knowledge with great care go unread from shameful apathy, and the food of life, which is the divine Scriptures, cools to tepidity. For this reason, I [God] now speak through a person who is not eloquent in the Scriptures or taught by an earthly teacher; I Who Am speak through her of new secrets and mystical truths, heretofore hidden in books, like one who mixes clay and then shapes it to any form he wishes. (III.11.18)

Is this pride or simply an author's conviction that she *has* seen mysteries others have obscured and explained them more fully than hitherto? Books that go unread "from shameful apathy," knowledge locked in "mighty books" that those more concerned about this life than the next do not take the time to read: it is easy to see how Hildegard gained her reputation for prophecy. Perhaps now we are in a better position to understand why, like John at the end of his revelation (Rv 22:18–19), Hildegard was so insistent, at the conclusion not only of the *Scivias*, but, indeed, of all three of her theological works, that "whoever rashly conceals these words written by the finger of God, madly abridging them, or for any human reason taking them to a strange place and scoffing at them, let him be reprobate; and the finger of God shall crush him" (III.13.16).[52] Structure, as well as content, mattered, for it was through structure—of creation, of the sacraments, of the human soul—that the Living God as Creator, Word, and Gift-giver made himself known. In God's words, as revealed to Hildegard, "Let the one who has ears sharp to hear inner meanings ardently love My reflection and pant after My words, and inscribe them in his soul and conscience. Amen" (III.13.16).

HERE ENDS THE READING.

NOTES

1. Hildegard of Bingen, *Scivias*, 1.1, ed. Führkötter and Carlevaris, 7–8; trans. Hart and Bishop, 67. Subsequent citations to the *Scivias* are given parenthetically in the body of the text in the form (pars.visio.capitulum).

2. Barbara Newman was one of the first to make this argument. See "Hildegard of Bingen: Visions and Validation."

3. Hartmann Schedel, *Liber cronicorum* (Nuremberg, 1493), fol. 201v; and *Das buch der croniken und geschichten mit figuren und pildnis* (Nuremberg, 1493), fol. 201v; reprinted as *The Nuremberg Chronicle*; cited by Constant Mews, "Hildegard and the Schools," 89, n. 1.

4. Pitra, *Analecta sacra Spicilegio Solesmensi parata. VIII: Sanctae Hildegardis Opera*, xii, xvii–xviii; cited by Mews, "Hildegard and the Schools," 90, n. 7. On Hildegard's title at Disibodenberg and Rupertsberg, see Mews, "Hildegard and the Schools," 95.

5. See Newman's introduction to Hildegard of Bingen, *Scivias*, trans. Hart and Bishop, 23. Compare Newman, *Sister of Wisdom*, 16.

6. Mews, "Hildegard and the Schools," 89–90.

7. McGinn, *The Growth of Mysticism*, 333, and *Visions of the End*, 97.

8. Hildegard of Bingen, *Epistola* I, in *Epistolarium I. I–XC*, 4; *The Letters of Hildegard of Bingen*, trans. Baird and Ehrman, 1:28.

9. Hildegard of Bingen, *Epistola* XLr, in *Epistolarium I. I–XC*, 104; *The Letters of Hildegard of Bingen*, trans. Baird and Ehrman, 1:111.

10. On Hildegard's objection to abridgment of her works, see Newman, "Hildegard of Bingen: Visions and Validation," 171.

11. For numbers of Hildegard's manuscripts, see Embach, *Die Schriften Hildegards von Bingen*, 76–77 (*Scivias*), 128–29 (*Liber vitae meritorum*), and 160 (*Liber divinorum operum*); and Kerby-Fulton, "Hildegard of Bingen (1098–1179)." On Gebeno, see Newman, *Sister of Wisdom*, 22; eadem, "Hildegard and her Hagiographers," 23; Kerby-Fulton, "Prophecy and Suspicion," 321; and eadem, *Books Under Suspicion*, 190.

12. Kerby-Fulton, "Prophecy and Suspicion," 338.

13. On Hildegard's reputation for obscurity as crafted by Gebeno, see Newman, "Hildegard and her Hagiographers," 27–28.

14. Flanagan, *Hildegard of Bingen*, 57.

15. Mews, "Religious Thinker," 57.

16. Hildegard of Bingen, *Epistola* LIIr, in *Epistolarium I. I–XC*, 127–30; *The Letters of Hildegard of Bingen*, trans. Baird and Ehrman, 1:128–30. For additional examples, see McGinn, "Hildegard of Bingen as Visionary and Exegete," 336.

17. McGinn, "Hildegard of Bingen as Visionary and Exegete," 327–32. For Augustine's discussion, see *De Genesi ad litteram*, bk 12. On the theology of Hildegard's visions more generally, see Berndt, "Im Angesicht Gottes." For the prevalence of Augustinian theories of vision, see Newman, "What Did It Mean to Say 'I Saw'?"

18. Augustine, *De Genesi ad litteram*, bk 12, chap. 8, in *The Literal Meaning of Genesis*, trans. Taylor, 2:189.

19. Augustine, *De Genesi ad litteram*, bk 12, chap. 9, in *The Literal Meaning of Genesis*, trans. Taylor, 2:189–90.

20. Nichols, *The Shape of Catholic Theology*, 32.

21. Ibid., 35.

22. Ibid., 36.

23. Ibid., 75–78, notes various objections often raised against the appeal to revelation: that human beings should rely on themselves for making decisions about how to live, not look for shortcuts in revelation; that human beings are not, in fact, free to determine their intellectual and volitional life, being "preprogrammed" by certain basic drives or needs (material, sexual, evolutionary, or the like), and therefore incapable of responding to a truth "coming wholly from outside themselves even if they wished to." Neither class of objection, however—and this is important—negates the *possibility* of revelation, only its utility or function. Indeed, it could be said that the only thing that such materialist arguments against the reality of revelation actually do is point all the more forcefully to its necessity, if we are to know anything about God.

24. Ibid., 42.

25. Ibid., 61.

26. Ibid., 94–95.

27. Mews, "Religious Thinker," 58.

28. McGinn, "Theologians as Trinitarian Iconographers," 188–90.

29. Mews, "Religious Thinker," 58; Mews, "Hildegard and the Schools," 105.

30. Hildegard of Bingen, *Scivias*, ed. Führkötter and Carlevaris, 3; trans. Hart and Bishop, 59.

31. McGinn, "Hildegard of Bingen as Visionary and Exegete," 337; Mews, "From *Scivias* to the *Liber Divinorum Operum*," 47.

32. Hildegard of Bingen, *Vita Hildegardis* II.xvi, ed. Klaes, 43; trans. in Silvas, *Jutta and Hildegard*, 179, with changes.

33. Hildegard of Bingen, *Scivias*, ed. Führkötter and Carlevaris, 4; trans. Hart and Bishop, 60, with changes.

34. Mews, "Religious Thinker," 211, n. 18.

35. Hildegard of Bingen, *Vita Hildegardis* II.xvi, ed. Klaes, 43–44; trans. in Silvas, *Jutta and Hildegard*, 179.

36. McGinn, "Hildegard of Bingen as Visionary and Exegete," 337.

37. Singer, *Studies in the History and Method of Science*, 1:1–55. For discussion, see Flanagan, *Hildegard of Bingen*, 185–204.

38. Hildegard of Bingen, *Scivias*, bk 1, vision 1, ed. Führkötter and Carlevaris, 8; trans. Hart and Bishop, 67; compare trans. in Mews, "From *Scivias* to the *Liber Divinorum Operum*," 47.

39. Rupert of Deutz, *In Apocalypsim Joannis*, prologus, PL 169:827–28. On Rupert's influence on Hildegard as a critic of the *status Christianitatis*, see Arduini, *Rupert von Deutz*, 308–24.

40. Rupert of Deutz, *De glorificatione Trinitatis*, bk. 1, chaps. 2–3, PL 169:15–16.

41. See Newman's introduction to Hildegard of Bingen, *Scivias*, Hart and Bishop, 31.

42. Flanagan, *Hildegard of Bingen*, 68.

43. Fulton, "Three-in-One."

44. Bernard of Clairvaux, Sermon 76, in *S. Bernardi opera omnia*, 3:482–83; trans. in *On the Song of Songs I–IV*, ed. Walsh and Edmonds, 4:115.

45. Hildegard of Bingen, *Epistola* XXXIr, in *Epistolarium I. I–XC*, 83–88; *The Letters of Hildegard of Bingen*, trans. Baird and Ehrman, 95–98, with slight changes.

46. On this motif, see Newman, *Sister of Wisdom*, 211–18.

47. On Hildegard's imagery and its correspondence with that of the *Shepherd*, see Dronke, "Arbor caritatis." On Rupert's influence, see Mews, "From *Scivias* to the *Liber Divinorum Operum*," 49–50; "Hildegard of Bingen: The Virgin, the Apocalypse and the Exegetical Tradition," 31–34; and "Hildegard, Visions and Religious Reform," 337–40.

48. Colish, *Peter Lombard*; Rosemann, *Peter Lombard*.

49. See Newman, "What Did It Mean to Say, 'I Saw'?" for a corrective on this question.

50. Newman, "Hildegard and Her Hagiographers," 27.

51. Ibid., 27–28.

52. Compare Hildegard of Bingen, *Liber vitae meritorum* 6.45, ed. Carlevaris, 292; and *Liber divinorum operum* 3.5.38, ed. Derolez and Dronke, 462–63.

JEREMY ADAMS

14 Returning Crusaders
Living Saints or Psychopaths?

Most cultures that practice Holy Wars tend to exalt those who have returned home from the fray as heroes touched by the numinous — unless there are some grounds to suspect them of cowardice. Latin Christendom certainly did so with those who returned triumphant from the First Crusade. Those suspected of cowardice, the "rope-walkers" like Stephen of Blois, were so tainted with opprobrium that most had to return to campaigns on behalf of the Holy Land, where Stephen appropriately met an honorable death at Ramba in 1102.

A prime example of First-Crusade hero worship was Count Robert II of Flanders (count 1093–1111), known to several writers of the twelfth century as Robert of Jerusalem. In his biography of King Louis VI, Robert's nephew, Abbot Suger of St Denis, called Robert "vir mirabilis, Christianis et Saracenis a promordio Ierosolimitane vie famosissimus."[1] Robert may well be the most famous of the returning heroes, seen by their contemporaries as numinous if not yet saintly, but he is far from the only instance one could cite.[2]

No part of this reaction is surprising, however. Immediately following that crusade, writers expressing the opinions of monastic culture produced a historiography declaring that the miraculous and wondrous days of the Old Testament had returned: God had once more activated his providential support of his people's military endeavors.[3] Obviously, those who had participated in the renewal of Exodus were very special individuals, deserving particular esteem.

What may be at first blush surprising, and is certainly instructive, is the pattern of reactions to those who returned from the First Crusade and became disedifying troublemakers. This type of social dysfunction is no surprise to our contemporary sensibility, by now well trained to sympathize with emotionally disturbed veterans of the Vietnam War, the current Iraqi and Afghan wars, and even in rueful retrospect recently admitted cases of such psychic trauma among veterans of World Wars I and II.[4]

One such dysfunctional veteran of the First Crusade was the monk-castrating crusader who in 1103 or thereabouts horrified Ivo of Chartres, provoking exceptional distress in that consensus-seeking reformer normally marked by equanimity. In a letter to Paschal II Ivo recounts the "unheard-of" atrocity (*inauditum apud nos*) of one Raimbold Creton (or Croton), a gentleman from the Chartrain, who got so enraged in an argument with a monk of Bonneval over property rights that he had him castrated. Ivo judged the case in his episcopal court, deprived Raimbold of the right to bear arms for fourteen years, and then mitigated the sentence, after Raimbold appealed to him, by sentencing Raimbold to make a pilgrimage to Rome and present his case to the pope. Ivo's Letter 135 is in a sense a letter of introduction of Raimbold to the pope, acknowledging that "in the siege of Jerusalem he fought vigorously" (*in obsidione Hierosolymitana strenue militavit*).[5] *Strenuitas* was definitely a virtue, not a vice, in the normal vocabulary of Ivo, Suger, other contemporaries. We know nothing of the outcome—how well or poorly the fury-prone Raimbold complied—but Bruce Brasington calls to the reader's attention the fact that this letter is the only one in which Ivo shares with his correspondent, the idealistic Paschal II, who did not recoil from extreme decisions, the exact penalty that Ivo had established in his court.

He also describes his own mitigation of his original sentence—living for fourteen years unarmed—as an *indulgentia*, for which he asks the pope's indulgence. Raimbold's crusading valor was no secret: the chronicler Albert of Aachen had called Raimbold a *miles Christianus* (a definite compliment, no mere description) and praised his specific valor in the storming of the Turkish citadel inside Antioch in June 1098;[6] he joined Orderic Vitalis and Ralph of Caen in crediting Raimbold with being among the first knights to step from the siege tower onto the walls of Jerusalem (July 15, 1099)—Ralph says he was the first.[7] At some point in the performance of these exploits Raimbold had lost a hand. Living unarmed in twelfth-century France must have been for him a special humiliation, as well as quite dangerous.

So what had happened to this *preux chevalier*, as many later authors would have considered the appropriate label? Ivo offers no psychological explanation, but it is clear to aficionados of Ivonian prose like Bruce Brasington that the case had troubled him deeply, producing one of his most intense reactions. That was not Ivo's wont: he is deservedly famous for his cool-headed search for pragmatic solutions, his steady record as a genuine idealist somehow at ease in his quite scandalous world. Brasington concludes that we see in Letter 135 a great peacemaker trying to find mercy within justice: "Here is harmony within the dissonance of life, even for this most fallen of men . . . a crusader turned criminal."[8]

What interests me most in this case is not the crusader's behavior (of whom we know next to nothing, and even that in two clearly biased accounts),[9] but that reforming prelate's reaction: this atrocity clearly fired Ivo's emotions, though it did not transform his mode of juridical behavior. Also of interest to anyone studying the crusades is Raimbold's mitigated punishment. A pilgrimage to Rome was presumably not too difficult an experience for one who had returned largely intact (at least physically) from a much more distant pilgrimage. Could it have been perhaps a therapeutic attempt to reform the miscreant by setting him back on the path of a pilgrimage to an exceptionally holy site, as though one might cure a sick holy warrior by reinserting him in the foundational experience of pilgrimage?

But Raimbold Creton pales beside Thomas de Marle, the bête noire of Guibert of Nogent, who provoked in that morally hypersensitive abbot a frenzy of outrage suspicious to the post-Freudian reader. Guibert's *Monodiae*, usually translated into the modern scholarly vernacular as *Memoirs* or *Autobiography*, was composed apparently in 1115 at the abbey of Nogent, a small but cultivated house uncomfortably close to the great castle of Coucy, long the seat of the paternal line from which Thomas de Marle claimed to be born.[10] Guibert disapproved of Thomas on practically every score, reacting with a loathing that Benton considered worthy of a modern psychiatric patient. To put it all too summarily, Thomas was as physical, violent, capriciously cruel, upper-class yet capable of political radicalism, and involved in sexual immorality as Guibert was not.[11]

It is interesting that Guibert, usually painfully class-conscious about himself and his relatives, does not make it clear (as does Jacques Chaurand)[12] that Thomas was closely related to the new royal family of Jerusalem as well as to several of the loftiest lineages of Picardy and its neighboring provinces. As Guibert was finishing the third book of his *Monodiae*, the least autobiographical part of that strikingly innovative work, Thomas had for several years been lending serious military aid to the rebellious commune of the neighboring city of Laon. The burghers had risen very bloodily in 1111 against Laon's corrupt bishop and hence the king (Louis VI, who could hardly tolerate such violence however much he may have shared the burghers' disgust at Bishop Gaudry). It is difficult to reconstruct anything like a political theory from the evidence, but Thomas may have had some truly radical notions about political order. Although free of explicit theory on this issue, the essentially conservative Guibert may have seen Thomas as practically a revolutionary threat to right order. In the years just before 1115, the tide had turned against Thomas: Louis had intervened, and Thomas had become debilitatingly ill and was suffering serious setbacks. He was still alive, unrepentant, and ornery, however, and Guibert must have feared what he might yet pull off.

Guibert's readers first meet Thomas in chapter 7 of book 3, where Guibert calls him "the most worthlessly evil man of any we have known in this age."[13] Bishop Gaudry wisely hates (and fears) Thomas, who has become close to one Gerard, a rural bailiff of the diocese. Gerard has good personal reasons to hate the bishop, but one wonders if he might not have had some dangerous thoughts about rightful rule in general. Bishop Gaudry has Gerard put in prison and then blinded by "his African man." The king is disgusted when he hears about this act of wanton cruelty, and perhaps the pope also, but these high authorities let Gaudry soft-talk and bribe his way out of trouble. So the burghers form a commune—which Guibert has already told us is an evil name for a new scheme enabling lords to exact more money from the people. The commune rises, kills several people, and generally runs amok; the king reacts negatively, as do some of the local nobles; sensing how deep is the trouble they are in, the commune appeals to Thomas; he responds with interest, and peace abandons Guibert's world. It had not returned when Guibert finished his book.

Guibert was so scandalized by Thomas that he had excluded him from the *Gesta Dei per Francos*, written 1109, even though he had in fact performed numerous exploits on the First Crusade. In his account of the storming of Jerusalem, Guibert declares his intent to suppress the names of "several of the young Franks whose pious boldness had made them preeminent" and who "rushed forward, unwilling to seem inferior to him who had preceded them" (Guibert gives the credit to one Lietaud) and climbed to the top of the wall. "I would insert their names on this page," Guibert continues, "were I not aware of the fact that, after they returned, they became famous for criminal acts (*tantorum eos flagitiorum ac scelerum infamiam incurrisse*); therefore, according to the judgment of men who love the name of God, my silence is not unjust."[14] It is very likely that Thomas was one of those young men.

So what were Thomas' *flagitia ac scelera?* Most strikingly, Guibert accused Thomas of cruelty, certainly deserving the clinical description of sadism.

> So unheard-of in our times (*nostris saeculis inaudita*) was his cruelty that men who are considered cruel seem more humane in killing cattle than he in killing men. For he did not merely kill them outright with the sword and for definite offenses, as is usual, but by butchery after horrible tortures. When he was compelling prisoners of any condition to ransom themselves, he hung them up by their testicles, and as these often tore off from the weight of the body, the vitals soon burst out. Sometimes he did this with his own hands. Others were suspended by their thumbs or by the male organ itself, and were weighted down with a stone placed on their shoulders. He himself walked below them, and when he could not extort from them what they did not have, he beat them madly with cudgels until they promised what satisfied him, or perished under this punishment.

No one can tell how many expired in his dungeons and chains from starvation, disease, and torture. It is certain that two years ago, when he had gone to Le Mont de Soissons to give aid to someone against some peasants, three of these men hid in a cave, and when he came to the entry of the cave with his lance, he drove his weapon into the mouth of one of them with so hard a thrust that the blade of the lance tore through his entrails and passed out through his anus. Why go on with instances that have no end? The two left in the cave both perished by his hand. Again, one of the prisoners was wounded and could not march. He asked the man why he did not go faster. He replied that he could not. "Stop," said he, "I'll fix things so you'll make speed with real trouble." Leaping down from his horse, he cut off both the man's feet, and of that he died. Of what use is it to recount these horrors when later there will be a major occasion for telling them? Let me return to the subject. . . .[15]

Another time he had thrust a leper into prison. When an assemblage of lepers in the province heard of it, they besieged the doors of the tyrant, crying out for their comrade to be returned to them. He threatened that if they would not go away, he would burn them alive. Fleeing in fright, when they had reached a safe place and had gathered together from every quarter, they called on God to take vengeance on him, and, lifting up their voices, they cursed him all together. That same day, the leper died in the same prison. . . . Also a pregnant woman was put to forced labour in that prison and died there.

When some of the prisoners traveled slowly, he ordered his men to pierce the place under the neck called the windpipe and had cords inserted in five or six people and made them march in terrible pain. After a little while they died in captivity. Why prolong the story? In that affair he alone killed thirty men with his own sword.[16]

Throughout his narrative, Guibert presents Thomas as bestially violent. He identifies the source of that cruelty as lust. One should expect no less from the son of the rampantly lecherous Enguerrand de Boves, who, while Thomas was quite young, tried to disown him as the illegitimate fruit of his "absolutely shameful" (though very nobly descended) wife Ade de Roucy.[17] Guibert calls Thomas' marriages "incestuous,"[18] although only one of his three marriages (to Ermengard, daughter of Roger of Montaigu) was canonically annulled on grounds of consanguinity.[19] This vice of lust, cause of so many others, Thomas inherited from his father, whose second wife ("concubine," according to Guibert) Sibylle was a monster of sexual depravity; she "had a spirit more cruel than that of any wild she-bear." She incited Enguerrand against Thomas, and he responded with cruelty after cruelty as Sybille turned him from a fool to a madman (*de stulto insanum facere*: Terence, *Eunuchus* 1.254), declaring that he had a right to treat men like beasts. Not surprisingly neither Thomas' wives nor his prostitutes could sate him. "In our generation we have never seen two persons come together anywhere under whose administration we have seen so many evils arise from a single cause. If he was the fire, she could be called the oil."[20] And these are just the most lurid incidents that Guibert alleges.

Thomas was also greedy for wealth, but could squander it as heedlessly as he acquired it. As Guibert might have said, "*Quid plura?*"

Such a story must have another side to it. Albert of Aachen and other crusade chroniclers supply a bit of that, at least as regards military valor. Albert probably wrote the first six books of his *Historia Hierosolimitana* about 1100–1102. In those books he mentions Thomas—usually as "Thomas de Feria (or Feriae) castro," "Thomas de La Fère," we might say—eight times. All references to him are either laudatory or neutral, and if neutral, Thomas is usually in good company. In book 1, chapter 42, reporting the siege of Nicea, Thomas is given his best notice: "Thomas de La Fère, Frenchman, keenest of soldiers" (*Thomas de Feria castro, Francigena, miles acerrimus*).[21]

It is true that Thomas first appears in rather dubious company: Count Emicho of Flonheim, the prime instigator of that deplorable precedent, the pogrom of the Jews of Mainz. Albert of Aachen makes it quite clear that he disapproves of that "very cruel massacre . . . *quod dictu nefas est.*" The chronicler later continues with a ringing denunciation of all such behavior, ending it with a classically Augustinian statement about the error of making anyone "come to the yoke of the Catholic faith against his will or under compulsion."[22]

Thomas appears in Albert's text just after the report of the Mainz pogrom, but definitely in association with Emicho and Clarembald of Vendeuil. May we surmise that the chronicler hesitated to lay full blame on this young associate, perhaps eighteen at the time (likely born c. 1078), and hence too easily influenced? Perhaps; if so, that would suggest some abiding sympathy on Albert's part. Thomas certainly gets credit for his valor at Antioch, where he marched out against Kerbogha in the contingent led by the venerable Count Hugh of St. Pol.[23] At the siege of Jerusalem in June and July of 1099, Thomas is first in a list of eight lesser barons who "settled on all sides around the city."[24] Albert does not assign him to the contingents of the great lords such as Godfrey of Bouillon, Raymond of Toulouse, Robert of Flanders, or Robert of Normandy, which suggests that he may have achieved some distinction warranting that modest but somewhat autonomous command status.

This picture of Thomas reappears more than half a century later in William of Tyre's *History of Deeds Done Across the Sea*, the first book of which utilizes Albert of Aachen.[25] These exploits were remembered and reported with great enhancement in the *Chanson de Jerusalem*, the epic put together perhaps in the generation following the First Crusade but recast in the form we have today sometime around 1200. Thomas has become quite a major hero in this version, and Raimbold Croton, though a lesser figure, does well, too. Analysis of that transformation is a topic of its own, well deserving the necessary time and space, but unfortunately only peripherally relevant to this paper. Its value to the present enquiry would be to gain a contrary perspective on Raimbold and Thomas' condemnation back home by Ivo, Guibert, and Suger. In Outremer these crusaders' reputations throve. For now suffice it to report a very few highlights. Thomas appears forty-one times in the 9891 lines (arranged in 281 rhymed laisses) of the *Chanson*. He is accorded a number of highly honorable epithets, such as *li bers, li preux et li senes* (l.894: the same epithet is accorded to no less a lord than Hugh of Vermandois in l.1212), *qui mult ot le cuer fier,* and much is said of his *corage* (as l.489 has it, *Tumas de Marle qui le corage or fier*). He is also in the highest company, frequently cited along with Godfrey, his brothers Baldwin and Eustace, Hugh of Vermandois, and especially Robert of Normandy and Robert of Flanders, who appreciate his several speeches, accept his advice, and charge into battle with him.[26] Here is one crusader who has risen in the world, or at least in the esteem of not only his peers but in the highest stratum of the ruling class. What does the heroic Thomas de Marle of the living memory of Outremer (based on Albert of Aachen) have in common with the criminal condemned and hounded to death in Francia? He is in both traditions *miles acerrimus,* who seems never to have lost his *corage*.

To assess Guibert's problem with Thomas, and simply to put Thomas in perspective, it is helpful to take a look at how he appeared to Suger of St. Denis who wrote about him ten or a dozen years after his death

(November 9, 1130). Suger's eulogistic royal biography, *Vita Ludovici Grossi Regis* was composed between 1138 and 1145, though it refers to some events three decades earlier.

Suger wrote with evident disapproval of several other returned crusaders, not only because they became obstacles to Louis VI's effort to bring order to the royal domain. Suger was not automatically impressed by having gone on crusade. He criticizes the motivation, for instance, of Everard III of Le Puiset, a man of "marvelous arrogance who had taken up arms at the outset of the expedition to Jerusalem"[27] (and perished quite honorably before Antioch on August 21, 1097, a fact Suger fails to mention) and is comparably unimpressed by the decision of his hatefully arrogant son Hugh—one of Suger's favorite villains—to go to the Holy Land in 1128 (or so). There he died (likely in 1132) in unheroic circumstances: one source suggests that Hugh succumbed to a dagger wound in a brawl occasioned by a game of dice; Suger says merely: "like many other worthless people, his viciousness inflamed by every poison ended only when his life was extinguished."[28] For Suger the mere act of crusading could not counteract really bad blood.

Another case of vainglorious crusading was Ebles de Roucy, a close relative of Thomas de Marle.[29] Suger writes dismissively of his pretentiousness covering mental imbalance and innate rapacity, which expressed themselves in acts of rapine and every kind of malice. Ebles, Thomas' uncle, eventually reconciled with Louis and joined Thomas de Marle's father Enguerrand de Boves in attacking Thomas' castle. It is pretty clear that Suger disapproves of the family dynamics of what Jacques Chaurand has called the "Roucy-Marle" lineage.[30] That was a lofty lineage in the rich land between Amiens and Reims: to cite just one connection, Thomas' grandfather Létard de Marle was the great-uncle of King Baldwin I of Jerusalem, the second cousin at whose side Thomas had in the summer of 1099 fought off Egyptian cavalrymen attacking the pilgrims who were trying to supply the besiegers of Jerusalem with wood for the siege-engines.[31]

A family of mixed virtue and mixed crusade performance was the house of Rochefort, very close to the Capetian family. Uncle Guy was admirable, and nephew Guy Trousseau was a rope-walker and proved himself *perditissimus* and *infestus* once back home.[32] The uncle was an experienced man and veteran soldier (*vir peritus et miles emeritus*): he had been King Philip's seneschal for ten years before going on crusade in 1101, and was made seneschal again when he returned; his daughter Lucienne de Rochefort was betrothed to Prince Louis, though consanguinity prevented their marrying. The worthless nephew had fled Antioch rather than face Kerbogha and thereupon lost all his bodily strength (surely a condign consequence). Nevertheless, he managed to arrange the marriage of his daughter to Louis' half-brother Philip (the son of King Philip's second wife—or concubine, in reformers' eyes—Bertrade of Montfort).

Thomas de Marle seemed to Suger a more serious offender than any of these, and got more attention. He appears in *The Life of Louis the Fat* in an episode that occurred while Louis' father King Philip was still alive, likely in the latter part of 1103. Thomas, whom Suger introduces as "most destructive of men, dangerous to God and Man" (*hominem perditissimum, Deo et hominibus infestum*) distinguished by an "intolerable rage, like that of an immense wolf,"[33] has just acquired by marriage to his cousin Ermengard, daughter of Roger of Montaigu, her family castle. Thomas' father, Enguerrand of Boves, lord of Coucy, easily gathers a coalition of local nobles (including his cousin Ebles of Roucy) to drive Thomas out of Montaigu; since that was a strong place, it required a time-consuming siege. Their plan was to condemn Thomas to perpetual imprisonment if he survived the siege.

Somehow Thomas slipped through the besiegers' lines and made his way to Louis' court, where he corrupted the courtiers and charmed the youthful king. Louis marched to Thomas' rescue with seven hundred knights. No one in Enguerrand's coalition wanted to fight their *dominus designatus*, whom they could not convince of Thomas' wickedness, so Thomas kept Montaigu until his marriage was annulled on grounds of consanguinity. Suger excuses Louis on the grounds of youthful flexibility; it is useful to note Lindy Grant's characterization of Louis as an "amiable thug," initially no friend of the reform-minded Suger.[34] Michel Bur opines that Louis found in Thomas another youth oppressed by his elders, and that the "valorous" Thomas had not yet become *ce scelerat enragé, ce loup cruel, ce coquin tyrannique*, who would soon horrify his contemporaries.[35]

Eleven years later (1114) he had thoroughly horrified respectable public opinion. Bloodily active in the general eruption at Laon, he had become the occasional champion of the commune, slaughtering in the process many a layman and cleric.[36] While the king was distracted by other military threats, Thomas had freely ravaged the territory of Amiens, Laon, and Reims ("butchering all, destroying all": *omnia trucidans, omnia perdens*) from his strongholds of Crécy and Nouvion. A council of the Church meeting at Beauvais excommunicated him, describing his character and crimes in language close to that employed in the following year by Guibert. Doubly enraged according to Suger (for reasons ecclesiastical and civil? or because Thomas had betrayed his earlier support?), Louis set out to deprive Thomas of his two castles, and accomplished that goal in short order. Both castles were destroyed, and the claim of Thomas' lineage to be counts of Amiens was abolished. Suger's description of the fire set to Crécy by the royal army suggests that he himself was present. It is interesting to see how he justifies the severity of the king's campaign: "he confounds the criminals, piously massacres the impious, mercilessly dismembers those who had mercilessly committed offenses"[37] — the central justification of holy war. The crusader turned criminal has now become the target of a domestic crusade.

Sixteen years later (1130) Thomas had still not learned his lesson.[38] His reverses at Crécy, Nouvion, and Amiens had been at least partly compensated by finally coming into possession of the mighty castle of Coucy, the ancestral seat of which his hateful father Enguerrand and monstrous stepmother Sibylle had so long deprived him. From that base he resumed his depredations, particularly capturing merchants for ransom. Louis sent his younger cousin Ralph of Vermandois to take care of Thomas, which he did efficiently. Thomas was seriously wounded in a skirmish, and brought in that condition to Laon, where he absolutely refused to free the merchants or pay any damages to the churches he had raided. The presence of his third wife Mélisende, from whom he had gotten the castles of Crécy and Nouvion, had no positive influence. When it was clear that he was dying, he was allowed to receive the Eucharist as viaticum despite his current excommunication, but refused. And so, unregenerate and unreconciled, "he breathed forth" (as Suger puts it) "his most repulsive spirit."[39] The date was November 9.[40] The merchants were freed, Enguerrand regained Coucy, and Louis rode off triumphantly to Paris.

We must admit that Suger was less hard on Thomas than Guibert had been. Like Guibert (perhaps consciously following him?), Suger does not mention that Thomas had gone on the heroic First Crusade. Nor does he praise Thomas' martial valor in so many words, but it is evident that Thomas was a redoubtable foe, whom Louis was proud to have overcome. Though he shares much of Guibert's vocabulary, Suger does not indulge in the paroxysms of condemnation Guibert seems unable to avoid or, once started, stop. Why was he so much less hard on this very criminal crusader? Was it just that Thomas at first won Louis over, and Louis was always the overriding focus of this work of Suger's? Was it that Suger was saner than at least Benton thinks Guibert was?[41]

I would like to think that it was more than that. It seems to me that the reactions of our three North French prelates living and writing during the first half of the twelfth century present an instructive spectrum of the reformist monastic attitude toward violence that affected decisively so much of medieval history in the aftermath of the millennium. It could be described as an ambivalent fascination, which shaped so many of that era's turbulent events: Gregory VII's necessarily bloody break with Henry IV; his and Urban II's decision to launch holy wars in 1074 and 1095, and the involvement of so many prelates, Cluniac and other, in defining that new form of attractive engagement in the affairs of the militant world; the zeal of all those vigilantes of God enforcing his peace or at least his truce on their violent society; and many others. In his repulsion at that mode of life, Paschal II tried to disencumber the church of those greed-inducing and violence-provoking temporalities. It makes sense that Guibert de Nogent, who voices the aspect of fascination that is repulsion, was critical even of Paschal's ethics, whereas Suger, who seems to embody the attractive side of this fascination, was a warm admirer of that utopian pope.

NOTES

1. Suger, *Vita Ludovici Grossi Regis*, chap. 19, 142.
2. For an overview of this subject, see Riley-Smith, *The First Crusaders, 1095–1131*, chap. 6, "Returning from Crusade" (144–68).
3. See Riley-Smith, *The First Crusade*, chap. 6, "Theological Refinement," 135–52, esp. 135–39.
4. See for instance, on Vietnam, Shay, *Odysseus in America*, and *Achilles and Vietnam*; and Tatum, *War and Remembrance*. For an early statement of traumatic experience, see Fussell, *The Great War*.
5. For this case, see Brasington, "Crusader, Castration, Canon Law"; the letter itself is on 381–82. Cf. Riley-Smith, *The First Crusaders, 1095–1131*, 155–56.

6. Albert of Aachen, *Historia Ierosolimitana*, 4.32 (294).

7. Ibid., 4.30. For these other statements of valor, see Kostick, *The Social Structure*, 175, 208; all of chap. 6, "Juvenes: The Glory-Seeking Knights of the First Crusade," 187–212, is useful for this topic.

8. Brasington, "Crusader, Castration, Canon Law," 381. This essay was written "In memoriam Stephan Kuttner," author of the lecture-essay *Harmony from Dissonance* (1960), a milestone in canon law studies.

9. As Jonathan Riley-Smith prudently observes in *The First Crusaders, 1095–1131*, "It is hard to penetrate the minds of the survivors" (153). But the minds of those who wrote about them in that articulate generation can sometimes be quite successfully penetrated.

10. On this work and this issue, see Benton's work in Guibert of Nogent, *Self and Society*, and Guibert de Nogent, *Autobiographie*.

11. Most of this assessment derives from Benton's introduction to Guibert of Nogent, *Self and Society*, something of a milestone in medieval psychohistory.

12. Jacques Chaurand, author of the curiously exculpatory interdisciplinary exercise *Thomas de Marle*, as well as entirely scholarly articles on Guibert, to be cited later.

13. Benton's translation in Guibert of Nogent, *Self and Society*, 170; Guibert of Nogent, *Autobiographie*, 328–29. Benton hardly does justice to Guibert's choice of vocabulary: "virum omnium quos novimus hac aetate nequissimum." "The most evil man of all we know in this generation" is how C. C. Swinton Bland, the translator Benton uses with some revisions, renders this absolute assessment.

14. Guibert of Nogent, *The Deeds of God*, 130. For the Latin text, see his *Gesta Dei per Francos*, 278.

15. Guibert of Nogent, *Self and Society*, 184–85, and *Autobiographie*, 362–65.

16. Guibert of Nogent, *Self and Society*, 201, and *Autobiographie*, 402–05.

17. Ade ("shameful" in Guibert of Nogent, *Self and Society*, 200) was the only daughter of Létard de Roucy, who was the son of Gilbert, Count of Reims and Roucy, who was the son of Reynaud, a Norman lord who married a niece of Otto the Great: Chaurand, *Thomas de Marle*, 15.

18. Guibert of Nogent, *Self and Society*, 184, and *Autobiographie*, 385.

19. Guibert of Nogent, *Autobiographie*, 363, n. 2.

20. Guibert of Nogent, *Self and Society*, 199, and *Autobiographie*, 398–99. The metaphor is Horatian, further testimony to Guibert's education.

21. Albert of Aachen, *Historia Ierosolimitana*, 1.42, 96–97.

22. For Thomas' first appearance, see ibid., 1.28, 52–53. Albert ends book one with an impassioned condemnation (end of 1.29, 30: 58–59) of the crusaders' errors, especially sexual license and monetary greed. He speculates with evident concern as to what could have been the cause of the "spiritual error" misleading so many of the pilgrims and those bearing the sign of the cross (*cruce signati*) to commit such horrible cruelty.

23. Ibid., 4.28, 320–23.

24. Ibid., 5.46, 404–05.
25. Ibid., xxiv–xxviii.
26. *The Old French Crusade Cycle*.
27. Suger, *Vita Ludovici Grossi Regis*, chap. 19, 130.
28. Ibid., chap. 22, 170–71.
29. Ibid., chaps. 10 and 19, 131.
30. Chaurand, *Thomas de Marle*, 18. Lindy Grant refers in her *Abbot Suger of St-Denis* to "the powerful and extended Marle-Roucy-Ramerupt-Rethel clan" (123) that would give Louis and his royal officers so much trouble in the area they dominated, opposing, for one example, royal policy in the Flemish succession crisis of 1127.
31. Albert of Aachen, *Historia Ierosolimitana*, 6.4, 208–9.
32. Suger, *Vita Ludovici Grossi Regis*, chaps. 6, 8. Cf. Riley-Smith, *The First Crusaders, 1095–1131*, chap. 7, "Crusading and the Montlhérys" (as he calls this lineage), 169–88.
33. Suger, *Vita Ludovici Grossi Regis*, chap. 24, 174.
34. Grant, *Abbot Suger of St-Denis*, 20.
35. Bur, *Suger*, 30–31.
36. Suger, *Vita Ludovici Grossi Regis*, chap. 24, 172–79.
37. ". . . sceleratos confundit, impios pie trucidat, et quos, quia inmisericordes offendit, inmisericorditer detruncat"; ibid., 176.
38. Ibid., chap. 31, 250–55.
39. ". . . et spiritum teterrimum divine expers Eucharistie exhalavit"; ibid., 254.
40. Ironically enough, the feast of St. Theodore, the martyred soldier often invoked by crusade preachers and contemporary sculptors, who thus, in full knightly armor, came to decorate many a church portal.
41. Before Benton published his Freudian analysis of Guibert's manifold insecurities, Chaurand had suggested a very different explanation for Guibert's acute rigorism, an entirely rational ethical schema affected by a tradition of Christian Neoplatonism: see Chaurand, "La conception de l'histoire de Guibert de Nogent."

FRANS VAN LIERE

15   Christ or Antichrist?
The Jewish Messiah in Twelfth-Century Christian Eschatology

In the twelfth century, a time of great cultural and educational renewal in Western Europe, the biblical prophets were studied as never before by both Jews and Christians.[1] Christians saw them as proof of the messiahship of Jesus Christ, and Jews saw them as messianic texts offering hope for redemption in an age that seemed increasingly characterized by Christian triumphalism. In the same period, Christian scholars such as Hugh and Andrew of St. Victor gave the study of the Bible a new direction by turning to Jewish exegetes for help with the textual interpretation of the Old Testament. This Christian-Jewish encounter over the interpretation of scripture is an exciting moment in history, an early exploration of the shared ground between Jews and Christians, marking the beginning of a new textual and historical approach to the biblical text within Christian scholarship.² But, as this chapter will show, the study of the prophetic texts in particular not only brought Christians and Jews together; it could also divide them sharply.

Christians, starting with the authors of the New Testament, have always read the Hebrew Bible, which they call the Old Testament, as a text that referred to and was eventually fulfilled in the messiahship of Jesus. The persistence of Jews who did not believe this was, of course, a theological problem. It led Christians to the conviction that Jews did not know how to read their own scriptures properly. This conviction can be seen in the personification of Judaism in the Middle Ages as Synagoga, a blindfolded woman, blind to the spiritual dimension of scripture. For Christians, the mystery of salvation through Jesus Christ was the hermeneutical key to unlocking the scriptures. Without this key, they argued, the Jews could not see the whole picture. This problem of Jewish blindness, however, had an eschatological solution. Augustine, for instance, was convinced that God himself had only blinded the Jews temporarily, to serve as a witness to Christian truth through their very presence, until at the end times they, too, would be converted and share fully in God's grace.³

With the conversion of the Roman Empire to Christianity, and the Christianization of Europe during the Middle Ages, Christians seemed to have history on their side. For many Christians, and even some Jews, the apparent triumph of the church through tribulations and persecutions, contrasted with the destruction of Jerusalem and the subsequent Jewish Diaspora, confirmed the notion that God favored the Christians and punished the Jews with eternal exile for their rejection of Jesus as the Messiah. The destruction of Jerusalem in 70 CE by the Romans was seen as an important "proof" of this divine punishment. The ruined Temple, for Christians, was a visible sign of God's wrath towards the Jews and favor towards the Christians.⁴

Jews, of course, had their own eschatological beliefs. They believed that a Messiah would arise from the posterity of David to liberate Israel from oppression and judge the nations for their wickedness. This Jewish eschatology included several historical elements: the end of the Roman Empire, or its successor, Christendom; the end of the Diaspora; and, not surprisingly, the rebuilding of the Temple in Jerusalem that the Romans had destroyed. Rabbinic Judaism even added a certain vengeful element to this messianism: the Messiah would take revenge on the present oppressors and turn them into the oppressed. For Jews living in Christian lands, the prospects for final redemption must have seemed bleak. At the time of the eleventh-century Gregorian reform of the church, Christianity had more reason to feel self-confident than ever before, and the crusades, which had brought disaster upon the Jewish communities of the Rhineland, seemed to underscore this idea of a triumphalist Christendom. In reaction (as stated above), Jews held on to the belief that the Messiah would bring about the end of the rule of Christendom, restore Jewish rule in Jerusalem, and wreak vengeance on the enemies of the Jews. This Jewish messianism drew on several prophetic biblical texts, the same texts that in Christian circles were often read as confirmation of the messiahship of Jesus. These texts could provide Jews with hope for the future, and even some glee over the future downfall of their present oppressors.[5]

Christians were aware of this Jewish eschatology, and this chapter will explore the various ways in which Christian scholars tried to come to terms with it. Some of these were friendlier to the Jews than others. Some Christian exegetes emphasized the traditional Augustinian idea that the Jews were blinded, but that they would be enfolded in God's grace at the end of time.[6] In contrast, Jerome took a fairly polemical stance against the Jews. He presented a Christological reading of these Old Testament prophecies as his alternative to the Jewish messianic reading, and he emphasized that Jews perpetuated their own blindness when they read these passages as prophecies about the coming of the Messiah.[7] Some medieval Christian exegetes, most notably Haimo of Auxerre (d. 875?) and the authors of the *Glossa ordinaria*, expanded Jerome's exegesis on this point. For them, this vengeful Messiah the Jews expected looked, suspiciously, not like Christ but like Antichrist. This notion seems to have become commonplace by the twelfth century. The purpose of this chapter is to explore some of the dynamics of Christian exegesis on this point, and show how it influenced the growing relations between Christians and Jews in this period.

The legend of Antichrist is as old as Christianity itself.[8] In its rudimentary form, it goes back to 2 Thessalonians 2:4, where Paul mentions a "final rebellion against God," "wickedness in human form," a man who "enthrones himself in the Temple of God." But this adversary would not be revealed until the "restraint that is holding him back" was removed from the scene. Christian interpreters commonly identified this "restraint" as the rule of the

Roman Empire. The Antichrist myth was given its basic narrative form in the seventh century by Ps.-Methodius, a Syriac Christian who lived at the time of the earliest Muslim conquest, and painted a compelling scenario, combining the notion of Antichrist in 2 Thessalonians with several other biblical apocalyptic elements, such as the invasion of the barbarian peoples Gog and Magog. He also added his own extrabiblical elements, such as the notion of the last emperor, who would yield his power in Jerusalem to the demonic adversary of Christ. This tradition appeared in the West in the tenth-century writings of Adso of Montmoutier-en-Der (d. 992) and found widespread resonance in apocalyptic writings and biblical commentaries.[9]

The role of the Jews in this Antichrist myth has been ambivalent. Although Jews were often associated with the Antichrist, or seen as his agents, the Antichrist himself was rarely Jewish. More popular was the idea of the Holy Roman emperor or (more often) the pope as the Antichrist.[10] The Augustinian idea that the Jews would convert in time before the coming of Christ is prevalent in most end-time scenarios. In the twelfth-century *Play of Antichrist*, this conversion even secures them martyrdom as they witness against Antichrist. After initially mistaking him for the expected Messiah, the Jews become the first ones to unmask Antichrist as a fraud, and they are subsequently martyred by his agents. Some have argued that the play's author had the recent martyrdom of the Jewish communities in the Rhineland in the wake of the Crusades in mind, and tried to come to terms with this atrocity.[11] Not all speculation about the end times was tolerant towards the Jews, however. Some authors, such as Peter Comestor (d. 1179), identified the apocalyptic peoples of Gog and Magog as Jews, namely, the ten lost tribes.[12] The most anti-Jewish variant of Christian eschatology, the idea that the Jewish Messiah was the very same as the Christian Antichrist, circulated for the first time in Jerome's commentaries. It was eagerly picked up and expanded on by the Carolingian exegete Haimo of Auxerre, and it resonated in twelfth-century exegetical sources as well. It represents a little-studied chapter in the history of Christian anti-Jewish polemic.

Haimo of Auxerre was a prolific biblical commentator. For a long time, the bulk of his work has been misattributed to Haimo of Halberstadt. Little is certain about Haimo of Auxerre's biography, and most of his work still awaits critical editions. He left commentaries on Genesis, Deuteronomy, the Song of Songs, and most of the prophetic books, as well as the Gospels,

Pauline Epistles, and the Apocalypse. His interest in Antichrist, as well as his anti-Judaism, have only received serious scholarly attention in the last decades.[13] In his commentary on the twelve Minor Prophets, Haimo shows himself clearly aware of the vengeful side of Jewish eschatological expectations. It is unlikely that he knew these ideas from firsthand experience, however. He could have easily found them in the commentaries of Jerome, which he used at length as a source in his commentary. In any case, the implications of the "vengeful messianism" of Jewish exegetes clearly troubled him. In response, he identified this Jewish Messiah with the Christian Antichrist, the evil ruler who would precede the second coming of Christ. As was said above, Haimo picked up this idea from Jerome's commentary on Obadiah. Obadiah 17 reads, "On Mount Zion there shall be a remnant which will be saved, and Jacob will possess those that dispossessed them." The entire book of Obadiah is a diatribe of revenge against Edom, which Obadiah predicts will be devoured by the house of Jacob; in common Jewish exegesis, as Jerome noted, Edom stood for Rome, or later Christianity in a more general sense. On verses 17–18, Jerome commented: "all these things . . . the Jews promise for themselves in the future, when they will receive the Antichrist as their Messiah."[14] In his own commentary on this passage, Haimo quotes Jerome almost literally:

> All the things we said before and which we are about to say, the Jews, dreaming up falsehoods, refer to the time of the Antichrist, and whatever we have interpreted as against Edom, they dream up against the Roman empire."[15]

There is a certain paradox in the Christian reception of the Jewish interpretation of these passages. Jerome, and Haimo with him, disagree that this passage actually refers to the end times at all: "We say that this happened according to the historical sense under Zerubbabel, or certainly is being fulfilled mystically in the church on a daily basis."[16] But, although they argue that these prophetic passages are not referring to future events at all, they do give credence to the Jewish belief in the future tribulation of Christians and destruction of the (Holy) Roman Empire. There would come a figure to bring about both; but this figure would not be the Messiah (who, after all, had already appeared, in the person of Jesus Christ), but his antithesis. The idea that Jews were expecting not the Messiah but Antichrist proved popular with Haimo; we see it surface elsewhere in his commentary as well. In those passages that Jewish exegetes read as evidence for their eschatological expectations, Haimo not only cited Jerome in his rejection of these expectations, but reiterated the notion that this "Messiah" was Antichrist more frequently than Jerome had done.

Two examples will illustrate how Haimo expanded on Jerome's notion. Zephaniah 3:8 reads: "Wherefore expect me, says the Lord, in the day of my resurrection that is to come; for my judgment is to assemble the Gentiles and to gather the kingdoms, and to pour upon them my indignation, all my fierce anger." Jerome comments: "The Jews refer this passage to the coming of the Christ [the Messiah] that they hope will come." In his opinion, however, Christians "who follow not the letter that kills, but that spirit that makes alive" interpret this verse as referring to the present, the time of the church. Haimo goes one step further in his rendering of the Jewish interpretation; he says that the Jews, and *nostri Judaizantes* ("the Judaizers among us," a term he most likely picked up from Jerome's commentary, to refer to Christians who believed in the coming of a thousand-year reign of Christ before the Last Judgment) refer this to the time of "their" Christ, who really is Antichrist.[17] On Zechariah 8:23, which describes how ten Gentiles will take hold of the robe of a Jew and say, "we will go with you, for God is with you," Jerome had commented that "some of the Jews believe that this was fulfilled under Zerubbabel and the time after Zerubbabel; but some delay this to the future, when they expect their Christ to come." Haimo follows Jerome's interpretation fairly closely, except that he replaced the words "their Christ" with "Antichrist": "Even though the Jews refer this to the time of Antichrist, we say that this happened at the time of the coming of our Lord, savior, when he was born of the Virgin Mary."[18] Thus, while Haimo did not want to give too much credence to these Jewish messianic interpretations, at the same time he seemed to have a nagging fear that the Jewish interpreters were not altogether mistaken in their notion that the future held some hard times for the Christian church; their desire for vengeance on the church made the Jews somehow fall into line with the Antichrist that Haimo expected would appear at the end of times.

It was through the inclusion of Haimo's commentary in the *Glossa ordinaria* that this idea became commonplace in the twelfth century. The *Glossa ordinaria* was a compilation of patristic commentary, neatly formatted to fit in the margin and between the lines of the biblical text. In the twelfth century, this *Glossa* was a relatively new tool in biblical exegesis; by its very layout it offered a new approach to the biblical text by making patristic exegesis directly accessible through the use of marginal and interlinear annotations.[19] The *Glossa* on the Minor Prophets was commonly ascribed to the French scholar Gilbert of Auxerre, or Gilbertus Universalis (d. 1135),[20] but it drew heavily on the work of the other scholar from Auxerre, Haimo. The passage in Obadiah, above, for instance, was incorporated into the *Glossa* straight from Haimo.[21] The *Glossa* did not always follow Haimo's interpretation strictly (the examples cited above, from Zephaniah and Zachariah, are closer to the wording of Jerome than Haimo: the Jews here are said to expect "their Christ," rather than Antichrist). But in many places, the *Glossa* expanded Jerome's interpretations in the same way as Haimo had done. In Hosea 2:21, for instance, "It will come to pass in that day; I will hear, says the Lord," Jerome concluded his exegesis with the observation that all the things described here "the Jews and our Judaizers expect after the coming of Antichrist, at the end of this world."[22] The *Glossa* paraphrases Jerome rather freely, using some phrases borrowed from Haimo:

> According to the literal meaning, one can understand that at the advent of Christ, these temporal goods are promised to the believers, so that, for the sake of him who is the seed of God, all things run their course, as they were established from the beginning, and serve the needs of mankind.

But then the *Glossa* adds the line: "And yet the Jews expect after all these goods the physical coming of Antichrist."[23] The self-evidence with which the *Glossa* equated the Jewish eschatological expectation of the Messiah with the coming of Antichrist seems to suggest that, by the twelfth century, Haimo's ideas had become commonplace. At the coming of Antichrist, so Christians thought, the Jews would flock to him in droves, because they mistook him for the Messiah that they had been expecting, due to their faulty interpretation of the prophetic texts.[24]

How did all these ideas affect the interactions between Jews and Christians in the twelfth century? One twelfth-century Christian exegete actually took the remarkable step of consulting Jews about the interpretation of the Old Testament prophets, and his own treatment of the Old Testament prophetic books may shed some light on this question. Andrew of St. Victor was a student of the well-known teacher and theologian Hugh of St. Victor (d. 1141), at the abbey of the same name just outside the walls of medieval Paris, and Andrew has traditionally been seen as a figure who bridged the divide between Christians and Jews in the Middle Ages.[25] He has left us a fairly limited oeuvre: his works include only commentaries on the Old Testament. In a world in which the meaning of scripture was largely established by an allegorical, mystical reading of the biblical text, Andrew dedicated himself almost entirely to a reading of scripture in its literal sense, limiting himself strictly to literary, and sometimes historical, comments on the biblical text, often using Jewish sources to make his point. He eschewed any allegorization or doctrinal interpretation of the text. Andrew's commentary on the Minor Prophets is partly an excerpt from Jerome's commentary on the same books, but in excerpting from Jerome, Andrew limits himself to Jerome's comments on the literal sense, and overlooks most of his more allegorical comments. Andrew also used the *Glossa ordinaria*, both to complement and to summarize Jerome.[26] At times, however, Andrew offered his own alternative interpretation of a passage to the one excerpted from Jerome or the *Glossa*. Often, these passages contained materials that he had obtained from Jewish sources. Many of them can be identified as coming from the commentaries of Rashi (d. 1105), and also from Andrew's contemporary Joseph Kara, while some of them were not written down until a generation after Andrew, in the commentaries of Radak (d. 1235). This indicates that Andrew must have heard this exegesis, rather than seen it in writing: most likely he derived his information by speaking directly with his Jewish contemporaries. The synagogue in Paris after all was a short walk from both the cathedral of Notre Dame and the Abbey of St. Victor.[27] Thus Andrew probably had firsthand knowledge of the Jewish eschatological traditions that Haimo and the *Glossa* knew only indirectly, through Jerome.

While pathbreaking in its exploration of the Jewish exegetical tradition, Andrew's commentary on the Minor Prophets is representative of the very ambivalent attitude of twelfth-century Christians towards Jewish learning. One of the most striking characteristics of Andrew's interpretation of the Minor Prophets is that he eschewed the more common Christian explanations, which looked for a Christological meaning in these texts. For Andrew, passages that his fellow Christians interpreted Christologically did not always necessarily refer to Christ according to their literal sense. There is plenty of evidence that Andrew's contemporaries were offended by this exegetical method. In the late 1150s, Andrew's contemporary Richard of St. Victor wrote a long refutation of Andrew's exegesis of Isaiah 7:14 ("A Virgin shall conceive"), which Andrew interpreted simply as a young woman, in this case, the young wife of Isaiah the prophet himself. To strip this passage of its Christological meaning, said Richard, was scandalous and dangerous.[28]

In the same way, when he came to interpret the Old Testament texts that Jerome had applied to Christ, Andrew often read them in a strictly historical sense. An example can be found in the Canticle of Habbakuk, Habbakuk 3:3: "God comes from the South; the Holy One from Mount Paran." For Jerome, this passage was a prophecy about the birth of the savior in Bethlehem and the coming of Christ incarnate in judgment against sinners. He even cited Jewish sources to support his Christological reading. The Ethiopians whose tents are crushed in verse 7 are the demons, defeated at the coming of Christ. Connecting verse 17 ("The fig tree has no buds") with the common interpretation of the parable of the fig tree in Matthew 21:19, where the fig tree stood for the unbelieving Jews, Jerome explained that this meant that, at the coming of Christ, the nonbelieving Jews would be ruined, while the believing elect would be saved.[29] Andrew, after excerpting this explanation from Jerome, offers two alternatives to Jerome's Christological reading. The first one is largely borrowed from contemporaneous Jewish sources, such as Rashi.[30] This reading interpreted the passage as a description of the liberation of Israel from Egypt. Mount Paran is Mount Sinai; the Ethiopians are the allies of the Egyptians; and the text mentions the rivers and waters being cleft, which are references to the crossing of the Red Sea and the Jordan. Verse 11, "The Sun forgets to run its course," refers to the time of Joshua, when the sun stood still (Jo 10:13). The reason that Habbakuk described God's liberating deeds of past times, Andrew says, was to console his audience about the coming evil that would be perpetrated by the Babylonian king Nebuchadnezzar. After rendering the common contemporary Jewish exegesis of this passage, Andrew offers a third alternative reading of the text, one that takes this passage to be prophetic but not messianic; it had already been fulfilled before the time of Christ. This canticle, Andrew argued, could be read as a prophecy about the coming defeat of the Babylonians by Cyrus and Darius. In an exegesis that, as far as I can see, is unique to Andrew, and based on a reading of Herodotus' *Histories*, he interprets it as a description of the siege and capture of Babylon and the end of the Babylonian captivity.[31] Andrew seems to say that there is no need to interpret these passages as referring to Christ in their literal and historical sense.

By choosing a strictly historical interpretation for passages like these, Andrew not only defused their messianic importance, but he seems to have wanted to deemphasize their Christological significance as well. This makes some of his commentaries surprisingly free of the polemical anti-Judaic tone that characterized so many of the other Christian commentaries on the Old Testament, Jerome's included. At times, Andrew seems to emphasize the Augustinian notion of a common eschatological future for both Jews and Christians. In Micah 2:11, for instance, "I will assemble and gather together all of thee," Andrew comments: "So far, we have not seen all of Jacob gathered together, but we expect it in the future, when Judah will be saved, and Israel shall live with confidence, and the rod of Joseph and Judah will be united, and out of two shall be one people, and they shall have one head, namely Christ, who is from the line of David, or, according to the Jews, David himself, who will rule over them."[32]

But when these Jewish messianic interpretations display a more vengeful attitude towards Christians, Andrew's attitude is decidedly more ambiguous than it first appears. Although he presents Jewish exegesis as alternative explanations, Andrew does not want to give too much credence to the Jewish eschatological reading of prophetic texts. Instead, he simply sets these prophetic texts in their own historical context and explain them as relating to events that happened during the prophets' own lifetime, or some time between the prophets' lifetime and the coming of Christ. His interpretation steers a "middle way" between Christology and messianism. Sometimes, Andrew did not have to look very far for this interpretation, since it was already suggested to him by Jerome. His exegesis of Obadiah 17–18, for instance, is remarkable mainly for what he left out, rather than what he said. Andrew here cited the *Glossa ordinaria*, which in turn had used Haimo, who had used Jerome. Thus for Andrew, this verse refers to the rebuilding of the Temple, but not the Temple destroyed by the Romans in 70 CE, as the Jews say, but the one destroyed by the Chaldeans in 586 BCE. This rebuilding took place in the time of the Persian Empire, under the leadership of Zerubbabel, and thus refers to a past historical event, not to a future messianic event.³³ Jerome's main point, however, that this prophecy was fulfilled in the church, Andrew left out.

Another example of the "middle way" that Andrew steered between Jewish messianism and Christological exegesis can be found in his interpretation of Joel 2:28–32 (in non-Vulgate versions, this is chapter 3), Joel's prophecy concerning the "pouring out of the Spirit of God on all Mankind" and the "great and terrible day of the Lord." According to Jerome's interpretation, which was probably inspired by the interpretation of this prophecy in the New Testament itself (Acts 2:17–22), these verses refer to events in the New Testament: the pouring out of the Spirit happened at Pentecost, the signs in heaven and on earth were the signs that accompanied the birth of Christ, and the "Sun turned to darkness and the moon to blood" refers to what happened at the moment of Jesus' crucifixion. That the chronological order seems to be a bit jumbled up does not matter, for, as Jerome states elsewhere (on Amos 2:9–11), in prophetic discourse, the order of history is not always maintained.³⁴ While Andrew faithfully excerpts Jerome here, he also offers an alternative interpretation, derived from Jewish exegetes. He observes that the Jews say that all this will happen in the future, at the end of times. To explain what will happen in those last days, Andrew summarizes an exegesis we can find in the Midrash Tanhuma, which is cited by Rashi: all will possess the spirit of God, and there will be no distinction between Jews and Gentiles. All people, young and old, will have the gift of prophecy. The day of judgment will surely come with mighty and fearful signs, but all who will call on the name of God will be saved.³⁵ Still, Andrew seems reluctant to give too much credibility to a messianic reading of this passage. In the following verse, "On Mount Zion there shall be salvation" (a verse that, incidentally, occurs in the same words in Obadiah 17), Andrew observes that here we have to find out whether this applies to the time of Christ or to the end of times; we cannot apply one part of the prophecy to one period, and another part to the other, because the prophet set everything within a single time frame. Jerome took this passage to be a reference to the small number of the Jews who converted to Christianity. The Jews, Andrew says, take this to refer to the end of the Jewish Diaspora, after the fall of the Roman Empire. The only way that all events fit within one time frame, however, Andrew says, is to interpret the verse as referring to the remnant of the ten tribes that fled to Jerusalem, after the destruction of Samaria in 722 BCE (2 Kgs 18:9).

While Andrew avoids the identification of the Jewish Messiah with Antichrist most of the time, the idea was not altogether alien to him. Despite his sympathetic stance towards Jewish exegesis, he probably did think that the Jews were ultimately deluded in their messianic interpretations. An example of this can be found in Hosea 13:13–15. The Vulgate reads: "I shall be your death, O death." The next verse says: "An east wind will come, a blast from the Lord, rising over the desert." Andrew offers no fewer than four contrasting interpretations of this text.[36] He first cites Jerome, who says that this refers to Christ, who died to defeat death so we might have life. The wind is Christ, says Jerome, with a reference to Habbakuk 3:3. Next Andrew says that according to the Jews, this wind refers to "their Messiah" (*helimenus suus*), who, he says, in our interpretation is the Antichrist, who will "overturn death," that is, the Roman Empire. While the interpretation of the "wind from the desert" as the Messiah can be found in the Targum Jonathan, the identification of this Messiah with Antichrist is Andrew's own addition, and thus he offers a strong rebuke of any hint at a messianic interpretation of this passage. Andrew refers to the Jewish Messiah here as the *helimenus*, a Greek word that is possibly derived from *elaio* ("to oil, to anoint"), or, less likely, *eleimenos* ("one who has received mercy"). Apart from one stray reference in Jerome's commentary on Isaiah, the word seems quite unique to Andrew.[37] It seems to indicate a reluctance to identify the expected Jewish Messiah with the second coming of Christ. Andrew closes his exegesis with two much more historical contextualizations. It is quite possible, he says, that this passage refers to one of the two past events: the "death" brought by the Assyrian army besieging the city of Jerusalem under Sennacherib, who were defeated by a plague sent by the Lord (2 Kgs 19:35–37). Or perhaps it refers to an even later period in history: the end of the Babylonian Empire at the hands of Cyrus and Darius, who "caused the springs to fail and fountains to run dry" (Hos 13:15), when they conquered the city of Babylon by diverting the course of the Euphrates.[38] In both cases, Andrew historicizes these passages; they are prophecies that already have been fulfilled before the coming of Christ, rather than future events. But, noting that Jews did read these as prophecies about the future, he did not seem uncomfortable with the suggestion that identified the coming Jewish Messiah with the Christian Antichrist.

Thus it was not so much the rejection of Jewish theology that set Andrew apart from his contemporaries; that was to be expected. The important difference is that, although some of the Jewish exegetical traditions he cited were derived from Jerome or the *Glossa ordinaria*, he knew others from firsthand experience. This use of firsthand sources sets Andrew apart from his medieval predecessors. For the modern scholar they provide an interesting insight into the beliefs of twelfth-century Jewish exegetes and their reception by Christian scholars. Andrew's rendering of the eschatological readings of Joel and Hosea, cited above, clearly show how Andrew's interpretations were not dependent on Jerome or the *Glossa*, but were derived from Jewish interlocutors who explained these ideas to him. Sometimes it is hard to ascertain the exact source for these exegetical traditions because we do not find them written down or printed in any Jewish sources that survive. For example, twice in his commentaries, Andrew states that the Jews believe that the coming Messiah would not be a descendant of David but the resurrected David himself.[39] No surviving Jewish exegetical source corroborates this tradition, and it is not certain whether Andrew here misheard or misinterpreted his source, or whether this is evidence for a Jewish tradition that is not otherwise recorded. In any case, not everything that was Jewish had undisputed authority to Andrew. He expresses clear skepticism about some of the traditions he encountered. In his Ezechiel commentary, for instance, Andrew responds to the Jewish tradition that at the end of times, after the resurrection of the dead, the Temple would be rebuilt. The notion seems absurd to him. Citing a popular saying of the day, found in Horace, Andrew exclaims, "May God prevent the pious minds of the saints from believing this! Let the Jew Apella believe this."[40]

Andrew's treatment of the prophetic texts is decidedly ambivalent. He combines appreciation for their exegetical tradition with skepticism towards their theology. The anti-Jewish tendencies of his Carolingian sources has been well established by scholars, and it does not seem surprising that Haimo would identify the Jewish Antichrist with the Messiah. The anti-Judaism of the *Glossa ordinaria* has also been well established.[41] But Andrew, by contrast, has been portrayed as much more open to Jewish exegesis, to the point of favoring Jewish interpretations of the Old Testament over more overtly Christian ones. To be sure, he often presents Jewish exegesis as a viable alternative to the common Christian Christological explanations of prophecies in the Old Testament. But his exploration of Jewish exegesis also brought him into contact with the "vengeful messianism" of common Jewish interpretations. Jews read these prophetic texts in an eschatological way, and the texts provided them with hope for the defeat of their current oppressors, and the hope of a reversal of the roles between Christians and Jews. This message was clearly disturbing for contemporary Christians. This Jewish Messiah, who would overturn the Roman Empire (identified by contemporaries with the Holy Roman Empire or Christendom in a more general sense) and establish a kingdom in Jerusalem, looked to them more like the Antichrist. Although twelfth-century exegetes such as Hugh and Andrew of St. Victor were pioneering in their exploration of the Jewish exegetical tradition, we should be careful not to make them more modern than they really were. They were more aware of Judaism as a living religion than their Christian predecessors, but it did not make them necessarily more tolerant. Where they encountered theological notions that contradicted their own, they felt compelled to refute them, using exegetical and theological concepts handed to them by the Christian tradition. It is ironic, and perhaps sad, that the discovery of a common interest in a shared scripture and theology should result in polemic rather than dialogue and reconciliation.

NOTES

1. This contribution is picking up a theme discussed by Michael Signer in "Consolation and Confrontation." I dedicate this article to the memory of Michael, in deep appreciation for his path-breaking work. I also wish to thank my wife, Kate Elliot van Liere, for her critical reading and constructive comments. An earlier version of this paper was presented at the Medieval Literatures Seminar, at the Centre for Medieval Studies of York University. I wish to thank the Centre for granting me the opportunity to pursue my research there in the spring of 2009.

2. Zinn, "History and Interpretation"; Dahan, "Juifs et Chrétiens en occident médiéval"; Signer, "Polemic and Exegesis."

3. For a more detailed discussion of this topic, see, for instance, Cohen, *Living Letters of the Law.*

4. See Brandon, *The Fall of Jerusalem,* and Yuval, *Two Nations in Your Womb,* 38–49.

5. Yuval, *Two Nations in Your Womb,* 92–123.

6. Compare Andrew of St. Victor and the *Glossa ordinaria* on Micah 2:11–13: Andrew of St. Victor, *Expositio super Duodecim Prophetas,* p. 192, lines 308–13, vs. *Biblia latina cum Glossa ordinaria,* 3:406a.

7. Jerome, *Commentarii in Prophetas Minores.*

8. On the development of this legend, see Bousset, *The Antichrist Legend*; McGinn, *The Antichrist*.

9. Bernheim, *Mittelalterliche Zeitanschauungen*. Adso's treatise is edited in Adso Dervensis, *De ortu et tempore Antichristi*, 20–30. On its reception in biblical commentaries, see Hughes, *Constructing Antichrist*, 115–238.

10. McGinn, *The Antichrist*, 114–72.

11. *Ludus de Antichristo*, 2:36–45; *The Play of Antichrist*, 57–61.

12. Gow, *The Red Jews*, 94–95; compare Peter Comestor, *Historia Scholastica*, PL 198:1446A.

13. Hughes, *Constructing Antichrist*, 144–67. For Haimo's position on the Jews, see Heil, *Kompilation oder Konstruktion?* and Savigni, "Il commentario a Isaia di Aimone d'Auxerre e le sue fonte." More recent studies on Haimo have appeared in Shimahara, ed., *Études d'exégèse carolingienne: Études autour d'Haymon d'Auxerre*. Unfortunately, Haimo's commentary on the minor prophets is not the subject of any of the studies mentioned here.

14. Jerome, *Commentarii in Prophetas Minores*, p. 369, lines 607–8.

15. Haimo of Auxerre, *Enarratio*, PL 117:126CD.

16. Ibid.

17. Jerome, *Commentarii in Prophetas Minores*, p. 700, lines 253–61; Haimo, *Enarratio*, PL 117:207D.

18. Jerome, *Commentarii in Prophetas Minores*, p. 822, lines 615–17; Haimo, *Enarratio*, PL 117:247C.

19. Smith, *The Glossa ordinaria*.

20. Smalley, "Gilbertus Universalis."

21. *Glossa ordinaria* in Ob 1:18.2 *marginalis*: *Biblia latina cum glossa ordinaria*, 3:396b.

22. Jerome, *Commentarii in Prophetas Minores*, p. 32, lines 556–57.

23. *Glossa ordinaria* in Hos 2:21 *marginalis*: *Biblia latina cum glossa ordinaria*, 3:357b. Haimo, *Enarratio*, PL 117:26CD.

24. See also, for instance, Rupert of Deutz, *Commentariorum in Duodecim Prophetas*, PL 168:158D, and Peter Comestor, *Historia Scholastica*.

25. Smalley, "Andrew of St. Victor," and *The Study of the Bible*; Berndt, *André de Saint-Victor*.

26. Van Liere, "Andrew of St. Victor, Jerome, and the Jews."

27. Andrew of St. Victor, *Expositio in Ezechielem*, pp. xxi–xxvii.

28. Van Zwieten, "Jewish Exegesis"; Van Liere, "Andrew of Saint Victor and His Franciscan Critics."

29. Jerome, *Commentarii in Prophetas Minores*, pp. 649–52, lines 1174–1247.

30. Rashi, *The Complete Jewish Bible with Rashi Commentary*.

31. Andrew of St. Victor, *Expositio super Duodecim Prophetas*, pp. 251–54, lines 733–834; Herodotus, *Historiae*, 1.191.

32. Andrew of St. Victor, *Expositio super Duodecim Prophetas*, p. 192, lines 308–13.

33. *The Targum of the Minor Prophets*, 102.

34. Andrew of St. Victor, *Expositio super Duodecim Prophetas*, pp. 98–99, lines 373–96; Jerome, *Commentarii in Prophetas Minores*, p. 237, lines 277–79. Compare Andrew of St. Victor, *Expositio super Duodecim Prophetas*, p. 119, lines 251–52: "ubi de laude Dei agitur non est curandus ordo historie."

35. Andrew of St. Victor, *Expositio super Duodecim Prophetas*, pp. 99–100, lines 397–413; Tanhuma Bar Abba, *Midrash Tanhuma*, 10.4.

36. Andrew of St. Victor, *Expositio super Duodecim Prophetas*, pp. 78–83, lines 2196–2339. The four alternative interpretations are introduced, respectively, with "potest et sic intelligi quod dicitur," "vel sic," and "potest et hoc legi de liberatione populi que facta est Babilone subuersa."

37. Ibid., p. 81, lines 2275–76. See also Jerome's commentary on Isaiah, PL 24:314A: "Antichristus, ut dicitur helimenus [or: helimmenus] suus." We find the term also in Andrew's Ezechiel commentary: Andrew of St. Victor, *Expositio in Ezechielem*, p. 140, line 112.

38. Andrew of St. Victor, *Expositio super Duodecim Prophetas*, pp. 82–83, lines 2334–36. Again, this interpretation seems to be based on the historical account of Herodotus, *Historiae*, 1.191.

39. Andrew of St. Victor, *Expositio in Ezechielem*, p. 152, lines 113–15 and p. 140, lines 113–14; Andrew of St. Victor, *Expositio super Duodecim Prophetas*, p. 192, lines 312–13.

40. "Auertet deus hec credere a sanctorum mente pia. Credat hoc iudeus Apella"; Andrew of St. Victor, *Expositio in Ezechielem*, p. 178, lines 114–15. Citing Horace, *Satyrae* 1.5.97.

41. Signer, "The Glossa Ordinaria."

RAYMOND CLEMENS

16 Medieval Women Visionaries in the Renaissance

Jacques Lefèvre d'Étaples' *Liber trium virorum et trium spiritualium virginum* (1513)

In 1513, the humanist Jacques Lefèvre d'Étaples published the first printed edition of Hildegard of Bingen's *Scivias* in a work entitled *Liber trium virorum et trium spiritualium virginum* at the press of Henri Estienne in Paris. Lefèvre's edition, reprinted by J.-P. Migne in 1855 in his *Patrologia latina* (vol. 197, cols 383–738), became the basis of modern scholarship on Hildegard's *Scivias* until Führkötter and Carlevaris' critical edition appeared in 1978.[1] Lefèvre published Hildegard's *Scivias* in a collection with the writings of five other visionaries, three men and two women. These texts, in the order they appear in the *Liber*, are: The *Shepherd of Hermas*, a second-century narrative Lefèvre believed to have been authored by a disciple of Paul; the *Visio Wettini*, written by Heito, abbot of Reichenau, sometime before 806, but which Lefèvre falsely attributed to Uguentino; two visionary books by the Dominican Robert of Uzès (d. 1296); Hildegard's *Scivias*; several books and letters of Elisabeth of Schönau, Hildegard's younger contemporary; and the *Liber specialis gratiae* of Mechthild of Hackeborn, one of the nuns of Helfta. A remarkable compendium of the medieval visionary corpus, Lefèvre's *Liber* was the first printed edition of all of these texts except for Mechthild's; most continued to be the only edition available in print until the late nineteenth century.[2] To understand why the humanists (especially Lefèvre) were interested in the visionary corpus and why Lefèvre made these texts available for others, we must examine his principal desire to reform the church and to put into circulation divinely inspired texts that illustrated spiritual regeneration. He also sought to provide fonts for spiritual knowledge to compete with the scholastic tomes produced by university trained theologians. Part of the appeal of these texts was, ironically for a humanist, their simple, at times corrupt Latin prose: their "rusticity" combined with the claim that the author had no (or little) formal education or knowledge of Latin made each of the visionaries a better vehicle through which the divine Word could speak. The topos of an unlettered woman dictating Latin or vernacular texts to a male cleric has been the subject of much scholarship that seeks to understand the relationship between the two figures (holy woman and educated man) and how the symbiotic relationship benefited both.[3] Despite his belief that Latin rusticity authenticated the visionaries and their message, Lefèvre can be seen silently emending the visionaries' Latin, fixing grammatical mistakes, Latinizing vernacular expressions, and clarifying meaning. Rusticity functioned only to validate the divine origin of the vision by demonstrating that God could make literate those illiterate in Latin. The actual Latin text, however, was not literally true in the way that the Bible was literally true, and so Lefèvre sought to make the vision's meaning clearer and the reading more profitable and pleasurable by correcting the visionary text. In this respect, Lefèvre acted in much the same way that the male amanuenses of many female visionaries did, preserving the meaning of their visions by making their language more acceptable and making the visions available for a wider audience by copying them.

 Little is known about the life of Lefèvre d'Étaples before he arrived at the University of Paris and began publishing. According to his own recollection, he was born around 1460. As a young man, he lived in the Collège du Cardinal Lemoine where he taught philosophy and the liberal arts until 1508, when he retired from active teaching to devote his attention to editing and translating. From 1509 to 1520, he lived and worked at the abbey of Saint-Germain-des-Prés supported by his patron, Guillaume Briçonnet, bishop of Lodèvre and later bishop of Meaux. His early publications were devoted to producing the most accurate Aristotelian translations and commentaries possible. Like his contemporary reformers, Lefèvre detested late medieval nominalism and sought to free texts from what he saw as scholastic sophistry.[4] He refined his method on Aristotelian texts and later applied those same editorial principles to patristic writings and the Bible. In 1521, Lefèvre went to Meaux at the request of his patron Briçonnet, now bishop of Meaux, to begin a program of reform.[5] He may also have left Paris because of a tremendous controversy over his *De Maria Magdalena et triduo Christi disceptatio* (1517), which argued that the woman known to the Middle Ages as Mary Magdalen was, in fact, three distinct women in the New Testament. This controversy, often called the *Querelle de la Madeleine*, continued to rage until Lefèvre's death and provoked hostile, almost violent reactions against Lefèvre and his work.[6] It is during his time at Meaux that Lefèvre produced a new French translation of the New Testament (1523) and Psalms (1525). In 1525, he fled to Strasbourg when he was called to the Parliament of Paris to answer questions about his writings and teaching. He was recalled by Francis I in 1526, and spent the remainder of his life under royal patronage and protection, first as librarian of the royal collection, then as tutor to the king's children. In 1530, he completed his French translation of the Bible (based on Jerome's Latin Bible). He died in 1536 or 1537. There is a clear break in the direction Lefèvre's work takes when he leaves Paris and arrives at Meaux. In Paris his publications were for an academic audience (Henri Estienne was the printer for the Sorbonne); in Meaux his publications were largely directed at the laity.

The reform program Lefèvre initiated before his time at Meaux centered on the humanist project of discovering lost texts and recovering and reforming texts that were forgotten or had become corrupt, either through bad copying, poor translation, or erroneous interpretation.[7] Lefèvre seems to have seen his primary role as a Christian humanist as establishing reliable, accurate copies of Aristotle, providing an accurate Latin version of the Bible, and discovering and recovering lost or under-utilized texts that described spiritual aspects of the Christian life.[8] Among the most important of this last group (many printed for the first time by Lefèvre) are the *Corpus Dionysiacum* (1499), several works of Raymond Lull (1499, 1505),[9] John of Damascus' *De orthodoxa fide* (1507),[10] Richard of St. Victor's *De Trinitate* (1510),[11] Berno's *De officio missae* (1510), and Ruysbroeck's *De ornatu spiritualium nuptiarum* (1512).[12] These works were part of a systematic program of instruction that led the reader from the profane knowledge of this world to the secret spiritual knowledge of God obtained through contemplation and purification. In 1506, Lefèvre proposed a curriculum for reading spiritual and mystical texts in his commentary on Leonardo Bruni's translations of Aristotle's *Politics* and *Economics*. According to Lefèvre, the study of Aristotle's natural philosophy prepared the reader for Aristotle's metaphysics and led to the reading of Holy Scripture and the church fathers, and eventually to more recent mystics such as Nicholas of Cusa: "Once these studies have purified the mind and disciplined the senses (and provided one has extirpated vice and leads a suitable and upright life), then the generous mind may aspire to scale gradually the heights of contemplation, instructed by Nicholas of Cusa and the divine Dionysius and others like them."[13]

In the summer of 1510, Lefèvre traveled to Germany in search of manuscripts for his edition of the works of Nicholas of Cusa, whose *Opera omnia* he published in 1514, one year after the *Liber trium virorum*.[14] The details of his trip are fragmentary; what we know comes from his letters and prefatory epistles to the works he discovered or was persuaded to publish while traveling. He spent some time with the Brethren of the Common Life in Cologne, where he was inspired to print the works of Ruysbroeck. At the Benedictine house in Rupertsberg, he was shown a manuscript containing Hildegard's *Scivias*. In July, at Mainz, he discovered the treatise on the office of the mass by Berno, abbot of Reichenau (d. 1048), and had it transcribed by Andrew Westhausen and printed by Henri Estienne in 1510.[15] Lefèvre was shown the manuscript of the *Visio Wettini* in the Benedictine monastery of St. Vincent du Mans (Metz).[16] Renaudet speculated that Lefèvre also discovered Robert of Uzès' prophecies in Metz, because that is where Robert died in 1296, although no manuscript of Robert's work survives from the region.[17] Lefèvre may have discovered Elisabeth of Schönau's writing through the manuscript of the *Scivias* that contained several of Hildegard's letters to Elisabeth, or he may have known about her through contacts in Paris, where he found the manuscripts he used in his edition of her works. Unlike Hildegard's *Scivias*, which, according to Anne Clark, survives in only ten pre-1500 copies, 145 manuscripts transmit some part of Elisabeth's text.[18] I do not know how Lefèvre learned of Mechthild's *Liber*, although he seems to have used two Paris manuscripts in his edition. Clearly Lefèvre considered these texts valuable enough to justify editing and printing them, and he believed they would be popular enough to sell to an eager public. Beyond the importance of each individual author, however, was the way Lefèvre saw the six works relating to each other, carefully and consciously balancing male and female authors within a single volume. On the most fundamental level, each author claimed to be transmitting the word of God directly, to be providing a revelation. Beyond that, most were critical of the contemporary church, revealing its abuses and calling for radical reformation.

Henri Estienne (the elder, active 1502–20), Lefèvre's publisher, was the printer for the Sorbonne and one of the first of the scholar-printers in Paris who worked alongside the humanists at the university there to promote ecclesiastical reform. From this remarkable press came most of Lefèvre's mystical and biblical works, and Lefèvre identified himself with the press in several instances, using the term *nostra officina* (our press) to describe the Estienne publishing house.[19] Beatus Rhenanus, humanist and friend of both Erasmus and Lefèvre, worked for the press as a proofreader and aided Lefèvre in gathering materials for *Liber trium virorum*.[20] Lefèvre relied on the press both to assist in the editing of the texts and in correcting them after publication, if necessary, a very unusual working arrangement in a world in which presses often did not last longer than the printing of a few books. In Lefèvre's edition of the *De trinitate* of Richard of St. Victor, for example, he included an appendix of corrections he had made to Richard's text, "errors," he wrote, "that were discovered and corrected through the diligence of the press."[21] Because of his close working relationship with Henri Estienne it is likely that Lefèvre had a great deal of control over the choice of texts, their length, and their arrangement. In the case of the *Liber trium virorum*, he authored the prefatory epistle and the biographical introduction, and he may have played a role in the creation of the remarkable woodblock print used on the title page.

While at first glance the writings by Hildegard, Elisabeth, and Mechthild seem very different from one another, what links them and distinguishes them from other female visionaries is that all three were cloistered women in either Benedictine (Hildegard and Elisabeth) or Cistercian (Mechthild) houses, whose work found significant male, ecclesiastical protection and promotion.[22] These women were, in other words, safe to promote as models of female sanctity and examples of theological orthodoxy. Lefèvre saw several common themes in the texts he grouped together, particularly the issue of church reform, but he may have arranged the texts within the *Liber trium virorum* not only to highlight their theological message, but also to offset the criticism that he foresaw would be directed at him for printing the writings of women visionaries. Lefèvre's anxieties about the reception of his text are revealed in his prefatory epistle and introduction to the *Liber*. He was well aware of the church's suspicion of women visionaries, made explicit in Jean Gerson's writings against the canonization of Birgitta of Sweden at the Council of Constance in 1415, which castigated female visionaries and their clerical advisers.[23] Gerson's primary concern was that women visionaries could easily be led astray by their visions, which could be phantasms produced either from their own fertile imaginations or through excessive fasting or mental illness; or worse, the visions could be sent by the devil to deceive the recipient. Gerson was especially suspicious if the vision was received in a state of ecstasy. If not carefully monitored by male clerics, these women might introduce heretical doctrine and lead the faithful away from the church and her teachings.

Before publishing *Liber trium vivorum*, Lefèvre published in 1512 a work by the Flemish mystic John of Ruysbroeck (1293/4–1381), *De ornatu spiritualium nuptiarum*, that had been condemned by Jean Gerson.[24] Ruysbroeck provided an interesting case for Lefèvre because his visions were received in the vernacular and only later translated into Latin. Ruysbroeck had no formal education beyond that required to be a priest, which left him free to receive revelations directly from God without the constraints of formal training in philosophy or theology. Even friends and supporters were worried that some of his revelations might be open to misinterpretation. The fact that the visions were recorded in the vernacular made them available to people without formal training who did not live in enclosed communities. Lefèvre published Ruysbroeck in Latin and indicates that, as a spiritual work, it should be used in the cloister. He also believed that Gerson may have had a corrupt copy of *De ornatu* or a bad translation of the work, two concerns that Lefèvre hoped to address with his new version. We see here three of his principles for spiritual authors: that their works be destined for an appropriate audience (in this case cloistered); that they be available in the best translation; and that they be free from the corruptions that can occur in copying. We also see that Lefèvre was not concerned about the fact that Ruysbroeck received his visions while in a state of ecstasy, and that the simplicity of the language complemented the profundity of the ideas contained within the text.

By placing the visions of the men before those of the women, and by selecting the apostolic Hermas to open the volume, he sought to validate the visionary voice and provide a context for a positive reception of the three women who followed. Hildegard's *Scivias* served as the centerpiece for Lefèvre's book. It provided a transition from the male-authored texts to the female. Hildegard was first among the women chronologically, but more importantly, she was the only one of the women whose visions were not received in ecstasy, and she was the only one whose visions were approved by the papacy. Thus, she provided a transition from the more secure visionary tradition to the less. She also provided a transition from one type of visionary experience to another—from prophetic to contemplative.

Despite their primary position in the book, the men and their visions do not seem to have been a central concern of Lefèvre's. Evidence of Lefèvre's overriding interest in the narratives of the women visionaries appears in a letter to Beatus Rhenanus dated June 24, 1511. In it, Lefèvre mentioned the work he was doing on Hildegard and Elisabeth and requested biographical information on Mechthild, but he did not mention Hermas, Wettinus, or Robert, an omission that cannot be justified by the amount of information he had gathered on the lives of the men. Although Hermas has a sufficient biography (his comprises half the biographical introduction and a good portion of the prefatory epistle), Wettinus and Robert are given a scant few lines in Lefèvre's biographical introduction and are not even mentioned in his prefatory epistle. Despite the primary placement of the men's visions in the title and the codex, they make up the smallest portion of the codex in terms of volume. Hermas' vision is the longest of the male visions, roughly thirty-four pages; the *Visio Wettini*, six pages; and Robert's, eighteen.[25] Hildegard's

Scivias, on the other hand, spans 182 pages; Elisabeth's writings are contained in 64 pages, and Mechthild's, 82.[26]

Lefèvre's most significant contribution to the *Liber* in terms of his own writing is an explanation of the various states in which visions were received. He answered an anticipated attack by offering Jerome's apocryphal letter to Paula and Eustochium validating her non-ecstatic vision as well as Ps.-Jerome's defense of his own ecstatic vision in his commentary on the Benedictine Rule written for nuns.[27] His principal concern with Elisabeth and Mechthild (but not with Hildegard) was the ecstatic nature of their visions, which he feared threatened their authenticity. When discussing Elisabeth's visions in his biographical preface, Lefèvre offered a taxonomy of visionary experience that served to validate even ecstatic visions. "Ecstasy," he writes,

> is when the mind has become separated from the body so that it arrives at a place where it is able to discern the good spirits which come to good people, and the evil ones which come to the wicked and curious; the latter are below nature, the former beyond. There is, moreover, an ecstasy which is below nature that is born from infirmity, called *Lipothymia* by the doctors, which is a defect of the mind and heart. Of these three states of ecstasy, the first is better than health, the second is worse than sickness, the third is simply a human illness.[28]

Lefèvre's concern here is to authenticate Elisabeth's visions, disentangle the "good" visions that she received from the "bad" (she was deceived in her first prophetic vision) and distinguish the ecstatic illness that often accompanied her visions from any physical or mental illness.

The remarkable woodcuts that serve as the title page for his book also demonstrate Lefèvre's concern to validate his visionaries (see fig. 16.1). These images are not stock woodcuts pressed into service for this volume; rather, they were cut specifically for the book and demonstrate a very close reading of the text contained therein. The visionaries are divided by gender into parallel columns that can be read chronologically from top to bottom. Hermas is presented receiving his vision from the angel. Wettinus is shown on his deathbed in his cell with eyes barely open, a spirit before him bearing an effigy of a priest. His is the only portrait to conform to the

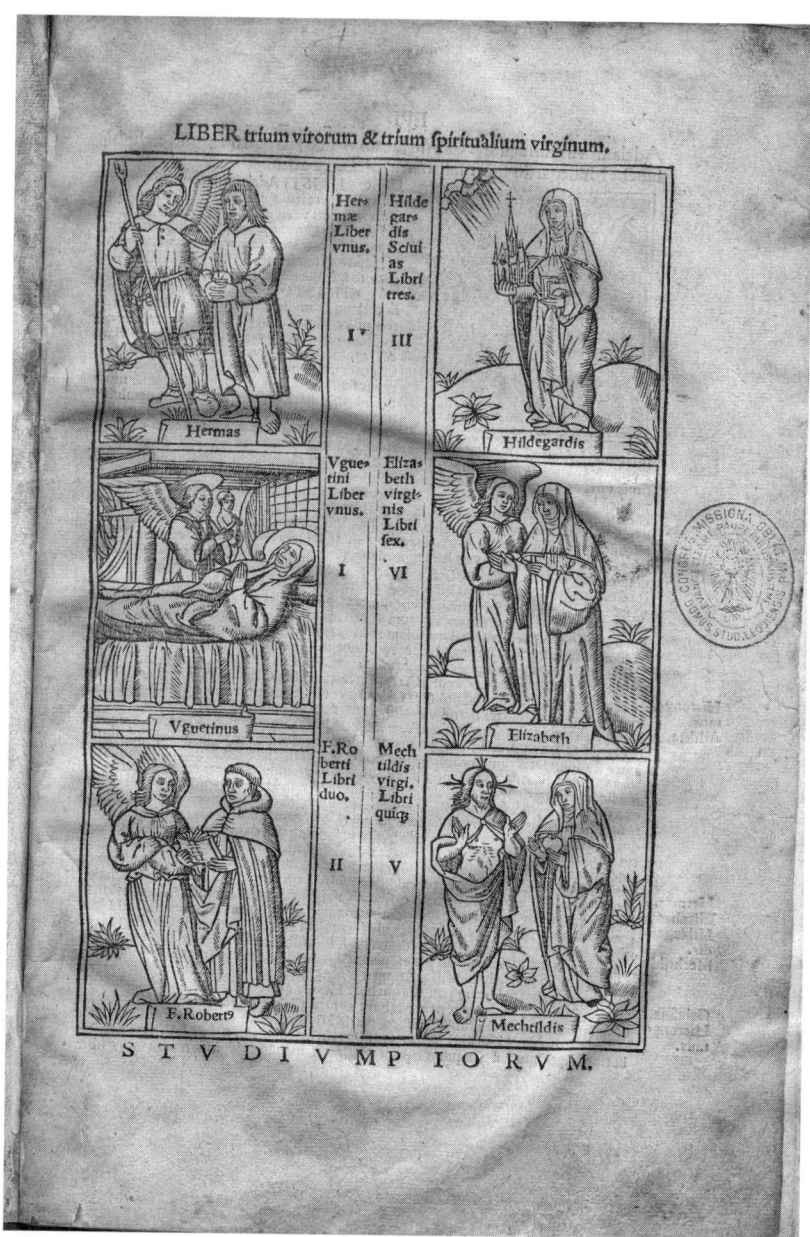

Figure 16.1. Title page from Jacques Lefèvre d'Étaples, *Liber trium virorum & trium spiritualium virginum.* Paris: Henri Estienne, 1513. Image courtesy of the Rare Book and Manuscript Library, University of Illinois at Urbana-Champaign.

traditional depiction of a visionary, lying on his back with the vision appearing before him. Robert is shown with an angel, in his hands the book he was ordered to write. Hildegard is the only one not shown receiving a vision through a human intermediary; instead, she is shown receiving her vision from the heavenly voice, "which she did not see with the eyes of the body, but only understood in her mind through the light of the spirit."[29] In her right hand, she carries her book (the *Scivias*, the only title on the page) and in her left, her monastic foundation (the Rupertsberg).[30] Elisabeth stands in front of her angel; she does not carry a book, perhaps a reference to her oral recitation of her visions to her brother Eckbert. Finally, Mechthild is shown with a vision of Jesus before her; she bears her devotion to his sacred heart in her hands and he reveals his wounds to her. She, too, is shown without her book, signaling the oral nature of her visions that were transcribed by her sisters. Neither of the women is shown in a state of ecstasy; each stands with eyes open looking directly at her apparition in a posture almost identical to that of Hermas. One would be hard-pressed to find another sixteenth-century image that puts women on a more equal footing with men or that argues so strongly for the orthodoxy of the visionaries.

Although Lefèvre had read Hildegard's *vita* and possessed some information about Elisabeth's life through her brother Eckbert's *De Obitu* (his account of Elisabeth's death), he knew little about Mechthild beyond the autobiographical material contained in her visions. His interest in her life indicates a concern for the context in which the visions were produced rather than a narrow interest in the text divorced from the individual who produced it. In a letter to Beatus Rhenanus, which among other things reveals much about the informal research networks on which humanists depended in their work, he wrote:

> I have the works of the virgin Elisabeth and the virgin Mechthild. Although it is certain she was a virgin, I have not been able to discover, despite diligent research, in what monastery or order she lived. And therefore ask (I pray you) in the monasteries of the sisters of St. Benedict and St. Bernard, which are near you, if perchance they know which Mechthild she was and where of the many, and make me more certain.[31]

It is important to note the emphasis Lefèvre placed on virginity, although in this context he almost certainly intended to indicate their status as nuns.

This was, no doubt, a further proof of the visions' authenticity, and Lefèvre repeats this designation in the title of the work, *A Book of Three Men and Three Spiritual Virgins*. He also repeats the designation at the beginning of Hildegard's *Scivias*. Sexually active or lay visionaries seem to have been beyond even Lefèvre's ability to rehabilitate.

As the woodcut demonstrates, the visionaries received their message in distinctly different ways, which had ramifications for the perceived authenticity of their prophecy in sixteenth-century France. Hermas received his vision in his dreams. He was shown a vision, which was then interpreted for him by an angel, initially an old woman symbolizing the church who then appeared younger in each vision as the narrative progressed. The woman was replaced by the angel of repentance in the guise of a shepherd who dictated the majority of the text. Hermas was ordered to write down the visions and their interpretation and compile them into a book to be disseminated. No mention was made of the language of the prophecy, and no suspicion was voiced concerning Hermas' ability to transcribe the divine vision without adulterating or distorting it. Dream visions were common in the ancient world, but were fiercely criticized by Jerome and Augustine. By the time Abbot Heito wrote the *Visio Wettini* (before 806), dream visions were no longer trusted because of the ease with which, it was believed, the devil could manipulate dreams. In the *Visio*, the author carefully notes that although on his deathbed, Wettinus was not asleep, but only had his eyes closed when he received his vision (*oculis tantummodo clausis et necdum in somnum*).[32] The apparition spoke in Latin, and his words were taken down exactly by Heito, who neither added nor deleted anything.[33]

Robert of Uzès, on the other hand, had multiple visionary modes, as he related in his preface:

> It pleases the Lord Jesus Christ to reveal in his mercy to me, the most vile of all sinners, at one time in dreams through imaginative visions, at another time in wakefulness these same visions, at still other times in exterior words or interior through many metaphors with their declarations.[34]

But in the woodcut, Robert is clearly shown receiving his vision fully conscious. He appears to have been reading his book to the angel, who stands with arms folded.

Lefèvre had several descriptions of the manner in which Hildegard received her visions. According to the preface to the *Scivias*, he knew that Hildegard received her visions while awake and fully conscious and never received them in ecstasy:

> But the visions I saw I did not perceive in dreams, or sleep, or delirium, or by the eyes of the body, or by the ears of the outer self, or in hidden places; but I received them while awake and seeing with a pure mind and the eyes and ears of the inner self, in open places, as God willed it.[35]

The visionary voice apparently spoke in Latin and commanded her to write (as the angel had commanded Hermas), although Hildegard states that she had little knowledge of composition. In fact, the voice chose Hildegard because she was "timid in speaking and simple in expounding and unlearned in writing."[36] For this reason, the voice commanded, she was to speak and write not according to the skills of human oratory, knowledge, and will, but, rather, according to the voice she received from heaven.[37]

Unlike her contemporary Hildegard, Elisabeth did receive her visions in a state of ecstasy, although the actual pronouncement of the vision occurred after the state of ecstasy had passed. Her brother Eckbert wrote in the short preface to her visions that the visions

> happened not without evident miracle, for frequently and as if by habit on Sundays and other feast days around the hours in which the devotion of the faithful was especially fervent, she was rapt in contemplation (*mentis excessum*) and after gradually being taken up by the spirit, suddenly she would pour forth divine words in Latin, which she had not learned from another, nor was she able to devise them on her own as she was uneducated, having meager learning [in general] and none in Latin pronunciation.[38]

Eckbert claims to be literally recording the words of God in Latin, with Elisabeth in a state of ecstasy acting as a human cipher. Like Hildegard, her ostensible ignorance of Latin composition validated her pronouncements, as Barbara Newman has demonstrated.[39] Elsewhere, however, Eckbert reveals a more complex process through which Elisabeth's visions were received and composed. In a preface to the visions, not found in Lefèvre's edition although very likely in his source, Eckbert writes:

> All who are about to read the words of this book should know without a doubt that some of the speeches that the angel of God is said to have made to Elisabeth, the handmaid of God, were uttered totally in Latin, some in German, and yet others he announced partly in Latin and partly in German. . . . Where the words of the angel were in Latin, I left them unchanged. Where they were in German, I translated them into Latin as clearly as I could, adding nothing from my own presumption, seeking nothing of human favor nor worldly advantage.[40]

This understanding of Eckbert's role—not simply as scribe but also as translator—opens the door to the possibility that the Latin text was not fully inerrant and that an editor such as Lefèvre could have some license to repair the text. Unfortunately we are not able to determine what changes Lefèvre made to Elisabeth's visions because we are not sure what manuscript Lefèvre used in his edition.

Despite the real differences that separate the visionaries in terms of gender, epoch, and visionary mode, what unites them, and what Lefèvre may have found most appealing about them, is their message. All six proclaimed the corruption of the church and its need for reform, always in prophetic, often apocalyptic, terms. Hermas' criticism of the church was for the corruption of its individual members who, if they did not reform, would not be part of the celestial tower of the church. He warned that after the tower was finished, the end of the world would be at hand. Abbot Heito was less concerned with the church at large and more concerned with the reform of monks and priests. The primary corruption he saw was sexual, particularly homosexual, and he presented dire consequences in the afterlife for those who indulged in sexual pleasures in this life. Although Robert's concerns were as broad and multifaceted as his modes of perceiving them, his primary anxiety seems to have been with the events surrounding the papacy initiated by the long vacancy of the see of St. Peter after the death of Nicholas IV in 1292, the abdication of the saintly hermit-pope Celestine V in 1294, and the ascension of the decidedly unsaintly Boniface VIII in 1295. Although a Dominican, Robert was strongly influenced by Joachite writing and was an early representative of the utilization and application of the Leonine prophecies to the thirteenth-century papacy. Hildegard also preached reform of the church, in her case Gregorian reform, and sought resolution of the conflicts between pope and emperor with a vivid depiction of the Antichrist and his attack on the church. Because, as Barbara Newman notes in her introduction to Hart's translation of the *Scivias*, Hildegard was vague in applying names and dates to her prophecies, they were open to use by later generations who saw in her visions the divine foretelling of contemporary events. Elisabeth, too, was critical of the church, but like Heito, emphasized individual sin and its ramifications (for example, both had visions of individuals in hell tormented for specific crimes).[41] Mechthild was less critical of the church, and her visions may have been attractive to Lefèvre because of their emphasis on the inner life, the soul's personal relationship with God, and devotion to the Virgin Mary.

Most of the visionaries in Lefèvre's volume employ the analogy of the church as a building built by the faithful but often under attack and in need of fortification. This was the religious reform in head and members that Lefèvre and other Christian humanists desired and sought to bring about through the printing of religious materials: most importantly the Bible (which Lefèvre translated into French), but also other mystical works (such as Ruysbroeck and Raymond Lull), manuals for the clergy, and even grammars and dictionaries to aid basic religious literacy.

In Hermas, Hildegard, and Elisabeth, the edifice was the church in the celestial Jerusalem. Hermas repeated the image in two places in his work, vision 3 and similitude 11. In both, the stones represent the various souls that make up the church; some fit together well without mortar, symbolizing the close relationship among the ministers of the church, apostles, bishops, deacons, and teachers who agree with one another in peace; in others stones have to be hammered and chiseled until they can be useful; these are those souls who have faith, but also possess riches. The riches must be cut away before the stone can be used. Some stones can never be used in the tower and thus must be discarded. Hildegard, as Barbara Newman has shown, was deeply influenced by Hermas, and most of her third book is based on a metaphoric building program in which she described a spiritual edifice of salvation, which became Jacob's ladder conveying souls back and forth to heaven.[42] Elisabeth, influenced by Hildegard, had a similar vision of souls along a mountain path, as Anne Clark has shown.[43] Wettinus and Robert also had metaphoric buildings, but their buildings and their meaning were somewhat different. In the *Visio Wettini*, the stone tower serves to purify monks:

> There was revealed to him there [Hell] an edifice in the manner of a castle, made of wood and stones that were joined unevenly (*inordinante*) and effaced by soot with smoke rising from the top of it. When he asked about it, the angel responded that it was the dwelling place of monks of diverse places and regions gathered into one place for their purification.[44]

If Hermas influenced Heito, it could be seen in the stones that had been joined unevenly, symbolizing the corruption of the monastic edifice and the blackened stones that represent sinners.

Robert of Uzès, who as Kathryn Kerby-Fulton has noted was strongly influenced by both Hermas and Hildegard, presented a building of the church covered in darkness, a sign of the church during the time of Antichrist.[45] He wrote:

> During the week of Easter, after I said Compline, I was seeing in the spirit of God and behold, there was a church before me made from white stones, above which stood a tall column in which there seemed to be apples the color of saffron. It was built on a stone mountain, having a tall and wide door on the west, which was cloudy and black, as were the windows. And the darkness flowed out from the church through the door just as a river, up to the north, and the waters mixed with the mist and flowed over the church, so that those within had to wait, but they were not able to ascend, although part of the column could be seen.[46]

Robert's vision of a church under assault and covered (although not entirely) by the darkness of Antichrist was more pessimistic about the state of the church than Hermas' vision of a solid, well-built church that excluded the unfit stones. Robert located the source of evil in the north, as Hildegard did in her third book of the *Scivias*. While Lefèvre does not seem to have an apocalyptic agenda, he was clearly drawn to authors who did, likely because of their strong feelings about corruption, both in the papacy and in the church more generally. These authors provided Lefèvre with a voice to articulate his own concerns about the church and its reform.

While the *Liber trium virorum* was the first printed work of each of these authors, it was to the abbess of Hildegard's foundation that Lefèvre dedicated his book; she has primacy of place among the female visionaries, and her text makes up the bulk of the printed codex. In shaping the *Scivias*, the cornerstone of his spiritual edifice, Lefèvre revealed his own understanding of Hildegard's prophetic voice and charted his own relationship to the visionary, the vision, and the text.

Lefèvre's edition of Hildegard's *Scivias* lies somewhere between a transcription and an edition as we understand them today.[47] Although he used only one manuscript for the *Scivias*,[48] he attempted to establish the best text by editing the manuscript according to humanist standards of textual criticism, correcting grammatical and factual errors but faithfully rendering the substance of the text. No page escaped his emendations. He used Wiesbaden, Hessische Landesbibliothek, Hs. 2, commonly called the Riesencodex, written between 1180 and 1190, which he rightly considered to be Hildegard's archetypal copy.[49] As mentioned earlier, he discovered the manuscript in the convent during his trip to Germany in the summer of 1510 and had it copied immediately, but publication was delayed because the unknown copyist omitted parts of the text.[50] In addition to Hildegard's *Scivias*, the Riesencodex contains the *Liber vitae meritorum*, *Liber divinorum operum*, letters, *Expositio evangeliorum*, *Lingua ignota* and *Litterae ignotae*, and the *Symphonia*, among others.[51] Lefèvre was aware of the existence of several of Hildegard's other books, either from a list that may have formed part of her *vita* (also in the Riesencodex) or through additional manuscripts he may have had access to while examining the *Scivias* in Rupertsberg.[52] Although we know which manuscript Lefèvre used and even where he copied it, we do not know how he first became acquainted with Hildegard's writings. He may have been informed of their existence by the Brethren of the Common Life while traveling in Germany. It is also possible that he knew of her reputation through chronicles; he claimed in his biographical preface that he knew of her works and life through Trithemius' *De scriptoribus ecclesiasticis*. Moreover, he may have known of her works through a miscellany of mystical or apocalyptic works; several contained Robert of Uzès' visions.[53] In 1220, Gebeno of Eberbach, a Cistercian monk, compiled Hildegard's apocalyptic visions into a collection that was copied until the Reformation and exists in more than one hundred manuscripts.[54] Several of the authors in *Liber trium virorum* wrote about the destruction of the church and the coming of Antichrist; perhaps Lefèvre possessed such a miscellany and sought out additional works by the authors of the fragments contained therein.

We know some of the reasons Lefèvre wanted to print Hildegard's *Scivias* once he had found it. In his 1511 letter to Beatus Rhenanus, he stated that he had a copy of the *Scivias* made *ad utilitatem posterorum* ("for the use of posterity").[55] In his prefatory epistle, he was more specific. He dedicated the book to Adelheid von Ottenstein, abbess of the convent of Rupertsberg near Bingen, the same community Hildegard founded with eighteen nuns from Disibodenberg between 1147 and 1150, and which she led until her death in 1179. Lefèvre repeated his intention to publish her works to make them known to future generations, but he also outlined a course of study for the nuns in Adelheid's care. Day and night, he exhorted them to read Holy Scripture, by day the New Testament and by night the Old. After this, they should pass on to the

> books of holy eloquence, hagiography, of such a sort are those now sent to you, for second study so that the desserts of the mind and (if I may say) the confections of spiritual exercise should not be displeasing, for they contain edification and lead one to God, the holy end of all desire.[56]

The message of spiritual instruction is also indicated on the title page in Roman block capitals: "STUDIUM PIORUM," which can be translated "the works of pious people" but in this context of a plan of study outlined by Lefèvre might be better translated "the school for pious people."

Lefèvre was a conscientious editor, who took pains to reproduce Hildegard's *Scivias* in its entirety, even when that meant considerably delaying the completion of the project. When he discovered the sections missing from his copy, he refused to allow the work to be printed until his associate, Kilian Westhausen of Mainz, restored the original text.[57] In comparing Lefèvre's edition with his exemplar, there are very few instances in which he misread Hildegard's text, and what misreadings exist can be attributed to any of the three men who worked on it: Lefèvre himself, the anonymous copyist who first transcribed the book for Lefèvre, or Kilian Westhausen. Lefèvre did not paraphrase or omit any sections, although he did insert a paragraph from Hildegard's *Explanatio symboli s. Athanasii* at the end of part 3, vision 5. He also significantly reworked the first and second visions in part 2. (Perhaps these were the missing sections supplied by Kilian.) We can say with some certainty, then, that what changes Lefèvre made to Hildegard's text he did with a certain intent, that is, to clothe her revelations in a more attractive Latin. His changes are numerous and systematic, but rarely do they affect the meaning of the text (or at least the meaning the text had for Lefèvre). Typically, his alterations functioned to classicize Hildegard's Latin or clarify her meaning according to his understanding of her text. Anyone familiar with Hildegard's Latin composition will empathize with Lefèvre's frustration with her difficult style, described by Barbara Newman as "suffer[ing] from redundancies, awkward constructions, and baffling neologisms; and her ideas often stretched her limited vocabulary to the breaking point."[58] Most often, Lefèvre's changes occur on the level of word forms or word choice and are, from a modern perspective, relatively innocuous by the standards of sixteenth-century textual editing. He routinely corrected case and tense, substituted synonyms for repeated words, and reordered words within a sentence for clarity. At other times, he substituted Latin words that he believed more concisely reflected Hildegard's meaning, and in some cases substituted a more impressive word for a common one to embellish her prose.

There were times, however, when Lefèvre's emendations significantly affected the meaning of Hildegard's words, changing the sense of a passage in subtle yet profound ways. For example, in *Scivias* I.2.29, Hildegard, explaining why God made man such that he could sin, indicated that humans needed to be tested just as gold is tested in the fire. She continued: "Spirit ought to be tested by spirit, flesh through flesh, land through water, fire through cold, battle through refraining," which Lefèvre changed to "Spirit ought to be tested by spirit, flesh through flesh, earth through air, fire through water, battle through peace."[59] Lefèvre's alterations here, although substantial, do not change the ultimate meaning of the passage; they do, I think, change its texture. In other places, he substantially changed the meaning of the text by simply rearranging the position of the words: for example, in *Scivias* I.2.33, he corrected his source, which read, "humility is like the soul and charity like the body" to "humility is like the body and charity is like the soul."[60] Given the standard value of soul above body and charity above humility, Lefèvre's reworking was probably, for him, simply a correction. For someone more familiar with Hildegard's soteriology and use of symbols, the emphasis on the body and humility would have made more sense. Lefèvre was not consciously altering Hildegard's theology; he was, in his own mind, correcting and clarifying incorrect or unclear text.[61]

What gave Lefèvre license to alter Hildegard's text? In part, the illiteracy topos functioned as a dichotomy for Renaissance editors. Because Hildegard was not trained in Latin composition, yet dictated or transcribed the visionary voice in Latin, the experience and meaning of her vision were authentic. But, unlike the biblical texts that Lefèvre was also editing at this time, Hildegard's visions were not considered by him to be literally the word of God, at least not in the form in which we have them. Her language was not divinely inspired, but the fact of its use was; that is, the fact that she was able to dictate in Latin meant that her vision was authentic.[62] Surely, Lefèvre may have speculated, Hildegard's divine voice could have dictated perfect, humanist Latin had it wished to. In fact, in his prefatory epistle, Lefèvre voiced his distrust of the intermediaries (he calls them translators, *interpretes*) through whom Hildegard's divine voice was transformed into writing:

> Something great should be conjectured from Hildegard and Mechthild, but their interpreters have represented it less, and they have substituted something beneath the dignity of the spirit, and sometimes they even mixed in something of themselves; nonetheless they are all piety and edification and consolation for pious minds.[63]

Lefèvre found justification for his concern about the transmission of Hildegard's voice while researching her life. The *vita* of Hildegard that he found at Rupertsberg (contained in the same codex as the manuscript of the *Scivias* that he used)[64] was a collaborative project: begun by Gottfried, a monk of Disibodenberg who may have succeeded Volmar as Hildegard's scribe after his death, it was expanded by Guibert of Gembloux, who left the *vita* incomplete, and then reluctantly brought to its final form by Theoderic of Echtenach, whom Barbara Newman has characterized as a literary hack.[65] In other words, there were many different views of Hildegard to be found in the *vita*, some of which were in conflict with her own description of the visionary experience found in the opening paragraphs of the *Scivias* itself. We know that Lefèvre knew her *vita*, and that his understanding of the nature of Hildegard's visions was informed by that text and not, as Rice suggests, solely by her description of them in the *Scivias*. Lefèvre mentioned in his biographical introduction that he had read the *vita*, which was held by the virgins of Rupertsberg, and he made statements in the *Liber trium virorum* that contained information only found in the *vita*.[66] In the second book of the *vita*, Theoderic explained Hildegard's visionary gift and the role that her scribe played in the redaction of her visions:

> How great a thing it is and worthy of admiration that whatever she saw or heard in spirit, with the same sense and in the same words, and with a careful and pure mind, she wrote down in her own hand, or orally dictated their content to one faithful male collaborator, who then rendered their cases, tenses, and conjugations according to the exactness of the grammatical art which she did not know, while he presumed neither to add nor subtract anything to their sense or meaning. Concerning this matter she even wrote to Pope Adrian [actually Anastasius] that in a heavenly vision she heard the following said to her: "Whenever something is shown to you from on high in familiar human form, you shall not publish it *in the Latin language* [italics added] yourself, for this familiarity is not given to you. Rather, let him who has a file not neglect to finish it off in a form pleasing to the human ear."[67]

The *vita* presented two possible modes of reception and redaction: Hildegard saw in the spirit and wrote with her own hand and recited orally *without any change in meaning and in the very same words* as were sent to her. Her companion (*symmista*) did not translate her words, but arranged them as grammar dictates, without altering their meaning, presumably working both with her dictation and her written text as depicted in the illumination in the Lucca manuscript (composed for Hildegard's canonization well after her death).[68] But the divine voice quoted in her letter to Pope Anastasius IV (1153–54) suggests a very different model. Here, Hildegard is unable to publish (*proferro*) Latin, so her redactor must translate and formulate her utterances according to human reason.[69] Interestingly, Theoderic (the last of the *vita* authors) added the phrase "in the Latin language" to the letter to Pope Anastasius; it is not present in the original letter.[70] What Barbara Newman's study of the *vita* of Hildegard reveals is that each individual who sought to present Hildegard and her writings did so with distinct motives that reflect his own agenda rather than Hildegard's ideas about the nature of the divine voice that commanded her to write.

There is no reason to assume that Lefèvre was any different in his handling of Hildegard's *Scivias* than any of her earlier collaborators. He wished to make her visions more polished and attractive. Lefèvre places the blame for any textual corruption on Hildegard's amanuenses rather than on Hildegard herself, and this justifies his interventions in the text. The highly problematic *vita*, which may reflect the intentions of several authors, may indeed have provided Lefèvre with the model of a male editor of an "illiterate" female visionary, even if his motivation for correcting her Latin was different than that of contemporary collaborators. Lefèvre's edition stands as testament to Hildegard's ongoing difficulties with her male interpreters, who continued to correct her Latin, often augmenting its meaning well after her death.

Lefèvre's *Liber trium virorum* brought the writings of several visionaries to the attention of a new generation. In an age that rarely valued women as highly as men, Lefèvre's collection established a rare parity between male and female visionaries. And while he continued the tradition of praising the simplistic writing of uneducated women as evidence of its divine inspiration, it should be noted that Lefèvre extended that tradition to cover male writers such as Ruysbroeck and Raymond Lull. For both the male and the female visionaries, he sought to convey the spiritual value that their writings revealed, and he was willing to polish their Latin to make their works more attractive to an educated audience. He genuinely valued the spirituality he found in the women visionaries and hoped their writing would provide an alternative to scholastic sophistry.

NOTES

1. Hildegard of Bingen, *Scivias*, ed. Führkötter and Carlevaris. I would like to thank Barbara Newman for her comments on an early draft of this chapter.
2. The first edition of Mechthild of Hackeborn's *Liber specialis gratiae* was published by J. Thanners in Leipzig, 1510. Renaudet, *Préréforme*, 602, n. 2.
3. Barbara Newman argues persuasively that the "unlettered" female visionary was a creation of the many biographers of Hildegard of Bingen. See Newman, "Hildegard and Her Hagiographers." There is a large bibliography on women visionaries and their male amanuenses, including several additional articles in Mooney, ed., *Gendered Voices*. For an excellent overview, including chapters on Elisabeth of Schönau and Hildegard of Bingen, see Coakley, *Women, Men, and Spiritual Power*. Less work has been done on female amanuenses, usually present only in female

monastic institutions such as Helfta, where two nuns and Gertrude the Great redacted much of Mechthild of Hackeborn's visionary output without her knowledge or consent until late in the process. For women's role in producing Latin manuscripts more generally, see Beach, *Women as Scribes*.

4. Charles Nauert notes that some of these humanist conflicts with late-medieval scholasticism, especially regarding biblical interpretation, which might seem like pedantic turf battles, were in fact direct challenges to the authority of the church because they called into question who had the authority to interpret the Bible. With their knowledge of Greek and Hebrew, the humanists had a great advantage when exploring the literal meaning of the Bible. See Nauert, "The Clash of Humanists and Scholastics," esp. 13–17 for Lefèvre's role.

5. There is still some debate over Lefèvre's relationship with the evangelical reform movement initiated in Germany and Switzerland in the early 1520s while he was at Meaux. See Heller, "The Evangelicism of Lefèvre d'Étaples," and Cameron, "The Charges of Lutheranism." One of the difficulties in analyzing the church's reaction against Lefèvre is distinguishing between hostility to his Magdalen writings and larger reform issues such as translating the Bible into French. He may have had great support among humanists for his biblical program had he not taken what surely seemed to him the next logical step in using a close and critical reading of the Bible to establish certain historical facts and rid the church of later, factually incorrect interpretations, even those made by such revered figures as Gregory the Great. The most important thing to note about Lefèvre's time at Meaux is, as Cameron notes, that he turned away from his earlier work that benefited academics and professional religious to focus on projects such as the translation of the Bible into French, which benefited the common people. See Cameron, "The Charges of Lutheranism," 121–23.

6. Lefèvre published several books following his original publication, refuting his critics and refining his argument. An edition of these texts with helpful introduction to the debate is Porrer, *Jacques Lefèvre d'Etaples*. It probably did not help Lefèvre's popularity with his critics when, in response to his first book, he denied that Mary Salome and Mary Jacobi were the Virgin Mary's half-sisters by men St. Anne married after she gave birth to the Virgin Mary. This occasioned great debate over the historical identity of "Three Marys" also known as the Holy Kinship.

7. Rice, "The Humanist Idea," 128–29.

8. His work on the Latin Bible, while immensely influential for the Reformation, was not without controversy. See Cameron, "The Attack on the Biblical Work."

9. On the production and reception of Lull's work and Lefèvre's role in both, see Victor, "The Revival of Lullism at Paris."

10. See Backus, "John of Damascus, *De fide orthodoxa*."

11. This was the first edition of Richard's *De trinitate*, which was accompanied by Lefèvre's commentary. Eugene Rice notes that Lefèvre used only one manuscript in his transcription, which has since been lost, but that Lefèvre "occasionally correct[ed] readings that seemed to him defective"; Rice, ed., *The Prefatory Epistles*,

224. Lefèvre included a list of his corrections at the end of the volume, in which he identified himself with the press: "Errata plerisque in locis Ricardi deprehensa et ex officina sedulo recognita"; ibid.

12. This was the Latin translation by Willem Jordaens (c. 1360) of Ruysbroeck's *Die gheestelike Brulocht*; see Rice, ed., *The Prefatory Epistles*, 276.

13. Rice, "Jacques Lefèvre d'Étaples and the Medieval Christian Mystics," 91.

14. Tyler, "Jacques Lefèvre d'Étaples," 25.

15. Rice, ed., *The Prefatory Epistles*, 234.

16. Jacques Lefèvre d'Étaples, *Liber trium virorum*, fol. 17r. See Renaudet, *Préréforme*, 635, n. 9.

17. Renaudet, *Préréforme*, 602, n. 3. Bignami-Odier used two manuscripts in her edition (Toledo, Library of the Cathedral, cod. 6–26, fols. 15r–25r, and Paris, BnF, lat. 2592, fols 53r–72r), neither of which was the manuscript that Lefèvre used, although Bignami-Odier conjectures that his manuscript was close to the Parisian manuscript. For her edition, see Bignami-Odier, "Les Visions de Robert d'Uzès." Kaeppeli indicates two additional manuscripts unknown to Bognami-Odier, one missing (Louvain, Bibl. can. reg. S. Martini) and one containing only a fragment, written after Lefèvre's edition (Vienna, ÖNB, 11413 [a. 1518], fols. 139r–140v): Kaeppeli, *Scriptores*, 3:327–28.

18. A. Clark, *Elisabeth of Schönau*, 49.

19. According to Tyler, Lefèvre printed sixty books with Henri Estienne. Henri Estienne only published just under 130 titles, so Lefèvre was responsible for almost half the printer's works. Tyler, "Jacques Lefèvre d'Étaples," 28.

20. For his involvement in printing humanist texts, see D'Amico, *Theory and Practice*.

21. "Errata plerisque in locis Ricardi deprehensa et ex officina sedulo recognita"; Rice, ed., *The Prefatory Epistles*, 224. It was extremely unusual for early printers to issue errata; Henri Estienne is considered to be among the first.

22. Helfta adopted the Cistercian constitution at its foundation in 1229, but it was an independent foundation, unaffiliated with the Cistercian order and strongly influenced by the Dominicans, who likely exercised *cura monialium* over the nuns at Helfta. Finnegan, *The Women of Helfta*, 6.

23. For the issue of testing women's visions, see Elliott, *Proving Woman*. For work on Gerson particularly, see Elliott, "Seeing Double."

24. For Lefèvre's defense of Ruysbroek see Rice, "Jacques Lefèvre d'Étaples and the Medieval Christian Mystics," 94–95. For Gerson and his impact, see Hobbins, *Authorship and Publicity*. The classic work on Gerson's condemnation of Ruysbroeck is Combes, *Essai sur la critique de Ruysbroeck*.

25. *The Shepherd of Hermas*: fols 1r–17r; Uguetinus' *Visio Wettini*: fols 17r–19r (densely presented); Robert of Uzès: fols 19r–27v (sparsely presented). The page length is slightly misleading: Uguentinus' visions have no initial letters or titles to break up the text and so are more densely presented. Robert has numerous rubrics

and large capitals beginning each vision, so his visions take up more printed space but are not significantly longer than Uguetinus'.

26. Hildegard: fols 28r–118v; Elisabeth: fols 119r–150v; Mechthild: fols 150v–190v.

27. Rice, "Jacques Lefèvre d'Étaples and the Medieval Christian Mystics," 92.

28. Rice, ed., *The Prefatory Epistles*, 317.

29. Jacques Lefèvre d'Étaples, *Liber trium virorum*, title page.

30. This is one of two images of the Rupertberg before its destruction in 1632 by the Swedes during the Thirty Years War. The other is an engraving by Daniel Meissner, executed before 1625. Maddock, *Hildegard of Bingen*, 97.

31. Beatus Rhenanus, *Briefwechsel des Beatus Rhenanus*, 38. Helfta was, in fact, a Cistercian foundation.

32. MGH, *Poetae Latini aevi Carolini*, 2.268.

33. Ibid., 2.269.

34. Bignami-Odier, "Les Visions de Robert d'Uzès," 272–73.

35. Hildegard of Bingen, *Scivias*, trans. Hart and Bishop, 60.

36. Hildegard of Bingen, *Scivias*, ed. Führkötter and Carlevaris, 3.

37. Ibid.

38. "Id autem non sine euidenti miraculo contingebat, frequenter enim & quasi ex consuetudine in diebus dominicis aliijsque festiuitatibus circa horas in quibus maxime fidelium feruet deuotio rapiebatur in mentis excessum, & resumpto paulatim spiritu, subito verba quaedam diuina latino sermone proferebat: quae neque per alium aliquando didicerat neque per seipsam inuenire poterat vt pote quae esset inerudita & latinae locutionis nullam vel exiguam habens peritiam"; Jacques Lefèvre d'Étaples, *Liber trium virorum*, fol. 119r. Anne Clark discusses Elisabeth's visionary states and her language in some detail providing a much more complex picture of her states than Lefèvre communicates. See A. Clark, *Elisabeth of Schönau*, 81.

39. Newman, "Hildegard and Her Hagiographers," 21, esp. n. 18. Anne Clark notes that Elisabeth's visions were a combination of Latin and German and that Eckbert transcribed the Latin and translated the German. A. Clark, "Holy Woman or Unworthy Vessel?" 37.

40. "The Preface of Abbot Ekbert to the Visions," trans. in A. Clark, *Elisabeth of Schönau*, 39. The preface appears only in the final version of the vision collections (278, n. 40).

41. Elisabeth saw family members and colleagues of her brother; Wettinus described a particular monk, abbot, and bishop, whom he saw punished. Interestingly, Wettinus reports that the abbot has not been sentenced to eternal damnation, but for his purification (*ad purgationem suam*), an earlier witness to purgatory than Elisabeth, whose visions were instrumental in establishing and defining purgatory. MGH, *Poetae Latini aevi Carolini*, 2.270, and A. Clark, *Elisabeth of Schönau*, 111–17. For the place of the *Visio Wettini* in the history of purgatory see Le Goff, *The Birth of Purgatory*, 24.

42. Newman, *Sister of Wisdom*, 216.

43. A. Clark, *Elisabeth of Schönau*, 118. The metaphor of souls ascending a mountain was important enough to devote an entire collection of visions to it. They are gathered in *Librum viarum dei* (in Lefèvre's *Liber trium virorum*). "The Book of the Ways of God," in A. Clark, *Elisabeth of Schönau*, 161–207.

44. MGH, *Poetae Latini aevi Carolini*, 2.270.

45. Kerby-Fulton, *Reformist Apocalypticism*, 101. For an interpretation of Robert's visions in crisis following Celestine's abdication and Boniface's election, see Clemens, "The Pope's Shrunken Head," 39–44.

46. Bignami-Odier, "Les Visions de Robert d'Uzès," 287, trans. in Clemens, "The Pope's Shrunken Head," 39.

47. It was customary practice to transcribe a single "best" (or "best on hand") manuscript when preparing a printed edition in the sixteenth century. Lefèvre and the Estienne publishing house were unusual in basing their editions on several codices when available.

48. Lefèvre may have had multiple sources. In his prefatory epistle he stated that he used the archtype, "bona pro parte," indicating the possibility of other manuscripts, but he may also have been referring to his insertion of non-*Scivias* material into the *Scivas* from elsewhere in the manuscript.

49. He remarked in his prefatory epistle to Adelheid von Ottenstein, abbess of the Benedictine convent of Rupertsberg, founded by Hildegard in 1147: "Nam cum in claustro vestro archetypos sanctae virginis Hildegardis legissem . . . unde hoc opus bona pro parte desumptum est" (Rice, ed., *The Prefatory Epistles*, 309). For a description of the Riesencodex, see Zedler, *Die Handschriften*, 3–17.

50. Rice, ed., *The Prefatory Epistles*, 313, n. 3.

51. Hildegard of Bingen, *Scivias*, ed. Führkötter and Carlevaris, 196. Lefèvre did not edit any of the texts other than the *Scivias*, although he did insert material from her *Explanatio symboli s. Athanasii* (from the Riesencodex) into the *Scivias* following bk. 3, vis. 5, chap. 33. See Hildegard of Bingen, *Scivias*, ed. Führkötter and Carlevaris, lix, n. 123, and 430–31.

52. Jacques Lefèvre d'Étaples, *Liber trium virorum*, n.p.

53. On apocalyptic miscellanies see Reeves, *The Influence of Prophecy*, 235, 255, 442, 495, and Kerby-Fulton, *Reformist Apocalypticism*, 98.

54. Newman, *Sister of Wisdom*, 22.

55. Beatus Rhenanus, *Briefwechsel des Beatus Rhenanus*, 38.

56. "Post hos autem sacrorum eloquiorum libros, agiographi, quales sunt qui nunc ad te mittuntur, pro secundo studio ut secundae quaedam animi mensae et quaedam (ut sic dicam) spiritualis exercitii bellaria non displiceant, nam aedificationem continent et sanctam ad Deum desideriorum omnium finem manuductionem." Rice, ed., *The Prefatory Epistles*, 310.

57. Beatus Rhenanus, *Briefwechsel des Beatus Rhenanus*, 38.

58. Newman, *Sister of Wisdom*, 23.

59. Hildegard of Bingen, *Scivias*, ed. Fürhkötter and Carlevaris, 33.
60. Ibid., 37.
61. For Hildegard's emphasis on "body" and "humility" see Bynum, ". . . And Woman His Humanity."
62. Hildegard and her contemporaries would surely object, believing that her words were literally from the mouth of God. See Newman, "Hildegard and Her Hagiographers," 21–22. We have many examples, however, of men who did not assign the same value to the words used by the visionary to describe their revelation. Brother A., for example, was unable to capture the texture of Angela of Foligno's words.
63. Rice, ed., *The Prefatory Epistles*, 310.
64. Hildegard of Bingen, *Vita Hildegardis*, 165*.
65. Newman, "Hildegard and Her Hagiographers," 27.
66. Details: *citra exstasis*, born near Gaul.
67. Hildegard of Bingen, *Vita Hildegardis*, 20–21; trans. Silvas, *Jutta and Hildegard*, 155–56.
68. See Klaes' discussion in Hildegard of Bingen, *Vita Sanctae Hildegardis*, 128–30. In the illuminations of Hildegard and Volmar, Hildegard is shown with wax tablets on her knees or desk while Volmar writes on parchment. In the Lucca manuscript (*De operatione Dei*, 1.1, Lucca, Biblioteca Statale, Cod. lat. 1942) Volmar concentrates on the written text; in the more popular Rupertsberg illumination he is shown looking at her mouth, presumably writing what she was saying. From Newman, *Sister of Wisdom*, ii.
69. In other writings Hildegard is described as dictating her visions partially in Latin and partially in German. Trithemius wrote: "Verum cum esset latini sermonis ignara, et praeter siplicem psalmodiam nihil ab homine didicisset, interno Spiritus sancti magiserio edocta, omnem scripturma positionem seu constructionem orationis perfect intellexit. Revelationes autem suas et visiones coelestes partin Latino parteim Teutonico protulit eloquio quas Gotfridus monachus S. Disibodi, capellanus et confessor eius, fecit latinas et congruas redigens in eum ordinem et form in qua hodie leguntur." Trithemius, *Chronicon Sponheimense ad annum 1179*, 257; quoted from Hildegard of Bingen, *Vita Hildegardis*, 130*, n. 262.
70. Silvas, *Jutta and Hildegard*, 156, n. 88.

E. ANN MATTER

17 Heart Calls to Heart
The Importance of the Love between the Lover and the Beloved in *The Mystical Ark* and *Wachet auf!*

Grover Zinn's scholarship has always been marked by careful attention to the relationship between medieval exegetical and theological formulations (especially among the Victorines) and medieval spiritual trends; that is, to the place where mystical theology begins. This is why the work of Richard of St. Victor has been such a natural, and excellent, focus of his scholarship. Richard was a masterful theologian and an insightful spiritual guide, the Victorine scholar who carried the combined intellectual and contemplative activities of that community to its highest point. This is especially evident in Richard's treatise *The Mystical Ark* (*Benjamin Major*), which was translated by Professor Zinn for the widely used series of English translations, The Classics of Western Spirituality.[1]

In the years Professor Zinn was working on this translation, I was fortunate to be one of his students at Oberlin College. I remember one snowy evening when he invited our Medieval Christianity class to meet for a special session to which each of us could bring a favourite piece of music to share. Already entranced by the Christian mystical tradition of commentary on the Song of Songs, I came armed with Johann Sebastian Bach's Cantata 140, *Wachet auf!* I played movements 3 and 6, two duets between a soprano and a bass (clearly understood as Christ and the soul), the first languid and poignant, the second brisk and joyful. I explained to my colleagues how this cantata, written for a Lutheran service in the eighteenth century, based on an equally Lutheran hymn by Philipp Nicolai composed at the very end of the sixteenth century, is a clear example of medieval mystical exegesis of the Song of Songs. I will never forget how, at the end of my remarks, my professor asked me one of the most devastating questions of my academic career: "That's very interesting, Ann, but, so what? What does it mean that Bach used this tradition?" I did not have an answer on that snowy night, but I pondered the question for many years, and finally, when I attended a conference on Bach in his Christian liturgical context, I had the opportunity to write an essay on the Song of Songs in *Wachet auf!*[2] That essay focused on the two duets as interpretations in Cassian's tropological or moral mode, in which the story of the approach of Christ to the longing but unready soul (Sg 2:10 and 5:2) is related twice, in slightly different versions. The first duet (movement 3 of the cantata) ends with the withdrawal of the Bridegroom Christ, leaving the soul/Bride in poignant sorrow, singing "Wann kommst du, mein Heil" ("When are you coming, my Savior?"), to which Christ answers "Ich komme, dein Teil" ("I come, your part"); whereas the second duet (movement 6) ends in the loving embrace of mystical union: the soul sings "Mein Freund ist mein" ("My Beloved is mine"), to which Christ answers "Und ich bin sein" ("and I am his").[3] Two passages of the Song of Songs resonate strongly in this second duet, namely, 2:16: "My beloved is mine and I am his," and 6:13: "I am my beloved's and my beloved is mine." It is interesting to note, though, that the rhetoric in Bach's duets suggests dialogue, whereas, in both cases, the biblical text puts both affirmations in the mouth of one speaker. However, neither the tradition of medieval Christian interpretation nor the rubricated medieval Bibles that assign voices to the verses of the Song of Songs make any effort to turn these affirmations into dialogues; the duetting voices of the cantata, then, is Bach's own choice.[4]

For all the fame (and aching beauty) of these duets, however, it must be noted that the foundational biblical passage of *Wachet auf!* is not from the Song of Songs at all. Instead, the cantata takes its title and its main exegetical orientation from the Nicolai hymn, which is based on Matthew 25, Jesus' parable of the five wise and five foolish virgins who sit with their lamps, awaiting the entry of the Bridegroom into the bridal chamber. In the parable, the foolish virgins neglected to bring oil for their lamps, but the wise virgins brought flasks of oil. When the Bridegroom is delayed, all ten virgins fall asleep. When, at midnight, the Bridegroom arrives to the cry "Behold the Bridegroom, come out to meet him" (Mt 25:6), they all awake. The foolish virgins ask the wise virgins to share their oil, but are rebuffed, and sent to the dealers to buy oil for their lamps. While they are gone, the wise virgins trim and light their lamps, and escort the Bridegroom into the marriage feast, shutting the door behind them. The foolish virgins return to find that they cannot enter the chamber and cry out "Lord, lord, open to us" (Mt 25:11), but the Bridegroom retorts: "Truly, I say to you, I do not know you" (Mt 25:12). The parable ends with Jesus' admonition "Watch therefore, for you know neither the day nor the hour" (Mt 25:13). The final warning brings an apocalyptic dimension to the parable: human beings do not know when Jesus will return, but it is our duty to have oil ready for our lamps and to be prepared to escort the Heavenly Bridegroom to his feast.

Bach used Nicolai's hymn as the backbone of the cantata, harmonizing three verses to make the rich chorales of movements 1, 4, and 7. The first hymn/chorale verse (*Wachet auf!* 1) repeats the admonition "Wake up!" specifically addressed by the watchmen to the city of Jerusalem at the midnight hour, when the Bridegroom is on the doorstep; the second verse (*Wachet auf!* 4) tells us that Zion (the wise virgins) hears the watchmen calling, and arise prepared for the heavenly guest, specifically identified as Jesus: "Herr Jesu, Gottes Son" ("Lord Jesus, Son of God"); and the third verse (*Wachet auf!* 7) ends the cantata with a hymn of praise.

The admonition of the title is addressed to the foolish virgins of Matthew 25; the warning is addressed to those who are awake, and who must be prepared to take up their lamps and go to meet the Bridegroom, since the time to the consummation grows short.[5] The implicit reference here is to the Eschaton, the apocalyptic end of time, when all things will be gathered up in the final embrace of the Christ who is to come again. Nicolai hints at this interpretation with a reference to the book of Apocalypse (Revelation).[6] The eschatological atmosphere is also evident from the liturgical context of this piece, the fact that the cantata was written for the twenty-seventh Sunday after Trinity, a Sunday that occurs liturgically very rarely, only when Easter falls unusually early and the Trinity season is stretched out longer than it usually is. For my argument that there is an apocalyptic dimension to *Wachet auf!* the most significant consequence of this chronological oddity is that it brings the end of the season of Trinity right up against the first Sunday of Advent, a season of eschatological anticipation. Indeed, the Gospel reading for the twenty-seventh Sunday after Trinity is Matthew 25, the parable of the wise and foolish virgins. This rare liturgical and exegetical concatenation did occur in 1731, probably the year in which *Wachet auf!* was written, and, since this made the Nicolai hymn an obvious choice for the liturgy, it was probably the inspiration for Bach's cantata 140.[7]

But it was left to Bach and his possible collaborators to compose the texts for the movements in between the verses of the Nicolai hymn, in this case, two short introductory recitatives and the two duets between Christ and the soul (*Wachet auf!* 2–3, and 5–6). This introduction of themes from the Song of Songs was thus quite an imaginative innovation, especially since the type of allegorical exegesis of medieval Christian Song of Songs interpretation was largely rejected by the Protestant theological tradition. As Carl von Winterfeld put it, "This was perhaps the first time that the Song of Songs was granted admission into the singing of the congregation in a Protestant church."[8] Bach must have played a major role in this decision, of course, but he was probably working with a local poet who helped compose the libretto for the cantata beyond the Nicolai hymn. This collaborator may well have been Christian Friedrich Henrici, a frequent collaborator who wrote under the pseudonym of Picander.[9] In any case, a decision was made in eighteenth-century Leipzig to use a medieval Christian interpretation of the Song of Songs to add another spiritual dimension to a Reformation interpretation of the parable of the wise and foolish virgins in Matthew 25. This is a significant exegetical move, if not entirely anomalous.

The way in which this selection was not surprising is related to the fact that the Song of Songs was one of the basic texts of medieval monastic literature, perhaps the most commented upon book of the Bible between the time of Origen of Alexandria in the third century and that of Martin Luther in the sixteenth. Although Luther's cry, "Sola Scriptura!" did not favor allegorical exegesis and its use in official theology, an allegorical reading of the

Song of Songs remained a strong force in Protestant spiritual writings. It was transmitted to Bach's world through the writings of Rhineland mystics such as Johannes Tauler and Lutheran Pietists like Philipp Jacob Spener and Johann Arndt.[10]

Most medieval Western (Latin) commentaries on the Song of Songs follow the modes of exegesis designated by John Cassian, a contemporary of Augustine who forged the "fourfold" method of allegorical interpretation that became the medieval Christian exegetical norm. According to Cassian, any biblical text could be interpreted in any or all of four separate modes of understanding:

1. "historical" (having to do with the literal sense of the text as it was written),
2. "allegorical" (having to do with Christ and the Church),
3. "tropological/moral" (understood as the relationship between Christ and the individual soul), or
4. "anagogical" (pertaining to the End Times).[11]

Most medieval Christian commentaries in the Latin tradition followed the allegorical or tropological modes.[12] One of the many interesting details of medieval Christian commentary on the Song of Songs is the fact that, in spite of the large number of commentaries written on this short book, and the variety of exegetical positions taken, there is not one (to my knowledge) written primarily in Cassian's "anagogical" mode, the type of interpretation that relates a biblical text to the eschatological end times.[13] As I have argued, this curious fact could make Bach's *Wachet auf!* a singular example of western Christian anagogical exegesis of the Song of Songs,[14] and thus may constitute an acceptable answer to Professor Zinn's challenging question, "So what?"

The present essay, however, gives me the opportunity to return to this question through study and comparison of a medieval text I did not consider in my first analysis of Bach's cantata, namely, one of the treatises translated by Professor Zinn, Richard of St. Victor's *The Mystical Ark*. In this remarkable work, Richard interprets God's instructions to Moses about the building of the ark of the covenant (Ex 25–27) as a guide to the contemplative life. First, Richard distinguishes contemplation from thinking and meditation. Contemplation is an intent beholding of and joyful adhering to the divine.[15]

Richard says: "Contemplation is the free, more penetrating gaze of a mind, suspended with wonder concerning manifestations of wisdom."[16] Although contemplation cannot be equated with thinking, Richard does consider it to have connections to imagination and reason. In fact, he distinguishes six levels of contemplation:

1. In imagination and according to imagination only
2. In imagination and according to reason
3. In reason and according to imagination
4. In reason and according to reason.
5. Above reason but not beyond reason
6. Above reason and seemingly beyond reason.[17]

Each of these kinds of contemplation is symbolized by one stage of the building of the ark of the covenant; as the ark is built, the contemplative soul moves from imagination (the first two steps, equated with the wood of the ark) to reason (steps 3 and 4, equated with the gilding of the ark), to understanding (the final steps, 5 and 6, associated with the pure gold crown of the ark).

The final two stages are discussed in detail in book 4 of *The Mystical Ark*, in which Richard describes the forging of the mercy seat (or "propitiatory"), which serves as the cover of the ark. It was crafted to the same length and breadth as the gold-sheathed wooden ark, but made of one piece of pure gold, with a cherub of pure gold at either end. The cherubim are to be of one piece with the mercy seat:

> Make one cherub on the one end, and one cherub on the other end; of one piece with the mercy seat shall you make the cherubim on its two ends. The cherubim shall spread their wings above, overshadowing the mercy seat with their wings, their faces one to another; toward the mercy seat shall the faces of the cherubim be.[18]

The fact that the cherubim face one another across the mercy seat gives Richard his clue for a lengthy discussion of the human yearning for God, a yearning for which the human soul is rarely prepared.[19] As Zinn describes this discussion:

few passages in mystical literature catch so well the subtleties of divine calling, human yearning, equally human procrastination and laziness, and the final outpouring of love in the mutual embraces of lovers that signifies mystic ecstasy for Richard.[20]

For this interpretation, Richard turns to several biblical passages outside of Exodus, passages that also refer to human diffidence in the face of God's love: to the hesitant "a little here, a little there" of Isaiah 28, to Abraham, who sat in the doorway of his tent (Gn 18: 1), and Elijah, who stood in the entrance to his cave (3 Kings 19:13) as the Lord approached; and especially to the coming of the lover to the unprepared beloved as described in Song of Songs 2 and 5, the same passages Bach chose to gloss Matthew 25 in *Wachet auf!*

In book 4, chapters 13–14, Richard ponders at length how the soul should be prepared for the coming of the Lord, but often, because of human weakness, hesitates to respond to God's call. He is clear about the fact that scripture speaks in various enigmas and figures:

> It often happens that one and the same passage of Scripture says many things to us in one thing when it is expounded in several ways: Expounded morally, it teaches us what our Beloved wishes us to do; taken allegorically, it reminds us what He has done for us through Himself; interpreted anagogically it proposes what He plans to make of us in the future.[21]

Richard's understanding and use of the Song of Songs here is basically according to the tropological mode, that is, having to do with the love between God and the soul, but he puts an interesting and original theological twist to this discussion later in book 4, when he turns to the question of why the cherubim face each other, across the golden expanse of the mercy seat.

The first cherub, Richard says, may be explained by the fifth level of contemplation, the level that is above reason but not beyond reason, while the second cherub equates to the sixth level, above reason and seemingly beyond reason. To Richard, this resonates with Trinitarian theology: the first cherub is the unity of God, and the second is the ineffable Trinity of the three persons.[22] The two cherubim turn their faces towards each other, but also towards the mercy seat, to show the unity of the triune God. For the human, the highest level of contemplation thus becomes the shared ecstasy of the three persons of the Trinity. Near the end of book 4, Richard reminds the reader that God spoke to Moses from above the mercy seat:

> We also ought neither to neglect nor to pass over without careful consideration of that which is promised by the voice of the Lord when it said to Moses: "I will speak to you from above the propitiatory," that is, "from between the two cherubim."[23]

Thus, the contemplative soul must rise up beyond reason, to join the ecstasy of God's embrace. In book 5, Richard specifically equates three levels of "alienation" of the contemplative mind (that is, alienation from sensible things) as "three anagogic modes of ecstasy described mystically in the Song of Songs."[24] I have noted elsewhere the close connection between the allegorical, tropological, and anagogical interpretations of the Song of Songs, found in the understanding that the love between the church or the human soul and the Triune God will be finally consummated at the Eschaton.[25] Richard was certainly sensitive to this connection, and, indeed, makes frequent reference to anagogy in the last book of *The Mystical Ark* and the *Allegories of the Tabernacle of the Covenant* that follows the end of book 5.[26] For example, Richard says:

> It should be noted that only Sacred Scripture uses
>   Allegorical and anagogical senses mystically.
> And among all the senses, it is crowned by this
>   Supereminent pair.[27]

A close study of the anagogical exegesis of Richard of St. Victor would be a worthy task for a student of medieval Christianity, something that could help scholars of medieval Christian biblical exegesis further our understanding of the subtleties of the senses of scripture.

In the meantime, it is interesting to note a few similarities in the role played by the Song of Songs in the two very different contexts I have been discussing, works by Richard of St. Victor and Johann Sebastian Bach. In each case, the main biblical text, the focus of the exegesis (be it liturgical or theological), was not the Song of Songs but very different biblical stories: for Richard, the instructions given to Moses for the building of the ark of the covenant in Exodus 25; for Bach, the parable of the wise and foolish virgins of Matthew 25, presented to him in a hymn from the Reformation period. In both cases, though, when certain themes arise, namely, the longing of the human soul for God and the baffling difficulty of human ability to respond to God's presence, the authors turned to the same passages of the Song of Songs to explain why this should be so and what it means about God's love and human spiritual potential. Obviously, the goals and methods of the two works are very different, but this fact only makes the shared references more striking. I would not try to even suggest that Bach read and was directly influenced by Richard of St. Victor. This would be difficult to prove, but it is also not necessary, since my argument, instead, hinges on the fact that Bach did not need to have read Richard to use those same passages from the Song of Songs in such a similar way. This is because both authors are participants in a more ample literary and theological culture in which the aching loss of the story of the ardent lover and the hesitant beloved in Song of Songs 2 and 5 was well known to signify the dilemma of human response to God's offered love.

Given the influence of late medieval mysticism on Luther and his colleagues, this should not seem surprising. What is less expected is the clear note of anagogical exegesis in both works, because, as I have noted, anagogy did not play a large part in the medieval Christian tradition of exegesis of the Song of Songs. Perhaps the challenge that arises from these observations on the love between God and the human soul in Richard of St. Victor's *The Mystical Ark* and Johann Sebastian Bach's Cantata 140, *Wachet auf!* should be seen as a need for a more focused consideration of what constitutes the divine present in Christian mysticism. Perhaps I was exaggerating when I suggested that the first anagogical Christian interpretation of the Song of Songs was crafted in eighteenth-century Leipzig, since that understanding is already abundantly present, if in a different but equally subtle way, in Richard of St. Victor's *The Mystical Ark*, written six hundred years earlier.

This still leaves some very interesting questions. To begin with, why should this be so? Why should the Song of Songs play such a useful, perhaps even vital, role in the Christian spiritual tradition? It is, after all, an anomalous book of the Hebrew Bible, a Hebrew text made up entirely of a set of love poems that contain no prophecy or sacred history, and do not even mention God, at least not by name. And yet, as many scholars have noted, its place in the canon of Sacred Scripture, in Jewish tradition as much as in Christian, is based on the assumption of an allegorical understanding in which one of the lovers/interlocutors of the poems is God. One Jewish tradition says that God gave the Song of Songs to Moses on Mount Sinai, thus making it part of the contents of the ark of the covenant along with the tablets of the law.[28]

But, of course, the Song of Songs is not law, it is poetry. Furthermore, the Song of Songs is poetry that, at least on the face of it, seems far more human than divine. This very humanity is exactly what makes it a precious tool of the Christian theological tradition over centuries, in many languages, and in conflicting theological contexts. This is because, ultimately, human beings can only know human things. All Christian theologians, beginning with Paul in 1 Corinthians 13, have lamented the fact that humans will not, cannot, know the ways of God in this world. This means that all that is left to us is knowledge through our own human senses. We cannot love God as God loves us. It is part of the human condition that we know that God's love surpasses human love, and that we can only yearn to love God face to face, and even this only by means of our human love, the only type of love we can know. The Christian theology of the Incarnation is key here, since by becoming a human being, Jesus Christ, the second person of the Trinity (and part of Richard's second cherub) experienced human love in a human form. The Song of Songs is such a powerful text for the Christian spiritual tradition because it dramatizes for us the love of the God/man, the Heavenly Bridegroom the devout soul will meet again at the wedding feast of the Eschaton, and it laments the human inclination towards inaction in this life, even in the face of a royal invitation to the loving bliss of God's embrace.

Since Richard of St. Victor wrote in the context of a clerical community of Augustinian canons in twelfth-century Paris, we can also assume that his intended audience understood a good deal of this complex association of meaning. The intended audience of *Wachet auf!*, and the three centuries of audiences who have been moved by Bach's poignant duets between Christ and the soul, in congregations and concert halls alike, may well not have understood the subtleties of this tradition. But the important thing about the use of this tradition, in both Johann Sebastian Bach and Richard of St. Victor, and ultimately about the tradition itself, is that its power lies more in the emotional than the intellectual side of the religious life. The fact that God calls to the human soul like a lover, even as the soul finds it so difficult to respond properly, is at the core of the Christian spirituality that Professor Zinn has studied, and the best possible answer to the question he posed to his student some four decades ago.

NOTES

1. Contained in Richard of St. Victor, *The Twelve Patriarchs; the Mystical Ark, Book Three of the Trinity*, trans. Zinn (hereafter *Richard of St. Victor*).
2. Matter, "The Love Between the Bride and the Bridegroom."
3. Ibid., 112–13.
4. Cf. Matter, *The Voice of My Beloved*, 56–57 and notes.
5. Apocalypse 21:21, "of twelve pearls are the gates of your city." See Matter, "The Love Between the Bride and the Bridegroom," 107–8, for further discussion of this point.
6. Matter, "The Love Between the Bride and the Bridegroom," 108 and 114 ff.
7. Herz, ed., *Johann Sebastian Bach, Cantata No. 140*, 51–54.
8. Winterfeld, *Der evangelische Kirchengesang*, 333. Translation by Gerhard Herz from the 1966 edition in Herz, ed., *Johann Sebastian Bach, Cantata No. 140*, 155.
9. Herz, ed., *Johann Sebastian Bach, Cantata No. 140*, 110.
10. See Heiko A. Oberman's preface to his *Johann Arndt*, xi–xvii, and Matter, "Buxtehude and Pietism?" The ongoing work of Johann Anselm Steiger on Arndt and his school will add much to this picture.
11. John Cassian, *Collationes* 14.8, ed. Pichery, 190.
12. For a summary of this tradition, see Matter, *The Voice of My Beloved*, 54–60.
13. Matter, *The Voice of My Beloved*, 109–11; see also Matter, "The Apocalypse," esp. 46–47.
14. Matter, "The Love Between the Bride and the Bridegroom," 117.
15. For Richard's distinction between thinking, meditation and contemplation, see *De gratia contemplationis libri quinque occasione accepta ab arca Moysis et ob eam rem hactenus dictum Benjamin Minor* 1.3–4, PL 196:66C–68C, in *Richard of St. Victor*, 155–58; and the essay of Dale Coulter in this volume.
16. "Contemplatio est libera mentis perspicacia in sapientiae spectacula cum admiratione suspense," I, 4, PL 196: 67D, in *Richard of St Victor*, transl. Zinn, 157.
17. "Sex autem sunt contemplationum genera a se et inter se omnino divisa. Primum itaque est in imaginatione et secundum solam imaginationem. Secundum est in imaginatione secundum rationem. Tertium est in ratione secundum imaginationem. Quartum est in ratione et secundum rationem. Quintum est supra, sed non

praeter rationem. Sextum supra rationem, et videtur esse praeter rationem." *The Mystical Ark* 1.6, PL 196:70B–72B, in *Richard of St. Victor*, 161–65, and discussed by Zinn, 23 ff.

18. Ex 25:19–20.

19. *The Mystical Ark* 4, PL 196:135A–168C, in *Richard of St. Victor*, 263–307.

20. *Richard of St. Victor*, 38.

21. "Et saepe fit ut una eademque Scriptura, dum multipliciter exponitur, multa nobis in unum loquatur, moraliter nos docens quid dilectus noster facere nos velit, allegoriter admonens quid pro nobis per semetipsum fecerit, anagogice proponens quid adhuc de nobis facere disponit." *The Mystical Ark* 4.14, PL 196:151B, in *Richard of St. Victor*, 283.

22. ". . . primum cherubin specialiter pertineant ea quae considerantur circa divinae illius summae et simplicis essentiae unitatem; ad secundum autem cherubin ea quae considerantur circa personarum Trinitatem." *The Mystical Ark* 4.17, PL 196:156B, in *Richard of St. Victor*, 289.

23. ". . . consideratione praetereundum, quod Dominica voce promittitur, cum ad Moysen dicitur: Inde loquar ad te desuper propitiatorio videlicet, et de medio duorum cherubin." Ex 25:22; *The Mystical Ark* 4.21, PL 196:163B, in *Richard of St. Victor*, 300.

24. "Hoc autem tres anagogicos excessionis modos eodem quo hic illos ordine posuimus, mystice quidem descriptos, in Canticis canticorum, ut arbitror, inveniemus." *The Mystical Ark* 5.5, PL 196:174D, in *Richard of St. Victor*, 317.

25. Matter, *The Voice of My Beloved*, 54–55.

26. *Nonnullae Allegoriae Tabernaculi Foederis Cum recapitulatione brevissima contentorum in praefato opere de gratia contemplationis*, PL 196:192C–202B, in *Richard of St. Victor*, 344–70; see especially 199C–D: "Per opus ligneum intelligimus sensum historicum; per labium tropologicum, per geminam coronam allegoricum et anagogicum," 364.

27. "Notandum quod sola Scriptura sacra allegorico et anagogico sensu mystice utitur sola inter omnes hac gemina supereminentia coronatur." PL 196:200D, in *Richard of St. Victor*, 367.

28. For the Jewish allegorical tradition, see *Midrash Rabbah*, vol. 9, and the discussions in Lowe, "Apologetic Motifs," and A. Green, "The Song of Songs." For a brief discussion of the impact of these readings on medieval Christian interpretation, see Matter, *The Voice of My Beloved*, 51.

Grover A. Zinn: Selected Publications

BOOKS

Medieval France: An Encyclopedia, edited with William W. Kibler. New York: Garland, 1995.

The Twelve Patriarchs; The Mystical Ark; Book Three of the Trinity. Translated and introduced. Classics of Western Spirituality. New York: Paulist Press, 1979.

CONTRIBUTIONS TO BOOKS

"*Vestigia victorina*: Victorine Influence on Spiritual Life in the Middle Ages with Special Reference to Hugh of Saint-Victor's *De institutione novitiorum*," in *L'École de Saint-Victor de Paris: Influence et rayonnement du Moyen Âge à l'époque moderne.* Colloque international du C. N. R. S. pour le neuvième centenaire de la foundation (1108–2008) tenu au Collège des Bernardins à Paris les 24–27 septembre 2008 et organisé par Patrick Gautier Dalché, Cédric Giraud, Luc Jocque, Dominique Poirel et Patrice Sicard. Edited by Dominique Poirel. Bibliotheca Victorina 22. Turnhout: Brepols, 2010.

"The Psalms at the Abbey of Saint-Victor: From the Novices' *schola* to the Heights of *contemplatio*," in *Transforming Relations: Essays on Jews and Christians throughout History in Honor of Michael A. Signer*, edited by Franklin T. Harkins. Notre Dame, Ind.: University of Notre Dame Press, 2010.

"Minding Matter: *Materia* and the World in the Spirituality and Theology of Hugh of Saint-Victor," in *Mind Matters: Studies of Medieval and Early Modern Intellectual History in Honour of Marcia L. Colish*, edited by Cary J. Nederman, Nancy Van Deusen, and E. Ann Matter. Turnhout: Brepols, 2009.

"Exile, the Abbey of Saint-Victor at Paris and Hugh of Saint-Victor," in *Medieval Paradigms: Essays in Honor of Jeremy duQuesnay Adams*, edited by Stephanie Hayes-Healy. The New Middle Ages 2. New York: Palgrave Macmillan, 2005.

"The History of Meditation on Jesus' Seven Last Words," and three meditations, in *Words from the Cross: Meditations on Franz Joseph Haydn's "The Seven Last Words of Christ,"* edited by Richard Young. Lanham, Md.: Rowman and Littlefield, 2005.

Introduction to *The Place of the Psalms in the Intellectual Culture of the Middle Ages*, edited by Nancy Van Deusen. Medieval Studies. Albany: State University of New York Press, 1999.

"Exegesis and Spirituality in Richard of St. Victor," in *Doors of Understanding: Conversations in Global Spirituality in Honor of Ewert Cousins*. Quincy, Ill.: Franciscan Press, 1997.

"Exegesis and Spirituality in the Writings of Gregory the Great," in *Gregory the Great*, edited by John Cavadini. Notre Dame Studies in Theology 2. Notre Dame, Ind. University of Notre Dame Press, 1996.

"The Influence of Augustine's *De doctrina christiana* on Hugh of St. Victor," in *Reading and Wisdom: The "De doctrina christiana" of Augustine in the Middle Ages*, edited by Edward D. English. Notre Dame, Ind.: University of Notre Dame Press, 1995.

"History and Interpretation: 'Hebrew Truth,' Judaism, and the Victorine Exegetical Tradition," in *Jews and Christians: Exploring the Past, Present, and Future*, edited by James H. Charlesworth. Shared Ground Among Jews and Christians: A Series of Explorations 1. New York: Crossroad, 1990.

"Greek Orthodox Theological Review," "Harvard Theological Review," and "Oberlin Quarterly Review," in *Religious Periodicals of the United States: Academic and Scholarly Journals*, edited by Charles H. Lippy. New York: Greenwood, 1986.

"Sound, Silence and Word in the Spirituality of Gregory the Great," in *Grégoire le Grand*, edited by Jacques Fontaine et al. Colloques Internationaux du Centre National de la Recherche Scientifique. Paris: CNRS, 1986.

"Regular Canons," in *Christian Spirituality: Origins to the Twelfth Century*, edited by Bernard McGinn and John Meyendorff, in collaboration with Jean Leclercq. Vol. 16 of *World Spirituality: An Encyclopedic History of the Religious Quest*. New York: Crossroad, 1986.

"Suger, Theology, and the Pseudo-Dionysian Tradition," in *Abbot Suger and Saint-Denis: A Symposium*, edited by Paula Lieber Gerson. New York: The Metropolitan Museum of Art, 1986.

"*Historia fundamentum est*: The Role of History in the Contemplative Life according to Hugh of Saint Victor," in *Contemporary Reflections on the Medieval Christian Tradition: Essays in Honor of Ray C. Petry*, edited by George H. Shriver. Durham, N.C.: Duke University Press, 1974.

"Book and Word: The Victorine Background of Bonaventure's Use of Symbols," in *S. Bonaventura 1274–1974*, edited by J. G. Bougerol. Rome: Collegio S. Bonaventura, 1974.

ARTICLES

"Hugh of St. Victor's *De scripturis et scriptoribus sacris* as an *Accessus* Treatise for the Study of the Bible." *Traditio: Studies in Ancient and Medieval History, Thought, and Religion* 52 (1997).

"Texts within Texts: The Exegesis of the Song of Songs in Works by Gregory the Great and Hugh of St. Victor," in *Studia Patristica 25: Papers presented at the Eleventh International Conference on Patristic Studies held in Oxford 1991* (1993).

"Hugh of St. Victor, Isaiah's Vision, and *De arca Noe*," in *The Church and the Arts*. Studies in Church History 28. Oxford: Blackwell, 1992.

"Personification Allegory and Visions of Light in Richard of St. Victor's Teaching on Contemplation." *University of Toronto Quarterly* 46 (1977).

"The Influence of Hugh of St. Victor's *Chronicon* on the *Abbreviationes chronicorum* by Ralph of Diceto." *Speculum* 52 (1977).

"*De gradibus ascensionum*: The Stages of Contemplative Ascent in Two Treatises on Noah's Ark by Hugh of St. Victor." *Studies in Medieval Culture* 5 (1975).

"Hugh of St. Victor and the Art of Memory." *Viator* 5 (1974).

"Mandala Symbolism and Use in the Mysticism of Hugh of St. Victor." *History of Religions* 12 (1973).

"Monasticism East and West: An Inquiry." *Japanese Religions* 7 (1971), with Prof. D. K. Swearer.

"Hugh of St. Victor and the Ark of Noah: A New Look," *Church History* 40 (1971).

Bibliography

MANUSCRIPTS

Arras
Médiathèque (formerly Bibl. mun.), 703 (622)

Cambrai
Médiathèque (formerly Bibl. mun.), 305

Cambridge
Corpus Christi College, 315
Trinity College
    B.1.1
    B.1.6
    B.1.10
    B.1.11
    B.1.12
    B.1.13

B.1.14
B.1.31
B.1.32
B.1.33
B.1.34
B.1.35
B.1.36
B.1.39
B.2.6
B.2.15
B.3.15
B.3.16
B.4.3
University Library
Dd.7.7–10

Durham
Cathedral and Chapter Library, A. III. 22

Karlsruhe
Badische Landesbibliothek, Aug. perg. 214

London
British Library
Arundel 275
Harley 3038

Lucca
Biblioteca Statale, Cod. lat. 1942

New Haven, CT
Yale University Library, Beinicke 640

Oxford
Bodleian Library
Bodl. 459
Bodl. 494
Canon. Bib. Lat. 70
e Mus. 62
Laud Lat. 9
Laud Misc. 156
Pococke 295

Brasenose College
    5
Corpus Christi College
    6

Paris
Archives Nationales
    K 21 no. 8a
    K 22 no. 4
    Museum AE III, no. 140
    NII, Seine 163
    Q², 121 liasse no. 7
Bibliothèque de la Chambre des Députés
    2
Bibliothèque Mazarine
    47
    729
BnF
    Arsenal 47
    Hebreu 161
    lat. 2165
    lat. 2592
    lat. 3438
    lat. 3848
    lat. 11561
    lat. 14515–14516
    lat. 14368–14376
    lat. 14395–14396
    lat. 14677–14683
    lat. 14881
    lat. 16702
    nouv. acq. lat. 1791
Bibliothèque de la Sorbonne
    16

Prague
Nàrodni Knihovna eské Republiky (National Library of the Czech Republic), XIV.
    D. 20

Salzburg
University Library, M. III. 24

Shrewsbury
Shrewsbury School, 12

Stuttgart
Württembergische Landesbibliothek, Bibl. fol. 23 (Stuttgart Psalter)

Toledo
Library of the Cathedral, cod. 6–26

Toulouse
Bibliothèque de Toulouse, 206

Tours
Bibliothèque municipale, 321

Troyes
Médiathèque de l'Aggolomération Troyenne, 544

Vatican City
Biblioteca Apostolica Vaticana
    Chigi B. VII. 106
    Lat. 1053
    Lat. 13014
    Reg. Lat. 277

Vendôme
Bibliothèque municipale
    23
    34
    61
    115

Vienna
ONB, Heb. 220

Wrocław
Bibliotheka Universytecka, IF 232 (259)

Zwickau
Ratsschulbibliothek, IV,1

INCUNABULA AND OTHER EARLY PRINTED EDITIONS

Hugh of St. Cher. *Postilla super totam bibliam*. Basel: Anton Koberger, Ioannes de Amerbach, 1498–1502.
Jacques Lefèvre d'Ètaples. *Liber trium virorum et trium spiritualium virginum*. Paris: Henri Estienne, 1513.
Mechthild of Hackeborn. *Liber specialis gratiae*. Leipzig: J. Thanners, 1510.
Nicholas of Lyra. *Postilla litteralis super totam bibliam*. Nuremberg: Anton Koberger, 1481.
Schedel, Hartmann. *Liber chronicarum*. Nuremberg: Anton Koberger, 1493; repr. *The Nuremberg Chronicle: A Facsimile of Hartmann Schedel's Buch der Chroniken*. New York: Landmark Press, 1979.

PRIMARY SOURCES

Achard of St. Victor. "On the Distinction of Soul, Spirit, and Mind." In *Works*, 357–74. Translated by Hugh Feiss. Cistercian Studies Series 165. Kalamazoo: Cistercian Publications, 2001
———. *Sermons*. In *Works*. Translated by Hugh Feiss. Cistercian Studies Series 165. Kalamazoo: Cistercian Publications, 2001.
———. *Sermons inédits*. Edited by Jean Châtillon. Textes Philosophiques du Moyen Age 17. Paris: Vrin, 1970.
———. *L'unité de Dieu et la pluralité des creatures*. Edited by Emmanuel Martineau. Saint-Lambert des Bois: Authentica, 1987.
Adam of St. Victor. *Quatorze proses du xiie siècle à louange de Marie*. Edited by Bernadette Jollès. Turnhout: Brepols, 1994.
Adam of Dryburgh (attrib). *Allegoriae in universam Scripturam sacram*. PL 112:851–1088.
——— (attrib). *Soliloquium de instructione animae libri II*. In *Thesaurus anecdotorum novissimus*, edited by Bernhard Pez. Venice: Augustæ Vindelicorum & Græcii, 1721–28.
Adamnán. *Adamnán's "De Locis Sanctis."* Edited by Denis Meehan. Scriptores Latinae Hiberniae 3. Dublin: Dublin Institute for Advanced Studies, 1958.
Adso Dervensis. *De ortu et tempore Antichristi, necnon et tractatus qui ab eo dependebant*, edited by D. Verhelst. CCCM 45. Turnhout: Brepols, 1976.
Alain de Lille. *Sermones octo*. PL 210:197–222.
Albert of Aachen. *Historia Ierosolimitana: History of the Journey to Jerusalem*. Edited and translated by Susan B. Edgington. Oxford: Clarendon Press, 2007.
Albertus Magnus. *Commentaria in II Sententiarum*. In *Opera omnia*, edited by E. C. A. Borgnet, vol. 27. Paris: Vivès, 1890–95.

———. *Summa de creaturis*. In *Opera omnia*, edited by E. C. A. Borgnet, vol. 35. Paris: Vivès, 1890–95.

Alexander of Hales. *Summa theologica*. Edited by Collegium S. Bonaventurae. 4 vols. Quaracchi: Collegium S. Bonaventurae, 1928.

Ambrose. *De Abraham*. Edited and translated by Franco Gori. SAEMO 2:2. Milan: Biblioteca Ambrosiana, 1984.

———. *De Iacob*. Edited by Karl Schenkl. Translated by Roberto Palla. SAEMO 3. Milan: Biblioteca Ambrosiana, 1982.

———. *De Isaac vel anima*. Edited by Karl Schenkl. Translated by Claudio Moreschini. SAEMO 3. Milan: Biblioteca Ambrosiana, 1982.

———. *Epistulae*. Edited by Michaela Zelzer. CSEL 82. Vienna: Hoelder-Pichler-Tempsky, 1982.

———. *Expositio Psalmi CXVIII*. Edited by Michael Petschenig. CSEL 62. Vienna: Hoelder-Pichler-Tempsky, 1913.

Andrew of St. Victor. *Expositio in Ezechielem*. Edited by Michael A. Signer. CCCM 53E. Turnhout: Brepols, 1991.

———. *Expositio super Duodecim Prophetas*. Edited by Frans A. Van Liere and Mark A. Zier. CCCM 53G. Turnhout: Brepols, 2007.

Augustine. *Confessiones*. Edited by Lucas Verheijen. CCSL 27. Turnhout: Brepols, 1981.

———. *The Confessions*. Edited and translated by Maria Boulding. Hyde Park, N.Y.: New City Press, 1997.

———. *De doctrina christiana*. Edited by Joseph Martin. CCSL 32. Turnhout: Brepols, 1962.

———. *De trinitate*. Edited by W. J. Mountain and Franciscus Glorie. CCSL 16. Turnhout: Brepols, 1968.

———. *Enarrationes in Psalmos 1–50*. Edited by Eligius Dekkers and Johannes Fraipont. CCSL 38. Turnhout: Brepols, 1956.

———. *Epistolae*. PL 33.

———. *The Literal Meaning of Genesis*. Translated by John Hammond Taylor. 2 vols. Ancient Christian Writers 41–42. New York: Newman Press, 1982.

Beatus Rhenanus. *Briefwechsel des Beatus Rhenanus*. Edited by Adalbert Horawitz and Karl Hertfelter. Hildesheim: G. Olms, 1966.

Bede. *Bede: A Biblical Miscellany*. Translated with notes and introduction by W. T. Foley and A. G. Holder. Translated Texts for Historians 28. Liverpool: Liverpool University Press, 1999.

———. *Bede: On the Temple*. Translated with notes by Seán Connolly and introduction by Jennifer O'Reilly. Translated Texts for Historians 21. Liverpool: Liverpool University Press, 1995.

———. *Bede: On the Tabernacle*. Translated with notes and introduction by Arthur G. Holder. Translated Texts for Historians 18. Liverpool: Liverpool University Press, 1994.

———. *De tabernaculo et vasis eius, ac vestibus sacerdotum.* PL 91:393–498.
Bernard of Clairvaux. *Apologia ad Guillelmum Abbatem.* In *S. Bernardi opera omnia,* edited by Jean Leclercq, C. H. Talbot, and H. M. Rochais, 3:61–117. Rome: Editiones cistercienses, 1963.
———. *Exordium magnum Cisterciense.* PL 185: 221–466.
———. *Lettres.* Edited and translated by Monique Duchet-Suchaux and Henri Rochais. SC 458. Paris: Cerf, 1997.
———. *On the Song of Songs I–IV.* Translated by Kilian J. Walsh and Irene M. Edmonds. Cistercian Fathers Series 4, 7, 31, and 40. Kalamazoo, Mich.: Cistercian Publications, 1981, 1983, 1979, and 1980.
———*S. Bernardi opera omnia,* edited by Jean Leclercq, C. H. Talbot, and H. M. Rochais, 9 vols. Rome: Editiones cistercienses, 1957–77.
———. *Sermones Super Cantica 36–86.* In *S. Bernardi opera omnia,* edited by Jean Leclercq, C. H. Talbot, and H. M. Rochais, vol. 2. Rome: Editiones cistercienses, 1958.
Biblia latina cum glossa ordinaria: Facsimile Reprint of the editio princeps; Adolph Rusch of Strassburg 1480/81. Edited by Karlfried Froehlich and M. T. Gibson. 4 vols. Turnhout: Brepols, 1992.
Boethius. *De consolatione philosophiae.* In *The Theological Tractates: The Consolation of Philosophy,* trans. H. F. Stewart, E. K. Rand, S. J. Tester. Loeb Classical Library 74. Cambridge, Mass.: Harvard University Press, 1973.
———. *In Porphyrium dialogi.* PL 64:9–70.
Bonaventure. *Commentaria in II Sententiarum.* In *Opera omnia,* edited by Collegium S. Bonaventurae, vol. 2. Quaracchi: Collegium S. Bonaventurae, 1885.
Bonfons, Pierre. *Les fastes antiquitez et choses plus remarquable de Paris.* Paris, 1607.
Caesarius of Heisterbach. *Dialogus miraculorum.* Edited by Joseph Strange. Cologne, 1851.
Cassian, John. *Collationes.* Edited by Eugène Pichery. SC 54. Paris: Cerf, 1958.
Cicero, Marcus Tullius. *Laelius de amicitia.* Edited and translated by J. G. F. Powell. Warminster: Aris & Phillips, 1990.
Corrozet, Gilles. *La fleur des antiquitez de la noble et triumphale ville et cité de Paris.* Paris, 1532; repr. Paris, 1874.
Donne, John. *Selected Poetry.* Edited by John Carey. Oxford: Oxford University Press, 1996.
de Breul, Jacques. *Le théatre des antiquez de Paris.* Paris, 1639.
The Durham "Liber vitae": London, British Library, MS Cotton Domitian A.VII. Edited by David and Lynda Rollason. London: British Library, 2007.
Epictetus. *Discourses: Book I.* Edited and translated by R. F. Dobbin. Oxford: Clarendon Press, 1998.
———. *Epictetus: The Discourses as reported by Arrian, the Manual, and Fragments.* Translated by William Abbott Oldfather. 2 vols. Cambridge, Mass.: Harvard University Press, 1928; repr. 1959.

Félibien, Michel. *Histoire de la ville de Paris*. Revised and expanded by G. A. Lobineau. 5 vols. Paris, 1725, abridged ed., 1735.

Gerald of Wales. *Symbolum electorum*. In *Giraldi Cambrensis Opera*, vol. 1, edited by J. S. Brewer. Rerum Britannicarum medii aevi scriptores 21. London: Longman, Green, Longman and Roberts, 1861.

Gertrude of Helfta, et al. *The Herald of God's Loving-Kindness*. Translated by Alexandra Barratt. 2 vols. Kalamazoo, Mich.: Cistercian Publications, 1991, 1999.

———. *Legatus divinae pietatis*. In *Oeuvres spirituelles*, edited by Pierre Doyère et al. SC 139, 143, 255, 331. Paris: Cerf, 1968–86.

Gesta abbatum monasterii Sancti Albani. Edited by H. T. Riley. Rolls Series 28.4a. London, 1867.

Godfrey of St. Victor. *Fons philosophiae*. Edited by Pierre Michaud-Quantin. Analecta mediaevalia Namurcensia 8. Namur: Éditions Godenne, 1956.

———. *The Fountain of Philosophy: A Translation of the Twelfth-century "Fons philosophiae" of Godfrey of Saint Victor*. Translated by Edward Synan. Toronto: Pontifical Institute of Mediaeval Studies, 1972.

———. *Le Microcosmus de Godefroy de Saint-Victor*. Edited by Philippe Delhaye. Vol. 1, *Texte*. Vol. 2, *Étude théologique*. Mémoires et travaux 56–57. Lille: Facultés catholiques; Gembloux: Duculot, 1951.

———. "The *Preconium Augustini* of Godfrey of St. Victor." Edited by Philip Damon. *Mediaeval Studies* 22 (1960): 92–107.

Gregory the Great. *Homiliae in Ezechielem prophetam*. PL 76:785–1072.

Guerric of Igny. *Sermo in festo Sancti Benedicti*. PL 185:99–116.

Guibert of Nogent. *Autobiographie*. Edited and translated by Edmond-René Labande. Paris: Belles-Lettres, 1981.

———. *The Deeds of God through the Franks: A Translation of Guibert de Nogent's "Gesta Dei per Francos."* Translated by Robert Levine. Woodbridge: The Boydell Press, 1997.

———. *Gesta Dei per Francos*. Edited by R. B. C. Huygens. CCSL 77a. Turnhout: Brepols, 1996.

———. *Self and Society in Medieval France: The Memoirs of Abbot Guibert of Nogent*. Edited by J. F. Benton. New York: Harper, 1970.

Guigo II. *Scala claustralium*. Edited by Edmund Colledge and James Walsh. SC 163. Paris: Cerf, 1970.

Haimo of Auxerre. *Enarratio*. PL 117:9–294.

Hildebert of Lavardin. *Epistolae*. PL 171:141–312.

Hildegard of Bingen. *Epistolarium I. I–XC*. Edited by Lieven Van Acker. CCCM 91. Turnhout: Brepols, 1991.

———. *The Letters of Hildegard of Bingen*. Translated by Joseph L. Baird and Radd K. Ehrman. 3 vols. New York: Oxford University Press, 1994.

———. *Liber divinorum operum*. Edited by Albert Derolez and Peter Dronke. CCCM 92. Turnhout: Brepols, 1996.

———. *Liber vitae meritorum.* Edited by Angela Carlevaris. CCCM 90. Turnhout: Brepols, 1995.

———. *Scivias.* Edited by Adelgundis Führkötter and Angela Carlevaris. CCCM 43. Turnhout: Brepols, 1978.

———. *Scivias.* Translated by Columba Hart and Jane Bishop. New York: Paulist Press, 1990.

———. *Vita Hildegardis.* Edited by Monika Klaes. CCCM 126. Turnhout: Brepols, 1993.

Hugh of St. Victor. *Adnotatiunculae elucidatoriae in threnos Jeremiae.* PL 175: 255–322.

———. *De amore sponsi ad sponsam (Eulogium).* PL 176:987–994.

———. *De archa Noe.* [*Libellus de formatione arche.*] Edited by Patrice Sicard, CCCM 176. Turnhout: Brepols, 2001.

———. *De arrha animae.* In *L'oeuvre de Hugues de Saint-Victor I*, edited and translated by H. B. Feiss, P. Sicard, D. Poirel, and H. Rochais. Turnhout: Brepols, 1997.

———. *De fructibus carnis et spiritus.* PL 176:997–1009.

———. *De institutione novitiorum.* PL 176:925–52.

———. *De institutione novitiorum.* In *L'oeuvre de Hugues de Saint-Victor I.* Edited and translated by H. B. Feiss, P. Sicard, D. Poirel, and H. Rochais. Turnhout: Brepols, 1997.

———. *De meditatione.* In *Six opuscules spirituels*, edited and translated by Roger Baron, 44–59. SC 155. Paris: Cerf, 1969.

———. *De quatuor voluntatibus in Christo.* PL 176:841–46.

———. *De sacramentis christianae fidei.* PL 176:173–618.

———. *De sacramentis legis naturalis et scriptae.* PL 176:17–42.

———. *De scripturis et scriptoribus sacris praenotatiunculae.* PL 175:9–28.

———. *De tribus diebus.* Edited by Dominique Poirel. CCCM 177. Turnhout: Brepols, 2002.

———. *De unione spiritus et corporis.* In "Il *De unione spiritus et corporis* di Ugo di San Vittore." Edited by A. M. Piazzoni. *Studi Medievali*, 3a ser., 1 (1980): 861–88.

———. *De vanitate mundi.* PL 176:703–40.

———. *De vanitate mundi.* In *Hugo von St. Viktor, Soliloquium de arrha animae und De vanitate mundi*, edited by Karl Müller. Kleine Texte für Vorlesungen und Übungen 123. Bonn: Verlag, 1913.

———. *Descriptio mappe mundi.* In *La "Descriptio mappe mundi" de Hugues de Saint-Victor.* Edited by Patrick Gautier Dalché. Paris: Études Augustiniennes, 1988.

———. *Didascalicon de studio legendi.* Edited by C. H. Buttimer. Studies in Medieval and Renaissance Latin 10. Washington, D.C.: Catholic University of America Press, 1939.

———. *Didascalicon de studio legendi.* Edited by Thilo Offergeld. Fontes Christiani 27. Freiburg: Herder, 1997.

———. *The Didascalicon of Hugh of St. Victor: A Medieval Guide to the Arts.* Translated by Jerome Taylor. New York: Columbia University Press, 1961.

———. *Elucidationes Variae in Scripturam Moraliter = De eo Quod Spiritualis Dijudicat Omnia, et de Judicio Veri Et Boni = Miscellanea I.* PL 177:469–588.

———. "Hugh of Saint-Victor: 'De tribus maximis circumstanciis gestorum.'" Edited by William Green. *Speculum* 18 (1943): 484–93.

———. *Hugh of St. Victor: Selected Spiritual Writings.* Translated by a Religious of the Community of St. Mary the Virgin. London: Faber and Faber, 1962.

———. *In hierarchiam coelestem S. Dionysii.* PL 175:923–1154.

———. *In Salomonis Ecclesiasten homiliae.* PL 175: 113–256.

———. *L'oeuvre de Hugues de Saint-Victor I.* Edited and translated by H. B. Feiss, P. Sicard, D. Poirel, and H. Rochais. Turnhout: Brepols, 1997.

———. *On the Sacraments of the Christian Faith (De sacramentis).* Translated by R. J. Deferrari. Medieval Academy of America 58. Cambridge, Mass.: Crimson Printing Company, 1951.

———. *Pro Assumptione Virginis.* In *L'oeuvre de Hugues de Saint-Victor II.* Edited by Bernadette Jollès. Turnhout: Brepols, 2000.

———. *Soliloquy on the Earnest Money of the Soul.* Translated by Kevin Herbert. Milwaukee: Marquette Christianity Press, 1956.

———. *Super Canticum Mariae.* In *L'oeuvre de Hugues de Saint-Victor II.* Edited by Bernadette Jollès. Turnhout: Brepols, 2000.

———. *Super Ierarchiam beati Dionisii.* Edited by Dominique Poirel. CCCM 178. Turnhout: Brepols. Forthcoming.

Ibn Hazm of Cordoba. *The Ring of the Dove.* Translated by A. J. Arberry. London: Luzac, 1953.

Ivo of Chartres. *Epistolae (Correspondance).* Edited by Jean Leclercq. Classiques de l'Histoire de France au Moyen Âge 22. Paris: Les Belles Lettres, 1949.

Jacobus de Voragine. *The Golden Legend: Readings on the Saints.* Translated by William Granger Ryan. 2 vols. Princeton: Princeton University Press, 1993.

Jacques Lefévre d'Ètaples. *The Prefatory Epistles of Jacques Lefévre d'Etaples and Related Texts.* Edited by Eugene F. Rice. New York: Columbia University Press, 1972.

Jacques de Vitry. *Historia occidentalis.* Edited by John Frederick Hinnebusch. Spicilegium Friburgense 17. Fribourg: University Press, 1972.

Jerome. *Commentarii in Prophetas Minores.* Edited by M. Adriaen. CCSL 76–76A. Turnhout: Brepols, 1969.

———. *Commentariorum in Hezekielem libri XIV.* Edited by Franciscus Glorie. CCSL 75. Turnhout: Brepols, 1964.

John of Kelso (attr. to Adam the Scot). *De Tripartito Tabernaculo.* PL 198:609–792.

——— (attr. to Adam the Scot). *Sermones.* PL 198 97–440.

John of La Rochelle. *Summa de vitiis.* Edited by Odon Lottin in *Psychologie et morale aux XIIe et XIIIe siècles,* 2:67–72. Louvain: Abbaye de Mont César, 1948–60.

Joseph, Hermann. "Iubilus de Domino Nostro Iesu Christo." In *Analecta Hymnica Medii Aevi*, edited by Clemens Blume and G. M. Dreves, 55:543. Repr. New York: Johnson Reprint, 1961.
Justin Martyr. *Iustini Martyris Dialogus cum Tryphone*. Edited by Miroslav Marcovich. Berlin: Walter de Gruyter, 1997.
——. *Justin, Philosopher and Martyr: Apologies*. Edited by Denis Minns and Paul Parvis. Oxford: Oxford University Press, 2009.
Libellus de diversis ordinibus et professionibus qui sunt in aecclesia. Edited and translated by Giles Constable and Bernard Smith. Oxford: Clarendon Press, 1972.
Liber ordinis Sancti Victoris Parisiensis. Edited by Lucas Jocqué and Ludovicus Milis. CCCM 61. Turnhout: Brepols, 1984.
Ludus de Antichristo. Edited by Gisela Vollmann-Profe. Litterae 82. Göppingen: Kümmerle Verlag, 1981.
Maimonides. *Maimonides Commentarius in Mischnam E Codicibus Hunt 117 et Pococke 295 in biblioteca Bodleiana Oxoniensis servatis et 72–73 Bibliotecae Sassooniensis, Letchworth*. Edited by Rafael Edelmann. Corpus Codicum Hebraicorum Medii Aevi 1–3. Haifa: E. Munkesgaard, 1966.
Marot, Jean. *L'architecture françoise, ou, Recueil des plans, élévations, coupes et profils des églises*. Paris, 1727.
Mechthild of Hackeborn, Gertrude of Helfta, et al. *Liber specialis gratiae*. In *Revelationes Gertrudianae ac Mechtildianae*, edited by the monks of Solesmes, vol. 2. Paris and Poitiers, 1877.
Mechthild of Magdeburg. *The Flowing Light of the Godhead*. Translated by Frank Tobin. New York: Paulist Press, 1998.
Des Minnesangs Frühling. Edited by Carl von Kraus et al. Leipzig: Hirzel, 1940.
Mérian, Gaspar. *Topographia Galliae*. 13 vols. Frankfurt, 1655; repr. as *Paris et l'Ile-de-France*, edited by M. V. Paris, 1986.
Midrash Rabbah. Translated by Harry Freedman and Maurice Simon. Vol. 9. London: Soncino, 1939.
Monuments historiques: Archives de l'Empire, Inventaire et documents. Edited by Jules Tardif. Paris, 1866.
The Old French Crusade Cycle, vol. 6, *La Chanson de Jerusalem*. Edited by N. R. Thorp. Tuscaloosa: University of Alabama Press, 1992.
Les Ordines Romani de Haut Moyen Âge. 5 vols. Edited by Michel Andrieu. Spicilegium Sacrum Lovaniense, Études et documents 28. Louvain: Spicilegium Sacrum Lovaniense, 1985.
Papsturkunden in Frankreich, Neue Folge, 9 Band, Diözese Paris II. Edited by Rolf Grosse. Abhandlungen der Akademie der Wissenschaften in Göttingen, Philologisch-Historische Klasse, Dritte Folge 225. Göttingen: Weidmannsche Buchhandlung, 1998.
Peter Abelard. *Historia calamitatum*. Edited by Jacques Monfrin. Paris: Vrin, 1959.
Peter Comestor. *Historia scholastica*. PL 198:1053–1722.

Peter Lombard. *Sententiae in IV Libris Distinctae*. Edited by I. F. Brady. Grottaferrata: Editiones Collegii S. Bonaventurae Ad Claras Aquas, 1971.
Philip the Chancellor. *Summa de bono*. Edited by Nikolaus Wicki. Bern: Francke Verlag, 1985.
Pinto, Hector. *Hieronymiani in Ezechielem prophetam commentaria*. Antwerp: P. Bellerus, 1582.
The Play of Antichrist. Translated by John Wright. Toronto: Pontifical Institute of Mediaeval Studies, 1967.
Plotinus. *Plotinus: Enneades*. In *Plotini opera*, edited by Paul Henry and Hans-Rudolf Schwyzer. Paris: Desclée de Brouwer, 1951–73.
———. *Plotinus: Enneads*. Translated by Arthur Hilary Armstrong. Loeb Classical Library, 7 vols. Cambridge, Mass.: Harvard University Press, 1966–1988.
Porphyry. *Porphyre: De l'abstinence*. Edited and translated by Jean Bouffartigue and Michel Patillon. 2 vols. Paris: Les Belles Lettres, 1977 and 1979.
———. *Select Works of Porphyry: Containing His Four Books On Abstinence from Animal Food; His Treatise On the Homeric Cave of the Nymphs; and His Auxiliaries to the Perception of Intelligible Natures*. Translated by Thomas Taylor. London: T. Rodd, 1823; repr. Ann Arbor: University Microfilms, 1965.
Ps.-Dionysius the Areopagite. *Hierarchia caelestis*, trad. Johannes Scotus Eriugena. PL 175: 923–1154.
Ps.-Hugh of St Victor. *Expositio regulae S. Augustini*. PL 176:881–924.
Ps.-Richard of St Victor. *De gradibus charitatis*. PL 196:1195–1208.
Rashi. *The Complete Jewish Bible with Rashi Commentary*. Translated by A. J. Rosenberg. New York: Judaica Press, n.d. Available at http://www.chabad.org/library/bible_cdo/aid/63255/jewish/The-Bible-with-Rashi.htm.
Recueil des Historiens des Gaules et de la France. 24 vols. Paris: Palmel, 1869–1904.
Regesta Pontificum Romanorum. Edited by Philip Jaffé and Wilhelm Wattenbach. 2nd ed. Leipzig: Veit, 1885–88.
Registrum Anglie de libris doctorum et auctorum veterum. Edited by R. H. Rouse and M. A. Rouse. Latin text by R. A. B. Mynors. Corpus of British Medieval Library Catalogues 4. London: British Library, 1991.
Richard of St Victor. *Apprehendet messis*. Edited by J.-B. Hauréau, *Notices et extraits de quelques manuscrits latins de la Bibliothèque nationale*, 1.112–20. Paris: C. Klincksieck, 1890.
———. *De arca mystica* [*Benjamin major*]. In *Contemplatio: Philosophische Studien zum Traktat Benjamin Maior des Richard von St. Victor*, edited by Marc-Aeilko Aris. Fuldaer Studien 6. Frankfurt am Main: J. Knecht, 1996.
———. *De contemplatione* [*Benjamin major*]. PL 196:63–202.
———. *De differentia sacrificii Abrahae a sacrificio beatae Mariae Virginis*. PL 196:1043–60.
———. *De exterminatione mali et promotione boni*. PL 196:1073–1116.
———. *De missione Spiritus Sancti*. PL 196:1017–32.

———. *De Trinitate*. Edited by Jean Ribaillier. Textes Philosophiques du Moyen Age 6. Paris: Vrin, 1958; partially translated into English by Grover Zinn, in *The Twelve Patriarchs; the Mystical Ark; Book Three of the Trinity*, 371–97. New York: Paulist Press, 1979.

———. *Les Douze Patriarches*. Edited by Jean Châtillon and Monique Duchet-Suchaux. Paris: Cerf, 1997.

———. *In visionem Ezechielis*. PL 196:527–600.

———. *Liber exceptionum*. Edited by Jean Châtillon. Textes philosophiques du Moyen Age 5. Paris: Vrin, 1958.

———. *Mysticae adnotationes in Psalmos*. PL 196:265–404.

———. *The Mystical Ark* [*Benjamin major*]. In *The Twelve Patriarchs; the Mystical Ark; Book Three of the Trinity*, trans. Grover Zinn. New York: Paulist Press, 1979.

———. *Les quatre degrés de la violente charité*. In *Épître à Séverin sur la charité / Ives. Les quatre degrés de la violente charité / Richard de Saint-Victor*, edited by Gervais Dumeige. Texts Philosophiques du Moyen Age 3. Paris: Vrin, 1955.

———. *Sermones centum*. PL 177:899–1210.

———. *Sermons et opuscules spirituels inédits*. Edited by Jean Châtillon and W. J. Tulloch. Translated by Joseph Barthélemy. Paris: Desclée, De Brouwer, 1951.

———. *La Trinité*. Edited and translated by Gaston Salet. SC 63. Paris: Cerf. 1959.

Rupert of Deutz. *Commentariorum in Duodecim Prophetas*, PL 168:9–836.

———. *De glorificatione Trinitatis et processione sancti Spiritus*. PL 169:9–202.

———. *In Apocalypsim Joannis apostolic commentariorum*. PL 169:826–1214.

Seneca. *Consolatio ad Marciam*. In *Dialogorum libri duodecim*, edited by L. D. Reynolds. Oxford: Clarendon Press, 1977.

———. *De beata vita*. In *Dialogorum libri duodecim*, edited by L. D. Reynolds. Oxford: Clarendon Press, 1977.

———. *De beneficiis*. Edited by François Prechac. 2 vols. Paris: Les Belles Lettres, 1926–29.

———. *De brevitate vitae*. In *Dialogorum libri duodecim*, edited by L. D. Reynolds. Oxford: Clarendon Press, 1977.

———. *De clementia*. Edited by François-Régis Chaumartin. Paris: Les Belles Lettres, 2005.

———. *De ira*. In *Dialogorum libri duodecim*, edited by L. D. Reynolds. Oxford: Clarendon Press, 1977.

———. *De tranquillitate animi*. In *Dialogorum libri duodecim*, edited by L. D. Reynolds. Oxford: Clarendon Press, 1977.

———. *Epistulae morales*. Edited by L. D. Reynolds. 2 vols. Oxford: Clarendon Press, 1965.

Das "*St. Katharinentaler Schwesternbuch*": *Untersuchung, Edition, Kommentar*. Edited by Ruth Meyer. Tübingen: Niemeyer, 1995.

Der Stuttgarter Bilderpsalter Bibl. fol. 23 Württembergische Landesbibliothek. 2 vols. Stuttgart: E. Schreiber, 1968.

Suger. *De consecratione.* In *Abt Suger von Saint-Denis: Ausgewählte Schriften: Ordinatio, De consecratione, De administratione,* edited by Andreas Speer. Darmstadt: Wissenschaftliche Buchgesellschaft, 2005.

———. *Gesta Sugerii abbatis.* In *Abt Suger von Saint-Denis: Ausgewählte Schriften: Ordinatio, De consecratione, De administratione,* edited by Andreas Speer. Darmstadt: Wissenschaftliche Buchgesellschaft, 2005.

———. *Ordinatio.* In *Abt Suger von Saint-Denis: Ausgewählte Schriften: Ordinatio, De consecratione, De administratione,* edited by Andreas Speer. Darmstadt: Wissenschaftliche Buchgesellschaft, 2005.

———. *Sugerii Vita.* In *Oeuvres,* edited by Françoise Gasparri. 2 vols. Les Classiques de l'Histoire de France au Moyen Âge 41. Paris: Les Belles Lettres, 2001.

———. *Vita Ludovici Grossi Regis (Vie de Louis VI).* Edited and translated by Henri Waquet. Les Classiques de l'Histoire de France au Moyen Âge 11. Paris: Les Belles Lettres, 1964.

Tanhuma Bar Abba. *Midrash Tanhuma ha-kadum veha-yashan: `al Hamishah Humshe Torah.* Edited by Salomon Buber. Vilna, 1885.

The Targum of the Minor Prophets. Translated by Kevin J. Cathcart and Robert P. Gordon. The Aramaic Bible 14. Collegeville, Minn.: Liturgical Press, 1989.

Thomas Aquinas. *Commentarium in IV Sententiarum.* Edited by Pierre Mandonnet and Maria Fabianus Moos. 4 vols. Paris: Lethellieux, 1929.

———. *Quaestiones disputatae de veritate.* Edited by Raymundi Spiazzi. 2 vols. Turin: Marietti, 1953.

———. *Summa theologiae.* Blackfriars edition and translation. 61 vols. New York: McGraw-Hill, 1964–76.

Thomas of Cantimpré. *Life of Lutgard of Aywières.* Translated by Margot H. King and Barbara Newman. In *Thomas of Cantimpré: The Collected Saints' Lives,* edited by Barbara Newman, 207–96. Turnhout: Brepols, 2008.

———. *Vita Lutgardis Aquiriensis.* Edited by Godfrey Henschen. AASS 16 June, 3:187–209.

Thoulouse, Jean de. *Abrégé de la fondation de l'abbaye S. Victor lez Paris.* Paris, 1640.

Udalrici codex. In *Monumenta Bambergensia,* edited by Philip Jaffé, 1–469. Berlin: Weidmann, 1869.

Walter of St. Victor. *Contra quatuor labyrinthos Franciae.* Edited by Palémon Glorieux. *Archives d'histoire doctrinale et littéraire du moyen âge* 19 (1953): 187–335.

———. *Sermones ineditos triginta sex.* Edited by Jean Châtillon. CCCM 30. Turnhout: Brepols, 1975.

William of St. Thierry. *Responsio Abbatum (Suessione, 1132) auctore Willelmo Abbate Sancti Theoderici.* In *Saint-Thierry, une abbaye du VIe au XXe siècle, Actes du Colloque international d'histoire monastique Reims-Saint-Thierry, 11 au 14 octobre 1976,* edited by Michel Bur, 334–50. Saint-Thierry: Association des Amis de L'Abbaye de Saint-Thierry, 1979.

SECONDARY SOURCES

Alexander, J. J. G., and Elżbieta Temple. *Illuminated Manuscripts in Oxford College Libraries*. Oxford: Clarendon Press, 1985.
Angelici, Ruben. *Richard of St. Victor: On the Trinity; English Translation and Commentary*. Eugene, Ore.: Cascade Books, 2011.
Antin, Paul. "Les idées morales de S. Jérôme." *Mélanges de science religieuses* 14 (1957): 13550. Repr. in *Receuil sur saint Jérôme*, 327-43. Brussels: Latomus, 1968.
Arduini, Maria Lodovica. *Rupert von Deutz (1076–1129) und der "Status Christianitatis" seiner Zeit*. Cologne: Böhlau Verlag, 1987.
Aris, Marc-Aeilko. *Contemplatio: Philosophische Studien zum Traktat Benjamin Maior des Richard von St. Victor*. Fuldaer Studien 6. Frankfurt am Main: J. Knecht, 1996.
Backus, Irena. "John of Damascus, *De fide orthodoxa*: Translations by Burgundio (1153/54), Grosseteste (1235/40) and Lefèvre d'Etaples (1507)." *Journal of the Warburg and Courtauld Institutes* 49 (1986): 211–17.
Baron, Roger. "Hugonis de Sancto Victore *Epitome Dindimi in philosophiam*: Introduction, texte critique et notes." *Traditio* 11 (1955): 91–148.
———. *Science et sagesse chez Hugues de Saint-Victor*. Paris: Thèse, 1957.
———. "Le style de Hugues de Saint-Victor." In *Études sur Hugues de Saint-Victor*, edited by Roger Baron, 91–120. Bruges: Desclée, De Brouwer, 1963.
Barratt, Alexandra. "'The Woman Who Shares the King's Bed': The Innocent Eroticism of Gertrud the Great of Helfta." In *Intersections of Sexuality and the Divine in Medieval Culture: The Word Made Flesh*, edited by Susannah Chewning, 107–19. Aldershot: Ashgate, 2005.
Barroux, Robert. "L'Abbé Suger et la vassalité du Vexin en 1124." *Le Moyen Âge* 64 (1958): 1–26.
Bates, David. "Les chartes de confirmation et les pancartes normandes du règne de Guillaume le Conquerant." In *Pancartes monastiques des XIe et XIIe siècles, Table ronde organisée part l'ARTEM, 6 et 7 juillet 1994 Nancy*, edited by Michel Parisse, Pierre Pegeot, and B.-M. Tock, 95–109. Turnhout: Brepols, 1998.
Bautier, R.-H. "Les origines et les premiers développements de l'abbaye Saint-Victor de Paris." In *L'abbaye parisienne de Saint-Victor au moyen âge*, edited by Jean Longère, 23–52. Biblioteca Victorina 1. Turnhout: Brepols, 1991.
———. "Paris au temps d'Abélard." In *Abélard en son temps: Actes du Colloque international organisé à l'occasion du IXe centenaire de la naissance de Pierre Abélard (14–19 mai 1979)*, edited by Jean Jolivet, 21–77. Paris: Les Belles Lettres, 1981.
Baylor, Michael G. *Action and Person: Conscience in Late Scholasticism*. Leiden: Brill, 1977.
Beach, Alison I. *Women as Scribes: Book Production and Monastic Reform in Twelfth-Century Bavaria*. Cambridge: Cambridge University Press, 2004.
Béguillet, Edmé. *Description historique de Paris et de ses plus beaux monuments*. 3 vols. Paris, 1779–81.

Beit-Arié, Malachi. *Catalogue of the Hebrew Manuscripts in the Bodleian Library: Supplement of Addenda and Corrigenda to Vol. 1 (A. Neubauer's Catalogue).* Oxford: Clarendon Press, 1994.

Bénatouïl, Thomas. *Faire usage: La pratique du Stoïcisme.* Paris: Vrin, 2006.

Bennett, Judith. "'Lesbian-Like' and the Social History of Lesbianisms." *Journal of the History of Sexuality* 9 (2000): 1–24.

Bergmann, Martin S. "Psychoanalytic Observations on the Capacity to Love." In *Separation—Individuation: Essays in Honor of Margaret S. Mahler,* edited by John McDevitt and Calvin Settlage, 15–40. New York: International Universities Press, 1971.

Berndt, Rainer. *André de Saint-Victor († 1175), exégète et théologien.* Bibliotheca Victorina 2. Paris and Turnhout: Brepols, 1992.

———. "Bibliographie." In *Schrift, Schreiber, Schrenker: Studien zu Abtei Sankt Viktor in Paris,* edited by Rainer Berndt, 321–62. Corpus Victorinum, Instrumenta 1. Berlin: Akademie Verlag, 2005.

———. "'Im Angesicht Gottes': Zur Theologie der Vision bei Hildegard von Bingen." In *"Im Angesicht Gottes suche der Mensch sich selbst": Hildegard von Bingen (1098–1179),* edited by Rainer Berndt, 269–90. Berlin: Akademie Verlag, 2000.

Bernheim, Ernst. *Mittelalterliche Zeitanschauungen in ihrem Einfluss auf Politik und Geschichtsschreibung. 1. (einziger Teil): Die Zeitanschauungen. Die augustinischen Ideen. Antichrist und Friedensfürst. Regnum und Sacerdotium.* Tübingen: J. B. C. Mohr (Paul Siebeck), 1918.

Bertola, Ermenegildo. *Il problema della coscienza nella teologia morale monastica del XII secolo.* Padua: CEDAM, 1970.

Bignami-Odier, Jeanne. "Les Visions de Robert d'Uzès O.P. († 1296)." *Archivum Fratrum Praedicatorum* 25 (1955): 258–310.

Biver, Paul, and Marie-Louise Biver. *Abbayes, monastères, et couvents de Paris: Des origines à la fin du XVIIIe siècle.* Paris: Éditions d'histoire et d'art, 1970.

Bloch, Peter. "Eine Dialogdarstellung des frühen 12. Jahrhunderts." In *Festschrift Dr. h.c. Eduard Trautscholdt,* edited by Heinz Ladendorf, 54–62. Hamburg: E. Hauswedell, 1962.

Blomme, Robert. *La doctrine du péché dans les écoles théologiques de la première moitié du XIIe siècle.* Louvain: Publications Universitaires de Louvain, 1958.

Bobzien, Susanne. *Determinism and Freedom in Stoic Philosophy.* Oxford: Clarendon Press, 1998.

Bonnard, Fourier. *Histoire de l'abbaye royale et de l'ordre des chanoines réguliers de St-Victor de Paris.* 2 vols. Paris, 1904, 1907.

Borgonovo, Graziano. *Sinderesi e coscienza nel pensiero di San Tommaso d'Aquino: Contributi per un "ridimensionameno" della coscienza morale nella teologia contemporanea.* Fribourg: Éditions Universitaires, 1996.

Boussard, Jacques. *De la fin du siège de 885–886 à la mort de Philippe Auguste.* 2nd ed. Nouvelle histoire de Paris. Paris: Diffusion Hachette, 1997.

Bousset, Wilhelm. *The Antichrist Legend: A Chapter in Christian and Jewish Folklore.* London: Hutchinson and Co., 1896.
Brandon, Samuel George Frederick. *The Fall of Jerusalem and the Christian Church: A Study of the Effects of the Jewish Overthrow of A.D. 70 on Christianity.* London: Society for Promoting Christian Knowledge, 1951.
Brasington, Bruce C. "Crusader, Castration, Canon Law: Ivo of Chartres' Letter 135." *The Catholic Historical Review* 85 (1999): 367–82.
Brice, Germain. *Description de la ville de Paris et de tout ce qu'elle contient de plus remarquable.* 4 vols. Paris, 1684.
———. *Description de la ville de Paris et de toute ce qu'elle contient de plus remarquable, reproduction de la 9e edition (1725).* Edited by Pierre Codet. Centre de recherches d'histoire et de philologie de la IVe section de l'Ecole pratique des Hautes-Etudes V. Hautes Etudes médiévales et modernes 12. Paris: Minard; Geneva: Droz, 1971.
Bruce-Mitford, R. L. S. "The Art of the Codex Amiatinus." *Journal of the British Archaeological Association* 32 (1969): 1–32.
Bur, Michel. *Suger, Abbé de Saint-Denis, Regent de France.* Paris: Perrin, 1991.
———, ed. *Saint-Thierry, une abbaye du VIe au XXe siècle, Actes du Colloque international d'histoire monastique Reims-Saint-Thierry, 11 au 14 octobre 1976, 299–350.* Saint-Thierry: Association des Amis de L'Abbaye de Saint-Thierry, 1979.
Burnaby, John. *Amor Dei: A Study of the Religion of St. Augustine.* London: Hodder & Stoughton, 1938.
Buschhausen, Helmut. "The Klosterneuburg Altar of Nicholas of Verdun: Art, Theology and Politics." *Journal of the Warburg and Courtauld Institutes* 37 (1974): 1–32.
Busson, Didier. *Carte archéologique de la Gaule 75: Paris.* Paris: Académie des Inscriptions et Belles-Lettres, 1998.
Byers, Sara. "Augustine on the 'Divided Self': Platonist or Stoic?" *Augustinian Studies* 38 (2007): 105–18.
Bynum, Caroline Walker. *Docere Verbo et Exemplo: An Aspect of Twelfth-Century Spirituality.* Harvard Theological Studies 31. Missoula, Mont.: Scholars Press, 1979.
———. *Jesus as Mother: Studies in the Spirituality of the High Middle Ages.* Berkeley: University of California Press, 1981.
———. "'. . . And Woman His Humanity': Gender Imagery in the Religious Writing of The Later Middle Ages." In *Gender and Religion: On the Complexity of Symbols*, edited by Caroline Bynum et al., 257–88. Boston: Beacon Press, 1986.
———. *Holy Feast and Holy Fast: The Religious Significance of Food to Medieval Women.* Berkeley: University of California Press, 1987.
Cabassut, André. "Coeurs, changement des." In *Dictionnaire de spiritualité ascétique et mystique, doctrine et histoire*, edited by Marcel Viller, 2.2:1046–51. Paris, 1932–95.

Cacciapuoti, Pierluigi. *"Deus existentia amoris": Teologia della carità e teologia della Trinità negli scritti di Riccardo di San Vittore († 1173)*. Turnhout: Brepols, 1998.

Cahn, Walter. "Architectural Draughtmanship in Twelfth-Century Paris: The Illustrations of Richard of Saint-Victor's Commentary on Ezekiel's Temple Vision." *Gesta: The International Center for Medieval Art* 15 (1976): 247–54.

———. "Architecture and Exegesis: Richard of Saint-Victor's Ezekiel Commentary and Its Illustrations." *Art Bulletin* 76 (1994): 53–68, repr. in idem, *Studies in Medieval Art and Interpretation*, London: Pindar Press, 2000, 369–406.

———. "Notes on the Illustrations of Ezekiel's Temple Vision in the *Postilla litteralis* of Nicholas of Lyra." In *Between Judaism and Christianity: Art Historical Essays in Honor of Elisheva (Elizabeth) Revel-Neher*, edited by Katrine Kogman-Appel and Mati Meyer, 155–67. Leiden: Brill, 2009.

———. *Romanesque Bible Illumination*. Ithaca: Cornell University Press, 1982.

———. *Romanesque Manuscripts. The Twelfth Century. A Survey of Manuscripts Illuminated in France*. London: Harvey Miller, 1996.

Cameron, Richard M. "The Attack on the Biblical Work of Lefèvre d'Étaples 1514–1521." *Church History* 38, no. 1 (1969): 9–24.

———. "The Charges of Lutheranism Brought against Jacques Lefèvre d'Etaples (1520–1529)." *The Harvard Theological Review* 63, no. 1 (1970): 119–49.

Carley, K.W. *The Book of the Prophet Ezekiel*. Cambridge: Cambridge University Press, 1974.

Carron, Delphine. "Sénèque, exemplarité ambiguë et ambiguïté exemplaire (IVe–XIVe siècle)." In *Exempla docent: Les exemples des philosophes de l'Antiquité à la Renaissance*, edited by Thomas Ricklin et al., 307–33. Paris: Vrin, 2006.

Carruthers, Mary. *The Book of Memory: A Study of Memory in Medieval Culture*. Cambridge: Cambridge University Press, 1990.

———. "Moving Images in the Mind's Eye." In *The Mind's Eye: Art and Theological Argument in the Middle Ages*, edited by J. F. Hamburger and A.-M. Bouché, 287–305. Princeton: Princeton University Press, 2006.

———. "'Pictures' of Jerusalem in Oxford, Bodleian Library, MS Laud Misc. 156." In *Imagining Jerusalem in the Medieval West*, edited by Lucy Donkin and Hanna Vorholt. London: The British Academy, 2012.

Casagrande, Carla, and Silvana Vecchio. *Les péches de la langue: Discipline et éthique de la parole dans la culture médiévale*. Paris: Cerf, 1991.

Cavalcoli, Giovanni. "Autoscienza e coscienza morale in S. Tommaso d'Aquino." In *Coscienza: Storia e percorsi di un concetto*, edited by Luca Gabbi and Vittor Ugo Petruio, 45–72. Rome: Donizelli Editore, 2000.

Ceglar, Stanislaus. "The Chapter of Soissons and the Authorship of the Reply to the Benedictine Abbots to Cardinal Matthew." In *Studies in Medieval Cistercian history II*, edited by J. R. Sommerfeldt, 92–105. Cistercian Studies Series 24. Kalamazoo, Mich.: Cistercian Publications, 1976.

———. "Guillaume de Saint-Thierry et son rôle directeur aux premiers Chapitres des abbés bénédictins, Reims 1131 et Soissons 1132 (avec l'édition des 'Acta primi capituli provincialis ordinis S. Benedicti Remis A.D. 1131 habiti')." In *Saint-Thierry, une abbaye du VIe au XXe siècle*, Actes du Colloque international d'histoire monastique Reims-Saint-Thierry, 11 au 14 octobre 1976, edited by Michel Bur, 299–350. Saint-Thierry: Association des Amis de L'Abbaye de Saint-Thierry, 1979.

Chadwick, Henry. *Boethius: The Consolations of Music, Logic, Theology and Philosophy*. Oxford: Clarendon Press, 1981.

Chase, Steven. *Contemplation and Compassion: The Victorine Tradition*. Maryknoll, NY: Orbis Books, 2003.

Châtillon, Jean. "Le contenu, l'authenticité et la date du *Liber exceptionum* et des *Sermones centum* de Richard de Saint-Victor." *Revue du Moyen Âge latin* 4 (1948): 23–52, 343–66.

———. "Une ecclésiologie médiévale." *Irénikon* 22 (1949) 115–38, 395–411, repr. in Jean Châtillon, *Le mouvement canonial au moyen age: réforme de l'église, spiritualité et culture*, ed. Patrice Sicard, Bibliotheca Victorina 3. Turnhout: Brepols, 1992.

———. "Richard de Saint-Victor." In *Dictionnaire de spiritualité*, edited by Marcel Viller, 13:616–17. Paris: G. Beauchesne, 1992.

———. "Sermons et prédicateurs victorins de la seconde moitié du xiie siècle." *Archives d'histoire doctrinale et littéraire du moyen âge* 32 (1965): 7–60.

———. "La transmission de l'oeuvre de Hugues de Saint-Victor: A propos d'un livre récent de Rudolf Goy." *Mittellateinisches Jahrbuch* 15 (1980): 57–62.

———, ed. *Trois opuscules spirituels de Richard de Saint-Victor*. Paris: Études Augustiniennes, 1986.

Châtillon, Jean, and W.-J. Tulloch, eds. *Sermons et opuscules spirituels inédits*. Translated by Joseph Barthélemy. Paris: Desclée, De Brouwer, 1951.

Chaurand, Jacques. "La conception de l'histoire de Guibert de Nogent." *Cahiers de civilization médiévale* 8 (1965): 381–95.

———. *Thomas de Marle, Sire de Coucy, Sire de Marle, Seigneur de La Fère, Vervins, Boves, Pinon et autres lieux*. Vervins: La Tribune de la Thierache, 1963.

Chenu, Marie-Dominique. *L'Éveil de la conscience dans la civilisation médiévale*. Montréal: Institut d'Études Médiévales, 1969.

Christe, Yves. "À propos de l'*Apologia* de Saint Bernard: Dans quelle mésure Suger a-t-il tenu compte de la reforme cistercienne." *Genava*, n.s. 14 (1966): 5–11.

———. *Églises parisiennes actuelles et disparues*. Paris: Éditions Tel, 1947.

Clanchy, M. T. "The Letters of Abelard and Heloise in Today's Scholarship." In *The Letters of Abelard and Heloise*, translated by Betty Radice, lxxv–lxxxi. Rev. ed. London: Penguin, 2003.

Clark, Anne L. *Elisabeth of Schönau: A Twelfth-Century Visionary*. Philadelphia: University of Pennsylvania Press, 1992.

———. "Holy Woman or Unworthy Vessel? The Representations of Elisabeth of Schönau." In *Gendered Voices: Medieval Saints and Their Interpreters*, edited by Catherine M. Mooney, 35–51. Philadelphia: University of Pennsylvania Press, 1999.

Clark, William. "Context, Continuity, and the Creation of National Memory in Paris, 1130–1160: A Critical Commentary." *Gesta* 45 (2006): 161–75.

Clemens, Raymond. "The Pope's Shrunken Head: The Apocalyptic Visions of Robert of Uzès." In *History in the Comic Mode: Medieval Communities and the Matter of Person*, edited by Rachel Fulton and Bruce Holsinger, 36–44. New York: Columbia University Press, 2007.

Coakley, John W. *Women, Men, and Spiritual Power: Female Saints and their Male Collaborators*. New York: Columbia University Press, 2006.

Cohen, Jeremy. *Living Letters of the Law: Ideas of the Jew in Medieval Christianity*. The Mark S. Taper Foundation Imprint in Jewish Studies. Berkeley: University of California Press, 1999.

Colish, Marcia L. *Ambrose's Patriarchs: Ethics for the Common Man*. Notre Dame, Ind.: University of Notre Dame Press, 2005.

———. *Peter Lombard*. 2 vols. Leiden: Brill, 1994.

———. "Stoicism and the New Testament: An Essay in Historiography." In *Aufstieg und Niedergang der römischen Welt*, edited by Wolfgang Haase and Hildegard Temporini, II/26/1: 334–79. Berlin: Walter de Gruyter, 1992.

———. *The Stoic Tradition from Antiquity to the Early Middle Ages*. 2nd ed. 2 vols. Leiden: Brill, 1990.

Collin, Hubert, et al. *Champagne romane*. La Pierre-qui-Vire: Zodiaque, 1981.

Combes, André. *Essai sur la critique de Ruysbroeck par Gerson*. 4 vols. Paris: Vrin, 1945–72.

Constable, Giles. "The Authorship of the *Epistolae duorum amantium*: A Reconsideration." In *Voices in Dialogue: Reading Women in the Middle Ages*, edited by Kathryn Kerby-Fulton and Linda Olson, 167–78. Notre Dame, Ind.: University of Notre Dame Press, 2005.

———. *The Reformation of the Twelfth Century*. Cambridge: Cambridge University Press, 1996.

———. "Suger's Monastic Administration." In *Abbot Suger and Saint-Denis: A Symposium*, ed. P. L. Gerson, 17–32. New York: Metropolitan Museum, 1986.

Cooke, G. A. *The Book of Ezekiel. A Critical and Exegetical Commentary*. Edinburgh: T & T Clark, 1985.

Coolman, Boyd Taylor. "*Pulchrum Esse*: The Beauty of Scripture, the Beauty of the Soul, and the Art of Exegesis in the Theology of Hugh of St. Victor." *Traditio* 58 (2003): 175–200.

Coolman, Boyd Taylor, and Dale M. Coulter, eds. *Trinity and Creation: A Selection of Works of Hugh, Richard, and Adam of St Victor*. Victorine Texts in Translation 1. Turnhout: Brepols, 2010.

Corsano, Karen. "The First Quire of the Codex Amiatinus and the *Institutiones* of Cassiodorus." *Scriptorium* 41 (1987): 3–34.
Coulter, Dale. *Per visibilia ad invisibilia: Theological Method in Richard of St Victor (d. 1173)*. Turnhout: Brepols, 2006.
Courcelle, Pierre. *Connais-toi toi-même de Socrate à saint Bernard*. 3 vols. Paris: Études Augustiniennes, 1974–75.
———. "La culture antique d'Absalon de Saint-Victor." *Journal des savants* (1972–73): 270–91.
Coyecque, Ernest, and Henry Debraye. *Catalogue général des manuscrits des bibliothèques publiques de France. Paris: Chambre des Députés*. Paris, 1907.
Crosby, Sumner. *The Royal Abbey of Saint-Denis from Its Beginnings to the Death of Suger, 475–1151*. Edited by Pamela Blum. New Haven: Yale University Press, 1987.
Cunningham, Stanley B. *Reclaiming Moral Agency: The Moral Philosophy of Albert the Great*. Washington, D.C.: Catholic University of America Press, 2008.
D'Amico, John F. *Theory and Practice in Renaissance Textual Criticism: Beatus Rhenanus Between Conjecture and History*. Berkeley: University of California Press, 1988.
Dahan, Gilbert. "Juifs et Chrétiens en occident medieval: La rencontre autour de la Bible (XIIe–XIVe siècle)." *Revue de synthèse*, 4 sér. 110 (1989): 3–31.
d'Alverny, Marie-Thérèse, ed. *Bibliothèque nationale, fonds latin: Catalogue des manuscrits en écriture latine portant des indications de date, de lieu ou de copiste*. Vol. 3, edited by Charles Samaran and Robert Marichal. Paris: Centre national de la recherche scientifique, 1974.
De Bruyne, Edgar. *Études d'esthétique médiévale*. 3 vols. Bruges: De Tempel, 1946.
De Hamel, C. F. R. *Glossed Books of the Bible and the Origins of the Paris Booktrade*. Woodbridge: D. S. Brewer, 1984.
———. *A History of Illuminated Manuscripts*. 2nd ed. London: Phaidon, 1994.
Delano-Smith, Catherine. "The Exegetical Jerusalem: Maps and Plans for Ezekiel Chapters 40–48." In *Imagining Jerusalem in the Medieval West*, edited by Lucy Donkin and Hanna Vorholt. London: The British Academy, 2012.
———. "Maps as Art *and* Science: Maps in Sixteenth Century Bibles." *Imago Mundi* 42 (1990): 65–83.
———. "Redesigning the Medieval Exegetical Map: The Desert Encampment and Ezekiel's Canaan in the Sixteenth Century." Forthcoming.
———. "Smoothed Lines and Empty Spaces: The Changing Face of the Exegetical Map before 1600." In *Combler les blancs de la carte: Modalités et enjeux de la construction des savoirs géographiques (xvii–viii siècle)*, edited by Isabelle Laboulais-Lesage, 17–34. Strasbourg: Presses Universitaires de Strasbourg, 2004.
———. "To Whom the Map Speaks: Recognising the Reader." In *Mappae Antiquae: Liber Amicorum Günter Schilder*, edited by Paula van Gestel-van het Schip and P. C. J. van den Krogt, 627–37. 't goy-Houten: Hes & De Graaf, 2007.

Delano-Smith, Catherine, and Mayer Gruber. "Rashi's Legacy: Maps of the Holy Land." *The Map Collector* 59 (1972): 30–35.

Delano-Smith, Catherine, and E. M. Ingram. *Maps in Bibles 1500–1600: An Illustrated Catalogue*. Geneva: Droz, 1991.

Delhaye, Philippe. *Christian Conscience*. Translated by Charles Underhill Quinn. New York: Desclée, 1968.

——. "Les sermons de Godefroy de Saint-Victor." RTAM 21 (1954) 194–210.

Delisle, Léopold. "Inventaire des manuscrits latins de Saint-Victor. BEC 30 (1869): 1–79.

de Lubac, Henri. *Exégèse médiévale: Les quatres sens de l'Écriture*. 4 vols. Paris: Aubier, 1959–64.

Dijon, Christian T. "La syndérèse selon Albert le Grand." In *Albertus Magnus: Zum Gedanken nach 800 Jahren; Neue Zugänge, Aspekte und Perspektiven*, edited by Walter Senner et al., 255–73. Berlin: Akademie Verlag, 2001.

Dinshaw, Carolyn. "Reading Like a Man: The Critics, the Narrator, Troilus, and Pandarus." In *Chaucer's Sexual Poetics*, 28-64. Madison: University of Wisconsin Press, 1989.

Diringer, David. *The Illuminated Book: Its History and Production*. London: Faber & Faber, 1958.

Dobson, C. A. *Maurice of Sully and the Medieval Vernacular Homily*. Oxford: Blackwell, 1952.

Dougherty, Michael V., et al. "40 Cases of Plagiarism." *Bulletin de philosophie médiévale* 51 (2009): 350–91.

Dove, Mary, ed. *Glossa Ordinaria Pars 22 In Canticum Canticorum*. CCCM 170. Turnhout: Brepols, 1997.

Dronke, Peter. "Arbor caritatis." In *Medieval Studies for J. A. W. Bennett: Aetatis suae LXX*, edited by P. L. Heyworth, 221–32. Oxford: Clarendon Press, 1981.

——. *Women Writers of the Middle Ages: A Critical Study of Texts from Perpetua († 203) to Marguerite Porete († 1310)*. Cambridge: Cambridge University Press, 1984.

Dufour, Jean, ed. *Recueil des actes de Louis VI, roi de France (1108–1137)*. 4 vols. Paris: Académie des Inscriptions et Belles-Lettres, 1992.

Duval, Noël, et al. "Paris." In *Topographie chrétienne des cités de la Gaule des origines au milieu du VIIIe siècle*, edited by Nancy Gauthier and J.-C. Picard, vol. 8, *Province ecclesiastique de Sens (Dugdunensis Senonia)*, 97–129. Paris: De Boccard, 1992.

Eco, Umberto. *Art and Beauty in the Middle Ages*. New Haven: Yale University Press, 1986.

Edwards, Catharine. "Self-Scrutiny and Self-Transcendence in Seneca's Letters." *Greece and Rome* 44 (1997): 23–38.

Ehlers, Joachim. "Arca significat ecclesiam: Ein theologisches Weltmodell aus den ersten Hälfte des 12. Jahrhunderts." *Frühmittelalterliche Studien* 6 (1972): 171–87.

Elliott, Dyan. *Proving Woman: Female Spirituality and Inquisitional Culture in the Later Middle Ages*. Princeton: Princeton University Press, 2004.

———. "Seeing Double: John Gerson, the Discernment of Spirits, and Joan of Arc." *American Historical Review* 107 (2002): 26–54

Embach, Michael. *Die Schriften Hildegards von Bingen: Studien zu ihrer Überlieferung und Rezeption im Mittelalter und in der Frühen Neuzeit*. Erudiri Sapientia 4. Berlin: Akademie Verlag, 2003.

Engberg-Pederson, Troels. *Paul and the Stoics*. Edinburgh: T & T Clark, 2000.

Erlande-Brandenburg, Alain. "Le grand dessein de Maurice de Sully." In *Notre-Dame de Paris: Un manifeste chrétien (1160–1230)*, edited by Michel Lemoine, 71–92. Rencontres médiévales européennes 4. Turnhout: Brepols, 2004.

Esmeijer, A. C. *Divina Quaternitas: A Preliminary Study in the Method and Application of Visual Exegesis*. Amsterdam: Van Gorcum, 1978.

Evans, M.W. "Fictive Painting in Twelfth-Century Paris." In *Sight and Insight: Essays in Art and Culture in Honour of E. H. Gombrich at 85*, edited by John Onians, 73–87. London: Phaidon Press, 1994.

Finnegan, Mary Jeremy. *The Women of Helfta: Scholars and Mystics*. Athens: University of Georgia Press, 1991.

Fish, Stanley. *Is There a Text in This Class? The Authority of Interpretive Communities*. Cambridge, Mass.: Harvard University Press, 1980.

Flanagan, Sabina. *Hildegard of Bingen: A Visionary Life*. 2nd ed. London: Routledge, 1998.

Fleury, Michel. "Communication sur les fouilles à l'émplacement de l'abbaye de Saint-Victor (5e)," séance du 1 avril 1968. In *Procès-verbaux de la Commission du vieux Paris*, 34–36. Paris, 1968–69.

Foley, Edward. *The First Ordinary of the Royal Abbey of St.-Denis in France, Paris, Bibliothèque Mazarine 526*. Spicilegium Friburgense 32. Fribourg: University Press, 1990.

Franklin, Alfred. *Les anciennes bibliothèques de Paris*. 3 vols. Paris: Imprimerie impériale, 1867.

Führer, Julian. "Suger et Bernard de Clairvaux." In *Suger en Question: Regards croisés sur Saint-Denis*, edited by Rolf Grosse, 81–93. Pariser Historische Studien 62. Munich: Oldenbourg, 2004.

Fulton, Rachel. *From Judgment to Passion: Devotion to Christ and the Virgin Mary, 800–1200*. New York: Columbia University Press, 2002.

———. "Three-in-One: Making God in Twelfth-Century Liturgy, Theology and Devotion." In *European Transformations: The Long Twelfth Century*, edited by Thomas F. X. Noble and John Van Engen, 468–98. Notre Dame, Ind.: University of Notre Dame Press, 2012.

Fussell, Paul. *The Great War and Modern Memory*. London: Oxford University Press, 1975.

Gardner, Stephen. "L'église Saint-Julien de Marolles-en-Brie et ses rapports avec l'architecture parisienne de la generation de Saint-Denis." *Bulletin monumental* 144 (1986): 7–31.

Gasparri, Françoise. "L'abbé Suger de Saint-Denis et la papauté." In *Suger en Question: Regards croisés sur Saint-Denis*, edited by Rolf Grosse, 69–80. Pariser Historische Studien 62. Munich: Oldenbourg, 2004.

———. *L'écriture des Actes de Louis VI, Louis VII et Philippe Auguste*. Centre de Recherche d'Histoire et de Philologie de la IVe section d'École pratique des Hautes Études 5, Hautes etudes médiévales et modernes 20. Geneva: Droz, 1973.

———. "Godefroid de Saint-Victor: Une personnalité peu connue du monde intellectuel et artistique parisien au xiie siècle." *Scriptorium* 39 (1985): 57–69.

———. "Philosophie et cosmologie: Godefroid de Saint-Victor." In *Notre-Dame de Paris: Un manifeste chrétien (1160–1230)*, edited by Michel Lemoine, 119–144. Rencontres médiévales européennes 4. Turnhout: Brepols, 2004.

Gautier Dalché, Patrick, ed. *La "Descriptio mappe mundi" de Hugues de Saint-Victor*. Paris: Études Augustiniennes, 1988.

Gaydon, A. T., et al., eds. *A History of the County of Shropshire*. Vol. 2. Victoria County History. London: Archibald Constable, 1973.

Ghisalberti, Alessandro. "Figure della coscienza nel pensiero medievale: Abelardo, Tommaso d'Aquino, Meister Eckhart." In *Coscienza: Storia e percorsi di un concetto*, edited by Luca Gabbi and Vittor Ugo Petruio, 29–43. Rome: Donizelli Editore, 2000.

Gill, Christopher. "Panaetius on the Virtue of Being Yourself." In *Images and Ideologies: Self-Definition in the Hellenistic World*, edited by Anthony Bullock, et al., 344–52. Berkeley: University of California Press, 1993.

———. *Personality in Greek Epic, Tragedy, and Philosophy: The Self in Dialogue*. Oxford: Clarendon Press, 1996.

———. *The Structured Self in Hellenistic and Roman Thought*. Oxford: Oxford University Press, 2006.

Giraud, Cédric, and Patricia Stirnemann. "Le rayonnement de l'école de Saint-Victor: Manuscrits de la Bibliothèque Mazarine." In *L'école de Saint-Victor. Influence et rayonnement du Moyen Âge à l'époque moderne*, edited by Dominique Poirel. Bibliotheca Victorina 22. Turnhout: Brepols, 2010.

Glorieux, Palémon. "Mauvaise action et mauvais travail: Le *Contra quatuor labyrinthos Franciae*." RTAM 21 (1954): 179–93.

Glunz, H. H. *History of the Vulgate in England*. Cambridge: Cambridge University Press, 1933.

Gorman, Michael. "The Diagrams in the Oldest Manuscripts of Cassiodorus' *Institutiones*." *Revue Bénédictine* 110 (2000): 27–41.

Gould, Josiah B. *The Philosophy of Chrysippus*. Albany: State University of New York Press, 1970.

Gow, Andrew Colin. *The Red Jews: Antisemitism in an Apocalyptic Age, 1200–1600.* Studies in Medieval and Reformation Thought 55. Leiden: E. J. Brill, 1995.

Goy, Rudolf. *Die handschriftliche Überlieferung der Werke Richards von St. Viktor im Mittelalter.* Bibliotheca Victorina 18. Turnhout: Brepols, 2005.

———. *Die Überlieferung der Werke Hugos von St. Viktor. Ein Beitrag zur Kommunikationsgeschichte des Mittelalters.* Monographien zur Geschichte des Mittelalters 14. Stuttgart: Hiersemann, 1976.

Grabois, Aryeh. "Le Schisme de 1130 et la France." *Revue d'Histoire Ecclésiastique Louvain* 76 (1981): 593–612.

Granboulan, Anne. "De la paroisse à la cathédrale: Une approche renouvelée du vitrail roman dans l'Ouest." *Revue de l'art* 103 (1994): 42–52.

Grant, Lindy. *Abbot Suger of St-Denis, Church and State in Early Twelfth-Century France.* London: Longman, 1998.

Green, Arthur. "The Song of Songs in Early Jewish Mysticism." *Orim* 2 (1987): 48–63. Repr. in *Modern Critical Interpretation: The Song of Songs*, edited by Harold Bloom, 141–53. New York: Chelsea House Publishers, 1988.

Green, William. "Hugh of Saint-Victor 'De tribus maximis circumstanciis gestorum.'" *Speculum* 18 (1943): 484–93.

Grimault, A. "Compte-rendu de la visite effectuée aux fouilles de la place Jussieu," séance du 9 mai 1931. In *Procès-verbaux de la Commission du vieux Paris*, 87–93. Paris, 1931.

———. "Rapport présenté sur les fouilles effectuées place Jussieu," séance du 28 fevrier 1931. In *Procès-verbaux de la Commission du vieux Paris*, 64–68. Paris, 1931.

Grosse, Rolf. "Remarques sur les cartulaires de Saint-Denis aux XIIIe et XIVe siècles." In *Les Cartulaires, Actes de la Table ronde organisée par l'École nationale des chartes et le G.D.R. 121 du C.N.R.S. (Paris, 5–7 décembre 1991)*, edited by Olivier Guyotjeanin, Laurent Morelle, and Michel Parisse, 279–89. Paris: École des chartes, 1993.

———. "Saint-Denis und das Papsttum zur Zeit des Abtes Suger." In *L'Eglise de France et la Papauté (Xe–XIIIe Siecle)*, edited by Rolf Grosse, 219–38. Études et documents pour servir à une Gallia Pontificia 1. Bonn: Bouvier, 1993.

Gruber, M. I. "Light on Rashi's Diagrams from the Asher Library of Spertus College of Judaica." In *The Solomon Goldman Lectures*, vol. 4, edited by Nathaniel Stampfer, 73–85. Chicago: The Spertus College of Judaica Press, 1993.

———. "The Sources of Rashi's Cartography." In *Letters and Texts of Jewish History*, edited by Norman Simms, 61–67. Hamilton, New Zealand: Outrigger Publications, 1998.

———. "What Happened to Rashi's Pictures?" *Bodleian Library Record* 14 (1992): 111–24.

Gsodam, Gertrude. "Welt, Fürst der Welt, Frau Welt." In *Lexikon der christlichen Ikonographie*, 4:496–98. Rome: Herder, 1972.

Gutmann, Joseph. "Return in Mercy to Zion: A Messianic Dream in Jewish Art." In *The Land of Israel: Jewish Perspectives*, edited by Lawrence A. Hoffman, 234–60. Notre Dame, Ind.: University of Notre Dame Press, 1986.

Guyotjeanin, Olivier, Jacques Pycke, and B.-M. Tock. *Diplomatique médiévale*. L'Atelier du Médiéviste 2. Turnhout: Brepols, 1993.

Hadot, Ilsetraut. *Seneca und die griechisch-römische Tradition der Seelenleitung*. Berlin: Walter de Gruyter, 1969.

———. "The Spiritual Guide." In *Classical and Mediterranean Spirituality: Egyptian, Greek, Roman*, edited by A. H. Armstrong, 436–59. New York: Crossroads, 1986.

Hadot, Pierre. *The Inner Citadel: The Meditations of Marcus Aurelius*. Translated by Michael Chase. Cambridge, Mass.: Harvard University Press, 1998.

———. *Philosophy as a Way of Life: Spiritual Exercises from Socrates to Foucault*. Edited by Arnold I. Davidson. Translated by Michael Chase. Oxford: Blackwell, 1995.

Harkins, Franklin T. *Reading and the Work of Restoration: History and Scripture in the Theology of Hugh of St. Victor*. Toronto: Pontifical Institute of Mediaeval Studies, 2009.

Harkins, Franklin T., and Frans van Liere, eds. *Interpretation of Scripture: Theory*. Victorine Texts in Translation 3. Turnhout: Brepols, 2012.

Harris, E. Kay. "Hildebert of Lavardin." In *Medieval France: An Encyclopedia*, edited by William W. Kibler and Grover A. Zinn, 450. New York: Garland, 1995.

Harrison, Anna. "'I Am Wholly Your Own': Liturgical Piety and Community among the Nuns of Helfta." *Church History* 78 (2009): 549–83.

———. "'Oh! What Treasure is in this Book?' Writing, Reading, and Community at the Monastery of Helfta." *Viator* 39 (2008): 75–106.

Hauréau, Jean Barthélemy. *Hugues de Saint-Victor: Nouvel examen de l'édition de ses oeuvres*. Paris, 1859.

Heil, Johannes. *Kompilation oder Konstruktion? Die Juden in den Pauluskommentaren des 9. Jahrhunderts*. Forschungen zur Geschichte der Juden. A. Abhandlungen. Hannover: Hahn, 1998.

Heller, Henry. "The Evangelicism of Lefèvre d'Étaples: 1525." *Studies in the Renaissance* 19 (1972): 42–77.

Henriet, Patrick. *La parole et la prière au Moyen Âge: Le Verbe efficace dans l'hagiographie monastique des XIe et XIIe siècles*. Brussels: De Boeck, 2000.

Herz, Gerhard, ed. *Johann Sebastian Bach, Cantata no. 140: Wachet auf, ruft uns die Stimme; The Score of the New Bach Edition: Backgrounds, Analysis, Views, and Comments*. New York: W.W. Norton, 1972.

Hiatt, Alfred. "The Map of Macrobius before 1100." *Imago Mundi* 59 (2007): 149–76.

Hill, John. "Aristocratic Friendship in *Troilus and Criseyde*: Pandarus, Courtly Love and Ciceronian Brotherhood in Troy." In *New Readings of Chaucer's Poetry*, edited by Robert G. Benson and Susan J. Ridyard, 165–82. Woodbridge: Boydell & Brewer, 2003.

Hobbins, Daniel. *Authorship and Publicity Before Print: Jean Gerson and the Transformation of Late Medieval Learning*. Philadelphia: University of Pennsylvania Press, 2009.

Hodder, A. G. "New Treasures and Old in Bede's 'De Tabernaculo' and 'De Templo.'" *Revue Bénédictine* 99 (1989): 237–49.

Hoffmann, Tobias, Jörn Müller, and Matthias Perkams, eds. *Das Problem der Willensschwäche in der mittelalterlichen Philosophie*. Leuven: Peeters, 2006.

Hubrath, Margarete. "The *Liber specialis gratiae* as a Collective Work of Several Nuns." *Jahrbuch der Oswald von Wolkenstein Gesellschaft* 11 (1999): 233–44.

Hughes, Kevin L. *Constructing Antichrist: Paul, Biblical Commentary, and the Development of Doctrine in the Early Middle Ages*. Washington, D.C.: Catholic University of America Press, 2005.

Hugonin, Flavien. *Étude critique des oeuvres de Hugues de Saint-Victor*. PL 175: 116–17.

Hurtaut, P.-T.-N. *Dictionnaire historique de la ville de Paris et de ses environs*. 4 vols. Paris: Moutard, 1779.

Ilkhani, Mohammad. *La philosophie de la création chez Achard de Saint-Victor*. Brussels: Ousia, 1999.

Inge, William Ralph. *The Philosophy of Plotinus: The Gifford Lectures at St. Andrews, 1917–1918*. 2nd ed. London: Longmans Green, 1923.

Ingham, Mary Elizabeth. "Practical Wisdom: Scotus' Presentation of Prudence." In *Duns Scotus: Metaphysics and Ethics*, edited by Ludger Honnefelder et al., 568–71. Leiden: Brill, 1996.

———. *La vie de la sagesse: Le Stoïcisme au moyen âge*. Fribourg: Academic Press, 2007.

Ingram, E. M. "Maps as Readers' Aids: Maps and Plans in Geneva Bibles." *Imago Mundi* 45 (1993): 29–44.

Inwood, Brad. *Reading Seneca: Stoic Philosophy at Rome*. Oxford: Clarendon Press, 2005.

Iser, Wolfgang. *The Act of Reading: A Theory of Aesthetic Response*. Baltimore: Johns Hopkins University Press, 1978.

Jackson-McCate, Matt. "The Stoic Theory of Implanted Preconceptions." *Phronesis* 44 (2004): 323–47.

Jaeger, C. Stephen. *Ennobling Love: In Search of a Lost Sensibility*. Philadelphia: University of Pennsylvania Press, 1999.

———. *The Envy of Angels: Cathedral Schools and Social Ideals in Medieval Europe, 950–1200*. Philadelphia: University of Pennsylvania Press, 1994.

———. "*Epistolae duorum amantium* and the Ascription to Heloise and Abelard." In *Voices in Dialogue: Reading Women in the Middle Ages*, edited by Kathryn Kerby-Fulton and Linda Olson, 125–66. Notre Dame, Ind.: University of Notre Dame Press, 2005.

———. "Humanism and Ethics at the School of St. Victor in the Early Twelfth Century." *Mediaeval Studies* 55 (1993): 51–79.

———. "A Reply to Giles Constable." In *Voices in Dialogue: Reading Women in the Middle Ages*, edited by Kathryn Kerby-Fulton and Linda Olson, 179–86. Notre Dame, Ind.: University of Notre Dame Press, 2005.

James, M. R. *A Descriptive Catalogue of the Manuscripts of Trinity College, Cambridge*. 4 vols. Cambridge: Cambridge University Press, 1900–1904.

Jauss, Hans Robert. *Aesthetic Experience and Literary Hermeneutics*. Translated by Michael Shaw. Minneapolis: University of Minnesota Press, 1982.

———. *Toward an Aesthetic of Reception*. Translated by Timothy Bahti. Minneapolis: Harvester, 1982.

Javelet, Robert. *Image et ressemblance au douzième siècle: De saint Anselme à Alain de Lille*. Paris: Letouzey et Ané, 1967.

Jeauneau, Édouard. "Le *Prologus in Eptatheucon* de Thierry de Chartres." *Mediaeval Studies* 16 (1954): 171–75.

Johnson, Penelope D. *Prayer, Patronage, and Power: The Abbey of La Trinité, Vendôme, 1032–1187*. New York: New York University Press, 1981.

Jocqué, Luc. "Les structures de la population claustrale dans l'ordre de Saint-Victor au XIIe siècle: Un essai d'analyse du 'Liber Ordinis.'" In *L'abbaye parisienne de Saint-Victor au moyen âge*, edited by Jean Longère, 53–95. Bibliotheca Victorina 1. Paris: Brepols, 1991.

Joyce, P. M. *Ezekiel: A Commentary*. London: T & T Clark, 2007.

Kaeppeli, Thomas. *Scriptores ordinis praedicatorum medii aevi*. 4 vols. Rome: S. Sabina, 1970–93.

Kamtekar, Rachana. "ΑΙΔΩΣ in Epictetus." *Classical Philology* 93 (1998): 136–60.

Karfíková, Lenka. *"De esse ad pulchrum esse": Schönheit in der Theologie Hugos von St. Viktor*. Bibliotheca Victorina 8. Turnhout: Brepols, 1998.

Kauffmann, C. M. *Romanesque Manuscripts 1066–1190*. London: Harvey Miller, 1975.

Kedar, B. Z. "Rashi's Map of the Land of Canaan, ca. 1100 and its Cartographic Background." In *Cartography in Antiquity and the Middle Ages: Fresh Perspectives, New Methods*, edited by R. J. A. Talbert and R. W. Unger, 155–68. Leiden: Brill, 2008.

Kerby-Fulton, Kathryn. *Books Under Suspicion: Censorship and Tolerance of Revelatory Writing in Late Medieval England*. Notre Dame, Ind.: University of Notre Dame Press, 2006.

———. "Hildegard of Bingen (1098–1179)." In *Medieval Holy Women in the Christian Tradition c. 1100–c. 1500*, edited by Rosalynn Voaden and Alastair Minnis, 343–69. Turnhout: Brepols, 2010.

———. "Prophecy and Suspicion: Closet Radicalism, Reformist Politics and the Vogue for Hildegardiana in Ricardian England." *Speculum* 75 (2000): 318–41.

———. *Reformist Apocalypticism and Piers Plowman*. Cambridge: Cambridge University Press, 1990.

Kirchenberger, Clare. *Richard of St Victor: Selected Writings on Contemplation.* London: Faber & Faber, 1957,

Kleinz, John Philip. *The Theory of Knowledge of Hugh of Saint Victor.* Washington, D.C.: Catholic University of America Press, 1944.

Klostermann, Erich. *Eusebius Onomastikon der Biblischen Ortsnamen.* GCS 11:1. Leipzig: J.C. Hinrich, 1904.

Kolbet, Paul R. "Athanasius, the Psalms, and the Reformation of the Self." *Harvard Theological Review* 99 (2006): 80–101.

Kolletzki, Claudia. "'Über die Wahrheit dieses Buches': Die Entstehung des 'Liber Specialis Gratiae' Mechthilds von Hackeborn zwischen Wirklichkeit und Fiktion." In *"Vor dir steht die leere Schale meiner Sehnsucht": Die Mystik der Frauen von Helfta,* edited by Michael Bangert and Hildegund Keul, 156–79. Leipzig: Benno, 1998.

Kominko, Maja. "New Perspectives on Paradise: The Levels of Reality in Byzantine and Latin Medieval Maps." In *Cartography in Antiquity and the Middle Ages: Fresh Perspectives, New Methods,* edited by R.J.A. Talbert and R.W. Unger, 139–53. Leiden: Brill, 2008.

Könsgen, Ewald, ed. *Epistolae duorum amantium: Briefe Abaelards und Heloises?* Leiden: Brill, 1974.

Kostick, Conor. *The Social Structure of the First Crusade.* Leiden: Brill, 2008.

Kramer, Susan R., and Caroline W. Bynum. "Revisiting the Twelfth-Century Individual: The Inner Self and the Christian Community." In *Das Eigene und das Ganze: Zum Individuellen im mittelalterlichen Religion,* edited by Gert Melville and Markus Schürer, 57–85. Münster: LIT, 2002.

Kries, Douglas. "Origen, Plato, and Conscience (*Synderesis*) in Jerome's Ezekiel Commentary." *Traditio* 57 (2002): 67–83.

Lalou, Elisabeth, Claudia Rabel, and Louis Holtz. *"Dedens mon livre de pensee...": De Grégoire de Tours à Charles d'Orléans; Une histoire du livre médiéval en région Centre.* Paris: Somogy, 1997.

Lamberts, Jef. "Liturgie et spiritualité de l'eucharistie au XIIIe siècle." In *Fête-Dieu (1246–1996): Actes du colloque de Liège, 12–14 septembre 1996,* edited by André Haquin, 81–95. Louvain-la-Neuve: Institut d'études médiévales de l'Université catholique de Louvain, 1999.

Lamy-Lasalle, Colette. "Saint-Victor." In *Les anciennes églises suburbaines de Paris (IVe–Xe siècles),* edited by Elisabeth Chatel et al. Memoires de la Fédération des sociétés historiques et archéologiques de Paris et de l'Ile-de-France 11 (1960): 17–282.

Langston, Douglas C. *Conscience and Other Virtues from Bonaventure to Macintyre.* University Park: Pennsylvania State University Press, 2001.

Lasteyrie, Robert de. *Cartulaire général de Paris I (528–1180).* Paris: Imprimerie Nationale, 1887.

Lebeuf, Jean. *Histoire de la ville et de tout le diocèse de Paris.* Revised by Adrien Augier and Fernand Bournon. 7 vols. Paris, 1883–93.

Leclercq, Jean. *The Love of Learning and the Desire for God: A Study of Monastic Culture*. Translated by Catharine Misrahi. New York: Fordham University Press, 1961.

———. "Pour l'histoire de l'expression 'philosophie chrétienne.'" *Mélanges de Science Religieuse* 9 (1952): 221–26.

Le Goff, Jacques. *The Birth of Purgatory*. Translated by Arthur Goldhammer. Chicago: University of Chicago Press, 1986.

Lemoine, Michel. "L'abbaye de Saint-Victor, reflet du renouveau spirituel." In *Notre-Dame de Paris: Un manifeste chrétien (1160–1230)*, edited by Michel Lemoine, 107–18. Rencontres médiévales européennes 4. Turnhout: Brepols, 2004.

Le Rouge, G.-L. *Curiosités de Paris, de Versailles, de Marly, de Vincennes, de St. Cloud, et des environs*. Repr. Paris, 1883.

Lexikon des Mittelalters. Vol. 8. Stuttgart: Metzger, 1999.

Lobrichon, Guy. "Chronologie des oeuvres de saint Bernard de Clairvaux." In *Bernard de Clairvaux, Histoire, Mentalités, Spiritualité, Colloque de Lyon-Cîteaux-Dijon*, 32–41. SC 380. Paris: Cerf, 1992.

Lochrie, Karma. "Mystical Acts, Queer Tendencies." In *Constructing Medieval Sexuality*, edited by Karma Lochrie et al., 180–200. Minneapolis: University of Minnesota Press, 1997.

Lohrmann, Dietrich. *Kirchengut im nördlichen Frankreich, Besitz, Verfassung, und Wirtschaft im Spiegel der Papstprivilegien des 11.–12. Jahrhunderts*. Pariser Historische Studien 20. Bonn: L. Röhrscheid, 1983.

Long, A. A. *Epictetus: A Stoic and Socratic Guide to Life*. Oxford: Clarendon Press, 2002.

Longère, Jean. "Maurice de Sully l'évêque de Paris, le predicateur." In *Notre-Dame de Paris: Un manifeste chrétien (1160–1230)*, edited by Michel Lemoine. Rencontres médiévales européennes 4. Turnhout: Brepols, 2004.

———. *La prédication médiévale*. Paris: Études Augustiniennes, 1983.

Lössl, Josef. "Intellect with a (Divine) Purpose: Augustine on the Will." In *The Will and Human Action from Antiquity to the Present*, edited by Thomas Pink and M. W. F. Stone, 53–77. London: Routledge, 2004.

Lottin, Odon. *Psychologie et morale aux XIIe et XIIIe siècles*. 6 vols. Louvain: Abbaye de Mont César, 1948–60.

Lowe, Raphael. "Apologetic Motifs in the Targum to the Song of Songs." In *Biblical Motifs: Origins and Transformations*, edited by Alexander Altman, 159–69. Cambridge, Mass.: Harvard University Press, 1966.

Madec, Goulven. *Saint Ambroise et la philosophie*. Paris: Études Augustiniennes, 1974.

Maddock, Fiona. *Hildegard of Bingen: The Woman of Her Age*. New York: Doubleday, 2001.

Magne, C. "Rapport présenté au nom de la 2e Sous-Commission," séance du 7 decembre 1912. *Procès-verbaux de la Commission du vieux Paris*. Paris, 1912.

Maines, C. "Good Works, Social Ties, and the Hope for Salvation: Abbot Suger and Saint-Denis." In *Abbot Suger and Saint-Denis: a symposium*, edited by P. L. Gerson, 77–94. New York: Metropolitan Museum of Art, 1986.

Maître, Claire, ed. *Graduel de l'abbaye royale de Saint-Denis, début XIe siècle: Paris, Bibliothèque Mazarine, ms. 384. Manuscrits notés 3*. Paris: Editions Actes Sud, 2005.

Mâle, Emile. *L'art religieux du XIIIe siècle en France: Étude sur l'iconographie du moyen âge et sur ses sources d'inspiration*. Paris: A. Colin, 1898. Translated by Dora Nussey as *Religious Art in France, the Thirteenth Century: A study of Medieval Iconography and Its Sources*. Princeton: Princeton University Press, 1984.

Malingrey, Anne Marie. *"Philosophia": Étude d'un groupe de mots dans la littérature grecque, des Présocratiques au IVe siècle après J.-C.* Paris: C. Klincksieck, 1961.

Manuscrits à peintures du VIIe and XIIe siècle. Paris: Bibliothèque Nationale, 1954.

Marenbon, John. *Boethius*. Oxford: Oxford University Press, 2003.

———. *The Philosophy of Peter Abelard*. Cambridge: Cambridge University Press, 1997.

Markschies, Christoph. *Gibt es eine "Theologie der gotischen Kathedrale"? Nochmals: Suger von Saint-Denis und Sankt Dionys vom Areopag*. Heidelberg: Universitätsverlag C. Winter, 1995.

Marrone, Steven P. *In the Light of Thy Countenance: Science and the Knowledge of God in the Thirteenth Century*. 2 vols. Leiden: Brill, 2001.

Martène, Edmond, ed. *De antiquis ecclesiae ritibus*. 3 vols. Antwerp, 1737.

Martène, E., and U. Durard, eds. *Veterorum Scriptorum et Monumentorum . . . amplissima collectio*. Paris: Montalant, 1724–33.

Martin, Henry. *Catalogue des manuscrits de la Bibliothèque de l'Arsenal*. Paris: E. Plon, Nourrit et cie, 1885.

Matter, E. Ann. "The Apocalypse in Early Medieval Exegesis." In *The Apocalypse in the Middle Ages*, edited by Richard K. Emmerson and Bernard McGinn, 38–50. Ithaca: Cornell University Press, 1992.

———. "Buxtehude and Pietism? A Reappraisal." *The American Organist* 21 (1987): 81–83.

———. "The Love Between the Bride and the Bridegroom in Cantata 140: 'Wachet auf!' from the Twelfth Century to Bach's Day." In *Die Quellen Johann Sebastian Bachs: Bachs Musik im Gottesdienst*, edited by Renate Steiger, 107–18. Heidelberg: Manutius Verlag, 1998.

———. "My Sister, My Spouse: Woman-Identified Women in Medieval Christianity." *Journal of Feminist Studies in Religion* 2 (1986): 81–93.

———. *The Voice of My Beloved: The Song of Songs in Western Medieval Christianity*. Philadelphia: University of Pennsylvania Press, 1990.

McGinn, Bernard. *The Antichrist: Two Thousand Years of the Human Fascination with Evil*. New York: Harper Collins, 1994.

———. *The Flowering of Mysticism: Men and Women in the New Mysticism, 1200–1350.* New York: Crossroad, 1998.

———. *The Growth of Mysticism: Gregory the Great through the Twelfth Century.* New York: Crossroad, 1994.

———. "Hildegard of Bingen as Visionary and Exegete." In *Hildegard von Bingen in ihrem historischen Umfeld: Internationaler wissenschaftlicher Kongreß zum 900jährigen Jubiläum, 13.–19. September 1998, Bingen am Rhein,* edited by Alfred Haverkamp, 321–50. Mainz: Philipp von Zabern, 2000.

———. *The Mystical Thought of Meister Eckhart: The Man from Whom God Hid Nothing.* New York: Crossroad, 2001.

———. "Theologians as Trinitarian Iconographers." In *The Mind's Eye: Art and Theological Argument in the Middle Ages,* edited by Jeffrey F. Hamburger and Anne-Marie Bouché, 186–207. Princeton: Princeton University Press, 2006.

———. *Visions of the End: Apocalyptic Traditions in the Middle Ages.* Records of Civilization, Sources and Studies 96. New York: Columbia University Press, 1979.

McKitterick, Rosamond. "The Carolingian Church and the Book." In *The Church and the Book,* edited by R. N. Swanson, 46–73. Studies in Church History 38. Woodbridge: The Boydell Press for The Ecclesiastical History Society, 2004.

Meersseman, Gilles G. "Seneca maestro di spiritualità nei opuscoli apocrifi dal XII al XV secolo." *Italia medioevale e umanistica* 16 (1973): 43–135.

Mews, Constant. *Abelard and Heloise.* Oxford: Oxford University Press, 2005.

———. "From *Scivias* to the *Liber Divinorum Operum*: Hildegard's Apocalyptic Imagination and the Call to Reform." *The Journal of Religious History* 24 (2000): 44–56.

———. "Hildegard and the Schools." In *Hildegard of Bingen: The Context of her Thought and Art,* edited by Charles Burnett and Peter Dronke, 89–110. Warburg Institute Colloquia 4. London: The Warburg Institute, 1998.

———. "Hildegard of Bingen: The Virgin, the Apocalypse and the Exegetical Tradition." In *Wisdom which Encircles Circles: Papers on Hildegard of Bingen,* edited by Audrey Ekdahl Davidson, 27–42. Kalamazoo, Mich.: Medieval Institute Publications, 1996.

———. "Hildegard, Visions and Religious Reform." In *"Im Angesicht Gottes suche der Mensch sich selbst": Hildegard von Bingen (1098–1179),* edited by Rainer Berndt, 325–342. Berlin: Akademie Verlag, 2000.

———. *The Lost Love Letters of Heloise and Abelard: Perceptions of Dialogue in Twelfth-Century France.* With translations by Neville Chiavaroli. New York: St. Martin's Press, 1999.

———. "Religious Thinker: 'A Frail Human Being' on Fiery Life." In *Voice of the Living Light: Hildegard of Bingen and Her World,* edited by Barbara Newman, 52–69. Berkeley: University of California Press, 1998.

Millard, A. R. "Cartography in the Ancient Near East." In *History of Cartography,* vol. 1, *Cartography in Prehistoric, Ancient, and Medieval Europe and the*

Mediterranean, edited by J. B. Harley and David Woodward, 107–16. Chicago: University of Chicago Press, 1987.

Molinier, Auguste. *Catalogue des manuscrits de la Bibliothèque Mazarine*. Paris: E. Plon, 1885.

Mooney, Catherine M., ed. *Gendered Voices: Medieval Saints and Their Interpreters*. Philadelphia: University of Pennsylvania Press, 1999.

Moore, Philip S., ed. *The Works of Peter of Poitiers*. Notre Dame, Ind.: University of Notre Dame Press, 1936.

Moore, Rebecca. *Jews and Christians in the Life and Thought of Hugh of St. Victor*. University of South Florida Studies in the History of Judaism 138. Atlanta: Scholars Press, 1998.

Moos, Peter Von. "Die *Epistolae duorum amantium* und die 'säkulare Religion der Liebe': Methodenkritische Vorüberlegungen zu einem einmaligen Werk mittellateinischer Briefliteratur." *Studi Medievali* 44 (2003): 1–115.

Morelle, Laurent. "Suger et les archives, en relisant deux passages du *De Administratione*." In *Suger en Question: Regards croisés sur Saint-Denis*, edited by Rolf Grosse, 117–39. Pariser Historische Studien 62. Munich: Oldenbourg, 2004.

Morrison, Karl F. *"I Am You": The Hermeneutics of Empathy in Western Literature, Theology, and Art*. Princeton: Princeton University Press, 1988.

Müller, Jörn. "*Agere contra conscientiam*: The Relationship between Weakness of Will and Conscience in Albert the Great." In *Intellect et imagination dans la philosophie médiévale, Actes du XIe congrès de philosophie médiévale, Porto, 26–31 août 2002*, edited by Maria Cândida Pacheco and José F. Meirinhos, 3:1303–15. Turnhout: Brepols, 2006.

Murdoch, J. E. *Album of Science: Antiquity and the Middle Ages*. New York: Scribners, 1984.

Mynors, R. A. B. *Durham Cathedral Manuscripts to the End of the Twelfth Century*. Oxford: Oxford University Press for Durham Cathedral, 1939.

Narkiss, Bezalel. "A Scheme of the Sanctuary from the Time of Herod the Great." *Journal of Jewish Art* 1 (1974): 6–15.

Nauert, Charles G. Jr. "The Clash of Humanists and Scholastics: An Approach to Pre-Reformation Controversies." *The Sixteenth Century Journal* 4, no. 1 (April 1973): 1–18.

Negri, Luigi. "Letture stilistica di Ugo di S. Vittore." *Convivium* 24 (1956): 129–40.

Nelli, René. *L'Érotique des troubadours*. Toulouse: E. Privat, 1963.

Neubauer, A. D. *Catalogue of Hebrew Manuscripts in the Bodleian Library and in the College Libraries of Oxford*. Oxford: Clarendon Press, 1886.

Newman, Barbara. *From Virile Woman to WomanChrist: Studies in Medieval Religion and Literature*. Philadelphia: University of Pennsylvania Press, 1995.

———. *God and the Goddesses: Vision, Poetry, and Belief in the Middle Ages*. Philadelphia: University of Pennsylvania Press, 2003.

———. "Hildegard and Her Hagiographers." In *Gendered Voices: Medieval Saints and Their Interpreters*, edited by Catherine M. Mooney, 16–34. Philadelphia: University of Pennsylvania Press, 1999.

———. "Hildegard of Bingen: Visions and Validation." *Church History* 54 (1985): 163–75.

———. "Liminalities: Literate Women in the Long Twelfth Century." In *European Transformations: The Long Twelfth Century*, edited by Thomas F. X. Noble and John Van Engen, 354–402. Notre Dame, Ind.: University of Notre Dame Press, 2012.

———. *Sister of Wisdom: St. Hildegard's Theology of the Feminine*. Berkeley: University of California Press, 1987.

———. "What Did It Mean to Say 'I Saw'? The Clash between Theory and Practice in Medieval Visionary Culture." *Speculum* 80 (2005): 1–43.

Nichols, Aidan. *The Shape of Catholic Theology: An Introduction to Its Sources, Principles, and History*. Collegeville, Minn.: The Liturgical Press, 1991.

Noone, Timothy. "Duns Scotus on *Incontinentia*." In *Das Problem der Willensschwäche in der mittelalterlichen Philosophie*, edited by Tobias Hoffmann, Jörn Müller, and Matthias Perkams, 285–305. Leuven: Peeters, 2006.

Oberman, Heiko, ed. *Johann Arndt: True Christianity*. Translated by Peter Erb. London: SPCK, 1979.

Obrist, Barbara. "Image et prophétie au XIIe siècle: Hugues de Saint-Victor et Joachim de Fiore." *Mélanges de l'Ecole française de Rome* 98 (1986): 35–63.

Ohly, Friedrich. "Du bist mein, ich bin dein. Du in mir, ich in dir. Ich du, du ich." In *Kritische Bewahrung: Beiträge zur deutschen Philologie: Festschrift für Werner Schröder*, edited by Ernst-Joachim Schmidt, 371–415. Berlin: E. Schmidt, 1974.

Old, Hughes Oliphant. *The Reading and Preaching of the Scriptures in the Worship of the Christian Church*, vol. 3, *The Medieval Church*. Grand Rapids, Mich.: Eerdmans, 1999.

O'Loughlin, Thomas. *Adomnán and The Holy Places: The Perceptions of an Insular Monk on the Locations of the Biblical Drama*. London: T & T Clark, 2007.

———. "Map and Text: A Mid Ninth-Century Map for the Book of Joshua." *Imago Mundi* 57 (2005): 7–22.

Oursel, Hervé, et al. *Nord roman*. La Pierre-qui-Vire: Zodiaque, 1994.

Ouy, Gilbert. *Manuscrits de l'abbaye de Saint-Victor: Catalogue établi sur la base du répertoire de Claude de Grandrue (1514)*. 2 vols. Bibliotheca Victorina 10. Turnhout: Brepols, 1999.

Pächt, Otto, and J. J. G. Alexander. *Illuminated Manuscripts in the Bodleian Library*. 2 vols. Oxford: Clarendon Press, 1966–73.

Pächt, Otto, C. R. Dodwell, and Francis Wormald. *The St. Albans Psalter (Albani Psalter)*. Studies of the Warburg Institute 25. London: Warburg Institute, 1960.

Panofsky, Erwin. *Herkules am Scheidewege und andere Antike Bildstoffe in der neueren Kunst*. Studien der Bibliothek Warburg 18. Berlin: Teubner, 1930.

———, ed. *Abbot Suger on the Abbey Church of St.-Denis and Its Art Treasures*. 2nd ed. Princeton: Princeton University Press, 1979.

Parisse, Michel. "Les pancartes: Étude d'un type d'acte diplomatique." In *Pancartes monastiques des XIe et XIIe siècles, Table ronde organisée part l'ARTEM, 6 et 7 juillet 1994 Nancy*, edited by Michel Parisse, Pierre Pegeot, and B.-M. Tock, 11–62. Turnhout: Brepols, 1998.

———. "Saint-Denis et ses biens en Lorraine et en Alsace." In *Bulletin philologique et historique (jusqu'à 1610) du Comité des travaux historiques et scientifiques*, 233–56. Paris: BnF, 1969.

Penkower, Joseph S. *Bible: Miqraot Gedolot HaKeter, Ezekiel* [Hebrew]. Ramat-Gan: University of Bar-Ilan, 1992.

Périn, Patrick, et al. *Collections merovingiennes*. Catalogues d'art et d'histoire du Musée Carnavalet. Paris: Musée Carnavalet, 1985.

Perkams, Matthias. "Gewissensirrtum und Gewissensfreiheit." *Philosophisches Jahrbuch* 112 (2005): 31–50.

Pitra, J. B., ed. *Analecta sacra Spicilegio Solesmensi parata*, vol. 8, *Sanctae Hildegardis Opera*. Montecassino, 1882; repr. Farnborough: Gregg, 1966.

Plagnieux, Philippe. "L'abbatiale de Saint-Germain-des-Prés et les débuts de l'architecture gothique." *Bulletin monumental* 158 (2000): 6–86.

Poirel, Dominique. "Alter Augustinus-Der zweite Augustinus." In *Hugo von Sankt Viktor und die Väter der Kirche. Ekklesiales Denken von den Anfängen bis in die Neuzeit*, edited by Johannes Arnold, Rainer Berndt, and Ralf M.W. Stammberger, 643–668. Paderborn: Ferdinand Schöningh, 2004.

———. *Hugues de Saint-Victor*. Paris: Cerf, 1998.

———. "Lire le monde sensible: Le sens d'une métaphore d'Hugues de Saint-Victor." In *Lire le monde au Moyen Âge: Signe, symbole et corporéité*, edited by Emmanuel Falque, 363–82. Actes du colloque organisé par le Laboratoire de philosophie patristique et médiévale de l'Institut catholique de Paris, 8–9 janvier 2009. Paris: Librairie Philosophique J. Vrin, 2011

———. *Livre de la nature et débat trinitaire au XIIe siècle: Le "De tribus diebus" de Hugues de Saint-Victor*. Bibliotheca Victorina 14. Turnhout: Brepols, 2002.

———. "*Mira pulchritudo*: de l'étonnement à l'émerveillement selon Hugues de Saint-Victor." In *La beauté du merveilleux: Pour une esthétique; Colloque organisé par l'EA 4195 TELEM, jeudi 5–vendredi 6 février 2009, Musée d'Aquitaine, 20 cours Pasteur, 33000 Bordeaux*, edited by Jean-René Valette and Aurélia Gaillard, 85–100. Bordeaux: Presses Universitaires de Bordeaux, 2011.

———. "'Symbolice et anagogice': L'Ecole des Saint-Victor et la naissance du gothique." In *L'Abbé Suger, le manifeste gothique de Saint-Denis et la pensée victorine*, edited by Dominique Poirel, 141–70. Turnhout: Brepols, 2001.

———, ed. *L'Abbé Suger, le manifeste gothique de Saint-Denis et la pensée victorine*. Turnhout: Brepols, 2001.

Polo de Beaulieu, Marie Anne. "La légende du coeur inscrit dans la littérature religieuse et didactique." In *Le "cuer" au moyen âge: Réalité et sénéfiance*, 297–312. Aix-en-Provence: Université de Provence, 1991.
Porrer, Sheila M. *Jacques Lefèvre d'Etaples and the Three Maries Debates*. Geneva: Librairie Droz, 2009.
Prache, Anne. *Ile-de-France romane*. La Pierre-qui-Vire: Zodiaque, 1983.
Poole, R. L. "The Masters of the Schools at Paris and Chartres in John of Salisbury's Time." In *Studies in Chronology and History*, edited by A. L. Poole, 223–47. Oxford: Clarendon Press, 1934.
Potts, Timothy. "Conscience." In *The Cambridge History of Later Medieval Philosophy from the Recovery of Aristotle to the Disintegration of Scholasticism, 1100–1600*, edited by Norman Kretzmann et al., 687–704. Cambridge: Cambridge University Press, 1982.
———. *Conscience in Medieval Philosophy*. Cambridge: Cambridge University Press, 1980.
Pugh, Tison. "Queer Pandarus? Silence and Sexual Ambiguity in Chaucer's *Troilus and Criseyde*." *Philological Quarterly* 80 (2001): 17–35.
Rabbow, Paul. *Seelenführung: Methodik der Exerzitien in der Antike*. Munich: Kösel-Verlag, 1954.
Reeves, Marjorie. *The Influence of Prophecy in the Later Middle Ages: A Study in Joachimism*. Oxford: Oxford University Press, 1969.
Renaudet, Augustin. *Préréforme et humanisme à Paris pendant les premières guerres d'Italie (1494–1517)*. 2nd ed. Paris: Librairie d'Argences, 1953.
Renz, Oskar. *Die Synteresis nach dem hl. Thomas von Aquin*. Münster: Aschendorff, 1911.
Reydams-Schils, Gretchen. *The Roman Stoics: Self, Responsibility, and Affection*. Chicago: University of Chicago Press, 2005.
Rice, Eugene F. "The Humanist Idea of Christian Antiquity: Lefèvre d'Étaples and his Circle." *Studies in the Renaissance* 9 (1962): 126–60.
———. "Jacques Lefèvre d'Étaples and the Medieval Christian Mystics." In *Florilegium Historiale: Essays Presented to Wallace K. Ferguson*, edited by J. G. Rowe and W. H. Stockdale, 89–124. Toronto: University of Toronto Press, 1971.
———, ed. *The Prefatory Epistles of Jacques Lefévre d'Etaples and Related Texts*. New York: Columbia University Press, 1972.
Rief, Josef. *Der Ordobegriff des jungen Augustinus*. Paderborn: Ferdinand Schöningh, 1962.
Riley-Smith, Jonathan. *The First Crusade and the Idea of Crusading*. Philadelphia: University of Pennsylvania Press, 1986.
———. *The First Crusaders, 1095–1131*. Cambridge: Cambridge University Press, 1997.
Robertson, A. W. *The Service Books of the Royal Abbey of Saint-Denis: Images of Ritual and Music in the Middle Ages*. Oxford: Clarendon Press, 1991.

Robinson, I. S. *The Papacy, 1073–1198: Continuity and Innovation.* Cambridge: Cambridge University Press, 1990.

Rochberg, Francesca. "The Expression of Terrestrial and Celestial Order in Ancient Mesopotamia." In *Ancient Perspectives: Maps and their Place in Mesopotamia, Egypt, Greece, and Rome,* ed. Richard J. A. Talbert, 9–46. Chicago: University of Chicago Press, 2012.

Röhrig, Floridus. *Der Verduner Altar.* 5th ed. Vienna: Herold, 1979.

Rorem, Paul. *Hugh of Saint-Victor.* Oxford: Oxford University Press, 2009.

Rosemann, Philipp W. *Peter Lombard.* Oxford: Oxford University Press, 2004.

Rosenau, Helen. "The Architecture of Nicholas de Lyra's Temple Illustrations and the Jewish Tradition." *Journal of Jewish Studies* 25 (1974): 294–304.

———. *Vision of the Temple: The Image of the Temple of Jerusalem in Judaism and Christianity.* London: Oresko Books, 1979.

Rudolph, Conrad. *Artistic Change at St. Denis: Abbot Suger's Program and the Early Twelfth Century Controversy Over Art.* Princeton: Princeton University Press, 1990.

———. "Bernard of Clairvaux's *Apologia* as a Description of Cluny and the Controversy over Monastic Art." *Gesta* 27 (1988): 125–32.

———. *"First I Find the Center Point": Reading the Text of Hugh of Saint-Victor's The Mystic Ark.* Transactions of the American Philosophical Society 94. Philadelphia: American Philosophical Society, 2004.

———. "The Scholarship on Bernard of Clairvaux's *Apologia.*" *Cîteaux: Commentarii Cistercienses* (1989): 69–111.

———. *The "Things of Greater Importance": Bernard of Clairvaux's Apologia and the Medieval Attitude Toward Art.* Philadelphia: University of Pennsylvania Press, 1990.

Rutherford, R. B. *The Meditations of Marcus Aurelius: A Study.* Oxford: Clarendon Press, 1989.

Saarinen, Risto. "Weakness of Will in the Renaissance and Reformation." In *Das Problem der Willensschwäche in der mittelalterlichen Philosophie,* edited by Tobias Hoffmann, Jörn Müller, and Matthias Perkams, 331–53. Leuven: Peeters, 2006.

Sandbach, F. H. "Ennoia and Prōlepsis in the Stoic Theory of Knowledge." In *Problems in Stoicism,* edited by A. A. Long, 44–51. London: Athlone Press, 1971.

Sansy, Daniele. "Chapeau juif ou chapeau pointu? Esquisse d'un signe d'infamie." In *Symbole des Alltags, Alltags der Symbole. Festschrift für Harry Kuhnel zum 65. Geburtstag,* edited by Gertrud Blaschitz, Helmut Hundsbichler, Gerhard Jaritz, and Elisabeth Vavra, 349–76. Graz: Akademische Druck- u. Verlagsanstalt, 1992.

Sassoon, S. D, ed. *Maimonidis Commentarius in Mischnam E Codicibus Hunt 117 et Pococke 295 in biblioteca Bodleiana Oxoniensis servatis et 72–73 Bibliotecae Sassooniensis, Letchworth.* Corpus Codicum Hebraicorum Medii Aevi 1–3. Haifa: E. Munkesgaard, 1966.

Sauval, Henri. *Histoire et recherches des antiquités de la ville de Paris*. 3 vols. Paris: Charles Moette, 1733.

Savigni, Raffaele. "Il commentario a Isaia di Aimone d'Auxerre e le sue fonte." In *Biblical Studies in the Early Middle Ages: Proceedings of the Conference on Biblical Studies in the Early Middle Ages (Palazzo Feltrinelli, Gargnano on Lake Garda, 24–27 June 2001)*, edited by Claudio Leonardi and G. Orlandi, 215–38. Firenze: SISMEL, 2005.

Saxl, Fritz. "Frühes Christentum und spätes Heidentum in ihren künstlerischen Ausdrucksformen. I. Der Dialog als Thema der christlichen Kunst." *Wiener Jahrbuch für Kunstgeschichte* NF 2, 16 (1923): 64–77.

Schenkluhn, Wolfgang. *Architektur der Bettelorden: Die Baukunst der Dominikaner und Franziskaner in Europa*. Darmstadt: Wissenschaftliche Buchgesellschaft, 2000.

Schlette, H. R. *Die Nichtigkeit der Welt: Der philosophische Horizont des Hugo von St. Viktor*. Munich: Kösel-Verlag, 1961.

Schoebel, Martin. *Archiv und Besitze der Abtei St. Viktor in Paris*. Pariser Historische Studien 31. Bonn: Bouvier, 1991.

Schröder, Jochen. *Gervasius von Canterbury, Richard von Saint-Victor und die Methodik der Bauerfassung im 12. Jarhundert*. Veröffentlichung der Abteilung Architekturgeschichte des Kunsthistorischen Instituts der Universität zu Köln 71. 2 vols. Cologne: Kunsthistorisches Institut der Universität zu Köln, 2000.

Scott, Kathleen. *Tradition and Innovation in Later Medieval English Manuscripts*. London: The British Library, 2007.

Sed-Rajna, Gabrielle. "Rashi's Diagrams to his Commentary in the Bible." *Jewish Quarterly Studies* 1 (1993/1994): 149–57.

Sedgwick, Eve Kosofsky. *Between Men: English Literature and Male Homosocial Desire*. New York: Columbia University Press, 1985.

Sellier, Charles. "Communication relative aux vestiges de l'ancienne abbaye Saint-Victor," séance du 13 avril 1899. *Procès-verbaux de la Commission du vieux Paris*, 113. Paris, 1899.

———. "Rapport sur les fouilles de démolitions exécutées du 10 octobre au 14 novembre 1901," séance du 14 novembre. *Procès-verbaux de la commission du vieux Paris*, 168–72. Paris, 1901.

Shakespeare, William. *Poems*. Edited by John Roe. Cambridge: Cambridge University Press, 2006.

Shay, Jonathan. *Achilles and Vietnam: Combat Trauma and the Undoing of Character*. New York: Scribner, 1994.

———. *Odysseus in America: Combat Trauma and the Trials of Homecoming*. New York: Scribner, 2002.

Sheppard, Jennifer. *The Buildwas Books: Book Production, Acquisition and Use at an English Cistercian Monastery, 1165–c. 1400*. Oxford: Oxford Bibliographical Society, 1997.

———. "Magister Robertus Amiclas: A Buildwas Benefactor?" *Transactions of the Cambridge Bibliographical Society* 9 (1988): 281–88.
Sherwin, Michael S. *By Knowledge and Love: Charity and Knowledge in the Moral Theology of St. Thomas.* Washington, D.C.: Catholic University of America Press, 2005.
Shimahara, Sumi, ed. *Études d'exégèse carolingienne: Études autour d'Haymon d'Auxerre; Atelier de recherches, 25–26 avril 2005, Centre d'Études médiévales d'Auxerre.* Collection Haut Moyen Âge 4. Turnhout: Brepols, 2007.
Sicard, Patrice. *Diagrammes médiévaux et exégèse visuelle: Le Libellus de formatione arche de Hugues de Saint-Victor.* Paris: Brepols, 1993.
———. *Hugues de Saint-Victor et son école.* Turnhout: Brepols, 1991.
Sieben, H. J. "Vanité du monde." In *Dictionnaire de spiritualité*, edited by Marcel Viller, 16:257–69. Paris: G. Beauchesne, 1992.
Signer, Michael A. "Consolation and Confrontation: Jewish and Christian Interpretation of the Prophetic Books." In *Scripture and Pluralism: Reading the Bible in the Religiously Plural Worlds of the Middle Ages and Renaissance*, edited by Thomas. J. Heffernan and Thomas E. Burman, 77–94. Studies in the History of Christian Traditions 123. Leiden: E. J. Brill, 2005.
———. "The Glossa Ordinaria and the Transmission of Medieval Anti-Judaism." In *A Distinct Voice: Medieval Studies in Honor of Leonard E. Boyle, O.P.*, edited by Jacqueline Brown and William P. Stoneman, 591–605. Notre Dame, Ind.: University of Notre Dame Press, 1998.
———. "Polemic and Exegesis: The Varieties of Twelfth-Century Hebraism." In *Hebraica Veritas? Christian Hebraism and the Study of Judaism in Early Modern Europe*, edited by Allison P. Coudert and Jeffrey S. Shoulson, 21–32. Philadelphia: University of Pennsylvania Press, 2004.
Silvas, Anna, trans. *Jutta and Hildegard: The Biographical Sources.* University Park: Pennsylvania State University Press, 1998.
Simson, Otto von. *The Gothic Cathedral.* 2nd ed. New York: Bollingen Foundation, 1964.
Singer, Charles. *Studies in the History and Method of Science.* 2 vols. Oxford: Oxford University Press, 1917–21.
Smalley, Beryl. "Andrew of St. Victor, Abbot of Wigmore: A Twelfth Century Hebraist." *RTAM* 10 (1938): 358–73.
———. "Les commentaires bibliques de l'époque romane: glose ordinaire et gloses périmées." *Cahiers de Civilisation Médiévale* 4 (1961): 15–22.
———. "Ecclesiastical attitudes to novelty c. 1100–c. 1250." In *Church, Society and Politics*, edited by Derek Baker, 113–31. Blackwell: Oxford, 1975. Repr. in Beryl Smalley, *Studies in Medieval Thought and Learning: From Abelard to Wyclif*, 97–115. London: Hambledon and Harper, 1981.
———. "Gilbertus Universalis, Bishop of London (1128–34), and the Problem of the 'Glossa Ordinaria.'" *RTAM* 7 (1935): 235–62; 8 (1936): 24–60.

———. *The Study of the Bible in the Middle Ages.* 3rd ed. Oxford: Blackwell Publishing, 1983.
Smith, Lesley. *The Glossa ordinaria: The Making of a Medieval Bible Commentary.* Commentaria 3. Leiden and Boston: Brill, 2009.
Sorabji, Richard. "The Concept of the Will from Plato to Maximus the Confessor." In *The Will and Human Action from Antiquity to the Present,* edited by Thomas Pink and M. W. F. Stone, 6–28. London: Routledge, 2004.
———. *Self: Ancient and Modern Insights about Individuality, Life, and Death.* Chicago: University of Chicago Press, 2006.
Southern, R. W. *Medieval Humanism and Other Essays.* Oxford: Blackwell, 1970.
———. "The Schools of Paris and the School of Chartres." In *Renaissance and Renewal in the Twelfth Century,* edited by Robert L. Benson and Giles Constable, 113–37. Cambridge, Mass.: Harvard Universitty Press, 1982; reprinted Toronto: University of Toronto Press, 1991.
Speer, Andreas. "Is There a Theology of the Gothic Cathedral? A Re-Reading of Abbot Suger's Writings on the Abbey Church of St.-Denis." In *The Mind's Eye: Art and Theological Argument in the Middle Ages,* edited by J. F. Hamburger and A.-M. Bouché, 65–83. Princeton: Princeton University Press, 2006.
Spieralska, Beata. "Les sermons attribués à Maurice de Sully." *Medieval Sermons Studies* 51 (2007): 95–98.
Spitzlei, Sabine B. *Erfahrungsraum Herz: Zur Mystik des Zisterzienserinnenklosters Helfta im 13. Jahrhundert.* Stuttgart-Bad Cannstatt: Frommann-Holzboog, 1991.
Stammler, Wolfgang. *Frau Welt: Eine mittelalterliche Allegorie.* Freiburger Universitätsreden NF 23. Freiburg: Universitätsverlag, 1959.
Sternagel, Peter. *Die artes mechanicae im Mittelalter: Begriffs- und Bedeutungsgeschichte bis zum Ende des 13. Jahrhunderts.* Münchener Historische Studien 2. Kallmünz Opf: Lassleben, 1966.
Stirnemann, Patricia. "Les manuscrits de la *Postille.*" In *Hugues de Saint-Cher: Bibliste et théologien,* edited by L.-J. Bataillon, Gilbert Dahan, and P.-M. Gy, 31–41. Turnhout: Brepols, 2004.
———. "Où ont été fabriqués les livres de la Glose ordinaire dans la première moitié du XIIe siècle." In *Le XIIe siècle: Mutations et renouveau en France dans la première moitié du XIIe siècle,* edited by F. Gasparri, 257–301. Cahiers du Léopard d'or 3. Paris: Le léopard d'or, 1994.
Stock, Brian. *Augustine the Reader: Meditation, Self-Knowledge, and the Ethics of Interpretation.* Cambridge, Mass.: Harvard University Press, 1996.
Stone, M. F. W. "Moral Psychology before 1277: The Will, *liberum arbitrium,* and Rectitude in Bonaventure." In *The Will and Human Action from Antiquity to the Present,* edited by Thomas Pink and M. W. F. Stone, 99–126. London: Routledge, 2004.
Strachan, James. *Early Bible Illustrations: A Short Study Based on Some Fifteenth and Early Sixteenth Century Printed Texts.* Cambridge: Cambridge University Press, 1957.

Swanson, R. N. *The Twelfth-Century Renaissance.* Manchester: Manchester University Press, 1999.
Tatum, James. *War and Remembrance from the "Iliad" to Vietnam.* Chicago: University of Chicago Press, 2004.
Teske, Gunnar. *Die Briefsammlungen des 12. Jahrhunderts in St. Viktor/Paris.* Studien und Dokumente zur Gallia Pontificia 2. Bonn: Bouvier, 1993.
Testard, Maurice. "Observations sur le thème de la *conscientia* dans le *De officiis ministrorum* de saint Ambroise." *Revue des études latines* 51 (1973): 219–61.
Thérel, M.-L. *Le triomphe de la Vierge-Église: À l'origine du décor du portail occidental de Notre-Dame de Senlis; Sources historiques, littéraires et iconographiques.* Paris: Éditions du Centre national de la Recherche scientifique, 1984.
Thiéry, L.-V. *Guide des amateurs et des étrangers voyageurs à Paris.* 2 vols. Paris, 1787.
Thomson, R. M. *Books and Learning in Twelfth-Century England: The Ending of "Alter Orbis."* The Lyell Lectures 2000–2001. Walkern: The Red Gull Press, 2006.
———. "The Library of Bury St Edmunds Abbey." *Speculum* 47 (1972): 617–45.
———. *MSS from St Albans Abbey 1066–1235.* 2 vols. Woodbridge: D. S. Brewer, 1982.
———. "Robert Amiclas: A Twelfth-Century Parisian Master and His Books." *Scriptorium* 49 (1995): 238–43.
Tock, B.-M. "Auteur ou impetrant? Reflexions sur les chartes des évêques d'Arras au XIIe siècle." *Bibliothèque de l'École des Chartes* 149 (1991): 215–48.
———. "La diplomatique sans pancarte: L'exemple des diocèses d'Arras et de Thérouanne." In *Pancartes monastiques des XIe et XIIe siècles,* ed. M. Parisse, P. Pégeot, and B.-M. Tock. Turnhout: Brepols 1998.
Tuell, Steven. "The Rivers of Paradise: Ezekiel 47:1–12 and Genesis 2:10–14." In *God Who Creates: Essays in Honor of W. Sibley Towner,* edited by W. P. Brown and S. D. McBride, 171–89. Grand Rapids, Mich.: Eerdmans, 2000.
Tyler, A. E. "Jacques Lefèvre d'Étaples and Henry Estienne the Elder, 1502–20." In *The French Mind: Studies in Honour of Gustave Rudler,* edited by Will Grayburn Moore et al., 17–33. Oxford: Clarendon Press, 1952.
Van den Eynde, Damien. *Essai sur la succession et la date des écrits de Hugues de Saint-Victor.* Spicilegium Pontificii Athenaei Antoniani 13. Rome: Pontificium Athenaeum Antonianum, 1960.
Van Liere, Frans A. "Andrew of Saint Victor and His Franciscan Critics." In *The Multiple Meaning of Scripture,* edited by Ineke Van 't Spijker, 291–309. Commentaria 2. Leiden: Brill, 2008.
———. "Andrew of St. Victor, Jerome, and the Jews: Biblical Scholarship in the Twelfth-Century Renaissance." In *Scripture and Pluralism: Reading the Bible in the Religiously Plural Worlds of the Middle Ages and Renaissance,* edited by Thomas. J. Heffernan and Thomas E. Burman, 59–75. Studies in the History of Christian Traditions 123. Leiden: E. J. Brill, 2005.

Van 't Spijker, Ineke. *Fictions of the Inner Life: Religious Literature and Formation of the Self in the Eleventh and Twelfth Centuries.* Turnhout: Brepols, 2004.

Van Zwieten, J. W. M. "Jewish Exegesis within Christian Bounds: Richard of St Victor's 'De Emmanuele' and Victorine Hermeneutics." *Bijdragen: Tijdschrift voor Philosophie en Theologie* 48 (1987): 327–35.

Vecchio, Silvana. "Peccatum cordis." In *Il cuore = The Heart*, edited by Nathalie Blancardi, 325–42. Micrologus 11. Firenze: SISMEL-Edizioni del Galluzzo, 2003.

Verbeke, Gerard. *The Presence of Stoicism in Medieval Thought.* Washington, D.C.: Catholic University of America Press, 1983.

Veyne, Paul. *Seneca: The Life of a Stoic.* Translated by David Sullivan. New York: Routledge, 2003.

Victor, Joseph M. "The Revival of Lullism at Paris, 1499–1516." *Renaissance Quarterly* 28, no. 4 (Winter 1975): 504–34.

Voaden, Rosalynn. "All Girls Together: Community, Gender and Vision at Helfta." In *Medieval Women in Their Communities*, edited by Diane Watt, 72–91. Toronto: University of Toronto Press, 1997.

Voelke, André-Jean. *L'Idée de la volonté dans le Stoïcisme.* Paris: Presses universitaires de France, 1973.

———. *La philosophie comme thérapie de l'âme: Études de philosophie héllenistique.* Fribourg: Éditions Universitaires, 1993.

Waldman, Tom. "Abbot Suger and the Nuns of Argenteuil." *Traditio* 41 (1985): 239–72.

Wolska-Conus, Wanda. *Cosmas Indicopleustes: Topographie chrétienne.* SC 141, 159, 197. Paris: Cerf, 1968, 1972, 1978.

Ward, John O., and Neville Chiavaroli. "The Young Heloise and Latin Rhetoric: Some Preliminary Comments on the 'Lost' Love Letters and Their Significance." In *Listening to Heloise: The Voice of a Twelfth-Century Woman*, edited by Bonnie Wheeler, 53–119. New York: St. Martin's Press, 2000.

Weber, Hubert Philipp. "The *Glossa in IV Sententiarum* by Alexander of Hales." In *Mediaeval Commentaries on the Sentences of Peter Lombard*, edited by Philipp W. Rosemann, 2:79–109. Leiden: Brill, 2010.

Weizmann, Kurt. *Ancient Book Illumination.* Cambridge, Mass.: Harvard University Press, 1959.

Wicki, Nikolaus. *Die Philosophie Philipps des Kanzlers: Ein philosophierender Theologe des frühen 13. Jahrhunderts.* Fribourg: Academic Press, 2005.

Wieland, G. R. "Gloss and Illustration: Two Means to the Same End?" In *Anglo-Saxon Manuscripts and Heritage*, edited by Phillip Pulsiano and E. M. Treharne, 1–20. Aldershot: Ashgate, 1988.

Wilkinson, John. *Jerusalem Pilgrims Before the Crusades.* Warminster: Aris & Phillips, 1977.

Willesme, J.-P. "L'abbaye de Saint-Victor." In *La montagne Sainte-Geneviève*, edited by Musée Carnavalet, 146–51. Paris: Musée Carnavalet, 1981.

———. "L'abbaye de Saint-Victor de Paris." Unpublished diss., 3e cycle, University of Paris-IV, 1979.

———. "L'abbaye Saint-Victor de Paris: L'église et les bâtiments, des origines à la Révolution." In *L'abbaye parisienne de Saint-Victor au moyen âge*, edited by Jean Longère, 97–115. Bibliotheca Victorina 1. Paris: Brepols, 1991.

———. "L'abbaye Saint-Victor de Paris sous la Révolution et la dispersion de son patrimoine." *Bulletin de la société de l'histoire de Paris et de l'Ile-de-France* 106 (1979): 133–53.

———. "Histoire et l'architecture de l'abbaye Saint-Victor de Paris du XIIe au XVIe siècles." Unpublished paper intended for presentation at the International Congress for Medieval Studies at Kalamazoo in 1984.

———. "Les origines de l'abbaye de Saint-Victor de Paris à travers ses historiens des XVIIe et XVIIIe si siècles." *Bulletin philologique et historique du Comité des travaux historiques et scientifiques* 58 (1977): 101–14.

———. "Saint-Victor au temps d'Abélard." In *Abélard en son temps: Actes du Colloque international organisé à l'occasion du IXe centenaire de la naissance de Pierre Abélard (14–19 mai 1979)*, edited by Jean Jolivet, 95–105. Paris: Les Belles Lettres 1981.

———. "Saint-Victor et la famille victorine (XIIe–XIIIe siècle)." In *Naissance et fonctionnement des réseaux monastiques et canoniaux*, 175–94. Travaux et recherches 1. Saint-Etienne: Centre européen de recherches sur les congrégations et ordres monastiques, 1991.

Wilmart, André. *Codices Reginenses Latini*. 2 vols. Vatican City: BAV, 1945.

Wischnitzer, Rachel. "Maimonides' Drawings of the Temple." *Journal of Jewish Art* 1 (1974): 16–27.

Wolter, Allan B., ed. and trans. *Duns Scotus on the Will and Morality*. Washington, D.C.: Catholic University of America Press, 1986.

Wulstan, David. "*Novi modulaminis melos*: The Music of Heloise and Abelard." *Plainsong and Medieval Music* 11 (2002): 1–23.

Wyss, Michaël, ed. *Atlas historique de Saint-Denis, des origins au XVIIIe siècle*. Documents d'Archéologie française 59. Paris: Éditions de la Maison des sciences de l'homme, 1996.

Yuval, Israel Jacob. *Two Nations in Your Womb: Perceptions of Jews and Christians in Late Antiquity and the Middle Ages*. Translated by Barbara Harshav and Jonathan Chipman. Berkeley: University of California Press, 2006.

Zedler, Gottfried. *Die Handschriften der Nassauischen Landesbibliothek zu Wiesbaden*. Beiheft zum Zentralblatt zum Bibliothekswesen 63. Leipzig: Harrassowitz, 1931.

Zier, Mark. "Sermons of the Twelfth Century Schoolmasters and Canons." In *The Sermon*, under the direction of Beverly Mayne Kienzle, 325–62. Typologie des sources du Moyen Âge occidental, Fasc. 81, 83. Turnhout: Brepols, 2000.

Zinn, G. A. "Exegesis and Spirituality in Richard of St. Victor." In *Doors of Understanding: Conversations in Global Spirituality in Honor of Ewert Cousins*, edited by Steven Chase, 127–44. Quincy, Ill.: Franciscan Press, 1997.
———. "*Historia fundamentum est*: The Role of History in the Contemplative Life according to Hugh of St. Victor." In *Contemporary Reflections on the Medieval Christian Tradition: Essays in Honor of Ray C. Petry*, edited by George H. Shriver, 135–58. Durham: Duke University Press, 1974.
———. "History and Interpretation: 'Hebrew Truth,' Judaism, and the Victorine exegetical tradition." In *Jews and Christians: Exploring the Past, Present, and Future*, edited by James H. Charlesworth, 100–122. New York: Crossroad, 1990.
———. "Hugh of St. Victor and the Art of Memory." *Viator* 5 (1974): 211–34.
———. "Hugh of St. Victor's *De scripturis et scriptoribus sacris* as an Accessus Treatise for the Study of the Bible." *Traditio* 52 (1997): 111–34.
———. "The Influence of Hugh of Saint-Victor's *Chronicon* on the *Abbreviationes chronicorum* by Ralph of Diceto." *Speculum* 52 (1977): 38–61.
———. "Mandala Symbolism and Use in the Mysticism of Hugh of St. Victor." *History of Religions* 12 (1972): 317–41.
———. "The Regular Canons." In *Christian Spirituality: Origins to the Twelfth Century*, edited by Bernard McGinn and John Meyendorff with Jean Leclercq, 218–28. New York: Crossroad, 1985.
———. "Suger, Theology, and the Pseudo-Dionysian Tradition." In *Abbot Suger and Saint-Denis: A Symposium*, edited by P. L. Gerson, 33–40. New York: Metropolitan Museum of Art, 1986.
———. "Vestigia victorina: Victorine Influence on Spiritual Life in the Middle Ages with Special Reference to Hugh of Saint-Victor's *De institutione novitiorum*." In *L'École de Saint-Victor: Influence et rayonnement du Moyen Âge à l'époque moderne; Colloque international du C.N.R.S. pour le neuvième centenaire de la fondation (1108–2008)*, edited by Dominique Poirel. Turnhout: Brepols, 2010.
Ziolkowski, Jan. "Latin and Vernacular Literature." In *The New Cambridge Medieval History*, vol. 4, c. 1024–c. 1198, edited by David Luscombe and Jonathan Riley-Smith, 658–92. Cambridge: Cambridge University Press, 2004.
———. "Lost and Not Yet Found: Heloise, Abelard, and the *Epistolae duorum amantium*." *Journal of Medieval Latin* 14 (2004): 171–202.
Zöller, Rainer. *Die Vorstellung vom Willen in der Morallehre Senecas*. Munich: K. G. Saur, 2003.

Contributors

Jeremy Adams is Altshuler Distinguished Teaching Professor in the Department of History, Southern Methodist University. His work employs the methods of intellectual and social historians to consider the history of human belonging and its obverse, exclusion. This has led him to publish on a wide variety of subjects, including Joan of Arc, Augustine and Jerome, and even modern, multicultural New Orleans.

Walter Cahn is Carnegie Professor Emeritus in the history of art, Yale University, and an authority on medieval art and architecture. His long publishing career has included specialized studies on topics such as *The Romanesque Wooden Doors of the Auvergne* (1974); *Romanesque Bible Illumination* (1982); *A Survey of Manuscripts Illuminated in France* (1996); and, on a more conceptual plane, *Masterpieces: Chapters in the History of an Idea* (1979).

William W. Clark is professor of art history at Queens College and the Graduate Center of the City University of New York, and author of many influential studies of medieval art and architecture. His publications include *Medieval Cathedrals* (2005); (with Charles M. Radding), *Medieval Architecture, Medieval Learning: builders and masters in the age of Romanesque and Gothic* (1992); *Laon Cathedral, Architecture* 1 (1983), 2 (1987); and (with Robert Bork, et al.), *New Approaches to Medieval Architecture* (2011).

Raymond Clemens is Curator for Early Books and Manuscripts at the Beinecke Rare Book and Manuscript Library, Yale University. His research interests particularly include the history of the book and late medieval hagiography. With Timothy Graham, he is the author of *Introduction to Manuscript Studies* (2007).

Marcia L. Colish, Frederick B. Artz Professor Emerita, Oberlin College, is currently lecturer in history at Yale University. A recognized authority on medieval intellectual history, her publications include the two-volume study, *Peter Lombard* (1994), winner of the Haskins Medal of the Medieval Academy of America, of which she is a past president.

Boyd Taylor Coolman is associate professor of theology at Boston College. His research centers on the Victorines and on early scholastic theology at the University of Paris. He has published a number of studies, including *The Theology of Hugh of St. Victor: An Interpretation* (2010), *Knowing God by Experience: The Spiritual Senses in the Theology of William of Auxerre* (2004), and (with Dale Coulter) *Trinity and Creation: A Selection of Works of Hugh, Richard, and Adam of St Victor*, in the Victorine Texts in Translation series (2010).

Dale M. Coulter is associate professor of historical theology at Regent University School of Divinity. He is an editor of the series Victorine Texts in Translation, and co-edited the first volume of the series, *Trinity and Creation* (2010). He has written two books and numerous articles primarily concerning pentecostalism and the history of Christianity. He is co-editor of PNEUMA: *The Journal of the Society for Pentecostal Studies*. In addition to his academic work, Dr. Coulter is involved in ecumenical discussions and is a participating member of Evangelicals and Catholics Together.

Catherine Delano-Smith is Senior Research Fellow at the Institute of Historical Research, University of London, and the editor of *Imago Mundi: The*

International Journal for the History of Cartography. She publishes widely on the history of maps and map-making, and is co-author (with R. J. P. Kain) of *English Maps: A History* (1999) and (with E. M. Ingram) *Maps in Bibles, 1500–1600: An Illustrated Catalogue* (1991).

Hugh Feiss is a Benedictine monk at the Monastery of the Ascension in Jerome, Idaho. His publications include translations, such as the *Works of Peter of Celle*, *Essential Monastic Wisdom*, and *Two Latin Lives of St. Winefride*, as well as studies of the theology of Frowin of Engelberg and the canons regular of St. Victor.

Rachel Fulton Brown is associate professor of medieval history at the University of Chicago. A cultural and intellectual historian, her work places particular emphasis on the history of Christianity and monasticism in the Latin West. Her publications include *From Judgment to Passion: Devotion to Christ and the Virgin Mary, 800–1200* (2002), and (co-edited with Bruce Holsinger) *History in the Comic Mode: Medieval Communities and the Matter of Person* (2007).

Franklin T. Harkins is assistant professor of theology and medieval studies at Fordham University in New York City. His research interests include the Victorines, Jewish-Christian relations, and Peter Lombard and the *Sentences* commentary tradition. He is the author of *Reading and the Work of Restoration: History and Scripture in the Theology of Hugh of St. Victor* (2009), and the editor of *Transforming Relations: Essays on Jews and Christians throughout History in Honor of Michael Signer* (2010). With Frans van Liere, he is editing two volumes on scriptural interpretation in the Victorine Texts in Translation series.

E. Ann Matter is William R. Kenan, Jr., Professor in the Department of Religious Studies at the University of Pennsylvania, Philadelphia. Although specializing in early medieval religion and mysticism, she has also written on women's history from the early Middle Ages to the early modern period. Her most recent publications are *The New Cambridge History of the Bible*, vol. 2, *600–1400* (co-edited with Richard Marsden), and two critical editions: *Una mistica contestata: La Vita di Lucia di Narni (1476–1544) tra agiografia a autobiografia* (2011, with Gabriella Zarri), and *Alcuin's De fide* (2012, with Eric Knibbs).

Barbara Newman is professor of English, religion, and classics and John Evans Professor of Latin at Northwestern University. Known for her work on medieval religious culture and women's spirituality, she is the author most recently of *Medieval Crossover: Reading the Secular Against the Sacred*. She is the author of *Frauenlob's Song of Songs: A Medieval German Poet and his Masterpiece* (2006), *God and the Goddesses: Vision, Poetry, and Belief in the Middle Ages* (2003), and *From Virile Woman to WomanChrist: Studies in Medieval Religion and Literature* (1995). She has also edited and translated works by Hildegard of Bingen and Thomas of Cantimpré.

Dominique Poirel is Directeur de recherche at the Institut de Recherche et d'Histoire des Textes at CNRS (Institut des sciences humaines et sociales), and a lecturer in religious sciences at l'École Pratique des Hautes Études in Paris. He specializes in the Parisian school of St. Victor, the Latin reception of Ps.-Dionysius, Franciscan authors, and the history of intellectual methods. In 2010, he was Doino Visiting Professor at the Franciscan Institute of St. Bonaventure University. With Patrice Sicard, he is co-director of the critical edition of Hugh of St. Victor's *Opera omnia* in the *Corpus Christianorum* series. Recent work includes his editorship of the proceedings of the international conference, *L'école de Saint-Victor de Paris: Influence et rayonnement du Moyen Âge à l'époque moderne* (2010).

Lesley Smith is Fellow and Tutor in Politics and Senior Tutor at Harris Manchester College, Oxford University. Her research centers on intellectual history in the twelfth and thirteenth centuries, often using the evidence of biblical exegesis at the University of Paris. Most recently, she has published *The Glossa Ordinaria: The Making of a Medieval Bible Commentary* (2009), and (with Conrad Leyser) *Motherhood, Religion, and Society, 400–1400* (2011).

Frans van Liere is professor of history at Calvin College, Michigan. He studies the history of biblical exegesis, with particular emphasis on the Victorine scholar Andrew of St. Victor. He has published editions of Andrew on Samuel and Kings and the Twelve Prophets, and with Franklin Harkins is editing two volumes on scriptural interpretation for the Victorine Texts in Translation series.

Thomas Waldman has written extensively on English and French ecclesiastical history, palaeography, and diplomatics, with a particular emphasis on the abbey of St. Denis. He is currently a visiting scholar at the University of Pennsylvania, Philadelphia. Recent publications include "Money, Stone, Liturgy, and Planning at the Royal Abbey of Saint-Denis," with William W. Clark, in *New Directions in Medieval Architecture* (2011). With Véronique Gazeau, he is editing the Acta of Hugh "of Amiens," Archbishop of Rouen (1130–1164) for the Presse Universitaire de Caen.

Index

Abelard, Peter
  on conscience, 244n26
  correspondence with Heloise, 283–85
  defining love, 283
  description of Trinity, 313
  Walter of St. Victor on, 171
Abrégé de la fondation de l'abbaye de St Victor de Paris, 76
Achard of St. Victor, sermons of, 157, 167–71
  for the Feast of All Saints, 168–69
  on the feast of the dedication of a church, 169–71
  on Lent, 167–68
  on the Trinity, 171
action (*operatio*), exercise of, 110

activity of men as element of beauty in universe, 252
Adamnán, 3, 6
Adam of Balsham, 174
Additiones (Paul of Burgos), 29, 41n84
Ade de Roucy, 333
Adelaide de Maurienne, Queen, 78
Adelheid von Ottenstein, 374, 382n49
adiophora, doctrine of, 239
Adso of Montmoutier-en-Der, 345
aesthetic, opposing views of Suger and Bernard of Clairvaux, 92, 94–97
Alacoque, Marguerite-Marie, 288
Alberic of Reims, 134
Albertano of Brescia, 117

Albert of Aachen
  on crusaders, 340n22
  on Raimbold Creton, 330
  on Thomas de Marle, 334–35
Albert the Great
  on *scintilla rationis*, 236
  on *synderesis* and conscience, 237–38
Alexander, J. J. G., 40n68
Alexander of Hales, 237, 245n27
allegorical interpretation
  Achard *versus* Richard of St. Victor, 171
  based on understanding of literal meaning, 8–9
  Cassian's fourfold method of, 388
  of church building, 161
  of Song of Songs, 387–88
  as superstructure of building, 104
Allegories of the Tabernacle of the Covenant (Richard of St. Victor), 391
allegorization, *distinctiones* as guides to, 167
altar and revelation of Trinity, 316–17
amanuenses of women visionaries, 378n3
Ambrose, 234
Amplonville, priory of, 156
Anacletus II (antipope), 86
anagogical exegesis, 388, 392
analogies
  of church as building in need of rebuilding, 371
  of seal impressed in wax, 116
Anastasius IV, Pope, 377
Andrew of St. Victor, 145, 348–55
  and Jewish exegetes, 342, 348
  use of firsthand sources, 349, 354
Angela of Foligno, 295

angels
  Hugh of St. Victor on fall of, 199n36
  knowledge of God by direct illumination, 213
  lower ranks of, 219
Annales (Jean de Thoulouse), 76
Anselm of Canterbury, 239
Anselm of Laon, 138, 150n1
Antichrist
  Jewish Messiah as
  —Andrew on, 353
  —Jerome on, 345
  legend of, 344–45
  in *Liber trium virorum*, 373
Antiquités (Jean de Thoulouse), 76
Apologia (Bernard of Clairvaux)
  aesthetic in, 92
  citing Psalm 25, 94
Apologists, 108
archaeology and church of St. Victor, 70, 72f, 80n6
"Architecture and Exegesis" (Cahn), 34n6
archival records and catalogues
  on non-narrative illustrations, 35n20
Argenteuil, priory of, 93
Aristotle
  Jerome's use of, 235
  Lefèvre on study of, 361
  logical writings arranged in scholastic order, 127n33
Ark treatises (Hugh of St. Victor)
  measure pertaining to desire and thought, 194
  on measurements of the Ark, 195
  moral-mystical reading of the symbol of Noah's Ark, 195
Arndt, Johann, 388
Arnulf (bishop of Lisieux), 156

450   Index

Augustine
  allegorical interpretation of Psalm 25, 93
  on *conscientia*, 234–35
  distinction between use and delight, 190
  doctrine of the divided self, 235
  doctrine of the *hegemonikon*, 234
  on Jews
  —blindness to meaning of Old Testament, 343
  —common eschatological future with Christians, 351
  on prophecy, 305
  read by students at St. Victor, 122
  on scriptural narrative and charity, 122–23
  spiritual association of cardinal points, 4
  symbolic significance of the Temple, 10
  transformation through Scripture reading, 123–24, 126n5
  use of Neoplatonism, 107

Bach, Johann Sebastian. *See Wachet auf!* (Bach)
baptism, revelation of Trinity in, 314–15
Bautier, R.-H., 76, 77–78, 79
Beatus Rhenanus, 362, 364, 367, 374
beauty
  difference between Hugh's and Greek concept of, 253
  elements of, 253
  as harmony between the part and the whole, 271, 272
  Hugh of St. Victor on spirituality and theology of, 247–80
  as object of love and affection, 263–67
  as radiance of wisdom, 258
  of the soul, Hugh of St. Victor on, 187–88
  —association with justice, 187
  —loss of original beauty as loss of measure, 189–91
  theophanic, 257
  ubiquitous theme in Hugh of St. Victor, 271
  visible, as image of invisible beauty, 262–63
Beck, Harry, 34n9
Bede
  plans in *De locis santis*, 6
  spiritual association of cardinal points, 4
  symbolic significance of the Temple, 10
Bennett, Judith, 295
Benton, John F., 331, 339
Bernard of Clairvaux
  attitude toward art and visual representation, 46, 92
  debates on Trinity, 313
  intervention with Pope Eugene III, 156
  laudatory letter to Suger, 92
  letter of Hildegard of Bingen to, 302–3
  and monasticism as philosophy, 109
  Suger and, 95
Berno (abbot of Reichenau), 361
Bible
  beginning of textual and historical approach, 342–43
  emphasis on the east in connection with the Tabernacle and the Temple, 4
  exegetical maps for New Testament, 41n81
  French translation by Lefèvre, 360
  See also scripture reading

Bible commentaries
  Canticle of Habbakuk
    —alternative readings by Andrew, 350–51
    —interpretation by Jerome, 350
  Hosea
    —Andrew's exegesis on, 353
    —*Glossa ordinaria* on, 348
  Joel 2:28–32
    —Andrew's exegesis of, 352
    —Jerome's interpretation of, 352
  Obadiah
    —Andrew on, 351–52
    —Jerome on, 346
  Zechariah, Jerome and Haimo on, 347
  Zephaniah, Jerome and Haimo on, 347
  See also Ezekiel, book of; Matthew 25; prophets, study of biblical; Psalms; Song of Songs
Bible manuscripts
  including four-river plan for chapter 12 of *In visionem Ezechielis*, 21–22
  Oxford, Bodleian Library, Ms Laud Lat. 9, 22, 24f, 25, 30
  Oxford, Brasenose College, Ms 5, 22, 23f, 25, 28, 40n68
Birgitta of Sweden, 363
Boethius
  commentary on *Isagogue* (Porphyry), 206–7, 208, 209
  on division of theoretical philosophy, 207–8
  influence on Hugh of St. Victor, 211, 218
  and term *animus*, 225n4
  and term *speculatio*, 206–10, 216
Bonaventure
  on conscience, 237
  integration of Aristotelian ideas into Christianity, 205
  scintilla rationis and, 236
  on *synderesis*, 237
Bonnard, Fourier, 76–77
Book of Three Men and Three Spiritual Virgins, A. *See Liber trium virorum et trium spiritualium virginum* (Jacques Lefèvre d'Étaples)
Brasington, Bruce, 329, 330
Briçonnet, Guillaume, 360
Bruni, Leonardo, 361
Bruno of Segni, 98n8
Buildwas, abbey of, 134–35
  library of (*See also* Glossed books of Robert Amiclas)
  —books in addition to Amiclas Glosses, 148–49t
  —Robert Amiclas's books part of, 132
  —surviving manuscripts from, 132
  retirement of Robert Amiclas at, 135
Bur, Michel, 337
Burnett, Charles, 139

Cahn, Walter, 9, 34n6
Calixtus II, 88
Calvin, John, 29
Cameron, Richard M., 379n5
Canaan, maps of
  cardinal points in, 4
  earliest exegetical map of, 6
  in Rashi, 7, 26, 28
  in *In visionem Ezechielis*, 25–28, 27f
canons of St. Victor
  combination of monastic way of life and ordained ministry, 154, 177
  influenced by Pseudo-Dionysius the Areopagite, 174
  literal concern with Ezekiel's Temple vision, 21
  ministry of, 154, 156, 180
  in priories, 157
  sermons of, 180–81
  See also St. Victor, abbey of

canons regular
  beauty in disciplined behavior of, 267
  customaries and constitutions of, 155
capitula in Mazarine Ms. 729, 51
cardinal points
  meanings of, 3–4
  north as source of evil, 372
Carlevaris, Angela, 358
Casagrande, Carla, 117
Cassian, John
  fourfold method of allegorical interpretation, 388
  tropological or moral mode, 385
Cassiodorus
  allegorical interpretation of Psalm 25, 93
  Tabernacle plan, 6, 36n23
Caterina de Ricci, 288
cathedral schools on desire for inner-outer correspondence, 115
Catherine of Siena, 288
Celestial Hierarchy (Pseudo-Dionysius), 262
  on lower ranks of angels, 219
  translation by Eriugena, 212
Chadwick, Henry, 207
Chambre des Députés Bible
  artist of, 61, 62
  David fighting the lion, *63f*
change as part of beauty, 253
Chanson de Jerusalem, 335
Charles the Bald, 92
Châtillon, Jean, 171–72, 184n50, 221
Chaurand, Jacques, 331, 336, 341n41
Christe, Yves, 95
Christianity as philosophy par excellence, 103
Christian Topography (Cosmas Indicopleustes), 6
Christocentrism of Walter of St. Victor, 173

Chronicon (Hugh of St. Victor)
  beginning of Hugh's pedagogical program, 114
  on challenge of moral reading, 125
Chrysippus, 232, 240n4
church building
  allegorical meaning of, 161
  tropological meaning of, 162
  See also metaphors: of building
Clarembald of Vendeuil, 334
Clark, Anne, 362, 371, 381n38, 381n39
Cligès (Chrétien de Troyes), 285
Codex Amiatinus, 5–6
cogitatio, 214, 215
coinherence, doctrine of
  in Abelard's letters, 284
  expressed by exchange of hearts, 282
  Gospel of John on, 282–83
  in mystical hagiography from Helfta, 290
  St. Hermann Joseph and, 286
Commentarius super tota bibliam (Hugh of St. Cher), 21
Commentary on Ezekiel (Richard of St. Victor). *See In visionem Ezechielis* (Richard of St. Victor)
Commentary on the Celestial Hierarchy (Hugh of St. Victor), 56, 192
  on formific beauty of God, 259–63
  influence of, 48
  use of *speculatio* in, 212–14
  views of beauty in, 248
Confessiones (Augustine), 122–23
confirmation, revelation of Trinity in, 315
conscience *(conscientia)*
  Abelard on, 244n26
  Albert the Great on, 238
  Ambrose on, 234
  Augustine on, 234–35
  Duns Scotus on, 238–39
  examination of, 230, 231

Jerome on, 235–36
  as mirror of sin, 234
  Seneca's use of term, 232–33
  Stoicism and, 229, 231
Consolation (Boethius), 208–9
contemplation *(contemplatio)*
  of the beautiful, 248
  close connection to *speculatio*, 205
  in *Expositio in Ecclesiasten*, 214, 215
  of God at St. Victor, 108
  as one of the elements of a devout Christian life, 158
  Richard of St. Victor's levels of, 389
contemplativi, 217–21
Contra Faustum (Augustine), 60f
  copy by Aubertus, 62
Contra quatuor labyrinthos Franciae (Walter of St. Victor), 171
Corpus Dionysiacum, 361
Cosmas Indicopleustes, 6
Crosby, Sumner, 93
crusaders, returning, 328–41
crusades and martyrdom of Jewish communities in the Rhineland, 345

Dante Alighieri, 230
dating of manuscripts, 151n15
De amore sponsi ad sponsam (Hugh of St. Victor), 50, 56, 57f, 59
De arca mystica (Richard of St. Victor), 218, 219
  on contemplation, 388–89
  —on three modes of, 220
  —and three modes of ecstasy in Song of Songs, 391
  speculatio in, 223–24
  translation of, 384
De archa Noe morali (Hugh of St. Victor), 55
  illuminations in Mazarine Ms. 729, 55f

De arrha animae (Hugh of St. Victor), 263–67
De Bruyne, Edgar, 247
decision making, etiology of conscientious, 233–34
De clementia (Seneca), 233
De Consecratione (Suger), 91
De contemptu mundi, as literary genre, 56
De differentia sacrificii Abrahae a sacrificio beatae Mariae Virginis (Richard of St. Victor), 218, 220
De duodecim patriarchis (Richard of St. Victor), 221–23
De exterminatione mali et promotione bona (Richard of St. Victor), 221
deference, practicing humble virtue of, 116
De Genesis ad litteram (Augustine), 305
De glorificatione Trinitatis et processione sancti Spiritus (Rupert of Deutz), 310
De institutione novitiorum (Hugh of St. Victor), 48
  aesthetic conception of virtue, 187
  on comportment, 192, 267
  contrast between humility and pride, 116
  as extended tropological commentary on Psalm 118:66, 112
  in Mazarine Ms. 729, 50
  practical instructions on leading a virtuous life, 104, 111–12
  use of the circumstances in, 117–18
  on ways to integrate knowledge in self, 114
De ira (Seneca), 233
De locis santis (Adamnán)
  measurements from the Church of the Holy Sepulchre in Jerusalem, 3
  plans used by Bede, 6

454   Index

De Maria Magdalena et triduo Christi disceptatio (Jacques Lefèvre d'Étaples), 360
De obitu (Eckbert), 367
De officiis (Ambrose), 234
De officio missae (Berno), 361
De ornatu spiritualium nuptiarum (Ruysbroeck), 361, 363–64
De orthodoxa fide (John of Damascus), 361
De sacramentis Christianae fidei (Hugh of St. Victor), 48
  on creation of rational creatures, 188–89
  in Mazarine Ms. 729, 50
  —illuminations, 51–55, *52f, 53f, 54f*
  and proper allegorical reading, 125
De sacramentis legis naturalis (Hugh of St. Victor), 56
De scriptoribus ecclesiasticis (Trithemius), 373
De tribus diebus (Hugh of St. Victor)
  on beauty of visible beings, 248
  on created perfections of the sensible universe, 249–50
  edition by Poirel, 50
  lists in, 251–52
  in Mazarine Ms. 729, 50
  as treatise on admiration, 254–55
De tribus maximis circumstancii gestorum (Hugh of St. Victor), 47
De tribus processionibus (Richard of St. Victor). *See Super exiit edictum* (Richard of St. Victor)
De Trinitate (Boethius), 207–8
De Trinitate (Richard of St. Victor), 361, 362
De vanitate mundi (Hugh of St. Victor), 50, 56, 58–59, *58f*, 61

diagrams
  use for demonstrative purposes by Hugh of St. Victor, 47
  use of term, 3
  See also drawing, exegetical; maps and plans in medieval exegesis
Dialogues (Gregory the Great), 179
Dictionnaire (Hurtaut), 74
Didascalicon (Hugh of St. Victor), 103–4, 272
  aesthetic conception of virtue, 187
  on author of Ecclesiastes, 61
  on contribution of saints to student's knowledge of virtue, 116
  on dignity of mechanical arts, 46
  influence on *Liber exceptionum*, 218
  on proper *ordo* of exercises, 110
  on *speculatio*, 210–12
  on trespassing measure, 192
Diplomatique Médiévale, 88
disciplina
  as type of education or formation, 109
  use of term by Hugh of St. Victor, 110
distinctiones, 167
divided self, doctrine of, 235
Dominicans, 238
Donne, John, 282
Dorothy of Montau, 288
Dove, Mary, 152n24
drawing, exegetical, 2–5
  keyed into the text
    —in *Postilla litteralis* (Nicholas of Lyra), 29
    —in *In visionem Ezechielis*, 8
  measurements, 3
  in *Postilla litteralis* (Nicholas of Lyra), 5
  significance of cardinal points in, 3–4
drawings, ichnographic, 9

Eberhard of Bamberg, 313
Ebles de Roucy, 336, 337
Eckbert of Schönau, 367, 369
education
    Lefèvre's curriculum for reading spiritual and mystical texts, 361
    program of Hugh of St. Victor
    —correct reading of scriptures and creation, 204–5
    —elements of, 125
Elisabeth of Schönau, 359, 365
    Clark on, 381n38, 381n39
    discovery by Lefèvre, 361–62
    Eckbert on, 367, 369–70
    on individual sins and the church, 371
    influenced by Hildegard, 371
    metaphor of souls ascending a mountain, 382n43
    visions
    —ecstatic nature of, 365, 369–70
    —illustration of reception of, 366f, 367
Emicho of Flonheim, 334
Enguerrand de Boves, 333, 336, 337
Enneads (Plotinus), 107
Epictetus
    on attention, 107
    compared to Seneca, 231
    on will, 232
Epictetus (Long), 241n4
Ernisius, Abbot of St. Victor, 175
Eschaton (apocalyptic end of time), 386–87
Eskriche, Pierre, 32
Estienne, Henri (the elder)
    Lefèvre and, 362, 380n19
    printer of *Liber trium virorum*, 358
    use of multiple codices in editions by, 382n47
Eugene III, Pope, 156
Eusebius (bishop of Caesarea), 5

Everard III of Le Puiset, 336
example, importance of providing and following, 115–16, 270
    Richard of St. Victor on, 164–65
exchange of hearts, metaphor of, 281–99
    as communal in Helfta writings, 290–95
    in mystical writings, 282, 287–88
    in saints' lives, 282
    in vernacular romances, 285
exemplarism, 258
Explanation of the Rule of St. Augustine (attr. Hugh of St. Victor), 186–87
explicits in Mazarine Ms. 729, 51
Expositio in Ecclesiasten (Hugh of St. Victor)
    meditatio, 214, 215
    use of *speculatio*, 214, 215–16
Ezekiel, book of
    Abelard on, 137
    Andrew's commentary on, 354
    Gregory the Great on literal understanding of, 8
    Hugh of St. Cher on Ezekiel 47, 21
    Jerome's commentary on, 235
    Nicholas of Lyra commentary on Ezekiel 47, 29–30
    —plan for, 30, *31f*
    visual thinking in, 9
    See also In visionem Ezechielis (Richard of St. Victor)

Fall, the, Hugh of St. Victor on, 190–91
fall of angels, Hugh of St. Victor on, 199n36
Figura terre repromissionis, 6
Fish, Stanley, 120–21, 121–22
Flamenca, 285
Flanagan, Sabina, 312
    on division of *Scivias*, 303–4

456   Index

Fleury-en Bière, priory of, 156
Flowing Light of the Godhead (Mechthild of Magdeburg), 288
Fons philosophiae (Fountain of Philosophy) (Godfrey of St. Victor), 175, 177–78
Francis I, 360
Franciscans, 238
friendship
  of Gertrude and Mechthild, 289, 292
  particular friendships, 292, 298n47
Führkötter, Adelgundis, 358

Gameson, Richard, 18
Gasparri, Françoise, 178
Gebeno of Eberbach, 323–24
  compilation of Hildegard of Bingen's writings, 303, 373
Geography (Ptolemy), 32
Gerard of Provins, 42n85
Gerson, Jean, 363
Gertrude of Hackeborn, 288
Gertrude the Great, 288. *See also* *Legatus divinae pietatis*
Gervasius von Canterbury (Schröder), 34n6
Gesta (Suger), 91
Gesta Dei per Francos (Guibert of Nogent), 332
gesture. *See* movement, discipline of
Ghellinck, Joseph de, 302
Gilbert de la Porrée
  commentary on the Pauline Epistles, 61, 62
  possible teacher of Robert Amiclas, 134
  Walter of St. Victor on, 171
Gilbert of Auxerre, 348
Gilbert of Poitiers, 313
Gilbertus Universalis. *See* Gilbert of Auxerre

Gilduin of St. Victor
  and church of St. Victor, 68, 77
  Indiculum, 48
Gill, Christopher, 240n4
Girard (bishop of Séez), 156
Glossed Bible (*Glossa ordinaria*), 131–52, 150n1
  anti-Judaism of, 354
  formats of, 140–41
  history of glossing of each book, 147
  inclusion of Haimo's commentary in, 347–48
  influence of Jerome on, 235
  on Jewish messianism, 344
  on Minor Prophets, 348–49
  as schools text, 147
  standardization of, 147, 152n24
Glossed books
  collections of, 138–39
  common groups of, 137
Glossed books of Robert Amiclas, 135, 136t, 137–38
  acquisitions of, 140–42
  annotations in, 142–47
  —changes for ease of use, 145–46
  —comments, 146
  —completing missing texts, 142
  —order of glosses, 144
  —and standardization, 143–44
  —textual clarifications, 144–45
  by date, 133t
  early date of, 140
  formats, 141–42
  as uncommon collection, 138–39
Glunz, H. H., 40n68
Godfrey of St. Victor
  Maurice de Sully compared to, 179
  self-portraits, 178
  sermons of, 157, 174–78
  —on All Saints' Day, 175–77
Golden Legend (Jacobus de Voragine), 287

Gothic architecture, origins of, 47–48
Gottfried of St. Disibod, 323
   and *vita* of Hildegard, 376
Grant, Lindy, 92, 337, 341n30
Gregory the Great
   on impossibility of a literal understanding of the book of Ezekiel, 8
   on parallel between procedures of biblical exegesis and stages of construction, 47, 104
   Richard of St. Victor on, 158
   as source for Maurice de Sully's sermons, 179
   spiritual association of cardinal points, 4
Grimault, A., 70, 72–76, 72f, 73f
Grosse, Rolf, 88
Gruber, Mayer, 7, 9
Guarinus of St. Albans and St. Victor, 51
Guerric of Igny, 109
Guibert of Gembloux, 376
Guibert of Nogent
   Chaurand on, 341n41
   treatment of Thomas de Marle, 330–34
   —compared to Suger's, 338–39
Guigo II, 158
Guillaume de Champeaux.
   See William of Champeaux
Guy de Rochefort, 336
Guy Trousseau, 336–37

Hadewijch, 295
Hadot, Pierre, 126n10
   on ancient philosophy as a way of life, 104, 109
   on modern understanding of philosophy, 104–5
   on philosophical meditation, 106
   on philosophy, 207

Haimeric, Cardinal, 88, 99n16
Haimo of Auxerre
   influenced by Jerome, 345–47
   on Jewish messianism, 344
Haimo of Halberstadt, 345
Harrison, Anna, 289, 291
hearing, joys of, 250–51
heart
   of Christ in vision of Mechthild, 290
   Hugh of St. Victor on, 114–15
   as location of ethical values, 230
   See also exchange of hearts, metaphor of; Sacred Heart
hegemonikon, doctrine of, 234
Heito (abbot of Reichenau), 358–59, 368, 370
Helfta, abbey of, 282, 380n22
   mystical hagiography from, 288–94
   theological culture at, 288
Heloise, 283–85
Henrici, Christian Friedrich, 387
Hermann Joseph, Saint, 286
Hermas
   analogy of church in, 371
   on corruption in the church, 370
   influence
   —on Hildegard, 322, 371
   —on Robert of Uzès, 372
   Shepherd of Hermas in *Liber trium virorum*, 358, 364
   vision reception by, 368
   —illustration of, 365, 366f
Herod's Temple
   destruction by Romans seen by Christians as divine punishment, 343
   importance in ancient Judaism, 10
   Mishnah's references to, 37n42
   profile by Maimonides, 3
Hildebert of Lavardin, 113, 182n21

Hildegard of Bingen
  as *alter Johannes*, 321
  analogy of church in, 371
  and Gregorian reform, 370–71
  images used to explain Trinity, 314
  influenced by Hermas, 322, 371
  influence on Robert of Uzès, 372
  as *magistra sententiarum*, 302
  obscurity in writings of, 303, 323–24
  status as prophet and visionary, 303, 307, 324
  structure of work, 322–23
  vision reception by, 369
  —illustration of, 366f, 367
  visions substantive to her theology, 307
  vita, 376, 377
  See also *Scivias*
Hilduin (abbot), 92
historia, internalization of, 118, 125
Historia calamitatum (Abelard), 137
Historia Hierosolimitana (Albert of Aachen), 334–35
Historia Ierosolymitana (William of Tyre), 134
Historia occidentalis (Jacques de Vitry), 154
historical interpretation, 388
Histories (Herodotus), 351
History of Deeds Done Across the Sea (William of Tyre), 335
History of the Vulgate (Glunz), 40n68
Homilies on Ecclesiastes (Hugh of St. Victor), 61
  on loss of measure in pursuit of knowledge, 192–93, 194
Honorius II, Pope, 94
Hugh of St. Cher, 6
  contradicted by Nicholas of Lyra, 29–30
  exegesis on Ezekiel 47 similar to Richard, 21

Hugh of St. Pol, 335
Hugh of St. Victor
  account of the Fall, 190–91
  on beauty
  —at the heart of his spirituality, 248
  —of the soul, 186–203
  —spirituality and theology of, 247–80
  on Christian philosopher, 110
  commentary on Pseudo-Dyonisius, 174
  created realities as God's language, 206
  on difference between Sacred Scripture and other writings, 165
  on dignity of mechanical arts, 46
  elements of education program, 125
  on fall of the angels, 199n36
  as gifted writer, 247
  images of, 49–50
  influenced by Boethius, 218
  influence on
  —Richard of St. Victor, 215
  —Suger, 48
  and Jewish exegetes, 342
  metaphor of painting exterior of an edifice with beautiful colors, 108
  and necessary correspondence of sacred reading and Christian living, 103–4
  Paris, Bibl. Mazarine, Ms 729, 50–67
  —illuminations, 51–62
  —irregularities in treatment of material, 51
  —texts included in, 50
  possible teacher of Robert Amiclas, 134
  rapid diffusion of writings of, 50
  reading in liberal arts and Sacred Scripture as a single *philosophia*, 104
  on scripture as honeycomb, 113, 114
  on status of original creation, 198n25

students of, 113–14
on tropology, 111
use of *speculatio*, 210–17
human being as most beautiful thing in creation, 258–59
human body
admiration of, 252
resemblance to human soul, 255–56
Hurtaut, P.-T.-N., 73–74

Ibn Hazm of Cordoba, 285
Ignatius, Saint, legends about, 286–87
Illuminated Manuscripts (Alexander and Temple), 40n68
illumination of the Mazarine codex Ms. 729, 51–62
artist, 62
construction of a church, 55f
creation of heaven and earth, 52f
creation of the angels, 53f
dialogue of the Soul and Reason, 58f
foliation of the manuscript, 65n17
Heavenly Bridegroom, 57f
marriage, 54f
ornamental initials, 51
imagery of Hildegard, 314, 323
imagination
rational *versus* bestial, 221–22
speculatio and, 222–23
incipits in Mazarine Ms. 729, 51
indefferenter, 284
Indiculum (Gilduin of St. Victor), 48
individual, medieval concepts of the, 243n24
indwelling, mutual. *See* coinherence, doctrine
iniustitia, *Scivias* on, 311
Innocent II, Pope
and France, 87
on *ordo* of St. Victor, 155
privilege for the abbey of St. Feuillien de Roeulx, 99n14
visit to abbey of St. Denis, 86–87
See also St. Denis, abbey of: Innocent II's privilege for
In visionem Ezechielis (Richard of St. Victor)
contradicted by Nicholas of Lyra on Temple stream, 29–30
dating of, 39n64
illustrations in, 44–45, 49
— dimensions in geometrical diagram, 3
— drawings, 7–9
incomplete at time of author's death, 16
manuscripts, 2, 42–43
— Cambridge, Corpus Christi College, 315, fol. 113r, 25–26
— Durham, A. III.22, 18–19
— with missing folios, 34n5
— Oxford, Bodleian Library, Ms Bodl. 459, 27f, 34n5
— Oxford, Bodleian Library, Ms e Mus. 62, 19, 34n5
— Paris, BnF, lat. 2165, 16, 17f, 18, 39n57
— Paris, BnF, lat. 3438, fol. 81r, 26
— Paris, BnF, lat. 14516, 19
— Troyes, MAT, 544, fols. 1–36, 19
— Vatican City, BAV, Reg. Lat. 277, 18, 39n57
— in Zwickau, 34n5
map of Canaan, 25–28, 27f
Temple plans, 9–25
— general layout, 11–12, 12f
— kitchens in, 15
— omission of four-river plan in many manuscripts, 19
— plan for chapter 12, 12, 13, 17f, 20f, 21–22
— plan for chapter 16, 14f
— varying complexity, 10–11
use of Rashi's map of the visionary Canaan, 7

460　Index

Isagogue (Porphyry), 206–7, 208, 209
Ivo of Chartres
　interpretation of Psalm 25, 93
　on Raimbol Creton, 329–30

Jacobus de Voragine, 287
Jacques de Vitry, 154
Jaeger, C. Stephen, 115
James, M. R., 132
Jauss, Hans Robert, 121
Javelet, Robert, 205
Jean de Thoulouse, 76–77
Jerome
　on conscience, 235–36
　influence on Haimo of Auxerre, 345–47
　on Jewish Messiah as Christian Antichrist, 345
　polemical stance against Jews, 344
Jewish exegetes
　Andrew of St. Victor and, 354–55
　on biblical prophets, 342
　influence of, 6–7, 342
　Nicholas of Lyra and, 29
Jews
　Christian exegetes on blindness to meaning of Old Testament, 343
　eschatological beliefs of, 343–44
　role in Antichrist myth, 345
　in Victorine theology, 183n35
John, Gospel of, 282–83
John of Damascus, 361
John of La Rochelle, 236–37
John of Séez, 155–56
John Scotus Eriugena, 174
Johnson, Penelope D., 62
Josephus, 37n42
Judaism personified as Synagoga, 343
Justin Martyr, 108

Kara, Joseph, 349
Karfíková, Lenka, 247
Kerby-Fulton, Kathryne, 372

Klosterneuburg altar (Nicholas of Verdun), 47
Koberger, Anton, 32

Lactantius, 234
Langmann, Adelheid, 288
language as source of harmony among men, 251
Lawrence of Westminster, 128n53
Leclerq, Jean, 302
　on connection between *philosophia* and *disciplina* in medieval monasticism, 109
Lefèvre d'Étaples, Jacques
　as Christian humanist, 360–61
　and church reform, 359
　—evangelical reform movement, 379n5
　Henri Estienne and, 362
　interest in life of women visionaries, 367
　on nature of visions in *Liber trium virorum*, 365
　on transmission of Hildegard's voice, 376
　works of John of Ruysbroeck printed by, 361, 363–64
　See also *Liber trium virorum et trium spiritualium virginum* (Jacques Lefèvre d'Étaples)
Legatus divinae pietatis (Gertrude the Great), 282, 288
　on intensity of friendship of Mechthild and Gertrude, 289, 292
Libellus de diversis ordinibus, 153–54
Liber de doctrina loquendi et tacendi (Albertano of Brescia), 117
Liber de formatione arche (Hugh of St. Victor), 48, 50
Liber divinorum operum (Hildegard of Bingen)
　manuscripts of, 303
　representations of the Trinity, 307

Liber exceptionum (Richard of
  St. Victor), 158–59
  as help for priests preaching to the
    people, 180
  as source for Maurice de Sully, 179
  speculativi versus *contemplativi*,
    217–18
Liber ordinis of St. Victor, 155
Liber ordinis Sancti Victoris Parisiensis,
  115
Liber scintillarum (Defensor of
  Ligugé), 139
Liber specialis gratiae (Mechthild of
  Hackeborn), 282, 288
  discovery of manuscript by Lefèvre,
    362
  in *Liber trium virorum*, 359
*Liber trium virorum et trium
    spiritualium virginum* (Jacques
    Lefèvre d'Étaples), 358–83
  dedication of work, 372–73, 374
  title page illustrations, 365, 366f
  women visionaries included in, 363
Liber vitae meritorum (Hildegard of
  Bingen), 303
Life of Louis VI (Suger), 337
  on visit of Innocent II at St. Denis, 86
listening, proper comportment when,
  267–68
list of circumstances
  Chronicon (Hugh of St. Victor) on,
    114
  in pedagogy of Hugh of St. Victor, 117
  success during the Middle Ages, 117
literal meaning
  Andrew of St. Victor and, 349
  canons of St. Victor and, 180
  as foundation of allegorical reading,
    104
  importance of visual exegesis for, 9
Lochrie, Karma, 295
Lohrmann, Dietrich, 88–89
Long, A. A., 241n4

Louis VI, 78
  foundation charter of St. Victor, 76,
    77
  on St. Denis, 93
  Thomas de Marle and, 337, 338
love as fusion, 282
  in letters of Heloise and Abelard,
    283–85
  See also exchange of hearts,
    metaphor of
Lull, Raymond, 361
Lutgard of Aywières, 287
Luther, Martin
  influence of medieval mysticism on,
    392
  use of illustration in exegesis, 29

McKitterick, Rosamund, 33
Maimonides (Moses ben Maimon)
  drawings of Herod's Temple, 3, 10
  plans in *Middot (Measures)*, 7
Mâle, Emile, 47
maps, modern example of
    diagrammatic, 34n9
maps and plans in medieval exegesis,
    1–45
  after Richard of St. Victor, 28–33
  before Richard of St. Victor, 5–7
  as topological constructions, 3
  in *In visionem Ezechielis*, 7–28
Marenbon, John, 208
Marot, Jean, 69, 70f, 71f, 75
Matthew 25
  Bach and, 390, 392
  commentary by Richard of
    St. Victor, 159
  Nicolai hymn and, 386
  reading in liturgy, 387
Matthew of Albano, 94, 95
Maurice de Sully (bishop of Paris),
  157, 178–80
  on Abbot Ernisius, 175
  sermons of, 179–80

McGinn, Bernard, on Hildegard
  as female version of John the
    Divine, 309
  representations of the Trinity, 307
  as theologian, 302
meaning, visible beauty conveying,
    255–56
measure *(mensura)*, Hugh of St. Victor
    on, 188–89
  associated with beauty and justice,
    187
  loss of, 192–93
  —and loss of creaturely integrity,
    194–95
  —and loss of original beauty, 189–91
  meaning of, 192–95
Mechthild of Hackeborn, 288
  amanuenses of, 379n3
  Liber specialis gratiae attributed to,
    289
  visions
  —ecstatic nature of, 365
  —illustration of reception of, 366f,
    367
Mechthild of Magdeburg, 288
meditation *(meditatio)*
  in ancient philosophy, 106
  defined by Hugh of St. Victor, 226n26
  in *Expositio in Ecclesiasten*, 214, 215
  as one of the elements of a devout
    Christian life, 158
  at St. Victor, 108
Mérian, 69, 70f, 71f
messianism, Jewish, 343–44
  Messiah as Antichrist
  —Andrew on idea of, 353
  —Jerome on, 345
  vengeful, Andrew and, 351–55
Metamorphosis Goliae, 134
metaphors
  of building, 104, 108, 371–72
  of sculpting, 107–8

  used by Hildegard of Bingen, 307
  See also exchange of hearts,
    metaphor of
Mews, Constant
  on Hildegard of Bingen
  —on importance of, 302
  —on *lux vivens*, 308
  —on metaphors of, 307
  on letters of Heloise and Abelard, 283
  on structure in *Scivias*, 304
Microcosmus (Godfrey of St. Victor),
    175, 178
Midrash Tanhuma, 352
Migne, J.-P., 47, 161, 358
Modes of Cognition Principle, 208
Molinier, Auguste, 50
monasticism
  as a philosophy, 108–9
  Suger's ordinances for the regulation
    of, 92
Monodiae (Guibert of Nogent),
    330–34
monumental arts, influence of Hugh of
    St. Victor on, 47
movement, discipline of, 119, 268–69
Mysticae adnotationes in Psalmos:
    In Psalmum 113 (Richard of
    St. Victor), 218, 219
  discussion of *speculativi*, 219
Mystical Ark, The (Benjamin Major)
    (Richard of St. Victor). *See*
    De arca mystica (Richard of
    St. Victor)
mystical writings, metaphor of
    exchanging hearts in, 282, 287–88

natural moral law, 230
nature
  as a book, 256–57
  parallel with scripture, 257
Nauert, Charles, 379n4
Nelli, René, 285

Neoplatonism
  on spiritual progress and degrees of virtue, 107
  theme of divine beauty in, 259
  theme of participation in, 259–60
Newman, Barbara
  on Hildegard
  —biographer, 323
  —importance of, 302
  —prophecies, 371
  —*vita*, 377
  —writing style, 375
  on order in *Scivias*, 312
  on Theodoric of Echtenach, 376
  on "unlettered" female visionary, 369, 378n3
"new," use of, 39n56
Nicholas of Cusa, 361
Nicholas of Lyra
  commentary on Ezekiel 47, 29–30
  —plan for, 30, 31*f*
  consultation of work by Gerard of Provins, 42n85
  on controversy about four-river plan in *In visionem Ezechielis*, 21
  on difference in exegesis on Temple vision, 29
  importance of literal meaning of scripture, 8–9
  maps and plans by, 41n83
  proportions in, 3
  spiritual association of cardinal points, 4
  and tradition of visual exegesis, 29
  See also *Postilla litteralis super total bibliam* (Nicholas of Lyra)
Nicholas of Verdun, 47
Nichols, Aidan, 304, 305–6
Nicolai, Philipp, 385, 386
Noah's Ark, reconstruction by Hugh of St. Victor, 47
Notre Dame, cathedral of, 179

Odo of Soissons, 303
Old Testament
  historical reading by Andrew of St. Victor, 350
  as read by Christians, 343
On the Distinction of Soul, Spirit, and Mind (Achard), 171
On the Instruction of Novices (Hugh of St. Victor). See *De institutione novitiorum* (Hugh of St. Victor)
"On the Place-Names in Holy Scripture" *(Onomasticon)* (Eusebius), 5
On the Sacraments (Hugh of St. Victor). See *De sacramentis Christianae fidei* (Hugh of St. Victor)
On the Unity of the Spirit and the Body (Hugh of St. Victor), 263
Opera omnia (Nicholas of Cusa), 361
order, beauty of, 252–53
Orderic Vitalis, 330
Ordinatio (Suger), 96
ordo of St. Victor, 155–56
original creation, status of, 198n25
Osanna of Mantua, 288
outward discipline
  beauty in behavior of canons, 267
  esthetic and ethical reasons for, 268, 269
  importance for Hugh, 119
  political reasons for, 269–70
  purposes of, 115
  and reestablishment of esthetic harmony of human person, 268
  taught to novices, 118

Panaetius, 239
Panofsky, Erwin, 47–48
Papsturkunden in Frankreich, 88
Paris, BnF, Ms 471, 62, 67n42
Paschal II, Pope, 329, 339

Patrologia latina (Migne), 47, 161, 358
Paul, Saint
  on conscience, 230
  on indwelling, 283
  and origin of the legend of Antichrist, 344
  Stoicism and, 240n3
Paul of Burgos, 29, 41n84
Pentachronon (Gebeno of Eberbach), 303
perception, four ways of, 208
performance *(actio)* at St. Victor, 108
Peter Comestor, 50, 345
Peter Lombard
  books of, 131, 138
  dependence on others' work, 322
  reception of, 50
  succeeded by Maurice de Sully as bishop of Paris, 179
  use of Glossed biblical texts, 138
  Walter of St. Victor on, 171
  See also Sententiae (Peter Lombard)
Peter of Poitiers, 171
Petit-Radel and Bénard ground plan of church of St. Victor, 69
Philip the Chancellor, 236
Philo, 37n42
philosopher, task of the ancient, 105–6
philosophy, ancient
  exercises of meditation and self-control, 106–7
  as way of life, 104, 109
  —Boethius on, 207
  —parallel in medieval monasticism, 109–10
Picander. *See* Henrici, Christian Friedrich
Play of Antichrist, 345
Plotinus, 107–8

Poirel, D., 50
Porcher, Jean, 62
Porphyry
  organization of Plotinus's *Enneads*, 107
  See also Isagogue (Porphyry)
porta, biblical meanings of, 38n48
Postilla litteralis super total bibliam (Nicholas of Lyra)
  diagrams in manuscripts of, 35n21
  first illustrated printed edition, 32
  illustrations in, 5
  —mistakes in reproductions, 30–31
  and tradition of visual exegesis, 29
prayer *(oratio)*
  as one of the elements of a devout Christian life, 158
  at St. Victor, 108
preaching
  as an element of devout Christian life, 158
  by canons of St. Victor, 157, 180–81 (*See also* Achard of St. Victor, sermons of; Godfrey of St. Victor; Richard of St. Victor; Walter of St. Victor, sermons of)
  as expression of compassion, 169
priories dependent of St. Victor, 156
prophets, study of biblical
  by Andrew, 354
  Andrew of St. Victor's commentary on Minor Prophets, 349
  by Jewish exegetes, 342
Psalms
  Achard's sermon on allegorical, tropological and anagogic sense of Psalm 18 (19), 170–71
  Psalm 25
  —interpretations of, 93
  —paraphrase in Innocent II's privilege, 93–94
  —Suger's references to, 96–97

Psalm 118
—commentary by Ambrose, 234
—*De institutione* on, 111–12
Psalter of St. Albans, 59
Pseudo-Dionysius the Areopagite
  influence on Suger, 48
  influence on Walter of St. Victor, 174
Pseudo-Methodius, 345
psychogenesis of ethical acts, 236
Puiseaux, priory of, 156
Pullen, Robert, 134

Querelle de la Madeleine, 360

Rabanus Maurus, 235
Radak, 349
Raimbold Creton (Croton), 329–30
  in *Chanson de Jerusalem*, 335
Ralph of Caen, 330
Ralph of Canterbury, 139
Ralph of Reims, 138–39
Ralph of Vermandois, 338
Ranulf of Buildwas, 135
Rashi (Rabbi Solomon ben Isaac)
  exegetical drawings, 7, 36n29
  —inconsistent orientation of plans in manuscripts, 40n74
  —lost knowledge of, 36n30
  on importance of literal meaning of scripture, 8–9
  influence on Andrew of St. Victor, 349, 350, 352
  as model for Richard's map of Canaan, 26
  on Solomon's Temple, 10
reader-response theory, 120–21, 125
reading, sacred
  and Christian living, 103–4
  exercise of *lectio*, 110
  meant to edify not preoccupy, 104
  as one of the elements of a devout Christian life, 158
  as a way of life, 103–30
reading or instruction (*lectio sive doctrina*) at St. Victor, 108
reason
  as exercise to integrate knowledge into self, 114
  versus will, in Roman Stoicism, 232
Reformation and exegetical maps for the New Testament, 29, 41n81
reform of the church
  Lefèvre and, 359, 379n5
  St. Victor and, 154–55
  Suger and, 91–92
  visionaries in *Liber trium virorum* on, 370–71
Registrum Anglie, 132
Renaudet, Augustin, 361
revelation, Hildegard's theology of, 300–327
Rice, Eugene, 376, 379n11
Richard of St. Victor
  concern with Ezekiel's vision of the Temple, 10
  on human diffidence in the face of God's love, 390
  importance of literal meaning of scripture, 8–9
  influenced by Hugh of St. Victor, 215
  on liminal status of abbey, 154
  refutation of Andrew's exegesis of Isaiah 7:14, 350
  sermons of, 157, 158–67
  —addressed to priests, 162–63
  —on allegorical meaning of church building, 161
  —for the feast day of saints, 163–64
  —for the Nativity of the Blessed Virgin, 165–67
  —on responsibilities of prelate, 164–65

Richard of St. Victor (*cont.*)
— on the Trinity, 171
— on tropological meaning of Jerusalem, 165
— on tropological sense of church building, 162
as source for Maurice de Sully's sermons, 179
use of *speculatio*, 217–24
See also *De arca mystica*; *In visionem Ezechielis*
Riesencodex, 373
right reason. See natural law
Ring of the Dove, The (Ibn Hazm of Cordoba), 285
Robert (dean of Arras), 138
Robert, Hans, 121
Robert II of Flanders, 328–29
Robert Amiclas, 131–52
biography, 134–35
books other than Glossed books, 139–40
ex libris of, 132
See also Glossed books of Robert Amiclas
Robert of Adington (Edington), Master, 138, 140
Robert of Jerusalem. See Robert II of Flanders
Robert of Uzès, 359, 364
application of Leonine prophecies to papacy, 370
building metaphor in, 372
discovery by Lefèvre, 361
influences on, 372
vision reception by, 368
— illustration of, 366f, 367
rose, allegorization of the, 167
Rosenau, Helen, 9
Rudolph, Conrad, 48, 93, 95
Rule of St. Augustine, 110
on spiritual beauty, 186

Rule of St. Benedict, 110
Rupert of Deutz, 309–10, 323
influence on Hildegard, 322
Rupertsberg, convent of, 374
Ruysbroeck, John of, 361, 363–64

sacraments
restoring man's original splendor, 266–67
revelation of Trinity through, 314–17
Sacred Heart
devotion to, 283
emanation of "golden reeds" from, 291–92
Schedel, Hartmann, 302, 323
Schönheit in der Theologie von Sankt Victor (Karfíková), 247
Schröder, Jochen, 19, 34n6
scintilla rationis (spark of reason), 245n27
Jerome on, 235–36
in twelfth century, 236
Scivias (Hildegard of Bingen), 300–327
diagrammatical structure of book three, 317
first printed edition in *Liber trium virorum*, 358, 364–65
Hildegard's visions compared to John the Divine's vision, 308–9
Lefèvre's editing of, 373, 374–75, 378
— effect on meaning, 375
manuscripts of, 303, 362
— Rupertsberg manuscript shown to Lefèvre, 361
order of topics in, 300–301
on Trinity
— representations of, 307
— on revelation of, 301
— on revelation of God as Trinity, 309
— revelation through Incarnation of the Son, 317

—revelation through sacraments, 314–17
—vision of the Trinity in Unity, 312–13
visions
—in book one, 310–12
—in book two, 312–17
—in book three, 317–22
Scotus, John Duns, 235
    and *scintilla rationis*, 236
    on *synderesis* and conscience, 238–39
scripture reading
    goal of internalizing the text, 121
    as honeycomb, 113, 114
    Hugh of St. Victor on difference from other writings, 165
    instructing concerning virtue, 118
    Liber exceptionum on benefits from reading, 159
    and *speculatio*, 221
sculpting, metaphor of, 107–8
self-examination, 114, 230, 242n5
Seneca
    on *conscientia*, 233
    reframing image of rolling cylinder, 232
    on the will, 231–32
Seneca morale (Dante), 230
Senece saepe noster (Tertullian), 230
Senlis Cathedral, 47
senses and experience of beauty, 250
Sententiae (Peter Lombard), 61, 62
    quoting Jerome, 235
    structure of elements of Christian doctrine in, 312
Sermones centum (Richard of St. Victor), 160–67
    dating, 227n36
    as source for Maurice de Sully, 179
Sermones de sacramentis (Ivo of Chartres), 139
Shepherd of Hermas. See Hermas

Sheppard, Jenny, 132, 141, 146, 150
Shrewsbury School, 132
Sicard, Patrice, 50, 251
silence, practicing humble virtue of, 116
Silvestre, 69
Simon of St. Albans, 141
Simson, Otto von, 48
sin
    according to Hugh of St. Victor, 191, 196
    of language, 117
Singer, Charles, 309
Smalley, Beryl, 39n56, 140
Smith, Lesley, 22, 40n68
Soliloquy on the Earnest Money of the Soul (Hugh of St. Victor), 188
Solomon's Temple, 10
Song of Songs
    allegorical reading of, 387–88
    Bach's understanding of, 392
    —anagogical exegesis in *Wachet auf!*, 388
    —themes introduced in *Wachet auf!*, 387
    as basic text of medieval monastic literature, 387
    in Christian spiritual tradition, 392–93
    medieval commentaries on, 385, 388
    Richard of St. Victor's understanding of, 390, 391–92
speaking, discipline in, 119–20, 267–68
speculatio
    difficulty of translation of, 205
    functioning of the mind in, 206
    as part of theoretical science, 211
    as process of "extraction," 223, 224
    use by Boethius, 206–10, 216
    use by Hugh of St. Victor, 210–17

speculatio (cont.)
   use by Richard of St. Victor, 217–24
   use in *De duodecim patriarchis*, 221–23
   Victorine use of term, 205
speculativa
   meaning of, 219
   use by Hugh of St. Victor, 211
speculativi, 217–21
   defined by Hugh of St. Victor, 219
Speculum historiale (Vincent of Beauvais), 286
Speculum temporum futurorum (Gebeno of Eberbach), 303
speech, vigilance concerning proper, 117
Spener, Philipp Jacob, 388
St. Denis, abbey of
   church of
   —Gothic architecture and, 47–48
   —Suger's reconstruction of, 92, 93
   Innocent II's privilege for, 86–102
   —contemporary endorsements on the back of, 97–98
   —language similar to Suger's writing, 90–91
   —possessions described in, 88–89
   —use of Psalm 25 in, 93–94, 95
   reform and construction at, 91–94
   restoration of objects given by Charles the Bald, 92
   visit of Innocent II to, 86–87, 93
St. Denis, Notre Dame, and St. Pierre, royal nunnery of, 78
St. Denis-de-l'Estrée, church of, 87, 93, 98n9
Stephen Langton, 6
Stephen of Blois, 328
Stephen of Tournai, 175
St. Germain-des-Prés, abbey church of, 74, 78

Stirnemann, Patricia
   dating of *In visionem Ezechielis*, 39n64
   dating of Mazarine Ms. 729, 50
Stoicism
   on acquisition of basic moral norms, 230–31
   doctrines retaining their identity, 230
   medieval transformations of, 229–46
   wise man, 105–6
St. Rémi, church of, 87, 93
Structured Self, The (Gill), 240n4
Stuttgart Psalter, literal illustrations in, 59
St. Victor, abbey of
   foundation charter, 76, 77
   important school, 155
   library of, 48–49
   —sermons in, 157
   Maurice de Sully's ties with, 179
   merger of the theology of the monasteries and the theology of the schools, 153
   monasteries affiliated with, 181n6
   pastoral ministry in dependencies of, 156–57
   preaching taught at, 157
   readings during the meals, 157
   as a *schola uirtutum*, 112, 187
   veneration of the Blessed Virgin at, 167
   See also canons of St. Victor
St. Victor, church of, 68–85
   1791 plan by Petit-Radel and Bénard, 69
   archaeology and, 70, 72f, 80n6
   architectural context, 78–79
   bell tower compared to others of same period, 69
   documents and dates, 76–78

estimation of dimensions of, 75–76, 78–79
plans by A. Grimault, 70, 72f, 73f, 74–76
visual evidence, 69–76
Suger
and Gothic architecture, 47–48
influenced by Hugh of St. Victor, 48
and Innocent II, 87
references to Psalm 25, 96–97
on Robert II of Flanders, 328–29
on Thomas de Marle, 335–39
—compared to Guibert, 338–39
and visual representation, 46
Summa Halensis (Alexander of Hales), 237
Super exiit edictum (Richard of St. Victor), 218–19
system of speculative, contemplative, and prophetic men, 220
Swanson, R. N., 126n10
symbols, contemplation of sensible, 213, 262
synderesis
Albert the Great on, 237–38
Bonaventure on, 237
as different from *conscientia*, 236
Duns Scotus on, 238–39
equated to *conscientia* by Jerome, 235
John of La Rochelle on, 236–37
Philip the Chancellor on, 236
Thomas Aquinas on, 238

Tabernacle, plans of, 6, 10
Tauler, Johannes, 388
Tegernsee correspondence, 285
Temple
Ezekiel's vision, 10 (*See also In visionem Ezechielis*)
—Nicholas of Lyra on different interpretations of, 29
—problem of sanctuary stream, 29–30

Solomon's Temple, 10
symbolic significance for Christianity, 10
See also Herod's Temple
Teresa of Avila, Saint, 288
Tertullian, 230
Theoderic of Echternach, 323, 376, 377
"Theologians as Trinitarian Iconographers" (McGinn), 307
theology
of beauty, Hugh of St. Victor, 247–80
definition of, 304–6
influence of Hugh of St. Victor on monumental arts, 47
of revelation of Hildegard, 300–327
at St. Victor, 153, 183n35
theophany of beauty, 257
Thérel, M.-L., 47
Thierry of Chartres, 109
Thomas Aquinas, Saint, 236, 238
Thomas Becket, 138
Thomas de Marle, 330–39
Albert of Aachen on, 334–35
in *Chanson de Jerusalem*, 335
and commune of Laon, 337
excommunication of, 338
Guibert of Nogent on, 330–34
Suger on, 335–39
Thomas Gallus, 174
Thomas of Cantimpré, 287
Thomas of St. Victor, 155
Thomson, Rod, 134, 139, 140, 147
"Three Marys," debate of historical identity of, 379n6
time in Hugh's concept of beauty, 253
Trinity, the
debates on, 313
as devotional and theological focus, 313

Trinity, the (*cont.*)
   Hildegard on
     —in *Liber divinorum operum*, 307
     —on revelation of, 301
     —revelation through Incarnation of the Son, 317
     —revelation through sacraments, 314–17
     —vision of the Trinity in Unity, 312–13
   Victorine sermons on, 171
Tristan (Gottfried von Strassburg), 285
Trithemius of Sponheim, Johannes, 303, 323, 373
Troilus and Criseyde (Chaucer), 285, 295
tropologia grounded in *historia*, 120
tropological/moral interpretation, 388
tropology
   as color on exterior of building, 104
   as method of moral training to be lived out, 111

universe, 260–61
   levels of seeing, 257

Vecchio, Silvana, 117
Vincent of Beauvais, 286
virginity, vow of, 315–16
virtues, moral, and measure, 193–94
visionary texts editing by Lefèvre, 359
visions
   in *Legatus divinae pietatis*, 292–94
   as underpinning theology of Hildegard of Bingen, 302
   as way of claiming authority, 302
   See also *Liber trium virorum et trium spiritualium virginum* (Jacques Lefèvre d'Étaples); *Scivias* (Hildegard of Bingen)

Visio Wettini (Heito), 358–59, 364
   manuscript of, 361
   metaphoric building in, 371–72
Vita Lutgardis (Thomas of Cantimpré), 287
Volmar, 304
   illustration of, 383n68

Wachet auf! (Bach), 385–86
   anagogical exegesis of the Song of Songs, 388
Walter of St. Victor, sermons of, 157, 171–74
   for Pentecost, 173–74
   for the solemnity of Easter, 172
Westhausen, Andrew, 361
Westhausen, Kilian, 374
Wettinus
   vision of purgatory, 381n41
   vision reception by, 368
   —illustration of, 365, 366f, 367
Whitgift, John, 132
will, the
   Duns Scotus on, 239
   versus reason, in Roman Stoicism, 232
   Seneca on, 231–32
   synderesis in, 236
Willesme, J.-P., 70, 77
William of Auvergne, 236
William of Champeaux, 77
   Christian philosophy of, 113
   foundation of St. Victor, 154–55
   praised for pursuit of beauty of virtue, 196n7
   teaching of, 112, 113
William of Ourscamp, 51
William of Savoy, 287
William of St. Thierry, 92, 94, 95
   interpretation of Psalm 25, 93
William of Tyre
   on Robert Amiclas, 134, 146
   on Thomas de Marle, 335

Wilmart, André, 18
Winterfeld, Carl von, 387
wisdom
    Boethius on, 206–7
    division by Hugh of St. Victor into understanding and knowledge, 211
    living according to, as ideal of ancient philosopher, 106
    relationship with beauty, 258
Wisdom, Book of
    Jerome's commentary on, 235

women visionaries, church suspicion of, 363
works of contemplative life *versus* active life, 158
Wren Library, Trinity College, 132

Yvain (Chrétien de Troyes), 285

Zinn, Grover, 48, 384
    on holistic vision of learning and living at abbey of St. Victor, 103